D1173992

THE CORDON COMPANY · PUBLISHERS · NEW YORK

agazine writing and editing by

MITCHELL V. CHARNLEY AND BLAIR CONVERSE

UNIVERSITY OF MINNESOTA · *DEPARTMENTS OF JOURNALISM* · IOWA STATE COLLEGE

Designed by Burnshaw

MANUFACTURED IN THE UNITED STATES OF AMERICA

Set up, printed, and bound by The Haddon Craftsmen, Inc., Camden, N. J.

Preface

THIS is a tremendously serious book—not in manner, its authors hope, but in purpose. Because its purpose may be not quite transparent, this word of guidance is offered.

Writing—almost any kind of writing—is more or less an art. That is to say, it can't be very well practiced out of a rule-book. With the proper instruments and the right rules one can learn to survey a field, construct a table, or repair an automobile. But one can't with instruments and rules learn to paint a picture, deliver a speech, or write an essay, poem, or article. These operations require so much of individual judgment, taste, and imagination, applied to ever-changing problems, that formulas, no matter how detailed, are inadequate.

The teaching of such work must, then, look to other devices than the handing out of formulas. It must endeaver, in short, to set up a program which will give the beginner the bases for building sound judgments for himself, which will make more sensitive and unerring his taste, and which will energize his imagination.

To the beginner the world of the magazine or newspaper is a distant, haze-hung land. But it is of that very land that he is asked suddenly to become a citizen. The bewildered immigrant does not know the language, the people, the government. That he is not able on the instant to become a useful, producing citizen is not strange.

To think accurately and acutely in any field (and one cannot produce the kind of work of which we are speaking without accurate and acute thinking), one must know one's way about, be thoroughly at home, familiar with the local idiom, the prevailing traits of mind and character.

These considerations have led the authors to follow what may strike the reader as an experimental procedure. But the book is, they believe, based very substantially on a sound conception of the learning process. They have attempted first of all to acclimate the beginner to the world of the feature article, to give him a vivid picture of the way magazines are made, to build his judgment, taste, and imagination on a close familiarity with the machinery of magazine production and the detailed methods and procedures of successful writers and editors.

To do this they have presented the story of how a magazine is made. With the extraordinarily hearty cooperation of the personnel of *Better Homes & Gardens* and the Meredith Publishing Company, they spent many days in the magazine plant, watching the processes of magazine making. They were given free access to the magazine's files, to correspondence with authors, artists, and photographers, to original manuscripts, to the work sheets which showed the processes of layout, editing, copy-fitting, proofing, and so on. Even more important, they discussed at length with every member of the staff the exact details of his work.

To the student who has worked his way through the first and second parts of the book, the world of the feature article is no longer a vague, foreign realm. He may not yet be a full-fledged citizen, but he has taken out his first papers. He has learned the language, he knows something of the people—he is beginning to feel at home.

And he is ready to go to *work*. The latter half of the book inducts him into the job of being a producer in the new land. It does not—can not—do his work for him, but it can guide, direct, and suggest.

Such a method as has been described is essentially inductive. It says, in effect, that the writing of articles is a task with creative aspects which cannot be reduced to formulas; that the student of article writing, given the language, the setting, and the atmosphere of periodical making, can and must think through for himself the problems of successful authorship.

This book strives to bridge the gap that yawns between the classroom and the writing world in which the student hopes to become a producer—to serve as a vital first contact with that world. Instead of writing in a vacuum of inexperience, the reader of this book can begin to function with something of the assurance of an initiate.

As a by-product of this initiation he is getting a training which will serve him well if he should find himself in a job behind the scenes.

The authors are sincerely grateful to Fred Bohen, president, and to E. T. Meredith, Jr., vice-president, of the Meredith Publishing Company.

Grateful acknowledgment is made to the following publications and authors for permission to reproduce material: *Country Home* and Mr. George Kent; the *Christian Science Monitor* and Mr. George Mullen; *Ceramic Industry*; *Successful Farming*; *Outdoor Life* and Mr. Robeson Bailey; *Stage* and Miss Patricia Collinge; *Harper's*; *Popular Science Monthly* and Mr. Robert E. Martin; *Engineering News-Record*; *New Republic* and Mr. Carleton Beals; *Household Magazine* and Miss Zorada Z. Titus; *Good Housekeeping* and Mrs. Constance J. Foster; *Esquire* and Mr. Paul W. Kearney; *Ladies' Home Journal* and Mr. Henry F. Pringle; *New York Times Magazine* and Mr. F. Raymond Daniell and Mr. H. L. Robbins; *Louisville Courier-Journal* and Mr. Peyton Hoge; *Scribner's* and Mr. Harland Manchester; *Country Gentleman* and Mrs. Genevieve Forbes Herrick; *Pictorial Review*; *Wallaces' Farmer and Iowa Homestead*; *Business Week*; *New Yorker*; *Liberty* and Princess Alexandra Kropotkin.

THE AUTHORS

Contents

These Got into Print

64 PAGES OF EDITORIAL MATTER REPRINTED FROM THE ORIGINAL PLATES OF "BETTER HOMES & GARDENS"

PART ONE

How Articles Get into Print

PART TWO

Writing the Article

PART THREE

Aids to the Writer

Magazine Writing and Editing

These Got into Print

64 PAGES OF EDITORIAL MATTER REPRINTED FROM THE ORIGINAL PLATES OF "BETTER HOMES & GARDENS"

IN THIS ISSUE

Cover Photograph by Charles Kuoni, Donnelley Studio

MEREDITH PUBLISHING COMPANY

E. T. MEREDITH, *Founder*, 1876-1928

President: Fred Bohen; *Vice-Presidents:* E. T. Meredith, Jr., E. F. Corbin; *Art Director:* Wallace F. Hainline; *Associate Editors:* Frank W. McDonough, W. L. Benson, Christine Holbrook, Paul F. Frese, Myrna Johnston, Helen Homer, John Normile, Fae Huttenlocher, Alfred Carl Hottes, Jean Guthrie; *Assistant Editor:* Anna Olson.

•

Home Offices: 1714 Locust Street, Des Moines, Iowa. Manuscripts submitted to the magazine must be accompanied by postage for their return, else we cannot be responsible for them.

Advertising Branch Offices: New York City, 420 Lexington Ave.; Philadelphia, 133 South Twelfth St.; Chicago, 333 North Michigan Ave.; Detroit, 5-145 General Motors Bldg.; San Francisco, 100 Bush St.; Los Angeles, 1212 Lincoln Bldg.; Atlanta, Georgia, 619 Grant Bldg.

Subscription: United States and Canada rates, one year, $1; two years, $1.50; three years, $2. Other countries, $1.50 a year. At newsstands, twentieth of the month, 10 cents a copy. Entered as second-class matter at the post office in Des Moines, Iowa, under act of Congress, March 3, 1879.

Change of Address: Report any change of address direct to *Better Homes & Gardens*, Des Moines, Iowa, rather than thru your local post office, giving old address as well as the new, and allow five weeks for the first copy to reach you.

ACROSS THE *Editor's* DESK

The Picture on the Cover: "Pansies for thoughts" . . . Bridal Wreath in snowy cascades . . . lilting May sunshine . . . and a charming little lady in a transplanting mood! If you can resist her you're a better man than I am, Mr. Din. And just to save you a stamp, that's not a bed of popcorn or even of babysbreath on which she kneels—lightly, I hope—but a crushed-rock garden path, soon to be completely bordered by the wise little faces of velvet-petaled pansies.

• • •

JUNIOR doesn't turn up his nose at spinach anymore. It's his favorite vegetable! This is the tradition-shaking fact disclosed recently in New York City when the results of a questionnaire filled out by 22,416 boys and girls between 6 and 16 were tabulated. Spinach was a close second with the girls, too. . . . What a tribute to our great canned-foods industry, including, especially, America's strained-vegetables-for-babies industry, and to Popeye!

▶ ▶ ▶ My friend Tom Wallace, editor of the Louisville Times, has discovered, in the mountain town of Pikeville, Kentucky, near the Trail of the Lonesome Pine, a bank that maintains extensive gardens from which come flowers for the bank and bouquets for depositors.

The bank also holds flower shows to encourage beautification of Pikeville (population 4,000), and gives away hollyhock seed. Last year it gave away 5,000 packages of it.

Increasing numbers of businessmen are recognizing that flowers pay them dividends in dollars and cents.

▶ ▶ ▶ Physicians of St. Louis for several months have asked the Missouri Botanical Garden of that city for fresh leaves from its tropical collection of aloe, the common houseplant.

The large leaves, which contain a copious supply of viscous fluid, are being used to treat severe X-ray and radium burns. The fresh leaves are split and their gelatinous inner surface applied directly to the burn, relieving the pain immediately.

Healing properties of aloe leaves came to the attention of the medical profession thru their use in Florida as a home remedy for severe sunburn. But I'm told the aloe is an old, old remedy used by the Mexicans.

▶ ▶ ▶ Double-feature movie programs are described by Samuel Goldwyn, film producer, as harmful to the health of children, as inducing gambling—thru the so-called "bank night," I suppose—and forcing production of deliberately mediocre pictures.

Dr. Herman N. Bundesen, well-known health writer and president of the Chicago board of health, says that our prolonged dose of the double feature is a detriment to the health of everyone.

Parents can eliminate the double feature promptly in their communities if thru their clubs, especially thru their Parent-Teacher Association, they make their demands known. In some parts of the country such agitation has already been felt, and exhibitors have responded with a return to single features. As buyers we get just about what we demand.

▶ ▶ ▶ Under "Magazine Features That Wouldn't Be Missed," Walter Winchell says, "About the time you're beginning to rely on a mag to tell you how to grow dahlias, it junks the series in favor of some new candid camera angles on Martha Raye."

You looked at the wrong magazine, Walter. Why don't you read your *Better Homes & Gardens?*

▶ ▶ ▶ Seven trees planted a century ago by Thomas Jefferson himself on his estate at Monticello, Virginia, are being saved by a number of "emergency operations" which correspond quite closely to "human" surgery as practiced today in our modern hospitals.

Infected areas in the trees are found by probing the bark. Sides of incisions then made aren't held back with clamps, as in human surgery, but the same objective is reached by painting the sides of the incisions with shellac; this also acts as an antiseptic in preventing harmful fungus cells in the air from lodging in the openings. Finally rubber blocks serving the same purpose as sutures employed by surgeons are used to close incisions.

Many other old trees on the grounds of the Jefferson estate are also being "operated upon," for they, like the house itself, are a national shrine.

It's to be hoped that the success of the unusual methods employed at Monticello will bring their more widespread use to save the lives of other historically significant trees thruout America.

Editor

♦ To make open-face sandwiches quickly, here's a **canape cutter** (Sketch **1**) with a sliding base. In the sketch you'll note the A-B-C process: cut your bread, spread while yet in the cutter and, to lift your canape, raise the cutter's base from below with your finger. [Standard cutter, 50 cents; stainless steel, $1, M. & M. Products, 163 South St., Pittsfield, Mass.]

♦ A one-piece smoothie (Sketch **2**) **for baby's crib** replaces large-size pad and lower sheet. It's a 27- x 50-inch pad (made of several thicknesses of the absorbent cotton weave called *Layettecloth*) softly seamed to a fine cotton-sheeting border to complete a 58- x 81-inch sheet. This combination design prevents lumping and, of large size, the piece anchors securely to stay smooth! [*Cribmaker*, $2.25 in your stores, Kendall Mills, Walpole, Mass.]

♦ Selling for a coin, the simple metal **hat-rest** (**3**) comes to be fitted together and slipped into its bracket on the closet door, wall, or shelf edge. [*Hi-hats*, 4 cost 50 cents, or 6 lacquered in blue, green, or red, $1, Thompson Mfg. Co., 64 New St., Naugatuck, Conn.]

♦ Push this **dandelion weeder** (in Sketch **4**) into the soil directly alongside the plant's roots. Half turn the weeder clockwise and pull out, removing the dandelion by the roots. The **cultivator** (also in Sketch **4**) has prong points streamlined, designed on the principle that they go thru the soil sleekly, no resistance set up. [*Dandelion puller*, 75 cents; *Cultivator No. 1563*, $1.80, Gardex, Inc., Michigan City, Ind.]

♦ Mud scraped onto the backbone of this black, hand-wrought iron horse (D in Sketch **5**) won't soil your carpets! This **foot scraper** is 10 inches wide over all, screws to the cement walk alongside your doorstep. [*Galloper*, $3.50 plus postage, Lewis & Conger, 45th St. & 6th Ave., New York City]

♦ The **entrance mat** (E in Sketch **5**) is made of strips cut from automobile tires. They are strung on a cross frame of steel spring wire, with beads of the rubber-and-fabric tire material used as spacers on the cross wires. [*Fabrix*, ½ inch thick, in standard sizes about 60 cents a square foot, Cincinnati Mat Co., 105 W. Court St., Cincinnati, Ohio]

♦ A new **laundering machine** is about 3 feet high, and in shape suggests a console radio. Nine pounds of dry clothes go in thru its front, round, glass window and—beyond your first brief preparations—you needn't even be on hand while it washes, rinses, and damp-dries the clothes, ready for the clothesline. Grand if you're delayed elsewhere, for it shuts itself off. The unit connects to your home's hot and cold water and drains automatically during the washing, 3 rinses, and damp-drying process. [*Bendix Home Laundry*, $169.50, Dept. B, Bendix Home Appliances, Inc., South Bend, Ind.]

♦ Indian Head is an inexpensive cotton material available in fast colors and refreshing this time of year for bedspreads, summer draperies, and luncheon sets. At yard-goods counters you may see a new handbook called a **Color Selector** that will help you to plan unique color schemes, using Indian Head. If your study club, or you individually, would like to have this handbook, it costs $1.50. [Nashua Mfg. Co., 40 Worth St., New York City]

♦ First of a new race of **dwarf chrysanthemums**, says Paul Frese, is Pygmy Gold. Its golden yellow pompon blossoms, an inch across, come on a foot-high bushy plant suitable for rock garden and hardy border. [50 cents each, $1.25 for 3, plus postage, Bristol Nurseries, Bristol, Conn.]

♦ After you've washed and rinsed your woolens (see the story, page 46), there's a powder that, dissolved in water for a last 15-minute soak, **moth-proofs your woolens** whether in use or stored away until they're again washed! The dime-size packet is enough for 3 sweaters or a single blanket. [*Rinsing Larvex*, in your stores]

♦ John Normile explains that a **silent electric switch** is offered, improvement on the kind that snaps when turned on and off. More important than its silence, the contact is made and broken by the movement of mercury, and there's literally nothing to wear out. [General Electric Company's *Mercury-Break Switch*]

♦ About to buy **garden roses?** "A good garden rose," says Paul Frese, "must have a strong, healthy plant, nicely shaped bloom, fragrance, and color." And these graces are claimed for the new *Saturnia*, a carmine hybrid tea rose flushed with scarlet and orange at the petal bases. [$1 ea. postpaid, Inter-State Nurseries, Hamburg, Iowa]

♦ McGredy's Pride is also your new **hybrid tea rose** if you like bright colors. Orange, salmon-pink, and saffron-yellow all blend in the one bloom. Paul Frese says it has a long bud, a full flower. [$1.50 from your seedsmen and nurserymen, or write for information to Jackson & Perkins Co., Dept. B., Newark, New York State]

♦ Paul Frese suggests that, charming for rock gardens and border edgings, there's a new little **annual**, Blue Cups (*Nierembergia hippomanica*). Its cushion-like plants, 6 inches high and a foot across, are smothered under lavender-blue cups all summer and autumn, and stand a lot of heat! [About 35 cents a packet from your seedsmen or Peter Henderson & Co., 35 Cortlandt St., New York City]

♦ A wood fiber, crepe-like, stretchable, **blanket insulation** interests John Normile because it has little bulk to deliver to the job and to handle, and manipulates easily. A workman can carry twin cartons—enough to insulate the top ceiling of a small house. Each section is 15 inches wide (fits the standard opening between studs) by 20 inches long. Because of the creping, when fastened at the top with a lath, this 20-inch length can be drawn gently downward to nearly 10 feet, and again lathed to anchor. [*Kimsul*, Kimberly-Clark Corp., 8 S. Michigan Ave., Chicago]

♦ For safe footing in bathtub or shower, an improved **rubber mat**, lightly ridged, has new, double-action vacuum cups on the under side to hold it, non-slip. [White and colors, 16 x 14 inches, $1.55, 18 x 32 inches (a center hole designed for shower drain), $2.50, Footsure Co., Inc., 1220 Maple Ave., Los Angeles, Calif.]

♦ The free booklet called *Upholstery Fabrics* shows clear drawings of smooth and pile weaves, tells what to expect of various materials, and defines **fabric names** (conquers such memory-teasers as matelassé. [Collins & Aikman Corp., 200 Madison Ave., New York City]

♦ A **paste furniture wax** now comes in 3 tints, maple, walnut, and mahogany, designed to polish a variety of woods. Not altering the wood's tone, the wax buffs out to transparency, but the color pigments fill into any slight mars or rough spots to make them less noticeable. [*Old English Tinted Furniture Wax*, ½ lb., 60 cents, A. S. Boyle Co., Inc., Jersey City, N. J.]

♦ To arch niches and nooks, and for the home-workshopman, ***Beaver Bent Board*** comes in half-curves, 6-, 12-, 18-, and 24-inch diameters, 8 feet long. John Normile explains these combine with 4- x 8-foot flat sheets. Both come in colors. [Available thru lumber dealers and builders' supply houses, Certain-teed Products Corp., 100 E. 42nd St., New York City]

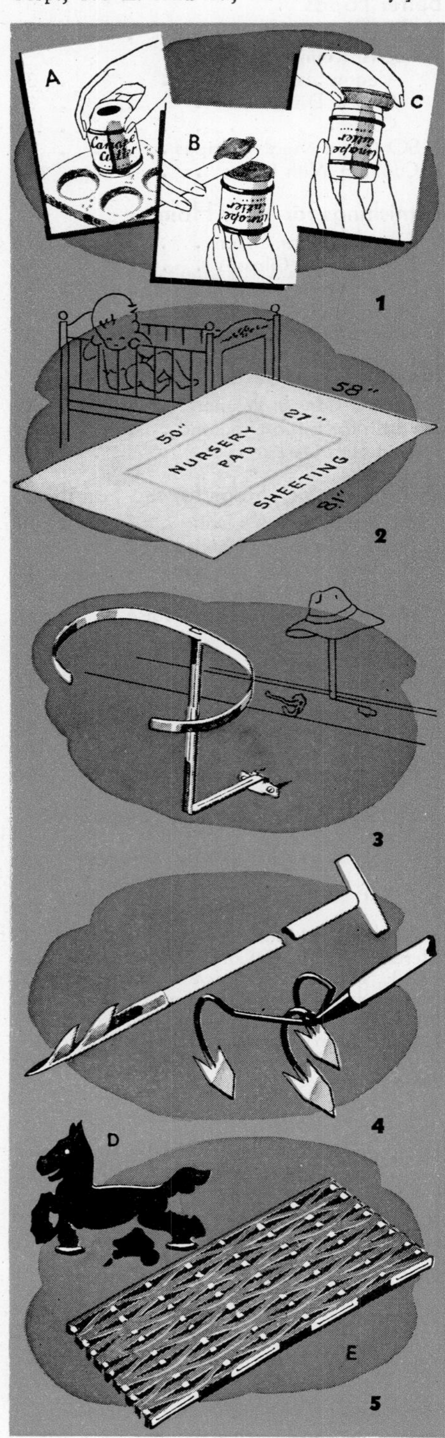

BETTER FOODS AND EQUIPMENT • *Helen Homer*

BETTER GARDENS • *Paul F. Frese*

BUILDING AND REMODELING • *John Normile*

HOME FURNISHINGS • *Christine Holbrook*

From Fairyland

WHAT are they waiting for? What will they find? Do you think real fairies will come out while they watch? Surely the fairies and gnomes are right there now—doing their work every minute.

A twig which had only six leaves yesterday has seven today. A fern frond unrolled last night and a harebell rang so hard it is broken this morning. Last week we called it a primrose; now it has gone to seed.

The scientist believes in elves, but he calls them atoms, electrons, and molecules. They dance in fairy rings, just as other things in the world of imagination do.

Surely there must be fairies in the garden at all times—mysteries—silent forces at work to cause growth, and flower, and continuance of life. . . .

. . . turn to page 16, read "Fairies Live in This Garden."

HE PASTURES HIS HOBBY-HORSE IN A *Garden*

A man you've heard lots about picked a hobby you know lots about

By Wainwright Evans

Gardening makes you saner and healthier, relaxed and contented with life, Earnest Elmo Calkins believes

". . . an old-fashioned garden with old-fashioned flowers to go with a century-old house!" "We use it as a sort of outdoor sitting room—a good place for luncheon or tea or loafing. Mrs. Calkins and I planned the garden after our own notions, with some suggestions from a clever landscape artist, a neighbor; and we think it's good"

A FEW years ago Earnest Elmo Calkins, whose name is one to conjure with in advertising, wrote an authoritative treatise that had nothing to do with advertising. He called it "The Care and Feeding of Hobby-Horses."

You may have seen it. It was published under the auspices of the Leisure League. A careful reading of it will show you how to run a whole stableful of hobby-horses if you so desire—how to tend, water, feed, groom, train and exercise them, and keep them in such fine condition that you will feel like a new man by contagion.

Mr. Calkins recommends concentrating on one or two of these amusing animals; and it seems a matter of no small significance that he pastures *his* favorite hobby-horse in a garden. But he still has a few "ponies" that he keeps indoors—making models of ships and covered wagons, and fashioning other things with tools and a power-driven lathe. Writing leisurely and delightful essays from a fund of ripe wisdom acquired in the course of a long and fruitful life is another. And his fingers itch so continually for the feel of type and the smell of printer's ink, that it is probably only a matter of time before he gets a small printing press and harks back to the days when he was everything on a small town newspaper.

MODERN advertising owes to Earnest Elmo Calkins much of what it is today. As president of the firm of Calkins and Holden, he pioneered in the development of modern agency practice. He brought about advances in the physical [*Turn to page 53*

"We are particularly fond of the water mirror," explains the famous author of "Louder Please." "We put it into a rather pretty frame by planting four Chinese Junipers in a square—joining them on opposite sides with narrow beds of roses which face each other, running the long way of the garden; and each bed is curved out, like a bow." (See sketch below)

The thing that feeds the soul of this pioneer in advertising is the hobby-horse that ranges a small and perfect garden. It whinnies every time he looks out the window; it crops the turf; keeps down the weeds, nibbles at the barberry 'til it looks like box, wades the pool, basks in the sun—and, when the sun gets too hot—slips into the shade of this old apple tree!

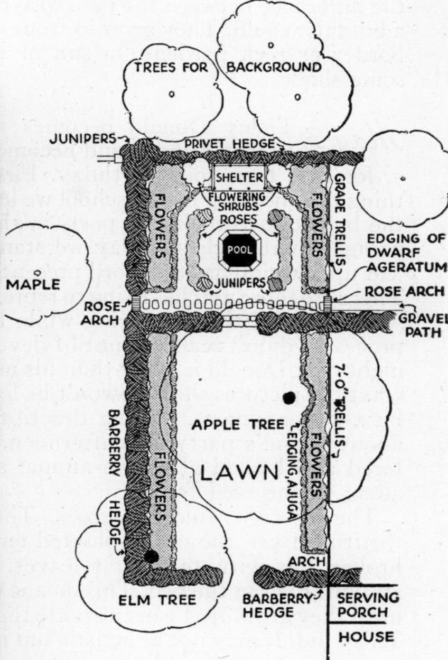

Ground plan of Calkins' garden, 85 feet long by 35 feet wide

". . . and there are the country moods, which one so rarely experiences in the city. A country mood is as sweet as country air," observes the celebrated owner of this trim old Connecticut home

PHOTOGRAPHS BY UNDERWOOD & UNDERWOOD

THE Diary OF A PLAIN DIRT GARDENER

By Harry R. O'Brien

CARICATURES BY TOM CARLISLE

"Maggie measured them; I took pictures"

May 1 Right after breakfast this Saturday morning we finished lawn-mowing and then the whole family went downtown to buy things. We are planning a trip to the Pacific Coast this summer. It will be six weeks before we leave but everybody is all excited about it. David wanted "a pair of pants, Daddy; something like explorers or Boy Scouts wear." He has visions of roughing it in the mountains. Maggie wanted a new traveling bag, and so on.

Back home, the horticultural news is that the row of nasturtiums David planted is up. The little plants need weeding, by now. But that isn't half as exciting as sowing the seed was. I suppose, if they're weeded, I'll have to do it.

May 2 The time of year has arrived when I go about the garden with notebook, making a record of what is in bloom. There are bluebells, white shadbush, single and double Russian violets, and the two saxifrage twins, *cordifolia* and *crassifolia*. These have clusters of pink blooms on thick succulent stems above the broad glossy leaves of the plants. I never can tell the difference between the two. Maybe a botanist could. They grow in front of border or rock gardens, in sun or in some shade.

"She began pulling a spray from my lilac"

May 3 Today Donald becomes 13 years old and David becomes 9, for it is their joint birthday. First thing this morning before school we led the boys out to their two posts in the garage where each birthday we stand 'em up, cut notches to record present height, and measure. There are those notches rising to represent the passing years.

Maggie did the measuring while I took pictures of the process. I didn't realize it until I developed the pictures tonight that Donald is taller than his mother. At least, that's what the pictures show. It won't be long now until he won't be a boy anymore. A long description could be written about David's party this afternoon. Or about how I watered and looked after the annual seedlings now coming along in the seed frame.

Then I cultivated the roses. These are now growing thriftily. Even the newly planted ones of this spring have broken out with their first leaves. I plant my roses in straight rows in the bed. This means that in the spring, and until they grow up, I can cultivate them with the wheel hoe. This I did. It may not be artistic but is a great saver of time.

May 4 Played a dirty trick on John, my neighbor, this evening. He's been making changes in his lawn and came over to borrow my roller. So with a smile on my face and a wicked grin on my soul, I pulled out our old family behemoth and turned it over to him. Helped him pull it down to the front pavement, in fact. Even offered to help him over to his lawn. But no, he said he could manage it.

I watched from afar, between turns at the lawn mower I was pushing myself, as he navigated up the pavement. I watched him pull it over his lawn. In a few minutes his wife came out and took hold. They both pulled. Then he gave up and came slowly dragging the old villain back here and put it away. I wasn't in sight just then, but I heard him stop at the back door and thank Maggie for it. I thought it best to remain *in absentia* for the moment, to avoid cuss words.

May 6 The call of our little ravine was stronger than lawn mower or spade. So after school this evening the boys and I put on old shoes and clothes and off we went with our cameras. Hepatica was gone and no Bloodroot could we find. But there were the little anemones, floor of ravine carpeted with blue, yellow, and white violets, and other things of spring. David set to work repairing the dam across the little brook. Donald and I took pictures, by different paths.

"Daddy, what kind of a wildflower is this?" I heard Donald call about 15 minutes later. I looked thru the trees and saw something lavender about 10 inches tall. I came running. It was a good colony of the little wild phlox of spring, *Phlox divaricata*. I had never found it in our ravine before. We found another large colony near by. Nature must have brought it in.

May 7 My double azalea, the only azalea I possess, is in full and gorgeous purplish-lavender bloom right now. This has managed to get along and really is thriving. When I planted it several years ago I prepared the spot by mixing with our usual clay some fine sand and some peatmoss, together with three or four trowelsful of aluminum sulphate, which is the trade form of alum. This chemical acidifies the soil, which is an essential for successful growing of azaleas, rhododendrons, and other similar plants. I set my azalea in this mixture.

Now once a year, usually in spring, I put about a trowelful of aluminum sulphate about this azalea and dig it in. Sometimes I give it another application in the fall. The azalea doesn't have shade but it is protected on the north and west by higher shrubbery. Maybe this all isn't the way the book says, but it seems to work. I bought my aluminum sulphate from a near-by landscape nurseryman.

May 8 Saturday and the big chore of the day was to sow a bed of annual seeds in the open. This included nasturtiums and other large-seed plants and some things which don't transplant well, as candytuft, Sweet Alyssum, and Ragged-robin.

I used to sow my zinnias in a frame and transplant them, but a well-known seed grower told me they did better if not transplanted. So last year I sowed my zinnia seeds where I wanted the plants, thinned them after they came up and I never had better zinnias. So this is how I sowed zinnias, too, this afternoon.

May 11 Last night's paper said frost, so with aid of Donald I put the sash cover back on my annual seedling frame. Sure enough, the ground was covered with white at early dawn this morning. It doesn't seem tho that any damage has been done here.

This afternoon a woman came in who introduced herself as a member of the XYZ garden club. As she was walking about, bless my soul if she didn't reach up and begin pulling off a spray from the President Grevy hybrid French lilac at the front corner of the house.

"Nobody will notice it, if I take it here," said she as she bent and pulled away. And to think I won't even let Maggie cut any of these for the house. Here I've worked for years to get those lilacs along so when they are in [*Turn to page 52*

"The boys played horse, pulling the mower"

BETTER HOMES & GARDENS
(COPYRIGHT 1938, THE MEREDITH PUBLISHING COMPANY)
VOLUME 16 APRIL, 1938 NUMBER 8

Good News WE ALL GET A BREAK!

The author (right) discusses the amended act with Stewart McDonald, FHA administrator

Here are the facts on the amended National Housing Act and what they mean to all of us who have a burning desire for a better home

By Gove Hambidge

BETTER HOMES & GARDENS WASHINGTON CORRESPONDENT

EVERYBODY, but especially the little fellow—who is most of us—is finally getting a break. The amendments recently written into the National Housing Act are primarily for his benefit. They're intended to make it easier for him to make the down payment on a home, and easier for him to carry the mortgage after he gets it.

IN A NUTSHELL, the two major financing changes, so far as the individual new-home wanter is concerned, affect all homes in this way:

First, mortgages of $5,400 or less are favored by the mortgagor's having to pay only ¼ of 1 percent insurance premium and by having the maximum length of his mortgage extended to 25 years, instead of 20, as heretofore. In other words, the total cost of the home doesn't matter so long as the mortgage doesn't exceed $5,400.

Second, the down payment on homes costing less than $6,000 is cut in half. Where you would have had to pay 20 percent down under the original Act, you now pay only 10 percent. Even for homes that cost $10,000 the necessary down payment has been cut as much as 30 percent.

Two other changes in the Act mean a monthly saving in dollars and cents. First, the service charge of ½ of 1 percent has been eliminated. The saving in the first year amounts to about $2 a month on a $5,000 mortgage, and it brings the total interest rate on all mortgages down to well under 6 percent. Second, the charge for FHA insurance is now based on the [*Turn to page 58*

Estimated Monthly Cost of Building or Buying a Home Under Revised National Housing Act

Value of House and Lot	Minimum Down Payment	Amount of Mortgage	Average Monthly Payment*		
			15 Years	20 Years	25 Years
$3,000	$ 300	$2,700	$28	$24	$22
4,000	400	3,600	37	33	30
5,000	500	4,500	47	41	37
6,000	600	5,400	56	49	45
7,000	800	6,200	65	57	....
8,000	1,000	7,000	74	65	....
10,000	1,400	8,600	91	80	....
12,000	2,400	9,600	103	91	....
15,000	3,000	12,000	129	113	....

*Based on maximum mortgage of 90% appraised value on first $6,000; 80% on amounts over $6,000. Figures include (1) payment on principal, (2) taxes—estimated at 2% of appraised value, (3) fire insurance—estimated at ½ of 1 percent of appraised value, (4) mortgage insurance premium—estimated at an average over the period, rather than on amortized remaining principal; in nearest approximate dollars. (Payments in beginning will be slightly higher than figures show; lower at end.) Appraisal and inspection fees, title search costs, etc., must be added to down payment. In some mortgage loans under FHA, the lot is taken as down payment, or partial down payment.

Now that genuine small-house financing has been made a reality, attention naturally is on the genuine small-home plan to team with it. Turn to the next page—see how one architect has proved that a modern, livable, architecturally desirable home for an average family can be built for less than $5,000, including cost of lot . . . .

TEN MINUTES FROM HOLLYWOOD

By Ethel McCall Head

IF IT isn't one thing, it's another. As soon as the architect mastered the skyscraper that rears 70 stories up and houses a city within itself, the little house that costs less than $5,000 popped up to plague him. At present the little house is his real problem child.

For a long time it wasn't anybody's child at all. From coast to coast, from Main Street to Country Club Drive, the little houses were built without benefit of architect. Most of them turned out as dull and unimaginative as the Jukes family. Occasionally someone added a swooping roof and a few chunks of stone around the front door, and then the house looked like Minnie the Moocher dressed for a party.

Now even the architect finds the small house pretty bratty. If he gives the outside a measure of come-hither, the inside is like as not unmanageable. And if he works out a solid, efficient interior, then the outside is utterly uninteresting. To make the house appeal to the eye, satisfy the demands of efficient room planning and modern living, and withal make it proof against the onslaught of the years is not easy. But it can be done.

FOR proof, tho this is by no means the only sample, we offer this little Cape Cod cottage in North Hollywood, California. It's the home of Mr. and Mrs. Paul Power, designed by Architect Leo Bachman. Tho small, it's no kin to the cracker box.

Look at the mellow brown roof of split shakes, and you'll note that it's divided into three major sections. Under the central one is the living-room. In the left wing are the kitchen and dining-room; in the right, two bedrooms and the bathroom. These roof sections show plainly that the house is divided. The effect is one of spaciousness and interest rarely found in the single-roof house.

Note how the roof rounds gracefully into the hood over the front door. Cute, isn't it? Practical, too, for it *does* rain in California. And note how the decorative frieze just below the eaves on the main section of the house gives it character. Other fine points are

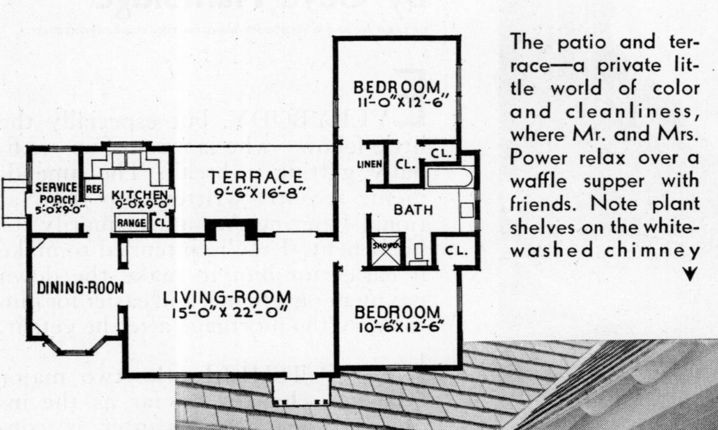

The patio and terrace—a private little world of color and cleanliness, where Mr. and Mrs. Power relax over a waffle supper with friends. Note plant shelves on the whitewashed chimney

BUILDER: WILLIAM MELLENTHIN

MOTT STUDIOS

Compact, immune to western sun and winter rain, built in 1935 for $4,100 including lot, this cottage is shining proof that Architect Leo Bachman licked his problem child

the nicely paneled front door, the simple latticework entrance detail, the excellent brass hardware of Colonial design, the solid-panel green shutters on the living-room windows, and the spacious bay of the dining-room windows. These give the street face a casual grace most becoming to any little house.

BUT what about the rear? Is the house phoney—an impressive front with nothing to back it up? We'd be ashamed to ask you if it was. Fact is, the rear is as charming as the front. You'll find a brick terrace, the chimney whitewashed, window ledges for flower pots, more dark-green shutters—the same careful detail and high quality noted in front. And you'll laud this: the service door was pushed from the back around to the side of the house where it belongs, and where it opens directly onto the driveway. This saves the rear of the property for garden and patio—for a lovely out-of-door living-room. Among the people who care, even those with little houses, the heyday of the backyard as a catch-all for the overflow from the house is over.

For the patio, the horizontal redwood siding used on the rest of the house was abandoned for vertical siding. Why? Why not, when this little variation cost no more and added a refreshing note. Mr. and Mrs. Powers rest in stillness and privacy on the patio.

SIMPLY studying the exterior of this cottage shows us what design can do for a little house without appreciably increasing the cost. Now go inside and find out if Architect Bachman has licked his problem child. See if there's plenty of closet room; if space is used economically. You enter the living-room directly. Yes, a hallway would be nice, but you can't have quite everything. The roominess of the living-room is surprising. It's no oversize dog house. Antique white plaster walls contrast with the darkly stained beams of the ceiling and with the soft dark color of the hardwood floors. For further interest, there's the fireplace set in a panel of knotty pine.

At the end of the living-room is the dining-room—small but adequate. The big bay window makes the room seem quite spacious. And the kitchen is a delight! Even the little woman who likes to eat out all the time would love to cook in this kitchen, paneled as it is with knotty pine. Best of all, look at the door leading to the patio, so that waffles on Sunday morning, tea for afternoon callers, or supper in the evening are managed without running a marathon.

Now cross to the bath and two-bedroom wing. The small hall there wastes no space. There's ample provision for linen storage and wardrobes, to say nothing of the separate shower stall, which certainly is rare in a small house.

CHECK the house plan for comfort and efficiency. From the bedroom hall you can go to the patio, or directly across to the kitchen without entering the living-room. From the living-room you can go directly to the patio and garden. And, as we said, it's only a few direct steps from the dining-room and kitchen to the terrace. Thus the three sections of the house are all tied together with the patio and the out-of-doors.

There are no tricky touches that boost costs without adding quality. Simple wainscots skirt the bedrooms, with wallpaper above. Wall heaters supply adequate heat. Plumbing is good quality, not showy.

All in all, the little Cape Cod cottage has settled down in the shadows of the mountains as if it had been there always. Could our austere New England forebears see it today, gleaming white behind its picket fence and rose bushes on a quiet, sunny street, they'd choke up with pride and admit they'd been pretty smart lads to have created anything so splendid.

1

Bridge If you can't read your mail or your handwriting, then here's your answer—a delicately scaled standing lamp for use at small table or secretary desk. The young lady is right-handed, so the lamp is located at her left.

Light
WHERE YOU NEED IT

By Mary Webber

YOU can't blame Abraham Lincoln for doing his work by firelight. He just didn't have anything better. But no flickering eyestrain for us! Banished, even, are the glaring, spotty lamps of yesterday. Instead, smart modern affairs like those pictured here offer soft, comfortable lighting and perfect protection for eyes and nerves. Except for numbers 3 and 8, all carry the certification tag showing that they've passed the high standard requirements of the Illuminating Engineering Society, organized to promote seeing safety. Each conceals a diffusing bowl to subdue and control light and reduce glare.

FOR just that right light for a particular place, different lamps call for different-size bulbs. Or a lamp may have a three-way switch to furnish various intensities with the same bulb. So when you buy, explain the use you'll make of your new lamp, and where it's to be placed. You'll be certain, then, that you've the lamp and the bulb for the purpose. There's no need, by the way, for a lamp to be on your left unless it's for desk work or sewing.

So here they are—nine types of lamps, suitably scaled, and developed to do duty with any sort of furniture grouping.

Co-operating With Better Homes & Gardens: 1 Lamp, Sandel; Furniture, Heywood-Wakefield. 2 Lamp, Colonial-Premier; Furniture, Karpen. 3 Lamp, Railley; Furniture, Drexel. 4 Lamp, Artistic; Table, Imperial. Courtesy, Marshall Field & Co. 5 Lamp, Mutual-Sunset; Furniture, Robert Irwin. 6 Lamp, Lightolier; Furniture, Tomlinson. 7 Lamp, Rindsberger; Piano, Musette. Courtesy, Lyon & Healy. 8 Lamp, Rembrandt; Furniture, Kroehler. 9 Lamp, Almco; Furniture, Tomlinson. All photographs made for *Better Homes & Gardens* by Hedrich-Blessing Studio.

2

Semi-Indirect Here's a charming blend of yesterday's furnishings with a lamp of today correctly placed toward the rear of rocker—the perfect setting for reading. The lamp has three-way switch, no candles.

3

Wall Type At last a reading-in-bed lamp that's kind to the eyes! It comes in so many styles of shades and period finish that one of them is bound to be lovely no matter what your bedroom's decorative scheme.

4

End-Table Generously tall and with just the right angle to its shade, this lamp for the little table sheds light where it's most needed. Use it in combination with other types of lamps in a room because it lights only one spot.

5

Table Study No danger of hand shadows and bothersome reflections with this modern lamp, designed for desk work. Place it at the left-center of the table where it can also serve a chair on the other side.

6

Floor Type In place of end-tables do you have a long coffee table in your davenport group? Then matching floor lamps, one at each end, will give you fine lighting for an evening of knitting or of reading.

[**Continued on page 30** ➤

HOW TO *Tile* YOUR BEDS TO YOUR LAWN

By Alfred C. Hottes

Associate Editor, Better Homes & Gardens

NEATNESS is one of the prime requisites of a good garden, and whether the beds are formal or informal it's very often desirable to edge them in some way to emphasize either the straight lines or graceful curves. We can edge the beds by merely cutting the sod to a neat line with an edging tool or a flat spade. Some persons even use a butcher knife or mason's trowel to tidy the edges.

Metal. Strips of sheet metal imbedded in the soil will last for a number of years and are particularly useful in edging paths which easily break down and become shabby. The use of wooden strips instead of metal is often a little too showy.

Tile, Bricks, or Rocks. Because of the expense of metal, we may use flat tile, bricks, or stratified rock, but it isn't wise to use the more or less globular cobblestones because they don't merge into the planting, but remain as individual conspicuous accents. Furthermore, it is very difficult to trim stray grass between such rounded stones.

Plants. Plant material may also be used for edging. Perhaps the most popular of annuals are the Sweet Alyssum, with its white flower, and the dwarf form of Ageratum in blue, in white, and in pink.

Among perennials the Carpathian Harebell is particularly useful, but I believe that my favorite edging plant is the Blue Fescue Grass (*Festuca glauca*) because it has no desire to stray from its original position. Dwarf iris, pinks, primroses, stonecrops, and Veronicas are used. One of the best, however, is a rather shrubby perennial known as Germander (*Teucrium chamaedrys*). It has tiny glossy leaves, a compact growth, and small purple flowers. For the front of shrubs in dry spots, the Goutweed (Aegopodium), with its green and white leaves, is popular.

For a hedge. Dwarf Boxwood, Box Barberry, Baby Cranberrybush (*Viburnum opulus nanum*), and Baby Wintercreeper (*Euonymus radicans minima*) are particularly popular for the closely clipped low edgings which can be kept from 8 to 12 inches tall. Such hedges take a great deal of care to keep them in close-cropped neatness.

In the semi-wild places, of course, it is undesirable to edge the beds either with a tool or by the use of any other line of demarcation. It is often desirable to let the sod run directly to the base of the informal shrubs or trees, but where order and primness are desirable, cutting the sod to a neat line will do much to make the garden look well tended.

For edging beds, an edging tool with a flat blade is superior to the spade because of its knifelike sharpness. Make the cut at a slight angle; otherwise the sod edge dries out too rapidly

Neat, compact edging plants shouldn't overflow their bounds and spread widely over the lawn. Many perennials are low growing but few are compact enough for an ideal edging

Low hedges of Dwarf Boxwood, Baby Wintercreeper, Baby Cranberrybush, and Box Barberry make neat, formal edgings but require a great deal of labor to keep them neatly clipped

For a formal, prim edging of grass paths nothing is superior to sheet metal strips deeply imbedded in the soil. They're inconspicuous and neat when set flush with the sod of the lawn

Tiles set on end may be ornamental when unusual kinds are chosen. Or they may serve a practical use only when deeply sunk in the soil. They may be recommended for flower beds

Bricks, placed on end, should be sunk at least half their length to make the edge firm and permanent. Unglazed brick, mellow in tint, is more attractive for garden work

Where there is a slight difference in level the use of stratified rocks is suggested for use along the sides of driveways, walks, or in front of a low terrace. Set rock plants in crevices

BAD. Globular field stones don't make a unified line. Each stone becomes a conspicuous mass in itself. Furthermore, stones are a nuisance when trimming the edge of the lawn

Why Families Leave Home

By Carl Sigman

Illustrations by the Author; Designs by Architect William J. Ward, Jr.

HERE are two *Better Homes & Gardens* cottages designed for families itching to get away from it all, but not so far away that father has to shave in cold water. They're compact as the most modern apartment, complete with showers, refrigerators, and ranges. Into their built-in storage units go books, linens, provisions, fishing gear, luggage, that stuffed owl you shot back in 1928. They're so simple you can build them yourself or trust inexperienced labor. They're adaptable to any background—woods, mountains, or the sea. Adaptable because they're so straightforward and sincere. Roofs aren't half pushed in to imitate a summer cottage in Bavaria or to "catch the picturesque charm of a fairy-tale house." No old wagon wheels or ship's timbers are used in their construction. They don't pretend to be anything other than what they are: clean-cut, personable, low-cost cottages designed for carefree living.

THIS smaller cottage is of the simplest rectangular frame construction, finished with clapboards outside, random-width pine inside. Windows and Dutch doors flanking the big native-stone fireplace, plus a door and eight other windows, send the slightest breeze rollicking thru. The fireplace is double: one hearth opens into the cottage, one onto the terrace. This permits outdoor cooking, and outdoor evenings, when the only sounds are the lapping of water, the thrumming of insects, the crackle of the fire.

DESIGN NO. 1

IN an alcove in one end of the living-room are all the comforts of a modern kitchen. The refrigerator, range, and sink, with storage cabinets above, flanking the window, come as a unit; the whole alcove is curtained off when not in use. To the right, left, and above are closets for supplies, general storage, and the tank that supplies hot water for kitchen, lavatory, and shower. At the opposite end of the living-room is a built-in china cabinet. And just off the living-room, as compact and efficient as the kitchen, are the bedroom and bathroom. In the bedroom are two closets and space for double-deck bunks.

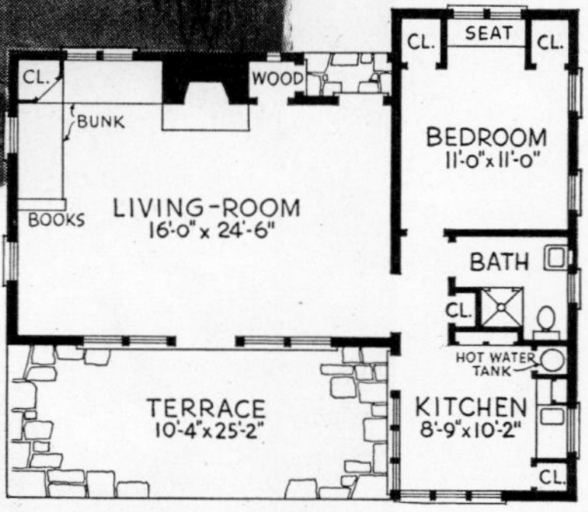

DESIGN NO. 2

LARGER, more imposing than the other, this cottage is still simply constructed of two rectangular units. The right unit houses the bedroom, bathroom, and combination kitchen and dining-room. Even on the sultriest days and nights, when those in towns and cities are swarming to apartment roofs and parks, and the air hangs still and oppressive, this cottage will be breezy and light. Twenty-one windows and four doors make it so. The living-room and kitchen are exposed on three sides, the bedroom on two. The living-room is so big that Butch and the boys can roughhouse in one end while the girls play a few tables of bridge in the other. French doors open from the living-room onto a 25-foot flagstone terrace, and another door opens from the kitchen to the terrace for outdoor dining. For the exterior finish, Architect Ward suggests vertical boards and battens.

THE living-room corner is further evidence ➤ of the compactness and utility of these cottages. Two built-in bunks for guests are sofas by day. Between them is a small bookcase and clothes closet, and beneath is storage space for bedding. Not shown, to the right of the fireplace, is a wood-storage closet that can be loaded from the outside. Kitchen and bathroom equipment is much like that in the other cottage. On the floor plan note the floor-to-ceiling kitchen cabinet and the closet space in the kitchen, hall, and bedroom.

● Each summer thousands of American families fork over whopping big rentals for inconvenient and ugly shacks called cottages or cabins, then spend the following weeks squirting insecticides at the life therein. For less expense in the long run, for something worth leaving home for, they might well consider self-owned cottages as well-designed as these.

Detailed working drawings of summer cottages—all the information you need for building—can be obtained from Better Homes & Gardens for $2 each

FAIRIES LIVE IN THIS GARDEN

By Helen Ramsey Fifield

PHOTOGRAPHS MADE ESPECIALLY FOR BETTER HOMES & GARDENS BY WILL CONNELL

In this garden dwell pink-eared rabbits, gnomes, a fawn, and all the little people of Fairyland. To enter the garden, push open the witch gate, made of crooked branches, and hear the Swiss bell ring

See additional photograph on page 3

Those who first see the garden must read these words, "There are fairies at the bottom of our garden"

DO YOU believe in fairies? I certainly do. Indeed, I'm so sure they exist that I've even made a little home for them in our garden.

It's just a little garden. It has only miniature trees and plants in it. The ground is all covered with soft green moss. In it are a little pool and a fairy river. There are also a fairy ring, a rustic bridge, a pink-eared rabbit, a little birdhouse, a pair of wee love-birds, a red-capped elf, and a lovely white fawn.

These charming little figures add greatly to the feeling of the garden. They don't look out of place as garden figures often do. They're in their natural environment and add charm instead of discord to the spot.

There is a tinkling bell on the gate which rings whenever you or the fairies enter the garden. Little violets and lovely small ferns grow in the corners. All thru the garden there is a host of small worms, many-legged bugs, busy ants, fuzzy caterpillars, short-legged spiders, and fairies! Indeed, it's true that "there are fairies at the bottom of our garden."

BECAUSE this little garden has brought such charm to our outdoors and because its spirit has so completely taken possession of me, I wish to share it with others.

My garden is about 12 feet square. It's built in two levels, formed by a small brick wall, four bricks high. The upper level is about 3 feet wide and serves as the "woods." A little path runs thru the woods and is made of "sand dollars" picked up along the seashore. These "sand dollars" have a peculiar marking on their round, flat shells which look as if fairy feet had lightly stepped upon them in the night. The lower level is about 9 feet square and forms the main part of the garden.

The fairies in our garden at "Copper Harbor," Los Angeles, California, are fortunate, for they have a natural environment as their home. It's secluded under a large Monterey Pine tree and surrounded on one side by English Holly bushes, on another by mockorange, and on the back by a purple wisteria vine which is tied to small, bare trunks of Monterey Cypress trees.

INCLOSING the entire garden is a little rustic fence made of weathered Manzanita branches over which dwarf ivy plants are growing. The fairy gate is made of these branches and the little Swiss bell rings as the gate shuts by its own weight on its wooden hinge. Forming a ceiling over the garden are long sprays of Cecil Brunner roses which have been tied to the branches of the large pine. Standing on the outside of this rustic fence is a black fox which waits patiently his turn to explore the land of fairies but which he has never been permitted to enter.

If you were invited to enter the Fairy Garden you would find many interesting things. The ground cover is of thick Curly Moss. The "Fairy Ring" is made of little stepping-stones, and in the center of the Ring is a dwarf Polystichum Fern. A little white china boat stands ready for a trip on the green glass pond. The yellow primroses, blue bellflowers, and violets add their bit of color to the background. The sweet-faced fawn looks tenderly over to the pink-eared rabbit and seems to say with Rose Flyeman: [*Turn to page 37*

By Arnold M. Davis

DURING the days of early spring ambition, when everyone wants to begin gardening, even on the smallest plot of land, garden questions pop up that need an immediate answer. Time is scarce; the days and weeks slip by too fast.

In anticipation of your questions, I have chosen a few that are timely and most frequently asked, and have answered them.

Caring for the Lawn

Q Should a lawn be burned over in the spring?

A No! Only lawns which have been badly neglected should be burned to remove last season's growth of grass. Normally, the lawn should be raked early in the spring and all foreign material removed. Then, with the lawn mower well oiled and correctly adjusted, the dry grass should be mowed off and the dry clippings raked up. Early burning of grass scorches the roots of grass plants, delays the growth, and is more injurious than neglect.

Q Why and when should a lawn be rolled?

A Lawns are rolled to compact the earth around the roots of the grass plants, thus offsetting frost action, and to smooth out irregularities in the lawn made during the winter. Rolling should be done when the lawn has dried out enough so that it is no longer soft and spongy. Rolling a lawn when the ground is wet will pack it too hard. Be systematic when you roll the lawn. Start from one side and go back and forth over the lawn in strips until the whole area has been rolled.

What to Do About Bulbs

Q When crocus in the lawn bloom the first year but fail to bloom after that, what is wrong?

A Crocus established in the lawn are a mistake unless you are willing to leave the grass unmown around the plants. This gives crocus leaves time to mature and die down naturally. Sometime during the first part of July (or when the crocus leaves are yellowing) these neglected patches of grass can be cut. Any spot where bulbs are naturalized should be allowed to grow as hay until the leaves of bulbs have finished their function of supplying food for next season's flowers. Then the grass can be cut.

Q Should tulips be dug up after they are thru blooming? How should they be cared for?

A I feel that tulips should not be taken up until the leaves begin to wilt and turn a grayish yellow. Take up the bulbs with the leaves and stem attached, if possible. Store them loosely in boxes, preferably kept in the shade, so that the leaves can dry out naturally. Clean the bulbs in August and sort them according to size, ready for October planting. Often, tulips can be left in the same place for several years and they will flower satisfactorily.

Q What treatment do narcissus that fail to bloom require?

A Bulbs which do not bloom usually need to be separated and reset in fertile soil and allowed to grow vigorously for a year or two, after which they will begin to bloom. In some cases, lack of water when the buds are forming will cause them to blast. Lack of food is also credited with doing this and so is disease. Hence, it may be wise to look at the bulbs, and to discard soft or diseased bulbs, or perhaps change to new and better varieties.

Q When planting gladiolus should the shucks be left on?

A If you live where gladiolus thrips is common, and you did not disinfect your corms in storage, by all means remove the shucks and disinfect the corms in any good disinfectant solution. Bichloride of mercury, or corrosive sublimate, is satisfactory and easily obtained. Use at the rate of one part to 1,000 of water, soaking the corms for 20 hours before planting. This will kill any thrips which live over winter on the corms. Corms free from insects and disease can be planted without removing the shucks.

Regarding Peonies

Q Are ants harmful to peony buds, as is often reported?

A No. It's probable that they are beneficial in removing some of the sticky sap common on peony buds, which seals them together. In general, ants found on any plant might indicate the presence of aphids. Ants take a sweet secretion from plant lice. Lice can be controlled with any good contact insecticide.

Q Is there any advantage in dividing peonies?

A Peonies can be divided frequently. However, you will get best results by letting the plants grow in one place for a long time. When this is done, plants which are well fed become large, bloom profusely, and produce magnificent results. I'm opposed to dividing peonies frequently unless you really need more plants.

Fruits and Vegetables

Q Will you suggest a fruit that I could grow on my property?

A You can grow all the strawberries you'll need for table use. A strawberry plant is the potential producer of a quart of good berries during the season. Hence, you can figure roughly how many plants you will need. Strawberries, incidently, can be grown in a flower border if they are used as edging plants. Of course, the ideal way to grow them is in rows.

BETTER FOODS & EQUIPMENT DEPARTMENT • EDITED BY HELEN HOMER

SPRING BREAKFASTS ENTERTAIN and it's fun when April's co-hostess and daffodils nod from a nest of Easter eggs! Add the frills and you've teasing spring menus for company breakfast or brunch. Doff the little extras and they're still a fine set of "good morning" ideas and praise-winners for hungry home folks. Miss something? Then it must be that cup of steaming hot coffee that's most certainly there—but just wouldn't fit into our meal plans.

FRUIT	MAIN DISH	ACCOMPANIMENT	BREAD	NICE TO SERVE
Fresh Rhubarb With Pineapple Cuts	Egg Scramble in Ham Nests on Rusks*	Grape Jelly	Hot Breads	Buttered Asparagus

How to Do: To keep rhubarb's true color and flavor—bake it. Sprinkle with sugar, cover, and bake in slow oven (325°) 1 hour. Chill and add fresh pineapple cuts. For scrambling, put all your eggs in a double boiler. Cooked this way they're moist, fluffy, tender, and digestible. For a late breakfast, serve asparagus.

Table Centerpiece: See "Old Designs for a New Easter," page 25

FRUIT	MAIN DISH	ACCOMPANIMENT	BREAD	NICE TO SERVE
Fruit Compote	Fluffy Omelet Frizzled Dried Beef	Crispy Whole-Wheat Cereal	Melba Toast	Breakfast Cocoa Conserve

How to Do: This is an eye-opener and easy, too. In a sherbet glass radiate cut pineapple spears; fill with chilled fruit cocktail. It's an omelet trick to preheat both the skillet and the lid. Before folding, slash the omelet 1 inch at opposite sides, and fold as it is rolled onto a hot platter. Fry dried beef lightly.

FRUIT	MAIN DISH	ACCOMPANIMENT	BREAD	NICE TO SERVE
Grapefruit With Sliced Strawberries	Poached Eggs in Minced Ham Cups	Fried Hominy	Raisin-Bread Toast	Hot Spiced Peaches

How to Do: Center grapefruit halves with a cluster of sliced strawberries. Use a store gadget for tailor-made poached eggs, but it's kitchen adventure to swirl almost boiling water round and round with a wooden spoon, then slip the egg into the maelstrom. Fry round minced-ham slices until they cup.

FRUIT	MAIN DISH	ACCOMPANIMENT	BREAD	NICE TO SERVE
Tomato Juice	Corn-Bacon Waffles* Honey Butter Sauce*	Pastel Easter Eggs	Toast Strips	Cheese Spread

How to Do: Pastel Easter Eggs: Dilute yellow, pink, and orchid food coloring or dissolve color tablets in cups of hot water. Prepare soft- or hard-cooked eggs, white eggs preferably. Dip into the color solution. Pastel eggs form an Easter rainbow on a crystal plate. Blend cream cheese with crushed pineapple.

FRUIT	MAIN DISH	ACCOMPANIMENT	BREAD	NICE TO SERVE
Orange-Lemon Bracer	April Soufflé* Vienna Sausages	Tossed Cereal	Hot Cross Buns*	Buttered New Peas

How to Do: The juice of half a lemon in a glass of orange juice will rouse any sleepy-head. Let the kiddies toss 2 or 3 kinds of ready-to-eat cereal. Serve with brown sugar or honey. "One-a-penny, Two-a-penny," bake hot cross buns. With scissors snip a cross before baking. Cool and mark cross with icing.

FRUIT	MAIN DISH	ACCOMPANIMENT	BREAD	NICE TO SERVE
Assorted Sliced Fruit Platter	Creamed Ham in Toasted Bread Cases*	Broiled Tomato Halves	No Bread	Hot Ripe Olives

How to Do: You'll sing before breakfast and after too, because there are no pans to do. Toast bread cases, broil tomato halves, and heat olives in their liquid in the oven. This plate is pretty and springy.

FRUIT	MAIN DISH	ACCOMPANIMENT	BREAD	NICE TO SERVE
Mixed Grape and Pineapple Juice	Eggs Individual Broiled Canadian Bacon	Glazed Fruits	Peanut-Butter Muffins	Breakfast Chocolate

How to Do: To brighten breakfast and plain muffins, fill pans one-third full, top with 1 teaspoon peanut butter, cover with remaining batter. There's childish delight when adults find their names printed on shells of 3-minute eggs. Use indelible pencil, print the name, and draw a funny face before cooking.

*Recipes for "So Good Meals" on page 56.

PLANNED FOR Miss Sixteen

By Penelope Hastings

PHOTOGRAPHS BY HEDRICH-BLESSING STUDIO

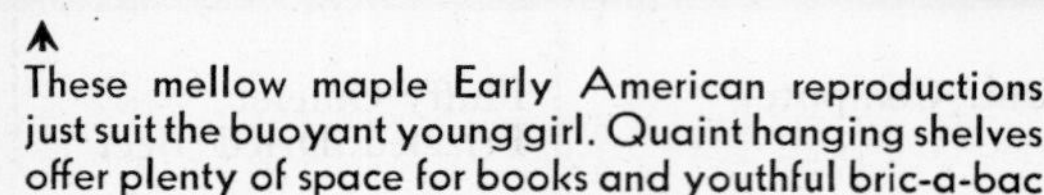

These mellow maple Early American reproductions just suit the buoyant young girl. Quaint hanging shelves offer plenty of space for books and youthful bric-a-bac

It never goes out of style—the chic, draped dressing table for the young daughter's room. And it's even more popular when, like this one, it's well placed, and skirted and topped with the same bright material that's used in the window draperies. A fitting sheet of glass over the dresser top gives the table a practical surface

WALLPAPER, DURAY; BORDER, IMPERIAL; CARPETING, MASLAND; GLASS CURTAINS, SCRANTON; DRAPERIES AND DRESSING-TABLE SKIRT, WAVERLY FABRICS; TRIMMING, MANSURE; FURNITURE, CONANT BALL; MIRROR, PITTSBURGH PLATE GLASS

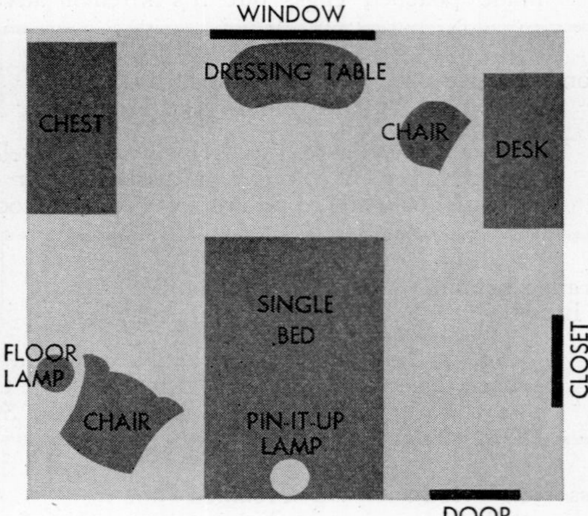

OUR Jean was just 16. Refurnishing her room was our birthday gift to her—and what young lady wouldn't thrill to this charmingly feminine room planned especially for her? Authentic furniture reproductions in mellow maple are lovely against lettuce-green washable wallpaper all scattered with white dots. For trimming there's a deep green ivy wallpaper border running around the sloping ceiling, the windows, doors, and baseboard. White was chosen for the woodwork, green for the simple floor-covering. Filmy net glass curtains flutter behind draperies of machine-quilted glazed chintz trimmed with white cotton fringe. The little skirt on the dressing table matches the draperies, and the gay note is caught up again in the white and red spread on the bed.

[See page 23 for suggestions for a boy's room]

Egg and Bacon Souffle Fry ¼ cup finely diced bacon until light brown. Brush 3 slices bread with bacon drippings; cut slice in small pieces to fit deep casserole; arrange in layers, sprinkling each with bacon. Combine 3 slightly beaten eggs, 1 cup milk, ½ teaspoon salt, ¼ teaspoon mustard, ¼ teaspoon paprika; pour over bread. Bake in moderate oven (350°) until puffy and mixture doesn't adhere to inserted knife, about 45 minutes. Serves 4.—*Mrs. F. A. Collins*, East Orange, New Jersey.

Egg Shortcake Sift 2 cups flour, ½ teaspoon salt, 4 teaspoons baking powder; cut in 4 tablespoons shortening; add 1 cup grated cheese, 1 beaten egg, ½ cup milk. Roll ½ inch thick on lightly floured surface; cut in squares or in rings; bake in hot oven (400°) 20 minutes. Split; serve with **Egg Sauce:** Make cream sauce of 3 tablespoons butter, 4 tablespoons flour, 2 cups milk. Add ½ teaspoon salt, 1/16 teaspoon red pepper, 1 tablespoon minced parsley, 6 chopped, hard-cooked eggs. Serves 6.—*Sidney Margaret Gardiner*, Topeka, Kansas.

For a luncheon serve Egg Shortcake with asparagus garnished with red pimiento, pickled peach, and hot chocolate.

Scrambled Surprise Beat 4 eggs; add 4 tablespoons milk, ½ teaspoon salt, ⅛ teaspoon pepper, ½ cup cooked, mashed carrots. Melt 1 tablespoon butter in double boiler; add egg mixture; stir until firm but not dry; garnish with watercress. Serves 4.—*Laura Frymute*, Somerset, Ohio.

For a child's lunch—Scrambled Surprise, apple-cabbage slaw, peanut cookies.

COOKS' ROUND TABLE

REG. U. S. PAT. OFF.

of Endorsed Recipes

Chocolate Cakes

FIDELIS HARRER

Grandma's Chocolate Cake

Heat 1 cup brown sugar, ½ cup milk, and 3 ounces grated, unsweetened chocolate in double boiler until chocolate melts. Cool. Cream ½ cup shortening and 1 cup brown sugar; add 3 beaten eggs; beat thoroly. Add alternately with ½ cup milk, 2 cups flour sifted with ¼ teaspoon salt, 1 teaspoon soda. Add chocolate mixture, 1 teaspoon vanilla extract; beat. Bake in two 9-inch pans in moderate oven (350°) 30 minutes. **Chocolate Frosting:** Combine 2 egg whites, 1½ cups sugar, 5 tablespoons water, 1 tablespoon light corn sirup in double boiler. Cook and beat 7 minutes; add 1 teaspoon vanilla extract; cool. Gently stir in 2½ ounces melted, unsweetened chocolate.—*Mrs. Irving Valentine, Sr.*, Erie, Pennsylvania.

Chocolate Dessert Cake Add gradually ¾ cup sugar to 4 stiff-beaten egg whites; fold in 4 well-beaten egg yolks; add 6 tablespoons cake flour sifted with ¼ teaspoon salt and ½ teaspoon baking powder; fold in 2 ounces melted, unsweetened chocolate, 1 teaspoon vanilla extract. Spread thinly in 11- by 16-inch pan lined with wax paper. Bake in hot oven (400°) 15 minutes. Turn out on cloth sprinkled with confectioners' sugar; trim edges. Remove paper; cool; cut in quarters. Spread 3 quarters with ¾ cup flavored whipped cream. Stack; top with plain layer; match edges. Spread top and sides with **Hungarian Chocolate Frosting:** Melt 2 ounces unsweetened chocolate in double boiler; add ½ cup confectioners' sugar, 1 tablespoon hot water; blend. Add 1 egg; beat; add 3 tablespoons butter.—*Mrs. E. H. Smith*, Dallas, Texas.

Oatmeal Chocolate Cake Cream ⅓ cup shortening and 1½ cups sugar; add 2 well-beaten eggs, 1 teaspoon vanilla extract; beat. Sift 1 cup flour, ½ teaspoon salt, 1 teaspoon soda, ⅓ cup cocoa. Add alternately with 1 cup buttermilk. Add 2 cups rolled oats, ½ cup chopped nut meats. Bake in 9- by 13-inch pan in moderate oven (350°) 35 minutes. **Peanut Butter Frosting:** Blend 3 tablespoons peanut butter, ¼ cup cream, 1 teaspoon vanilla extract; add ¾ cup sifted confectioners' sugar.—*Mrs. H. S. Gailey*, Collyer, Kansas.

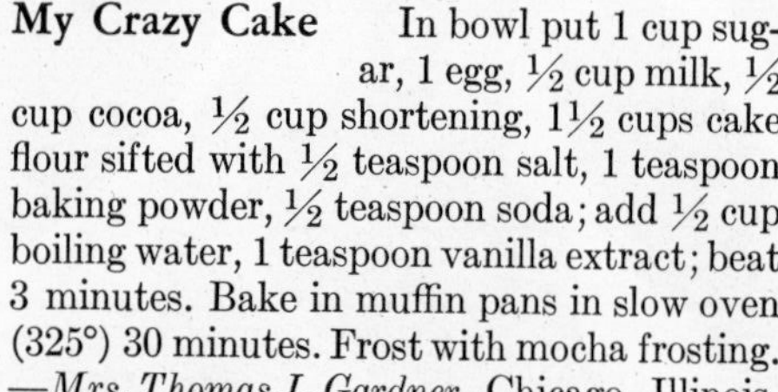

My Crazy Cake In bowl put 1 cup sugar, 1 egg, ½ cup milk, ½ cup cocoa, ½ cup shortening, 1½ cups cake flour sifted with ½ teaspoon salt, 1 teaspoon baking powder, ½ teaspoon soda; add ½ cup boiling water, 1 teaspoon vanilla extract; beat 3 minutes. Bake in muffin pans in slow oven (325°) 30 minutes. Frost with mocha frosting. —*Mrs. Thomas J. Gardner*, Chicago, Illinois.

COOKS' ROUND TABLE

REG. U. S. PAT. OFF.

of Endorsed Recipes

Egg Dishes

Fluffy Omelet Tomato Sauce

Beat 5 egg yolks until thick and lemon colored; add 5 tablespoons tomato juice, ¾ teaspoon salt; carefully fold in 5 stiff-beaten egg whites. Melt 1 tablespoon butter in heavy skillet. Pour in omelet; spread evenly; cover with heated skillet lid. Cook over very low heat 15 minutes. Crease thru center; fold. Serve with tomato sauce between layers and around omelet. **Tomato Sauce:** Combine 2¼ cups tomatoes, 2 tablespoons quick-cooking tapioca, ½ teaspoon salt in double boiler. Cook 15 minutes; add ½ cup diced cheese; cook until cheese melts. Serves 6.—*Mrs. Jeanette Pressley*, Long Beach, California.

Note: Use 1 No. 2 can tomatoes for sauce, reserving 5 tablespoons juice for omelet. For breakfast serve chilled canned figs, ready-to-eat cereal, Fluffy Omelet With Tomato Sauce, bacon muffins, milk, and coffee.

TOMMY'S ROOM IS Washable

← For Tommy a comfortable couch-bed and drop-leaf table with drawers. BELOW: No matter if feet are on the bed-cover, it's washable. See page 34 for suggestions for an attractive girl's room]

THIS ROOM DECORATED BY MARSHALL FIELD & COMPANY

CURTAINS, SLIP-COVERS, RUG—FIELDCREST; WALLPAPER—IMPERIAL; PHOTOGRAPHS BY HEDRICH-BLESSING STUDIO

By Helen Brooke

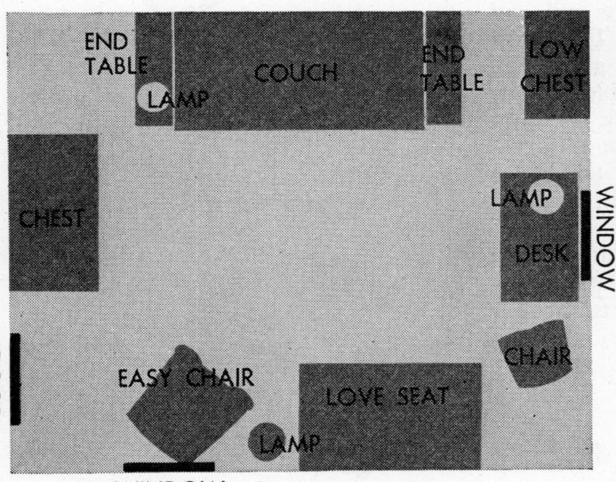

"TOMMY! Get your feet off that bed, and don't spatter the ink!"

Such parental explosions no longer spoil the good times of this young man. Everything in his room is washable!

First there's the masculine bedroom suite with none of those silly feminine gewgaws a fellow's always falling over. The pieces are unfinished Modern, shellacked and waxed, but they could be painted or stained any color. Either way, they're washable with soap and water. That gaily striped bedspread and all the upholstery in the room come off to be laundered, as do the zip-up slip-covers on the armchair. Even the carpet can be sponged with a good carpet cleaner to keep it fresh and clean.

Smudges shouldn't matter on the washable wallpaper which covers three sides of the room. The fourth wall is a thin sheet of cork—the grandest set-up for dart games, map-tacking, and such. The lamps (both built according to Illuminating Engineering Society specifications, with switches for low, medium, or strong light) boast parchment shades, easily wiped clean with a moist cloth.

A GOOD deal of ingenuity went into Tommy's bed. The head and foot are two long end-tables, with two open-end bookcases at the back corners. Behind the big, loose cushions is a chest for bedding and pillows. The bed base, which slides back under the bedding chest, fits flush against the wall. The small chest in the corner beneath the map does admirably for a seat and at the same time houses toys, shoes, and what not.

Result—the perfect room for the real boy.

First Aid to Turf

By Frank J. McGregor

YOUR lawn can be damaged at any season of the year, even when it's snow-covered. Have you been careless about it during the winter by backing the family car over the edges? If you have, you'll discover this spring that some repair work is necessary.

Rutted turf can be brought back to the proper level by using two broad-tined spading forks. Two people should work together. Each one thrusts his fork into opposite sides of the rut, and then pulls the handle away from the rut. This loosens the soil below and raises the turf to its normal position. Then pull out the forks and continue the process along the entire length of the depression.

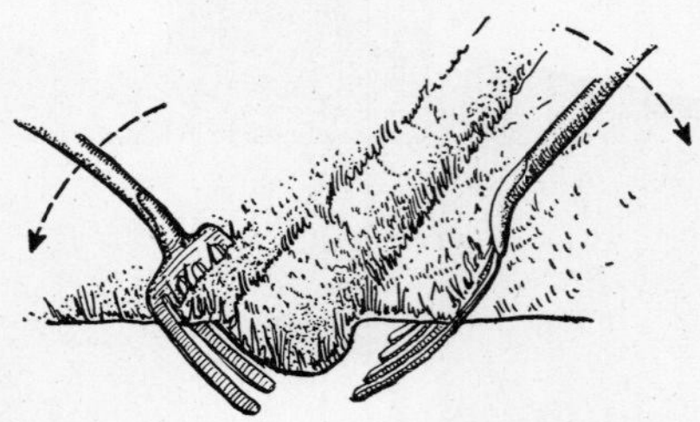

Raise ruts in turf with spading forks

Badly chewed-up turf may be beyond repair. Some people make a practice of filling in ruts or damaged sections of the lawn with new soil and sowing grass seed on top. This isn't advisable because the new grass will invariably be a light green color and of softer growth, and will mark the spot where the repairing was done all summer long. Furthermore, if the layer of new soil is shallow, it will dry out quickly, forming a crust.

Therefore, badly rutted turf should be removed. By stretching string between stakes and by using a turf-edger the damaged grass can be rolled out in strips with a spade. Loosen the soil below and replace the old turf with new turf of the same kind as the rest of the lawn. Tamp it down with the back of the shovel or by laying a board over it and walking on it, and water well.

New grass in ruts stays light colored

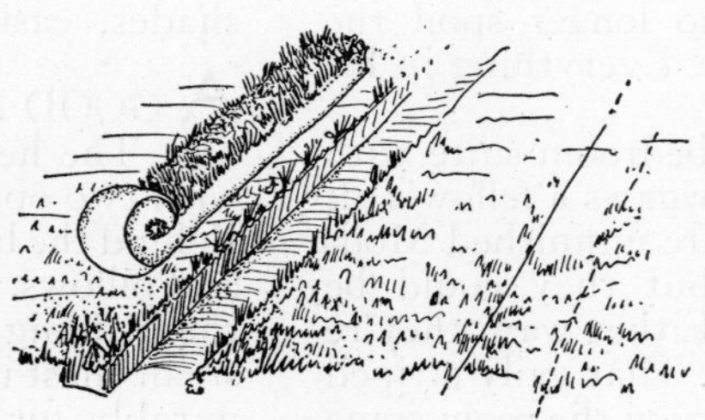

Lift out damaged turf in strips and put in good sod of the same kind

It's possible to fill in a shallow rut gradually by putting on thin layers of soil every few months or as soon as the grass grows thru. Scatter soil over the spot, rake it in between the grass plants, and repeat when the turf has grown thru the soil.

If you edge your walks and driveways with a turf cutter or edger to make them straight or even, the raw edge you leave exposes grass roots to the drying summer wind and sun. To overcome this, remove a slice of soil from under the turf with a spade. This done, the grass can be brought down to the walk or drive level. Then gently roll the turf, and water well for 10 days until the grass roots become established.

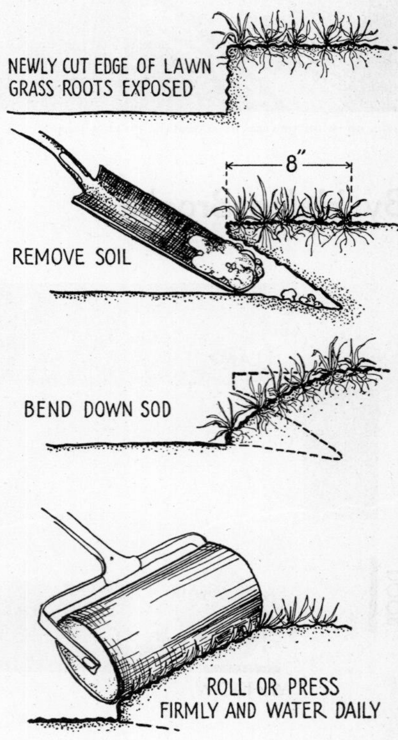

ILLUSTRATIONS BY GRETCHEN HARSHBARGER

After winter, lawns need raking to remove debris and dead grass. You can use an iron rake, but don't rip out the grass roots. Early spring feeding with a balanced plant food thickens the turf and so chokes out the weeds. Peatmoss gives the grass a rooting medium. Where the grass is thin, stir the soil with a rake as soon as it's dry enough to work and scatter fresh seed. Roll the surface or tamp it with a shovel or board to firm the soil over the seed.

OLD DESIGNS FOR A New Easter

By. Christel Huttenlocher

TO ANCIENT races the egg was symbolic of new life and of the new year—an occasion celebrated in the spring which became the Easter festival of Christian peoples. Many of the customs of the old celebration became associated with the new, and today in middle Europe you will find Easter eggs decorated with the designs of the ancient Persians.

THE SIMPLEST of the old designs use flower forms to symbolize new life on earth. Put the hard-cooked or blown egg on a folded cloth to keep it from rolling about. On each half outline the design and border (see picture) with a hard pencil, drawing the flower freehand and tracing the border round a small scallop cut out of stiff paper. Here you'll need a steady hand. Leave the lily white. Use water colors for dark green leaves, black outlines and background, and for yellow and fuchsia. Combine black, white, and yellow in border. When using pastel colors it is best to select white-shelled eggs.

YOU WILL FIND this purely geometric design either more difficult or simpler to do, depending upon your ability to make accurate measurements on an oval surface and the steadiness of your hand in the fine brush work. Try your colors on paper first, remembering that large black areas will accent them beautifully. You may enjoy creating your designs by cutting folded paper with very sharp scissors, unfolding, placing it over the egg, and tracing stencil fashion.

IN THIS GEOMETRIC design the flower forms are still evident altho the symbolism and the design are more complicated. Straight paper edges, a compass and cut-out scallops will help with the pencil outlines. The Persians used dyes made from berries and roots in yellows, orange, and bricky reds; and the royal purple from a sea mollusk. Combine several colors for the design, with black for the larger areas.

THE Question BEFORE THE HOUSE

A department of answers to building and remodeling questions you ask us

By J. F. Carter

JOHNS-MANVILLE CORPORATION

Asbestos-shingle siding is good-looking, economical. See "Popularity Deserved," at left, above

Popularity Deserved

We're going to remodel, and have considered shingling the exterior walls of our house. Is this asbestos-shingle siding a good bet?

For finishing the exterior of either new or old houses, asbestos shingles are both economical and permanent. Perhaps that accounts for their growing popularity everywhere. They're easily applied over any type of finish on houses being remodeled (see picture at right), and the improvement in appearance is notable. A number of asbestos building-material manufacturers are producing these shingles.

Will Knotty Pine Cup?

Our builder says knotty pine boards for interior walls will cup and perhaps crack open. Does this always occur?

Cupping is caused by shrinkage of boards. If the boards are thoroly kiln-dried and are actually kept dry until nailed into the job, they won't crack or cup. However, mere placing of an order for kiln-dried boards isn't sufficient. See that they're delivered dry and kept dry. Almost every lumber retailer has means of measuring the moisture content of lumber.

To Waterproof Concrete Basement

How should I go about waterproofing a concrete basement?

The "membrane" method is effective. Sheets of waterproof material are stuck to the outside of the walls with asphalt, pitch, or similar adhesive. For best protection the membrane is stuck to the top of the concrete footing before the wall is poured, and the part that extends outside is lapped over the wall-covering. Various types of felt, cloth, and other fabrics are used as membranes. Copper so thin it weighs only two ounces a square foot is now available in rolls. This makes an excellent waterproofing material; it's strong, rustproof, and only slightly more expensive than other materials. Two layers are used, bound with pitch or asphalt.

Termite Insurance

When building a new home, is it necessary to guard against termite attack? If so, how?

Termite protection is good insurance. In new construction cut off all avenues of entry with sheet-copper shields. Authorities agree that such structural methods of control as this, which introduce actual barriers, are best because they're sure and permanent. Be sure the shields are properly designed and sufficiently thick to hold their shape, and are installed by a competent man.

Clinkers in Stoker?

We're considering installation of a stoker but are worried about clinkers. How much of a nuisance are they?

It's the unburned residue of bituminous coal that fuses into clinkers. Burning a hopperful of coal will usually leave about a bucketful of clinkers, each about the size of a man's fist. Clinkers are removed with tongs every day or two; the operation takes only two or three minutes. Anthracite coal doesn't clinker, leaves behind a powdery ash which, in most anthracite stokers, is automatically conveyed to cans.

Paint for Basement Floors

Is there any paint product especially adapted to use on concrete floors, particularly basement ones?

Concrete basement floors are a problem because of dampness, but one of the leading cement manufacturers has produced a concrete floor coating in which the binder is a rubber derivative. When carefully applied over a thoroly cleaned concrete floor, it becomes a durable and handsome floor covering. It comes in black, white, or any of six colors.

CONVERTED TO *Colonial*

AFTER

For $834 another mongrel turns thorobred—and wins a first in our remodeling contest

HERE'S a striking example of the importance of architectural features to the appearance of a house. A new porch, a couple of dormers, and a roof trim did more for this Greensboro, North Carolina, place than a plastic surgeon and a masseuse can do for a dowager.

The old house was a typical small house of the late twenties. The owners, Mr. and Mrs. Homer R. White, weren't exactly satisfied. So carpenters whacked off two feet of the awkwardly overhanging roof and rebuilt it of stock materials so it extends over only six inches. They set in two dormers and built a new porch with good Colonial detail. And they put on a new roof—using copper valleys and flashings.

Cost of the whole job, which, incidentally, won first prize in Class 2 of *Better Homes & Gardens'* 1937 remodeling contest: $834.

BEFORE

HE ANNEXES THE Attic

Alden I. Clark turned carpenter to escape his havoc-spreading three-year-old

AFTER

BEFORE

WHEN the Clarks' offspring reached the hurricane stage, Handy-man-about-the-house Clark, no carpenter, climbed to his attic and built himself this 12 x 14 studio den. His books and magazines are now safe in three recessed cases, and he can retreat there when the hurricane gets to roaring too much.

From the picture of the old attic, with the storm sash and Rochester pennant in one corner, you gather how useful it was. Now, in the the opposite corner, are Clark's desk, three recessed files, a couple of handy drawers, and a drop shelf for his typewriter. Walls are knotty-pine wainscoting over half inch insulation board, and the ceiling is insulation board. In the small entryway there are clothes and linen closets.

The whole job, without the furniture and draperies, cost $174. And this Rochester, New York, man's good taste won him the $100 first prize in Class 1 of *Better Homes & Gardens'* remodeling contest.

Early-Bird Bargains

No. 19 of a Series of Family Life-Insurance Stories by Ray Giles, Author, "Your Money and Your Life Insurance"

SAYS B. L., father of one son of 20 and another just turned 25:

"Of course I knew that rates for life insurance go up for every year you wait, but it was only last month that some figures startled me into talking the matter over with my boys and deciding that it was worth some sacrifice to get them insured immediately."

B. L. fished from his billfold a scrap of paper carrying important figures. These show that at age 20, any given amount of money—whether $50 or $500—will buy 12 percent more life insurance than the same money will purchase at 25. At 25 every dollar will buy 13 percent more insurance than you can get by the time you're 30. Between 30 and 35 there's another rousing difference of 15 percent in favor of the younger man. And the man of 35 makes his hard-earned dollars go 17 percent further than his brother of 40.

B. L.'S other comments on early birds will interest every person in the twenties as well as every parent.

"By taking insurance five or ten years sooner, Frank and Mason will be assured of much bigger cash values for conversion into life income at 55, 60, or 65. If they need money for unforeseen emergencies they'll be able to borrow larger amounts. This greater borrowing capacity may be a business life-saver at some unexpected crisis, for their insurance will be the best possible collateral for a bank loan.

"If, after their children are grown, they don't need so much insurance and want to stop paying premiums, their cash values will buy much larger amounts of paid-up insurance than they could have gotten from insurance taken later.

"I'm convinced that life insurance begun early develops earlier skill in money management. It helps a young man to grow up financially to participate in these greatest co-operative financial institutions of our times, just as it helps him to grow financially to have a savings bank account or carry a check book. And as an early start is more likely to give the young married man adequate coverage and protection for his family, he's freer to use daring and initiative when opportunity beckons to him in his career."

TO THESE excellent thoughts, I would add another. Many a man of 30 or 40 who can't today secure life insurance because of physical impairment, would have passed the same medical examination with flying colors when he was in his 20's. So if you want to be *sure* of having life insurance when you may need it badly, remember—you can't apply too early.

Miracle

The pink rose grows so full and proud
I'm wondering if maybe
That lovely, tiny, dew kissed bud
Could be the rose's baby.

—Eleanor Scates Smith

Light Where You Need It

[*Begins on page 10*]

7

SWIVEL FLOOR. With its folding arm it reaches out to you with light, whether you're at the new console piano or the near-by wing chair. For a grand or upright you'll want a larger lamp (shown in picture 9) which can be placed also at the left or the right of the keyboard.

8

INDIRECT ILLUMINATOR. Very modern and effective are these simple upturned bowls, a pair of them lending an air of distinction to the dining alcove, gameroom, hall, or even the more formal, candle-lit dining-room. They add needed light without detracting from the beauty of the tapers on the table.

9

SEMI-INDIRECT WITH CANDLES. A good chair, a book, and a pipe call for the best in the lamp line. For reading, this one should be close behind the chair or at one side or the other. It's an ideal floor lamp for placing near davenports and large chairs.

Safe AT HOME BUT Are YOU?

By Estelle H. Ries

ACCIDENTS at home don't just happen. They're caused. This puts a mighty serious indictment on our doorstep, but the ugly truth is that the majority of mishaps, from cuts and bruises to stark tragedies, happen because some household detail has been poorly planned, some dangerous economy practiced, or some piece of equipment left out of order.

We talk a lot about the dangers of the road, but very little about the perils of being at home. Yet within a year 5,000,000 persons are temporarily disabled in home accidents, 150,000 permanently put out of commission, and 39,000 killed. A safety survey recently estimated that this year, in nearly 30,000 homes, a life would be snuffed out because of household carelessness.

"... elusive cake of soap somewhere underfoot"

Are you interested in being the next victim?

First there's the matter of sure footing. Nearly half of the more serious household accidents occur because of falls. Yet there are few of them that couldn't have been avoided. Too little light or none at all, especially at the head and foot of stairs, above porch steps, or in cellarways, gives you a good opportunity to break your neck. Or if it's only a couple of legs, your doctor won't object, for the average stair fall has been figured at $132. For probably no more than $5 you could have installed an outlet with a proper light.

Your son may brand you "spoil sport," but don't let that keep you from anointing your walk, steps, and driveway generously with sand, gravel, or ashes with the first icy weather and repeating the job whenever needed. The sidewalk in front of your house is a public thorofare, and you should keep it safe.

Or you can join the parade and fall down in your bathtub. Over 120,000 people do it every year, which is also a good thing for the doctors and undertakers. Obviously a soap dish attached to the wall or tub is a lot safer place for the elusive cake than somewhere underfoot. If you're clever enough to slip in a tub or shower without soap, get a vacuum mat to stand on—and be sure it's not one which also slips just when you've one leg in the air. A firm handrail is a good safety device to assist large, heavy people in rising.

"... silly habit of climbing on unsteady chairs"

The embarrassed swain who slips on the hall rug and lands at his lady's feet may make good copy for the short story, but it's no joke when it's your own spinal column that's been injured for life. Small, nimble rugs on polished floors and curled edges or worn spots that catch heels and toes have no excuse whatsoever. Mend the breaks, weight the edges, and introduce under every small rug a non-skid pad of cork to hold it stationary.

Even when there are no rugs, falls happen every day because of overheavy waxing and insufficient polishing of the floor. It doesn't look or wear any better, it walks off on the nearest carpet, and it makes a hurriedly taken corner a real menace.

"... embarrassed swain who lands at his lady's feet"

If you're one of those who believe children should be allowed to manage themselves and their possessions without interference, you'll change your mind the first time you slip on Junior's skates at the top of the stairs and go rocketing down to the tune of a tidy hospital bill. Orderliness is a safety rule you can't afford to ignore. Objects left in unexpected places and things parked at the head or foot of stairs to be taken care of later are just plain dangerous.

The silly habit of climbing on unsteady chairs and [*Turn to page 43*

This spring I'm sneaking out into the b. w.'s garden again to plant a row of corn, as I did the spring we were married, and pretend when it comes up that it's a new kind of lily. I'll bet she falls for it all over again.

\+ + +

After-dinner reverie of a million husbands: "If food were as appetizing as the colored pictures of it in the magazines; we'd all weigh 200 pounds; so heaven forbid."

\+ + +

My whimsical neighbor to the north vows that he's always happier in May if he relies on garden magazines and gossip over the garden gate instead of news dispatches for tidings of fundamental importance.

\+ + +

At the age of seven the b. g. has skipped half a grade in school, and her parents are putting on a few airs; this may turn out to be an intellectual family after all.

\+ + +

By this time the WPA has become an established and honorable part of the government service, something like the Army and the Navy, and some of the spring brides and bridegrooms ought to walk out from their nuptials under an archway of spades and pickaxes.

\+ + +

As the winter ended it dawned on me that we've been buying our heater oil from the same gentleman who sold us the heating plant, and I can't help but wonder (as I study the fuel bills) whether that isn't like patronizing a doctor who's also in the undertaking business!

\+ + +

What, after all, puts a damper on romance so completely as to have a wife wander into the bathroom while her husband is using dental floss on his teeth?

\+ + +

We think we're going to like our new neighbor. . . . When we moved in she brought in the phone numbers of her grocer, laundry, baker, milkman, yardman, shoe shop, and flower store; in fact, the fruit of years of research.

\+ + +

A dozen American men and women have been married to seven or more spouses. . . . Luckily, they never had time enough to get so familiar with the name of one to run the risk of calling a later mate by the wrong name at the wrong time.

\+ + +

Every time I hear some of the more inane palaver on the radio I add another quarter to the fund for my automatic phonograph, so some day I can listen to a dozen of my favorite tunes without interruption by somebody's nickel-plated sales personality. Without changing records—and without dialing.

\+ + +

A good time to diet, of course, is when the cost of living is advancing 30 percent while your salary advances only 10 percent; then the pain is virtually cut in half.

\+ + +

Upon moving halfway across the country, we discover that the cost of transporting our furniture to our new home is only about $5 less than the furniture is worth—if you include its sentimental value.

\+ + +

When I lived in my own house I could drive a nail fairly straight . . . But now halfway thru the hammer stroke I remember "This isn't my house!" and the result is a hook or a slice.

\+ + +

"Another objection to hiring a pretty housemaid," complains Phyllis Gowan, "is that you have to find a relative to stay with your baby on her extra nights out, and then you run into her at the same restaurants and dancing places you go to!"

\+ + +

Charlie McCarthy, of course, isn't the only ventriloquist's dummy on the air; most of the radio comedians are in a certain sense sitting on the knee of some bashful humorist who writes their wisecracks.

ILLUSTRATIONS BY GEORGE CALLAHAN

"Charlie McCarthy, of course, isn't the only ventriloquist's dummy on the air"

As a stern parent, I am slightly outraged when my tot's grandparents are vastly amused by some of his antics that would have brought me a brisk spanking at the same age.

+ + +

Well, it's high time to be moving the porch and terrace furniture outdoors, and certain corners of the interior will acquire that empty look again. . . . Perhaps this summer we'll actually get to a furniture store before autumn brings that furniture indoors once more!

+ + +

"Yes, we met a lot of celebrities down at Washington," muses Les Gowan, "and they all seemed to be ordinary human beings who were wondering how they were doing."

+ + +

In almost every "young married crowd" there seems to be one young wife who's so sisterly to the other girls' husbands that she must sit in their laps occasionally.

"So sisterly to the other girls' husbands she must sit in their laps"

Newlyweds are a little surprised and hurt by the recent assaults against buying on the installment plan. . . . They had supposed that next to a preacher, installment buying was the most important preliminary to married life.

+ + +

The young husband around the corner says that the best food he ever eats at his house are the leftovers the evening after his wife has entertained her bridge club.

+ + +

One American mother in three seems to think that when her daughter becomes a bride, she should keep divorce in mind as a way out . . . Would they want the vow changed to " . . . until death or divorce do us part?"

+ + +

My prosperous neighbor in the next block confides that the only way he can discipline his 14-year-old boy nowadays is by cutting $5 off his weekly allowance or refusing to let him take the car more than five nights a week.

+ + +

Why is it that husband and wife seldom feel more relaxed or closer to each other than immediately after some tedious guests have left?

—HARLAN MILLER

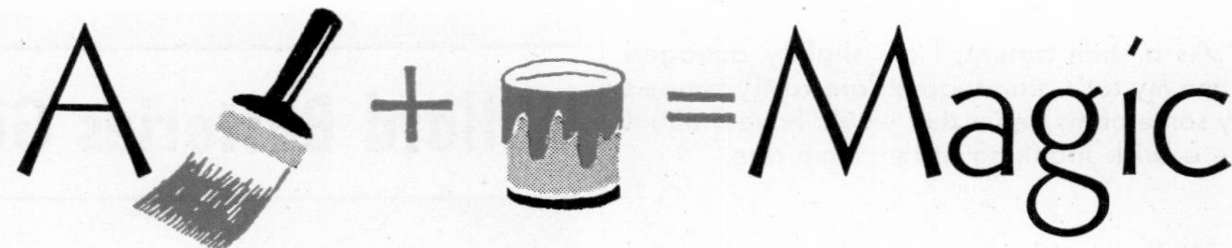

By Jessie S. Pflanz

TO MY mind there's nothing more fascinating, on a rainy afternoon, than playing magician with brush and enamels. An amazing variety of odds and ends can be endowed with new beauty by a few simple brush strokes.

Your brush and broom closet will look ever so orderly and attractive if all the handles of cleaning accessories, hanging neatly in a row, are of one color. And for your utility cupboard, why not a soldierly array of sizable cans for reserve soap powder, starch, steel wool, oiled stove-cloths, and sweeping compound, all painted to match the broom and mop handles?

Then there's that collection of kitchen gadgets, handles chipped.

Resurrection: Stored away in your attic, perhaps you've an odd lamp or an old-fashioned fern-holder finished in once resplendent polychrome, bronze, or paint. Don't you see the possibilities for your front porch or sunroom? A few strokes of your brush —using Chinese red, green, or tan enamel—and back these discarded pieces come into practical service.

And while we're viewing the front porch, haven't you some flower pots covered with faded crêpe paper? Rip it off, hunt up an extra pot for each of them, just a size larger than the one in which your plant is growing, and turn the big ones into colorful jardinieres. Being porous, flower pots require at least two coats of enamel. The idea is, of course, that growing plants should live in porous pots. Your enameled jar thus serves as a camouflage for the pot proper.

Finally, doll carriages, doll beds, and a long list of other "invalids" are just waiting in line to attend your clinic.

More Resurrection: Let's assume that you've several small cans, each containing but a spoonful of paint. Scrape them all into one large can and mix and mix. They'll blend perfectly! Next place a double fold of cheese cloth over the top and strain the mixture in a clean can. If it's still too thick, add turpentine to thin it properly. Mix again. You know, of course, that no matter how many colors you combine, if you add the right amount of black or white to the mixture you'll have a soft, neutral shade of gray, tan, or taupe as a result. And what could be more perfect for the refuse container, watering can, garden-tool handles, and perhaps that bushel basket for the laundry? No paint left now to harden in cans—and all over the house the harmony of fresh new colors.

Gay Stay Our Kitchens: Let's hope the gay reds and yellows now smiling from our little kitchens aren't going out of style. Decorators do seem to be becoming beige-and-brown-minded again, and I shudder to think of the old brown wainscoting coming back.

So why not a compromise? Let's use light beige on the walls; maroon, red, and brick-tile linoleum for the floor; and a lighter beige with red pin stripes for woodwork and furniture. Red canister sets, pot-holders with red binding, and curtains with red dots supply the gay notes.

Sunshine Below Ground: Even basements are going in for color—live, warm tones that seem to bring the riches of sunshine below ground. If you don't incline toward a playroom, what about a modern, sunny laundry? Yellow calcimine walls and burnt-orange cement paint on the floor, shelves edged with orange above the tubs, orange cheese-cloth curtains at the window—these will do wonders to even the darkest corner of the basement. A bright light with a reflector, and a mat or rubber pad to stand on while you work will add to your comfort, while an old table covered with yellow oilcloth to hold your starch basins and dyeing paraphernalia completes the magic. Beige-color dishes will be lovely if you can find one with red poppies and wild grasses patterned all over them. Or use blue or orange in place of red.

Your Garden Tools: Are they always in confusion? Then rig up a rack on which to hang rakes, hoes, and spading fork; a shelf or two for watering cans, trowels, and catalogs. Astonish your furnace room. A fine spring coat of black stove enamel will work annual magic on the cast-iron portions of your furnace, and aluminum paint will spruce up your water tank and pipes. Keep your basement proud of itself and at the same time preserve the life of equipment.

Among Ourselves

The Reeves' fireplace. "We used native fieldstone; chimney is about 7 feet high, draws splendidly. We built a rock wall out from the arbor, plus a built-in woodbox. With the rock floor it makes almost an outdoor room. Our house is on a hilltop overlooking entire town"

THE following was addressed to *Better Homes & Gardens:* "It was with a great deal of pleasure that I have read Gladys Denny Shultz' story on the Quintuplets. It is the best magazine story I have seen on the Toronto Symposium, and the entire theme is excellently handled." It was signed ALLAN ROY DAFOE. Your editors liked that immensely.

The Clifford Pressors of Haddon Heights, New Jersey, are responsible for this delightful reproduction of the Manger pictured on the December cover of BH&G. It was made by Mr. Pressor of prune-box wood from the grocery and figures from the 10-cent store

Mrs. O. B. C., of Battle Creek, Michigan, postscripts about an incident concerning last September's cover, "Our daughter and her husband were expecting a visit from the stork and were happily making plans . . . selecting names seemed difficult . . . when my September copy of *Better Homes & Gardens* came, I saw the color photograph of that adorable child and turned to read concerning it. Thereupon both my mother (now the great-grandmother!) and myself suggested the name Patricia, and when the darling baby came she was called Patricia Louise McB——. . . . Thanks for such a fine magazine, splendid thru and thru."

+ + +

With an expression of thanks for the pictures of outdoor fireplaces which appeared in *Better Homes & Gardens* last June, Mr. & Mrs. Henry Reeve, of Menard, Texas, inclose snapshots of theirs, first of its kind in that community, built as a result of the impression made by the *BH&G* outdoor fireplace feature. Explains Mr. Reeve: "Texas, as you know, is the home of the barbecue, and many have built barbecue pits. Ours is a stove as well. The top is from an old ranch stove; has four removable plates. Midway in firebox is the barbecue grill. Only cost was for firebrick to line the stove, three bags of cement, one of lime, and a dollar at a blacksmith shop for the grill.

"It was my first one—really good fun. Not a soul lent a hand in the work. The only drawback is that after seeing what we accomplished, Mrs. Reeve is flooded with ideas for even more activity on my part." (Right, above)

+ + +

Mrs. Katherine Riehl, Pittsburgh, Pa., spent last summer in Provincetown, Massachusetts. She was pleasantly surprised, she relates, to see looking out at her from last August's *Better Homes & Gardens'* feature on New England, pictures of two houses she lived in while there. . . . "The one on the left with the low roof is known as the Sibley Cottage and is over 100 years old. Mrs. Sibley, now well over 70, was born there and has lived there ever since. The house was moved to its present location many years ago. One of the parlor doors has upper panels shaped like a cross, an old superstition that a door so marked kept the witches away. . . . House on the right, with the arbor, was my home for five weeks. The summer was so fascinating I shall never forget it. As you started downtown in the morning, an artist might be setting up his easel on the corner; when you returned there would be a delightful picture of the sea or the quaint entrance to one of the old houses. Many picturesque shops, different types of people, and the never-ending fascination of the sea makes Provincetown a delightful place indeed."

+ + +

To Mrs. James J. Tynan of Milton, Massachusetts, speaking of how pantries have given way to built-in cabinets and cupboards, the swinging-out cupboard doors are inconvenient when trying to work on the cabinet tops. She points out that to [*Turn to page 63*

WHIMS and HOBBIES

Charles Horace Mayo, youngest of the two famous surgeons who head the great Mayo Clinic, in Rochester, Minnesota, designed a Swedish fireplace for the home of his daughter, Mrs. George T. Trenholm, also of Rochester. The distinctive feature of the fireplace is that the base is built up about a foot above the floor and Mr. and Mrs. Trenholm therefore do not even have to bend their backs to place a log in the fireplace. On his own home grounds, "Doctor Charlie," as he is affectionately known in Rochester, has a herd of deer, both American and Japanese.

▼ ▼ ▼

Cornelia Hopper Terheun, of Hackensack, New Jersey, last survivor in a direct line of one of the first families settling in that vicinity in 1670, owns one of the ancient landmarks of that state. It consists of the house in which she lives, the land surrounding it, and a 600-year-old elm. These have been in the sole possession of the Terheun family for 263 years.

▼ ▼ ▼

Dr. Ella K. Dearborn of Portland, Oregon, has collected 2,560 spoons from all parts of the world; said to be the largest and most valuable collection of its kind.

▼ ▼ ▼

Mrs. H. E. Loring, of Ottumwa, Iowa, expresses interest in the fact that the celebrated Albert Payson Terhune's hobby is not dogs, but collecting famous authentic pieces of old historic armor.

▼ ▼ ▼

If accompanied by satisfactory proof, Better Homes & Gardens will pay $2 each for each Whims and Hobbies paragraph accepted for publication. No entries will be returned.

SAMUEL GOTTSCHO

THE garden fireplace lets you be a woodsman like Dan'l Boone or Kit Carson without getting your white shoes dirty. Pretty handy, we think; all the fun of a picnic without even getting smoke in your face.

Mr. and Mrs. Ritchie Brooks, of West Englewood, New Jersey, think it's handy too. They lugged rocks from a little of everywhere to build this fireplace. The coral came from Bermuda, the ivy from Canterbury Cathedral. Construction was simple. First built was the concrete base. Then the stones were laid on an arched wood form. Rough joints accent the rustic effect. The grate, made by a local blacksmith, is removable. After supper it's taken out and logs put on the charcoal fire, and then friends sit around and reminisce—and what rare and wonderful stories such a setting brings forth.

GARDEN FIREPLACE NO. 11

HAVE YOUR Picnics at Home

GARDEN FIREPLACE NO. 12

Meals in your garden are easy and pleasant with inexpensive home-built fireplaces like the two here

← WITH the spirit of fine bird dogs after quail, the H. L. Weatherbys and their auto trailer went ranging for miles out from their home in Montgomery, Alabama, to gather rocks for this fireplace. So the grille would be conveniently high for cooking, the ash compartment was raised from the ground and the area under it filled with tamped cinders to support the concrete floor.

BEHIND the firebox the Weatherbys built this brick-lined oven for heating rolls and keeping other foods warm while steaks are broiling. An oven rack doubles the capacity. The oven door and rack and the firebox grate came from a Montgomery foundry, and the plate for the oven bottom came from the junk yard. ↓

Detailed building plans for fireplaces are available for 25 cents each. Also available, for 4 cents, is an illustrated leaflet (No. B-J-2) describing 9 garden fireplaces. Address 5904 Meredith Building, Des Moines, Iowa.

Fairies Live in This Garden

[*Begins on page 16*]

"To all kind folk who make delightful gardens
Where we may live
Enjoying days and nights of busy leisure
Amid devices fashioned for our pleasure
Our thanks we give."

TREES in the Fairy Garden are all miniature, none being over one foot high. There are a dwarf yew tree, a dwarf Canary Island Pine (*Pinus canariensis*), an interesting Monkey-Puzzle tree, a dwarf Austrian Pine, and a small Pfitzer Juniper. Small Myrtle bushes are green and attractive in the corners, and Ajuga forms a satisfactory groundcover on the upper level where there is a green glass river with a rustic bridge, homemade from branches of mockorange. Sword Ferns form a high background for the upper level when the wisteria isn't in bloom. Small Maidenhair-Ferns (*Adiantum pedatum*) add daintiness to the "Fairy Woods."

COMING down on its web out of the large pine tree is an old black spider which is the guardian of fairies at night, for concealed in its stomach is an electric light which casts an almost unreal, truly fairy-like, light over the entire Fairyland.

Perhaps you'll get as much satisfaction from a Fairy Garden as I do when the school children visit it with their teachers from time to time. Perhaps you have children in your home and feel the urgent desire to bring into their lives something of the wonder and beauty of Nature and the garden. The stately perennial garden in the rear is a place where these children may not play, for the flowers demand particular care and careful treatment. The rose garden is full of beauty, but it's also full of thorns, and so the allurement there is lessened.

BUT a Fairy Garden! It isn't necessary to have a large space for it. It's within the reach of everyone's space and purse. Here is a place where the children may first experience the wonderment and thrill of a garden. The plants are small and easily cared for in a Fairy Garden so that it may be truly the child's very own. If a doubting adult would but supply the space and plants, any little child could bring a Fairyland of his own into his own backyard!

Fair Warning

You have bad manners, Mister Wind!
I wish you'd please tell me,
When I am so polite to you,
Why do you "boo" at me?

I walk along and never try
To strike or fight with you
Although you pull and jerk my coat
And even push me too.

Some day I shall be grown up tall,
And then you'd better mind
And watch your P's and Q's or I
May be a bit unkind!

—Blanche Lea Walden

WATCH THOSE "Children's Diseases"

They're still top-ranking enemies of childhood, but a few of them are falling before the onslaught of science

By Gladys Denny Shultz

Child Care and Training Director
Better Homes & Gardens

PHOTOGRAPHIC ILLUSTRATIONS, INC.

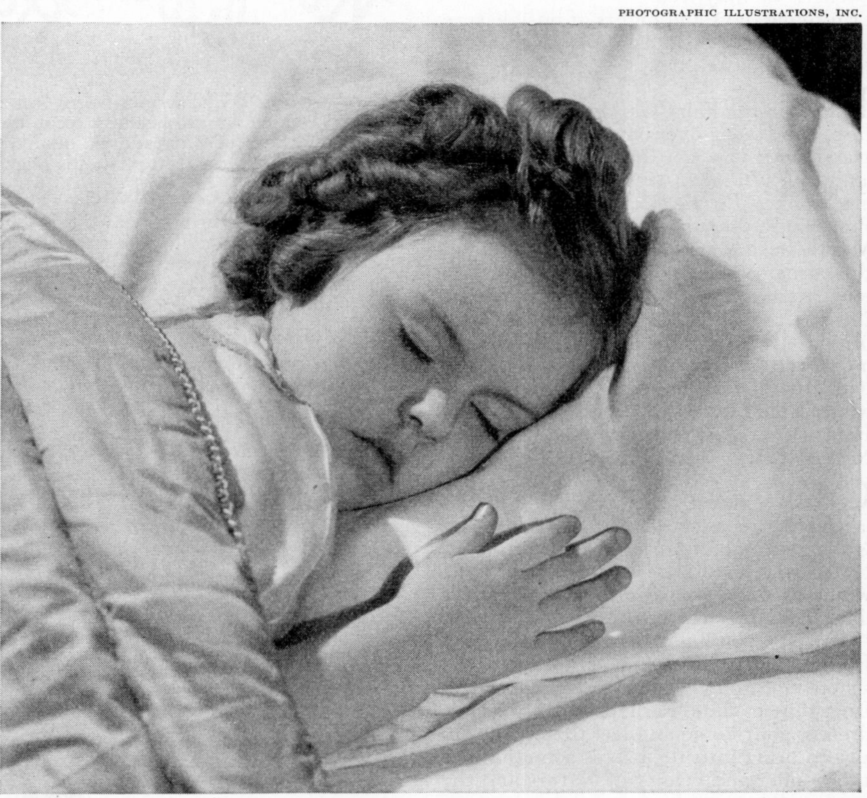

Bedrest and light diet are very important—serums must be given early to be most effective

ALL set for my interview, I arrived at the office of the director of the division of preventable diseases of the state department of health, just as that gentleman was holding a cryptic and rather gory long-distance telephone discourse.

"I'm sorry, Doctor," he was saying, "but we can't send you serum for purely preventive purposes. We can supply it only for patients who actually need it. The epidemic is just starting, and not many potential donors have developed yet.

"By the way, do you have enough donors to hold a bleeding clinic in your town? Splendid! Then you can get plenty of blood to immunize your own people and you'll be helping us as well. Let us know when your potential donors are ready and we'll arrange for the clinic."

Clicking down the receiver, the director caught my puzzled look and laughed a bit wearily. "That ought to be a good start for your story. Let me interpret it for you; then give you a picture of our latest methods for putting the so-called children's diseases out of business."

An epidemic, he explained, was beginning—one of those waves of contagion which attack the child population so regularly that the health department can chart them much as a meteorologist charts the weather.

THE season starts with infantile paralysis, which appears in late summer and vanishes usually with cold weather. It claims comparatively few victims but is more feared than any other disease. Scarlet fever enlivens the holiday season for many families, and whooping cough, measles, chicken pox, and mumps keep seats empty in the lower grades until school closes in the spring.

Thirty years ago diphtheria and smallpox would have headed this list, but the development of permanent immunizations has rendered them almost negligible in communities which respect and carry out preventive measures. Not so with the other diseases. Until quite recently there has seemed nothing to do except to protect children from exposure as long as possible.

New serums have changed all this. Interestingly enough, they're made from human blood, drawn from persons recently recovered from the disease. Hence the name "convalescent serums."

THRU their use, scarlet fever and measles, two diseases which have had a high mortality rate and a bad record of after-effects, can be largely controlled. There's also a vaccine for whooping cough which lessens its severity. The health officer went on to say that undoubtedly chicken pox and mumps could be held in check, too, if they were serious enough to warrant it. Poliomyelitis (infantile paralysis) serum, taken from former sufferers, remains the best weapon developed so far against that infection which differs from the so-called children's diseases in that many people seem naturally immune to it, whereas a large proportion of those exposed to the others contract them.

The idea behind the serum treatment is that there are certain protective substances in the blood of a person recently recovered from one of these diseases. If this blood is injected in time into the veins or muscles of others it will either prevent the illness entirely or at least do away with serious after-effects.

Perhaps this all seems very sober and scientific, but the way in which the se- [*Turn to page 40*

We Parents

How We Cope With Everyday Child-Training Problems

An Open Forum for Mothers and Fathers

Conducted by

Gladys Denny Shultz

BETTER HOMES & GARDENS' CHILD CARE AND TRAINING DIRECTOR

Some mothers put their children in the corner when they cry or sulk. I put mine down in front of a mirror for five minutes. It always works! I also use a mirror to remind them to clean up before coming to the table. It's also placed so they can see themselves while eating, and has done a lot toward improving table manners without spoken corrections.—Mrs. B. E. English, Pasadena, California.

Spotlighting Careers

SOMETIME ago I started for my children a scrapbook entitled "What Shall I Do?" In it I've pasted many magazine articles pertaining to careers. Sometimes I've obtained only typed or penned comments from personal experiences, but the book is rich in help and interest. In this way I hope to guide my children in deciding which lifework they wish to follow and to avoid deciding too late; and my 12-year-old daughter and her companions greatly enjoy the career scrapbook.—*Mrs. R. W. Matthews*, Seattle, Washington.

Children Have Guest Night

IN SPITE of a wildly soaring grocery bill, we use this scheme to keep that divine spark of hospitality which our children have exhibited: One evening of the week each of our three children may invite a guest for dinner. The children do the planning, most of the work, and all the entertaining. We now have one guest evening a week instead of seven, and know how many to plan for it. We have a few quiet evenings to ourselves. Everyone's happy. —*Mrs. F. M. Wood*, Lincoln, Nebraska.

Pride of Possession

SMALL daughter observed the "mine and thine" rule in regard to most things; only when it came to magazines it didn't seem to make any impression upon her. She joyously attacked every new magazine that arrived. But we found a way. Our magazine rack has two sections. I put all my magazines in the rear and her books and old magazines in the front. Now that that part of the rack is hers, she's content to play with the books and articles in her section, leaving ours alone.—*Mrs. Mabel L. Zeisser*, Royal Oak, Michigan.

In Defense of Cutting Up

WE'VE three children and most of our friends have several. When the families dropped in for a visit, all those children with nothing in particular to do were really a problem. So we bought a canvas 4 by 6 feet, half a dozen boxes of colored crayons, small scissors, paste, colored paper, and drawing books. Now when they arrive we spread the canvas on the basement floor or up in the attic, pass around the material, and leave the youngsters to amuse themselves. When they're thru, they fold up the canvas and put it away with the other things in their special box. —*Mrs. Nellie Loper*, Thomson, Georgia.

What! No Crusts?

OUR 5-year-old daughter loves peanut-butter sandwiches, but decidedly doesn't love to eat the crusts. "No," she says, "we'll give them to the blackbirds."

This was nice for the blackbirds, but not very good training for the young lady. So one day I put extra butter and peanut butter on the crusts and rolled each one in a lettuce leaf. They stayed rolled surprisingly well but could have been held even more securely with toothpicks. The crusts now disappear like magic.—*Mrs. K. C. Hague*, Los Angeles, California.

Time-Wasting Corrected

OUR daughter Jane is of average intelligence, quick, capable, and does her tasks well—but *formerly only when we worked together*.

To leave Jane alone with some task was to court failure. It took her too long to clean a room; to get a meal was out of the question. She seemed to have no sense of time. Responsibility bewildered her.

But we determined to overcome this problem and we've succeeded. We simply piled responsibility after responsibility upon her shoulders. If Jane didn't get dressed in time, she was left at home. Nobody hurried her, no one seemed to notice. When she cooked a meal, no one rushed in at the last moment to give her a hand. She was left to do things by herself, and if she had time for her own pleasures and privileges it was because she managed her own work.—*C. M. F.*, Meadow Grove, Nebraska.

A Vocabulary-Builder

ISN'T it a pleasure to hear a child talk who has at his command more than the average child's limited vocabulary? We've hit upon this plan to enlarge our children's vocabularies and keep our conversations above the commonplace.

Father begins: "Children, let us take the word S-M-A-R-T. How many different meanings has this sentence, 'She is a SMART girl'?"

Jean answers quickly, "She is an intelligent girl." Don says, "She's an industrious girl."

[*Turn to page 45*

Watch Those "Children's Diseases"

[*Begins on page 38*]

rums are obtained has a touch of the theatrical, even the bizarre. When an epidemic is raging, you may see in your daily paper an invitation to citizens to attend a "bleeding clinic" at a certain time and place. This is intended for those over 12 years of age who have just had scarlet fever, measles, or infantile paralysis; have had a doctor's care thru it; been reported to the board of health; endured quarantine; and in other ways carried out the rules of the game. They are now willing, in the interests of mankind, to part with some of their blood.

THE potential donor for measles or scarlet fever must be out of quarantine but must have recovered from the disease not more than four months previously. For infantile paralysis, anyone is eligible who has ever had the disease, for the protective substances produced by poliomyelitis are believed to be more lasting than the others. The immunity given by all these serums, however, is of only two or three weeks duration and must be renewed with each epidemic.

Let's suppose that you accept this unusual invitation and come to the bleeding clinic. If your name checks with the list in the department of health and you're in good physical condition, a doctor will drain a cup of your blood into an 8-ounce flask and pay you $5 for it. If you're a very husky specimen, you can give two cups and get $10. I was told that some soldiers at the army post, convalescents from scarlet fever, made a tidy bit of Christmas money in this way. A vigorous person can give blood once a month without ill effect.

BUT it's in the infantile paralysis bleeding clinic that human interest abounds.

"The donors come from all over," explained the health officer, "perhaps even from other states. Often the small sum they receive can't begin to pay their expenses. They're simply drawn by a desire to help others. You may see the lame. Often several have to be helped up on the table, but all are happy because they feel they may be preventing the crippling of someone else."

Your blood, tightly stoppered and chilled, is sent to a serum center along with other containers from your community but it's kept separate thru the entire processing until it's passed the Wasserman and other tests, given to make sure it contains no harmful bacteria. All the blood cells are then removed and only a clear, yellowish liquid remains, about 40 percent of the original bulk. This is incubated, sterilized, a preservative added, filtered, and finally put into vials and kept under refrigeration until needed.

GIVEN as a preventive, the scarlet fever serum can protect 97 percent of all those exposed to the disease. It's taken without discomfort, for being made from human blood there's none of the painful reaction some people receive from serums made with horses' blood.

If the disease has developed, with the characteristic sore throat and rash, within 24 hours after the serum has been injected the throat will be better and the rash disappearing. Best of all, it does away with the after-effects dreaded in scarlet fever, ear complications, and kidney trouble.

MUCH the same results are obtained from measles serum, with the difference that when the child is old enough and strong enough to stand it, he's usually allowed to contract the disease, then given the serum so that he can have a light attack. Thus permanent immunity is gained, an important point, for measles is a disease that people are bound to get as adults if they escape it as children.

Measles serum injected four days after exposure prevents the disease and is a help with babies or children with any chronic condition such as diabetes, tuberculosis, or malnutrition. When my own son, Peter, was two months old and Eleanor got the measles, the doctor took blood directly from her and injected it into the baby, saving him from what might have been a disastrous illness at so tender an age.

If the exposed youngster is strong and past infancy, however, the doctor will likely wait until six or seven days after exposure, when the symptoms have appeared, to give the serum. This immediately lightens the attack.

FOR infantile paralysis, nothing has yet been found which all authorities are satisfied either confers immunity or can be depended upon to do away with the ill effects of the disease. But health authorities do believe that if the poliomyelitis convalescent serum is given before paralysis sets in, serum may in some cases avert the paralysis. The procedure in suspected cases is to drain the spinal fluid, examine it, and if infantile paralysis is found, to inject the serum. Fortunately this serum remains potent much longer than the others and the serum center will have it on hand even at the beginning of an outbreak. Early diagnosis is of the utmost importance, for if paralysis once attacks a victim, little can be done.

Pertussis, the vaccine made from whooping cough patients who have recovered, is not a certain preventive but is believed by many doctors to build up the patient's resistance to the disease and thus make for a lighter attack. It's an excellent plan to give it to an infant or young child who has been exposed, for fatalities in this disease come from their ranks.

SO WIDESPREAD has been the education for vaccination against smallpox that in some states no cases are ever reported. Parents must remember, however, that any relaxing in vigilance would soon bring back this scourge with all its horrors. Every baby should be vaccinated before he's a year old, revaccinated before entering school, and once more between junior and senior high, the health officer says. He guarantees that there'll be no discomfort or scar after one vaccination has taken, providing succeeding ones are properly administered.

Diphtheria immunization has been greatly improved. Toxoid, requiring only one treatment, is given widely in place of toxin-antitoxin which required three. The latter, incidentally, is made now from sheep's blood instead of horses's, which does away with the allergic reaction mentioned before.

Every baby should be immunized against diphtheria [*Turn to next page*

Watch Those "Children's Diseases"

before his first birthday and then be given the Schick test six months later to be sure the treatment has taken.

QUARANTINE is changed, too, from what it used to be. The rules differ in different localities, but in general 21 days from the onset of symptoms is used for scarlet fever and infantile paralysis, and only two weeks for diphtheria, smallpox, and meningitis.

Remember the dismal "pesthouse," calling forth a shudder by its very name, and usually located in some desolate and deserted spot? It has taken on a more gracious aspect, too, and is now called a contagious diseases or isolation hospital. Many of my friends, devoted parents all, have sent their children thither when they caught quarantinable germs. The youngsters had excellent care and a grand time with other convalescents while getting well.

But back to the serums. To be effective they must be given early. That's why it's important, when any epidemic is raging, to get in touch with the doctor at the first sniffle, cough, stomach upset, or throat soreness. He may be able to turn a possibly serious siege into a light session, and keep other members of the family from having the disease at all.

LIGHT diet and bedrest, as long as there's any fever, remain the best treatment when one of the children's diseases has been contracted. If there's a rash or itchy breaking out the doctor has several schemes for making the young patient more comfortable. Ask him about them. He will want you to keep the child warm and quiet and have him engaged only in non-strenuous activities for a while after the fever is gone and the youngster is out of bed. Should the fever hang on or come up again call the doctor at once, for this may be the sign of ear inflammation or one of the other after-effects which must always be watched in children's diseases.

If it's chicken pox or mumps and your child is a husky, the doctor may not even bother to come to the house, but you'll want to be in touch with him just the same. They're tricky, these diseases.

"A Pool Is So Full of a Number of Things!"

GARDEN pools, we're talking about; and in next month's *Better Homes & Gardens* will be a feature on pools and what goes in them. You'll find it absorbing whether your garden has a pool or not.

Safe at Home—But ARE You?

[*Begins on page 31*]

over-reaching from such an insecure base as an open drawer, a wobbly table, or a narrow shelf hardly deserves sympathy. The tumbles that usually result net the medical profession around $300 per spill.

THERE are a great many easy ways to set fire to your clothes, hair, home-furnishings, or your whole house. Try drying your towels or laundry close to a hot stove, if possible with a nice draft whipping them. Reach over a burner or adjust the logs in the fireplace while wearing long flowing sleeves. Get your head down intimately over stove while lighting it. Let the curtains blow gaily over the range burners. Don't bother to see that the candles are firmly planted in their holders or that the holders themselves have substantial bases. Put them in windows where drafts can blow the flame up the curtains, and leave them burning when you depart from the house. Don't bother about metal cans for hot ashes, coals, and oily rags: wooden barrels and baskets will make a fine blaze. Omit the hearth screen and let the embers pop out on rugs, chairs, and people's laps.

OR YOU can start a good fire and spread it by sloshing water on burning fat, tho some timid souls recommend smothering the flames with a metal cover or handfuls of salt. If you don't mind being scorched, clean your stove with a wet cloth while it's still hot. The same sort of fun can be had by starting the furnace, hearth fire, or coal stove with gasoline, hunting for leaks with a match rather than a flashlight, alternating candles and cotton balls on the Christmas tree, or scrubbing silks with inflammable liquids.

Cigarets can always be laid over the edge of shallow ash-trays and allowed to drop off onto the runner or the rug. As a pleasant diversion, practice smoking in bed when you're drowsy—with the number of the fire department somewhere handy. Or get in the naughty habit of striking matches toward you, with the folder open just to show you don't believe in signs. Since children and mice have a liking for matches, you might leave them around handy, tho you'll find some who prefer to put extra kitchen matches away in closed fruit jars or metal boxes.

And then there are the matters of furnaces and electric lighting. If you'd like to be in the market for a new house, don't bother to have your flues and furnace cleaned and your wiring checked each year. Stick to your old, untreated roof shingles and put in new electrical fixtures without official inspection. You'll probably not be able to collect on the insurance, but, after all, what you wanted was a new house.

I think you get the point.

IN CASE of fire—keep your head. A hand fire-extinguisher—one that will do the least damage possible to furnishings—should be a part of the equipment of every home. Know how and when to use it.

Cuts are invariably a matter of carelessness—yours or somebody else's. Wield a knife away from you. Keep all sharp implements in slots in a rack, not jum-

Safe at Home—But ARE You?

bled in a drawer. Hang up your scissors or sheath them. Broken glass, bent pins, and old razor blades don't belong in the waste basket. Put them in a box for discard. Keep pins and such non-digestible things out of your mouth. If you've small children, see to it that the things they can reach, or dislodge, are reasonably sure not to hurt them. Treat guns as tho they were loaded—but make sure that they aren't. Label poison bottles loudly. Put pins in the cork or tie bells on them if you're the kind that gropes in the medicine chest in the dark.

MORE people die every day by mixing electricity and moisture than it's pleasant to contemplate. The bathroom, the kitchen, and the laundry are the danger points. One person with a pain decided an electric vibrator and a hot bath would help. Applying the vibrator while in the tub killed both the pain and the patient. Another woman reached out from the bathtub to turn the electric heater off. She's dead, too. *Never* touch an electrical appliance or a metal light pull while standing in water, on the damp floor, or while your hands or feet are wet or even damp. To protect yourself and others, keep these potential death-dealers out of reach from the tub.

Rule out brass sockets for bathroom, kitchen, and laundry and install porcelain ones instead. Add a length or loop of string to the end of metal pull chains in these places so that the chain will never be touched by damp hands. And remember, even if your hand is moist only from perspiration, it can form a conductor for a fatal charge of electricity. Good electric pads are equipped with rubber cases intended for use, not decoration.

ANOTHER rule important to your health—never touch two electrical fixtures at the same time. Don't pull on a light with one hand while holding an electric iron with the other. Don't attempt to manipulate the toaster and the percolator together.

Defective electric cords can blow fuses and ruin electric equipment even if they happen not to electrocute you at the same time. Make certain before you buy a piece of electrical equipment or a separate cord that the cord is listed as standard by the Underwriters' Laboratories. If a cord becomes frayed, throw it away; don't try to patch it. Replace a burnt-out fuse with a new one. Never court tragedy by inserting pennies in the fuse socket. If cords must run under rugs or thru doorways, buy insulated rubber cords or protect them with insulated guards sold for the purpose. Never hang cords over nails or fasten them to mouldings with uninsulated staples.

Now make a tour of your home, looking for small danger spots. Jagged edges, exposed nails, weak table and chair legs, and sharp or splintered surfaces are things to repair before accidents happen, not afterward.

And finally, since we're all human and therefore have mishaps no matter how careful we try to be, have ready for prompt action a good first-aid kit, a clear head, and a working knowledge of how to use both of them.

We Parents

[*Begins on page 39*]

Marguerite adds, "She's a well-dressed girl."

Little Cecil pipes up, "She's a smart-aleck!"

And so on until someone misses, whereupon it's the turn of the maker of the first sentence to suggest a new word. Perhaps it will be "sharp," "fine," "splendid," "nice." There are so many misused words or words that have various meanings. This game not only improves the vocabulary but keeps the children alert for new words to introduce at the next family session.—*Mrs. May H. McEachern*, Jacksonville, Florida.

They're Young Consumers

EACH year I add to my daughters' allowances enough money to enable them to buy thruout the year some item of their wardrobe. They not only buy it but are responsible for its care and upkeep. For example, Roberta at 8 began buying her handkerchiefs and ironing them. Eleven-year-old Betty is buying her stockings and washing and darning them. By adding an item each year eventually the girls will buy their entire wardrobe. It requires guidance, but it's a most valuable way to teach wise spending, careful selection, and care of clothing.—*Mrs. E. L. Dixon*, Eagle River, Wisconsin.

Trees Get Thirsty, Too

OFTEN a child's fears can be corrected in a simple way. Our little 5-year-old was desperately afraid of rain. Finally, one clear day I took him to the window and asked him, "How do you think the trees, grass, and flowers get drinks of water? You know they get thirsty, just as you do. You can have a glass of water, but they have to ask God for water. Then He sends the rain down to them and they drink and drink."

I never had any more trouble. His fear was gone.—*Roberta Horn*, Horn Springs, Tennessee.

Button! Button!

MY NEIGHBOR'S little girl likes to come over to my house to visit. Since we've no toys, she's often quite a bother. One day I asked her if she would sort the buttons in my sewing-machine drawers. I showed her how to put the very small buttons in one kind of box, the medium-size in another, and the large coat and sweater buttons in a big tin one. Since then I always have some easy task for her to do—arranging the small "gadgets," putting clean papers on shelves, or watering plants. It's fun for her and a big help to me.—*Mrs. Eugene Chrisman*, Scottsbluff, Nebraska.

LETTERS about problems you've met and solved—concerning any age group between 6 months and 18 years—will be welcomed; $3 will be paid for each one accepted for publication. Limit letters to 200 words or less. *No material can be acknowledged or returned.* Address 7404 Meredith Building, Des Moines, Iowa.

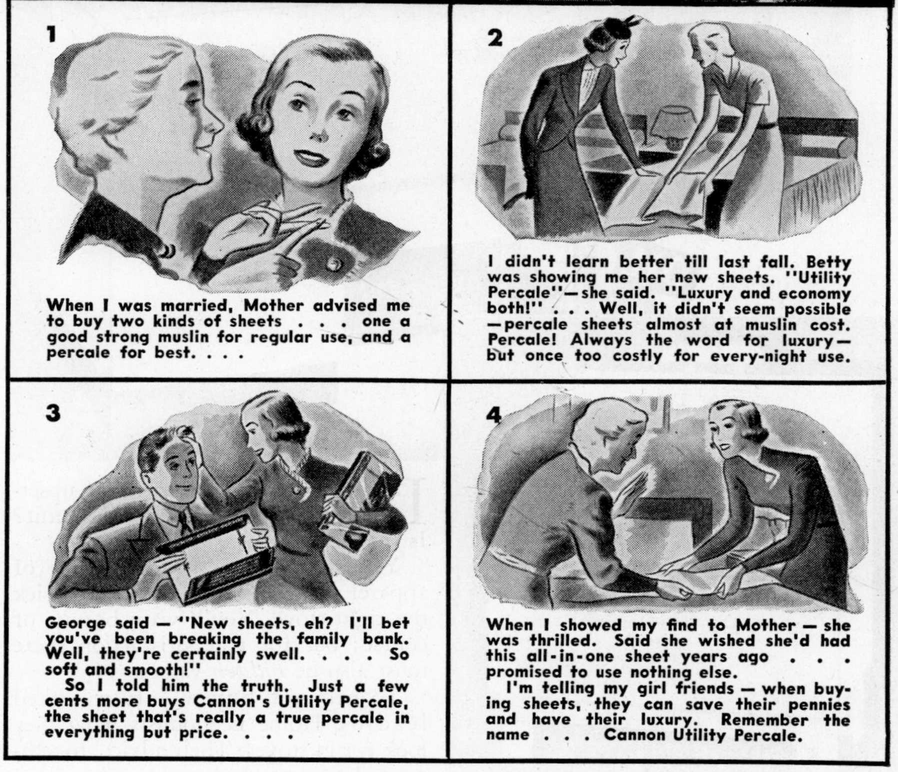

Great-Grandma's Cake Brings Home the Bacon

See Cooks' Round Table of Endorsed Recipes on pages 21 and 22

IT'S REALLY as old as that—the luscious chocolate cake that made off with first place in our recent Chocolate Cake and Egg-Dish Contest! And to Great-Granddaughter, Mrs. Irving Valentine, Sr., of Erie, Pennsylvania, goes top prize of $5 and the honor of authoring our Dish of the Month for April (page 21).

"It's a cake with centuries of history," writes Mrs. Valentine. "First there was Great-Grandma Sherwood serving it after her singing concerts, and Grandma Sherwood feeding it to Grandpa's guests. (He was town mayor.) Then, of course, Mother made it for Dad in their courting days, and all of us seven children have baked it to show off when there was company. And now I suppose our youngsters and their offspring will joyfully carry on the tradition!"

AS FOR the runners-up in the contest, there were plenty—both cakes and egg dishes—that made us lick our judicial lips as we tested and tasted. A few of the best you'll find on pages 21 and 22. Dessert Cake—there's something different. The little walnut-crowned cup cakes are rightly called Crazy Cakes, they're that simple to make. The Oatmeal Chocolate Cake is an everyday favorite. It's a good keeper if given a chance. And that big can of tomatoes lends a fine tang to the Fluffy Omelet. The good cooks who sent them are among the winners on our April Honor Roll which follows.

Honor Roll

Herman F. Ackerman, Candelaria, Nev.
Elah Chapman, Spencer, W. Va.
Mrs. F. A. Collins, East Orange, N. J.
Laura Frymute, Somerset, Ohio
Mrs. H. S. Gailey, Collyer, Kans.
Sidney Margaret Gardiner, Topeka, Kans.
Mrs. Thos. J. Gardner, Chicago, Ill.
Mrs. DeWitt C. Gottry, Pine City, Minn.
Mrs. A. Lane, Nanaimo, B. C., Can.
Theresa M. Lessmeister, Peru, Ill.
Evelyn C. Lien, Volin, S. Dak.
Samela Kay Parkhurst, Seattle, Wash.
Mrs. Harry Petersen, Ames, Iowa
Mrs. E. A. Pickarts, Humboldt, Kans.
Mrs. L. J. Piller, Great Bend, Kans.
Olive May Sickenberger, Okanogan, Wash.
Mrs. E. H. Smith, Dallas, Tex.
Mrs. Walter O. Wallin, Iron Mountain, Mich.
Mrs. E. A. Wise, Cedar Rapids, Iowa
Mrs. Ruth H. Wise, West Terre Haute, Ind.

Presenting—

"The Chocolate Cake Clan"

One of our best families, culinarily speaking, has gathered to make up the Cooks' Round Table News for April. Present are Red Devil Special, Nugget Cake, Old-fashioned Marble, and members favoring variously sour cream, sour milk, sweet milk, and water. For "The Chocolate Cake Clan," send a 3-cent stamp to *Better Homes & Gardens*, 8404 Meredith Building, Des Moines, Iowa.

It's the Kid in Us

—that goes for apples and gingerbread when October starts putting pep in the air. And since we believe in humoring that part of us that stays young—and hungry, our April Cooks' Round Table Contest, with its winners breaking into print next October, is a double-header on Gingerbreads and Apple Desserts. The ever popular apple pie is in order here along with dumplings, applesauce cakes, and puddings; in fact we're out to get all the big apple desserts. To the best will go the Dish-of-the-Month award of $5. Senders of each of the 20 next tempting will win $1 and a place on the Honor Roll of the month.

Remember, $5 is awarded for the recipe that's outstanding in dependability, interest, and downright goodness, and 20 $1 prizes for Honor Roll Winners.

As before, the winners of these 21 prizes, *if they specify in their recipes one or more of the products advertised in this or in the past six issues of Better Homes & Gardens*, will receive a package of each advertised product they mention, the *Better Homes & Gardens* Certificate of Endorsement for framing, and *six copies of the endorsed recipe.*

1. Write your recipe clearly on one side of the paper. Send but one recipe at a time and mark it "October Apple Dessert Recipe" or "October Gingerbread Recipe."
2. Give measurements in *level* cups, tablespoons, and teaspoons, never in heaping or scant measurements.
3. Be sure to specify in your recipe the brand names of the *nationally* known food products you use as ingredients—products available everywhere. We must know them so we can test your recipe with the same brands you use.
4. All recipes submitted become the property of *Better Homes & Gardens.*
5. Contest closes midnight, April 30.
6. Address recipes to 7204 Tasting-Test Kitchen, *Better Homes & Gardens*, Des Moines.

• FOR GARDENING: This sturdy, gay awning-stripe outfit—the same material used in your outdoor chair or glider—keeps you trig. Knee-length apron with two 7-inch pockets, crownless hat, cotton work gloves, and a kneeling pad are all bias-tape bound. [$1.95; The P. R. Mitchell Co., Station B, Cincinnati, O.]—A. J. O.

Potpourri

Dear Editor: I'd like to see these two suggestions developed in some future issue of *Better Homes & Gardens.*

How about some directions for making potpourri or fragrance jars? An interesting hobby and comes right in line with gardening and homemaking. The history of the art, adaptations to the small garden, what the most appropriate flowers are to use, recipes, formulas, all would be appreciated.

Another suggestion! Herb-gardening. Again the history of the art, suitable plans for a small garden, the use of various herbs for the health of an individual, kitchen-tested recipes, all are suggested.—*Mrs. F. W. Traylor, Stanwood, Wash.*

Participated to a Sufficiency

Dear Editor: Have had about enough "We Buy a Puppy." What has that got to do with homes and gardens? The last two issues were very poor.—*Mrs. H. L. Haase, Cedar Rapids, Iowa.*

● **It would be interesting to have comment from other readers. What about it, you dog-lovers? Want more, or less, about dogs?**

For a Big Red Apple

Gentlemen: I very much appreciate your cover for last February. I refer particularly to the fact that while the gentleman in the picture is helping his wife make up the seed order, he is munching a nice red apple. The idea is fine.—*H. L. Mantle, Pres., Ohio Apple Institute, Painesville, O.*

Cheshire Population

Dear Back Talk: By their teeth you shall know them is right! Bravo, Mrs. S. W. P.! [BH&G, Jan. '38, p. 51] It's about time the righteous women's clubs or somebody descended in a body on those advertisers who spread grinning mouths all over their pages. I don't like them glum, but one would think professional models' offspring would be born with permanent grins affixed. Are we to have a descendant population of Cheshires?—*L. W. Boxman, Los Angeles, Calif.*

Cowsheds and Cider

Dear Editor: Heaven help us if we have to live in barns such as that pictured in your January issue, page 38.

Architect Wills apparently is a foremost (sic) architect, but apparently also this was done on "one of those days."

I have a very good theory about the origin. Please check me. Cowsheds in New England are plentiful. So is cider. Double them and what do you get? I mean, double the cider and sometimes it makes one shed seem as two—with rose bushes growing all around.

Ah! An idea. Recipe for a Wills Cape Cod house: Throw two sheds together; fold in a milk-trough. Garnish with roses.

Talk!

Toss in a cranberry bush for the "added touch." Cape Cod, here we come!—*H. B. Wellborn, Brookline, Mass.*

● **Now won't some New England reader tell this fellow where to get off?**

On Grooming

Dear Editor: Why doesn't *Better Homes & Gardens* have a department on good grooming? After our homes and gardens and menus have all reached near perfection, that isn't all of it. Of course, according to psychologists and sociologists, how we look and feel depends much on our environment. Granted. But for a lot of us it takes a little more than a square meal and a good snooze to bring beauty and charm. Frankly, we're a wee bit disappointed to find you completely omitting such a department. Everyone recognizes your authority, dependableness, and timeliness, and certainly any hints and suggestions you could relay to us in such subjects as style (not fashion!), good health, and good grooming would be practiced with equally as much faith as to where to plant the peonies. Do I hear an objection stating that this is a man's magazine, too? All right—he can stand a few suggestions along with the rest of us.

Maybe the Child-Training Director could help me win my point. How about it, Mrs. Shultz? Just as one woman to another, you know.—*Mrs. T. N. G., Ithaca, New York.*

Community Lungs

Editors: A salute to Mr. Righter! [BH&G, Jan. '38, p. 51] And what a grand thing it would be if *Better Homes & Gardens* took the lead in encouraging clubs and other community groups all over the United States to donate and collect money to present their own hospitals with respirators (Iron Lungs) for the use of the communities.

A respirator in every community would save a great many lives now lost as a result of the infantile-paralysis plague.

I learn there's now being introduced in this country, from Sweden, a relatively low-cost "rubber aluminum-lung" which performs the same functions of the expensive iron lung now in use for keeping alive patients whose breathing apparatus is paralyzed by infantile paralysis. This new device utilizes a plate of aluminum which is made to fit the patient's body closely by means of rubber fittings. It covers only the thorax and abdomen. Differences in air pressure within raise and lower the patient's breathing muscles.

Community groups not able to buy the more elaborate apparatus could supply these. Why not start the ball rolling?—*Mrs. Harry Wood, Philadelphia.*

● A splendid suggestion.

They Want Hobbies

Gentlemen: For the last ten or twelve years I've borrowed *Better Homes & Gardens* and read them hungrily. Now I'm a subscriber and proud possessor of your

Back Talk!

perfect cook book. Wish I could let you taste some of my old-fashioned sugar cookies which just came from my oven.

If you want a suggestion for your excellent magazine: We mothers and daddies appreciate busy-work suggestions for boys and girls. Our 9-year old has joined a hobby club. Here's one favorite of hers: A ten-cent ball of variegated wool, woven among the meshes of a five-cent dishcloth. When finished, sew sides together, forming a most attractive bag. Will be anxiously awaiting those pages.—*Mrs. Wm. Rahning, Madeira, Ohio.*

Dear Sirs: There are several articles I'd like to see eliminated. The first of these is "The Man Next Door." Why waste two whole pages of that sort of nonsense and go to the bother of changing type three times to get it printed! I'd far rather see a topic like "Hobbies" treated at considerable length in every issue. Too much emphasis nowadays can't be placed on honest work and play.

If every young girl, boy, man and woman had a hobby there would be fewer crimes. Hobbies are stabilizers. They mean play every day and represent an ideal. Isn't a subject like that, which is conductive to better living and better homemaking, worth consideration?

With "The Man Next Door" I'd like to see "We Buy a Puppy" pass into oblivion.

Usually it's the man next door who owns a puppy which makes his neighbor say, "Dog-gone it, if those dogs don't keep out of my yard I've a notion to poison them all." Why waste pages and printer's ink on how to raise better puppies when that very same space could contain much helpful material written for the betterment of the adolescent child?—*Mrs. J. A. D., Vermillion, South Dakota.*

Liked the Baby

Editors: I resented many of the criticisms of your January issue. That darling baby face on the November cover was to me a great inspiration. I loved it so much I decided to put it in a blue and black frame and hang it in our bathroom.

For the most part I feel *Better Homes & Gardens* is the most constructive family magazine I know of. I have only one criticism. I think *Better Homes & Gardens* is too clean to cater to tobacco interests.

We do not want our American women, mothers especially, threatening the lives of their infants by cigaret smoking.—*Mrs. I. M. S., Camden, New Jersey.*

Suggestion Page

Editorial Dept.: Why not have a "Home-Saving Suggestion" page in your magazine each month; that is, suggested by subscribers? At present you have a page to cover new gadgets on the market, but I see possibilities in a prize page or the like.—*Roy F. Swenson, Worcester, Mass.*

Please address letters of comment and criticism to "Back Talk," *Better Homes & Gardens,* Des Moines, Iowa. Unless requested to use only initials, readers' names will be printed in full. Please confine letters to 150 words or less.

CONFESSIONS
OF GOOD COOKS

● If you're ever in too much of a hurry to roll bread or cracker crumbs for a veal loaf or for hamburg patties, add rolled oats instead. You'll love the fine new flavor!—*Mrs. Mary C. Newman*, Columbus, Ohio.

● Nobody likes "old maids" in his popcorn, so get rid of them this way! Cover the bottom of your wire popper with corn, then drench with water and shake out just before placing over the heat. Every grain will pop, and in a hurry, too.—*Lida Maze*, Los Angeles, California.

● I despise this business of running cracker crumbs around on a plate when rolling croquettes and things in them. Instead, I now turn the cracker meal into a round-bottom bowl. It takes less crumbs and works much faster.—*Mrs. E. M. Ball*, Bloomingdale, New Jersey.

● Bacon is such a messy thing to cut up when you're wanting it in bits for an omelet or waffle batter. I use the kitchen scissors, which do the job speedily, easily, and tidily.—*Mrs. M. J. Beister*, Cleveland Heights, Ohio.

● Just in case you want extra-delicious flavor in your fried chicken, southern style, dip each piece in buttermilk to which has been added a pinch of soda. Then dredge with seasoned flour and fry as usual.—*Mrs. Julian Watters*, Atlanta, Georgia.

● Instead of lining bread pans with wax paper for molding refrigerator cookies, I merely use one-pound butter cartons. They're already paraffin-lined, can be easily unwrapped, and won't stick to the dough.—*Mrs. H. Timmerman*, Grand Rapids, Michigan.

● When juicing lemons for punch for the crowd this is an economy tip worthy of note. It's a hot lemonade from start to finish. Ever try slightly warming the lemons either in the oven or in the double boiler before squeezing them? You'll get about twice as much juice!—*Mrs. Sherman Dickinson*, Columbia, Missouri.

● When I make hamburg patties I roll the seasoned mixture into the right thickness on oiled paper, then cut it into uniform patties with a biscuit cutter.—*Mrs. Eugene Chrisman*, Scottsbluff, Nebraska.

● If you've a moderately hot oven (375°) when you're ready to cook bacon, place the bacon strips on a cake rack over a cake pan or pie plate. Bake in the oven 10 to 15 minutes. The bacon will be deliciously crisp, unsoaked by grease.—*Margaret S. Mosteller*, Los Angeles, California.

● You've certainly made toast and crisped bacon, but have you ever tried combining the two? Use either an electric toasting-and-broiling device or your oven-broiler. Toast the bread on one side, turn, put on thin slices of bacon, then keep turning the bacon until both toast and bacon are delicately browned.—*Mrs. Lucy W. Mitchell*, Mount Claire, New Jersey.

● Baking "company cakes" is easy. While the white frosting on your pet creation is still warm, take a sharp paring knife and shave slivers from a piece of unsweetened chocolate, letting them fall casually over the white top.—*Olive Leeper*, Albert Lea, Minn.

● Our folks think fried green peppers as a garnish for steaks or omelets make a pleasant change from fried onions. Just drop the peppers into boiling water for 5 minutes, drain, take out the seeds, and cut the peppers in lengthwise slices half an inch wide. Cook in fat or salad oil until tender and a little browned.—*Neva Lacey*, Vandalia, Missouri.

● Nothing's worse than a dull food chopper! A good way I've found to sharpen it is to run a piece of sand soap or cake-cleanser thru it. It sharpens and brightens the blades and at the same time removes any grease that may be hiding on them.—*Mrs. R. C. Yeager*, Braddock, Pennsylvania, and *Justine G. Eberhardt*, Dubuque, Iowa.

● If you're the proud possessor of two oven-glass pie plates—and your recipe calls for a "baked pie shell"—you can get a nice, flat, brown one this way: Roll out the crust and press lightly into the first pie plate. Flute the dough, then set the second glass plate into the pastry-lined one and bake. The weight of the top plate keeps the crust from humping and shrinking.—*Esther M. Maugh*, Marine City, Michigan.

● My very shortest short cut is a maple frosting. I simply add maple sirup to confectioners' sugar until it's of spreading consistency, stir in a pinch of salt, and cover the cake with it. It's just as good for a cake filling, too.—*Mrs. William H. Wye, Jr.*, Belmont, Massachusetts.

The Diary of a Plain Dirt Gardener

[*Begins on page 6*]

bloom, they will give me a few days of beauty. But to have a stranger pick them without even waiting to ask whether or not she could! —*—*—* !!

May 14 Another of life's big mistakes is now apparent and I set it down as a warning to other negligent cusses. One of my favorite shrubs is the lilac. Several years ago I planted a number of French hybrid varieties at the back border of the garden. These have made good growth and are now coming into bloom.

When I set them out there was a label on each. I didn't make a planting record in my notebook at the time—make it later, thinks I. Do it in a few days, when I have the notebook out.

Days, months, years went by. The labels have long since dropped off. So I don't know which is which.

This afternoon I learned another lesson. I was trying to get the jump on Saturday by mowing some of the lawn. Out came David.

"Daddy, let's play horse and I'll pull the lawn mower," said he. I thought he would be just a bother but a little fellow has to have some fun. So we found a piece of light rope about 10 feet long, fastened it onto the middle of the mower, and he pulled on it as I pushed.

And would you believe it—that little bit of extra pull made all the difference in the world in getting that mower thru the tough grass. Donald saw and out he came, wanting to do it too. So the boys teamed

"Flowering Dogwood spread before us"

up. It was play to them and a great blessing to me. But I'll bet that when I ask them to do it next time, I won't get a bit of encouragement from either of them.

May 15 Saturday, and I got out my arsenal of pruning and clipping shears and took to pruning the shrubs. Now I know that all those bright chappies who write the garden books and the articles in the garden magazines always get this pruning done on a warm day in March. But a plain dirt gardener gets it done when he can. Also, by waiting until the shrubs are out in leaf, I can more easily see which is dead wood.

So one thing I did was to take out all the dead wood I could find. In some cases, too, I took out a few of the older, outworn canes in the center, cutting right at the ground, to give the new growth more room. I lopped off any branches that had grown where they weren't wanted.

I didn't prune back for shape otherwise, for with a good many things such pruning now would cut off this year's bloom. However, this was the right time for pruning forsythia, which is just thru blooming. Next year's bloom will be on new growth to be made later. It is also time to prune Japanese Quince.

May 16 The Bexley Garden Club was making an all-day tour today to the state parks down in Hocking County and has invited us to go along. So this morning we packed up our cameras, with other essentials, and, dressed in hiking clothes, we drove off. Down there where we went Nature has carved out wonderful beauty spots—caves, wooded hills, gorges, and high cliffs.

The Redbud was gone but the white Flowering Dogwood was spread for mile after mile in panorama before us. Then underfoot were the wildflowers.

I saw thousands of trilliums, the familiar *Phlox divaricata* and another brighter reddish-purple phlox that I learned was *Phlox stolonifera*. In places whole hillsides were covered with a deep crimson form of catchfly that someone identified for me as *Silene virginica*.

By midafternoon these half-dozen little state parks near each other were filled with literally thousands of people in all. But I saw only two people who had picked any of the dogwood.

May 22 With the help of the boys, I began this Saturday one spring chore, long neglected, of trimming the edges of the grass paths in the garden and around the shrubbery on the lawn. We'd measure the edges straight with twine and stakes. Then I'd cut them with the half-moon edger. Donald would dig up the cut sod with a hoe. David would pile it in his little wheelbarrow and haul it away. We were busy as bees until a rain came dashing down to put a stop to it.

This work, along with weeding and cultivating, will be our work for the rest of the month. There will be transplanting of annuals and mums. Meanwhile the oncoming iris, peonies, daylilies, and roses bring promise of a flood tide of bloom.

Small House for Narrow Lot

COMING in next month's *Better Homes & Gardens* is one of the small houses for which many of you have been waiting. "Alternate front" design makes it equally adaptable to wide or narrow lots. . . . Also next month—2 native-log cabins, along with many other features in which builders, remodelers, and furnishers will glory.

He Pastures His Hobby-Horse

[*Begins on page 4*]

appearance of advertising thru better use of art and typography. He pioneered in the movement for better design in packages and improved product. First published record was his article in the *Atlantic Monthly* in 1927, entitled "Beauty, the New Business Tool."

The significance of the title of his delightful autobiography "Louder Please!" is that Mr. Calkins has had, many times, to say just *that* to the world in which he has managed to live so successfully. He has made excellent lemonade out of one large lemon that life handed him while he was a child—deafness.

"Louder Please!" is the whimsical, humorous, candid story of how one condemned to dwell in the midst of a great silence has made an asset of that silence, and a springboard of his loneliness.

OUR meeting was in his New York office. He leaves his Salisbury, Connecticut, place in late fall; winters in town; goes back to the country in early spring. But does he stable his favorite hobby-horse out there in the country for the winter? By no means! There was the animal romping about and amusing itself right on top of that big flat-topped desk, galloping up and down that desk at full speed, and leaping business papers and other city-generated junk as if they hadn't been there. One suspected that Mr. Calkins was quite capable of hiding a seed catalog behind some ponderous advertising tome, after the manner of boys reading dime novels behind the geography at school.

The minute I said "garden" Mr. Calkins reached for a yellow pad and a black pencil and began to make a drawing—and then I knew he was still an advertising man even when a gardener. He plunged, *in medias res*, another advertising trait. "You see," he began, as if we were merely resuming an interrupted conversation, "the difficulty of constructing a garden in Connecticut soil is one of the things that makes it interesting."

"WHAT part of Connecticut?" I interposed.

"Litchfield County. You can't just put something in the ground and let it grow. In our section we have only about 8 or 10 inches of topsoil. Under that is a bed of clay so compact a pick will hardly do more than dent it. Plants which put down a long taproot give that clay up as a bad job. Take the hollyhock, for instance. Instead of going on down toward China, its roots spread out thru the topsoil. That applies to most anything you may plant.

"So one of the first things Mrs. Calkins and I had to do when we bought our place eight years ago was to dig out the clay and fill the whole with topsoil and manure to make a bed where deep-rooted plants would prosper.

"No," he added with a smile, "I'm a dirt gardener all right, but I didn't do my own hauling. I have a handy man on the place, and he gets part of the exercise. I do as much of the work, however, as I have time for. It gives me exercise.

"If it were practicable, I'd like to do it all. As it is, with the feel of the sun on my

He Pastures His Hobby-Horse

back, I like to go after the weeds myself, and to stir the soil around the roots so the air will reach them. I like to see the almost immediate effect on the plants. It seems to make some subtle change in their appearance and bearing; and I like to fancy that they are grateful for what one has done for them."

"DO YOU feel that gardening is the best of the hobbies?" I asked.

"It would almost have to be," he answered. "For one thing, it's racially old—one of the earliest things man ever did. Thought and feeling flow more easily along those ancient channels of the mind than thru any others. Gardening gets one away from the unnatural stresses and strains that are part of the price we pay for being civilized. It's spontaneous. It takes nothing out of you. It puts strength into you; makes you saner and healthier, relaxed and contented with life. For me, it's a particularly effective release from the limitations of a deafened person. The garden is one place where deafness matters least."

"Do you do any vegetable gardening?"

"Once. In Westchester County I raised about every vegetable you'd find listed in a seed catalog. That was before the depression. I had a gardener. But later I sold my big place and got me something less pretentious. Suddenly I realized that I had been hiring somebody to have a lot of fun I might have been appropriating to myself; and so I became my own gardener.

"IN OTHER words, I do all the planning, the directing; and I put in considerable physical labor along with it; leave the rest to a handy man. As a result I'm getting more fun and vastly more benefit.

"But of course I do things on a smaller scale; and I've abandoned most of the vegetable gardening. Besides," added Mr. Calkins with a chuckle, "we are surrounded by neighbors with *big* vegetable gardens, and they raise so many vegetables they don't know what to do with them. We allow them to acquire merit by giving us some. You know a vegetable gardener with nobody to give some of his vegetables away to would feel that life wasn't treating him right!

"And so we raise a few strawberries and some small fruit, and Golden Bantam corn, which the markets don't have for sale, but that's about all."

"DO YOU keep bees?" I asked, as one beekeeper to another. And when I saw the flash that came into his eye—the true beekeeper flash—I knew part of the answer before he spoke.

"I did on my other place," he said. "And I would like to start an apiary where I am. I have put it off for one reason or another; but bees and flowers ought to be watched and studied and cherished as one. They go together."

While Mr. Calkins talked, in quick, sure strokes he was drawing a map. Evidently this was Hobby-Horse's pasture. I could fairly see the animal prick up his ears and flare his nostrils as he stopped to look at it. And what a pasture! Over all, it would be a rectangle, 85 feet long by 35 wide, with a division in the middle, at about 50 feet from one end and

35 feet from the other. In short, a square and an oblong, laid end to end. (*Eleanor Robertson Paepke suggested the garden plan.*)

"Now—take a look at this," said Mr. Calkins as the pencil flew. "In the first place, here's the outside border, a barberry hedge, clipped so that it looks something like boxwood. I do most of the clipping, a little at a time, so that the growth never gets out of hand.

"Inside the barberry we have a flowering border of perennials and annuals. The perennials form a kind of skeleton for the design, and we fill it in with annuals. Chief background planting is made up of delphiniums, peonies, lemon daylilies, *Lilium henryi*, Japanese iris, columbine, bleedingheart, and phlox. The annuals are mostly petunia, verbena, ageratum, calliopsis, scabiosa, snapdragon, stocks, and salpiglossis."

NOW the pencil moved to the 35-foot square. "This square," he explained, "is separated from the rest of the garden by a couple of flagstone steps and a row of barberry, edged with perennials and annuals. At the far end, opposite these steps, is a recess, flagstone paved, with a big umbrella in the middle, and some iron seats. Here we can have tea with our friends and look down the whole length of the garden close.

"When we sit there, there lies at our feet something we are particularly fond of. It's a *water mirror*—an octagonal pool about 8 feet across. Of concrete, and with a border of flagstones on the outside, the whole inside is painted black, making a mirror of it. If you've ever looked into a shop window, the space behind the glass covered with black velvet hangings, you'll get the idea. The effect of our water mirror is really very lovely. I like to fancy that the dryads and wood nymphs come there to look at themselves when we're not around. At any rate, the frogs do."

WITH that the pencil walked down the two flagstone steps into the other, larger section of the garden, and made a vigorous, black circular scrawl in the near left-hand corner.

"That's the apple tree. It's as old as the hundred-year-old house. I suppose both were planted together. That tree is the most glorious thing on the place, especially in spring when it's in bloom. We could replace the house—but not that tree. The trunk has a diameter of 3 feet, and the branches have an enormous spread. There's a circular bench around the trunk. In a good year the old tree has produced 18 barrels of Baldwins. Often I have to pick a considerable portion of them while still small and green for fear the weight will break the tree."

"And this big, blank space in the middle?"

"Turf—thick, smooth, and green."

So this was where the hobby-horse had his pasture, when he wasn't nibbling the barberry, pawing out weeds, looking into the water mirror, and cropping roses!

A LITTLE later I took my leave of Earnest Elmo Calkins. As I went out the door I seemed to feel something brush by me; and there, believe it or not, was the hobby-horse, streaking down the hall —apparently in the general direction of Connecticut. But doubtless he'll come back to keep Mr. Calkins company.

In the meantime, I think you'll agree that Earnest Elmo Calkins, as a master of the art of living, knows how to ride 'im.

RECIPES FOR So Good Meals

[*The meals themselves appear on page 19*]

Egg Scramble in Ham Nests

[A TASTING-TEST KITCHEN ENDORSED RECIPE]

¾ pound smoked ham
¼ pound round steak
¼ pound fresh pork
½ cup bread crumbs
½ tablespoon chopped green pepper
½ tablespoon chopped onion
½ teaspoon salt
1/16 teaspoon paprika
1 beaten egg
½ cup tomato pulp

Thoroly mix meats and add remaining ingredients. Fill greased individual ring molds. Bake in moderate oven (350°) 30 to 40 minutes. Unmold on heated rusks and fill centers with scrambled eggs. Serves 8.

Corn and Bacon Waffles

[A TASTING-TEST KITCHEN ENDORSED RECIPE]

2 cups flour
½ teaspoon salt
3 teaspoons baking powder
1 tablespoon sugar
2 well-beaten egg yolks
1 cup milk
¼ cup melted shortening or salad oil
1 cup drained whole-kernel corn
¼ cup chopped, crisp bacon
2 stiff-beaten egg whites

Sift together dry ingredients. Mix egg yolks, milk, and shortening and add to dry ingredients; stir just until blended. Stir in corn and bacon; fold in egg whites. Bake in hot waffle iron. Makes 8 waffles.

Honey Butter Sauce

[A TASTING-TEST KITCHEN ENDORSED RECIPE]

1 cup honey
¼ cup melted butter
¼ teaspoon cinnamon
Dash of nutmeg

Warm honey slowly over hot water and stir in remaining ingredients. Serve warm.

April Souffle

[A TASTING-TEST KITCHEN ENDORSED RECIPE]

1 tablespoon fat
1½ tablespoons flour
½ cup milk
½ teaspoon salt
⅛ teaspoon chili powder
½ cup grated cheese
3 beaten egg yolks
3 stiff-beaten egg whites

Make cream sauce of fat, flour, and milk; season with salt and chili powder; cool slightly. Add grated cheese and egg yolks, mix well, and fold in egg whites. Half fill greased baking cups. Bake in slow oven (325°) 25 minutes. Serves 6.

Creamed Ham in Toasted Bread Cases

[A TASTING-TEST KITCHEN ENDORSED RECIPE]

2 tablespoons chopped green pepper
½ cup sliced mushrooms
4 tablespoons butter
4 tablespoons flour
2 cups milk
2 cups cooked ham, cubed
4 hard-cooked eggs, chopped
Salt to taste
1 loaf unsliced, day-old bread

SO Good Meals Recipes

Slightly brown green pepper and mushrooms in butter. Blend in flour, add milk and cook until thick. Add ham and hard-cooked eggs, season with salt, stirring carefully. Remove crusts from bread, cut into 2-inch squares, and with sharp knife remove center. Brush outside of bread cases with melted butter or salad oil. Toast in moderate oven (325°) until light brown. Fill bread cases with creamed ham mixture. Serves 8.

Hot Cross Buns

[A TASTING-TEST KITCHEN ENDORSED RECIPE]

2 cakes compressed yeast
1/3 cup sugar
2/3 cup milk, scalded
3 1/2 cups flour
1/2 cup melted shortening
3/4 teaspoon salt
3 eggs, unbeaten
2/3 cup currants
1/2 teaspoon cinnamon

Soften yeast and dissolve sugar in milk cooled to lukewarm. Add 1 cup flour and beat. Add shortening, salt, eggs, and 2 1/2 cups of flour. Beat 3 minutes. Cover and let rise until double in bulk—about 1 hour. Mix currants and cinnamon, add to dough, and mix lightly. Roll 1 inch thick and cut with 2 1/2-inch floured cutter. Shape into buns, place 2 inches apart in greased baking pans, and brush tops with slightly beaten egg white. Allow to rise until very light. Using scissors, snip tops of buns at right angles to form cross. Bake in moderate oven (350°) 12 minutes. To the remaining egg white, add confectioners' sugar to make a frosting; with pastry tube form a cross on each bun. Makes 2 dozen.

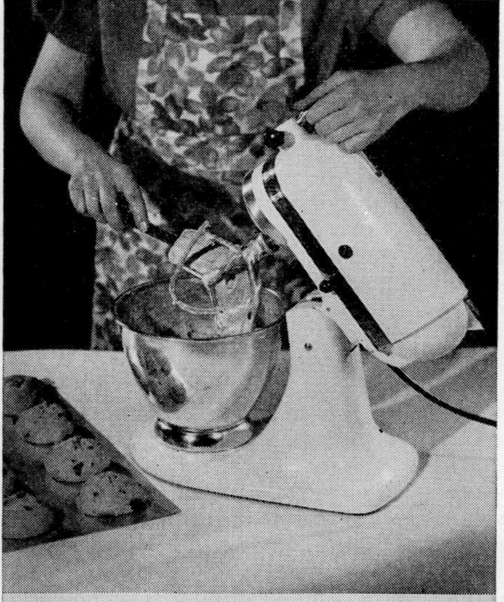

● VERSATILE! This heavy-duty electric food preparer mixes even the stiff yeast doughs for hot cross buns, light rolls, and homemade bread as easily as it whips an egg white. As the beater turns it's also traveling clockwise *around* the bowl for thoro, double-action mixing. A wire whip replaces the flat beater for whipping or lighter beating. You may buy extra attachments—a pea sheller, food chopper, vegetable slicer, ice-cream freezer, and others to do, electrically, a large number of tasks. [*KitchenAid, Model K,* $49.50, Dept. BH, The Hobart Mfg. Co., Troy, Ohio]—*A. J. O.*

Good News! We All Get a Break

[*Begins on page 7*]

unpaid balance of your mortgage instead of on the whole amount, so that the more you pay off, the less the charge becomes.

Suppose you're ready right now to start the ball rolling toward the new home. In general, what does the Act now say you can do?

The Interest and Monthly Payments

On a mortgage of $5,400 or less you'll pay 5 percent interest plus a ¼ percent mortgage-insurance premium, or a ½ percent premium on a mortgage above this amount. Interest and premium are both figured on the unpaid balance and, as mentioned previously, there's no longer a service charge to the home-builder. You make monthly payments thruout the life of the mortgage. The monthly payment includes (1) interest, (2) payment on principal, (3) mortgage-insurance premium, (4) taxes, and (5) fire insurance. Thus all these charges are taken care of automatically and you don't need to bother about them individually.

In addition to a down payment, *in advance* you pay the fees for initial service, title search, mortgage recording, and appraisal by the FHA. These fees may total $50 to $200, depending on locality and value of property.

The Small Home

You can build a new single-family home, with a total mortgage not over $5,400, to be occupied by yourself and inspected by the FHA during construction, by making a down payment of 10 percent of the appraised value of the property ($6,000) and signing a mortgage for 90 percent.

The project must be approved before construction is begun. You can, however, buy an existing house for your own occupancy on the same terms if construction was begun after January 1, 1937, and before February 3, 1938, and if it has neither been sold nor occupied since completion.

The mortgage for $5,400 or less may run for a maximum period of 25 years, payable in monthly installments. It's the only one that may run for as long as 25 years (maximum period for all the others is 20 years). It's also the only mortgage on which the down payment may be as low as 10 percent.

If you pay 20 percent down and take a mortgage for 20 years, the house needn't be owner-occupied; nor need it be new.

The Medium-Size Home

You can build a home with a total mortgage of not more than $8,600 by making a down payment of 10 percent on the first $6,000 of appraised value plus 20 percent of the amount of appraised value over $6,000. If a home costs $10,000, this would amount to a down payment of 14 percent and a mortgage for 86 percent. For a home costing $8,000, it would amount to a down payment of 12½ percent and a mortgage for 87½ percent. This, too, must be a new, single-family, owner-occupied home, approved before the beginning of building operations and inspected during construction by the FHA.

Again, however, you may buy an existing, unsold, unoccupied house, built between January 1, 1937, and February 3, 1938, on the same terms. This mortgage would run for a maximum of 20 years, payable in monthly installments.

If you pay a straight 20 percent down, the house needn't be owner-occupied or newly built.

The Large Home

You can build or buy a home with a total mortgage not over $16,000 by making a down payment of 20 percent and getting a mortgage for 80 percent of the appraised value on the property, running for a maximum of 20 years, payable in monthly installments. Total cost of the home doesn't matter so long as the mortgage doesn't exceed $16,000 and is no more than 80 percent of the appraised value.

The house needn't be single-family or owner-occupied, but it mustn't be designed for use by more than four families.

Remodeling Loans

You can borrow up to $10,000 to modernize, repair, or alter an existing property so long as the improvements are permanent in nature. This includes fixed equipment, such as automatic-firing heating plants or devices, doors and storm doors, driveways, fences, landscaping, linoleum that's cemented to the floor, walks, a water heater when it's part of the water system, a water softener when it's part of the water system, and practically all types of built-in equipment. It doesn't include movable equipment, such as ranges or refrigerators. The charge can't exceed $5 for every $100 you borrow, and is deductible in advance; that is, you receive $95 on a $100 one-year note. The loan must be paid in equal periodical installments over a maximum period of 5 years. Discount, in advance, would be equivalent to a true interest rate of about 9¾ percent.

Subject to certain restrictions, the same kind of loan may be obtained to finance new construction, such as a summer camp or cottage; but here the advance is limited to a maximum of $2,500, the deduction is only $3.50 per $100, and the loan may run for a maximum of 10 years, payable in periodical installments. This provision expires July 1, 1939.

Refinancing a Mortgage

You may refinance an existing home, securing a mortgage up to $16,000, to represent not more than 80 percent of appraised value on the same terms as for a new home—that is, 5 percent interest, ½ percent premium, 20-year payment. After July 1, 1939, however, no mortgages will be acceptable unless they cover houses constructed since July 1, 1937.

Rental-Purchase Plan

Finally, it's possible for you to buy a home without any down payment, by what is called the *rental-purchase plan*, in some housing developments. This applies usually to homes in a development of 10 or more houses financed by an operating builder or real-estate company thru a FHA insured group-mortgage. You rent the house, and when you've paid enough rent to satisfy requirements, for either a 10 or a 20 percent down payment (depending on appraised value), the mortgage is released and refinanced in your name as owner-occupier. Very often, however, the developer may require a small down payment as evidence of good faith.

Where to Get Money

As for money to finance your mortgage—that you obtain from a FHA approved mortgagee—banks, building and loan associations, insurance companies—in your community or near by. If you don't know where to find one, a local bank, architect, building contractor, building-supply dealer, realtor, or your state FHA director will be able to tell you.

When the Housing Act was originally passed, there was hesitation on the part of loaning agencies to grant mortgages as high as 80 percent. There may be similar hesitation over the new 90 percent mortgages. Much will depend on conservative appraisal of properties, the acceptance only of sound risks, and freedom of mortgage money in the community.

Of course, you may not want to use the FHA. You may be able to pay down 40 or 50 percent and get a lower interest rate than the 5¼–5½ percent, which is the total FHA charge. In some communities there's plenty of mortgage money available right now at rates down to 4½ percent, when borrowers can afford a bigger down payment. Be cautious, however, about the house on which you're asked to pay very little down (say 5 percent) and also get a very low interest rate. The price of the house may have been written up to compensate for the extraordinary terms on which it's offered. *Also, no matter how much you borrow, be sure to get an amortized loan.*

Reducing the Cost of Home Ownership

Why is the amended National Housing Act so *significant* to men and women who want a new or better home?

First, the FHA program reduces costs of financing. The actual lowering of the interest rate is only a part. Just as important is the fact that secondary financing is eliminated. The prospective home-owner gets a whole loan on a first mortgage, at a standard and reasonable rate of interest.

A reduction in financing costs means much more to the [Turn to next page

Lovely Kitchens!

EFFICIENT kitchens. . . . Livable kitchens. The kind of kitchens you like, modern and convenient, from resilient floor to work-saving equipment — PRIZEWINNERS, if you please!

Pictures of them will greet you, words will explain, from the printed pages of next month's *Better Homes & Gardens*—the Better Kitchens Contest winners, best of the country's 1937 crop of new and remodeled kitchens.

Good News! We All Get a Break

home-owner than is apparent on the surface. One percent less in interest charges doesn't sound so huge. But 1 percent a year for 10 years is 10 percent. On a long-term mortgage, a small reduction in interest rate means the same as a large reduction in the cost of the house, even tho actual interest payment is gradually reduced as the principal is paid off.

Making It Easier to Buy

Second, the small down payment, now as low as 10 percent for properties costing $6,000 or less, makes it possible for a great many more people with moderate incomes to become home-owners.

There'll be those who'll say that if a man wants a home, he ought to have at least 20 percent of the cost, and preferably more, saved before he starts to buy or build. This is the old thrift argument—don't spend what you haven't got. Certainly it has validity; we've had a lesson in what happens when large numbers of people over-extend themselves on installment-buying with small down payments. Yet there's a difference. A family can't get along without a roof over its head. In other words, you have to spend money on rent anyway. The real question is whether it's better to continue putting this money into rent or to let it slowly count toward owning your home.

Mortgages With Less Headache

Third, the long amortization period makes for *security*. This, too, will be disputed. How can a man be secure in possession of his home when there's a mortgage on it for 20 or 25 years? The answer is that there's no such thing as absolute security. As some wise man said long ago, *the only sure things are death and taxes*. The whole picture must be faced realistically; it's silly to look at it in any other way. And speaking realistically, the man who has any kind of mortgage on his home doesn't own the home; if the mortgage runs for 20 or 25 years—or one year or two years—he practically leases the place from the mortgagee for that period. Suppose he loses his job. Then he's likely to lose his home. In great economic crises many do lose their jobs—and their homes.

But a realistic view also compels us to ask ourselves these questions:

Am I more secure with a long-time mortgage on which I make small monthly payments that, under normal circumstances, are well within my means—or with a short-time mortgage on which I have to make heavier payments than I can really afford? In which case am I more likely to lose my home in event of a minor financial upset? (Granted that I may lose it anyway in a widespread economic catastrophe.) And which kind of mortgage is easier on the nerves?

If I should lose, thru foreclosure, what I have actually paid on my home, will I lose more if I've paid only 10 percent down and small monthly installments, or a large amount down and heavy installments? In the former case, does the equity I lose amount to much more than I'd have had to pay for rent, anyway?

In case I must sell my house, will I have a better chance if it carries a long-term mortgage requiring only a small down payment from a buyer, or if it carries a short-term mortgage requiring a heavy down payment?

Again, in event of misfortune, I may be able to sell my house and get back at least part of what I've put into it. To do this advantageously, it may be necessary to refinance the mortgage and bring it back to somewhere near the original figure—especially if I've been making payments for a long time. Will this refinancing be easier if the house is one that has already met the rather strict requirements for FHA mortgage insurance, or if it isn't?

To Own or to Rent?

There are plenty of people who insist that a man puts his head into a noose in buying a home at all—that it's better to rent and be free of entangling alliances. We must acknowledge that there's at least one very strong argument for this point of view. It's summed up in the word uncertainty—uncertainty of staying in one place, uncertainty of employment, uncertainty of life in general. Life does play us strange tricks. But on the other hand, there's no known method of completely escaping these uncertainties. We're compelled to take some chances.

For my own part, I've felt very strongly that the satisfaction of having a home I could call my own, and of working with it creatively over many years, was worth the risk. I've known what it is to have a home—never free of mortgage, by the way—and be compelled by painful circumstances to leave it. I wouldn't exchange the joy and creative effort of those years for any amount of playing safe, even if I'd known how to play safe. Who did, during the depression?

A Good Time to Build

So this is the story so far as the individual new-home wanter or remodeler is concerned. Regardless of whether the cost of building materials is due to go down or up, the prospective home-owner—particularly the little fellow—is now enormously benefited. There's a shortage of decent homes. Land prices, according to experts, are still comparatively low, with a rise ahead if real-estate history repeats itself. So many improvements have been made in building methods, materials, and equipment that the house built today gives considerably more value for the same amount of money than the house built 10 years ago. All in all, it looks like a good time to think seriously of getting that little gray home in the West—or in the East, South, or North.

Editor's Note: The foregoing article has been reviewed and authenticated by the Federal Housing Administration, and the table of average monthly payments on page 7 has been compiled from figures supplied by the Federal Housing Administration.

Naturally it will be understood by all _Better Homes & Gardens_ families that because of the many variables, it's possible to give only estimated and approximate figures, to the nearest even dollar. Exact figures and information in respect to financing the particular home you're going to build can be obtained from authorized FHA financing agencies in your community and from state offices of the Federal Housing Administration.

ALONG THE Garden Path

WITH THE WEEK-END GARDENER

ILLUSTRATIONS ALSO BY THE WEEK-END GARDENER

75 PERCENT OF THE SECRET

NOT long ago I had occasion to check the time consumed in cultivating the 200 feet of finished border in my Long Island garden. It was just under an hour.

Now that's pretty good going. The border averages some 6 feet in width. All sorts of perennial shoots are popping up in it. Consequently, in manipulating even the fastest of modern tools, a certain *finesse* is indicated. The job can't successfully be tackled in the spirit of a one-armed paper hanger with the hives. In view of the required delicacy and carefulness, to cover that much territory in less than 60 minutes—if not a course record—is certainly a stroke or two under par.

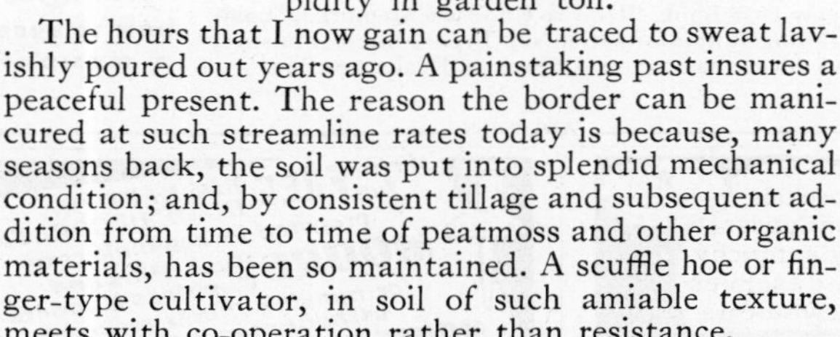

"—all sorts of perennial shoots pop up in it"

Naturally, members of *The Week-End Gardeners' League* are keen to discover methods whereby energy may be conserved. Cluster round, then, and make yourselves comfortable, while I let you in on a handsome proportion of the secret of rapidity in garden toil.

The hours that I now gain can be traced to sweat lavishly poured out years ago. A painstaking past insures a peaceful present. The reason the border can be manicured at such streamline rates today is because, many seasons back, the soil was put into splendid mechanical condition; and, by consistent tillage and subsequent addition from time to time of peatmoss and other organic materials, has been so maintained. A scuffle hoe or finger-type cultivator, in soil of such amiable texture, meets with co-operation rather than resistance.

Did you ever stop to consider what soil is? It's interesting, living stuff, you know—not merely a compound employed as a symbol of immaturity by small boys. Topsoil is the thin upper crust of the earth's surface. By action of sun and rain and by inclusion of matter which once possessed life—organic matter, both vegetable and animal—it has been rendered capable of supporting a crop. Subsoil is the stratum, usually lighter in color, beneath it. The main difference between the two lies in the subsoil's organic lack. Subsoil has been defined as rotting rock, and topsoil as rotting subsoil.

If you should examine under a powerful microscope a pinch of soil, what you'd see would somewhat resemble a pile of marbles. These marbles would be the soil-grains, bits of rock which might vary in size from the finest particles of clay to coarse sand or gravel. Mixed in with them would be bits of organic matter. Between them would be atmosphere, like the air we humans take into our lungs, except that it includes more carbon dioxide and nitrogen; and water, containing chemicals. Also, living in the compost would be tiny organisms, the bacteria.

In all good soils these five things are present. All of them are important. The size of the soil-grains largely determines the consistency of the soil. If they're too small, it packs; if they're too large, moisture is lost overreadily. Organic matter helps soil hold water and lightens and aerates it as well.

"A scuffle hoe meets with co-operation"

Air, as well as water, must be at hand so that roots may breathe and bacteria may be busy breaking down organic tissue into forms convertible to plant use. The soil solution carries the liquid diet upon which plants thrive.

Accordingly, we attempt to build up in our gardens a rich loam, simultaneously heavy enough to hold water and light enough to hold air. The physical attributes of soil, you see, are more vital to the gardener than its chemical properties. The average soil contains most of the elements needed for plant growth. With the land in what farmers call "good heart," those elements will be available. If there are chemical deficiencies—and there may be in nitrogen, phosphorus, or potash, and other elements—an application of complete plant food is a simple, and usually an immediate, cure.

Some fashioners of gardens are extremely slow and methodical in their soil-conditioning. I confess I lean to that school myself. But, really, the rules of the game boil down to two: (1) dig deeply, and (2) add humus. That's all there is to it. If the land on which either a vegetable or flower garden is being made is halfway decent, it will react to those two fundamentals as amazingly as an old bachelor responds to a debutante's smiles.

". . . soil carries the liquid diet which plants thrive on"

Digging is as old as the Garden of Eden, as unavoidable as taxes. It breaks up compacted earth, separates soil particles, makes possible thereby the increased retention of moisture, and lets in air to stimulate bacteria. The farther down we loosen the soil and add to it humus-making materials, the lower will hungry roots tend to penetrate, the greater the food area they'll tap, and the more protected from the blistering August suns will be your plant companions.

Humus is decaying vegetative matter. We introduce it in the form of leafmold; or a green crop (like rape or red clover) turned under when young and succulent; or the flower-gardener's pal, peatmoss. If the soil is too sandy, humus will thicken it. If it contains too much clay, humus will make it looser. It's a miracle-worker, all right. Before long, you'll find it has turned your unpromising ground into a substance, which, under average rainfall, will hold its shape when you squeeze a handful and pulverize when you toss a ball of it against your trowel. Humus and deep digging will create for you, in short, that priceless horticultural product—good garden loam.

There are times, admittedly, when existing soil is so uncompromising that there's nothing to do but discard it and haul in fresh topsoil. Sometimes a whole bed may have to be imported. More likely, tho, planting a single specimen—a magnolia, perhaps, or a choice yew—will call for such treatment. A generous hole, a thick layer of new soil beneath and around the root-ball, a thoro soaking—and that's that.

Time spent in spring preparation is time saved on summer cultivation. Leap to it, then, while the world is new and the mood is upon you. Seize your spade, seed of Adam; thrust straight and dig deep!

Among Ourselves

[*Begins on page 35*]

give necessary, reachable shelfroom many of the doors are only 14 or 15 inches above "counter" level. "We must either work with them open, which is a nuisance, or continually open and push them while at work. Therefore, on the principle of the Venetian blind, I would face my cupboards with thin, wide-lathed blinds that could slide up while I'm at work and slide down into place when the kitchen is in order. I would carry out my color scheme of light buff and yellow by having laths buff, lower edges rimmed in yellow. Here's hoping someone may enjoy using my idea even tho I must wait awhile before using it myself!"

+ + +

Mrs. Harold A. Hughes of Fort Wayne, Indiana, writes that the prize for the best brickbat letter "helped to serve a very large buffet supper the day after Christmas for a wide circle of relatives and friends."

+ + +

He Chose a Garden

He chose a peaceful garden
When he longed to pray,
Upon the lonely eve
Of crucifixion day.

He knew the quiet healing
That growing things impart,
The balm a garden offers
To soothe a troubled heart.

—Kathrya Kendall

+ + +

Marcella T., *Better Homes & Gardens* reader, Orange, New Jersey, takes pen in hand to whisper that she feels the Plain Dirt Gardener's articles are so human—that he's like a personal friend. "My garden, rather large, is my playground—it's my only recreation," she says. "My mother is 91 years old and has had to be waited upon, hand and foot, for the past six years. My sister, who was a teacher, retired three years ago. I am still teaching. So you see why my garden is a real necessity. It is here I rest my nerves; work out my more serious problems. The while I am sorting and pulling out and casting away the weeds that choke my flowers, I find it so easy to sort out and cast away mental weeds that clutter up the mind and stunt the growth of clear, progressive thinking."

For an interesting letter go Christine Holbrook's thanks to Mrs. L. S. Bell of Pasadena, these excerpts from which we think you, too, will like: "I used to be a subscriber; then old man depression hit us. . . . Three years have gone past and we are getting ahead again—bought a lovely home in a lovely setting and am dashing hither and yon, buying paint and paper, varnish and curtain material. . . . I do everything myself (I used to be a commercial artist and dress designer). I paint, pa-

Better Homes & Gardens HOLIDAY MENU WINNERS

First Prize, $50, Mrs. John R. Wilkes, Lewisburg, Tenn.; Second Prize, $25, Mrs. Louise Davis, Stigler, Okla.; Third Prize, $15, Norma Hardwick, Rochester, N. Y.; Fourth Prize, $10, Aquina G. Shea, Glyndon, Minn.; Fifth Prize, $5, Mrs. George Mecham, Omaha, Nebr. And 20 Prizes of $1 each to: Mrs. Robert Ritz, Valparaiso, Ind.; Mrs. James M. Schroder, Pittsburgh, Pa.; Mrs. Ralph Milne, Chiloquin, Ore.; Mrs. H. Randolph Jackson, Winona, Minn.; Mrs. Scott Cliff, Nampa, Idaho; Mrs. Herman Schmidt, Portsmouth, Ohio; Mrs. John L. Davis, Lynchburg, Va.; Miss Jessie Rutherford, Knoxville, Tenn.; Mrs. Marshall J. Smith, Memphis, Tenn.; Mrs. Frances Parrot, Newton Center, Mass.; Mrs. H. L. Vernon, Peoria, Ill.; Mrs. A. W. Maydwell, Eminence, Ky.; Mrs. J. M. Brown, Coral Gables, Fla.; Mrs. J. F. Steinmiller, Toledo, Ohio; Mrs. Floyd Berry, Pittsburg, Texas; Mrs. W. H. Nicks, Riverton, Wyo.; Mrs. Helen M. Kent, Kansas City, Kans.; Althea Marshall, Shreveport, La.; Mrs. Emma Maxwell, Zanesville, Ohio; Mrs. J. E. Tucker, Los Angeles, Calif.

per—that's lots of fun—and make all my crisscross curtains. I love them!

"Today I went downtown for the first time in three months (we live right up against these inspiring mountains) . . . stopped in the drugstore to wait for my husband, and right in front of me lay *Better Homes & Gardens*. I extravagantly dived into my purse for a thin dime, and settled down to renew old acquaintances. Did I have fun! First I read about the Quints. That was a nice article. The Plain Dirt Gardener tickled me as of yore. I have had three years of bitter and blessed experience since. Bitter because of gophers; blessed because of flowers and trees. My long, beautifully kept nails are a thing of the past; my hands are toil-worn, but most interested in finding out whether seed is going to grow up or not! It's a shame to dig them up to see, but we *will* do it. What was it someone wrote—'He who plants a seed beneath the sod, and expects to see it come thru the clod—believes in God.' That isn't right, but the idea is there. I must have a strong faith in God, because they certainly come up!

"I was so absorbed in my old friend *BH&G* that I didn't see my husband walking around the store several times looking for me. . . . Then I dashed home to get his lunch and couldn't wait (have not even done the luncheon dishes!) to go on reading. There's so much. In other magazines you look at the pictures and thrill at the color ads, but seldom do I just pore over them from cover to cover, jealously saving bits that are most interesting for last reading . . . I'm going to try Lily Strickland's salad recipe for supper.

"My wallpaper just came; blue for the front room—really lovely paper—and plain white for the east room and hall. Am painting the woodwork white, as the kitchen and bedroom. You should see them! Everyone just gasps—they're lovely; and now I'm going to have some fun doing the bedrooms. I got white scrim for the blue room (crisscross), with round ball fringe in blue; peach for the white room. . . .

"You can tell the Plain Dirt Gardener I'll bet I can put him to shame when it comes to raising zinnias!"

Horse in His Garden?

SURE! He pastures it there!

It whinnies to him (so says Wainwright Evans), crops the turf, keeps down the weeds, nibbles at the barberry hedge, wades the pool, basks in the sun, and when the sun gets too hot, slips into the shade of the old apple tree!

What kind of a horse is this!

Ah—it's the kind *you* like to ride, and the man who owns him is an interesting celebrity you've heard lots about. It's all explained in next month's *Better Homes & Gardens*.

PART ONE

How Articles Get into Print

The "Why" of This Book

MAGAZINES are as much a commonplace in America today as neckties. Millions of copies of them appear in millions of mail boxes and on thousands of news stands. Reading them is an American habit almost as firmly fixed as taking time off for lunch. Occasionally they break into the news: the *American Mercury* when the police of Providence, Rhode Island, decide to ban it, the *Saturday Evening Post* when it publishes a revealing article by an ex-President, *Life* when it ceases to be a comic and becomes an expensive-looking picture magazine. Usually their readers take them in stride, expecting of them brief periods of entertainment, instruction, or stimulation but rarely asking or thinking more of them.

Because they are a habit, it is not surprising that their readers seldom pause to think how they grow. The *Esquire* reader, accustomed to *Esquire's* bland pictures and vigorous prose, takes half an hour's relaxation from an article concerning Ernest Hemingway's skill as a fisherman and passes on. He finds suggestions that may be of use to him in a *Nation's Business* discussion of retailing methods, perhaps makes mental notes or clips the article—and goes down to the basement to shake up the furnace. He does not halt to wonder how the piece he has just read came into being, who the writer is, on what experience or research he based it, or how it reached the magazine editor's hands. Still less does he consider the processes through which it passed after the editor decided to publish it, or the possible problems of making it fit the space available for it, or the relations of the editor's task to those of other departments of the magazine.

All of this is as it should be. A basic principle of modern magazine-making is that the reader must find each issue, and each part of it, so easy to take that he will be conscious of none of the mechanics of presentation. To reach this goal, magazine-making today has had to become a highly technical and involved process. It employs the services of many thousands of workers, most of them highly skilled. It is faced with a maze of problems of writing, editing, illustration, finance, circulation, and production. Publishing is one of the country's biggest businesses.

This has not always been the case. Magazines have developed to their present status from beginnings no more impressive than those of the transportation industry, which contrasts shiny streamlined trains to ox-carts and mule-back; or the printing industry itself, with its scores of methods of lightning-quantity reproduction the outgrowth of the genius of Gutenberg and Caxton.

Periodicals in the modern sense began only a little more than 200 years ago in the English-speaking world with *The Tatler* and *The Spectator* of Addison and Steele. Comparatively speaking, Addison and Steele had an easy time of it. Their handset printing was slow and crude; their circulation was small; their sources of manuscripts—largely their own writings—were limited. But such limitations were advantages of a sort. Though printing was slow, it was simple. It did not offer scores of type and illustration and reproduction possibilities; there was but one way of doing the job, and that way was eminently satisfactory for their purpose. Small circulation meant not only a simple job of getting the magazine to its readers but also a narrow and well-defined circle of tastes to appease. And the fact that they and their friends wrote their own copy was a very different story from that of today's magazine, for which the entire globe may furnish material.

In 1935 only two American industries, food products and textiles, had more than publishing's 22,606 establishments; seven employed more than its 304,842 workers; five paid more than its $446,372,062 annual wages; eight had larger material bills than its $498,768,924; and seven produced material of greater value than its $2,164,995,207. In the same year the United States had 2,009 monthly periodicals with a circulation of 102,193,704, and 1,778 semi-monthly, quarterly, and "other" (newspapers excluded) periodicals with a circulation of 73,593,498.—*Figures from 1938 World Almanac.*

This is not the place to present even a brief history of the changes that have made today's magazine what it is. It is enough to say that it is a big business, presenting a many-sided set of problems that its reader-audience rarely suspects and never entirely visualizes.

Basically, these problems are of two closely-related kinds:

1. The editorial problem: Understanding the audience and discovering how to reach and please it; obtaining material and presenting it effectively; overcoming obstacles of production and reproduction.

2. The business problem: Gaining circulation suitable to the magazine's purpose, and holding it; selling advertising space on the basis of circulation; promoting, producing, and circulating the magazine.

The purpose of this book is to present a rounded picture of the first problem, to the end that prospective writers and makers of magazines may gain a realistic knowledge and understanding of it. It is not a simple problem. It is a complex of scores of factors, some within its own confines but many growing out of the business problem. Editorial problems cannot be considered merely in their relation to the editorial room; they are inextricably bound to the work of the business office. Consequently this "rounded picture" must take into account the impingements of business, circulation, production, and promotion on editorial practice. It will not attempt to include complete discussion of the business problem. But it will show how the second relates to the first.

It may be asked why the prospective writer for the magazines should spend his time delving into the editor's job. The answer is simple: Today's magazine is not a *Tatler* or a *Spectator*. Its writers are not its editors. Yet to write for it an author needs to understand it almost as thoroughly as if he were to edit it. A general knowledge of editorial problems and techniques will help him to a knowledge of specific magazine needs and purposes; it will enable him to direct his writing at the bull's eye rather than take pot shots aimed at nothing in particular and usually hitting nothing.

That the knowledge of the writer's task is vital to the editor needs no proving. Magazine editors frequently get their jobs because they have written acceptably for publications and have thus shown appreciation of editorial needs. Some magazines refuse to select new editors on any other basis.

The method by which this book offers information about magazine editing and writing is the case method. It is highly specific. It purposes not to tell *how to edit and write for the magazine,* but *how magazines are edited and written.* In other words, it is inductive rather than deductive: It presents detailed accounts of actual editing and writing jobs, points them up with as much specific explanation and example as may be necessary, and draws or suggests general conclusions.

To aid in this approach, the authors have thought it desirable to use an intimate and minute study of an actual magazine and its actual articles as a starting point. The magazine chosen is *Better Homes & Gardens,* published in Des Moines, Iowa, by the Meredith Publishing Company. Any of scores of other magazines might have been selected. The choice fell on *Better Homes & Gardens* because, a periodical of broad appeal and variety, it offers concrete examples of many types of editing and writing problems; because its wide circulation makes it generally available to readers of this book who may wish to examine it more thoroughly than the book permits.

A magazine rather than a newspaper has been chosen for detailed description for these reasons: (1) The magazine furnishes a wider variety of feature-article material than the newspaper; (2) the feature article is relatively much more important in the magazine than in the newspaper; (3) the behind-the-scenes picture of the magazine is not generally so well known as that of the newspaper.

Sixty-four pages from issues of this magazine are presented in facsimile reproduction as part of the case method. They have been selected to illustrate a variety of editing and writing problems and solutions, and many of the book's suggestions make direct reference to them. Further, the editorial practices of the magazine and even the personalities of the executives have been made an integral part of the book. The authors offer these specific details because, though they apply in their entirety to no other single periodical, they are typical of thousands. Where essential departures from *Better Homes & Gardens* practices may occur, they are suggested or described.

What follows has been divided into three sections:

PART I. The setting in which magazines are made. This pictures the magazine organization, the daily routine of the editorial staff, the mechanics of the editorial office; how manuscripts are handled, what the tasks are of readers, copy editors, proofreaders, art and make-up editors; the work of the circulation, advertising, promotion, production, and research departments as they impinge on editorial tasks and duties; the evolution of magazine policies.

Part II. The sources, gathering of information, planning and writing of principal types of magazine articles. This section takes the novice back of the curtain to give him a view of all the factors that enter into the making of a successful piece of editorial matter; from examination of a wide variety of case studies it leads him to the formulation of concrete suggestions on subjects for articles, search for materials, "policy angles," article writing, illustration, and so on.

Part III. Detail of the practical problems of the magazine writer. The study of magazine markets, the use of printed and other sources of information, relations with editors, copyright laws, and allied topics form the subject matter of this section.

Practice suggestions and supplementary reading lists are included from time to time. Of the two, the practice suggestions are of the greater value. Nobody ever learned how to edit a magazine or how to write for it by reading about it; the supplementary reading must have something to supplement. The hope of the authors, however, is that practice and study based on the suggestions and information in this book will aid young men and women to undertake either of two types of work: as magazine editorial assistants, or as commercially successful writers.

11

What Happens to a Manuscript?

FIFTEEN OR TWENTY bulky gray bags of mail arrive each week-day morning at the big red-and-white plant of the Meredith Publishing Company in Des Moines. Unloaded from the mail truck, they are carted to an elevator, hoisted to the third floor, and carted again to a long table in the mailing department on the west side of the building.

The porter dumps the contents of the bags onto the table, and a group of girl mail-clerks goes to work on the thousands of envelopes, parcels, boxes. These pieces of mail have come from every part of the world to this bottle-neck; here they are sorted and sent in hurried order to some scores of offices throughout the building. The clerks pour expertly through them and toss them into the assorted pigeon-holes just across the table. The pigeon-holes are labeled under two general headings, "Successful Farming" and "Better Homes & Gardens," and under many sub-classifications. One of the larger holes bears this label: "BH&G—Editorial."

Into this hole each day go scores of pieces of mail. Most of them are of standard letter sizes, but more than thirty a day—200 a week, 10,000 a year—are larger. From them comes most of the material that will fill the pages of each month's issue of nearly two million copies.

The letters go to a whirring mail-opening machine that neatly slices an end off each envelope. A clerk takes the manuscript mail and stamps each envelope with a time-and-date-recording device. Then she slits the envelopes with a paper-knife (they are too bulky for the mail-opener), removes from them enclosed stamps, notes their amount (or their lack, if none is enclosed) on the envelope, and credits the total amount to the *Better Homes & Gardens* editorial postage account.

Next the envelopes go to a girl in the "central stenographic division." For each envelope she goes through the following procedure:

Writes on a salmon-colored 3″ x 5″ card the author's name and address, title of manuscript, number and nature of illustrations submitted with it, and date received.

Addresses and mails to the author a postcard which says:

> Dear Friend:
> We acknowledge, with thanks, the receipt of your material. You'll hear from us within a week or ten days.
> Sincerely yours,
> THE EDITORS
> BETTER HOMES & GARDENS

If the manuscript is verse, her job is finished. If, however, it is an article of any nature, she continues the routine:

She makes out a yellow 4″ x 6″ card which is to bear not only all the information carried by the salmon card but also to record precisely what happens to the manuscript from that moment to its acceptance or rejection. She notes at the top of the card the amount of postage on the envelope (which she then destroys), and in the "remarks" space the amount of postage enclosed; and she estimates the number of words and records the estimate.

	Uses 12¢ postage
MANUSCRIPT RECORD	Assigned to: Publication BHG Issue Ms. No.
Author's Title Every Inch a Home	Date Rec'd 5-13-38
Author Brown, John	Address 4216 West 4th St. Chicago, Ill.
Classification bldg Refer to Normile	
Illus. Received 3p 4dr Illus. Returned	Price Each $25
Ed. OK. [illegible] Ed. Rej.	Sug. Price Ms. 75
Accepted by Words 1200	$100
Remarks: Enclosed 9¢ postage	Price 100=
1,511—J.O.-7738	

She examines enclosed illustrations and other content carefully. If photographs are broken or damaged, she notes the fact under "remarks."

She clips all record cards, photographs and other material to the manuscript.

The office mail carrier (a gangling boy with a big V-shaped pouch hanging from a shoulder) comes along, picks up the stack of manuscripts, and carries them down to the second floor. He deposits them on the desk of a dark-haired secretary in an editor's office.

They are now "in the mill," and their fates are in the hands of the editors.

A counterpart of this picture appears, at least in general outline, in every magazine office in America. The differences are chiefly in scale. Some publishing houses are larger—receive more manuscripts, issue more magazines, present more complex circulation, advertising, editorial, and production problems. The Curtis Publishing Company, with its *Saturday Evening Post, Ladies' Home Journal,* and *Country Gentleman,* operates on a larger scale. So do Crowell (*Collier's, Woman's Home Companion,* and others) and Hearst (*Good Housekeeping, Cosmopolitan,* and others).

Most magazines are less elaborate enterprises. Many issue from "one-publication houses," and often the one publication is a monthly magazine of a few hundred or thousand circulation, with limited editorial, production, and business needs and possibilities.

But the problems follow like patterns, and an understanding of one situation is an introduction to all.

The Magazine's Organization

The work of editing *Better Homes & Gardens* each month, of producing it anew every thirty days, centers in the office of Editor Frank McDonough. To his office come the departmental editors to discuss projects and plans, and the circulation, promotion, advertising, and production managers to confer on their closely-related problems. Here are laid down the editorial policies by which forthcoming issues are to be guided; here the efforts of the scores of men and women who combine to produce the magazine are coordinated so that a hundred threads reach the right length at the same time. Little of the actual production takes place in the editor's office; but all of it has its nerve centers here.

Mr. McDonough is slow-spoken and always affably calm. The job of bringing all the threads of production to their monthly conclusions calls for calmness; for no two months offer entirely similar problems, and the end-of-the-month rush always presents new difficulties. Yet the top of his desk is as clear as that of the first vice-president of a bank.

Part of the blankness of the desk top and the calmness of the office are traceable to Mr. McDonough's efficient secretary, Miss Mary Sullivan. Miss Sullivan not only handles stenographic duties but also maintains records of manuscript acceptance and payment and sees to it that routine flows smoothly day by day and issue by issue.

A phenomenon of the American magazine office is that it always has a super-efficient secretary, one of whom the editor says, "I'm not the boss. She is." Which is another way of saying that the modern magazine-editing job is so complex that ultra-efficient routinization is a universal necessity.

What are the chief editorial threads that center in this office?

A door opposite Mr. McDonough's desk leads into the office of W. L. Benson, associate editor in charge of the general division. "General" means just that—all of the material in *Better Homes & Gardens* that cannot be classified under the four other division headings comes from this office. Broadly, this means material dealing with family interests, nature (when it does not deal directly with gardens and gardening), editorial discussion, recreation, travel, poetry, and the like. In Mr. Benson's office is Miss Elizabeth Acri, the dark-haired secretary to whose desk that pile of manuscripts is delivered each morning.

Down the hall and on the other side of Mr. McDonough's office is a third—that of Mrs. Christine Holbrook, associate editor in charge of home furnishings and decoration, and John Normile, associate editor for building, remodeling, and home maintenance. Mrs. Holbrook is often absent, for her work calls for frequent trips out of the city. Mr. Normile, a practicing architect, comes to the office only at stated intervals during the week. When they are not present, the work goes forward under Miss Arlene Jacobson, secretary.

Beyond this office and at the end of the hall is a big room with four big desks. Two of them are for associate editors—Alfred Carl Hottes, in charge of the garden division, and Mrs. Fae Huttenlocher, editor of the Garden Club Exchange and expert on table-setting and flower-arrangement. At the third sits Walter Adams, editor's assistant, who works with Mr. Hottes in the presentation and editing of garden pages and of garden-service leaflets and booklets. The fourth is the desk of Charles H. Swain, manager of the club program department. The office also accommodates two secretaries. At one end a door leads to the office of Lee Goode, director of Better Homes & Gardens Home Service Bureau, and his staff.

Back down the long hall, past the editor's office, are the quarters of the second Meredith publication, *Successful Farming*. Beyond them is a luxurious large conference room. At the corner, where the hall turns, is the art department. In the inner office sits Wallace Hainline, art director; in the adjoining room, bending over drawing boards, his three assistants. Their special charge is the physical appearance of the magazine: Layouts, page arrangements, cover design, typographical plan, decoration, color.

To the right is the office of "Helen Homer," associate editor in charge of foods and equipment. "Helen Homer" is a pen name. Actually she is Mrs. Myrna Johnston. Not only foods and kitchen equipment but also household arts and child care and training are under her supervision. She directs the work of the "Tasting-Test Kitchen" across the hall, a practical foods laboratory in which hundreds of recipes are tested each month. "Jean Byers" (whose real name is Helen Johnson) has immediate charge of the kitchen.

In another office is Anna Joyce Olson, assistant editor in charge of the "It's News to Me" page and other special equipment features. Associate Editor Jean Guthrie, whose home is in South Dakota, has no regular office space, but comes to Des Moines periodically for consultation.

From these offices come the editorial threads that lead to Mr. McDonough's desk. Another set of them, however, comes from the floor below, the site of the business offices—a set as important in the monthly job of magazine production as those from the editorial desks.

President of the Meredith Publishing Company is Fred Bohen. General manager and vice-president is E. T. Meredith, Jr. Another vice-president, E. F. Corbin, is director of sales and promotion and editorial work. Advertising manager for *Better Homes & Gardens* is Peter Ainsworth. Lester H. Mugge is circulation manager; Rex Stark promotion manager. L. E. Smith is production manager, and Glen Boylan manager of the methods department. Director of the important research division, which directs both advertising and editorial research, is J. T. Miller. Each has a corps of assistants.

And this is not to mention the roaring composing, press, and bindery rooms, with their expensive machinery hungry for copy, for plates, and for paper; the air-conditioned basement, crammed with hundreds of tons of paper; the big general stenographic office; the department on the third floor where millions of names are filed, where expirations are noted and new subscriptions entered, where stencils for the addressing machines are cut; the paper-testing laboratory; the business office on the main floor; the cafeteria on the second, where hundreds of employes are served low-cost, scientifically-prepared meals each noon; the considerable force of janitors and engineers who keep the big plant clean, properly heated, and in smooth running order.

Every morning more than 600 men and women come to work in the red-and-white building. Every day the presses grind out a hundred thousand magazines. And every day, so the editors say, problems in what seem comparable numbers come crowding across their desks.

The Manuscripts Go to the Editors

What happens to that pile of manuscripts deposited each morning on Miss Acri's desk in the general editorial office on the second floor?

Much the largest number of them are verse—poems, their authors would fondly call them. Of the more than 10,000 manuscripts that come to *Better Homes & Gardens* each year, nearly 75 percent is verse. At the rate of almost twenty-five a day they pour into the office; and they pour out at almost precisely the same rate, for the magazine has use for only about fifty a year—one a week.

Miss Acri disposes of the "poems" easily. Mr. Adams is the verse editor, and as fast as verse manuscripts with their salmon cards come to Miss Acri she carries them to him. That disposes of three-fourths of her daily mail, in number of pieces if not in deadweight.

The remaining one-fourth, however, bulks larger both in size of individual manuscripts and in importance. And the handling of it is more involved.

First Miss Acri sorts the daily grist—eight to ten a day—according to their nature. To assist Miss Acri in this job, Mr. McDonough has prepared a detailed schedule of subjects that come into the especial province of each of the magazine's five editorial divisions. Among those in the purview of the garden division, for instance, are:

1. How-to-do-it articles (soil culture, plant foods, irrigation, etc.)
2. Plant variety discussions (Oriental poppies, peony varieties, etc.)
3. Landscape design
4. Garden accessories (walks, stepping stones, fences, pergolas, gardenhouses, etc.)
5. Hedges
6. Lawns
7. Evergreens.
8. Bulbs
9. Shrubs
10. Trees

The list goes on with dozens of other topics that belong in the garden division. It means that, when Miss Acri comes across an article dealing with the layout of a rock garden, or plants that can easily be grown indoors, or control of garden pests, she places it in the stack destined for the garden editor's desk. More manuscripts come under this heading than under any other—it appears that most readers of the magazine wish to tell others how they made petunias bloom where only quack grass had grown before.

The sorting is not always easy. "All articles that are obviously published for the benefit of the gardener are to be listed under this head," say the instructions. But "a home greenhouse article, even though it contain building instructions, should be delivered to the garden division" and not to the building editor. On the other hand, a civic-beautification article goes to the general division unless it deals mainly with effective roadside planting or something else that is obviously the gardener's interest.

To Mr. Normile of the building division go the manuscripts concerned with new home construction of whatever nature, from the 18-room mansion to the brick-chimneyed fireplace for the seaside bungalow. This division also gets articles on built-in equipment—millwork, hardware, plumbing and wiring, heating and air-conditioning equipment; on architecture and its relation to landscape; on painting; and on accessories such as insulation, weather-stripping, clothes chutes, built-in bookcases, and ventilators. Again there is an exception: "An article on built-in features . . . would come under this heading unless such features were considered in their relationship in a decorative scheme." In this case the article would go to Mrs. Holbrook of the furnishings and decoration division.

What else goes to Mrs. Holbrook? All articles that have to do with colors used in interiors, or the composition of interior features, or the arrangement of furniture. An article on "The Problem of the Corner Fireplace" would be hers to consider if it viewed the fireplace as an element in room arrangement; it would be Mr. Normile's if it told how to construct the corner fireplace to keep it from smoking. Wall and floor coverings, interior painting, lighting, hangings and curtains, furniture—all these are subjects for this division.

To the better foods and equipment division goes everything dealing with the preparation and serving of food: Recipes and menus and food planning, of course, but also kitchen utensils, tableware, linens, care of refrigerators. To Mrs. Johnston also go the articles on washing machines, bedclothes, vacuum cleaners, irons—every kind of home equipment. And her division includes child care and training, health, parent education, clothing, styles, needlecraft, and artcraft.

To the general division goes—everything else.

For a considerable portion of the magazine's content fails to fit readily under any of these four heads. And so to Mr. Benson's desk Miss Acri routes manuscripts dealing with books, music, and the arts—"family improvement," according to the breakdown; articles of inspirational nature; articles on family relationships, education, recreation, budgets and finance; travel articles, nature material not in the garden division's area, discussion of legal problems of the home, of how to keep pets and how to start a civic beautification campaign. This desk also receives all material that might fit into the magazine's editorial column and other special departments not handled by other editors.

How Manuscripts Are Rejected

Once Miss Acri has sorted the manuscripts into five piles, she goes through this procedure:

Removes all salmon cards and files them alphabetically in a filing cabinet marked "Manuscripts Received."

Types on each yellow card the classification and the editor's name and re-attaches it to its manuscript.

Carries each stack of manuscripts, once a day or at least several times a week, to the editor whose name appears on its yellow cards.

Thus the 10,000 manuscripts a year reach the editors who are to decide on their disposition. Factors that influence the decisions are to be discussed in Chapter IV. For the present, follow the course of the scripts as the machinery continues to grind.

Once the manuscript has been read and its merits weighed by the editor to whom it has been referred, one of three dispositions may be made of it:

Rejection

Recommendation for purchase, in whole or in part

Return to author for revision

The first of the three possibilities is the most likely, for less than 1 percent of all verse submitted proves suitable, and not more than 10 percent of other manuscripts. What happens in case of rejection?

If the editor decides to reject a manuscript without passing it on for further consideration, his secretary attaches to it that bane of the free-lance, a rejection slip. Often the editor would like to write a detailed letter describing reasons for rejection, and sometimes—when the author is one who has sold other material to the magazine, or who has been selling to other magazines, or who has barely missed making a sale in this particular case—he does. Usually, because his time is all too limited, he must use the rejection slip.

To bridge the gap between the harsh impersonality of such a slip and the more kindly personal letter, however, the *Better Homes & Gardens* rejection slip (like that used by scores of other magazines) is more than a mere card of regret. It is a four-page folder. Its first page bears the formal statement of rejection and an invitation to try again; its second contains a list of twelve of the more common reasons for rejection which the editor may check as they apply to individual manuscripts; and its third a set of eight "suggestions" which are really rules that every free-lance writer should know and follow but that many ignore.

The secretary removes from the rejected manuscript the yellow card, on which the editor has initialed the space "Ed. Rej.," and sends it to Miss Acri. Miss Acri then takes the salmon card for the manuscript from the "Manuscripts Received" file, stamps the return date on it, and transposes it to a "Manuscripts Returned" file (the first file is a centralized record of manuscripts in the building for consideration, the second a permanent record of rejections). She destroys the yellow card.

> With a view to being helpful we wish you to know why we have to return your material. The specific reason is indicated below:
>
> ☐ Supplied. We have, or have recently used, articles on these subjects.
>
> ☐ Not enough "how to." We are not as much interested in mere description or *why* you make a garden, for instance, as *how* you make it.
>
> ☐ Outside our field. *Better Homes & Gardens* is published for gardened-home families in cities, towns, and suburbs—and material we accept must all be adapted to such families.
>
> ☐ Length. Articles should approximate 1,500 words.
>
> ☐ We use no fiction, fashions, or beauty aids; poetry only for special purposes.
>
> ☐ Too technically written.
>
> ☐ Cannot be applied by many *Better Homes & Gardens* families in their own homes.
>
> ☐ Must be more delightfully informative.
>
> ☐ Untimely. Because issues are planned far in advance, seasonable material should be in our hands at least five months before date of issue in which it should appear. Many good articles arrive too late to appear in the issue for which they are suitable.
>
> ☐ Material submitted to exploit a specific brand of merchandise to the exclusion of other brands among that class of commodities is not acceptable.
>
> ☐ Photographs must be at least 5x7, clear with good detail, sharp contrasts, and on glossy paper.
>
> ☐ Does not meet our present needs.

The secretary now puts manuscript, illustrations, and rejection slip (or letter) into a return envelope and, if the author has submitted enough postage, sends it upstairs to the "promotional mailing" department. This department attaches the stamps needed, makes sure that the manuscript and enclosures are protected with enough cardboard, seals the envelope, and tosses it into the mail bag.

If the author has failed to send within six cents of enough postage, the secretary sends out a grayish postcard with this message:

> Thank you for letting us see your manuscript. We have given it a very careful reading and find that it is not adapted to our present needs.
>
> Because you did not send postage for its return, we ask that you do so now, inclosing ..... cents so that we may return it to you promptly.

If the return postage is less than six cents short of the required amount,

Better Homes & Gardens pays the difference—it is less costly to do so because of time and handling saved.

The rejection of poetry is simpler. The salmon card is attached to verse manuscripts, and a special rejection slip without the spaces for comment is used. Otherwise, however, the procedure is substantially the same.

Sometimes editors make woefully wrong decisions when they reject manuscripts. When Walter Hines Page was editor of the *Atlantic Monthly*, one of his sub-editors reported to him, "This is a vulgar manuscript and smells of the stable." Mr. Page read half the script and approved its rejection. It was "David Harum," one of the best-selling books of all time.

This procedure disposes of most of the manuscripts. For the more fortunate ones—those that editors wish to purchase—the course is different.

How Manuscripts Are Accepted

First the editor may consult with his associates as to the desirability of buying a script. If furnishings show in a photograph the garden editor wishes to buy, for instance, he gets the home furnishings editor's approval of them. If an article is on the border-line, he asks for the opinions of others. Then he notes on the yellow card the suggested payment for illustrations and manuscript, and sends it to Mr. McDonough with a memorandum, or takes it in person to him.

Now Mr. McDonough reads the manuscript and considers the editor's recommendation. If he decides against its purchase—his decision is final—it follows the same path as the others rejected, except that it is likely to go home with a letter instead of a rejection slip. If he approves it, he notes the purchase price suggested on the yellow card and confirms or alters it (payment is figured basically on the amount of space the feature is expected to occupy. But the author's rank as an authority or his skill as a writer may boost the price). He initials the yellow card, which is now stamped "paid," and the manuscript and illustrations go back to the editor who recommended their purchase.

In one case *Better Homes & Gardens* bought for $150 a manuscript and pictures expected to take two pages. Later it was decided to devote four pages to the material. An additional check for $75 was sent to the author.

Miss Sullivan, Mr. McDonough's secretary, removes the salmon card from the "Manuscripts Received" file and places it in another, "Manuscripts Paid For." The yellow card she puts into an "inventory box," where it becomes a record of unused manuscripts on hand.

Once a week Miss Sullivan sends a "payment record" downstairs to the business office. This is a request for the business office to make out checks for the material bought that week—usually six to ten items. The checks come back to Miss Sullivan, and she dispatches each with a form letter that says "accepted material is subject to such editorial changes as the policy of our publications may require" and "acceptance of the inclosed check" is the author's guarantee that the manuscript is original and unpublished.

Miss Sullivan has other duties connected with manuscript purchase:

For each major feature bought she makes a permanent "record of contributor" on a printed form punched for filing in a loose-leaf binder. This record shows the writer's name and address, dates on which manuscripts from him have been bought, the number of words in them, the prices paid.

She keeps a record of the ten or a dozen recipes bought each week, at the standard rate of $1, and lists them on her weekly "payment record." The $1 checks she sends to contributors with special simplified form letters.

She keeps track of royalties due architects who furnish plans for houses offered to *Better Homes & Gardens* families through the building division, and sees that royalty checks go out (see Chapter IV).

Once a month, after each issue has appeared, she "charges off" the manuscripts used in the issue. She goes through two copies of the magazine and writes boldly across each feature the price paid for it. She keeps one copy for the editorial department's record, and sends the other to the art department, where one of the art director's assistants adds the cost of the art work in the issue. This copy then goes to the business office, where the amounts spent are charged to the editorial and art departments. After "charging off" an article, Miss Sullivan removes the corresponding yellow card from the "inventory box" and destroys it.

All of this is the basic mechanical routine of the *Better Homes & Gardens* editorial department. It demands only a fraction of the editors' and secretaries' time. But it is the foundation on which the scores of other editorial operations are laid.

In Other Magazine Offices

Similar routines form similar bases for the procedure of every magazine office in America. No two are precisely alike; not many, unhappy to relate, are as efficient in manuscript handling. But all have their set machinery for the receipt, consideration, and disposition of the incredibly large amount of grist that clogs their daily mails.

As a rule, only large and highly-organized magazine offices have plans for the receipt, disposal, and dispatch of manuscripts so systematic as that just described. In many magazine offices all incoming mail is dumped onto the desk of a secretary whose job it is to sort and distribute. Sometimes it is also her task to open mail, to record manuscripts' receipt in some form of record system, to put them on first readers' desks, and eventually to return most of them.

Again few magazines are so highly departmentalized as is *Better Homes & Gardens*. Usually first readers—junior editors—take charge of weeding out the impossibles, the 90 or 95 percent (in some cases the figure is 99 plus) that is unsuitable, and of passing on to other editors the articles and stories that are possibilities or better.

Keeping records by the card system is not usual. Most magazines employ big loose-leaf ledgers that show date of manuscripts' receipt, their authors' names and addresses, their titles and lengths, whether they are accompanied by illustrations, and their disposition. All magazines maintain systems for record of purchased manuscripts. Often, as in *Better Homes & Gardens,* these records are kept under authors' names, either in loose-leaf ledgers or on filing cards.

Reports on manuscripts vary widely. *Modern Mechanix* uses a 9" x 12" envelope for each manuscript. On this envelope is printed a form with spaces for necessary information about receipt and disposition of the manuscript and, in addition, a space in which each editor who reads it may state his opinion. These opinions vary from a flat "yes" or "no" to an elaborate discussion of the manuscript's merits and shortcomings, suggestions for its revision or editing, justifications for the editors' opinions that it should or should not be purchased. If its purchase is approved, the envelope is used to file it in a fire-proof vault until it is withdrawn for use. If it is not bought, the record on the envelope's face is filed as a memorandum of the script.

In most magazine offices editors' memoranda on manuscripts are written on small sheets of paper that are clipped to the manuscripts. Sometimes manuscripts go to the executive editor in whom the power of final decision is vested, with only one such memorandum; others bear as many as half a dozen. Some magazines make it a rule that all material must be examined by at least two editors before it may be rejected. Rarely is a manuscript purchased, on the other hand, on the recommendation of but one editor, except in the case of the small magazine for which the entire editorial job is handled by one man. The *Ladies' Home Journal* usually buys material only after five or six editors have seen it; *Collier's* three to five; *Rotarian* four to six; *Esquire* two; *Atlantic Monthly* four; and so on.

Inexperienced writers often fume under the delusion that the magazines do not welcome their efforts. Nothing is farther from the truth. The statement of one magazine editor on this score has become a truism: "No manuscript is rejected until it has disqualified itself." This means that any story or article that seems to have the dimmest chance of meeting a magazine's requirements will be passed by the first reader to other editors for further consideration. The fact is that every magazine editor in the United States is begging for material—that he is eternally on the lookout for new writers, new talent, fresh points of view. A bad manuscript from an accepted writer—one known either from previous sales to the magazine considering his script or from sales to other markets—will have, it is true, a better chance to get to the executive editor than a bad manuscript from an unknown. But a manuscript from a novice with no more than a glimmer of promise is likely to get consideration out of all proportion to its worth simply because it gives editors hope that they may be on the trail of new talent. This is true not alone because the supply of well-qualified writers seems never to equal the demand, but also because good manuscripts can often be bought from little-known writers at lower prices than can pieces of no more merit from writers with established names. It may be that this fact does not check with the writer's notion of justice; but it fits nicely with established business practice.

Moreover, the first reader on a magazine is not always a junior editor. When William Kostka, later executive editor of the Fawcett publications, was editing *Modern Mechanix,* he always insisted on reading every manuscript that came to his office. This assured him of getting a chance at every article that had the remotest chance of meeting his needs. Not a usual practice, it is employed by a few editors.

Most magazines publish statements that they will not be responsible for the return of manuscripts for which authors have failed to provide return fare. In some cases such scripts, after a waiting period, are deposited summarily in the waste basket. A few periodicals, however, return all manuscripts regardless of return postage—a practice that often costs them some hundreds of dollars in a year's time.

Rejection slips are most commonly mere formal statements of the editors' polite regret at the manuscript's failure to meet current needs, sometimes coupled with an invitation not to give up: "We appreciate your thought of us, and hope you will let us see other material." Scores of magazines, however, use the type with a list of common faults which editors may check as a partial substitute for personal letters of criticism. A few, such as *Esquire,* promise personal comment on all material submitted to them. But it is only fair to say that this "personal comment" is sometimes disappointing. Usually it is no more than a hastily-scratched note on a memorandum slip: "Sorry—not for us," "well-written but too long," "old stuff," or the like.

How Long Does "Consideration" Take?

How long a time is usually required for consideration of a manuscript? To this question, asked querulously by so many writers who have waited weeks and months to get manuscripts back, there is no pat answer. The factors that govern the waiting-period are, chiefly, two: Size of staff and efficiency of staff organization. As a rule the magazines holding manuscripts for longer periods are those with staffs so small that they find it difficult to keep up with reading and clerical duties (yet *Mill and Factory,* a relatively small trade publication, reports with great promptness). Unquestionably most magazines desire to hold manuscripts as briefly as is consistent with fair consideration.

Promptness in payment for accepted material varies as widely as does promptness in reporting. Some periodicals send out checks immediately on decision to purchase; others, like *Better Homes & Gardens,* at stated intervals—once a week or once a month; others on publication. A scattering few pay as soon after publication as they are able—if they are able. This generalization may be drawn: Most of the successful, well-established magazines pay on acceptance, or within a short interval after acceptance.

Of twenty-six widely varying magazines asked, "How promptly do you ordinarily report on unacceptable non-fiction?" ten responded that they need 1 week, seven asked 2 weeks and four 3 weeks. Two said that they report in 2 to 4 days, and three that they manage it in 24 hours. No standard key explains these differences: The three with the shortest consideration periods were *American Mercury, Field and Stream,* and *Mill and Factory*; those with the longest were *Asia, Esquire, Sports Afield,* and *Theatre Arts Monthly*. The nature or magnitude of the magazine, obviously, has nothing to do with it, though those in the 1-week division are for the most part such firmly established and well-organized periodicals as *Woman's Home Companion, Harper's, Collier's, Nation's Business,* and *Forum*.

Such a policy is both good business and fair play. The *American Boy* is one of the magazines paying most promptly for material; and its one-time managing editor, George F. Pierrot, has explained the policy thus: "We have two major reasons for wanting to pay promptly for manuscripts. One is that we believe we have no right to hold an author's property any longer than we absolutely must without either coming to a decision to reject it and returning it to him, or paying him for it. Most free-lance writers depend on their checks for their living, and they have as much right to expect reasonably prompt payment as have the shoe dealer and the grocer who may be dunning them.

"The other is that we find the prompt-decision-and-payment policy wins us friends and gets us manuscripts we might not otherwise have a chance at. The *American Boy* cannot pay as high rates for its material as can some of the larger general magazines; but it wants as good writing, and from some of the same writers. We have found that authors frequently send manuscripts to us rather than to other magazines because they know they can count on quick decision and quick payment."

Many of the pulp magazines make quick decision and prompt payment a standard policy for precisely the same reasons, and they find the policy advantageous. Sometimes, however, authors accustomed to long waits for scripts' return are inclined to suspect too-prompt action. When one inexperienced writer received a manuscript back from a magazine two days after he had mailed it, with a note from the acting managing editor, he at once shot off a heated letter stating that the time elapsed made it physically impossible for the magazine to have given his work fair consideration—and that he wasn't going to accept criticism from anybody less than the managing editor (who, it chanced, was in Europe) anyway! The magazine accepted with admirable equanimity his threat never to offer it another script, and replied with complete reports from two editors on his story.

This magazine, however, realizing that such prompt action may frequently be suspect, thereupon put into effect a rule that no returns should be made until three days after the date of receipt, even though decision had been reached immediately.

Figuring Rates of Payment

Rates of payment vary from pole to pole. Not a few publications are unable to make any payment for contributions. Some of these are obscure, struggling class and trade magazines published on very frayed shoe-strings. Others are those backed by specialized groups, such as the *Journal of the American Medical Association* and the *Journalism Quarterly*. Rate of payment is a false guide to a magazine's "quality" or standing. When *Story* first appeared, it made no payment for the manuscripts it accepted; even after it was put on a commercial basis its rates were not considered high. Yet it was ranked by critics as a leader among American "literary" magazines. Many of the "best" magazines, either on the basis of literary and artistic merit or that of authority in their fields, have never been able to compete in rates with the big-circulation popular magazines. Nevertheless they command first-rate talent because of the prestige attached to the names of authors on their table of contents pages, or because of authors' interest in the causes they espouse.

To newspaper editors the free-lance feature article is relatively unimportant. Some metropolitan newspapers buy a few such articles for Sunday (rarely for week-day) use; but most long newspaper features are prepared by staff writers. This is doubtless the reason newspapers receive only a few articles a week from free lances, and it probably explains the sad lack of systematic handling of manuscripts, characteristic of most newspapers. When Sunday or feature editors buy free-lance articles, they usually pay at space rates a week or so after publication.

On the opposite side of the picture are the tremendous sums offered by wealthy magazines for material (or, in some cases, names) they desire. The *Saturday Evening Post* usually pays $300 to $500 for a normal-length contribution from a "new author," and several times that for stories or articles by successful writers or well-known names. One big popular weekly is said to have bid and paid $55,000 for a serial story by one of America's best-known writers (a writer who, being business man enough to realize his value, had offered his story to a number of magazines on a best-bid basis).

And between these extremes are the hundreds of publications that pay moderate sums for material.

Rates are usually determined on one of two bases: So much per word for a story or article as it is to appear in print; or so much per story or article with little regard to the precise word-count. Magazines offering payment on the first basis usually announce a minimum rate of 1/3 to 3 cents a word (the going base rate is listed in the current manuscript market guides, and it may change from time to time). This minimum rate, however, is by no means the only rate at which a magazine pays. It is commonly understood that the minimum will be paid to a writer new to the magazine, unless he has already established a reputation that will enable him to demand, and get, a higher rate. As a writer continues to sell, and as his skill and his reader-following increase, his rate usually rises. Most magazines have not only minimum but also maximum rates. A publication with a 2-cent base seldom goes above 5 cents. . . . Magazines that pay on page- or column- instead of word-rates follow similar rules.

And the same practices apply to publications with lump-sum base rates. *Esquire,* according to writers' reports, usually pays $75 for an article from a new writer. It pays a good deal more to a writer with an established name.

Many magazines have set rates for specific classifications of material. *Better Homes & Gardens* pays $1 for each recipe it accepts. *Collier's* pays $5 for any acceptable contribution to its "Keeping Up With the World" column. *Scribner's* at one time was paying $100 for each usable manuscript for its "Life in the United States" section.

Magazine rates, be it noted, are as subject to the whims of economic law as are stock-market figures. Rates for most periodicals hit new highs in the booming days of the late twenties. A number of pulp magazines, usually listing 2-cent bases, paid as high as 15 cents a word for material from men whose work was in demand. Since that time sky-high rates have become less common, and magazine editors have expressed the opinion—and the hope—that such towering fees will never again be anything but rare exceptions.

The word-rate basis for payment offers this difficulty, from the magazine's point of view: That authors sometimes, consciously or not, pad their manuscripts to enlarge their checks. For this reason many editors always estimate the number of words that will appear on the published pages, rather than that in the typed manuscript, and pay on that basis. More than one writer in the golden days of high rates and keen competition lost markets because they refused to accept payment on the basis of edited and pruned manuscripts.

Some form of guarantee by an author that a manuscript is original is demanded by most editors. This usually takes the shape of a statement sent with the check that its cashing is the author's acceptance of the magazine's conditions: That the material is his to sell, that he will not duplicate it, that certain rights are irrevocably transferred to the buyer. These rights may include "first serial rights," which means the right to first periodical publication, and sometimes all other publication rights, book rights, motion picture, radio and dramatic rights, the privilege of copyright, and so on. Though an author give up all such rights, most magazines are willing to re-assign to him what rights he may desire after publication—permission to put the material into book form, for instance.

Another form of sales contract is exemplified by that of the *American Mercury.* The *Mercury* sends to an author whose work it wishes to purchase a "writer's acceptance" slip, the signing of which agrees to the purchase price suggested by the editors and confirms the magazine in the publication rights it desires.

That writers are not as good as their word is always an outside possibility. Occasionally a magazine buys a manuscript in good faith, only to learn before or after publication that the whole thing has been "lifted." Such cases are usually net losses; magazines rarely wish to carry them to court, and often a court order would gain nothing anyway, for "writers" who employ plagiarism do not customarily have attachable assets or earning power. The cases arise infrequently, partly because few persons are so stupid as to become involved in them and partly because magazine editors make it their business to know virtually everything that is being or has been published in their fields. They are not often caught sleeping.

Practice Suggestions

1. From an examination of an issue of each of three departmentalized magazines—say *McCall's*, *Country Gentleman*, and *Mademoiselle*—make up lists of the subjects that appear to be the especial province of each department (including the general or miscellaneous).

2. Write an "editor's report" on each non-fiction feature in one issue of a magazine at least half devoted to non-fiction material. Make each report the kind of comment you would offer if you were the article's "first reader" and were passing it on to the executive editor for consideration.

3. Examine all the material that appears under the same departmental heading of three successive issues of a magazine. Then write a paragraph of comment on each article or feature, stating the qualities that, you think, led the editors to decide on its use.

REFERENCES

Magazine Making, by John Bakeless. Viking Press, New York. 1931.

Magazine Publishing, by Lenox R. Lohr. Williams & Wilkins Company, Baltimore. 1932.

III

The Story of an Issue

DEVELOPING a finished issue of a magazine from the welter of manuscripts, photographs, drawings, blurbs, departments, and advertisements that must go into it is a job not unlike putting together a Ford on the River Rouge assembly line.

The parts that go to make the finished Ford are built to blue-print and machined to the fraction of a centimeter. Once the dies are cut and the lathes set, the process is not much more than the routine of putting the parts together. All of this is true of magazine production. Its parts must be machined to fit, and when they have been suited to the pattern the "models" may be turned out in hundreds, thousands, or millions.

But the Ford factory has this advantage: When its patterns are finished it may turn to production for a season or a year; indeed, it may make none but superficial changes over even longer periods. The magazine, however, is remade once a week or once a month. It is producing from two to six "models" at the same time—in different parts of the shop the jobs of blue-printing, of machining parts, of seeking new raw material, and of planning future patterns are all going on simultaneously.

System makes it possible.

A precise system or routine—a kind of editorial assembly line—is a necessity for every magazine. In some shops, those of magazines with simple make-up and production problems and with relatively simple departmentalization, the routine is simple. For the more elaborate and involved magazines—especially the "slicks," those printed on coated paper and using many illustrations and color work—the routine too must be elaborate and involved.

Typical of the latter routine is that of *Better Homes & Gardens,* a magazine with problems of illustration, color, high-speed presses, and intricate departmentalization. Part of the routine, for the consideration, selection, and purchase of raw material, has been described in Chapter II.

At the base of the *Better Homes & Gardens* editorial production routine is what is called the "lead-feature and color-feature plan." By this plan every editor knows months in advance what major features he must provide, and he can select material (or take steps to get it) and start it into production according to a definite schedule.

Briefly, the lead-feature plan lays down for about a year in advance a schedule of the major features—by type of subject matter, not by specific article—for each month's issue. Major features are those occupying the first two positions in the front of the book. *Better Homes & Gardens,* according to the lead-feature plan here portrayed, regularly opens the front of the book on Page 13. On this page opens the first "lead feature."

"Front of the book" in any magazine office means the main editorial section—the section between the advertisements opening the magazine and those that bring up its rear. Some editorial material, placed among the opening advertisements, may precede the "front of the book": table of contents, or departments, or editorial page, or frontispiece. But this material is not, in magazine jargon, "front-of-the-book" material. "Back of the book," of course, is the section that follows the main editorial section. The first advertisement that appears as the reader pages through this section usually signals that he has reached the "back of the book," though he may be less than half way through the magazine's total pages. Magazines like *Readers Digest,* with no advertisements, are all "front of the book"; *Liberty* has neither "front" nor "back," for it intersperses advertisements at intervals throughout.

The outline of the lead-feature plan for a typical year is shown on Page 89. The usual opening feature, under this plan, is of three pages; "lead feature No. 2" of two pages. The first always opens on Page 13, a righthand page; the second on Page 16. The first, therefore, ordinarily gets an opening page plus a "spread"—two facing pages. The second gets a spread. Each may have runover to the back of the book, but this is not important in original planning.

The year's plan shows that the general division gets five and a half lead features (the June lead is shared with the garden division); gardens get four; home furnishings two and a half. Of second leads five go to gardens, three to building, remodeling, and maintenance, two to home furnishings, one to general, and one to a special gift section. Thus the largest share of opening space is accorded to general material, which is planned for the widest possible reading audience; the second largest share to gardens, which the magazine's editors have found to be the strongest single specialized interest of its readers. As a further concession to this interest, gardens get almost half of the second leads. Home furnishings come third in total share of opening space; the building division, with no lead features but a generous share of second leads, fourth.

The magazine's fifth division, better foods and equipment, is granted none of the lead positions. But its needs are not ignored. Seven pages of each issue go to this division; and it gets almost half of the year's four-color pages. More of this later.

The lead-feature plan, then, gives each department editor warning long in advance that he must have on hand material for timely major features for specific issues. It does not, however, invariably assign space under mere divisional designations. The year's plan here outlined calls for ten lead features under divisional assignments. But two are assigned more precisely: June to garden and general because a seasonable article was on hand when the plan was designed, December to garden and furnishings because an article-idea had been proposed by one of the editors.

And the plan is open to change if good reason appears. An example: The plan here given called for an April home-furnishings lead feature. But Mrs. Holbrook, division editor, gave up this preferred position because the cover and two inside four-color pages were to be devoted to her material. Then came a news break. Congress made important amendments to the National Housing Act, and the editors decided that an article explaining what the revised act would mean to homebuilders should take precedence over everything else. The article was rushed into shape, and "Good News" (see Page 7) appeared on Page 13, the first front-of-the-book page. "Ten Minutes From Hollywood" (see Pages 8, 9) was altered to fit the spread following.

BETTER HOMES & GARDENS

LEAD-FEATURE PLAN

1938

Issue	*Lead Feature*	*Pages*	*Lead Feature No. 2*	*Pages*
January	General	3	Garden	2
February	Garden	3	Garden	2
March	General	3	Garden	2
April	Home-Furnishings	3	Garden	2
May	Garden	3	Building or Maintenance	2
June	Combined Garden and General Story (Edw. Steichen and His Delphiniums)	3	Remodeling or Maintenance	2
July	General	3	Home-Furnishings	2
August	General	3	Building	2
September	Garden	3	General	2
October	Home-Furnishings	3	Home-Furnishings	2
November	General	3	Garden	2
December	Garden and Furnishings; that is, decorating the house, inside and out, for Christmas	3	Gift Section	2

Mr. McDonough explains the lead-feature plan: "Although the lead feature calls for three pages, division editors are at liberty to use them as a one-page lead feature with a second story on the following spread. Usually, however, a lead feature should treat a subject important enough to display in three-page form."

A further provision of the plan is that each editorial division, whether it has a lead position or not, is to provide at least one spread for every issue.

The color-feature plan operates similarly, and is coordinated with the lead-feature schedule. It plans for a year in advance the full-color pages to be allotted to the editorial departments, so that each editor may arrange months ahead of time for suitable material. The plan on Page 90 provides for twenty-three four-color pages. Eleven of these—one in each month except January—go to the foods and equipment division. Six of the remaining twelve go to furnishings and decoration, two in April and four in October. Thus furnishings are given both lead-feature positions in October as well as four color-pages—October is the time of year when housewives think of renovating, refurnishing, and redecorating. The same division gets "special play" in April, the opening feature and two color-pages. Gardens are given four color-pages, two in February in conjunction with both lead features—this is the year's big garden-planning issue—and two in September, with an opening feature. The last two color-pages go to the special December gift section.

BETTER HOMES & GARDENS
COLOR-FEATURE PLAN
1938

Issue	*Department*	*Pages*
January		0
February	Better Gardens	2
	Better Foods & Equipment	1
March	Better Foods & Equipment	1
April	Home Furnishings & Decoration	2
	Better Foods & Equipment	1*
May	Better Foods & Equipment	1
June	Better Foods & Equipment	1†
July	Better Foods & Equipment	1†
August	Better Foods & Equipment	1†
September	Better Gardens	2
	Better Foods & Equipment	1
October	Home Furnishings & Decoration	4
	Better Foods & Equipment	1
November	Better Foods & Equipment	1
December	Better Foods & Equipment	1
	Gift Section	2‡
	Total	23

* May combine table settings with foods
† Combines foods and table settings
‡ Possibly. Tentatively set down because of the December staff conference, at which color pages were suggested for opening the gift section pages

The foods and equipment editor, Mrs. Johnston, has a more definite guide for needs each month than the lead- and color-feature plan alone provides. She has to have seven pages in each issue, a solid front-of-the-book section. It opens with a spread, a four-color page on the left with a black-and-one-color page facing. This is a meal-planning spread. Next comes a spread on household equipment, or perhaps two single pages on equipment or methods. The fifth page, on the left, may be devoted to table settings, recipes, diet, child care and training—almost any subject she chooses within her field. And the last two pages are always the "Cooks' Round Table of Endorsed Recipes" insert.

There are other standard guides which each editor follows each month. "The Diary of a Plain Dirt Gardener" and "Along the Garden Path" are regular monthly garden departments. The building division always furnishes plans, description, and pictures of a "Bildcost gardened-home" and "The Question Before the House," a monthly question-and-answer service. The general editor provides a whole portfolio of regular features: "Across the Editor's Desk," editorial notes (written by Mr. McDonough) that lie alongside the table of contents on Page 4; the frontispiece on Page 7; "Back Talk," the letters-to-the-editor department; "Among Ourselves," a chatty column of hints from gardeners and householders, containing within its own columns another monthly feature, "Whims and Hobbies"; and a humor column, "The Man Next Door." Miss Olson must supply "It's News to Me" for Page 10.

Ordinarily every issue of *Better Homes & Gardens* includes all these features, unless a change in plan or unexpected lack of space excludes some of them. And each editor plans for his share of them, sometimes as much as a year ahead of publication. Moreover, Mr. McDonough, laying his plans month by month, counts on them.

One more dependable guide must be listed: The never-ending need for seasonable material. Each February the garden division must present a quantity of garden articles and features suitable to the coming season: Plans for spring landscaping, newsy articles about new flowers for spring planting, and so on. In the summer issues Mrs. Johnston must plan for articles on hot-weather menus. Mr. Benson seeks for December or January an article on winter travel or one suggesting winter sports to be enjoyed near home. Seasonable material is always in high demand, and editors always welcome it.

In Other Magazine Offices

Most magazines have comparable monthly "must lists" whereby to build the skeletons of their plans. A minority has as many regular features as *Better Homes & Gardens,* for few are so highly departmentalized and few assign to themselves so many subjects to be covered regularly. But all have schedules, explicit or implicit, that vary in detail and practice rather than in purpose or effect.

Systematized schedules like the lead- and color-feature plan are not common. They are especially rare in magazines part of whose contents is fiction. Such magazines may in one issue open the front of the book with a short story or the first installment of a serial, a "one-shot" article the next, the first of a biographical series the third. Where the magazine is departmentalized, however, there is usually at least an informal schedule that requires each editor to furnish certain standard types of material for each issue.

And almost all magazines have regular departments. They vary from "contributors' columns" to stamp pages, book reviews to beauty hints, letter departments such as *Esquire's* "The Sound and the Fury" to theater and entertainment guides such as the *New Yorker's* "Goings on About Town." Though their natures are identical in no two publications, they have these common aspects: They act as compulsion on editors to seek certain types of material month after month, and they give to editors rules of thumb to govern at least a part of their jobs.

To most magazines the need for seasonable material is of top rank. The *Saturday Evening Post, Collier's,* and *Liberty* each spring or summer make concessions to their readers' heightened interest in baseball. The women's magazines each fall publish articles to help school girls select their fall and winter wardrobes. Thanksgiving, Christmas, Easter, and Fourth of July features are as important to *Boy's Life* as they are to *Vogue. Harper's* and the *Atlantic Monthly,* less amenable to the seasons' demands than most periodicals, nevertheless like to publish wintry articles in winter; and they present their "summer fiction numbers" in August. The *Nation* has its special book-review issue shortly before Christmas. And the *Northwestern Druggist* tries, in summer, to publish articles telling readers how to sell more ice cream sodas and more mosquito-bite remedy.

A common guide to planning the issue is that of proportion. Precise proportions by which editors allot their space are, however, often carefully-guarded secrets. This is because of editors' belief that the success of their publications may very well lie in the scientific propriety of their balance. "It is true that anybody can dig out the facts of a magazine's proportional scheme," they say. "Mere analysis of contents of several issues will tell anybody who cares to take the trouble that an editor gives so much space to this kind of material, so much to that, and so much to the other. But there's no reason why an editor should gratuitously offer such information to a possible competitor. Let him find out for himself!"

In the all-fiction magazine the proportion rule means that there must be proper ratio of rough-and-tumble adventure to young love. In the general magazine seeking a broad audience there must be a balance between the heavy and the light, between fiction and non-fiction. Some magazines have readily-visible patterns by which such balance is attained: *Collier's* usually offers one or two light love stories, one Western or action story, one or two serial installments, one humorous story, one short short; and one social or political article, one "glamor" article on a celebrity of stage, screen, or other special-interest field, one sports article or story.

Such guides to proportion apply more commonly to the individual issue than to the magazine over a long period. They may change with the seasons: Usually a higher percentage of fiction is printed in the magazines in the summer than in the winter.

How the Machinery Works

On the first day of each month Mr. McDonough throws the lever to start the machinery that, three and a half months later, will turn out a finished issue of *Better Homes & Gardens.*

On that day a memorandum goes to all the editors of the magazine —not only to the heads of the strictly editorial divisions, but also to Mr. Hainline, art director, and to other associate and assistant editors— giving them a forecast of the probable size of the issue on which they are to start active work. The memorandum lists the anticipated number of editorial pages (spreads, single pages, double and single column spaces) and breaks these spaces down into divisional allotments. (How he knows what these spaces are to be is described in Chapter V.) The arrival of that memorandum in each office is the signal that each editor is to turn his material in to Mr. McDonough by the tenth of the month. Mr. McDonough, in turn, is to present all material, or as much of it as possible, to Mr. Hainline for layout and other art work by the fifteenth; and all copy is due in the composing room by the thirtieth of the following month.

Precisely how does this machinery operate?

Take a typical April issue as an example. Mr. McDonough's memorandum asking for material for this issue goes to the editors on December 1, three and a half months before the first copy will reach its subscriber on March 15. The memorandum forecasts an issue of 190 pages, with a breakdown that gives the editorial department fifty-two full pages, twenty of them singles and the remainder in sixteen spreads. In addition, twenty-two double-column back-of-the-book spaces are expected. Mr. McDonough allocates this space so as to give home furnishings, the featured department in the issue, 26 percent; gardens 24 percent; building 18 percent; and general and foods and equipment 16 percent each—a fairly even distribution.

This done, he prepares two layout books. One is a large book with pages of exact *Better Homes & Gardens* size, the second a small 4-by-6 dummy. The first is his guide to Mr. Hainline and the art department for the placing of each feature; the second his own informal memorandum by which to keep tab on the growth of the issue.

As the manuscripts start to come in (Mr. McDonough and the division editors have talked them over and decided on editorial changes some time in the past), he enters their names in the two layout books. By December 10, the due date, much of the material is in his hands. By this time, the estimate of the probable size of the issue has decreased—not as much advertising as had at first been expected seems to be forthcoming, and the issue will be smaller than 190 pages. Because there is a relation between the amounts of editorial and advertising space, the space open for editorial material is smaller; but this does not change the front of the book appreciably. (Sometimes the estimate must be revised upward, and more material is demanded.)

The lead-feature plan for April calls for three opening pages devoted to home furnishings, followed by a garden spread. A staff conference has somewhat altered this plan. Mrs. Holbrook is to have a home furnishing cover picture and five spreads, and she has deeded her claim to the opening feature to Mr. Normile (associate editor for building and remodeling, and home maintenance). He plans a two-page opening story, "Ten Minutes From Hollywood," and a single-page story on a remodeled home for his third page. Lead feature No. 2, a garden spread on Pages 16 and 17, thereby becomes the third instead of the second title in the front of the book.

Mr. McDonough outlines the remainder of the issue in the two layout books as the manuscripts pour in. On December 15 he sends to the art editor a list of seventy layouts that will probably be needed. A number of these are "holdovers"—articles planned for previous issues, hence already in type and ready to be put into the magazine without further work; others are articles for which layouts have already been made. Most are new material.

By December 15 the division editors complete most of their work for the issue. They have furnished manuscripts, illustrations, and cut-lines (captions for illustrations) for the spaces they have been asked to fill. They have edited manuscripts so that they will approximate the allotted space; but exactness is often impossible, for they cannot know just how much room the art department will need for head-lines, pictures, and the all-important white space.

Now the April issue is, temporarily, in the hands of the art department. Here the layouts, the working drawings for page make-up, are made, and often remade half a dozen times before precisely the right ones are developed. In the weeks between December 15 and February 1 all of this work is completed, most of it by mid-January.

Once the layouts receive Mr. McDonough's approval, he turns them over to Mr. Adams, his assistant. It is Mr. Adams' responsibility to see that the manuscript pages are turned into type and the photographs and drawings into engravings—and that both type and engravings fit the space assigned to them. Manuscripts for the April issue start to come to his desk on December 21; by New Year's Day one spread and four two-column layouts go from him to the composing room. Layouts continue to dribble through until January 12; then a flood of them between January 14 and 22. After that a few more come in, some as late as the first days of February. Last on the list is "Good News," the last-minute article that is to open the front of the book.

Now comes the monumental task of making the type fit the space. Printers are fond of telling novice editors that "type is not made of rubber," and the dozens of changes that must be made in every magazine office are proof. Though editors try to submit manuscripts adapted to their allotted space, they are often too long, sometimes too short. Moreover, space allotments are sometimes changed—a spread may be

---

A common method of estimating the space an article will take is to count the words in it, then divide the total by the number of words in an average column of the type in which the article is to be set. The result is not precise, but it is a reasonably accurate guide. A more precise method is to estimate the number of typewritten characters in your manuscript (by taking the average of a few lines). Then count the average number of characters in a typical line of type in the magazine. Count a blank space as a character.

---

cut to one page with a one-column runover, a page to two columns. This often means the elimination of illustrations; more frequently it necessitates heart-breaking slashing of copy. Authors, seeing their works in print, sometimes become caustic at editors' expense because they miss their pet phrases; but the loss saddens the editors as much as it irritates the authors. Nevertheless, type won't compress nor space stretch.

From Copy to Type Page

First step in the mechanical process is typesetting. When a manuscript goes to the composing room, it carries with it the art department's layout sheets—actually blue-prints which show the compositors how they are to translate typewritten pages into type. In the composing room the foreman or an assistant "marks up" the layout for type sizes and lengths of lines of type. The layout sheets for "Ten Minutes From Hollywood" show these instructions.

"Ten Minutes From Hollywood," as has already been said, was originally planned as the lead feature, to occupy Pages 13 and 14. Page 13 was to include color, Page 14 to appear in black and white only. Note that on the layout for Page 13 the two copy blocks under the title bear the pencilled notation "17/18 pi." Translated, this means to the machine operator that he is to set each of these blocks in 17 lines of type, 18 picas long. That means 34 lines of 18 picas each (a pica is one-sixth of an inch). The Page 14 layout calls for 60 lines of 19 picas, 24 in one block and 36 in the second. The layout sheets give other instructions: the *Better Homes & Gardens* title at the head of Page 13 (the title on the layout sheet is clipped from a previous issue and pasted on); an initial letter at the start of the article and two others on Page 14; placement of cuts and cut-lines; an arrow on Page 14 to connect cut-line and illustration below.

A block of proof of cut-line type is pasted onto the layout sheet for Page 14. This proof consists of line upon line of the familiar "The quick brown fox jumped over the lazy dog." By counting the letters and spaces, or units, on the block pasted on the layout sheet the editor can figure just how long to write the cut-line so that it will fit.

With these layout sheets and the copy, the typesetters go to work. They set the type according to instruction—34 lines of 18 picas, 60 of 19, with the last of the 19-pica lines concluding with the italicized words (*Turn to page oo*. They then set the remainder of the copy in 13½-pica lines—the width of a column in the back of the book, where the runover must appear, is 13½ picas. The figures in the italicized "continuation line" are *oo* because the runover page is not yet known.

Once the type is set, galley proofs are pulled and union proofreaders check them carefully. Errors are corrected. Then the type goes to a printer who, with layout sheets before him, proceeds to put type and cuts together to make two one-page forms as the layouts direct. (The cuts have been made by a commercial engraver to whom the copy for them—photographs, drawings, and other illustrations—was sent by the art department.) Again the proofs are read in the composing rooms, and errors are marked but not immediately corrected. Then the proofs, on yellow paper, go upstairs to Mr. Adams' desk.

The copy for "Ten Minutes From Hollywood" had gone to the composing room on January 6; page proofs come back to Mr. Adams just one week later, January 13. Now he and the other editors get their first chance to see how effectively their plans are working out.

Page 13, Mr. Adams finds, needs two typographical corrections. Otherwise it is satisfactory. But he applies two rubber stamps to the proof: "COLOR on this page" and "Please Submit Another Proof." Then it goes to the art department, which finds little wrong but also asks for another proof with another rubber stamp: "Another Proof—Art."

The Page 14 proof needs more attention. A line of type has to be written in; a "was" changed to a "were" and an "outsize" to an "oversize." An initial letter must be inserted in column two, and this forces the insertion of a blank line and the moving of nineteen words from the bottom of the column to the head of the runover. Mr. Adams doesn't bother to stamp this with the demand for another proof—it's obvious that he will want to see one.

The corrections are made, and the revised proofs come back within a day or so. Page 13 gets Mr. Adams' initialled OK at once. But Page 14 still needs typographical corrections, a little editing to improve the effect, and a revision of the cut-line. This last change is made because the cut-line does not "come out even"—its last line is shorter than the lines above. And all *Better Homes & Gardens* cut-lines are "squared up," so that they make even rectangles of type. So Mr. Adams chips off the last sentence and writes another, carefully counted to fit. He asks for another proof. And the art department wants third proofs of both pages.

Ordinarily three proofs are enough. In the case of "Ten Minutes From Hollywood" one more proof of Page 14 would likely have finished the job. Then a page proof would have come to Mr. Adams—a proof of the finished page, taken just before it is to go to the foundry for casting and electroplating—and it would have been quickly checked and approved.

But in this case a new difficulty arises. It is decided to open the issue with "Good News" instead of with "Ten Minutes From Hollywood," and much of the job must be done over. First the art department makes a new layout—one that will be suitable as a spread instead of as a left-hand and a following righthand page. This is comparatively simple. The new layout transposes the two cuts—the big cut of the house goes on the second page, that of the patio and terrace on the first. The title and byline are moved to the top of the first page, and the magazine title is removed. All of the body matter is set 19 picas; and enough space is gained by removal of the magazine title to get almost the entire article into the spread.

Now the whole process is repeated. The opening page of the spread, now Page 14, again gets its OK on the second proof. The second page, 15, is again more troublesome. It develops that there are nine lines of type more than the two pages will accommodate, and Mr. Adams "cuts back" nine lines from Page 15 so as to make the article fit. When the

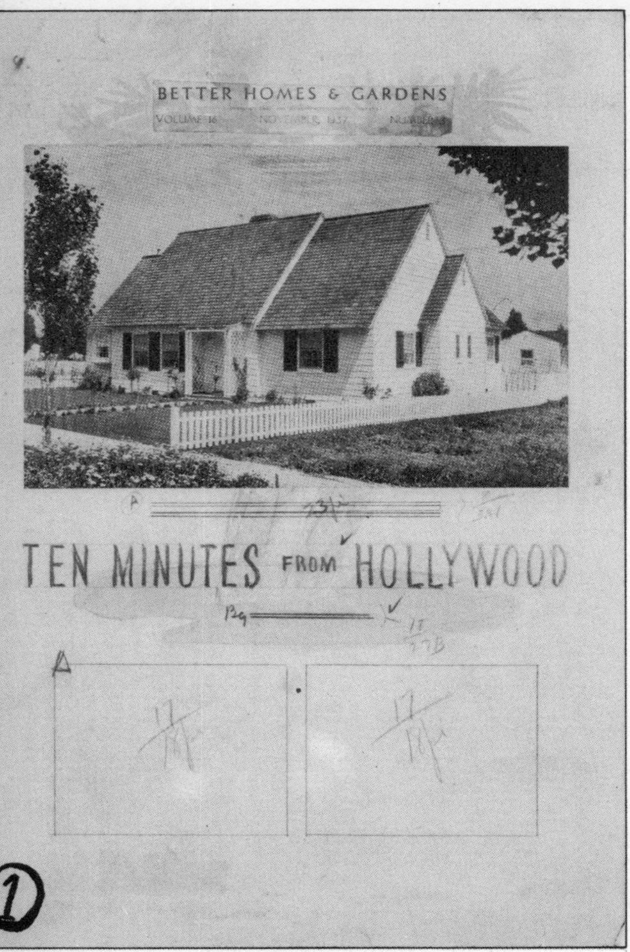

BETTER HOMES & GARDENS

VOLUME 16 NOVEMBER, 1937 NUMBER

TEN MINUTES FROM HOLLYWOOD

BETTER HOMES & GARDENS

VOLUME 16 APRIL, 1938 NUMBER 8

Low-cost, compact, immune to western sun and winter rain, yet fetching, this cottage is shining proof that Architect Leo Bachman licked his problem child

TEN MINUTES FROM HOLLYWOOD

By Ethel McCall Head

IF IT isn't one thing, it's another. As soon as the architect mastered the skyscraper that rears 70 stories up and houses a city within itself, the little house that costs less than $5,000 popped up to plague him. At present the little house is his real problem child.

For a long time it wasn't anybody's child at all. From coast to coast, from Main Street to Country Club Drive, the little houses were built without benefit of architect. Most of them turned out as dull and unimaginative as the Jukes family. Occasionally someone added a swooping roof and a few chunks of stone around the front door, and then the house looked like Minnie the Moocher dressed for a party.

Now even the architect finds the small house pretty beatty. If he gives the outside a measure of come-hither, the inside is like as not unmanageable. And if he works out a solid, efficient interior, then the outside is utterly uninteresting. To make the house appeal to the eye, satisfy the demands of efficient room planning and modern living, and withal make it proof against the onslaught of the years is not easy. But it can be done.

FOR proof, tho this is by no means the only sample, we offer this little Cape Cod cottage in North Hollywood, California. It's the home of Mr. and Mrs. Paul Power, designed by Architect Leo Bachman. Tho small, it's no kin to the cracker box.

Look at the mellow brown roof of split shakes, and you'll note that it's divided into three major sections. Under the central one is the living-room. In the left wing are the kitchen and dining-room;

Better Homes & Gardens, April, 1938

CASE HISTORY

OF THE LAYOUTS AND PAGE-PROOFS OF "TEN MINUTES FROM HOLLYWOOD" . . .

1. Art-Department layout of first page of "Ten Minutes from Hollywood" designed as a one-page layout for a right-hand page, the story to be continued on the following left-hand page.

2. First page-proof. (Galley proof of the type matter had been previously pulled, read, and corrected.) This proof follows the layout shown in (1).

3. Revised page-proof. It is still not satisfactory, and another page-proof is called for. Before this could be provided, plans were made to move the article back a page in the book, and a new scheme had to be worked out. [OVER]

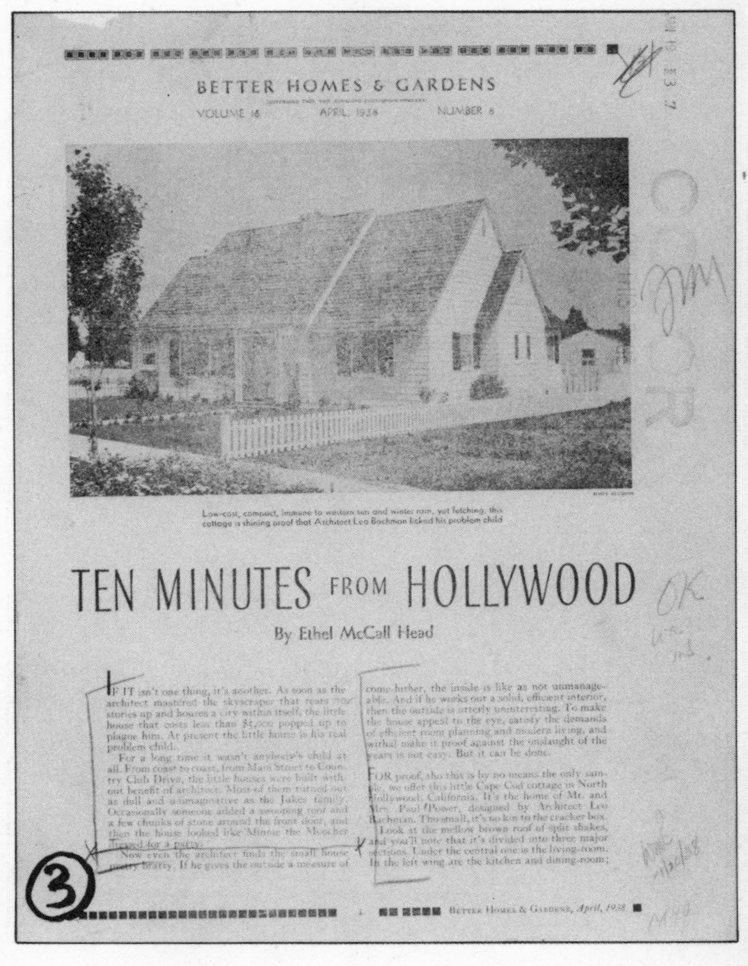

BETTER HOMES & GARDENS

VOLUME 16 APRIL, 1938 NUMBER 8

Low-cost, compact, immune to western sun and winter rain, yet fetching, this cottage is shining proof that Architect Leo Bachman licked his problem child

TEN MINUTES FROM HOLLYWOOD

By Ethel McCall Head

IF IT isn't one thing, it's another. As soon as the architect mastered the skyscraper that rears 70 stories up and houses a city within itself, the little house that costs less than $5,000 popped up to plague him. At present the little house is his real problem child.

For a long time it wasn't anybody's child at all. From coast to coast, from Main Street to Country Club Drive, the little houses were built without benefit of architect. Most of them turned out as dull and unimaginative as the Jukes family. Occasionally someone added a swooping roof and a few chunks of stone around the front door, and then the house looked like Minnie the Moocher dressed for a party.

Now even the architect finds the small house pretty beatty. If he gives the outside a measure of come-hither, the inside is like as not unmanageable. And if he works out a solid, efficient interior, then the outside is utterly uninteresting. To make the house appeal to the eye, satisfy the demands of efficient room planning and modern living, and withal make it proof against the onslaught of the years is not easy. But it can be done.

FOR proof, tho this is by no means the only sample, we offer this little Cape Cod cottage in North Hollywood, California. It's the home of Mr. and Mrs. Paul Power, designed by Architect Leo Bachman. Tho small, it's no kin to the cracker box.

Look at the mellow brown roof of split shakes, and you'll note that it's divided into three major sections. Under the central one is the living-room. In the left wing are the kitchen and dining-room;

Better Homes & Gardens, April, 1938

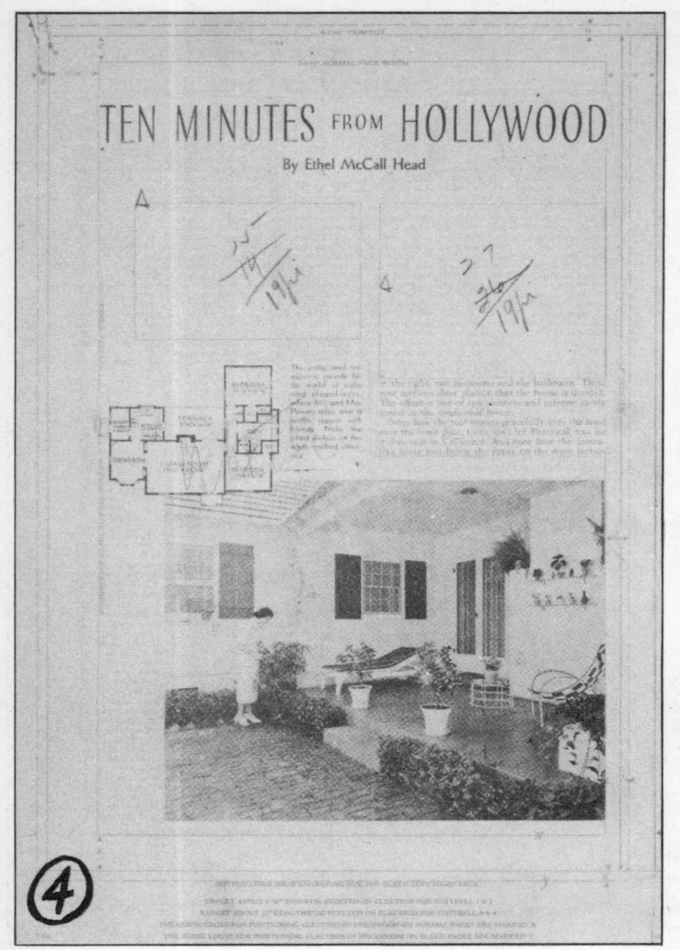

TEN MINUTES FROM HOLLYWOOD

By Ethel McCall Head

TEN MINUTES FROM HOLLYWOOD

By Ethel McCall Head

TEN MINUTES FROM HOLLYWOOD

By Ethel McCall Head

CASE HISTORY

OF THE LAYOUTS AND PAGE-PROOFS OF "TEN MINUTES FROM HOLLYWOOD" . . .

4. Revised layout of first page of "Ten Minutes from Hollywood", which, it is decided, shall be a two-page spread. This is now a left-hand page. (See Pages 8 and 9.)

5. First page-proof of the revised layout. It has a typographical error, and so a "revise" is called for.

6. Final page-proof. It is marked "O.K." by the Art Department and the Editorial Department.

second proof comes back, there are still three lines extra. More cutting, more resetting, more corrections. Even the third proof shows a few errors; but this gets an "OK with corrections," and finally the page is ready for the foundry.

Other "Paging Up" Problems

"Light Where You Need It," another article in the April issue, goes through even more proofs. The first title on the article, planned for a spread with a two-column runover, is "Perfect Lighting." The art department decides on a hand-lettered head-line, and one of the artists draws it in attractive script. The copy goes to the composing room on January 26, and the first proof comes back February 2. Many changes are necessary—typographical errors, lowering of the byline, alteration of cut-lines, reduction by a shade in the size of the numerals in the list of "cooperating firms."

Copies of these first proofs, meanwhile, have been sent to the feature's author, Miss Webber. A wire comes back objecting to the title. The feature does not describe "perfect lighting," Miss Webber says—in fact, she adds, lighting engineers do not think they can produce perfect lighting! So the editors go into conference and select a new title, "Easy on the Eyes." The art department makes a new hand-lettered heading.

While this is going on second and third proofs have come through and the third has received a final OK. But Miss Webber has suggested several changes in cut-lines and body matter, and fourth and fifth proofs are necessary. The fifth proof bears the new title.

Now a new complication arises. Proofs of full-page advertisements for the issue come to the desk of Mr. Adams, who pastes them in the editorial dummy. He notices a full-page General Electric advertisement using a script head-line—and it says, "Easy on the Eyes!" So a third title is evolved. And finally, on February 19, the sixth proof receives the approval of both art and editorial departments.

A different problem arises in a holdover article, set in type and approved before work on the April issue had started. Planned for two columns on a lefthand page and one on a right, with a short runover, it bears the title "Gloxinia Wants Applause." It is decided to change the title to "Gloxinia Stages a Comeback" and to save space by eliminating the runover. But the article has already been pared to the bone; in order to get it into three columns, it is necessary to reset it in 9-point instead of 10-point type (the runover is already in 9-point). Omission of a one-column cut planned for the righthand page also becomes necessary. These changes fit the article precisely into its three columns. But when the issue appears, the opening two columns are on Page 74, the third column on Page 151; no facing pages with the right spaces are available.

Every article, every picture layout, every special department or feature that goes into *Better Homes & Gardens* must go through a similar process. Basically, each is very like all the others; yet each may present its peculiar problems. When the last page proof has been sent back to the composing room with its "OK" or "OK with corrections," however, the editorial department has virtually finished its work on the issue.

Careful and detailed though the process is, it does not always prevent slip-ups. Sometimes errors are discovered after the final proof has been approved. If the electroplate for the page has been made, it is often more desirable to patch the plate than to correct the error in type and make a new plate. A special "makeover instructions" memorandum sheet is provided on which Mr. McDonough, Mr. Adams, or another editor in whose province the job falls, may order such patching.

An unusual case requiring makeover after the presses had "started to roll" was this: It developed that the brown towel in an illustration for "Safe at Home—but ARE You?" (see Page 31) was making a defacing shadow in an illustration in an advertisement on the other side of the sheet. Makeover instructions went to the composing room calling for the shifting of this feature to another page bearing a two-column feature with similar color combination (see "A Brush Plus Paint Equals Magic," Page 34), and the shifting of the second feature to the first page. Changes in continuation and table of contents lines had also to be made. The two pages that were interchanged were recast and electroplated again. The other lesser changes were made with patches.

Long before all such problems are solved, the magazine's staff is deep into the next issue. The April copy has only begun to reach the composing room when the call for May material goes out. April proofs are still being approved as June copy starts to come in. The first call for July may be issued before final makeover instructions for the April issue have been followed out. A chart of a typical month's work—say February—would look like this:

February 1 ...... First call for June copy
February 1-5 ..... Final makeover for March issue
February 1-28 .... Change and approval of April proofs
February 10 ..... June copy due
February 15 ..... March issue mailed to subscribers
February 10-28 ... Change and approval of May proofs
February 15 ..... June copy goes to art department
February 20 ..... March issue on sale on news stands
February 24 ..... April issue goes to press
February 28 ..... Last May copy goes to composing room
March 1 .... First call for July copy

Work on the production of at least four issues, in other words, is going on during each month. And this is not to mention all of the planning, the manuscript reading and other editorial duties that continue endlessly throughout the year, often looking not four but eight, ten or twelve months ahead.

In Other Magazine Offices

What goes on in the *Better Homes & Gardens* office each month is being enacted, with greater or smaller variations, in every other magazine office in the United States. In mass-production editorial offices the procedures are even more highly systematized than those just described. In plants with long lists of magazines it may be that one editor has general supervision over half a dozen publications. To keep all the strings in his hands he relies on the most rigid kind of routinization—routinization that, in some cases, produces careless editing, hasty selection of material, bad proofreading, and shoddy work in general.

Collier's faces an unusual production problem in its unique plan for simultaneous worldwide publication. Its final page proofs (mechanically perfect reproduction proofs), ready four weeks in advance, are sent by air express to twenty-one cities in all parts of the world. There local representatives have plates made from the proofs, and supply localized copy for "Any Week," the editorial page. By these methods it is possible to put each issue into circulation in London, Moscow, Tokyo, Sydney, Buenos Aires, and sixteen other cities at exactly the same time it reaches readers in the United States.

The other side of the picture is the magazine that boasts an editorial staff of but one or two workers. There are many such; and, to the credit of the editors, their products are often among the most carefully edited of all that reach an audience. With all the duties from manuscript reading through make-up to proofchecking—and, sometimes, solicitation of advertising and addressing of wrappers for subscriptions—on the shoulders of these low-man-power staffs, the jobs are "killers." But they not infrequently enlist enthusiasm and loyalty that make possible surprisingly effective work.

The make-up job for a magazine like *Harper's* or the *American Mercury* is simple. These magazines have no illustrations; they rarely use the runover device, preferring to let each article run "straight" from start to finish. Once they have decided approximately what material they wish to use in a given issue, they have little difficulty beyond the choice of a lead feature and the task of cutting a few lines from the end of matter that runs only a little beyond a full final page. Magazines made up like these do not object to pages that are partly blank.

Another obstacle they overcome is the one occasioned by the demand some editors make that all major titles appear on righthand pages. The reason for this demand is that the righthand has higher attention value than the lefthand—it is the page the reader sees first as he thumbs through the magazine. Most editors agree with the principle, and some make extra effort to give choice features righthand openings—it may be done by juggling the order of titles and perhaps a little extra cutting to eliminate concluding righthand pages. But the periodicals that depend not on eye-appeal to catch readers but rather on reader-faith in the merit of the editors' judgment make little concession to this factor. Slavish adherence to the righthand-opening rule would offer two major disadvantages: It would become monotonous, and it would eliminate many possibilities for the use of spreads as make-up units.

Most magazines place regular features in the same relative positions—sometimes on the same pages—issue after issue. This serves, from the editor's point of view, to simplify the make-up problem. More important is the fact that readers like to find familiar features in familiar, hence easy-to-find, positions. Every regular reader of *Time* knows that its popular "Letters" department begins on Page 2 in the front advertising section, and that "Books" is always the closing section. *Saturday Evening Post* partisans can count on finding "Postscripts" on the last front-of-the-book page. In *Editor & Publisher* the "Shop Talk at Thirty" page is always the last in the magazine (even when its length forces its runover into a position ahead of its beginning).

In the carefully-planned magazine the placing of runover is as important as the placing of any other back-of-the-book feature or department. *Better Homes & Gardens,* every page of which is planned in the editor's office, goes so far as to allot to each article its precise runover space, usually in full-column segments. Runover and other back-of-the-book matter, by this magazine as by many others, are placed when possible on pages bearing advertisements with subject matter of a closely related nature.

A common practice in the placement of runover, however, is to make a rough estimate as to the amount of space needed for it and then to leave that much back-of-the-book space free. It then becomes an easy matter to fit the runover into this space, one block of it after another. Most magazines employing this method make no violent effort to end each runover at the bottom of a page. Rather they end one runover where its length happens to bring it, and start another. If the end of a runover is near the end of a column or page, they may use a short filler—a poem, a picture or cartoon, a "blurb" for a forthcoming feature—to plug the hole. Head-lines, even on runover matter, are ineffective both in attention value and in appearance if they fall too far down on the page.

Such fillers may be dropped into the hole at the end of the runover. But if the space is of more than one column it is often more effective to "make it up" in two or more columns, perhaps well up on the page instead of at the bottom. This necessitates some resetting, but only a little.

The simplest method of fitting runover into the back of the book is that used some years ago by the make-up editor of *Pacific Ports,* a defunct monthly. His plan was this: Take the runover from the first article in the issue and start filling editorial space at the extreme back; take runover from the next article and place it just ahead of the first; and so on. Thus he worked from both ends toward the middle, and ended—if he were lucky—with blank space in the center for other features he had on hand.

But both of these last two methods deny the make-up editor the opportunity of genuine planning for the back of the book, and they often result in slipshod appearance. They fail to observe the principle that the back of the book is entitled to as much attractiveness (from the reader's point of view and from the advertiser's) as careful layout can give it. And they do not give the editor who outlines the issue's contents a workable basis for deciding on back-of-the-book features. They are easy methods, but they are not good editing.

"Cutting Back" the Proof

"Cutting back" to eliminate the extra lines that cannot be crowded in at the end of a page, a process inherent in careful make-up, is a job that requires scrupulous skill. If only a few lines—ten or so—are to be "saved," the trick is usually to cut out words and phrases in several paragraphs so as to shorten each by a line or two. The experienced editor cuts words as near the end of a paragraph as possible, in order to avoid more than a minimum of resetting. If, for example, he had to cut *this* paragraph of type to shorten it by two lines, he could do it by eliminating most of the first sentence: "To eliminate the extra lines that cannot be crowded in at the end of a page, a process inherent in careful make-up." He could, but he wouldn't. For removal of those words would mean resetting the entire paragraph. Instead he would cut the last two sentences. There would be little resetting—no more than a few words—and the paragraph's meaning would be unchanged.

If the "cutting" back involves more than a few lines—and sometimes it may involve as much as a column—the editor has no choice but to slash out whole paragraphs. Often content and even meaning must be sacrificed in such cutting. But type that can't be used is of no value; the editor must labor to say as much as he can in fewer words.

Proofreading is usually an editorial job, even though every printshop has its own expert proofreaders, men and women unbelievably skillful in detecting errors. There are at least two good reasons why magazines assign editors to proofreading. One is insurance—the more proofreaders, the fewer errors (few magazines go to their readers 100% clean; if this book does so, the earnest hopes and efforts of its printers, its publishers, and its authors will have achieved a miracle of publishing). The other is that the final reading of an article or story when its editor goes over the proof may turn up last-minute editorial changes that will improve the copy. Editors, like proofreaders, do not always hit the bull's eye at the first shot.

A common practice is to submit galley or page proof to its author, in sufficient time so that he may make corrections or suggest changes before the final page is locked up. Some magazines do this only when extensive editorial changes from the original manuscript have been made in the office; others send proofs as a matter of routine.

The more of these editorial practices a magazine follows, the longer the period it will need to accomplish them. Magazines whose make-up problems are simple may start work on their issues only a month or so (supposing them to be monthly magazines) before they are to go to press. Those that plan each page carefully, that have many departments and many titles in each issue, that have difficult color problems, require longer periods. The *Better Homes & Gardens* routine, beginning three and a half months before an issue reaches its readers, is typical of magazines of its complexity.

Other magazines that need relatively long periods for planning and make-up are *Ladies' Home Journal,* which is planned three months before publication and made up seven weeks in advance; *McCall's,* five and four months; *Pictorial Review,* four and two; *Esquire,* four months and six weeks. The problems of most of these magazines are similar to those of *Better Homes & Gardens.* The *Rotarian,* a simpler magazine, lays its plans six months in advance and makes up two months before issue.

Such magazines as *Harper's* and the *Atlantic Monthly,* on the other hand, usually need less time for make-up—*Harper's* make-up deadline is five weeks ahead of publication, the *Atlantic Monthly's* only twelve days. *Harper's* begins its planning "six days to six months" ahead, the *Atlantic Monthly* six weeks. The simplicity of the mechanical problems of magazines like these, and their shorter press runs, combine to give them considerably greater leeway than many periodicals enjoy.

The weekly magazines follow comparable schedules. *Collier's* is planned six to ten weeks in advance, made up four weeks. The *Saturday Evening Post's* schedule is similar. But periodicals like the *Nation* plan their issues on a much more compact routine, for timeliness is their essence. And *Time* and *News-Week,* to which newsiness is primary, close their forms only about three days before publication.

A special problem is involved in the not uncommon case of the magazine printed at a point distant from the editorial offices. The *Farm Journal,* a monthly magazine with editorial headquarters in Philadelphia, is printed in Chicago. Copy for the printer is prepared in Philadelphia not on the usual copy paper, but on special sheets ruled so that a line of typewriter type contains approximately the same number of characters as a one-column line set on the linotype. Thus the editors, knowing the number of type-lines available for a given article, can edit it so that the typewritten copy will almost exactly fit the space. Further, the special copy paper numbers each typewritten line so that, if the editors need to revise after the copy has gone to Chicago, they can send to the printer instructions to change line 7 on page 2, or any other specific lines, as directed.

To speed last-minute copy changes and to send late copy, the Philadelphia office is connected to the Chicago printer's headquarters by a teletype machine, the kind used by Associated Press and other news services. A stenographer in Philadelphia types out instructions for changes, or new copy, and within a few moments the teletype in Chicago is typing out identical material.

The *Farm Journal* closes its forms in Chicago only four days before the date of issue. Thus such special devices as the teletype and the ruled copy paper are vital. They mean that, when one of the editors arrives in Chicago on closing day to supervise last-minute work, his job is simplified to the last degree.

The emphasis on speed in the making of those magazines which are primarily concerned with news, news commentary, and news interpretation has not, of course, carried over to magazines of other types, although there has been a general tightening up of schedules in the past few years. Many magazines play up news interpretation articles in a way that was not common before the news-magazines came into the picture.

Practice Suggestions

1. From a year's issues of a monthly magazine, or three months' of a weekly, make a list of the "lead features" and draw whatever conclusions you can as to the method by which they are chosen.

2. From three consecutive issues of any highly-departmentalized magazine make up a table to show the percentages of total editorial space allotted to different departments or subjects.

3. Suggest at least five topics each for seasonable articles for the January issue of (a) a women's magazine; (b) a non-fiction outdoor sports magazine; (c) a grocers' trade magazine.

4. Count the number of words on three pages of ordinary double-spaced typewritten copy. Estimate how many columns and parts of columns they would fill if set in the type-size and line-length used in the body matter of this book.

5. "Cut back" the last two columns of the runover of any article printed in a current magazine so as to shorten them by ten lines.

6. Take a page from a popular magazine and pad it out to run over three inches.

REFERENCES

Manuscripts and Proof, by John Benbow. Oxford University Press, New York. 1937.

See also *Magazine Making* (Bakeless) and *Magazine Publishing* (Lohr).

IV

The Editors at Work

MAGAZINE-MAKING, with all its rejection slips, layout, scheduling, "cutting back," and the rest of the endless routine described in Chapters II and III, is a great deal more than mere system. Were it only that, it would be a simple business. A candidate for a Ph. D. degree in magazinology, with a minor in statistics, could very nicely tabulate and graph the routines of a score or two of periodicals and produce a fool-proof working plan for all magazines everywhere. They would all come out on time, letter perfect and neat as new collar buttons—and probably about as varied and exciting. An airtight plan works both ways—it keeps air from getting in as well as out.

The routine is exacting and necessary, but it is not the heart of the magazine. Just what the heart is is not easy to say. Oswald Garrison Villard once wrote that the success of the *Nation* grew out of the fact that to its backers the profit motive was always secondary; as evidence he pointed to its outliving the *Independent*, the *Outlook*, *Leslie's Weekly*, and other contemporaries. O. O. McIntyre ventured an opinion that "the editors whose tenures are longest are those who strike a policy in which they believe and to which they cling despite the surrounding changes." He presented George Horace Lorimer of the *Saturday Evening Post* as an example.

These points of view suggest that the essence of any magazine is primarily the genius of the men and women who edit it. Certainly the *New Yorker* could not be the *New Yorker* without E. B. White, Harold Ross, James Thurber, and their incredibly deft cohort. *Esquire* is the skill of Arnold Gingrich, *Time* the inventiveness and breezy freshness of Luce and Hadden, *Nation's Business* the mirror of Merle Thorpe. And each of these men has had able assistants to catch his spirit and reflect his ideas.

No less is *Better Homes & Gardens* a reflection of the thought, effort and energy put into it by men and women. The magazine's conception and basic formula are credited to E. T. Meredith, who died in 1928; they have been carried on by Fred Bohen, the company's president, and Vice-Presidents E. T. Meredith, Jr., and E. F. Corbin. But neither these men, nor Editor Frank McDonough, would claim responsibility for the entire character of the magazine. Rather they would point to the editorial and business staffs whose combined efforts produce it.

All of this is not to say that a successful pattern may not be set up. Such a pattern is, indeed, frequently established by one editor or one editorial board and followed by successors as well as by any number of imitators. But the emulation is always with a difference. Firm as is the imprint of Mr. Lorimer on the *Saturday Evening Post,* the *Post* is no longer the magazine he left at his retirement. The pattern is there, but the frills are new and constantly changing. In time they will, no doubt, set an entirely renovated model.

And it is not enough to gather a group of editors of character, articulateness, cleverness, imagination, and conviction and say, "Set up a pattern that will achieve success." Such a group might invent a magazine of shimmering brilliance that would prove to be a dismal flop. The pattern must have direction. It must be a pattern that will have reader-appeal—that will form a framework into which the editors can fit articles, stories, and pictures that will fill a reader-need. The pattern may be as broad as that conceived by Mr. Lorimer—one that will justify the use of almost any kind of material of general interest—or it may be as narrow as that of *Mill and Factory,* with its attempt to reach only a highly-specialized group. Either type of pattern, if it be not entirely esoteric, may be successful.

In the word "success" lies an important qualification of a pattern's effectiveness. "Success" usually means that a magazine, in addition to interesting a fairly large percentage of those to whom its pattern is suited, also draws enough advertisers so that its ledgers can be written in black ink. There are for most magazines these two aspects to the pattern:

1. It must actively interest readers.
2. It must actively interest advertisers.

A few magazines, it is true, ignore the second aspect. *Look,* the second of the big picture magazines to appear, put virtually all its emphasis at first on attracting readers, and succeeded to the extent that it showed profits without advertising revenue. *Readers Digest,* dependent entirely on subscription and single-copy sales, has been a money-maker from the start. Most of the pulp magazines make their money largely from circulation income. But these cases are in the minority, and most of them develop from the fact that, for whatever reason, the nature of the material they offer to attract readers does not lead advertisers to think that the readers would be good markets for their products.

But most magazines seek double-purpose patterns. The large low-price weeklies that reach for readers in all classes are devised on the theory that their advertising as well as their editorial pages will interest all classes. More-specialized magazines would rarely pass the Volume I, Number 1 stage if they had not developed formulas to bring advertisements between their covers. *Fortune* was established on the belief that a magazine with authoritative, searching articles on the interests of big industry would appeal to big industrialists and others with allied points of view (and similar incomes), and the corollary that if such an appeal were achieved the advertisers would take advantage of the opportunity to reach these same readers. The *Southern Lumber Journal* operates on a theory that, vastly different in its expression, is precisely the same in general outline.

Better Homes & Gardens has, like any other going magazine, its pattern; and it is a dual-purpose pattern. Broadly stated, it is the purpose to interest and help as many average American home-owners as possible. When Mr. Meredith established it, it was with the belief that a very large reader-audience would be interested in reading material designed for that purpose, and that a large group of advertisers would desire to lay their products before this same audience.

So every line that goes into the magazine's editorial columns is put there first to interest and help readers, and second to make the publication an attractive advertising medium. The first always comes first: Few magazines achieve real success if they are edited for the advertisers. But the magazine that reaches and holds an audience is pretty sure to be of value to advertisers. Consequently *Better Homes & Gardens'* editors select material for their readers; if they do not believe that a line—or a page, article, or section—will attract readers, out it goes.

The routines outlined in Chapters II and III are merely machinery to aid in the accomplishment of that ultimate objective. How the machinery is used depends on the individuals at the controls. The best road toward an understanding of the direction the editors seek to give to the magazine, and of the methods by which they work, is an examination of the special duties and responsibilities of each.

The Executive Editor at Work

Much of Mr. McDonough's work has been described. His primary responsibility is to keep the editorial machinery running. This means not only the monthly planning of the magazine, issuance of the call for material and follow-up to see it through the plant to completion, but also the sometimes-difficult task of coordination. For there are as many production and service lines in the editing and distribution of a magazine as in the manufacture and merchandising of a Plymouth or a Frigidaire. It is the executive editor's duty to serve as go-between among all divisions of the editorial department, and between his and the many other departments—advertising, circulation, promotion, research, mechanical, and so on.

In *Better Homes & Gardens,* as in most magazines, the job of keeping the editorial mechanism turning smoothly is not difficult. The basic routines are thoroughly enough developed that few insoluble problems arise. Occasional staff conferences iron out tangles or lay plans for campaigns, special projects, special issues.

Perhaps 25 percent of Mr. McDonough's time goes to relations with non-editorial departments. Mr. Mugge, circulation manager, perhaps wants to confer about a new idea for solicitation of subscriptions. R. G. Wright, comptroller, reports that the next issue must be eight pages smaller than at first planned. The production manager, Mr. Smith, proposes a new routine for handling four-color inserts. Each such situation calls for a conference, for, perhaps, hours of consideration and re-planning. Sometimes Mr. McDonough can refer these problems to one of the division editors; many he must supervise or solve himself. (Detail of inter-department relations appears in Chapter V.)

Second only to the tasks of supervision and coordination is the eternal search for ideas. The magazine must be ever fresh. Next January's issue must resemble last January's in no more than the date-line and the adaptation of both to winter interests. What was new and vital last year becomes old stuff in twelve months. The editorial contest that drew thousands of entries in its first use would not get a score in a second unless it were so disguised that nobody would recognize it for more than a distant cousin. New and timely topics, new methods of treatment, new writers, new layout devices—for all of these the executive editor must be on the constant hunt. The fundamental pattern may alter little in ten years; but its window dressing must always seem new.

Scribner's reports the birth of an article-idea thus: Gilbert H. Burck, an editor of *Railroad Magazine,* submitted an article on transportation. It went back to him with a note quoting one sentence from it. "Take this sentence," said the note, "and develop it. Get all the facts, examine them and then, probably, you'll have an article for Scribner's." Mr. Burck did. The result: "The Great Speedup," *Scribner's,* July, 1938.

Where do ideas come from? Many out of the editor's head, and from the heads of other editors. A staff conference develops a new treatment for next year's Christmas gift section. A letter from a reader asks for an article telling how to put children's play-equipment into the backyard without shattering its landscaping plan. Mr. Ainsworth, the advertising manager, brings word of a new kind of wallboard that will make certain building problems easier. A friend at a casual luncheon says, "Why don't you print a piece telling me something about growing old-fashioned flowers indoors in the winter?"

From such sources and a thousand others come the ideas that eventually turn into fodder for the magazine's pages (and for every one that works out successfully half a dozen are considered and discarded). But Mr. McDonough does not rely on chance suggestions, nor does any other magazine editor. Every magazine works hard and systematically at seeking out new ideas and new approaches.

One method is wide reading. In his office and in his study at home—where he puts in many hours a week, free from the inescapable interruptions of the office—Mr. McDonough combs through scores of magazines, and through newspapers which come to him from every section of the United States. From these he culls not only tips for stories but also up-to-date knowledge of his audience's interests. Often he makes clippings from them and refers them to other editors for investigation or follow-up. And all the editors read with great care the letters from readers—not alone those that come in spontaneously, but those often solicited from readers. From these they get the "feel" of what people want.

Better Homes & Gardens subscribes for or exchanges with about thirty magazines of especial value to its editors. Received and catalogued by the librarian, each magazine is supplied with a perforated series of tags. Each tag bears a name. The office mail carrier takes the magazine to the official or editor whose name is on the bottom tag; he reads it within the specified time (2 or 3 days), crosses out his name and throws it into his outgoing-mail basket. The mail carrier then delivers it to the next name on the list, and returns the bottom tag to the librarian so that she can keep track of the magazine's circulation. Some magazines may go to every editor in the office, others to no more than two.

Frequently Mr. McDonough and division editors make trips east, west, north, and south, not alone to confer with writers and other editors, illustrators, and advertisers, but also to visit *Better Homes & Gardens* families. They find that these visits, to reader-families in their own homes, are among their most productive sources of ideas.

Keeping Track of Costs

One of the executive editor's tasks on any magazine is the constant checking of editorial costs. This is a before-and-after problem: Adoption of a budget for expenditures before an issue appears, balancing against the budget afterward. *Better Homes & Gardens'* editorial budget is made up annually. Each spring Mr. McDonough prepares for submission to Mr. Corbin, editorial director, a detailed estimate of the probable cost of operating his department for the next 12 months. Based on the cost-experience of preceding years and the probable need for expansion or possible reduction of expense, the proposed budget covers not only the cost of manuscripts and illustrations but also salaries, postage, telephone and telegraph, travel, and every other item involved in the editorial department's operation. The budget is checked, perhaps altered, and finally approved as a basis for the coming year's work.

The cost of manuscripts and illustrations is figured on a budget base of so much per page. Likely no individual page in an issue costs precisely this amount; perhaps one issue, or two or three issues in a row, will run to a cost beyond the budgeted figure. Mr. McDonough keeps his finger on this cost through the monthly "charge-off" made by his secretary, Miss Sullivan (see Chapter II). He is informed of the monthly costs under other budget items by a report from the business office. If the editorial cost of an issue, or several of them, is beyond the budget, he makes plans for composing future issues of material of lower cost. At times he may ask for a budget increase.

But costs never depart widely from budget estimates. Adjustment, therefore, is rarely difficult.

In addition to all these duties are scores of others not so easily classified. There are always new campaigns to plan, new projects to consider. The before-and-after remodeling contest may be ending, but another is beginning. There are readers to receive—bent either on delivering oral tribute or oral brickbats. An important advertiser of garden seeds asks, perhaps, for "a list of your best writers on garden subjects." This request must be courteously rejected, both because the writers' privacy is to be protected and because *Better Homes & Gardens* doesn't care to risk releasing so valuable and carefully-built a property to anybody. There is the daily batch of correspondence to answer—often a stack of gargantuan dimensions. There are countless other distractions, even to the queries of a couple of authors who are working at a book on how to write for and edit magazines.

The task of the executive editor of *Better Homes & Gardens* is not much different from that of almost any editor in a comparable position. Every such editor finds his primary functions those of coordinator and idea man. He must keep his organization operating so smoothly that deadlines will be met; and he must continually pour onto his assistants' and associates' desks a flow of suggestions, plans, and possibilities for making the magazine more attractive to readers. Probably only a small percentage of his suggestions will take root. But if one in ten flowers his effort will justify itself.

The first function is one largely governed by the establishment of a workable office routine and the application of a certain amount of diplomacy. But the second requires not only lively imagination and curiosity, but the closest kind of contact with readers and those who may become readers, and with editors and writers as well.

Consequently most editors spend much of their time in "contacts." Most leading American magazines find it expedient to have their offices in New York City because it is the cross-roads of the nation: There their editors can get almost instantly into touch with almost anybody the need of the moment suggests. More writers live in the Middle Atlantic states and New England than in any other sections of the country; more magazine illustrators as well. The advantage, therefore, works both ways. Free-lance workers live in the East because the magazines are there; magazines stay there rather than move to places where they might lower costs because the men and women who supply their fodder are handy.

New York is not always, however, the ideal location for a magazine. *Sunset,* "a practical magazine for Western families," finds San Francisco a most convenient site. The *Rotarian* chooses Chicago because its parent organization, Rotary International, has headquarters there. Sectional and regional magazines naturally locate in the centers of their sections and regions. *Better Homes & Gardens* finds Des Moines a suitable location because "it can do the best national job from the center of the country. If the editorial offices were in New York, the magazine might be in a position of unreality. In a word, it is closer to home and garden and what the masses of people really want because of its location." Its original establishment in Des Moines was, of course, influenced by the fact that the city was the site of the Meredith Publishing Company.

Other Editors at Work

Working closely under Mr. McDonough is Mr. Adams, assistant to the editor and junior member of the staff. One of his major duties has been described in Chapter III—seeing copy "through the shop," from the editor's desk to the casting foundry. He is a "writing editor"—he rewrites many manuscripts that, suitable in subject matter, need to be recast to get the *Better Homes & Gardens* "slant" or to save space; in some cases, to achieve the dignity of good English. For many experts who furnish admirable information are sadly lacking in the ability to present it so as to be pleasing, interesting, or even intelligible to readers.

Mr. Adams handles the daily flood of verse—7,500 hopeful "poems" a year. Most of it is bad. Much of it is offered on a basis other than merit; letters accompanying verse not uncommonly take a tone like this:

> I think your use of my poem would be an advertisement for the magazine, for my husband would be so proud he would carry *Better Homes & Gardens* to many places and many homes. His friends are countless and your magazine would be on display quite a while with him. He is held in esteem by all classes and my character is above reproach.

Unfortunately the character of the verse thus introduced wasn't, and it had to go back. The fifty poems a year that get checks are those suitable in subject, brief enough to serve as filler if need be, cheerful in tone, and, if not altogether expertly done, at least susceptible to correction at Mr. Adams' hand.

The number of "poems" in the mailbags of the United States each year reaches astronomical figures. Most verse spends most of its life in the mailbags, going or coming. Most of it is incredibly bad—if it isn't sentimental tribute to the moon or "my dog Rover," it rhymes "home" with "alone" or flatly ignores the metrical niceties. Often good poetry is sent to publications that never use it, or to markets for which its subject or treatment makes it quite unfit.

In the office adjoining Mr. McDonough's sits Mr. Benson, general editor. The general division is set up to care for all editorial material not included under other specialized classifications. This rule-of-thumb means that not only a number of major and minor articles but also many of the magazine's departments pass through Mr. Benson's hands. To help him in studying his needs, he has classified material into seven subdivisions:

1. Family relationships, which includes all material about family life not directly in the field of child care. An article on how to get along with those touchy neighbors falls in this division. So does one on buying books for the whole family, or another on the use of a garden as a lure for 'teen-age children and their friends.

2. Homecraft and handicraft, so long as such material doesn't tread on the toes of other divisions. "Build Your Own Playhouse" would be such an article—one that falls neither in building nor gardens, though it is related to both.

3. Human interest material, such as light biographical articles about notables who do their own gardening. Articles about hobbies, especially if they relate to the magazine's several fields, are of this sort.

4. Nature articles—birds, bees, pets. These articles are often baited with tie-ins with well-known names.

5. Semi-regular features on dogs: How to feed them, how to train them, how to select and care for them.

6. Travel material, especially travel with a garden or architectural angle. An article on travel in Japan might fit *Better Homes & Gardens*

if its author described Japanese gardens and the intimate connection between Japanese homes and home-building and the environment.

7. Humor, mild satire, or almost anything that strikes a pleasantly contrasting note. Poetry comes under this classification, as does one of the regular departments, "The Man Next Door."

Limited definitions such as these do not make allowance for all types of material. "Washington in Bloom," an April article, fits none of the seven heads precisely (it tells the landscaping story of the national capital, with especial emphasis on the famous Japanese cherry trees surrounding the Tidal Basin). No more does "Good News! We All Get a Break" (see Page 7). Yet both were prepared by the general division.

Other articles may come under several of the seven heads. "He Has Collect-itis—But I Love Him!" is such an article. The humorous account of a wife's trials with her collectomaniac husband, it is part family relationships, part hobbies and part satire.

Correspondence and Other Columns

No less than six of the monthly departments of the magazine are the responsibility of the general editor. One of these, "Across the Editor's Desk" (see Page 1), is prepared by Mr. McDonough. Another, "It's News to Me" (see Page 2), is prepared by Miss Olson; but it too is a general division responsibility.

"Back Talk" (see Pages 48, 49, 50), the correspondence column, is a third. A box at the end of the "Back Talk" section asks that correspondents hold letters to 150 words, and suggests that they permit use of their names. Writers do not always observe either suggestion. Eight of the eleven letters on Pages 48, 49, and 50 are signed by full names; three by initials.

It is never hard for a widely-circulated magazine to find enough letters to fill such a column; but "good" letters are not always plentiful. "Good" does not mean "favorable." A good letter is one that will interest a considerable body of readers. Space in the letter column is precious, and a letter of highly-specialized interest is not often considered worth printing.

Few magazines consider it wise editing to print in correspondence columns only favorable letters. A column composed entirely of floral wreaths will convince none but the most gullible. Editors of letter columns prefer to publish brickbats along with bouquets, preferably in fairly even proportions. Sometimes they reply in "editorial notes" to the brickbats; sometimes they prefer to let the reader draw his own conclusions. If a flood of letters expressing displeasure with a feature comes in, the editor sometimes publishes a good many of them with explanation or, on occasion, apology.

Getting "Back Talk" letters ready for the printer is more than merely sending him the original letters. Mr. Benson puts a brief and appropriate title on each; he edits each letter carefully. Sometimes editing means no more than the change of a comma. It may involve cutting a long-winded letter to bring it within the word-limit. Not infrequently it means rephrasing, repunctuating, and respelling to make comment intelligible—few editors let correspondents appear so illiterate as their letters sometimes show them to be. When either type of editing is necessary, utmost care is exercised that the writer's meaning is not altered.

"The Man Next Door" (see Pages 32, 33) is written for *Better Homes & Gardens* by a well-known newspaper columnist, Harlan S. Miller. Mr. Miller lived in Des Moines when he started doing this department, and in it he followed a highly personalized manner that had proved popular in his *Des Moines Register* column. He moved to Washington, D. C., however, and a difficulty arose: His first "Man Next Door" copy after the move was so much about Washington, Mr. Benson and Mr. McDonough agreed, that it lacked its former flavor. Whereupon they pasted on one sheet headed "This Is What We Don't Want" the Washington paragraphs and on another, "This Is What We Do Want," the remainder, and sent both sheets to Mr. Miller. He returned at once to his former manner, and the trouble was dispelled.

Editing "The Man Next Door" is easy. It involves checking the copy and perhaps cutting it to fit the space assigned to it. A copy of the edited manuscript is furnished to the artist who makes its illustrations. Suggestions as to which paragraphs might well be illustrated are given.

"Among Ourselves" (see Pages 35, 63, 64), the fifth department under Mr. Benson's supervision, takes more time than any of the others. Based largely on correspondence, its scope is as wide as the interests of all of the magazine's readers put together. Essentially it is a gossip column in which the readers talk about the magazine and themselves. But each paragraph in it calls for careful selection and a smooth job of knitting quoted material to brief comment. Usually it is illustrated with photographs.

Included in this department is a brief feature, "Whims and Hobbies" (see Page 35). Each short item in this feature describes some hobby or activity, often of a noted individual, that is likely to interest the magazine's readers. Material for "Whims and Hobbies" is not easy to get; hence the four-line appeal at the bottom of the column. Shortly after the feature was started, Mr. Benson sent to departments and schools of journalism and to chapters of Sigma Delta Chi, professional journalistic society, a form letter asking journalism students to submit "brief squibs" suitable for it. The letter said that "sketches about the home and garden hobbies of *well-known persons* will be preferred, although this is not a prerequisite to consideration. . . . Payment will be made on acceptance. No manuscripts can be acknowledged or returned."

The frontispiece of the magazine is another general division responsibility. The frontispiece, Page 7 in the magazine, is usually a photograph selected for beauty and timeliness. Not often does it tie in with other material in the issue, as it does in the case illustrated in this book (see Pages 3, 16, 17). In this case Mr. Benson put a small boldface notation in the lower righthand corner of the frontispiece to call attention to the tie-in.

Mr. Benson's task, briefly described, is to see that all of the material that he needs to satisfy the editor's monthly call for manuscripts is on hand, and ready to go. The lead-feature plan tells him of major articles he is to provide; the schedule of departments is another guide. But he does not know until the monthly space-budget reaches him just how much or how little additional material he will need, and so he carries in his desk drawer a considerable quantity of already-purchased material.

Some of this material, if he is lucky, is ready to send to the art department for layout almost "as is." But most of it has to be rewritten, pruned, re-arranged. Sometimes it needs new photographs or drawings. Often Mr. Benson consults Mr. McDonough about treatment of an article or the space it should occupy, and Mr. Hainline about elements that should receive emphasis in layout and illustration.

Many "general" articles are the result of Mr. Benson's planning. The daily grist that comes across his desk unsolicited provides a few; but he cannot rely on the chance that they will suit his needs. So he develops dozens of article-ideas and selects the right writers to produce the manuscripts. Not infrequently such manuscripts are revised several times before their salmon cards go in the "Manuscripts Paid For" file. And perhaps he rewrites them himself after their purchase.

Preparation of the table of contents for most magazines is more of a chore than merely listing titles and appending page numbers. For *Better Homes & Gardens* it involves proper departmentalization of titles and decision on their order. In the table on Page 1, from a May issue, "Better Gardens" leads; but in an April issue "Furnishings for Your Home" is given top position. Articles prepared by the general division are not listed as "General," but under a more attractive suggestion: "A Number of Things for the Family."

Departmentalization in the table of contents is a common practice, though there is little agreement on meanings of terms. In *Scribner's* "Features" mean verse, pictorial material, and certain monthly features; "Articles" mean non-fiction that is neither "Features" nor "Departments." In the *American Boy*, "Features" are non-fiction titles. . . . Many magazines include on contents pages editorial columns or announcements of forthcoming articles and stories.

A behind-the-scenes department to introduce or identify authors is a favorite with editors. The *Atlantic Monthly* has its "Contributors' Column"; *Harper's*, "Personal and Otherwise"; the *Saturday Evening Post*, "Keeping Posted"; the *American Boy*, "In the Morning Mail," which combines author-biographies with letters from readers and other miscellany (the "Morning Mail" editor is identified as Pluto, the Office Pup). Such departments vary from terse biographical notes to breezy, loitering informality. That the attempts at informality sometimes result sadly is indicated by a satire on such departments in the *New Yorker* (February 19, 1938) entitled "Our Fascinating but Neglected Contributors." Here the *New Yorker* reported Frank Sullivan to be in Ceylon covering the sponge divers' strike, Editor E. B. White as writing from a Natchez jail, and James Thurber as a Chinese born in Altoona, Pa.

An anti-climax to this satire appeared in *Harper's* "Personal and Otherwise" (April, 1938). Herein *Harper's* commented on the *New Yorker's* ribbing, quoted three of its "barefaced fraudulences" and said, "Anyone can play at this sort of game." As evidence it presented a fantastic "biography" of Louis Adamic. But it failed to prove its point. The *New Yorker's* technique in other hands is something less than the *New Yorker.*

Editing the Garden Section

Largest of the four specialized divisions in *Better Homes & Gardens* is that devoted to better gardens. As guides to his monthly needs the garden editor has a series of rules-of-thumb:

He always has a minimum of six pages, and he may have a maximum of seventeen.

The bulkiest issues—made so by heavy seasonal advertising—are those of March, April, May, June, and October.

The February number is a "garden planning issue," with its first ten or twelve pages devoted to gardens. In addition there may be many garden "shorts."

Seasons are of utmost importance. Garden material is useless if it appears at the wrong time of year. If a strictly seasonable article is crowded out of the issue for which it is intended, it must be held over for a year. A rock-garden article intended for the April, 1935, issue and already laid out, set into type, and approved was forced out at the last moment by unexpected space shortage. Plates for the article (it involved a four-color illustration on a full page and two single columns of runover) were filed away through 1936 and 1937. A four-color page with two columns of additional space became available as the April, 1938, issue was being put to bed, and the rock-garden article was dropped into the hole.

The problem of holdover material often causes editors to call for aspirin. In 1922 a magazine bought from a Washington writer an article entitled "The Day's Work of a President." It was based largely on incidents from President Harding's day. Before the magazine found the right spot for it, President Harding died and the article was at once out of date. The writer had meantime left Washington, and the magazine had to send a staff member to the capital to get material about Coolidge to substitute for the Harding incidents. . . . Most editors attempt to hold their inventories of material on hand only a little above anticipated needs for a few months in advance. But when the *Youth's Companion* ceased publication in 1929, it had more than 2,000 manuscripts in its file—some more than 30 years old, most no longer usable.

One of the garden editor's problems is to assure a balance of subject matter each month. He tries to treat flowers, shrubs, vegetables, rock gardens, and half a dozen other garden subjects in each issue—it would not do to have several articles on hedges and none on transplanting bulbs in an early spring issue. And because of this need for variety and balance, he can rely on unanticipated incoming mail no more than can Mr.

Benson. He has a list of reliable writers in his several fields, and often he asks them for specific articles for specific issues. He seeks pictorial features—photographs showing skillful flower arrangement, for instance, are hard to get; snapshots of attractive gardens with seasonable flowers; unusual climbing-vine pictures; and so on.

Two regular departments come under his care, "The Diary of a Plain Dirt Gardener" (see Pages 6, 52) and "Along the Garden Path" (see Page 62), always the last page in the magazine. The "Diary" is prepared by an experienced gardener living near Columbus, Ohio, Harry R. O'Brien, who travels widely to procure material for this column and for garden articles he writes for *Better Homes & Gardens* and other magazines. The department always occupies five columns; they may consist of a full page and a two-column runover, as illustrated, or of two columns facing each other across the "gutter" (see "Back Talk," Pages 48, 49) plus three single columns, or of other combinations. Caricatures in pen and ink are made by an artist to whom this task is always delegated, Tom Carlisle.

"Along the Garden Path" is also prepared by a regular contributor who writes from his Long Island garden and who furnishes not only copy but also pen-and-ink sketches to illustrate it. Its informal, highly personalized manner blends anecdote with seasonable gardening hints.

Where does garden material originate? Much of it in the imaginations of Mr. Hottes and his associates; much in those of free-lance writers. "How to Tie Your Beds to Your Lawn" (see Pages 12, 13) was prepared by Mr. Hottes as a means of showing in pictures something hard to put into words. The drawings were done first by a Des Moines artist, then remade by a New York artist when it was decided that the first set did not tell the story.

"The Quickest Garden," another spread, was submitted unsolicited by a free-lance writer who had frequently sold to *Better Homes & Gardens*. A box headed "Annual Flower-planting Guide," though it tied in with the "Quickest Garden" article, resulted from an editor's conversation with a seed dealer in Philadelphia; the dealer wrote it.

"Fairies Live in This Garden" (see Pages 3, 16, 17, 37) was also an unsolicited free-lance article. The article itself was usable, with some revision and editing; the original photographic illustrations were not satisfactory, and new ones had to be taken. The results of the retake were so striking that it was decided to use one as a frontispiece.

Only part of the material furnished by Mr. McGregor for "First Aid to Turf" (see Page 24) was used in the two-column article. The author, a florist, had been asked for a batch of "semi-pro tips" on gardening. He submitted them with rough sketches, the basis for the illustrations on Page 24; some were used, others held for later issues.

A short article, "We Grow Iris From Seed," grew out of a long list of subjects suggested by a free-lance writer. The editor selected one, and when the article came in it was prepared for one page in a March issue. Space limitation prevented its use; it was revamped to make a two-column opening page plus runover for April.

Other typical article-developments in the garden division:

"Starting Tuberous Begonias" was written "in the shop" by an editor. Photographs for it were made under his direction.

A tip for an article on lupines, lovely old-fashioned flowers, came from a note in a trade paper about an Englishman who had had unusual success with them. The article came in "cold"; a new opening was written for it, with a brief note about the English gardener to add a human-interest touch. Pictures were procured separately.

"Gloxinia Stages a Comeback" was ordered from a California garden writer.

A personal-experience article, "I Can't Resist a Vegetable Garden," arrived unsolicited. It was welcomed, for articles on vegetables are hard to get.

Each issue, in addition to articles and departments, may contain special features such as a column called "Thanks for the Tip," a collection of hints from readers, or "Answering Your Spring Garden Questions," a series of one-paragraph solutions to common problems. A feature like this last is usually prepared by the garden staff. Fillers, too, are constant needs—short pieces with or without illustrations that will fill the bottom of a column. Those on Pages 47 and 57 are lifted bodily from Miss Olson's "It's News to Me" copy. On Page 64 is another type—the "blurb," or announcement of a forthcoming feature (in this case the blurb announces "He Pastures His Hobby-Horse in a Garden," reproduced on Pages 4, 5, 53, 54, and 55). Other blurbs appear on Pages 42 (for a garden article), 52 (building), and 59 (foods and equipment).

Handling Special Services

Additional demands on Mr. Hottes' time are made by two other especial charges: The garden service publications and the lecture service bureau.

Service publications are of two kinds: Leaflets and booklets. Some scores of leaflets in all of the magazine's special fields are furnished to readers for 4 to 8 cents each, and the largest group of them, dealing with gardening subjects, is prepared under Mr. Hottes' direction. This task involves selection of timely garden questions that puzzle enough readers so that leaflets on them would be of service (letters from readers, garden news, and such sources provide tips for subjects); seeking authorities to write the leaflets, sometimes rewriting them, procuring the right illustrations; supervising their printing (each is punched in the left margin for insertion in a scrapbook furnished by the magazine at nominal cost);

All four of the *Better Homes & Gardens* specialized departments—home furnishings, gardens, home building, and foods and equipment—provide such booklets and leaflets. They are listed from time to time in the magazine, and they go out in thousands. Orders for them are filled through the Home Service Bureau, an editorial-department adjunct that also handles the magazine's question-and-answer service, its Bildcost home-building plans and other services.

BETTER HOMES & GARDENS
FLOWER CULTURE LEAFLET

NO. GC **1**

HOW TO PRUNE
Trees, Shrubs, Evergreens and Fruit

by Victor H. Ries and Ralph R. Rothacker

OUR yards and gardens must have some care each year if they are to maintain a vigorous, thriving, and prosperous appearance. This care, in addition to proper fertilization, disease and insect control, will consist largely of a little intelligent pruning.

One of the big problems confronting the home owner and possessor of ornamental trees and shrubs is, therefore, when and how to prune, altho in many cases it is even more important to know

realizing that they will eventually grow into trees. Here again it is not a question of pruning, but the improper use of these plants. So, before we decide to do drastic pruning, we should make sure we do not need a new planting of the proper varieties.

What Is Pruning?

Pruning is the removal of surplus or undesirable growth at the proper time of

retiring out-of-date leaflets as they lose their usefulness and replacing them with new ones; and occasionally even redesigning their format.

Booklets are more elaborate. Usually of larger page size, they run to as many as 168 pages; they sell to readers at from 10 to 50 cents. Some of their material is written especially for the purpose; some reprinted from the magazine ("How to Tie Your Beds to Your Lawn" appears in a booklet called "See How to Plant Your Home Grounds").

The lecture service bureau offers three types of service:

Lectures by Mr. Hottes on garden subjects, made during regularly scheduled tours to all parts of the country. Clubs engaging him for these lectures pay a moderate fee.

"Better Homes & Gardens lectures" on flowers and gardens, available to garden clubs that agree to campaign for subscriptions to the magazine (the clubs retain a 40 percent commission for their treasuries). These lectures consist of manuscripts of the talks and sixty or more colored slides each; they cost the club only postage or express both ways. The lectures are prepared by members of the editorial staff.

"Illustrated lectures," furnished in the same form and on the same basis as the second type, except that no subscription campaign is involved. These lectures are prepared by the magazine's editors and approved by them at the request of advertisers, who pay the costs of preparation and slides. General Electric, for example, supplies a lecture called "Light Is the Key to Secret Gardens"; the International Silver Company one on "The Art of Table Arrangement."

The detail of handling lectures is assigned to Mr. Swain, whose desk is near that of Mr. Hottes. Demand for the lectures is heaviest in the winter and early spring months, lightest in the summer when club activities slow up. In a typical March Mr. Swain circulated thirty-three *Better Homes & Gardens* lectures and 112 commercial lectures. At the same time he was arranging a seven-week lecture tour to the Pacific coast for Mr. Hottes.

In the same office is the desk of Mrs. Huttenlocher, another associate editor. She is charged with the editing of all material on table settings and flower arrangements. Most of her features tell their stories in photography, and she spends many hours "posing" gladioli or other flowers in precisely the right arrangements, precisely the right containers and—if the photography is to be in color—precisely the right colors; or in disposing table- and silverware, linens and exquisitely prepared dishes so that no Emily Post can find anything wrong.

She has other duties that show but little through the pages of the magazine. She edits the monthly Garden Club Exchange, an eight-page publication sent free to the presidents of America's 16,000 garden clubs and the advisers of more thousands of junior garden clubs. This little publication has editorial problems just as definite, though not as involved, as those of *Better Homes & Gardens* itself. It presents news of garden clubs and garden shows, book reviews, descriptions of *Better Homes & Gardens* club services and other matter.

Mrs. Huttenlocher also prepares illustrated lectures for the lecture service bureau, and occasionally travels to give lectures. An important part of her job is to cooperate with the advertising department, to advise and aid advertisers seeking information in her specialties.

Editing for the Home Planner

John Normile, editor in charge of building, remodeling, and home maintenance, sets as his monthly goal presentation of four types of material: Illustrated houses, remodeling, accessories such as plumbing and heating, and Bildcost home plans. A fifth classification, "miscellaneous," is usually made up of short filler material—about the only type Mr. Normile procures unsolicited from free-lance writers.

For most of this department's manuscripts are planned in advance. Mr. Normile's usual procedure is to lay out plans for an issue, then to seek the material from authorities whose qualifications he knows.

His monthly "must" is a new Bildcost plan. Under this copyrighted title the magazine offers each month photographs and floor-plans of a small home. A brightly written description of the home (usually the writing is done by Mr. Adams) is followed with an offer of a list of materials for its construction to any reader who sends a 3-cent stamp. An additional paragraph says:

> This list of materials is only one part of Bildcost Service. If the cost (as figured by a local builder) is right and you decide to build this house, we'll send you the necessary plans, specifications and contract forms for the nominal price of $5 for one set, $1 for each additional set. For all practicable purposes, three sets are necessary—one each for your architect, contractor and yourself.

That in brief is the plan. But it involves arduous search by Mr. Normile for new houses and new plans that will fit his rigorous specifications. The house should cost, complete, about $5,000; it should have distinctive appearance, sound architecture, modernity; it should conform to Federal Housing Administration specifications. And the twelve Bildcost homes in any one year must fit a number of special circumstances—one for a narrow lot, one for a lake setting, one for a warm climate, and so on. Sometimes the house is one that has already been built, in which case actual photographs of it are used; sometimes Mr. Normile has to call on an expert model builder to reproduce the house in miniature for the purpose of illustration.

Architects whose plans are used for these Bildcost homes receive royalties on each set of plans sold. In the six years since *Better Homes & Gardens* first offered the Bildcost plan 13,533 sets of plans and 125,606 lists of materials have been furnished to prospective home-builders. A booklet with forty-five "Bildcost Gardened-Home Plans" is available for 25 cents.

Articles under Mr. Normile's other classifications need no detailed description. "Ten Minutes From Hollywood" (see Pages 8, 9) and "Why Families Leave Home" (see Pages 14, 15) are examples of the first type, illustrated houses. Under remodeling come "Converted to Colonial" (see Page 27) and "He Annexes the Attic" (see Page 28). "Have Your Picnics at Home" (see Page 36) is "miscellaneous." Articles on accessories, usually solicited by the editor, often deal with seasonable topics: Heating equipment and insulation in the fall, how to put a shower into the old-fashioned bathroom in the summer.

"The Question Before the House" is a monthly question-and-answer department prepared for the building division by J. F. Carter on the basis of inquiries received by the magazine.

Contests play an important part in the building division's editorial plans. "Before-and-after" contests which called for photographs of a house before and after remodeling, together with brief description of the project, brought thousands of responses and provided many columns of excellent editorial material. Other contests have dealt with new homes, kitchen remodeling, and similar subjects.

Two of *Better Homes & Gardens'* editorial divisions aim their efforts directly, and almost exclusively, at the housewife. These are the home-furnishings and decorating division and the better foods and equipment division, the latter of which includes child care and training.

Mrs. Holbrook, furnishings and decorating editor, writes some of her own articles. But most of them she obtains from other authorities—men and women whose word on specific subjects is unquestioned. An article on home lighting is needed; it is procured from Mary Webber, an expert (see Pages 10, 11, 30). An article on window shades comes from information furnished by the Window Shade Institute. And so on.

Her subject matter includes "everything inside the home except the kitchen." This means color, rugs, curtains, vacuum cleaners, lights, furniture, decoration. It includes topics as widely separated as home safety (see "Safe at Home—but ARE You?" on Pages 31, 43, 44) and the washing and storing of woolens. Seasonableness is important in this field as in others. January and its post-Christmas white sales call for an article on linens. In the spring Mrs. Holbrook talks about house-cleaning; in August and September she makes suggestions about furniture.

Most such articles, long or short, front- or back-of-the-book, are extensively illustrated with photographs or, less often, diagrams. But Mrs. Holbrook does not rely too much on pictures. A survey of readers has showed that they want "a little meat" with their illustrations. Mrs. Holbrook supervises the photography for most of her articles, often making trips to Chicago and New York to do so. The pictures for "Light Where You Need It" were made in this manner, with the cooperation of a number of lighting and furniture firms. The color photograph on the cover was made under her supervision and the art director's in a reader's home.

Article-ideas come to Mrs. Holbrook from many sources, and few of them by chance. She maintains constant touch with home-furnishing firms and department stores, so as to keep up with the most recent in home equipment news. She goes frequently to New York to consult with advertisers, manufacturers, and dealers. She sometimes goes with *Better Homes & Gardens* advertising salesmen when they call on prospective advertisers, both for her own editorial purposes and to help the salesmen "tell the Better Homes & Gardens story."

A number of retailing and equipment trade journals comes to her desk regularly.

A question-and-answer service for the furnishings division is conducted by an interior decorator. From 150 to 200 letters a month are received and answered; the number is largest in the spring months.

The Work of the Foods Editor

Editor of the better foods and equipment division is Mrs. Johnston (she appears in the by-lines as "Helen Homer"). Mrs. Johnston's list of responsibilities is a long one. Her regular seven-page front-of-the-book section has been outlined in Chapter III; in addition she furnishes a number of back-of-the-book articles, "shorts," and fillers. The breakdown of subjects under her supervision shows:

1. Meal planning
2. Equipment
3. Foods and nutrition
4. "Cooks' Round Table"
5. Child care
6. Artcrafts
7. Miscellany

A meal-planning spread under the title "SO Good Meals" (see Page 19) usually opens the seven-page section. The page, in two colors, faces a four-color photograph. The "SO Good Meals" on Page 19 are spring breakfasts—the page comes from an April issue. Those for March might deal with Lenten dishes; those for July with cold meats and salads. Seasonableness is always important. Recipes for the unusual dishes on this page are given in back-of-the-book space (see Page 56). Occasionally other meal-planning features may be used.

The spread that follows (it may be used for one or two features) is devoted to equipment and methods. This space may be used for an article like "Kitchen Energy-Savers," prepared with the cooperation of Mrs. Holbrook; or for a discussion of skillful dish-washing and another of "kitchen gadgets that pay their way"; or for a spread on table-setting by Mrs. Huttenlocher. Equipment shorts for the back of the book are also needed.

The fifth page is usually devoted to an article under the third subject on Mrs. Johnston's list. Such an article may be one on cake-baking, one on quick luncheons, one on after-theater suppers.

The "Cooks' Round Table" takes up the final two pages of the section (see Pages 21, 22, 46, 47). It is always an "insert"—a page printed separately and inserted in the bindery—because it must be punched for use in the *Better Homes & Gardens Cook Book.* The recipes printed on it come from readers as the result of contests, one each month, announced six months ahead of publication time (results of the April contest appear in the October issue). The long six-month period is necessary because of the *Better Homes & Gardens* rule that all recipes must be judged on actual tests in the Tasting-Test Kitchen.

In addition to preparing these pages and such "shorts" as "Confessions of Good Cooks" (see Page 51), Mrs. Johnston also issues a monthly four-page leaflet, the "Cooks' Round Table News," with additional recipes yielded by the contests. These are offered to readers (see Page 46) for insertion in the *Better Homes & Gardens Cook Book.*

Mrs. Johnston supervises the Tasting-Test Kitchen, a modern foods laboratory of shining porcelain and tile. Under the direct charge of "Jean Byers" (Mrs. Johnston graduated from this *nom de plume* to become "Helen Homer"), this kitchen tests every recipe that appears in the magazine or its leaflets and *Cook Book,* and tries out new kitchen equipment as well. Thousands of dishes of every conceivable variety are produced here each year; and many of them—the successful ones—are offered to Meredith employes for lunch, on the counter of the big cafeteria.

Articles on child care are also Mrs. Johnston's responsibility. Typical examples are "Watch Those 'Children's Diseases' " (see Pages 38, 40, 41, 42) and "We Parents" (see Pages 39, 45). Both are written by Gladys Denny Shultz, the magazine's "child care and training director." The first is a straightforward article, the second a compilation of hints on solution of parents' problems from the parents themselves. The hints come as response to an offer to pay $3 for each usable letter (see bottom of Page 45).

"Artcraft" articles are those on needlework, hooked rugs, simple toy-making, and the like. Sometimes usable material under this heading comes to Mrs. Johnston unsolicited; but she goes after much of it. Not infrequently she presents artcraft ideas to skilled workwomen whose ability she knows and asks them to work out finished products and simple patterns and directions for them.

The chief responsibility of Miss Olson, assistant editor, is the monthly "It's News to Me" page (see Page 2). Usually placed on Page 10 in the magazine, this feature is devoted to home and garden news of endless variety. It is news in the strict sense—brief items about new lawn mowers, high chairs, electric egg beaters, garden tools, curtain rods. Though there is direct mention of the manufacturer in each item, no commercial tie-up exists. When the page was designed the magazine's executives decided that it would have greatest reader-value if prices and names of producers were presented.

Miss Olson checks each paragraph backward and forward. When she gets word of a new gadget suitable for the page—tips come from newspapers, advertisements, trade journals, members of the staff, readers, visits to home furnishings and equipment shows, and other sources—she sends a questionnaire to the manufacturer, asking complete information. She examines the device if possible. She obtains comments from users and from other editors. She investigates the manufacturer's commercial standing. She sometimes holds up mention of it for months, pending its actual proof in use.

In addition to her work on the "It's News to Me" page, Miss Olson writes household-equipment and household-shopping articles, most of them based on the same kind of investigation. Much of her time goes to trying out gadgets sent to her by manufacturers who hope to "make" the magazine; at times she is flooded with them. A paragraph describing a new type of window shelf brought two other shelves from competing manufacturers before the issue had been in circulation a week.

Associate Editor Jean Guthrie, her home in South Dakota, works largely by mail. She makes frequent trips to Des Moines for conference and assignments, develops articles on foods and household furnishings, and serves as a rewrite editor.

Practice Suggestions

1. Suggest sources for article-ideas for the following magazines: *Current History, Fortune, Liberty, American Girl, Prairie Farmer, Sunset, Esquire, Forum.*

2. List the magazines you think should be read regularly by the editor of each of the following periodicals: *New York Times Magazine, Scribner's, New Yorker, Vogue, Country Gentleman, Business Week, Motorboat, Northwest Farm Equipment Journal, Nation.*

3. Analyze the contents of the "Letters" column in *Time,* and write a statement of your conclusion as to the type of letter *Time's* editors like to publish.

4. a. Analyze the foods material in *Good Housekeeping,* and make

a list of the types of material you think are in demand under this heading.

b. Analyze the non-fiction in the *American Magazine,* and set up a list of the types of material you think the *American Magazine* seeks.

c. Analyze the material in a trade magazine, and make a list of the types of subject matter you think it likes to offer.

5. Examine eight or ten photograph-illustrated articles in the *Saturday Evening Post.* State your conclusions as to whether most of the photographs have been supplied by the authors of the articles, or procured from other sources by the editors.

6. Some magazines departmentalize their tables of contents, some do not. State the factors that you think may influence editors to decide on one treatment or the other.

7. Study all the non-fiction in one issue of the *Cosmopolitan,* and state what clues you find as to which articles are assignments, editor-inspired, and which are probably unsolicited.

8. Suggest for each of the following magazines an editorial contest that would provide valuable editorial material for it: *Story, Pictorial Review, Advertising and Selling, Open Road for Boys.*

9. Suggest authoritative sources for articles for the *American Boy* on each of the following subjects: How to improve your tackling (football); how to build a tree-house; how to collect stamps; what college should I choose?; selecting a vocation; making summer vacation profitable; a home chemistry laboratory; high school courtesy.

REFERENCES

BOOKS

The Business Paper Editor at Work, by Douglas G. Woolf. McGraw-Hill Book Company, Inc., New York. 1936.

Pulpwood Editor, by Harold B. Hersey. Frederick A. Stokes Company, New York. 1937.

See also *Magazine Making* (Bakeless) and *Magazine Publishing* (Lohr).

PERIODICALS

"The Readers Digest," *Fortune,* November, 1936, Page 121.

"Over the Tops" by Gilbert Seldes, *Saturday Evening Post,* April 25, 1936, Page 20.

"What Makes a Book a Best Seller?" by Edward Weeks, *New York Times Book Review,* December 20, 1936, Page 2.

"The New Scribner's," *Scribner's,* October, 1936, Page 25.

" 'Time' and Henry Luce" by Dwight MacDonald, *Nation,* May 1, 1937, Page 500; " 'Fortune' Magazine" by Dwight MacDonald, *Nation,* May 8, 1937, Page 527; "Time, Fortune, Life" by Dwight MacDonald, *Nation,* May 22, 1937, Page 583.

"Meet the Magazine Editor" by George F. Pierrot, *Quill,* November, 1932, Page 4.

" 'Ken'—the Inside Story" by George Seldes, *Nation,* April 30, 1938, Page 497.

See also the series on "Magazines That Sell" in *Scribner's* beginning with "Sex, Esq." by Henry F. Pringle, March, 1938, Page 33.

See also the series on policies, growth, and operation of many American magazines in the *Quill* beginning with "Behind the Scenes at Collier's" by William L. Chenery, May, 1934, Page 8.

PAMPHLET

"A Short History of the Saturday Evening Post." Curtis Publishing Company, Philadelphia. 1936.

V

How Will It Look?

All these editors of *Better Homes & Gardens,* and those in comparable positions on most magazines, are concerned with their periodical's content—subject, breadth and authority of material, and its suitability to the tastes and needs of the reader-audience. A final division of the editorial department, that headed by the art director or make-up editor, is charged with the delicate task of effective visual presentation—which is a ten-syllable way of saying that its job is to lead the reader into each successive article by the attractiveness of its impression on his optic nerves.

For it is a maxim in most magazine offices that mere excellence of content is not enough to lure the reader into a periodical. This maxim may be only mildly applicable to such magazines as *Harper's,* the *Nation,* and others whose readers are limited groups attracted to them by experience that guarantees excellence. But it is of primary importance to the majority of magazines, especially those with a "popular" or somewhat casual audience. Ninety percent of magazine readers pick up the periodical on their reading tables or on drug-store news stands in a most casual manner, and their first act is to leaf casually through the pages with a stop-me-if-you-can air. It is the task of the art director (or of whoever else controls the magazine's physical appearance) to do precisely that, and to do it with every page of every issue.

A writer on advertising has pictured the advertisement reader as a man floating aimlessly downstream in a canoe, his interest mildly intrigued by the signboards along the shores. The signboards are the advertisements, and the man in the canoe is strong in sales-resistance to all of them. He will make the effort to paddle his craft to the shore only when a signboard is so compelling as to overcome his essential lethargy. And unless the sign (and what lies behind it) becomes more interesting as he examines it more closely, he will give up the effort and start floating away again.

This picture is almost precisely that of the magazine reader. Perhaps his resistance is not as stubborn as that of the man floating past the ads, for the probability is that he will not have steered himself into a magazine's pages unless he has hope of finding occasional pleasant stopping-places. But the resistance is there nevertheless, and it is up to the art director to overcome it.

In effect every feature in a magazine is in competition with every other feature. Each is competing for the reader's interest; each is attempting not alone to halt him as he pages along, but to hold him after he is halted until he has read it in its entirety. The holding job is the editor's responsibility—he must present the text of an article or story so that the opening seizes the reader firmly. And the body of the article must follow smoothly and interestingly enough so that the reader cannot get away. But the signboard must be set up by the art department (subject to the editor's approval).

Three major elements constitute the signboard: The title itself; the illustrations, decorations, and color; and the layout or arrangement of elements. Usually the title is dictated by the editorial staff, though the art department may propose changes if it is too long, or too short, or otherwise unsuited to effective visual presentation. Illustrations, especially if they are photographic, are sometimes provided by the editors; they too may be subject to change if the art department thinks they will not reproduce well or are otherwise unsatisfactory. The other elements—decorations, color, and layout—are entirely in the art department's bailiwick.

That there are few set rules for effective presentation is shown by a glance at the pages of any half-dozen modern magazines—indeed, at the pages of one issue of one magazine. Some pages and some spreads offer general similarities; no two are precisely alike, and many are rules unto themselves. Not all do their jobs well. Sometimes, in their straining for variety, art editors attain it at the cost of freakishness, absurdity, or complete loss of interest. But more and more, especially as, in recent years, conventions of make-up have been cast aside, have magazines grown to be things of interest, if not always of beauty, to the most casual of readers.

A few basic rules hold in most magazines, even those that reject conventions:

The righthand page is more effective than the left, since it is the one on which the eye falls first as a reader turns a page.

The two pages in a spread, whether they offer one feature, two or more, should present a degree of balance and unity.

Simplicity consonant with effective display is always a virtue.

The tone of a magazine's layouts should reflect the tone of its contents.

The tone of the layout for an article should reflect the tone of the article.

Laying Out the Magazine

How do Wallace Hainline, art director of *Better Homes & Gardens,* and his assistants go about their work?

On the fifteenth of each month Mr. McDonough discusses with Mr. Hainline a stack of features. With some of them are photographs, with others sketches or diagrams; some have no illustrations whatsoever. With each is a statement of the space it is expected to occupy in the completed issue—a page, a spread, a page and a spread, two columns plus runover, two single columns across a gutter, a single column or several of them, or any of several other possible arrangements. The accompanying layout book shows not only how this will work out but also which pages are to bear color. The art department has forty-five days—until the thirtieth of the succeeding month—to do its job.

If the article is to appear on black-and-white pages without color and if its illustrations are photographs already available, the job is relatively simple. The problem is merely to decide on arrangements of the major elements—head-line and by-line, bodies of type, pictures and possibly boxes and additional decorative matter—so as to achieve a pleasing effect. Mr. Hainline or one of his assistants—Dick Ramsell, Bert Dieter, and Leslie Baridon—studies manuscript and photographs, then makes a rough sketch of a suggested layout on thin paper. Often he makes a second and a third, and sometimes eight or ten, before he produces the one that seems right. He may consult Mr. McDonough, or the division editor responsible for the manuscript, as to which pictures to emphasize, which to play down or discard.

When a satisfactory layout is evolved, it is drawn with extreme care on layout pages—sheets with a solid page of *Better Homes & Gardens* body matter printed in pale green ink so that the precise size of the type page is presented. Proofs of the halftone cuts (the photographs are sent to the engraver, a Des Moines commercial firm, as soon as the sizes of their reproductions are decided) are pasted carefully in exact position. The title is penciled into position, as are other display lines. Proofs of cut-line type are pasted into place. The space to be occupied by body matter is indicated by penciled rectangles, and the positions of initial letters are spotted. Then the layout goes with the copy to the division editor involved and to Mr. McDonough for approval; thence to the printer. Thereafter follows the process described in Chapter III.

When the art department considers reproduction qualities of photographs unsatisfactory, the editor in charge seeks new ones, often as suggested by the layout man (those on Pages 3, 16, and 17 were a second set). Diagrams or drawings may have to be made over (as were those for "How to Tie Your Beds to Your Lawn," Pages 12, 13. See also Chapter IV). Often rough sketches must be turned into finished work by the layout man, or by a free-lance artist.

When manuscripts are unillustrated, the art director and the division editor confer as to the best medium and the best available artist for the specific work. Then the pictures are procured.

A "decoration" is an ornamental drawing or other device used to enhance the effectiveness of a page, spread, or smaller unit such as a blurb or filler. The drawing of the woman working in her garden, on Page 12, and the sketches accompanying "Along the Garden Path" on Page 62 are decorations. An "illustration" is a picture that not only adds to the visual effectiveness of the page but also helps to tell the story. Art editors often use the term "spot" for the small decorative pictures like those on Page 62.

If color is to be used on a page, the artist making the layout indicates the elements on a page that are to be colored, and often makes drawings for such elements. For the frontispiece on Page 3 not only the small sketches but also the title line, "From Fairyland," were made by the layout man. Hand-lettered titles are common art-department jobs (see "Good News" on Page 7, "Light" on Page 10, "Children's Diseases" on Page 38).

Half to two-thirds of *Better Homes & Gardens'* illustrations are photographs, a fact that eases the art department's problem. Of the remaining illustrations, about half are made by the four men in the department and the others by free-lance illustrators on Mr. Hainline's "call list." About 80 percent of these artists live in New York City, most of the rest in Chicago.

The magazine's artists have specialties of their own: Mr. Ramsell makes the "spots" for "Back Talk" (see Pages 48, 49); Mr. Baridon is especially skilled at drawings for garden articles, Mr. Dieter at pictures of dramatic quality. The four-man staff does the art work not only for *Better Homes & Gardens* but also for *Successful Farming.* It also lays out and illustrates leaflets, booklets, and other publications issued by the Meredith Publishing Company.

There are two broad classifications of layout: the symmetrical and the asymmetrical. In a symmetrical layout there is an equal and balanced amount and arrangement of type and illustration on either side of a vertical axis. In an asymmetrical layout there are unequal amounts and arrangements of type and illustration with respect to the vertical axis. While both the symmetrical and the asymmetrical layouts seek a unity of design, the symmetrical is considered static composition, the asymmetrical, dynamic composition. Example of the symmetrical, Page 11 when viewed as a single page; example of the asymmetrical, Pages 16 and 17. Characteristically the more conservative magazines use a symmetrical layout, and the more popular magazines an asymmetrical layout.

Mr. Hainline has one principal guide for layouts. "They must have change of pace. If one spread presents a quiet, dignified effect, the next should be designed with life and motion. If one is in 'formal balance,' with precisely-weighted cuts and type panels on its facing pages, the next may well be 'informal.' Variety is the goal." Formal balance is presented by "Ten Minutes From Hollywood" (see Pages 8, 9). The two photographs have almost precisely the same tones or weights, and occupy almost the same space, 30 and 31½ inches; and the larger type panel on the right is balanced by a smaller panel plus head and by-line plus diagram on the left. Informal balance appears in "He Pastures His Hobby-Horse in a Garden" (see Pages 4, 5), where one photograph breaks unevenly across the gutter and three photographs and a diagram on one page are weighted against head, sub-head, by-line, two photographs, and two type panels on the other.

The art department also supervises all four-color illustration, including the cover. Most four-color work is in color photography, done by Chicago, Los Angeles, and New York color photographers on order from and in consultation with Mr. Hainline and the division editor concerned. *Better Homes & Gardens,* like most illustrated periodicals, maintains a list of expert photographers, strategically spotted throughout the country, who can furnish pictures on almost any subject on short notice.

Added to Mr. Hainline's supervision of the production of each issue of the two magazines are the responsibilities of long-range plans. When it was decided to change the size of *Better Homes & Gardens* to a larger page, he spent nine months experimenting with new types and type faces, new layout devices, and new departmental arrangements before arriving at a satisfactory plan.

Practices of Other Magazines

For many magazine art directors and make-up editors the illustration problem is complicated by the fact that most of their pictures come from "outside the shop." Especially is this true of the slick-paper fiction magazines, which purchase almost all their fiction illustrations from free-lance artists, often at a cost equal to or exceeding the cost of the stories themselves. Magazine tradition has it that the high point in art

---

The successfully-illustrated magazine is the one whose pages not only interest and please its readers but also reflect in unmistakable terms the publication's character. *Ken's* sensational pictures and gaudy colors say instantaneously to the man leafing through its pages that it is dynamic, explosive, resentful, startling, at times even a little hysterical. The restrained black-and-white of the *New Yorker* and its equally temperate typographical plan describe it as urbane, subtle, unwilling to strain for effect. *Scribner's* interest in the "best in contemporary American life" is portrayed quite as definitely in its heavy coated paper, its quiet but never uninteresting make-up, its careful art work, and its superior photographs as in the things its articles and stories say.

---

cost was reached some years ago by one of the big-circulation women's magazines that paid $24,000 to a well-known painter of sea pictures for a series of illustrations for an eight-part serial bought at about a quarter of the pictures' cost.

Usual procedure in obtaining illustrations from free-lance artists is something like this: After the manuscript is edited and put in final form, the make-up editor allots it space, then sends a carbon copy to the artist selected. The matter of selection is important, for most illustrators have specialties—humorous pictures, Westerns, sea, sports, pen-and-ink drawings, costume pictures, aviation, and so on. The artist is told the space the story is to have—spread, spread plus a page, single page—and the colors in which reproduction is to be made. Sometimes he is asked to make his main illustration to break across two pages, or to supply "two square-ups, a vignette, and some spots." Infrequently is he told precisely what incidents to illustrate, for artists usually work more effectively when they select their own picture-possibilities.

The artist submits rough sketches of the pictures he plans, and the art director and the editor in charge of the story consider them, approve or suggest changes, and send them back. The artist then makes the final drawings or paintings. Most finished pictures are in color, even though they are to appear in black and white; most are in grease pencil or lithographer's crayon. Many techniques, however, are employed—oils, pen-and-ink, charcoal, water color, wash drawing.

"Headaches" for the art directors come chiefly from two sources:

Mistakes by the artist, and his failure to meet his deadline. Art editors may beat deadline trouble by asking for pictures weeks or months ahead of time; but they can't be sure that artists will exercise due care. One of America's best-known—and highest-priced—humorous artists once sent to a magazine two wash drawings for an account of a harebrained transcontinental auto tour; in one he pictured the car with disc wheels and righthand drive, in the other with artillery wheels and lefthand drive. Another made a set of football pictures that were marvellously effective in action and vitality, but that showed the white lines running longitudinally down the field. A third, picturing a duel described in the manuscript as fought with rapiers, had his combatants hacking away at each other with sabres. Editors learn to check every finished drawing with utmost care to catch such slips of the brush.

Larger magazines with elaborate layout problems have art directors and staff artists; small publications frequently rely on commercial artists "on call." Layout, make-up, and illustration problems are essentially the same for all publications, however. They vary in degree, but not in kind.

Practice Suggestions

1. Using the five photographs and the diagram on Pages 4 and 5, make three other possible layouts for this spread.

2. Analyze the front-of-the-book layouts in three issues of any one of the big-circulation women's magazines.

3. Suggest three other possible layouts for the material on Page 6.

4. The two articles on Pages 8, 9, 10 and 11 appeared in the same order in an issue of *Better Homes & Gardens*. Write a discussion of their "pace," or lack of it, as defined by Mr. Hainline in Chapter V.

VI

Relations with Other Departments

ONCE upon a time a group of ultra-skillful magazine editors, one of whom was also (and to the regret of his confrères) a practical-minded person, decided to edit the most beautiful, the most interesting, and the most important magazine in the history of the world. This they did. They assembled a collection of manuscripts which, in artistic merit as well as in fame of authors' names and in world-wide appeal, has not before or since been equalled. They added to them illustrations that would have graced the walls of the Louvre. They laid out their pages with diabolical cleverness, and the cover they planned was a thing beyond imagination.

"Now," said the practical-minded editor, "we must see about getting all of this incredible beauty into print ——"

"What!" said the others in chorus, albeit somewhat vaguely. "That isn't the editors' job ——"

"——and we, or some one, will have to arrange circulation, and promotion of the magazine, and advertising to pay for it ——"

But by this time the other editors had collected themselves. They fell on him and soon had beaten him to a pulp. Feeling that his advice was not desired, he went down the street and, picking up a couple of other practical-minded persons on a corner, founded a confession magazine that soon attained seven hundred thousand circulation.

"Good riddance," said his erstwhile colleagues. "We must have none of his ilk." (That was their very word.) "A magazine of such merit as ours requires no promotion. And as for circulation and advertising, readers and merchants will flock to us as soon as they hear about us. Why, in two weeks our publication will be a collector's item. . . ."

As indeed it would have been, had anybody ever heard of it. But nobody ever did, and that is the reason that nobody can prove that this tale is untrue. For truth is inherent in it.

Today's successful magazine is a compound of skillful editing with skillful circulation and advertising management. All three are necessary; in precisely what proportions no one can say. It is not even possible to declare positively that good editing is more important than good management of the circulation and advertising departments, or vice versa. Magazine history is full of examples of periodicals that pleased considerable groups of readers and would have continued to please them long after bad business practices forced them to the wall; and of cases in which sound circulation and plentiful advertising disappeared because editors failed to continue to do their jobs well enough to hold their readers.

It is probably true that sound editing is the primary requisite. The editorial content of a magazine, its appearance, and its effectiveness—all are editorial responsibility—must be such that it will serve a considerable group of readers significantly enough to make them want it. If it does this, able management will be able to capitalize it to the extent of building a circulation sufficient to draw a body of advertising; and the two combined will pay the bills and make a profit. Good editing will even enable a magazine to survive business depressions and periods of mismanagement, if neither is too tenacious. But the best editing in the world will not write checks.

It is also true that skillful promotion and vigorous salesmanship of advertising space may either tide a magazine over a period of inferior editing or, for a short time, "put across" one inferior from the start. There is no record, however, of the magazine nobody wants kept alive unless it is subsidized. And there have been scores of examples of magazines operated unexceptionably from the advertising and circulation points of view which have been either complete fiascos or have made only a temporary flash because they have filled no vital, long-time reader need.

Not only is the successful magazine one in which each of its major subdivisions is capably operated. It is also one in which the subdivisions have the most intimate of relationships, in which each keeps constantly in mind the needs of the others, in which the efforts of the men and women "on the business side" are at all times coordinated with those of the editorial staff. The function of the editorial department is to bring together a body of material of service and interest to a given group of readers; that of the business department to finance editorial operations and its own through sale of circulation and sale of advertising space. The two functions are sharply distinguished; but they are as interdependent as the buying and selling operations of a corner grocery.

The Interplay of Departments

Just as no two magazine editorial departments are exactly alike, neither do any two business departments, in organization or operation, resemble each other precisely. Nevertheless their basic purposes and methods are similar enough so that a knowledge of one situation is a key to the understanding of all. Specifically, the relation of the *Better Homes & Gardens* business department to the editorial department is a clue to what goes on in hundreds of other periodical-publishing offices.

The principal subdivisions of the business department with which the editorial department maintains constant contact, largely through the editor's office, are five: Advertising, circulation, promotion, production, and research. Consider them in order.

All departments of a magazine are responsible to the publisher or to his representative. In large organizations such executives are not often intimately concerned with details of operation, business or editorial. Their department heads confer with them on matters of policy, on major steps.

On smaller magazines they may also be their own editors or business managers; in some cases they are everything but office boy and mail clerk.

Peter Ainsworth is advertising manager of *Better Homes & Gardens*. His job: To fill as many pages as possible each month with advertisements of reputable products of interest to *Better Homes & Gardens* readers. Quite aside from the fact that his success in this task is one of the principal measures of the magazine's prosperity, it is of essential interest to Mr. McDonough because the amount of advertising in each issue governs the number of pages in it, and consequently the amount of editorial space available.

Months before an issue is ready to go to press, Mr. Ainsworth estimates the amount of advertising it will probably carry, basing his estimate on the commitments, orders, and other data in his files. By use of a mathematical formula worked out by the magazine's management—one that takes into account columns of advertising and the number of necessary "supporting editorial columns," plus the main editorial pages (the front of the book, the frontispiece, the table of contents page, and so on)—the total number of pages to be expected in the issue is determined.

On the wall of an office in the advertising department are three "make-up boards" which show graphically the outcome of this figuring. Each board represents one of the next three issues to go to press (an issue "closes" on the first of the second month preceding its date of publication: The April issue closes on February 1). Little colored tabs on each board, each on the proper hook for its page number, represent the pages anticipated for the issue. A red tab means a four-color full-page advertisement; a red with white center a four-color editorial page; a white a full editorial page; a green an advertising page; two-thirds green and one-third white a page with two columns of advertising and one of editorial matter; and so on. The tabs are arranged on their hooks so that no spread in the issue, unless it is one with both pages devoted to one advertiser, is without two columns of editorial matter; so that each four-color advertisement is faced by a full editorial page, each full-page black-and-white or black-and-one-color advertisement is faced by at least two editorial columns.

Most magazines set up minimums below which the number of pages in any issue may not go. The *Better Homes & Gardens* minimum is 78 pages; if the formula produces a number lower than this, enough editorial pages to bring it to 78 may be authorized by Mr. Wright, the company's comptroller. Few magazines use the formula method of figuring issue-size. Instead they maintain a ratio of editorial to advertising columns, usually varying from 60-40 to 40-60.

These tabs, changed from day to day as advertising prospects change, show precisely what the forthcoming issue is expected to be. Before Mr. McDonough, on the first of each month (see Chapter III), prepares his call to editors for material, he studies the make-up board. From it he learns how many full pages, color pages, one- and two-column spaces, he may count on. His December 1 forecast for the April issue described in Chapter III was 190 pages; the issue as it finally appeared was cut to 156.

As the issue progresses through the month, Mr. McDonough consults the almost-daily changes of the make-up board. Reductions in the number of tabs on it mean elimination of editorial matter; additions mean provision of more features. Of course, manuscripts are kept on hand to meet such emergencies. But in spite of this, last minute additions of pages give magazine making some of the excitement of newspaper editing.

When the issue is being made up, the advertising order-handling division furnishes to Mr. Adams, make-up editor, a list showing the placement and nature of full-page, two-column, and one-column advertisements. Mr. Adams then places related editorial matter alongside the ads, insofar as possible. A one-column garden article, in other words, may be placed on a page with a two-column advertisement for garden tools. *Better Homes & Gardens* editors and other executives, like those on most magazines, agree that it is "good magazine making to group related editorial matter and advertising, viewing the matter purely from the standpoint of readers."

Editorial-advertising conferences on other matters are daily affairs. For example: An advertiser offers an advertisement for a new kitchen cabinet. Mr. Ainsworth asks the opinion of Mrs. Johnston and Miss Olson. Are they familiar with the cabinet? Is it properly designed? Is it priced right? What do they know of the manufacturer's responsibility? Their answers will have much to do with his decision on acceptance of the advertisement.

Not infrequently he may ask Mrs. Holbrook, Mrs. Huttenlocher, or other editors (see Chapter IV) to act as consultants with advertisers or advertising agencies. Editors know the magazine's readership and the needs of readers. They are in position to give advertisers information that is helpful to them in designing merchandise to suit these needs.

If Mr. Ainsworth gets help, he also gives it. Frequently he learns from advertising copy, or from talks with advertisers, of new devices that suggest editorial features. A seed advertiser announces a new breed of peony: Is there a tip for a garden article in it? Mr. Ainsworth talks with the garden editor, who weighs the suggestion and accepts or rejects it according to his editorial judgment.

What about "compulsion"? Does this kind of suggestion by the advertising manager put pressure on the editors? Do they favor articles that may "give a break" to advertisers? By no means, say both editorial and advertising departments. "Any suggestion I make," says Mr. Ainsworth, "is just that and nothing more. If I presented it as anything more, Frank McDonough would kick me downstairs—and I would deserve it. No magazine can afford to give an advertiser 'plugging' for at least two major reasons. First, every other advertiser in the field would have legitimate objection. Second, such a practice would soon break down reader-confidence in editorial integrity, and shortly neither circulation nor advertising salesmen would have anything to sell."

Circulation and Editorial

Perhaps more direct than the relationship between advertising and editorial departments is that between circulation and editorial. The essential job of the editorial department is to offer material that will serve and please as many potential readers as thoroughly as possible. The essential job of the circulation department is to sell as many copies of the magazine as it can economically to the potential readers the editorial department is working to please. The two work with many of the same

> Too much circulation is something few magazines can afford. The reason is that the sum paid by the reader for the publication, if it is of the "slick" variety with expensive illustration and production, almost never pays the actual cost of putting the finished copy into homes or onto news stands. Especially is this true after subscription agents' commissions—40 to 70 percent—are subtracted. The deficiency is made up by advertising revenue. But advertising revenue, though it may make up such a deficiency on a normal issue of a magazine, might not do so if the number of copies printed and sold were suddenly enlarged. For advertising rates cannot be jumped overnight, nor extra advertising space sold at the last minute.

tools. Prominent among circulation efforts are the mailings that follow each expiration—thousands occur each month—to bring ex-subscribers back into the fold. Lester H. Mugge, *Better Homes & Gardens* circulation manager, confers with editors to obtain information for such mailings—attractive descriptions of forthcoming features of the magazine make the best possible copy for renewal letters. Sometimes the circulation department, though it bears responsibility for the production of subscription mailings, seeks editorial help not only in planning but also in writing them. It may seek similar help in preparation of circulation advertisements in the magazine itself or in other media. Mr. Mugge may come to Mr. McDonough and other editors for advice on timing a campaign to take advantage of special issues or special features.

The plan described in Chapter IV whereby women's clubs are provided lectures in return for carrying on subscription efforts is typical of other special campaigns that editorial and circulation departments cooperate to arrange.

Related in some respects to the work of the circulation department is that of the promotion department, headed by Rex Stark. The circulation department handles the general promotion and enormous detail of selling the magazine by subscription and through newsdealers; the promotion department is interested in ideas and devices that will make the magazine more attractive, both to readers and to advertisers.

Occasionally *Better Homes & Gardens* editorial features are suggested by Mr. Stark and his assistants. The growth of the "Endorsed Recipe" plan is an example. Seeking a new and distinctive method of presenting foods material, promotional and editorial heads were put together. They evolved the editorial plan that became the "Cooks' Round Table" in its present form. By this plan any woman may send her pet recipe to the magazine for testing in the Tasting-Test Kitchen. If it passes the test, the woman gets a certificate and six printed copies of

How do circulation departments get mailing lists? Usually the lists that bring the highest percentage of returns (2 to 4 percent on a new-subscriber mailing is considered very high) are those made up from their own files—former subscribers, persons who write to the magazine, and so on. But they may buy lists from firms that make a specialty of preparing them—the R. L. Polk Company, specialists in city directories, for instance. Such lists are often broken down according to economic or social classes; and a list of two-car families, or of yacht owners, costs more than a general or non-selective list, for its proportional buying power is higher. Many other sources of lists may be used: Telephone and city directories, social registers, lists of club members, directories of specialized organizations.

the recipe; and the best recipes each month are printed in the magazine.

The results of the plan: The foods division of the magazine gets a monthly feature that is authoritative, distinctive, and high in reader-interest. Some 2,000 readers a month take the trouble to send recipes to Des Moines. The "Cooks' Round Table of Endorsed Recipes" interests food advertisers in the magazine. And many a newspaper considers that the award of a *Better Homes & Gardens* certificate to a local woman is worth a news story in its columns.

The *Better Homes & Gardens Cook Book,* prepared by the better foods division and enlarged each month (see Chapter IV), was first suggested to members of the magazine's staff by Mr. Bohen, Meredith president. Mr. Corbin, vice-president and editorial director, and other officials turned the matter over in their minds for several years, seeking a way of doing the unusual rather than merely getting out another standard cook book. One evening Hadar Ortman, former director of operation and finance of the Meredith company, was discussing the problem with Mr. Corbin at his home. Mrs. Corbin said, "I have a cook book that I want to show you."

She brought out a ring binder note book that one of her sons had been using at school. In it was an accumulation of recipes, menus, pictures of table settings, and so on; Mrs. Corbin planned to paste the clippings on sheets and file them by subject. The next day Mr. Corbin took the idea to the office. A conference followed, and the loose leaf cook book was under way. . . . In its first eight years 900,000 copies of the book were sold.

The moral of incidents such as these, obviously, is that ideas may come from unexpected sources, and that anyone connected with an organization is likely to produce them. Sometimes they must be adapted; sometimes ideas that glitter on the surface may have to be discarded after probing.

The promotion department is closely concerned with editorial contests. For a home-remodeling contest, promotion men prepared the announcements that appeared as "house ads," wrote a remodeling booklet offered to readers, and followed up with advertising promotion to bring building advertisers into the magazine. The department furnished news of contest winners to newspapers. The editorial material prepared in connection with the contest and the judging of the contest entries were responsibilities of the editorial department.

The promotion department also aids in planning the format of leaflets and in conducting such other editorial services as lectures and question-and-answer bureaus. Among promotional duties is the preparation of the announcements of these services for editorial and advertising columns.

Open Letter to Program Chairman

Dear Chairman:

If you want to give your club programs new zest, if you want to add color, inspiration and genuine helpfulness to your entertainment, then you'll want to present the newly revised *Better Homes & Gardens* Illustrated Lectures at your club meetings.

Your club members will be delighted with these lectures and they are available at no actual cost to your club. There are four lectures, each consisting of sixty slides naturally colored and a manuscript that describes each lecture.

Send today for complete details on how you can show the *Better Homes & Gardens* Illustrated Lectures to your club. Simply drop a card or letter to Dept. 6305 Meredith Building,

BETTER HOMES & GARDENS
Des Moines, Iowa

BILDCOST
REG. U. S. PAT. OFF.

Better Homes & Gardens' Bildcost Service is a regular feature of the magazine. No matter where you live—East, West, North, or South—there's a Bildcost Gardened Home for you and your family. Send 25 cents for the *Better Homes & Gardens'* Book of Bildcost Gardened-Home Plans. It contains descriptions of 45 other homes designed by outstanding architects.

Better Homes & Gardens
5404 Meredith Building
Des Moines, Iowa (Please Check)

☐ Please send me the List of Materials which will enable me to learn the exact cost to me to build Bildcost Home No. 804 (described on page 109) in my own community. I inclose a 3-cent stamp.

☐ Please send me Better Homes & Gardens' Book of Bildcost Gardened-Home Plans and the List of Materials for Bildcost Home No. 804. I inclose 28 cents.

Name.................................

Address.................................

City................State..............

NOW READY!

New Landscaping Picture Book

THEORY is all very well, but for downright helpfulness in landscaping, there's nothing like photographs of gardens and home grounds that have made good. That's *Better Homes & Gardens'* first principle.

"See How to Plant Your Home Grounds," a new *Better Homes & Gardens* book just off the press, covers modern landscaping for your needs thoroly—and it knows you can better digest words of wisdom with illustrative accompaniment.

Here's a brief taste of what you get in this big 52-page picture book: Appropriate plantings that invite you in, pictures of informal gardens, sketches of formal gardens, suggestions for garden nooks, new ideas for the outdoor living-room, practical how-to-do tricks of the landscape architect, how to grade lawns and terraces, how to build a proper rock garden and lily pool, successful evergreens, attractive fences and gates, intriguing garden-houses, useful outdoor fireplaces, plus 22 common landscaping errors, which warn you what *not* to do!

Whether you are planning a new yard or just doing things to an old one, this book will help you. Order your copy today! Price, only 25 cents.

Address all orders to:

BETTER HOMES & GARDENS
6304 Meredith Bldg., Des Moines, Iowa

In Other Magazine Offices

Magazines with less elaborate organizations than those of the Meredith, Curtis, Hearst, Crowell, Macfadden, and Butterick publications—especially periodicals that come from one-publication houses and those that have limited reader-audiences (*Modern Medicine, Motor Boat*)—often do not enjoy the luxury of a promotion department or a promotion manager. But every one has its promotional activities.

Writing a letter to a "prospect," either for advertising or for subscription, is promotion. So is the common practice of sending copies of specific issues to individuals whose attention to special features is desired. So is keeping up-to-date the magazine's listing in the writers' publications. So are speeches made by editors and other executives, and contests, and efforts to obtain material from new authors. Not a day passes in the office of any magazine in America without activity that is essentially promotional, no matter what it may be called.

Country Home's annual selection of America's champion country newspaper correspondent has the same virtues. *Collier's* annual All-America football team, the movie star popularity contests of the motion picture magazines, *Harper's* and the *Atlantic Monthly's* frequent contests for fiction or article writers, all provide editorial material. And this material is frequently the source of free publicity in newspapers.

Sometimes promotional efforts grow out of beginnings innocent of any intent but that to procure editorial matter. When the *American Boy* bought a series of articles on building model airplanes, its editors saw at first merely a series of articles. But within a year there had grown an Airplane Model League of America with 400,000 members (more than the magazine had subscribers), a direct tie-in with sixty newspapers using *American Boy* material and carrying the magazine's name every day for a four-month period, and a national contest that became a nation-wide newspaper and news magazine story.

Among the best-known of organized promotional efforts is the Good Housekeeping Institute. The Institute, which tests commercial products and, if it approves them, permits use of its seal, has proved of untold value to the magazine. It attracts advertising, it adds authority to editorial material, and it carries mention of *Good Housekeeping* onto millions of commercial labels each year.

Wallaces' Farmer and Iowa Homestead has a "service editor" whose job is essentially promotional. He visits farm groups, gives talks, conducts a question-and-answer service, judges contests, supplies a department for the magazine. Another *Wallaces' Farmer and Iowa Homestead* promotional effort was its series of annual low-cost tours to American show places and vacation spots, arranged for readers.

When magazine men learned of the staggering fees reputedly paid ex-President Coolidge by the *Saturday Evening Post* for a series of articles, they shook their heads. Not even the taciturn Mr. Coolidge expressing himself in 8,000-word batches, they agreed, was worth that much money. But when they saw his articles appearing as news in most of the nation's dailies, always with mention of the *Saturday Evening Post,* they changed their minds.

The production manager of *Better Homes & Gardens,* L. E. Smith, and Glen Boylan, manager of the methods department, work with Mr. McDonough and the other editors toward one end: To turn out the best-looking magazine possible with high-speed production methods.

The term "high-speed" is significant. If a monthly magazine circulates but a few thousand copies, it can use the comparatively slow flat-bed press, it can print from original type and photo-engravings, if it wishes (thus avoiding possible loss in sharpness of reproduction, the constant problem of making plates for rotary presses), it can run presses at low speed. *Better Homes & Gardens* has to print 100,000 copies of an issue each working day for more than three weeks, and other big circulation magazines have the same problem (the *Saturday Evening Post* prints about 600,000 each day in a five-day week). This complicates production problems; sometimes it means that big-circulation magazines cannot hope to obtain as fine printing as low-speed presses produce. What, specifically, are the major problems that editors, art directors and production men have to solve?

For many years pressmen thought that four-color printing could never be achieved without four press-runs—one each for yellow, red, blue, and black. Were this true, full color illustrations and advertisements could never appear in magazines printed on rotary presses except through the costly insert method. But invention has followed invention until, today, high-speed presses produce full color practically as well as they produce black alone.

Use of color is one of the most troublesome. Major difficulties in black-and-white printing have been solved. But color printing, despite technical advances, is beset with "angles." Has the ink-mixing room blended inks so as to produce precisely the tints desired by the art department? Will a deep green be more effective than a light one? Can a page designated for a black-and-orange run be switched to a black-and-red? Is color on a page showing through and spoiling an effect on the reverse?

The modern high-speed rotary color press is designed so that colors other than black must be used in four- or eight-page lots—not consecutive pages, but pages arranged according to the placing of plates on the press (imposition). If it is planned to use Nile green in an illustration on Page 16, the same green—and no other—may be used on Pages 20, 21, and 25. Halftone and Benday screens make it possible to use this green in a variety of values.

As an aid to the solution of color problems, Mr. Hainline sends to the press room at make-up time—between the tenth and twentieth of the month—a list showing color pages for the issue. The list shows also which pages are to carry "bleed" illustrations—illustrations, that is, that extend through page margins to its edge (see Pages 3, 21, 22). It is necessary also to decide in advance the positions for insertion of four-color and other special pages.

There are scores of minor problems. The production men ask the editorial department to get copy to them earlier; to make fewer changes in proof; to seek photographs with sharper contrast. The editors ask for "cleaner" proof—proof with fewer errors; for improvement in engraver's plates; for checking on color inks to be sure that they maintain the same tones throughout an issue.

Research and the Editor

Finally, the research department. Under J. T. Miller, this department serves advertising and circulation departments as well as editorial. Frequently information it digs up for Mr. Ainsworth—data on the sale of electric refrigerators, for instance—has value for the editorial department as well.

Essentially the research task is fact-finding—facts about readers, about effectiveness of editorial features or advertisements, about desires and tastes of prospective readers. Facts, too, that will aid in the preparation of articles under way in the editorial department.

Every year the research department conducts a general investigation among *Better Homes & Gardens* readers, sending to 10,000 subscribers picked at random a questionnaire seeking answers to scores of questions: Questions to reveal the economic status of readers, their preferences in home equipment, their social and cultural interests, the kinds of automobiles they drive. This investigation is aimed at providing information for advertising salesmen to pass on to clients about the precise nature of the reader-public they may reach by buying *Better Homes &*

Gardens space. But it is obvious that the information is of value to the editors as well as to the advertisers. Such a survey helps editors to select and prepare material on a basis of fact instead of by guessing.

A further service to the editorial department is the reader-survey made two or three times each year. This survey, directed at discovery of reader-response to material in a specific issue, is conducted by the so-called Gallup personal interview method. A corps of interviewers (employed through a firm that specializes in such surveys) goes to subscribers evenly divided among ten widely-scattered sections of the United States. A printed form lists each editorial feature in the issue under survey (one that has been in the subscriber's hands about two weeks), with check-blanks marked "read completely," "partly read," and "not read." The interviewer, armed with a copy of the issue, checks a blank for each feature according to the subscriber's response to questions. Then he procures other information: Economic status of the reader, whether he is a home owner, whether he would like more or fewer pictures in the magazine, what his major household and garden interests are, and so on.

This direct, specific comment on the magazine is a significant guide to the editors in planning future issues. Certain features may be losing reader-attraction, others gaining; the survey will tell the story. It shows when an old department is outmoded, or a new one needed to meet new interests.

Knowing in advance what issue is to be the subject of a survey, editors may put into it two contrasting features of the same general classification, as a check on the possible superiority of one treatment over another. The result may be exceedingly revealing; or it may be puzzling. In such a trial involving "We Parents" and "Watch Those 'Children's Diseases' " (see Pages 38, 39, 40, 41, 42, 45) the survey showed percentages of readership high enough to justify continued use of both types of treatment.

It is the task of the research department not only to conduct such surveys but also to analyze and tabulate their findings. The department serves the editorial department in other ways: It may undertake an analysis of reader-interest in a regular feature whose value the editors question. It may investigate reader-acceptance of a new form of kitchen equipment which has been advertised in the magazine, or described in its editorial columns, or both. It may analyze the departmental contents and subject-percentages of other magazines. It is often called on for aid in the compilation of statistics for editorial use: The table accompanying "Good News" (see Page 7) was compiled by the research department.

Other Types of Research

Every successful magazine, whether it maintains a department labeled "research" or not, engages in a good deal of fact-finding and fact-analysis. Advertising departments have made greater use of research, until recent years, than have their editorial colleagues. The lengths to which magazines have gone to dig out facts that aid in telling the advertising story are often astonishing. For the modern advertiser wants to know, before deciding how to apportion his advertising dollar, everything about a magazine's readers from their income to their average attitude toward female addiction to nicotine, and everything about the magazine's effectiveness in reaching them as well.

Modern magazines are too competitive, however, for editorial departments to edit by dead reckoning. Editors have to work by methods as nearly scientific as may be; and the scientific method calls for facts. Consequently editors have learned not only to make wide use of the findings of advertising surveys but to conduct all kinds of research themselves.

Often the surveys are of the type used by *Better Homes & Gardens* in its frequent check-ups—the Gallup method. Several fact-finding organizations have developed in the United States in recent years to carry out such investigations, and many magazines without their own research departments spend thousands of dollars through them.

There are, however, many other methods of learning reader-tastes, reader-preferences, and reader-habits. Some of them are far more subtle than the direct-survey method. Among them:

1. Contests directed at getting readers to write critical letters to the editor. Such contests have value; but editors have learned not to place too much confidence in them, for experience shows that contest entrants often say what they think the judges want them to say. The *American Boy* found in every such contest that its editorial page was ranked at or near the top in reader-interest. But it also discovered that in unsolicited, non-contest letters the editorial page was rarely mentioned. It decided to eliminate the page, and the number of protests was negligible.

2. Visits by editors to reader-groups, where the editors may ask direct questions and get direct, and often surprisingly honest, answers. Editors of the *Farmer's Wife* spend months on the road each year, sometimes to procure material or make talks, but always with a purpose to establish intimate contact with readers.

3. Use of "ballots" in the magazine on which readers may send in their choices of favorite features and stories.

4. Letters to authorities asking criticism of specific features. A women's magazine, for instance, may ask home economics teachers to comment on foods, clothing, and other home-making features or departments.

5. Omission from one issue of a department of questionable value to discover whether its lack brings reader-objection.

6. Use of the aged advertisers' device, suggestion that readers write for a leaflet or some other inexpensive "premium," to test the readership and drawing power of the feature in which the suggestion is placed.

7. Contests aimed at getting readers to describe themselves. Such contests may ask for short essays on "What I Like to Read," or "My Hobby," or "I Had the Best Time of My Life When ——."

Practice Suggestions

1. a. Count the number of columns of editorial matter and of advertising matter in at least three non-consecutive issues of a magazine and figure the usual percentage of each.

b. Study in at least three issues of a magazine the relation of editorial to advertising matter. Is care taken to suit "reading matter" to advertisements? Is there apparent any rule as to the minimum amount of editorial matter per spread?

c. Study the apparent relation of editorial matter to advertising (is there evidence of attempt to favor advertised material?) in a women's magazine, a sports magazine, and a trade magazine.

2. a. Suggest effective mailing lists for subscription campaigns for the following magazines: *Harper's Bazaar, Automobile Trade Journal, News-Week, Cosmopolitan, Pictorial Review.*

b. From periodicals current on the news stands, select five that you think have "good news stand covers" and tell why.

c. Study a copy of the *Saturday Evening Post, McCall's, Boy's Life,* or *Scribner's* and write a report on the evidences you find in it of editorial effort to aid the circulation department in procuring renewals of subscriptions that expire with the issue you study.

3. a. Suggest for each of the following magazines a "promotion stunt" that you think would have the twin virtues of providing good editorial material and bringing the magazine to general public attention: *Forum, Liberty, Readers Digest, Nation's Business, Life.*

b. List as many magazine promotional efforts similar to *Better Homes & Gardens Cook Book* and the Good Housekeeping Institute as you can. Write a one-paragraph evaluation of each.

4. a. What are the particular "production problems" of a magazine like *Vogue*? *National Geographic*? *New Republic*? *American Mercury*? *Country Home*?

b. Study in a magazine using color printing the sequences of pages bearing the same colors. Write a discussion of any production problems you discover involved therein.

5. a. Suppose yourself to be research manager of a new magazine to be aimed at the audience reached by, and with essentially the same characteristics as, *Harper's* and the *Atlantic Monthly.* Make up a questionnaire the aim of which is to procure information about the audience's tastes, desires, and needs, the results to be used by your editorial department in seeking the right kind of material.

b. From three copies of general magazines make up a list of all the evidences you can find of efforts to obtain knowledge of readers' tastes, preferences, likes, and dislikes.

REFERENCES

Magazine Circulation, by Phillips Wyman. The McCall Company, New York.
See also *Magazine Making* (Bakeless) and *Magazine Publishing* (Lohr).

VII

Creative Editing

BY THIS time it is obvious that magazine-editing is more than a swivel-chair job—a very great deal more. Should the editors decide to sit back and depend on hope that the daily mail would bring the stuff of which "good" magazines are made, your library table would soon be as bare of periodicals as it is of ostrich eggs.

For two reasons: The editors would shortly find themselves without anything they'd care, even dare, to publish. And you would find their magazines things you wouldn't give a snap of your fingers to read.

To repeat, hope doesn't produce usable scripts. If it did, the editorial job would be easy. For most magazines receive in a year twenty to thirty times as much material as they can possibly cram into their pages; the average "take" from manuscripts submitted is three percent or less. And of this three percent of usable material, no more than half is unsolicited—hoped for but not asked for. In sample figures, it works out this way:

Manuscripts received in a year	10,000
Manuscripts needed for a year	300
Manuscripts rejected	9,700
Manuscripts needed for a year	300
Usable unsolicited manuscripts	150
Additional manuscripts needed	150

This is a statistical way of saying that, since less than half of a magazine's needs will be met by the arrival of unplanned material, it has to satisfy the remainder through steps of its own devising. And such steps are "creative editing."

Creative editing does not begin, however, with the planning and solicitation of manuscripts and other features. Its first manifestation appears in the basic plan of the publication—the "story" it proposes to tell. This story, whether it be aid and entertainment for the housewife or furtherance of the boot-and-shoe industry, reflection of the nation's best thought and literary craft or appeal to shopgirl sentimentality, is always the primary editorial creation. But the editors responsible for telling and retelling the story issue after issue find that they can do so successfully only by continuous application of creative imagination, initiative, and energy. For each issue they must produce a new batch of article and feature ideas that will suit their purpose; and, once having evolved the ideas, they must see them through to fruition.

Why is it that, once a magazine's story is as firmly established as that, say, of the *American*, its editors cannot rely on the thousands of writers who would give their eye-teeth to sell to it to furnish them enough suitable material? Why is not the daily influx of manuscripts loaded with articles and stories that meet the needs so clearly, if implicitly, stated in each issue? Why must the editors seek beyond the scripts sent by men and women who theoretically have opportunity to learn what the magazine wants? Two reasons:

1. Fewer than 10 percent of aspiring free-lance writers realize the necessity or take the trouble to find out what their market's story really is.

2. Special editorial needs, changes in policy, and the like are often things that writers cannot know, no matter how sedulously they study markets.

In a number of representative magazine offices the percentages of unsolicited material that draw checks instead of rejections are given as: *Hotel Management, McCall's,* and *Pictorial Review,* 0; *American Mercury,* .001; *Ladies' Home Journal,* .01; *Collier's* and *Harper's,* 1 or less; *Scribner's,* 1; *Rotarian* and *Sports Afield,* 2; *Better Homes & Gardens, Good Housekeeping,* and *Theatre Arts Monthly,* 5; *Dry Goods Economist,* 5 to 8; *Etude* and *Nation's Business,* 10.

How Do Editors "Create"?

What are the "creative" steps that editors take to procure the material that free-lance writers won't or can't furnish?

A full-length answer to this question as it concerns *Better Homes & Gardens* appears in Chapters IV and VI (with some additional detail in Chapters IX-XIII). *Better Homes & Gardens* editors spend many hours developing article, department, and contest ideas and turning them into publishable realities. In the broad their solution of the problem is typical of magazine procedure everywhere. But procedures vary in detail, just as do magazine purposes. Examination of the creative editing in another magazine office will show what some of the variations are.

Take the *American Boy*. Its average reader is 16 years old, a junior in high school. His interests are sports, adventure, science and mechanics, school life. He hopes to go to college. He drives or wants to drive a car; he likes to use tools, to "make things"; his interest in girls is as yet latent, carefully unexpressed. The magazine's editors must furnish him material to follow (or lead) his seasonal interest in athletics, to give him a wide variety of adventure, to appeal to his hobbies, and so on. The 7,500 manuscripts that come to the office each year furnish less than half of the material the editors need; they must "create" the remainder. Here are some of the ways they do it.

In the fall they plan to use two or possibly three football stories and two or possibly three articles on how to play (or how to watch) the game. Among unsolicited manuscripts they may find one or two of the football stories they need, but usually they have to ask experienced writers of sports stories who know the magazine's slant for stories written specifically to fill the holes. The articles are a more difficult problem. They must have authority, they must be colorfully and clearly written, they must be well illustrated. Commonly they are staff assignments:

A member of the editorial staff accompanied a Southern university team on its long trek to Pasadena for the Tournament of Roses game, watched the game, interviewed coaches and players, and wrote a series of articles for the next fall.

A staff member sat in the stands at a Yale-Princeton game, interviewed the rival quarterbacks afterward, got from each an analysis of his strategy, and wrote a highly specific article, one that combined the color of the contest with a look behind the scenes.

A staff writer interviewed every member of an All-American football team and turned out eleven brief how-to-play articles.

A staff writer interviewed George Hauser, line coach of the University of Minnesota team, and wrote a series of tips on how a national championship line learns and performs its job.

When six-man football was becoming boomingly popular in small high schools of the West, Franklin M. Reck, managing editor, made a month-long trip to watch and study the game, talk to its inventor and its coaches, and obtain material for a series of articles. The articles, he decided, were inadequate as a means of introducing the game to high school boys. So he and other editors initiated the following additional efforts:

They took the existing rule book—incomplete, of small circulation, and selling for 50 cents—and had it enlarged, and the magazine sold 10,000 copies in a year at 20 cents. They appointed an official rules committee. They arranged for "six-man clinics" for coaches all over the country, and persuaded summer coaching schools to include the new sport in their curricula. They made a survey of the cost of the sport to a school, and advised hundreds of teachers and coaches how to undertake it economically. They picked an All-American Honor Roll at the end of the season—and 2,000 newspapers and forty radio stations announced the selections. They aided in the preparation of three motion pictures of the game. What started as an attempt to build up an interesting, serviceful series of editorial articles became not only that but also a first-rate promotion venture.

How much of a magazine's non-fiction content is ordinarily staff-planned? A representative group of editors, asked this question, responded: *McCall's* and *Pictorial Review,* all; *American Mercury,* 99 percent plus; *Atlantic Monthly,* overwhelming majority; *Harper's,* most; *Rotarian,* well over 90 percent; *Collier's* and *Nation's Business,* 90 percent; *Good Housekeeping,* all but five articles a year; *Mill and Factory,* 70 percent; *Sporting Goods Journal,* 60 percent; *Better Homes & Gardens, Country Gentleman, Dry Goods Economist,* and *Hotel Management,* 50 percent; *Scribner's,* 40 percent; *Field and Stream, Forum,* and *Theatre Arts Monthly,* 25 percent; *Modern Mechanix,* 20 percent; *Esquire,* 10 percent.

Similar practices produce similar articles about other sports: Interviews with big-league baseball players, tennis stars, swimming coaches, skating champions. Occasionally these planned articles are assigned to newspaper sports editors or other writers with whose work the editors are acquainted.

Meanwhile articles to meet other needs are under development:

High school boys need vocational advice. An editor of the magazine traveled to many sections of the country to procure competent information for a series of articles. Among those from whom the information came were William Allen White of Kansas on journalism, Dan Casement of Colorado and Kansas on farming, Dr. W. J. Mayo of Minnesota on medicine.

A series of brief, bright tips on manners is desired. Its style must be just right, for high school boys usually turn up noses at "manners stuff." Finally it is decided that an editor of the magazine must write the series.

Understandable, boy-language explanation of modern investment and finance has a place in the magazine. To fill it the editors engage a skillful free-lance writer who knows the subject, and talk over with him the presentation problem. At length a personification of money—"Mr. John C. Hundred"—is evolved, and a series of twelve short articles show his adventures in banking, insurance, stocks, bonds, mortgages, real estate, and so on.

How to interest boys in politics, citizenship, and civic responsibility? To answer this question the editors assign a fiction writer to do a series of stories on high school politics and citizenship, tie in with it contests for editorial writers of high school newspapers. No articles urging readers to take interest in the subject are included in the campaign, for boys don't like to be preached to.

Interest in travel is spurred by elaborate contests in which the prizes are trips to many parts of the United States and to Europe and the Orient.

In Other Magazine Offices

Thus one staff works so that its editorial product will be precisely what the editors think it ought to be. And thus work the staffs of most other magazines. Some other examples:

The *Saturday Evening Post,* in the spring of 1935, wanted a series of authoritative articles on the Brazilian cotton boom. Col. James E. Edmonds, New Orleans cotton expert, was commissioned to go to Brazil and return with information to set at rest the contradictory reports reaching this country.

At about the same time it became evident that Italy was to invade Ethiopia. Gordon MacCreagh, a leading American authority on Ethiopia, was asked to write an article for the *Saturday Evening Post.* It appeared just as Mussolini's troops went into the African empire—not by chance, but by design. The end of the Ethiopian rainy season set a virtually certain date for the beginning of the invasion.

Professionalism in intercollegiate athletics was a few years ago a subject for general speculation. A *Saturday Evening Post* editorial conference rejected the plan of treating the subject in article form; instead it assigned a writer to do a fiction serial which, possessing the value of a good story, would also present all the angles of the problem.

Editor-planned articles in American magazines are written more commonly by free-lance writers engaged for the jobs than by staff members. Of twenty-five magazines asked whether they use staff or non-staff writers for this kind of work, fourteen responded that they employ non-staff writers, nine that they assign it to staff members. One said, "Fifty-fifty"; another, "Both."

The *Forum* uses a monthly debate on a timely topic. Any important current topic may do; but not any writers. Many hours of thought and effort are necessary to get John Thomas Taylor and Gerald P. Nye to debate the profits-in-war question, or Edward L. Bernays and Ferdinand Lundberg to take sides on propaganda as a menace to democracy. In a July issue the debate subject is a light one, and the debaters skillful light writers, Alfred Uhler and Margaret Fishback, discussing "Are Men Mice?"

When *Liberty* editors learned that President Franklin Roosevelt had a pet plot for a serial story, they obtained permission to use it and assigned six well-known fiction writers to the writing job, one to an installment.

Ralph Peters, editor of the *Quill,* wanted a series of articles on newspaper comic strips and their artists. He got plentiful cooperation from the artists or the syndicates that managed them because the articles, appearing in a journalistic magazine, had publicity value for the strips.

Successful Farming wanted an article about a farm in Iowa on which experimental work in weed eradication was under way. Editor Kirk Fox asked a free-lance writer at Iowa State College, where experts in charge of the experiment were located, to gather material for the story and write it.

In the 1936 elections the Democrats carried forty-six states although most of the nation's newspapers talked Republican. The *New Republic* desired an analysis of newspaper attitudes during the campaign and of their apparent effect on voting. The editorial staff itself went to work to make the analysis, and its findings appeared in a supplement to the magazine.

Collier's sent a staff writer, Jim Marshall, to the Orient early in the Sino-Japanese war to get material for a series of interpretative articles (and Mr. Marshall had the simultaneous good luck and misfortune to be on the United States gunboat Panay when Japanese planes fired on her).

Like many popular and general magazines, *Collier's* makes a feature of personality articles, and usually assigns subjects to specific writers. Kyle Crichton is the magazine's screen and feature writer; Quentin Reynolds its sports writer; Robert McCormick its Washington correspondent. Much of the work of staff writers like these men is the preparation of personality articles, for such articles may be made to do double duty. Mr. McCormick's story on Senator Reynolds of North Carolina, for instance, not only gives to readers an interesting, easy-to-read human interest article about a colorful public figure, but also provides them an intimate view of aspects of the national political scene. Mr. Crichton's interview with Deanna Durbin tells them things they want to know about Hollywood as well as the young movie star.

These examples are picked at random from among thousands. Every issue of every magazine tells the story of other such efforts to get material that would never come to life if the editors merely hoped. Not often do such articles and features tell the readers in so many words that they have been "created," however. More commonly they appear as impersonally and casually as any of the material supplied without editorial stimulation. But sometimes a clue shows in an editorial footnote, or in a phrase in the article itself, or—as in the case of the *Forum* debates—in the very nature of the feature. Obviously these debates don't just grow.

Long feature stories in newspapers are, nine times out of ten, more apparently inspired than are magazine articles. A newspaper publishes a Sunday feature describing the work of the "sand hogs" digging a sewage disposal tunnel a hundred feet below the city's streets: It is obvious that the city or feature editor "thought up" the idea and assigned a man to it. The same thing is true of the feature that gives an inside view of the dog pound at a time when dog-muzzling is in the local news; and of the feature which tells the immense amount of detail concerned in clearing the streets after a heavy snow.

How Contests Grow

Another creative editing tack is that which results in the production of contest ideas. Most magazines use contests to stimulate reader-interest, or to procure editorial material, or both. The *New Yorker*, sophisticated in approach and careful never to demand anything difficult of its readers, eschews contests. So do *Fortune*, the *Saturday Evening Post*, and a number of other periodicals. But most use them, usually at the expense of badly-furrowed editorial brows. Examples:

Harper's conducted a contest for essays on "The American Way," open to professional as well as amateur writers. The result was a series of brilliant discussions of American social, political, and economic philosophy that became leading articles in the magazine (and, eventually, a book published by Harper and Brothers, who also publish the magazine).

From the day its first publishers announced a $25,000 prize for a title for it, *Liberty* has used many contests. Most are of the "trick" variety, like that offering prizes in miles of travel for solution of 100 anagrams and a short essay on "Where I Would Like Best to Spend My Vacation, and Why."

Scribner's offered cash prizes varying from $1,000 to $100 for personal experience articles suitable for its "Life in the United States" section.

Saddest contest in *American Boy* editors' experience was a "what's-wrong-with-this-cartoon" contest. The artist thought he had put forty-nine errors in the drawing. One of the 18,000 entrants submitted a list of 1,400 errors; many had lists of 200 to 1,000. All had to be checked, even that listing "Errors 427 to 444—nobody in the picture has any rubbers on." Eventually the editors had to allow seventy-two "legitimate errors"; the first prize winner had sixty-nine right in a list of several hundred. He won $10! The editors took a rest cure.

Almost every women's magazine conducts recipe contests and others similar to them, often with very small prizes. Confession magazines regularly offer prizes for confession stories. Most magazines design contests that touch the special interests of their readers—hobby contests, puzzle contests, contests asking for letters on popular or seasonable topics. The list is endless, and it would be elaborating on the obvious to extend it.

Most contests, as has been said, are of two kinds: Those that aim at production of useful editorial material, such as *Harper's* "American Way" essays, and those the purpose of which is to tie the reader more closely to the magazine. How may they accomplish this second purpose? In two ways. Any reader who writes a letter to a magazine feels himself somehow personally tied to it. And any reader who doesn't himself enter the contest but who is interested in its subject will look forward to the announcement of its result. It serves its purpose completely when, in order not to miss the final announcement, the reader renews his subscription.

Do contests ordinarily furnish "good copy"? Usually not. Of twenty-five magazines asked, "Have you found contests useful for obtaining publishable non-fiction?" nineteen responded, "No"; one, "Only occasionally"; two, "Never use them"; and three—*Sports Afield, Atlantic Monthly,* and *Rotarian*—"Yes."

Helping Writers Write

Another aspect of creative editing is the work of editors to help their writers write.

Let's look again at the things the *American Boy's* editors do. For this magazine the problem of obtaining exactly the right material is especially difficult, for relatively few writers have taken the trouble to understand the "slant" of the older-boy periodical (*Boy's Life* and the *Open Road for Boys* are the other leaders in the field). And sometimes it is necessary that the editors send writers off on new tacks, or even put new wind in their sails.

The *American Boy* wanted fictionized material that would show the operations of modern retail business. It arranged for William Heyliger, a regular contributor, to spend a month in Gimbel's department store in New York City and to write a series of stories showing a boy against the background of the store.

It sent Mr. Heyliger to the iron mines of upper New York State to procure material for a mining serial.

It arranged for Frederic N. Litten, another free lance, to go through the course of training of a cadet in the United States Army aviation school in Texas, so that he could write a series of stories with this background. It sent him to Puerto Rico to gather material for another series, and assigned him to a study of commercial aviation for another.

Desiring circus fiction, it made arrangements with a big circus for Thomson Burtis to travel with it for a summer. Mr. Burtis did so, actually performing as a clown for a time, and got material not only for an *American Boy* series but also for a dozen other stories that he sold to other magazines. The magazine sent Mr. Burtis to Tampico, Mexico, for a series of stories about the Mexican oil fields; and to Hollywood for a movie series.

Other magazines follow the same technique. When J. P. Marquand had finished a *Saturday Evening Post* serial and had no other in mind, the *Saturday Evening Post* sent him to the Orient; he returned with material for a whole book-shelf of serials (one of which was the well-known "Thank You, Mr. Moto"). It persuaded Katharine Dayton, intent on a trip to Geneva, to go instead to Washington, get herself a newspaper job, and procure background for a series of satirical skits on the Washington scene.

Another time-consuming task of the magazine editor is that of working with the writer who has almost but not quite arrived, or who has temporarily "gone dry" after years of successful writing. Examples of this kind of work are abundant (those here are for obvious reasons presented anonymously):

One magazine, receiving a manuscript that announced itself as a novice's attempt not only by its own deficiencies but by the frank letter that came with it, found in it evidence that the author might learn to write. The editors sent him lengthy criticism, asked him to rewrite the piece. He did so—not once, but six times; and each time the editors criticized further. At length their response was not a criticism, but a check. His next manuscript was rewritten only once. Since that time he has become a regular writer for the magazine that gave him his first boost, and for thirty others.

Another magazine found that one of its star writers had suddenly taken to sending it third-rate material. Objecting to this, the editors learned that the author knew his scripts were bad. "But I can't do anything about it," he said. "I work as hard as I ever did—harder—but I can't turn out a decent story." The editors went into a six-hour conference and developed a plot for a serial story laid against a background the writer knew thoroughly. One of them turned out a 15,000-word synopsis. This went to the writer, and shortly he came back with a first-rate story based on it. Moreover, the editors' effort bridged the bad spot for him, and he went ahead to produce salable stories again.

Editors of a third magazine found a usable plot for an imaginative pseudo-science story in a manuscript itself unusable. They bought the plot from the author for a comparatively small fee, then sent the script to another author known for his skill at the pseudo-science story. He turned out a finished manuscript, and was paid full price for it.

How much creative editing—idea-development, assignment of subjects to writers, invention of new contests, work with writers—any magazine does is limited by only one factor: The size of the editorial staff and consequently the time available for such work. The one-man magazine, or that with a small staff, cannot go extensively into the editorial luxuries. But not even the largest, best-equipped, least hurried magazine staff ever achieves satisfaction with what it turns out. Few readers' criticisms are as devastating as those the editors themselves level at their finished products.

When will the perfect magazine appear? The answer can only be something like this: When a combination of all the right manuscripts, all the right illustrations, all the necessary editorial time and skill, all the finest production methods, magically becomes available. This editorial millennium has not yet put in its appearance, and there is no evidence that it is around a distant corner. Too many hurdles exist, and they are too closely spaced, for any magazine to take them all without a falter.

The day may come. The perfect magazine may some time appear. If it does, it will be the day when all the obstacles described or suggested in Part I of this book have been overcome. And even when the day arrives, there is pretty sure to be one obdurate editor in the office who will say, "If only we had made the cut on Page 20 a shade larger. . . ."

Which is one of the things that keep editors forever at their desks.

Practice Suggestions

1. From three consecutive issues of any monthly magazine make a list of articles you think are staff-planned, and tell why you think so.

2. Suggest for the coming year's issues of the *American Boy* five articles that would make suitable how-to-play sports features, and state in each case how or by whom you think the feature should be prepared.

3. Suggest several possible treatments for a September women's magazine article aimed at telling freshman co-eds what kind of clothes to take with them when they go away to college.

4. Study the contests in several issues of a magazine that uses at least one an issue. Then suggest three contest-ideas that might be suitable for the magazine.

5. Study several issues of a magazine that does not use contests. Then write an explanation of what you believe to be the editors' reasons for not including the contest device in their editorial scheme.

PART TWO

Writing the Article

VIII

The Eternal Triangle

In this part of the book we are to look at a large number of "cases"—get their histories, feel their pulses, take their blood-pressures, put them through a thorough clinical examination. But first a little polishing of our instruments.

Why did the editor of *Better Homes & Gardens* use the particular stories that are reproduced in the front of the book? Why did Mr. and Mrs. Gould use the story (Chapter XII) "What Do the Women of America Think about War," in the *Ladies' Home Journal*? Why did Mr. Kelley pick the story, "Mountain King" (Chapter IX) for *Country Home*? Why, out of the thousands of stories that come to a magazine, are only *certain* stories bought and used?

The answer, over-simplified, is carried in this formula: Number of readers + intensity of reader interest = value of article.

There are 130,000,000 people or thereabouts in the United States—to say nothing of Canadians, English-speaking and -reading people in other countries, and American expatriates. The ideal magazine—from one point of view—would be one that was read with goggle-eyed avidity by all of the literates—and the pictures devoured by the illiterates.

Illiteracy figures, which range (by states) in the United States from 14.9 percent to .08 percent, are of considerable interest to magazine and newspaper circulation departments.

But there is no such magazine. The reason: People aren't all alike. There is no one theme—no common denominator of interest—that will hold all of the readers all of the time against the competitive pull of other interests.

These millions of people, or some part of them, are the magazine's and the free lance's customers. If it is mass circulation that the magazine is after, then it must discover and continuously exploit a "theme" which has a very widespread interest.

And to be sure there are such themes. One is health. Everybody wants to keep well. Another is money, another romance, another entertainment—commodities for which we are all avid. But all of us are not always, preeminently, and exclusively interested in any *one* of these themes. The reasons are that people are individually too complex and that there are too many differences between people.

People differ in their occupations. There are lawyers, housewives, mechanics, artists, merchants, teachers. They differ in their social situations and outlooks. They differ in temperament. They differ racially and in the parts of the globe that they occupy.

And so the customer market for the magazine is tremendously varied. No magazine has yet succeeded in cornering this market—and it is a safe prediction that no magazine will.

The strategy of the magazine is to find, out of the broad market—all of the people—a sector that is fairly homogeneous and to devise a theme which will have for the people who comprise this sector a high degree of interest.

The best way to see how magazines have chosen for themselves "selected" markets out of the broad market of all of the people is to refer to standard classifications of magazines and to illustrate the chief classification with typical magazines.

Classification of Periodicals

The classification given by *Standard Rate and Data Service,* a monthly publication which gives detailed data on all American and Canadian daily newspapers and magazines, is as follows:

Daily newspapers (English language)

Agricultural Publications
- General:
  - *Examples: Capper's Farmer, Country Gentleman, Country Home, Farmer's Wife, Rural New Yorker, Successful Farming, Wallaces' Farmer and Iowa Homestead.*
- Dairy:
  - *Examples: Hoard's Dairyman, California Dairyman.*
- Fruit:
  - *Examples: American Fruit Grower, Northwest Fruit Grower.*
- Live Stock (General):
  - *Examples: Chicago Daily Drovers' Journal, National Live Stock Producer.*
- Breed Publications:
  - *Examples: Holstein-Friesian World, American Hereford Journal, Poland China Journal.*
- Poultry:
  - *Examples: Poultry Tribune, Plymouth Rock Monthly.*
- Pigeons and Pet Stock:
  - *Examples: American Pigeon Journal, American Rabbit Journal.*
- Bees:
  - *Examples: American Bee Journal, Gleanings in Bee Culture.*
- Specialized Farming:
  - *Example: Cotton Digest.*
- Power Farming:
  - *Examples: Agricultural Engineering, Farm Machinery and Equipment.*
- Farmer's Associations:
  - *Examples: Farm Bureau News, National Grange Monthly.*

General Magazines (includes all magazines of importance published in the United States)
- Antiques
- Art
- Athletics
- Aviation
- Baseball
- Billiards
- Birds
- Birth Control
- Boxing
- Business (executives)
  - *Examples: Nation's Business, Fortune, System, Business Week.*
- Clubs
- Collegiate
- Dogs
- Dramatic and Theatrical
  - *Examples: Theatre Arts Monthly, Stage.*
- Educational
- Fashions
- Florists
- Fraternal
- General
  - *Examples: American, Atlantic Monthly, College Humor, Cosmopolitan, Current History, Forum,*

General (*Continued*)
- *Harper's, National Geographic, Parents' Magazine, Redbook, Scientific American, Scribner's, Sunset Magazine, Survey Graphic, True Confessions, Vanity Fair, Nation, New Republic, Collier's, Liberty, New Yorker, Saturday Evening Post, Time.*

Golf
Home and Landscape
- *Examples: American Home, Better Homes & Gardens, House and Garden.*

Horse and Hunting
Juvenile
- *Examples: American Boy, Boy's Life.*

Literary
- *Examples: Writer, Saturday Review of Literature.*

Mail Order
Matrimonial
Military, Naval and Service Men
Miscellaneous
Motion Picture
Motoring
Music
Needlework
Radio and Wireless
Railroad Employees
Society
Sports
- *Examples: Field and Stream, Outdoor Life.*

Tennis
Travel
Women's
- *Examples: Good Housekeeping, Household Magazine, Farmer's Wife, Ladies' Home Journal, McCall's, Pictorial Review, Woman's Home Companion, Vogue.*

Yachting and Motor Boating

Business Papers:
- *Examples: Advertising and Selling, American Journal of Surgery, American Restaurant, Brick and Clay Record, Coal Age, Dry Goods Economist, Foundry, Musical Digest, Oil and Gas Journal, Printers' Ink, Public Safety, Editor and Publisher, Quill, Railway Age, Textile Review, Journal of the American Medical Association, Journal of Bacteriology, Journal of Home Economics.*

Religious Publications

This classification is based largely on subject matter. A simpler classification that is frequently used is as follows:

Weekly Newspapers
Daily Newspapers
Sunday Newspapers
General Magazines
Weekly Magazines
Women's Magazines
Home Service Magazines
Farm Journals
Religious Magazines
Business and Trade Publications
Juvenile Magazines
Technical and Scientific Journals

The purpose of studying these classifications is to get as clear a conception as possible of the varied reader-groups and subject-matter fields covered by American periodicals. Each newspaper and magazine is different from all the rest. It has chiseled out for itself a niche. It may differ in the area it covers, in the readers it tries to reach, in its subject matter, and in its style of presenting material. A study of such a list as that from *Standard Rate and Data Service* should give one a picture of the range of magazine writing possibilities.

Newspaper features, published in the regular columns and magazine sections of daily newspapers, are blood cousins of many of the articles that appear in general magazines. The chief differences between the newspaper feature and the popular magazine article are that the former may (although it need not) deal with subject matter that is local to the newspaper's territory; and it may lean more heavily than does the magazine on current news events.

Editorial—Circulation—Advertising

Every magazine has a "philosophy" and two "stories." Its philosophy is the germinal conception of the magazine, involving its theme, the audience it will attempt to reach, and the niche it hopes to hold in the world of advertising.

One of its "stories" is the circulation story. It is the magazine's own interpretation of why and how it should interest those readers whom it wishes to bring into the circulation fold.

The other is the advertising story. It recounts with never-ending refinements the ways in which the magazine can serve effectively as an advertising medium.

To illustrate. The idea or philosophy of *Better Homes & Gardens* envisages a publication directed at the numerically large group of middle-class home owners and prospective home owners. The central theme is the hearth-side. The emotions evoked are those associated with the hearth, the home, the family. This idea is the focal point of a broad group of related interests: the house, the garden, children, food, interior decoration, interior and garden furnishings.

The circulation story recounts to prospective subscribers the practical and inspirational benefits that they will get from a magazine which tells them, in popular and attractive form, how to build, garden, prepare food, decorate and furnish their homes, rear children, etc.

To the advertiser the magazine can offer a group of readers who, precisely because they are readers of such a publication, have demonstrated that they have the need for building materials, nursery stock, foods, furniture, etc.; have the ability to buy; and the willingness to spend.

Time has had a very deep effect on magazine and newspaper making during the past fifteen years. The idea of *Time* is, essentially, to dramatize and humanize the significant news events which are given only a summary and factual treatment in the newspaper. To subscribers it says that you can keep posted on the events of the world and pleasurably titillated at the same time by a weekly perusal of *Time's* pages. It will select, collate, and embellish so that, on an investment of thirty or forty minutes a week, you can be as well (or better) informed as the next man. *Time* discovered what had been suspected from time to time through the ages, that intelligence does not have to be stodgy. To its

Typical circulations of magazines:

American	2,202,686
Saturday Evening Post	3,026,129
Woman's Home Companion	2,981,826
Atlantic Monthly	105,250
Business Week	97,692
Printers' Ink (weekly)	17,803
Chemical and Metallurgical Engineering	14,897
Journal of Bacteriology	2,111

(Data from N. W. Ayer and Son's "Directory of Newspapers and Periodicals, 1938.")

advertisers *Time* offers 670,000 readers who are interested in worthwhile things, therefore intelligent, and, by the final step of logic, supported by indubitable statistics, better endowed with the world's goods and the ability and desire to buy from advertisers than the run of folk.

And so on with every magazine that exists: an editorial concept, an editorial content conceived to attract a specified type of reader, and an advertising medium with advantages demonstrable to manufacturer and merchant.

Time has had paid to it the highest compliment, that of sedulous imitation. Scores of magazines have adapted the *Time* formula to their own needs. Even the characteristic *Time* makeup has been widely imitated. Some of its more important influences have been: the use of human-interest background, interpretation of news to give it historical and human setting, and condensation in writing.

What does all this mean? It means that the very first step in the business of becoming a writer of articles or an editorial worker is for one to get into his very bones the conception of the editorial point of view. It means that all editorial thinking must basically be in terms of the eternal editorial triangle: the reader, the advertiser, and the editorial content.

Looking at the whole business from this basic point of view, we are ready to examine our "cases." We shall discover a good many things about them, but above all we shall want to discover why they were printed, why people should want to read them, what devices they employ to attract and hold readers, how they fit into the magazine's "policy."

Practice Suggestions

1. Study a number of issues of some magazine. Write out a statement of what you think are: (a) the editorial strategy of the magazine; (b) its circulation story; (c) its advertising story.

2. Do you think there is a place for a new magazine about cats? Analyze the circulation and business possibilities of such a magazine. Outline an editorial program for it, including specifications as to the kind of material you would use, format, and illustrations.

3. Why do you think *Harper's* and the *Atlantic Monthly* do not use illustrations?

4. What do you think of a department of letters-to-the-editor in such magazines as: *Time, Country Gentleman, Woman's Home Companion, Scribner's*?

5. Take five articles from a single current magazine and rate them on the number of magazine readers to whom you think they will appeal and on intensity of the reader interest in them.

6. Take a story out of *Saturday Evening Post* or *Collier's*. List other magazines that might be interested in the same article.

REFERENCES

BOOKS

Magazine Making, by John Bakeless. Viking Press, New York. 1931.

Magazine Article Writing, by Ernest Brennecke, Jr., and Donald Lemen Clark. The Macmillan Company, New York.

Modern Feature Writing, by Harry F. Harrington, and Elmo Scott Watson. Harper and Brothers, New York. 1935.

Magazine Articles, by Robert P. Crawford. McGraw-Hill Book Company, New York. 1931.

Writing Journalistic Features, by P. I. Reed. McGraw-Hill Book Company, New York. 1931.

Writing for Profit, by Donald Wilhelm. McGraw-Hill Book Company, New York. 1937.

Magazine Circulation, by Phillips Wyman. The McCall Company, New York.

The Business Paper Editor at Work, by Douglas G. Woolf. McGraw-Hill Book Company, New York. 1936.

PERIODICALS

"Controlled Magazines and How They've Grown," by Roy Sheldon. *Advertising and Selling,* May, 1937, Page 29.

IX

The Experience Article

Largely with the purpose of supplying handles for lifting them about, newspaper and magazine articles are classified in this book as belonging to one or another of the following types:

1. Experience articles
   a. Third person experience articles (experiences not the author's and told in third person)
   b. Personal experience articles (experiences of the author, told in the first person)
   c. Confession articles
2. News features
3. Process articles
4. Information articles
5. Personality articles

[*a. Third Person Experience Article*]

Hobby-Horse in a Garden

Before you go any farther in this chapter, turn back and read the story "He Pastures His Hobby-Horse in a Garden" by Wainwright Evans (Page 4). Read the story with a mind that bristles with questions. Prominent among them should be: Why did *Better Homes & Gardens* buy and pay good money for this article? Why was it given a prominent place in the magazine? Why were these particular illustrations used? Why does the story begin as it does? Is the style appropriate? Is the story too long or too short?

A year and a half ago, Mr. McDonough was leafing through a magazine. He saw a picture. It was of Ernest Elmo Calkins. A picture of Mr. Calkins would stop a magazine man because for many years Mr. Calkins had been very prominent in the advertising business. Mr. McDonough did more than look, however, because the legend to the picture told of two of Mr. Calkins' hobbies. One of them is woodworking, the other, gardens. So the editorial shears came out of the drawer, and picture and legend were snipped from the magazine. They went into an idea file which reposes in the bottom right-hand drawer of Mr. McDonough's desk.

That picture went through a process of incubation—not in its nest in the desk drawer, but in the editor's mind. A year later Mr. McDonough wrote a letter to Wainwright Evans at New York City. Mr. Evans was not a stranger. He was known to Mr. McDonough—as well as to a host of other editors—for the hundreds of articles and stories he has written during the past twenty-five years, and more particularly because he had already done a number of things for *Better Homes & Gardens.* Why was it Mr. Evans to whom Mr. McDonough wrote? Mr. McDonough's answer is: "Because Wainwright Evans has the gumption to know just what we want and the skill to turn it out."

And that letter told about the clipped picture, asked Mr. Evans if he wouldn't call on Mr. Calkins, survey the possibilities of the story about Calkins' garden hobby, and report back.

Following a visit with Mr. Calkins, Mr. Evans wrote to Mr. McDonough that the story was obtainable and described what he saw in it.

Mr. McDonough decided he wanted the story and instructed Mr. Evans to write it. The next step was the arranging of an interview with Mr. Calkins—not in his New York office, but in the garden of his summer home in Connecticut.

The story locates Mr. Calkins' home as in Salisbury, Connecticut. Frequently the exact location of a garden or home which is the subject of a magazine article is not given because of the danger that the people concerned will be bothered by swarms of curious readers of the magazine who want to see the place and its inhabitants.

That visit to Salisbury, Connecticut, plus the previous interview with Mr. Calkins, plus the material that he got about him from Calkins' own books constituted Mr. Evans' material for the article.

Sixteen months after Mr. Evans' article came into the office of *Better Homes & Gardens,* it appeared in the magazine. A good part of those sixteen months it lay in the "manuscript paid for" file. It wasn't forgotten, however. While the story wasn't essentially seasonable, it was by all odds best for a spring issue of the magazine. And the spring issues of 1937 were already too definitely planned, when this story came in, for a place to be made for it. So it rode around the calendar until another spring.

With the manuscript came a number of photographs that Mr. Evans, himself, had taken. They were pulled out of the envelope and spread on Mr. McDonough's desk. An editor is apt to look at pictures a long time. First of all, are they good enough—sharp, clear, with contrasting darks and lights—to make good halftones? (The art director is, of course, consulted.) Second, do they really add to the story they are supposed to illustrate? Third, do they have the character, the tone, the "feel," that are wanted in the illustrations for a particular story? One or two of these pictures measured up. For example the one which shows Mr. Calkins kneeling beside one of his flower beds. But most of them wouldn't pass muster.

Next was a detailed memorandum from the editor to the art director who, in turn, wrote to Underwood & Underwood—one of the largest photographic services in the world. The letter contained detailed instructions as to the pictures that were wanted to illustrate the story.

For one thing it was desirable to show both Mr. and Mrs. Calkins using, enjoying, and living in their garden and home. Another was the great-limbed, old apple tree, and another the mirror pool. As a result of this letter and its detailed instructions, some eight or ten pictures were taken by an Underwood & Underwood photographer, who specializes in garden and outdoor pictures, and from these the ones finally used to illustrate the story were selected.

A blue print showing the design of the Calkins' garden had been secured by Mr. Evans and submitted with the manuscript.

Some five or six months before the story appeared in the magazine, it was taken out of the file and started along the road to publication. There wasn't a great deal of editing to do on the manuscript. It was in pretty good shape as it stood, but it got a careful going-over just the same, and a few changes were made. For example, the first two paragraphs appeared in the manuscript as a single paragraph. Several paragraphs of the manuscript were lifted out entirely and used as legends to the pictures. In one place the hobby horse instead of "going up and down that desk at full speed" was made to "gallop" up and down. A little excess wordage was squeezed out and the whole manuscript was made to conform to the editorial style followed by *Better Homes & Gardens.* At this stage in the proceedings, the copy of the edited manuscript and all the available pictures were sent to Mr. Hainline, head of the art department, so that layouts and art work could be planned. With them went a sheaf of penciled notes from Mr. Benson. For example:

"Please make drawing of garden plan from blue print, does not need to be large—in fact, small as possible to be legible and clear, will be ducky.

"*No* caption (legend to you!) is to be shortened. All are to be almost exactly the length you find them now. Reason: part of the story is told in pictures and captions. The remainder in text. That part in the captions is *not* duplicated in the text (the captions are paragraphs deleted from the text); therefore, the feature will fall short if captions do not appear much as they are now. Please plan layout so that there will be plenty of space for the legends (captions to me!)."

There followed a list of the illustrations with the legends (or captions) which were to be used with them.

Layouts were made, the copy was marked for the composing room, and the final steps toward seeing the story into the magazine were taken in the way described in Part I.

But our concern with hobby horses is not yet exhausted. We need to go back to the questions you were supposed to have asked yourself as you read over the article. Let's throw the answers to these questions and other observations that need to be made about this story into a series of notes.

Notes: If we want to give this story a label it can be called an experience story. This means that the information which the story is designed to convey is cast in the form of an actual experience. There are a number of advantages to this form. First of all, the things described really happened. If you don't believe it, you can go to Salisbury, Connecticut, and see for yourself. In other words the story has the weight and impressiveness of direct testimony. It is in the nature of an affidavit. And this sense of reality carries such implications as these: If Calkins could do it, I can do it too; if Calkins gets so much satisfaction out of his gardening hobby, it may be that I could get the same kind of satisfaction out of the same kind of hobby. Second, because the story is not hortatory—does not preach, but rather demonstrates—it avoids setting up that psychological rebelliousness which most humans feel when they are told that they "should" or that they "ought." Third, the experience story by its very nature introduces people—human interest. This is no place for a discussion of the psychology of human interest, but this much is obvious: None of us, living in a world of men, with our strongest and deepest emotions stirred by love and hate and envy and admiration of our fellowmen, can escape the sense of warmth and color which inheres in a real and living account of other people.

The story is slanted for *Better Homes & Gardens* in these regards: Its subject matter hits at the very heart of the editorial theme of the magazine, and the style of writing is skillfully tuned to the magazine's audience. (A possible objection to the story is that it deals with a man who, probably, is economically several rungs higher up the ladder than the average reader of the magazine. Note that every effort is made to avoid the impression that Mr. Calkins is a rich man. His place in Connecticut is *not* referred to as a summer home. Mr. Calkins does *not* employ a gardener—merely a handy-man.)

The story was not a particularly difficult or intricate one to report. Essentially there were only two sources of material: Mr. Calkins' own writings, particularly his autobiography, and Mr. Calkins himself. Every story has "source of material zones." (See Chapter XVI.) In this case the zone is highly restricted, being limited to a single man. In other cases the zones may comprise a neighborhood, a group of people or institutions, a city, a state, a section of the country, a country as a whole, or even the wide round world. The important thing for the writer is to make sure that, if the story belongs to a particular zone, say zone three, he does not handle it as if it belonged to zone one.

The central theme of this story is the pleasure and satisfaction that a prominent man derives from his garden hobby. The whole story structure revolves around the necessity of projecting that central theme into the reader's mind. The devices used to accomplish this are: first, to establish the identity of the central figure in the story, and to arouse our curiosity about him; second, to make the Calkins experience live before the reader's mind through realism of incident and conversation; third, to make everything included in the story contribute to the essential theme.

The hobby-horse device is particularly worth noting. It is used in two ways: as a refrain which, like the refrain of a ballad, gives to the story a sense of unity; and as a way of putting into the story a very real feeling of action and movement. We can be sure that Mr. Evans knew he "had something" when he came across the title of Mr. Calkins' treatise, "The Care and Feeding of Hobby Horses." In a sense that phrase "made" the story, and what remained to be done was largely to fill in around it. The hobby horse, you will note, not only trots breathlessly through the story but he appears as well in the title and in the lead.

Questions:

Why is the word "garden" put in different and larger type in the title of the article?

There isn't a good camera "portrait" of Mr. Calkins with the article. Why not?

There's nothing much about gardens in the first 300 or 400 words. Why didn't Mr. Evans bring the garden theme in earlier?

There is some first person in the story ("What part of Connecticut?" *I* interposed). Is this desirable or not? Why?

Do you believe that Mr. Calkins said the things he is quoted as saying—do the quotes sound real and life-like? If you think they do, try to put your finger on exactly those turns of phrase or idiom which give that effect. If they don't sound real, point out why.

A word about the magazine and newspaper articles which have been selected for reproduction and study in this book. They are in no sense the twenty or twenty-five "best" stories in American magazines. Rather they are "successful" in that they have met the requirements of editors of various periodicals. Taken as a whole they represent a typical cross-section of the magazine and newspaper feature market. The basis of selection has been the utility of each piece in illustrating a type of feature article and in pointing up the various problems of article writing.

It is hoped that the reader will endeavor to "understand" these articles, to argue their editorial merits and demerits in his own mind, to recognize any weaknesses that they may have, and, above all, to see in them the values which the editors who bought them saw.

In short the reader is *not* told to "write like this" if he would be successful—to *copy* the matter or the manner of any other writer. He *is* told to think through the problems that each of these stories raises, and to learn to apply the same processes of thought to his own work.

Country Home is a rural magazine. It isn't a dirt-copy farm paper, like *Wallaces' Farmer and Iowa Homestead* or the *Prairie Farmer*, but rather a general magazine slanted toward a farm audience. While it publishes material with the purpose of helping the farmer and the farm wife with the practical details of their business, it puts greater weight on articles that will entertain and inspire. Toward the first of these two aims it publishes fiction; and, in its articles, it strives for a tone and a treatment that will make them highly readable, amusing, and easy to digest. The inspirational strings are harped on by the frequent publication of success stories about farm men and women.

"Mountain King," which follows, is an example of the kind of story *Country Home*—and many other magazines—likes to get and use.

Mountain King

By George Kent

How a master salesman makes $25,000 a year from a farm which had been abandoned as worthless

MOUNTAIN KING

By George Kent

Reprinted by special permission from Country Home

It was the biggest moment of Austin Blakeslee's career. He had just been proclaimed one of the greatest potato growers of Pennsylvania—a member of the famous 400-Bushel Club. He was proud and he had a right to be. In two short years he had turned a worthless mountaintop farm into a "vegetable factory" which produced 438 bushels of potatoes to the acre. Now he sat at a table with fifty-four fellow 400-bushel men, with the governor of the state presiding. It was enough to turn the head of any tyro farmer. But then and there, with oratory ringing in his ears, and with those about him resolving to raise bigger and better potatoes, Austin Blakeslee made up his mind to raise no more potatoes at all. There were too many other good potato growers, he figured—enough to glut the market. He would try another crop.

Decisions like this are typical of Blakeslee. I have just visited him on his hilltop farm where, good times and bad, he wrings an annual profit of $25,000 from the once-barren land, and I think I have discovered the secret of his amazing success. He makes big money out of what he himself calls a "rock pile," simply because he possesses two great qualities—lightning business judgment and daring.

In these days when many farmers go blindly on, year after year, feeding cattle or planting their habitual crops in the face of overproduction, Blakeslee plants only those crops that will be in demand on the day of harvest. From his mountaintop he spies on the market like a field marshal directing a battle from a lofty lookout post. When he sees a scarcity, he attacks. When supplies are high, he retreats.

I had heard many stories of this extraordinary farmer and expected to see a man of action, but when I went to meet him at Stroudsburg, Pennsylvania, nothing had prepared me for a human whirlwind. A red truck pulled up with a scream of brakes in front of the local bank, and Blakeslee, a thin man in a sports jacket, jumped down and hurried through the door. He slapped a guard on the back, waved to the teller, and gripped me with a hard hand.

"Please wait," he said quickly. "I'm a director here and have to attend a board meeting."

Evidently he rushed affairs to a quick and businesslike conclusion, because he was out of the meeting again in a few moments, motioning me to the truck. As we thundered out of Stroudsburg, shot around curves at sixty miles an hour, and climbed to his farm in the Pocono hills, he explained to me that he had a couple of pleasure cars, but liked a truck because it made a noise. People noticed you when you rode in it. He has a boyish, enthusiastic way of looking at life. He's the kind who would go for a red truck.

The farther into the hills we sped, the more they looked like a fine place for a summer resort, but perdition for farmers.

On all sides were tumble-down houses, overgrown fields. At last, twenty-five miles from the nearest town, we entered a hard road walled with trees. This was where his land began; this was his private road. On the mountaintop, surrounded by 1,800 acres of timber, was a 200-acre rectangle of farm land. It was covered this day with the soft green of tied cauliflower heads and tawny billows of barley.

A four-year-old boy on a velocipede was in the driveway when we arrived. This was his youngest son. He has six other children, three boys and three girls, the eldest sixteen. A mass of flowers nodded gaily on both sides of the doorway as we entered the house. Mrs. Blakeslee, a tall dark woman, college bred, put down her knitting to greet us and we sat down to the long banquet-sized table. The hired girl sat down with us after she brought out a roast chicken, wild strawberry jam, three vegetables, two different kinds of pie and a demijohn of milk, which was pretty good, I thought, for a pick-up meal for an unannounced visitor.

Here, deep in the mountains, an electric toaster popped, and from the kitchen came the fitful purr of a refrigerator. On the wall a thermostat regulated the heat. Outside, I could see a small village of slick, newly painted farm buildings, and an open shed in which stood two cars and four trucks.

This was the farm and home which Austin Blakeslee built from a run-down profitless enterprise. He was thirty-two years old when the death of his father left his mother alone on the mountaintop farm. For twelve years Austin Blakeslee had been a successful lumber salesman, but his family needed him on the old place. He chucked his sample case under the bed, put on his overalls and faced the facts. Here he was on a dilapidated farm. Down the mountainside in every direction were abandoned farms, dismal evidence that the stubborn rocky land had won victory after victory over those who tried to make it yield. He had no training as a farmer. He was a salesman—a sales organization without a commodity to sell. So he looked at the rocky land as a potential factory. He knew he could find markets and sell goods, but first he had to find out how to produce them.

One bright day he answered the question by registering at the State College of Agriculture. He went there for two winters, and if I know anything of the man, the instructors must have been in a sweat of giving all the time. There never was a man who could ask so many questions, who could go longer without getting tired.

The spring after his first winter in college he was ready to start his "rock-pile vegetable factory." It was at the end of his second year in school that he put in his prize-winning potato crop, decided he had launched himself in a crowded profession and looked around him for a product in which there was no threatened surplus.

He studied the local markets. There was, he noted, a three-weeks period in which cauliflower was scarce and brought a high price. He set out to learn how he could bring it to market during those strategic three weeks.

All he knew about cauliflower was that local farmers, who had invested $7 a pound in seed, had invariably failed. He heard that the best cauliflower seed in the country was raised in Texas. To Texas he went, and returned with seed for which he had paid forty dollars a pound.

After he sowed the precious purchase, he had his doubts. Would the seed produce? He eagerly investigated every phase of the business and employed the best of cultivating methods and fertilizers he could find. His crop came through. He was ahead of time on eastern markets. There were no heavy freight charges to be paid by near-by buyers. Today Blakeslee has pushed his production up to 200,000 head, and sells them all at top prices.

Austin Blakeslee noted that many big hotels were in the market for broilers. He also heard that chicken manure would hasten the growth of his cauliflower. He tried a small experiment in a hothouse. It worked. On the basis of this test he built two brooder houses at a cost of $3,000 and began raising broilers.

The manure brought his cauliflower in eight to ten days earlier. He delivered chickens and cauliflower in the same trucks to big New York hotels.

Then the depression came over the hill with steadily lowering prices in its wake. One year Blakeslee's broiler business showed a loss. Did he hang on to it? He did not.

Once more he scaled his lookout for a product which did not surfeit the market. This time he saw a dearth of rhubarb. Not ordinary kitchen rhubarb which in summer is worth a cent a pound, but hothouse rhubarb, which fetches fifteen cents a pound. It was a crop he could grow in the winter. There was a virgin market in his region.

But no one could tell him how to grow rhubarb. He toured the country. In Michigan he found a few farmers who knew how but they wouldn't tell.

One day a friend who had returned from Canada told him he had seen a wagon loaded with rhubarb roots in Waterloo, Quebec. Two weeks later Blakeslee was in Waterloo, talking with a Mr. Frank Slack, rhubarb farmer.

"I've driven 800 miles to ask you one question," he said. "Tell me, how do you grow rhubarb?"

Slack, unable to get his rhubarb across the border, told him. Three days later Blakeslee was rolling home.

Today his brooder houses produce rhubarb which rides to market in long green boxes, each fitted with a small window through which peep the neatly aligned cherry-red stalks. And they go on the kind of market on which Blakeslee sells—a market without a surplus.

Austin Blakeslee decided he was paying too much for crates. His annual bill was $1,500, which he thought was a crazy sum for a man to spend who lived in the middle of a pine forest. He bought a secondhand sawmill, put it up on his land, and today he makes his own crates.

When Blakeslee climbs onto a truck of produce and roars off to market he changes, chameleon-like, from farmer to salesman. When he took his first load of cauliflower to the New York market, he pulled off the ferry boat into a thundering herd of trucks. He asked a cop where he could sell some cauliflower from Pennsylvania. The cop, who thought he was sort of touched, said, "Cauliflower from Pennsylvania! There ain't no such thing."

"Here's a load of it," said Blakeslee, "and you're going to see lots more of it." Blakeslee was right. Today Pennsylvania cauliflower is listed on the New York Produce Exchange Board and Blakeslee supplies most of it.

Aus never ceases trying to please buyers. He

Questions:

On what elemental human emotion does this story base its appeal?

Should the story give more detail than it does about the cultural practices Blakeslee used in growing his crops?

Why is this a good *Country Home* story?

Note the almost rhythmical alternation of short and long sentences in the first paragraph of the story. Is it intentional? What effect does it produce?

How would you phrase the theme of this story?

---

observed one day that the ordinary crate brought the cauliflower to market wilted and dog-eared. He tried this and that, and finally punched an old hatbox full of holes. It kept the vegetables fresh.

Thereafter, he shipped in pasteboard boxes. No one had ever done it before. Later he found that a crate with a parchment paper liner did an even better job. You may say it's not a farmer's job to worry about markets, salesmanship and packages. You may say he is just a grower. Austin Blakeslee would disagree. "The trouble with farmers nowadays," he said to me, "is that they don't know enough about business. If farmers were businessmen, there wouldn't be any farm problem."

MAINE POTATOES PUT ON AIRS TO ATTRACT MORE CONSUMERS

By Robert R. Mullen

Reprinted by special permission from the Christian Science Monitor

In the case of the following story from the *Christian Science Monitor*, the experience reported is not that of an individual but of a whole community—the potato growers of Aroostook County, Maine.

Presque Isle, Maine—They aren't exactly wrapping their potatoes up in tissue paper and boxing them like apples and oranges up in Aroostook County, Maine, the nation's biggest potato bin; but something has happened to make the growers look on their product a little less as though they were just spuds and a little more as if they were something extremely good to eat.

Until this year, potatoes went into 100-pound gunny sacks and were unceremoniously dumped in a grocery store bin where they made a rather drab appeal to the shopping housewife. It was easy for potatoes to be pushed aside, especially when unkind talk went the rounds that Sir Francis Drake's favorite tubers gave one that Henry VIII look.

In Aroostook County they happen to raise some 50,000 carloads of these tubers every year, planting in May and harvesting through October. This is nearly twice the total of any other state. Nearly all the County's 6,700 farms are engaged in potato growing. So when Mr. and Mrs. America suddenly start cutting down on potatoes, the effect up here is just one of those things. Gross income drops from $60,000,000 to $30,000,000.

The Potato Situation

But Maine folk are traditionally reserved. They don't get excited even when the auctioneer's flag flies. Up in Aroostook County there is still some very good fishing. This section is up so far that sportsmen have to really mean business before they will embark for an expedition into Aroostook, all of which makes it nice for the local farmers. When things got bad back in '31 they went fishing.

But when you fish (even in Maine waters) you have plenty of time to think. In the winter you can't fish, so you sit around the base burner with the boys and talk. When it suddenly develops in the talk that you have all been thinking about the same thing while you fished, well, it gives conversation a pause.

With a bit of imagination we might reconstruct it this way:—

"Yes, when you get right down to it," said Andy Beck to Harry Grinnell, taking up the conversation, "there really is nothing better to eat than a big dish of mashed potatoes that's been fixed right."

Mashed Potato Recipe

"Take 'em and boil 'em soft," advised Harry, "then smooth them out fine with something like a cream bottle, then put in some cream and butter and whip them with a fork 'til they look like ivory and are as light as whipped cream. Serve them hot with salt and pepper and butter . . . There's nothing better."

"And I don't believe they are any more fattening than lots of other foods," chimed in Tom York. "The Irish just about live on them, and they're not notably hefty. It's bosh, like a lot of other food fads."

"What we should do," summed up Andy Beck, "is advertise. We ought to tell folks about potatoes. We ought to put them up so they look good, give some recipes. Now, look at Charlie Teagle. He's from right up here at Caribou. He went out to California, now he is head of the California Fruit Growers' Association. And wherever you go, you see these big signs and advertisements, 'Eat California oranges' or 'Try California lemons.' If they can do it for fruit, we can do it for spuds, and I'm for doing it."

Well, that is how such things start. As early as

1931 they were talking about a state branding law to mark potato sacks so people would know they were getting Maine potatoes, but it was 1935 before a law was actually enacted. Then the state appropriated $25,000 for advertising and research.

Many of the growers by last year had become enthused with the possibilities of such a campaign and co-operated with the Development Commission in packing a large part of their crop in the red, white and blue peck paper bags that now form such a colorful section in the grocery stores of the Atlantic seaboard and as far inland as Ohio and Illinois.

Another bright idea was to put six jumbo baking potatoes in a long pasteboard box. These have had ready sale, especially in the larger cities.

These merchandising ideas have been largely directed by G. C. Stone, who left his native Aroostook County as a lad to serve a national chain grocery firm in various parts of the nation.

Mr. Stone is closely interested in the chemurgic possibilities for potatoes (uses other than for food). About 20 per cent of the advertising appropriation is set aside for this purpose and work is progressing at the University of Maine in Orono. Of course, such things as starch and potato flour have been produced in Maine for years, but new and more extensive consumption outlets are being energetically sought.

Short Experience Stories

Short experience stories are an important part of the contents of a good many magazines, particularly farm papers and trade journals. In three or four hundred words or less, these stories tell how farmer, merchant, or manufacturer has solved some problem of his business. And they imply—but do not say—that these successful methods or devices can be profitably adopted by the reader. For the beginning writer, such stories present an opportunity to undertake comparatively simple writing tasks—and usually receive a warm welcome from magazine editors.

GRASSLAND FARMING GAINING

Reprinted by special permission from Country Gentleman

New Jersey dairymen are rapidly recognizing the merits of grassland farming. According to Prof. C. B. Bender, who has been conducting demonstrations of the system, 5000 acres of pasture in the state are now under intensive fertilization and rotation management and in addition several thousand acres are being used for ensiling of various green crops with molasses.

As an example of what is being done, Fairlawn Farms, in Monmouth County, has completed its first year under the grassland plan. This farm contains 300 acres and carries 225 head of Guernseys. Sixty acres of grassland adjacent to the barn were set aside as pasture for 110 milking cows. This area was divided into twelve five-acre fields by means of electric fence for rotational grazing. Six of these plots received commercial fertilizer, three as an early and three as a medium-early application. The balance of the pasture area was untreated. Three plots were grazed at one time because of herd management. The pasture furnished by the first six plots carried the herd for seven weeks, so that the herbage produced on the other six was mowed for grass silage by June first, yielding better than eight tons per acre.

As soon as the first six plots had been grazed the second time, 200 pounds of nitrate of soda were applied per acre. In addition to the grass silage produced, the sixty acres supplied sufficient pasture for the milking herd until the end of August. Oat silage was then fed once a day. With the help of the silage, the pasture carried the herd until time to keep the cattle in the barn. Thirty additional acres of fertilized pasture were provided for the young stock. These young cattle also grazed second-growth timothy hay fields.

The balance of the land was used to produce grass silage and hay. Six hundred tons of alfalfa, timothy and clover, oats and pasture grass were ensiled. In addition to the grass silage, 150 tons of clover and alfalfa hay, 90 tons of timothy hay and 40 tons of oat hay were stored for the winter.

According to Harry Norton, the manager of the farm, the results of this program were beyond expectation. Since the cows have been on this program they are milking better and their condition and breeding health are superior to any previous time. The milk produced on the grass silage and hay roughage has a high color and a good flavor. —E. J. PERRY.

(Mr. Perry is extension dairyman, New Jersey Experiment Station.)

COUNT YOUR PEACHES

Reprinted by special permission from Country Home

Grant Fox, large fruit grower of Normadale, Ontario, has originated a system of peach thinning that takes out the guesswork and cuts costs 30 per cent.

Instead of the usual method of spacing fruit at selected distances on the branches, Fox determines the production capacities of his individual trees. If, in his judgment, a tree is capable of producing five bushels of No. 1 fruit, he thins it to 900 peaches, the number in five bushels of top-grade fruit.

Workers leave only one peach on bearing wood less than six inches in length, and leave two on wood that is twelve to fifteen inches long. Fruit remaining on the tree is counted. If there are still too many peaches on the tree, according to its production capacity, more are taken off the longer wood. Should some limbs have a number of small spurs, all peaches are removed on every third spur.

Removal of peaches by thinning, best done after the June drop, allows full development of those remaining and reduces culls.

[Unsigned article]

FIRE 1,400 DOZENS OF DINNERWARE PER DAY IN ONE-MAN ELECTRIC KILN

Reprinted by special permission from Ceramic Industry

Although only 58 feet long the one-man electric decorating kiln at Harker Pottery Co., Chester, W. Va., turns out the surprising production of 1,400 dozens of dinnerware per day. One man does all the placing and drawing.

The kiln is of the roller hearth type—that is, the ware is placed on heat resisting alloy trays which are moved through the kiln on rollers. A small electric motor drives the rollers by means of ratchets attached to a long oscillating bar. The pawls on this bar engage ratchet gears on each roller, moving the trays forward a short distance at each stroke.

Trays are of alloy metal built up with a rigid framework supporting an expanded metal setting surface. They are extremely light so that they can be readily handled and absorb a minimum of heat. They move through the kiln in adjacent pairs and there are 58 of them in the kiln at one time.

This kiln built by the Electric Furnace Co. differs from other designs in one important particular. It is actually a kiln folded back upon itself in the center. That is to say, the ware moves forward in one direction on two adjacent lines of trays until it reaches the point of maximum temperature, at which point the trays are automatically lowered to the return conveyor bringing them back to the starting place. The operation of transferring the trays from the top conveyor to the bottom is entirely automatic and requires no manual attention whatever. Even though the two lines of trays may not reach the end at exactly the same time, the elevator will not move downward until both are in line. Each line of trays engages switches and the elevator does not function until all switches are engaged. After depositing the trays on the return line the elevator again automatically moves back into position for the next load.

Since the two lines of ware movement are not closed off from each other the kiln becomes recuperative, heat being transferred from the outgoing cooling ware on the lower deck to the incoming ware on the upper deck.

Electric heating makes possible the automatic control of any desired temperature within plus or minus 5° F. The temperature is automatically controlled by means of Leeds & Northrup recording and indicating controllers. The kiln is enclosed with a steel shell and is, of course, completely insulated. According to the Harker officials the temperature above the kiln, even on warm summer days, does not exceed 90 degrees. It may be seen, therefore, that little heat is lost.

Ware completes its firing cycle in 8 hours, although 7 hours is possible. An average of 8 dozen pieces is set per tray.

This type of kiln may be heated either electrically as described in the present instance, or may be gas-fired. In either case the operating cost, due to the recuperative feature, will be comparable with similar costs obtained on non-recuperative kilns. Whether to fire the kiln with gas or electrically, therefore, is dependent upon local costs for either fuel. It may be pointed out, however, that with ordinary electric and gas rates which obtain in the average size pottery, the operating cost per day of the recuperative electric kiln will not vary greatly from the cost per day of the non-recuperative, gas-fired kiln. In making this computation consideration must be made of the fact that electric fans and other auxiliaries are used in the non-recuperative kiln, the cost of which must be added to the cost of the fuel for combustion.

Due to the convenience of placing and drawing the recuperative type kiln, labor conditions are very favorable for its operation as compared to non-recuperative kilns.

In many respects this kiln is similar to the electric decorating kiln installed some years ago at the Edwin M. Knowles China Co. plant, Newell, W. Va., described in CERAMIC INDUSTRY for March, 1932.

[Unsigned article]

183-PERCENT LAMB CROP!

Reprinted by special permission from Successful Farming

Forty-two lambs marketed from 23 ewes won a gold medal and the Marion Williams trophy for Garth Nelson of Blackford County, Indiana. The trophy is annually engraved to the flockmaster producing the largest percentage of market lambs.

When ready for market, Nelson's 42 lambs balanced the scales at 3,219 pounds, or an average of 76.64 pounds per lamb. The grain they nibbled was nix. "Well, then," you ask, "how did Nelson handle his ewes and lambs to get such results?"

To begin with, they were large, broad-backed grade Shropshire ewes, from 3 to 6 years old, bred and flushed on new alfalfa pasture during the fall. During the winter and before lambing, silage, oats, and soybean hay were their ration, fed in a barn with openings to the south and with no other livestock present to injure or annoy them.

The lambs were dropped about the second week in March, and the ewes were generously fed with silage, oats, soybean hay, and corn until grass came. What grain the lambs ever got was what they picked up with their mothers.

But Nelson did have an appetizing pasture stirred by the first warmth of spring; it was a seeding of English clover, sweet clover, alfalfa, and alsike clover.

"I believe the variety of feeds I rationed out to the ewes before and after lambing and the variety in the pasture mixture promoted top-notch health," Nelson said. "Heavy-milking ewes hustled the lambs along, and, even without grain, their gains were both fast and economical."—I. J. M., Ind.

[*b. Personal Experience Article*]

Fairies Live in This Garden

The experience-story family has three brothers. They are quaintly christened Third Person, Personal, and Confession. They are all good fellows and are welcome in any magazine office. Third Person gets around the most. You are apt to meet him anywhere. Personal, while less ubiquitous, is still frequently to be met up with in the pages of magazines. Confession, the baby of the family, is something of an introvert. He is shy and not a very good hand-shaker. He goes his own way. When the mood takes him, he can be charming and genteel in the best of company. But, sad to relate, he sometimes gads with the demi-monde. You have met Third Person in the stories that have just preceded. Here waiting to be introduced is Personal.

Helen Ramsey Fifield, who wrote the story "Fairies Live in This Garden" on Page 16, was an utter stranger to the editors of *Better Homes & Gardens*. Unheralded and unsung her story came to the magazine in an undistinguished envelope among hundreds of others.

It was fished out of the stream of incoming and backgoing manuscripts, because the editors saw in it certain possibilities.

These possibilities were suggested as much or more by the pictures which accompanied the manuscript as by the manuscript itself. They weren't good pictures, there was no chance of using them in the magazine, but to the roving and speculating editorial eye, they held out the possibility that retakes (new photographs of the same subject) might make something charming and unusual. So letters went off to the author and to Will Connell, a photographer in Los Angeles, known to the art director for his exceptionally fine out-of-doors pictures.

Whether or not the story would ever be used depended on what Mr. Connell was able to do with his camera. If his lens could catch the fairy quality of this miniature garden—if it could reproduce the subtle other-worldliness, the quaint imagination of this fairyland—the story would be used. Without such pictures there would be only another mediocre account of a "stunt" garden.

When the pictures came back, they were more than the editor had hoped for. They were unique and charming, lovely in detail, and mysterious with subtle lights and shades. Here *was* a fairy garden. Here was inspiration for others who wanted to seek release from the strain and pressures of modern living, in the making of a fairy spot of their own. The pictures showed them that it had been done, that it could be done again.

The frontispiece of the magazine was a by-product of the article. One of the pictures was borrowed from the article and turned over to the art department. The frontispiece layout was the result.

Notes: Mr. McDonough explains why he used the story in this way: "First of all, it was a dramatization of the central theme of the magazine, that in the heartfelt things of home and garden are a release and a haven from the strain of a too turbulent and harassing life. But, more than that, the suggestions in the story are practical and there isn't a reader of the magazine who couldn't, if he wished, adopt them. In the third place the story is unusual. Another like it won't come along in years. And, finally, it is a real experience told in the first person."

Conservation and RESTOCKING

TROUT from Your Personal Pond

TROUT FROM YOUR PERSONAL POND

Reprinted by special permission from Outdoor Life

The fish story—"that long, and if you don't believe it"—is always a personal experience. (There's not much incentive to lie to the glory of another person.) The gossip of their accomplishments with reel and gun is red meat and strong drink to sportsmen—and, therefore, to outdoor magazines. A large proportion of the material in such a magazine as *Outdoor Life,* consists of personal experiences.

Everything was arranged. George was to meet me in Portland, Me.; the camp and guides would be ready. All I had to do was to telegraph him, and he would complete the details. "And so," his letter urged, "I expect a wire from you tomorrow. The whole trip won't stand you more than fifty bucks, and boy! how those square-tails are hitting."

It sounded swell. The North woods, the long June twilights, and giant trout swirling up through the dark waters. I started for the 'phone to call the telegraph office, and, in my mind's eye, I could already see the sun climbing above the pine spires. I could smell the wonderful aroma of coffee and frying bacon, could taste the delectable trout.

Then my eye fell on my open check book. I flipped back the pages, running over the month's checks. Not for the life of me could I stretch the pitifully small "Bal. Car. For'd." My dollars were not rubber, but any $50 check I cashed was sure to bounce. I came down to earth with a dull thud.

No fishing trip for me. For two days, I moped about the house, thinking of George and his fabulous square-tails. The trout virus, once it gets into a man's blood, is not a thing that can be lightly shaken off. On the afternoon of the third day, I walked over to the pond in my neighbor's cow pasture. Idly, I tossed pebbles onto the smooth sheet of water.

Then something clicked. Maybe the splash of the pebbles did it. Perhaps it was merely the sight of placid water. Anyway, I began to wonder if trout could live in that pond. I plunged my arm in up to the elbow. The water was cold! There was plenty of insect life about. Why not?

"Why, yes," my neighbor said that evening, "there used to be trout down there. Unfortunately, I foolishly tried to enlarge the pond, and dug it deeper. I must have got down to the hard pan, for about 8 or 9 years ago, when we had a bad drought, the pond dried up entirely, and there wasn't enough water to keep a minnow alive—much less trout. Lately I've noticed the pond holds up pretty well through the summer. Probably enough silt has washed down the brook to plug up the leaks."

Would he mind if I put a few trout in that pond? He would be delighted.

Well, I had no equipment, little money, and no experience in such delicate matters. But I wanted trout fishing and I went to work.

No hatchery would deliver the three dozen trout I could afford. And there was no hatchery near enough for me to go and get them. At last, however, I learned that one of the large hatcheries was delivering several thousand 9-inch fish to a pond owned by a sportsmen's club about 40 miles from my home. If I would be there at the time of the delivery, and furnish my own cans, I could have three dozen fish. The hatchery doubted, however, that I could get them into my water alive. But I was willing to gamble. After all, I had little to lose.

I had only one day in which to prepare. The first essential was to obtain suitable cans. Then I remembered the two ash cans I had bought the fall before. I lugged them up from the cellar, and my garden hose proved them watertight. Luckily, they fitted neatly and solidly into the space available for them in the rumble seat of my little roadster.

But how to keep the water from sloshing out on the 40-mile dash across country over rough roads? I recalled seeing pictures of inverted funnels over the tops of cans used to transport live fish. These funnels would probably catch most of the splash. The local tinsmith supplied these for $1.50.

There was one more serious problem. The cow pond lay nearly a mile from a hard road, across swampy meadows. No car could possibly cross those wet spots, and there was no other approach. The cans would be much too heavy to carry any distance. I could not use a helper, if one had been available, as I did not want to advertise my experiment. No sense putting temptation in the way of honest folk!

I thought I was licked. I tried a wheelbarrow, but it was no use. The wheel sank into the marshy muck, and I couldn't budge under the weight of even one of the cans. Only a horse or a tank could navigate the ooze of those marshy places. And where, in this busy time of the farmer's year, could I borrow a horse?

A tank! How about that little utility tractor and high-wheeled wagon my neighbor owned? Could he possibly lend them to me? He could. Now I was all set, so far as equipment was concerned. Perhaps I had been lucky, but, with a little more time, I believe I could have solved any of these problems half a dozen ways.

The hatchery trucks pulled up to the club and found me waiting. It was the work of a few moments to transfer the trout to the cans in my rumble seat. It was a hot, sunny day, and I was warned to stop occasionally to see if the fish were coming to the surface. If they were, I was to aërate the water by bailing it from one can to the other. But, once underway, excitement forbade my stopping. As I crested sharp rises or took sudden bumps, the water sloshed up through the caps. That, I thought, would provide more aëration than mere spilling from a bucket. Time was the precious factor!

That was one of the most intense drives I've ever had. I expected to hear a motor cop's siren screaming behind me any moment. The sun blazed on the road and beat on the unprotected cans in the rumble. I should have put a cake of ice in each can. Would my fish all be belly-up and bloated by the time I reached home? It would take another hour to transfer the fish from car to tractor to pond. Could they hold out in the warm, soupy water of the cans?

At last, I swung into our driveway, jumped out, and peered into the cans. The fish were all alive. A few were nosing about at the top, distinctly listless. If I could only get them down to the pond before they rolled their bellies up!

And then I tried to lift one of the cans. Even though half the water had sloshed out, it simply was not possible. They were wedged in, and much too heavy. I should have thought of this difficulty before.

What to do? Hurry! Think! Keep them alive, keep them alive at all costs! Ah!

I suddenly remembered that my garden hose was already connected. I backed the car up to it, screwed down the nozzle to give the water all the force possible, and plunged it into the bottom of one of the cans. The effect was almost immediate. The fish returned to the bottom of the can. Then, using my landing net, I put all the fish in one can, leaving the hose running. The water overflowed into the bottom of my car, but I didn't care about such trifles! Then I bailed out the other can and worked it out of the rumble seat. I put it on the wagon, filled it, and transferred all the fish. Soon, I had both cans on the wagon, full of fresh, cold water, and the fish evenly divided between them.

Tanklike, the little tractor wallowed through the marshy meadows, and came at last to the edge of the pond. With infinite satisfaction and relief, I watched those trout swim into their new home. Not one was sickly; each darted off into the mystery of strange water.

I sat on the bank a while, smoking and basking in a comfortable feeling of accomplishment. By and by, I noticed a moth struggling across the water. Snap! A curving streak of bronze and silver had flashed up and devoured it. Trout water!

Fishing a pond like this is not wilderness fishing, and I don't pretend that it is. But, as a substitute, it offers the trout fisherman a far pleasanter way to spend those long, quiet afternoons and summer twilights than batting a golf ball around a crowded course.

Try it. It isn't expensive. It can be done almost anywhere, even in the suburbs. Most owners of suitable waters will be glad to coöperate in keeping off poachers, and making any necessary improvements to streams and ponds. For there is something about water that has trout in it that appeals alike to angler and landowner. You have opportunity to study at your leisure the curious and often baffling habits of trout, and you may learn something that will come in handy on your next trip into the wilderness.—ROBESON BAILEY.

Questions:

Is this article too long? Does it drag?

If you wanted to cut out 500 words, how would you go about doing it?

Do you believe the incident of the checkbook, or is it merely a device to start the story?

What merits do you see in the article, which recommended it to the editor of *Outdoor Life?*

EXPLANATION FOR ALBERT

In which Albert gets a brief lesson in how to tell the bird from the flowers

By Patricia Collinge

Reprinted by special permission from Stage

There may very well be an argument as to whether "Explanation for Albert" is an article at all. Maybe it's an informal essay (it has been said somewhere in these pages that essays and articles may, at their fringes, blend and blur). But there is a good deal of substantial flesh under the lace and the ribbons—enough to justify the inclusion of the article (or essay) as an example of a personal-experience story.

Seasons come and seasons go and opening nights go on forever. And some of these openings are successful and some are very unsuccessful indeed, and the only trouble is that you can't always tell the difference right off. That is, not unless you stay firmly out front. But if you go backstage after anything but an out-and-out debacle, you will find that the general ritual is pretty much the same.

The moment the curtain falls for the last time, the little door back of where they keep the electrical equipment and all those ropes bursts open and eight million people in tails and ermine and silver fox fall over the cables and knock down the electrician in an effort to be the first to fling themselves on the actors and tell them that it was too, too divine. When it has been really pretty good there are twelve million instead of eight, and when there has been a genuine hit hell breaks loose. I may be a little out on my figures. There may not actually be eight million, but they make a good deal of noise and they sound like eight million. And here the lay mind, whom I will call Albert, may ask why. "Why," inquires Albert, "do they do that? If they haven't liked the play why do they go backstage at all?"

Well, Albert, it is a little difficult to explain. Some of them have to go back, being friends and relatives of those concerned. And some of those who haven't liked the play are afraid that if they don't say they *did*, someone will think they didn't. And if that isn't clear to you, Albert, I'm terribly sorry. And then the people who go backstage are apt to be pretty bright and cheery about it, and that is infectious. On the way back someone is sure to say that the sets were *darling*, and someone else says that it was awfully well done, and *didn't* Mary look too *enchanting*. And then they get to telling each other that they had an awfully good *time*, and there is always someone who saw one of the critics laughing like anything. No one ever asks what he was laughing *at*, but after that it is only a matter of moments till they are embracing the actors and screaming the place down.

"But, why?" asks Albert again, "why all this screaming and nonsense? Why, if they *must* go back, don't they just say that they were awfully sorry, but they didn't think it got over, or something like that? Why can't they be honest?"

Well, Albert, in an odd perverted way they are. They don't attack without warning; the signs are there if you can recognize them. Come backstage with me a moment, Albert my pet, and tell me what the lady over there is saying.

"She seems to be saying 'Darling' a good deal," says Albert.

"Pay no attention to that, Albert. What does she say next?"

"She says . . . you were *won*derful."

Perfect, Albert. We couldn't have a better example. She isn't saying that she thinks the actress was wonderful in her part, is she? Nor is she mentioning the play. "Wonderful" has many meanings, Albert, and the actress involved could have been lousy and still wonderful. It's more like a code than a compliment, Albert, and perfectly honest because both sides understand it. Take the simple phrase "I liked it." What does that mean?

"It means that he or she liked it, meaning the play," Albert will probably answer. And I answer, not at all. At least, it depends on how it is read. If the visitor says she liked it, very probably she did. But if she says, "*I* liked it," the actress can take warning. And if the visitor says earnestly, "I LIKED it," the actress can prepare for the worst. And if the visitor has to be pinned down to this mild opinion then the actress can begin thinking of summer stock right away.

One of the simplest ways to clear a dressing-room after an unsuccessful premiere is to ask straight out what everyone thinks of the play. Before you can say "Cain's warehouse" everyone has thought of someone else he *must* see, or somewhere else he *must* go, and the next thing she knows the actress is all alone with her thoughts, which are apt to be on the dark side.

"But, look," says Albert, "doesn't anyone ever tell the truth?"

Yes, Albert, but only the very close and the very sure, because except in rare cases there is always the element of doubt. The visitors may have hated the whole thing, but they can also be wrong. And so until the press and public have pronounced a definite verdict they feel diffident about expressing themselves. It wouldn't be much fun to go back and tell everyone that they might as well start packing, and then find out that they had just seen the play of the century, would it?

Of course, Albert, sometimes a play fails so disastrously that even the actors know it, and then there is no need for anyone to say anything. The truth is there, naked and smirking, for everyone to see. And the behavior of the visitor doesn't enter into that at all, because in such cases there are no visitors and the whole thing is rather grim and, if you don't mind, I would rather not discuss it.

"But," Albert might say, "I would think that that would be the time when everyone would *want* to go back, and rally round, and be at least kind."

Yes, Albert. Very probably you would.

"But," Albert would persist, "I still don't understand. First you say that the behavior of the visitor gives no clue to the fate of the play, and then you say it does. And then you say that everyone has to wait for the professional verdict, anyway. Surely the *actors* know where they stand. I can understand about the visitors, but I can't understand about the actors."

Well, in the first place, Albert, no one understands about actors. As for the waiting and so on, well . . . that is because of an element that I omitted to mention which is really another matter altogether and comes more under the heading of hope.

And now, Albert, how would you like to shut up?

Questions:

Why did you (assuming that you did) like this story?

Of what would the story consist if only the bare bones of fact were presented?

Instead of "Albert *would have* said" would "Albert said" have been better?

How much of the value of the story do you attribute to the fact that Patricia Collinge is a famous actress?

[*c. Confession Article*]

The confession article is an anonymous personal-experience story. The fact that the story is not signed (either not signed at all or with a pseudonym) makes it possible for the author to deal with subjects that he might not want to handle under his signature. The peculiar effect of the confession story is to give the reader the sense of being taken behind the scenes, of being "let in" on material about which it would be dangerous or impolitic or in poor taste to speak out loud.

The confession story, which has its perfectly legitimate uses, has been brought into disrepute by its exploitation in cheap, sensational magazines.

The following titles of confession stories that have appeared in various magazines will give some idea of material that can be legitimately handled in this form: "What's Wrong with Banking," by an anonymous bank president; "Out of the Dark," by a woman who had been temporarily insane; "Why I Resigned from My Fraternity," by an ex-Greek; "It Doesn't Pay," by an ex-bank-robber.

There are fewer confession stories than stories of any other type. But that doesn't mean that editors aren't eager to buy such stories.

A PROFESSOR QUITS THE COMMUNIST PARTY

By Stuart Browne

Stuart Browne is not the real name of the author of this article. For obvious reasons the author did not choose to sign the piece. But his anonymity is not merely a protection. It makes it possible for him to go into much more intimate and revealing detail than he would want to do over his own signature. And, further, it gives the reader the feeling that he is getting a full, uncensored "low down" on the subject of the article.

It was four o'clock in the afternoon, and I had just begun to revise my lecture notes on the Industrial Revolution (my special field is English History in the Eighteenth Century), when my wife came into my study.

"Someone 'phoned. Said he was coming over." As she spoke she gave me a queer look and sat down as if waiting for me to reply.

"Who was it?" I asked.

"He wouldn't give his name."

"No? Well, what does he want?"

"He didn't tell *me*." She stressed the pronoun to indicate a rather definite disapproval of the kind of people who sought my company.

"All right, dear, and please don't look so worried. I'm sure he's not from the President's office."

"Well, I hope not," she said and left me to the quiet of my study. I looked down at my notes again and saw: Burke "Thoughts and Details on Scarcity." Following the title I had written: cf. T.L. p. 198ff. "T.L.," I muttered to myself. "Now why in hell do I always use these abbreviations and then forget what they stand for. T.L.?" I was still puzzling over the letters when the doorbell rang. A moment later my wife opened the study door to admit my caller. She closed the door behind him, leaving us alone.

"Hello, Benson," I said as I arose to shake hands with him. He was a short, heavy-set man whose nervous hands were never still except for brief moments when they were poised in some dramatic gesture. He spoke in a voice that suggested secrecy, and when he finally took a seat he sat forward on his chair, tense and restless.

"My wife said you 'phoned, but did not give your name."

"Yes. I did not tell her my name because you never know who may be listening. I came on a special errand, direct from the Party Headquarters."

Two hours later, when he left my study, I had given my word that I would be a member of the Communist Party of America. I had also signed a card, but not with my real name. No man in the Party who wishes to be protected uses his own name. He has a party name under which he registers and by which he is known to other party members.

But I must not give the impression that my decision was the result of an instantaneous conversion. For three years preceding this meeting in the spring of 1934, the recent economic depression had been very active on our campus. We had received three separate salary cuts totaling a reduction of thirty-five per cent. Our class hours had been increased to eighteen a week, with an increase of students in the classes. We no longer were allowed assistants to read class papers. Mortgage companies were asking money on the line. In fact, the professors were beginning to feel the pressure of a real world outside the campus. This in itself was bad, but even worse was the vicious propaganda against the professors which almost daily headlined certain newspapers. Our University President made no effort to defend us. We even believed that he was secretly aiding the forces that were encroaching upon our intellectual freedom.

To meet these conditions, certain leaders among the faculty liberals had organized groups for the consideration of action to meet the policies of the Administration. It was in one of these groups that I had met Benson, who was invited there to lead the discussion on some phase of Marxism. Through him I was led to sign some anti-Fascist protest, then to speak before the Central Labor Council on the development of Trade Unions in the late Eighteenth Century. Following that speech, I was in constant demand for speaking engagements at labor union meetings, liberal professional groups, and other organizations such as Townsend Clubs and Technocrats. I talked myself into the Party without knowing that I was doing it. At the time I joined, it seemed clear to me that only by the united action of all liberal groups, under the leadership of the Communists, could we possibly stem the Fascist waves that were sweeping over the country, stifling freedom and liberty. It seemed then as though our University was ready at any moment to capitulate to the fierce demands of Fascist newspapers, and that before long University professors would be muzzled in America as effectively as they are in certain European countries. I joined the Party because I believed it would foster and protect that precious freedom which we Americans believe is so necessary to life.

As I look back on it now, I feel sure that I believed myself a martyr in a noble cause. My Communist friend made me feel that at last I had become a man, not just a narrow, cloistered parasite on the Capitalist System. Now I could join hands with the workers, I could call them Comrades, and then, after the Revolution, I and the other professors who were Comrades would run the University.

"Since I have signed the card perhaps you'll tell me who else on the faculty are members," I said.

"No. We never reveal the name of a Comrade," he answered. "Tomorrow night at eight o'clock a Comrade whom you know will call for you. Your unit meets every Wednesday night."

At the first meeting of my unit I found that two other faculty men and their wives had preceded me into the party. In addition to these four, there were eight other professional workers. We were classed by the Party as a professional unit attached to a larger section made up of industrial workers.

The Organizer who had recruited me was present to welcome me and to explain certain duties and responsibilities to the Party. In the first place, he covered briefly the organization of the United States into twelve regions. Each region is ruled by a District Organizer, affectionately referred to as the D.O.

"Some day you will meet our D.O.," a nervous little man with a hairline mustache whispered to me. Comrade Benson had paused to show his displeasure at the whispered interruption. His strong, restless hands were poised in mid-air, tense and still. Next followed the explanation of how each region was divided into sections, with a Section Organizer and an Agitprop.

"The unit is the backbone of the Communist Party. It is in the units that we make the true Bolshevist. We teach you in the unit to exercise true Bolshevist initiative." And here he expounded on fundamental theory, the essence of which seemed to be loyalty to the Party program, once it had been established in true Bolshevist manner, through the channels of Democratic Centralism.

"What is an Agitprop?" I asked after this speech was over.

"He is the Comrade in charge of Agitation and Propaganda," said the organizer. "He takes care of your reading material, examines you in theory, indicates what you should read, sees that you subscribe to the *Daily Worker*, and that you buy pamphlets, magazines, Russian and American, that are essential to your growth and development."

"I am the Agitprop," said the little man with the hairline mustache.

I looked at him, and then recognized him as a bookkeeper in a downtown furniture store. Perhaps it was at this point that my fundamental unfitness for the Party first asserted itself. I admit that I may be guilty of snobbery, but somehow I resented it that this bookkeeper, whose intellect and background had never impressed me when I came to make my monthly furniture payments, should now have charge of my reading and further intellectual development. I smiled a little insincerely and nodded acquiescence.

The next procedure was introductions all round by our new Party names. Everyone was urged to use the prefix Comrade, and to address the members of the unit by their Party names. After that I was given my Party Book in which my new name was inscribed. The Agitprop then showed me how I could figure my dues from the table given in the back. That there would be dues, I had known, but I was not quite prepared for what I found—with the help of the bookkeeper. My yearly salary was $3600 or, since we were paid on a ten-month basis, $360 a month. The scale of dues ranged from two cents a week for unemployed members, to three dollars and fifty cents a week for me. To this was added an extra week's dues every month for the International, plus an occasional extra levy of a month's dues for the American Party Convention in New York. In the two and one-half years I was a member only two of these extra levies were made. Then there was literature to buy: books, pamphlets, magazines, and newspapers. Often we were required to buy bundles of these, which we were permitted to resell, but which no professor or professional worker could possibly sell. Once each year we were requested to contribute a day's salary to the *Daily Worker* drive. In all, my financial obligation to the Party amounted to approximately nine hundred dollars in two and one-half years. This in itself became a serious matter with me as time passed, because my standard of living was "wrong, middle-class, and bourgeois." All very true, but there wasn't a great deal I could do about it and retain my university position. Like most professors, I was living up to the full capacity of my salary. Each year I saved out enough money for a vacation, but after I had been in the Party for a year I was forced to give up the usual two weeks' auto trip with my wife and child.

II

The fact that membership in the Party cost me nearly four hundred dollars a year was not an insuperable obstacle, but the psychological reaction was the source of endless worry. I began to save in all the places where I knew I should not save. I discontinued membership in two historical associations, I stopped subscriptions to three different magazines, I stopped buying books in my field. One of my chief literary interests had been gathering together a good library of novels and poetry of the Eighteenth Century, including modern novels with a setting in that period. I continued to look through the pages of English secondhand book catalogues, carefully marking books I wished to own and then filing the catalogues away in my library without ordering the items checked.

This was a minor worry compared to others that came to disturb my waking hours and haunt my tortured sleep. I didn't like the atmosphere of the Party. There are some people who thrive in a conspiratorial atmosphere. To them the most innocent remark suggests endless dark and sinister meanings. Every unit meeting was permeated with a conspiratorial undertone. Fascists were lurking in every corner of the city. Roosevelt was leaning toward Fascism, our University President was clearly a Fascist, in almost daily communication with Hitler and Mussolini. There was an air of profound secrecy surrounding our movements. If someone in the excitement of a discussion should raise his voice he was immediately hushed. Imaginary enemies lurked outside our doors. If some innocent caller rang the doorbell a dead silence fell over us, as we waited with fluttering hearts for the caller to depart. Then in whispered tones, the discussion would begin again.

These unit meetings were held in the homes of members, except in cases where the wives were not Comrades. I went through the first year without letting my wife know that I was a member. This added further complications. At least twice every week when I attended a secret Party meeting I had to lie to her about my absence from home. This in itself became so intolerable that it almost resulted in a serious quarrel in my family, not because she doubted the various meetings and professional responsibilities I had suddenly assumed, but because I grew so sick of myself and my endless lies that I began leaving night after night without a word of explanation. Then at breakfast the toast stuck in my throat as I saw how my behavior worried my wife.

It was not the two secret meetings that caused all the trouble. A Party man must give everything to the Cause. After I got well into the routine of Party work I was fortunate if I had two nights a week free to devote to my family and ordinary social engagements. On such nights I was often so exhausted that I went to sleep at a movie or dozed in my chair at a social gathering. Quite often after I had promised to take my wife to the theater I would receive a 'phone call from my unit organizer saying that the strategy committee of the Farmer-Labor party was meeting. Would I please attend in an advisory capacity? I could not answer, "I should be pleased to but, you see, I have promised to take my wife to the theater." Nothing could be more ridiculous for one who has asserted his belief in the class struggle and the ultimate triumph of the workers' revolution. I would go to the meeting, knowing all was not well at home.

This situation came to a sudden dramatic conclusion when I returned home at three o'clock one morning to find my wife sitting by the fire. She had been crying.

"Please come here and talk to me," she said.

I sat down by her side, more unhappy than I had ever been before in my life.

"Tell me," she said, "what is wrong. I have waited a long time for you to explain, until now I am desperate." After a brief pause she said very softly, "Do you love someone else?"

Like a fool, I had never thought she would doubt my love. I answered by telling her that I had joined the Party. We talked till dawn. I shall never forget the joy I experienced during the next few days as I moved free from the endless lies that had filled my home.

A week later my wife said, "If the Party is good enough for you it's good enough for me. I'll join with you. If we have to lie and deceive, let's do it together." The Party accepted her, somewhat doubtful of her "political maturity," but the little man with the hairline mustache promised to give her some special education. I was congratulated by my unit organizer for my splendid work in recruiting a person into the party who had such "a definite bourgeois background."

My wife is the daughter of a man who has an owner's share in a small factory employing non-union workers. Hence the pointed reference to her background. Her schooling proceeded rather slowly because of her sense of humor. At one of her first unit meetings she made some light, joking reference to Stalin's mustache. This remark produced a profound silence. She found that only Hitler, Roosevelt, and such people were subjects for jokes. "This is war, class war," said our organizer, "and if we don't defend the Soviet Union we are traitors to the working-class movement."

That night, after we had gone to bed and finished reading a pamphlet on the share-croppers' union, I put out the light. For a long time there was silence. I turned on my right side very carefully so as not to awaken my wife, when she suddenly burst into a fit of laughter. When I asked her what was so funny she answered, "Stalin's mustache. It's part of the working-class movement." Then I laughed too, and both of us felt very friendly to Stalin and his disciples. We wished them all well, and slept in peace.

The greatest devotion, loyalty, and honor were expected from every Comrade. Our ethical standards were very high. It soon became apparent, however, that ethics may harbor strange practices. After my wife had been in the Party a month we were given a joint assignment. We were asked to get my wife's father to tell us what plans were being made by the executives in his factory to oppose unionization of the workers in his plant. Would the officers put up a fight? Whom are they planning to fire? What do they know about the Chamber of Commerce's attitude toward the union meetings? These things we were to worm out of my wife's father while we sat as guests at his dinner table or entertained him in our home.

One day the Section Organizer came to my house asking me to contribute twenty dollars to an emergency fund. A crisis had arisen. (Crises arise frequently in the Party.) I explained that I didn't have twenty dollars. "If you had come an hour earlier, I'd have given it to you," I said. And then very foolishly I made the following explanation: "An old friend of mine came here this afternoon. He is a farmer and his wife is expecting a baby. He did not have the money for hospital expenses and asked me to loan him fifty dollars, and I did."

The Organizer's face grew red. "You gave him fifty dollars and you deny twenty to the Party. That is not Bolshevist behavior."

"But he told me his wife's condition was critical and that she must be delivered in a hospital."

The Organizer looked disturbed. "I suppose," he said, "we can't expect middle-class ideology to adjust itself to the higher loyalty of the Party. I'd cheat my grandmother if by so doing I could further the cause of the revolution."

These examples could be multiplied endlessly. From a purely rational point of view it may be argued that the Party is right and that I am wrong. It is probably far more important to aid the workers in their struggle for a just wage than it is to help save the life of some poor farmer's wife. Let someone else answer that. All I know is that I could make no other choice than the one I made.

One of the "concentration tasks" of our unit was to raise money. At every meeting we discussed the names of well-to-do people who might be made to contribute under one guise or another. The possible sources of contribution were spoken of in the most scornful tones as contemptible and bourgeois, and then we were asked to use our social position to win their favor and get them to make contributions. We were asked to get them to contribute to organizations that existed only in the minds of Party members and then turn over the money to the Party. We were asked to sponsor dinners, picnics, and excursions in the interest of workers and then get people to contribute to these affairs. We were requested to have parties in our homes and charge our friends admission. "This is war," said our Organizer. "When the enemy is storming your trench you don't say, 'Pardon me, but you'll have to wait till I get my machine gun ready for action.' No! You don't stop to see if your pants are pressed. You meet the emergency." Thus our Organizer inspired us to action.

In addition to raising money and exploiting our middle-class friends, those of us who were faculty members were to recruit others from the faculty. We were to discover who were sympathetic, invite them to our homes, lead them into a discussion of Marxist theory, and thus by a simple, logical process lead them to the Party. Anyone can see how reasonable a request that is. All you have to do is to abandon the friends you have usually entertained in your home—all except one or two who may be Party material—and then embark upon a new social life with a group of people who may be radical. The fact that you may not like the radical English Professor, who thinks he should run the faculty meeting, makes no difference. You may not like the Psychology Professor's wife, who talks in a high-pitched voice about the wonderful things her four-year-old son can do. That doesn't matter. Her husband has signed a petition in favor of Spanish Democracy, therefore he must be cultivated even though your wife thinks him a bore. "You are a Comrade, and a Comrade knows how to sacrifice for The Cause. Lenin endured all sorts of people whom he hated personally because he put The Cause above himself."

During the thirty months that I was in the Party I recruited my wife and a graduate student in History who had failed in his preliminary doctor's examination. I was doomed to enjoy the fruits of this great victory for only a brief period. After he had attended three unit meetings he received an appointment as an instructor in a normal school out West. He promised to write for his Party Book when he got settled, but the letter never came.

Others in our unit fared not much better. When I entered the unit there were thirteen members. When I withdrew there were sixteen. We had recruited six and lost three.

III

Part of our ineffectiveness was due to our leaders. During my period as a Communist I met a great many of the officials in the Party including one member of the Central Committee. Tiresome as the average politician may be, he is a wonder of ingenious perspicacity when contrasted to the Communist Party leader. The Party leaders are all alike. This is a strange statement to make about any group of people, but with minor reservations, everyone is willing to accept this statement as true of certain selected groups. If you have heard one lecturer from a certain church Board of Lecturers, if you have talked to one member of the House of David, if you have seen one Doukhobor meeting, you have observed the pattern to which all the others are cut. Perhaps in all the cases I have mentioned this is a sign of strength from which flows their power and their virtue. I would not deny that, but I would make the purely individual remark that to me they are very, very dull.

The Communist leaders fit a pattern more perfectly than any other human beings I have ever known. They are all dogmatic. So dogmatic that they are not even conscious of their dogmatism. If a Comrade disagrees with a D.O. he is told about his error and the "true line" is explained to him. If he still persists in opposition he is told what to believe, and if that doesn't work he is assigned to a study unit where he is instructed in Marx and Lenin.

The leaders move in an atmosphere of sanctity that requires a humorless devotion to appreciate. One slight deviation from the true faith brings forth fiery denunciation. I had not been in the Party very long when I took the "mistaken position" that Villard's article in *The Nation* on the first Moscow Trial was sound reasoning from a democratic point of view. I was told of my error, and the contemptible character of people who did not see this trial as a triumph of Working Class justice was emphasized. When I murmured a comparison to Hitler's purge I was told to read Olgin's pamphlet on Trotsky and I should see the difference. I read Olgin and I still don't see the difference. I was once a completely submerged and *bona fide* member of the Baptist Church, but I never encountered a Baptist preacher more certain and smug about his knowledge of the one and only road to salvation than the Party leaders are of the one and only true revolution.

The Party leaders talk about democracy, but the only democracy they practice is that defined within the limits of Comrade Stalin's dictates. The answer to anyone who objects is simple and clear. "The party line was laid down by the Seventh World Congress. In Comrade Dimitroff's speech you have a clear Marxist-Leninist analysis of the working-class struggle against Fascism. The answer is the United Front. This is our guide." No evangelist ever pointed with greater pride to a Bible text than do the Party leaders to the text of Marx as amended by Lenin, defiled by Trotsky, and practiced by Stalin. To deny this, or even to speak lightly of it, is heresy.

The Party leaders are often confused in their reasoning, and substitute passion for common sense. In their last campaign in the interests of Mr. Browder they devoted their whole energy to defeating Mr. Landon. This was following the party line laid down by Comrade Dimitroff. Mr. Landon was excoriated as the arch fiend of growing Fascism, and our duty was to defeat him. But as Communists, we were to vote for Mr. Browder. If we asked, "But how can we defeat Landon by voting for Browder?" we heard more talk about Landon, but no answer to our question. On this issue I saw one man from my unit "read out" of the Party. He had persisted in saying that if the Party wants Roosevelt elected, why don't they say so, instead of beating about the bush.

He was summoned before the D.O., the Section Organizer, and his Unit Organizer, and I was permitted to go with him to the hearing. It was in the form of a trial in which the judges did all the talking. He was asked if he believed in the class struggle, in the dictatorship of the proletariat, in the Marxian interpretation of history, and all the other sacred articles of faith. The man answered in the affirmative, but with a stubbornness born of American love of independence, reiterated that the party line on defeating Landon by supporting Browder was wrong. Then he added, "Furthermore, I believe in the danger of Landon so much that I'm going to vote for Roosevelt."

A hushed silence fell over the group. The officials looked so serious that for a moment I felt as though we were in Moscow and not the United States. I should not have been surprised had I heard this man labeled as an enemy of the working class, a wrecker of true socialism, a spy and a traitor, a vermin whose doom would be "Execution before a firing squad." At last the D.O. spoke. "Turn over your book to your Unit Organizer, and from now on you are no longer a member of the Party." I wiped my brow and went over to the window for a breath of fresh air. The sun was shining on a familiar American city. At that moment I admitted to myself for the first time that I wished I were out of the Party.

IV

Just exactly what can a professor under the direction of the Communist Party do to help the cause of a working-class revolution? The best I can do to answer this question is to give an account of my activities for one week. I shall begin with Sunday. At the previous Wednesday unit meeting we were instructed to send representatives to a plenum. A plenum is something that an American would call a party convention. To this plenum all units in our section sent representatives. We met at a private home at nine o'clock on Sunday morning to consider the following program:

1. Middle-class position in the workers' revolution.
2. How to broaden the base of the finance committee.
3. New tactics in the *Daily Worker* drive.
4. The Comrades' work in the trade union.
5. Bolshevist strategy in strike-leadership.
6. Fractionating:
   The Socialist Party
   The Central Labor Council
   The Women's Republican Club
   The Women's Democratic Club
   The University Branch of the American Association of University Professors. (This with special reference to University people in the Party.)
   The Faculty Wives' Club
   (This list was long, including almost every organized group except the D.A.R. and W.C.T.U.)
7. How to bring forth the party line.
8. Self-development and required reading.
9. Criticism.

The purpose of the plenum was to coordinate the work of the various units, prevent wasteful duplication and the dangers of over-fractionating any group; to base the Party policy upon the action of the units; and to develop self-criticism.

The plenum which met to deal with the above topics lasted from nine o'clock in the morning till midnight. Each topic was presented by a person who had prepared a speech on the subject. After each speech came specific recommendations and then debate. The plan sounds very democratic, yet it soon became clear to me that any suggestion which did not fit into a preconceived plan of the Party leaders would receive no consideration. I'll be specific. The women who reported on fractionating the Faculty Wives' Club recommended that my wife should begin taking an active part in club work. She should strive for definite objectives, such as:

1. Get *The New Masses, Health and Hygiene, The New Theater* into the club reading room.
2. Penetrate the drama section and get them to sponsor a workers' drama.
3. Get a committee organized to sponsor radical speeches on the campus.
4. Get support for left-wing candidates in local elections.

My objection, voiced on the floor, was that such a program would fail because no woman could advocate these reforms among a group of highly selected conservatives such as the members of a Faculty Wives' Club without exposing herself as a radical. My objection was overruled and I was instructed to inform my wife of the decision of the plenum. It is true that a vote was taken whenever it was demanded by a member of the group, but no balloting was secret, and the selected group was entirely under the influence of the Party leaders.

The meeting droned on endlessly with rules, regulations, plans, and the whole generously interspersed by laudatory testimonials of Party achievements in the past. Mistakes were admitted and analyzed in such a way that one felt that if it were human to err it was godlike to admit it.

Six months later at a plenum meeting I felt convinced that not a single objective of the previous plenum had been carried out, with one exception: definite progress had been made in developing left-wing leadership in the trade unions.

Thus I had passed my Sunday. On Monday I attended a union fraction meeting. We spent three hours trying to decide how to get mass support for a motion to endorse the Farmer-Labor Party. At the union meeting later we did not get the endorsement.

On Tuesday afternoon, from four to six, I attended a very dull meeting of the American Association of University Professors. I tried in vain to get them to pass a resolution announcing to the press that they openly opposed the dismissal of Professor Granville Hicks.

Wednesday was free until eight o'clock, when my wife and I went to our unit meeting. The meeting began promptly. We listened to a poorly written paper on Volume One of Webbs' *Soviet Communism.* We heard reports on the activities of the various Comrades, how one had gone to a Socialist meeting but had not seen fit to move anything; how another had attended a public meeting of the Women's Republican Club. This Comrade gave a long account of what the speaker had said. The report was as monotonous as it was painstakingly accurate. Everyone who listened could be sure he knew what the speaker had said at this large open meeting. The speech had been expertly reported in the daily press three days before. So we went round the circle.

After that we took up our proposed activities for the coming week, again going round the circle, one by one. Next came the talk by the Agitprop on our reading, and then the sale of the so-called literature. We all bought extra copies of the *Sunday Worker* and *Soviet Russia To-day* because our Agitprop had shamed us by pointing out that many units made up of workers in the lower wage brackets had a better record for buying literature than we had. I wanted to remind him that my Sunday School Superintendent years ago had told that story, but I kept still. You learn to keep still if you are in the Party.

Thursday was a free day. We had a little dinner party at our home to which we had invited two professors and their wives in order that we might sound them out on their attitude toward Corey's *The Crisis of the Middle Class.*

Friday at three o'clock I came home from my last class. As I came in the door, the phone rang.

"For God's sake don't touch it!" I shouted to my wife, in a tone so loud that she turned pale with fear. Before she could question me I hastened to explain. "It's nothing except I want to get out of here before something does happen." We hurriedly got our wraps, jumped into the car, picked up our son at his school, and then drove into the country for dinner. We stayed away until ten o'clock. No Party work that day.

On Saturday night we attended a *New Masses* party, where we paid admission, and then paid for cocktails and talked in little groups about *The Coming Struggle for Power.* Tired and a little sad we went to bed at midnight. A typical party worker's week was over. I also taught some classes at the University that week.

V

There was no dramatic trial when my wife and I dropped out of the Party. We were not summoned before the D.O. or threatened with dire punishments. Our withdrawal was a little sad, a sort of weary cessation of useless activity. Our Unit Organizer had a downtown office. I called on him and told him that I could no longer consider myself a member of the Party. He looked worried and disturbed. After we had talked for a time he asked me to come to the unit meeting and explain why I was leaving. I replied that I would gladly do so, but that I didn't think he would want me to tell the group what my objections were.

"Certainly I should. We want intelligent criticism," he replied. "Just what are your reasons?"

I had prepared them very carefully and proceeded to explain. "In the first place, I believe that I am not temperamentally fitted for the Party. The rigorous routine, the stifling of individual initiative, the necessity for secrecy, the inevitable deception which forces one to live in two worlds, these disturb my peace of mind. It may be my fault, but I have lost contact with my old friends outside the Party, and those in the Party have no time for friendship. Before I entered the Party no one could predict the subjects that might come up for discussion when a group of us met. Now every discussion follows a pattern that is monotonous—perhaps worse than monotonous. I feel that my intellectual life, poor as it may have been, is stifled. I have no time to read the books and magazines that are free and unfettered, that give joy and adventure to the art of reading. My intellectual life has become dull. My teaching, which used to be interesting, has not flourished under the dictates of the Party Line. Instead, it has become stereotyped. I have come to hate my classes. The solemnity with which the Party treats every problem weighs upon my spirit. I cannot believe that the economic conditions in our country warrant an attitude which implies that the revolution is imminent. Every unit meeting is as serious in tone as though it were being held in a cellar near University City, Madrid. The interference with my personal liberty is no longer endurable to me. I'll give you one example. I am simple enough to take joy in the feeling that when I enter a voting booth in the United States no one, in spirit or in fact, goes with me. I may vote wrong, and I may have to pay for my mistake, but I vote as a free man. As a Communist I voted according to the *line* laid down for me and all Communists by the Seventh World Congress in Moscow. These are a few of the reasons why I must withdraw, and of course my wife is also leaving the Party."

In the silence that followed my statement I could not help wondering why I had stayed in the Party for two and a half years. The objections I had just enumerated did not dawn upon me suddenly. I had felt them more or less clearly after the first few weeks in the Party. I believe that one reason I remained a member after I had come to hate Party activity was that I was ashamed to admit defeat; I did not want to be a quitter. For a long time I tried to make myself believe that the Party could organize an effective protest against the worst aspects of labor exploitation. It was not until I had actually seen the Party at work in many different situations that I came to believe that its interest in revolution often led the unions into taking a stand that was so unreasonable as to invite disaster. As time passed, I felt quite certain that often the Party leaders aimed at creating a strike situation for its own sake, and not primarily in order to gain advantages for the workers. The Party wins, according to its theory, even though the individual worker may lose, because it is the development of strikes and more strikes that brings the day of revolution nearer.

These objections developed slowly. Day by day there were certain compensations to which a

Party man clings. I believed that my work was helping the cause of labor, that I was closer to the living problems of history in the making. I also felt that I was doing something unselfishly to help remedy the evils in my own profession. The idea of all workers united in a common cause appealed to me. When I realized that my activities were furthering a dictatorship with the name of democracy used as bait for the unwary, the one hope that had supported me over many specific disappointments was lost.

My friend sat staring out of the window. It was a long time before he answered. "Do you then mean to say that everything is wrong that the Party does?"

"No, I won't say that; but before it can enlist any genuine support from the majority of Americans, it will have to abandon its Russian-born practices. It will have to become an American Party before it succeeds in America."

"Did you bring your book?"

"Yes, and I also brought my wife's. You don't want me to come to the unit meeting then?"

"No. I think it best to accept your books to-day."

On my way home I thought of how I had joined the Communist Party of America in the interests of freedom, and how I had withdrawn in order to be once more a free citizen of the United States.

Questions:

Why does this article follow a chronological arrangement of material? (Note, also, the same arrangement in "Trout from Your Personal Pond.") Would some other order have been more effective?

To what basic human emotions does this article appeal?

This article caused quite a stir. Why?

The story has very little "window-dressing," as compared, for example, with "Mountain King." The tone is straightforward, rather subdued, unspectacular. Why was it written this way?

Practice Suggestions

1. Look through ten different magazines and make an estimate of the proportion of their editorial matter that consists of experience articles.

2. Analyze as well as you can why these magazines use much or little of this type of material.

3. In the course of about a week accumulate ten tips for third-person experience stories that you think you could get; ten for first-person experience stories; five for confession stories.

4. Why is the experience story particularly prominent in many trade publications and farm journals?

5. If you wished to get farm-experience stories, to what people might you go for suggestions? for a trade paper; for a women's magazine?

6. One danger in the writing of a personal-experience story is that the use of the first person may give the piece an air of boastfulness. Look at several personal-experience stories and note in detail how this impression is avoided.

X

The News Feature

NOT many issues of many magazines go to press without one or more articles that are "news features." And in many magazines—particularly trade journals, news-magazines such as *Time* and *News-Week*, and journals of comment such as the *New Republic* and *Nation*—the news feature may occupy a sizable proportion of the editorial space.

The prime characteristic of such an article is that its central theme is a contemporary news event or situation.

How does the magazine treatment of a news event—the passage of a piece of legislation, a convention, the death of a prominent person, a political campaign, a war—differ from the treatments of the same events in the newspaper? Of course, today's newspaper gives only the account of today's or yesterday's happenings. But most significant stories are longer-lived than a single day. A war may last for months or years, a single battle may go on for days, a piece of legislation is debated and fought over for weeks and months. Today's newspaper story, then, of today's aspect of these long continuing events must inevitably be fragmentary, often one-sided and incomplete. The magazine on the other hand, because of its less frequent publication, cannot keep so closely on the heels of the news; but it can survey a major news event in its entirety or in one of its major aspects. It has the leisure, not only to report what happened, but to set the news event in its historical, social, or economic setting. The newspaper account, usually anonymous, is written with a conscious effort to keep out the personal point of view of the writer, to eliminate partisanship, bias, and special pleading. These restrictions do not necessarily apply to the magazine article. It is usually signed, and it is the accepted consensus that in it the author may comment, interpret, analyze. It is even desirable that he slant the story with the special interests of the magazine readers in mind.

On Page 7 is the news feature, "Good News," by Gove Hambidge. The story behind this story is as follows:

During the winter of 1937-38, a piece of "must" legislation in Congress was the revision of the National Housing Act. Naturally the editors of *Better Homes & Gardens* followed like hawks every move in the legislative battle. In January the bill was passed by Congress and sent to the President.

Mr. McDonough, in New York late in January, bought an evening paper that announced that President Roosevelt had signed the bill. Mr. McDonough saw the story about 4 o'clock. Within an hour he had completed two long-distance telephone conversations. One was to Mr. Corbin in the home office. They discussed across 1,200 miles what

Better Homes & Gardens should do with the story—particularly whether or not they should try to cover it in the April issue, which was already completely in type, dummied, and only two weeks away from the presses.

The other call was to Gove Hambidge in the Press Service of the Department of Agriculture at Washington. Mr. McDonough called Mr. Hambidge for two or three reasons: One, he knew him as a thorough and brilliant writer, an author of several books, and a contributor to *Better Homes & Gardens*. Second, *Better Homes & Gardens* had within the past few weeks bought an article from Hambidge on the home-building situation—an article which was now junked because of the new developments introduced by the passage of the FHA act. The third and most pressing reason was that he wanted Mr. Hambidge, on the scene at Washington, to begin without a moment's delay the planning of a new housing story.

These telephone calls out of the way, Mr. McDonough caught a train for Washington. The next morning he and Mr. Hambidge talked over plans for the article. Mr. McDonough hurried back to Des Moines to take charge of the revisions in the April issue which would be made necessary by the inclusion of the FHA story.

Within three days Mr. Hambidge's manuscript was received by air-mail in Des Moines. What happened next is revealed in excerpts from a letter from Mr. McDonough to Mr. Hambidge:

"Dear Gove: I spent all yesterday afternoon going over your article. I am returning your original article and would like to have you re-arrange the material and make revisions. We have been working against time, but I feel that both you and I tried to hurry this job too much.

"First, about what we plan to do: the pictures you obtained from FHA, I agree, are completely out of question. They aren't very good photographs, and, moreover, they all come from Idaho. We have a number of excellent photographs of houses ranging in price from $5,000 up to $15,000 and $16,000 which we might use to illustrate your article. However, the better plan now seems to be to confine your story to a single-page lead feature and use a spread on a perfect small house ($5,000 to $6,000) on the following pages. On the lead feature, single-page, then, we'd use a legend or box at the bottom of the page with an arrow pointing to the next two pages as a good example of what we mean when we talk about the 'small' house. It will be illustrative of the greater market which is, of course, the under-$6,000 home. This house will be as good and about as small as the one shown on the attached tear sheets.

"This morning I received the photograph from Underwood & Underwood. [This is the picture of Stewart McDonald, FHA administrator, and Mr. Hambidge which appears with the story.] What we will try to do is to use this photograph on the lead-feature page, and, if we can, the tabular material at the bottom of the page, perhaps putting a color tone over it to get attention. If we can't get the tabular material on the feature page we will carry it to a two-column runover layout farther in the back of the book.

"What I'm getting at, Gove, is that we want to use the picture as a strictly *news* photograph with a *news* style article on the new financing situation.

"This is to suggest then that you rearrange and re-do the article to give it strictly a *news* slant and to click off, paragraph after paragraph, all the news of the amendment.

"To do this we'll assume that *Better Homes & Gardens'* families know all about the Federal Administration Act up to the present time. We then leave out the paragraphs I have crossed out and begin with material under the title 'What You Can Do Under the New Law,' and continuing on through to 'A Good Time to Build.' In giving these comparisons and explanations, the biggest news, in our opinion, to people taking *Better Homes & Gardens,* is the $6,000-and-under house, so we should start with that. I think, too, that we should give comparisons everywhere throughout the manuscript; that is, give costs before the amendment compared to costs now, after the amendment. This 'before' and 'after' illustration will be extremely effective, in our opinion. [There follows a page of detailed suggestions for altering the original manuscript to the end of emphasizing the news angles of the story.]

"Sincerely yours,
"F. W. McDonough"

In the meantime the necessary changes and plans for the April issue were under way. The article "Ten Minutes From Hollywood," which had been scheduled as the lead-off article, was moved back one page and made into a double-spread to follow the FHA story. This necessitated the elimination of a one-page article and readjustments in the runover pages in the back of the book.

At the same time the research department was at work preparing the table of estimated monthly costs of building or buying a home under the revised National Housing Act. This is the table which is reproduced with the story on Page 7. When the research department had completed the table, off it went to FHA in Washington, for checking.

Hambidge completed the revision of his manuscript and got approval of it from FHA. It took two or three telegrams from Des Moines, however, to get FHA's approval for the table.

Notes: As this story shaped up, it became more and more apparent to all concerned—Mr. McDonough, Mr. Hambidge, Mr. Corbin, Mr. Benson, associate editor, Peter Ainsworth, advertising manager, who happened to be in Washington while Hambidge was revising his story and had an opportunity to make some suggestions about it—that it should be handled as a news feature. This plan was especially important because, in the nature of the case, newspaper and news-magazine reports of the legislation and its effects were incomplete and unaccompanied by thorough interpretation. Further, they were not specifically directed toward the audience represented by *Better Homes & Gardens'* readers.

The job of reporting this story, while comparatively simple, was still considerably more complex than that of the hobby-horse piece. The bulk of the data, out of which the story was built, was contained in the text of the FHA act, but the interpretation of the act and the analysis of its significance had to be secured by interview from members of the Federal Housing Administration.

The story deals with very exact, intricate material. Note the extreme care with which the author and the magazine checked every phase of the data. Hambidge's original article was gone over by FHA executives and approved; the revised article was similarly checked; and the table, although developed from FHA data, was sent, at the expense of valuable days, to Washington for approval.

How the conception of the story changed and crystallized as author and editors worked with it and thought about it is illustrated by a comparison of the opening of Hambidge's original article and the opening of the article as it was printed. This is the way the story started in its original form—before the idea of a strictly news treatment came in to dominate the situation.

> One of the favorite melodramas when I was young was the mortgage on the old homestead. This mortgage was always held by the villain of the piece. At the great moment he crackled the document menacingly before the eyes of the beautiful young heroine. "Aha," he cried with a sinister laugh. "Will you mar-r-ry me, or will you see your aged parents turned out to wander, homeless in yon r-r-raging storm?"
>
> And the audience understood and shuddered. Oh, yes. They knew what a mortgage was. It was an absolute lien on your house, owned by a sort of Shylock who exacted heavy interest. Every two or three years you had to renew these fateful papers. If you had defaulted in any way, you were at the mercy of the mortgagor. By sweating blood and making large payments, you might some day be free of him. Until then, the mortgage sword of Damocles hung over your head.

This is a leisurely, entertaining, and witty introduction to a discussion of home financing. But it is utterly out of key with the article as it finally developed.

The beginning that was used does primarily two things: It throws us headlong into the discussion of the National Housing Act, and it indicates the slant of the whole story toward "the little fellow."

There is no place here for literary embellishment, for incident, or anecdote, or conversation. The style is direct and hard and simple. The highlights of the story are brought out not by literary but by typographical devices—by italics, boldface type, and paragraph indentations.

Questions:

How do you like the title? Is it, with the subtitle, sufficiently descriptive of the story? If you disapprove, try your hand at some substitutes.

Do you judge that the cost of pushing this story into the April issue was worth-while?

Why, since he was in Washington anyway, didn't Mr. McDonough handle this story himself? (There are at least two good answers.)

Do you think the table showing estimated monthly costs of building under the revised act was worth all the bother that was taken to get it? Why?

Wall Around Hell

HOW SCIENCE IS FIGHTING THE WORLD'S BIGGEST FIRE

By ROBERT E. MARTIN

WALL AROUND HELL

How Science Is Fighting the World's Biggest Fire

By Robert E. Martin

Reprinted by special permission from Popular Science Monthly

To elaborate on current news of science, invention, engineering, industry, politics, government, is one of the jobs of the magazine or newspaper news-feature article. "Wall Around Hell," from *Popular Science Monthly,* is such an elaboration. Newspapers have from time to time carried accounts of the fight to throttle "the world's costliest fire." These have told of the inception of the WPA project and, subsequently, of the progress of the struggle. Now the magazine or Sunday-newspaper article comes along and presents in one piece the whole story.

Carefully and systematically, engineers and miners are closing the dampers of the world's largest fire, a conflagration that has smoldered for fifty-four years beneath some of the richest hills of southern Ohio. The fire fighters may know in a year or two whether their efforts have been successful, or it may not be known for another half century.

The "Valley of Ten Thousand Smokes" in Alaska, Dante's Inferno, and other real or imaginary regions of fire and brimstone have nothing on the parts of Perry and Hocking counties in the vicinity of New Straitsville, Ohio. In an area covering twenty-four square miles, roughly a rectangle running six miles east and west and four miles north and south, a visitor can, in a few hours, obtain a fairly complete picture of what the domain of Satan must be like. From the summits and slopes of beautiful wooded ridges, hundreds of columns of steam and smoke shoot into the air, many of them as high as a city office building. Steaming cracks, some no wider than a pencil and others too wide to jump across, and fiery craters big enough to drive a truck into, make the ground a treacherous place on which to walk. Steam and hot gases that sear the skin belch from many of the craters, and the acrid smell of sulphurous gases is everywhere. If the visitor is fortunate, he may witness the results of an underground explosion that sends sheets of flame from one of the craters to a height of perhaps 200 feet. These geysers of fire last for only a short time, then die down. Even if no outward flame is visible, the glow of white heat usually can be seen, deep down in some of the holes and crevasses.

Now and then a tree leans over at a crazy angle, and finally crashes to the ground or into one of the fiery pits, its blazing roots showing plainly why it toppled. A spring from which ice-cold water once gushed now steams, its water scalding hot. Thousands of acres of rolling hills are pock-marked by sink holes that indicate the area where fire once raged but has since died out.

This underground inferno is caused by the burning of valuable coal deposits. Started over a half century ago during a strike of mine workers, the fire has destroyed an estimated $50,000,000 worth of coal. Should it continue to burn indefinitely, it would spread through vast areas of Ohio's rich coal lands.

But now, after a number of private companies have spent fortunes trying to put the fire out, and after a great many people have become convinced that nothing can be done to stop it, its conquest is in sight.

For nearly two years, stopping the world's costliest mine fire has been a project of the Works Progress Administration. Under the direction of James R. Cavanaugh, veteran mine-fire fighter, about 340 men, mostly unemployed miners, have been building barriers that will prevent the spread of the fire to rich coal fields. If left alone, the fire eventually will burn itself out inside the barriers. However, Cavanaugh believes that the fire can be extinguished within three years and at a cost of less than $1,000,000, by stopping up all holes and cracks in the earth through which air reaches the burning coal.

The coal in the New Straitsville area lies in horizontal veins that are contained in the hills. Wherever there is a valley, the coal deposits are broken, so that fire cannot cross from one ridge to another. However, there are three coal-bearing ridges that connect with outside coal fields, including the rich Hocking Valley district. It is to sever these three paths that the new project was undertaken.

The barriers are essentially earth-filled gaps in the coal veins. The Plummer Hill barrier west of the village of New Straitsville has been completed, and already is holding back the subterranean fires. It is 640 feet long, and cuts the ridge at its narrowest part. The Lost Run barrier, south of the village, in Hocking County, is approximately a mile long, and in some places is 200 feet underground. The Shawnee barrier, east of New Straitsville, is about 6,000 feet long, and averages 175 feet deep.

Construction of one of the larger barriers will require about two years of work. At the time this is being written, the Lost Run barrier is about three-fifths finished, and the Shawnee barrier better than a third. The underground fires are sufficiently far away to prevent their reaching the barriers before the work now under way is done.

The smallest barrier, already finished, will save more than 1,000,000 tons of coal from the fire, and will pay for the entire project several times over.

Imagine that you are visiting one of the barriers, say the one at Lost Run, while it is being constructed. This barrier gets its name from the Lost Run mine, which has not been worked since about 1902.

You drive the short distance from New Straitsville wondering what a barrier looks like, anyway. When you descend the last steep hill, and pull up at the west end of the project, you think that you have made a mistake and that you have come upon another mine instead. But you haven't, for the barrier, at this stage of its development, is essentially a mine consisting of a single tunnel running from one side of the hill to the other.

In fact, this barrier, like that near the village of Shawnee, consists chiefly of old mine workings. Your guide, Adam J. Laverty, general superintendent of the work, and one of the few men living who remember the hectic days when the mine fires were started, can point out to you where a man was killed, back in 1901 or thereabouts, by falling rock. He can tell you about some of the old miners' lamps, bottles of lamp oil, and other relics found in the long-abandoned tunnels.

The first step in the construction of the Lost Run barrier was to bore through the hill and cut a twelve-foot gap through the coal vein, which varies in thickness from four to twelve feet and is nearly a mile wide at that point. Whenever possible, the old mine tunnels have been used, to simplify the work and keep down expense. These tunnels were, for the most part, filled with loose rock, earth, and fire clay that had been washed in. All this was removed. Elaborate timber bracing, which is one of the most costly items of the project, was installed. Rails were laid to carry coal cars used in removing debris and in hauling the coal that was taken out in extending new sections of the tunnel. From the old mine tunnels, side tunnels had been bored. These have been walled with stone and clay. Electric pumps carry off the water that seeps in.

As you slosh along through the tunnel in your rubber boots, sometimes crouched low to clear the cross timbers where they are only four feet from the floor, you become aware of a change in temperature. When you first enter the tunnel, the air is icy cold, and you shiver. The exertion of walking in a strange environment and in unfamiliar boots soon overcomes that. But after a while, you pass through a canvas-curtained opening into a section of tunnel where the temperature seems very high. Your guide explains that the increase in temperature is caused by burning coal a scant 200 feet from the tunnel. A thermometer indicates that the temperature is in the fifties, but the humidity makes it seem much higher.

After the tunnel is completed, the next step in construction of the barrier is to fill it with earth. This will be a dangerous job, because all the bracing and every other piece of wood or other combustible material have to be taken out. A single stick of wood left accidentally might carry the fire across the barrier, and thus destroy the value of the project.

To fill the tunnel, earth is flushed into it through vertical pipes driven down from the surface at 100-foot intervals throughout its length. While the water flows off through cracks in wooden bulkheads, the earth is deposited to form a solid plug across the face of the coal vein.

Filling the barrier will not end the fire-stopping work. The earthen plug will be inspected regularly, and watched for signs of failure. To make this possible, a parallel tunnel, which is in part an old mine entry, will be kept open. At intervals, connecting tunnels will permit the barrier to be reached. The main tunnel is protected by a right-of-way extending for 100 feet on each side. No coal may be mined inside this distance.

The project at New Straitsville is not wholly an experiment, for a similar barrier, erected to stop a mine fire near Pittsburgh, Pa., proved entirely successful. The barrier design was worked out by the U. S. Bureau of Mines, which is supervising the work, and which also is safeguarding the lives of workmen with all the known safety and first-aid devices.

The underground fire has produced a great many odd happenings. A woman living in a house near the spot where the Plummer Hill barrier now stands went into her cellar one day to get something. She struck a match to make a light, but it went out. She tried another, and it refused to burn. Later she found it impossible to keep a fire burning in her stove, or her oil lamp going. She was advised to move out at once, because her house was being filled with gases from the underground fire, which drove out the oxygen. Other residents nearby have been driven from their homes by gases time and again, but insist on remaining as long as possible.

One man had a well into which he used to

lower buckets of snow, to be melted for drinking water. A woman used the water from her well for doing her washing, without further heating. Cisterns and wells have been destroyed by their bottoms dropping out, or by cracking in the heat. One farmer was able to dig roasted potatoes from his patch. Plants grow in winter and blossom out of season, in ground kept warm by the fire. Farm animals have lost their lives by falling into pits.

The fire-fighting project at New Straitsville is considered the most dangerous mine job in the country. Yet, because of high safety standards, no life has been lost to date, and but few injuries reported. Mine-rescue instruction is given constantly, and special rescue squads stand in readiness for emergencies.

Great caution is necessary because of the nature of the work. In utilizing tunnels of abandoned mines, many risks are encountered. Water, seeping into the old workings, had been dammed up by cave-ins to form large accumulations that had to be drained or pumped out before the work could proceed. In removing these underground lakes, care had to be taken to prevent a flood of water rushing into other parts of the project where men were working. Among the poisonous or otherwise dangerous gases encountered are fire damp (marsh gas), white damp (carbon monoxide), "stink damp" (hydrogen sulphide), and black damp (carbon dioxide). Huge fans, with capacities of 55,000 cubic feet of air a minute, force fresh air through the tunnels to remove such gases.

Since 1884, when the fires started, numerous efforts have been made to halt the underground inferno. Several of the mining companies went broke fighting it. A creek was diverted into a mine in the hope that the water would put out the fire, but this proved a boomerang. When the water struck the hot coal, it flashed into steam. The resulting pressure opened cracks that produced added draft and made the fire worse than before.

These and other failures endangered all the coal deposits in the vicinity of New Straitsville. Unless something could be done to halt the blaze, it became evident, all unmined coal over an area of hundreds of square miles might be consumed.

But it now looks as though the underground inferno has at last met its master. The first barrier seems to be holding perfectly, and there is reason to believe that the others will prove equally successful.

The objective of the present work is not to put the fire out, but only to build fences against it, and confine it to the twenty-four square miles where it is now raging, until it burns itself out. This may take a few years, maybe a century. And until the last spark has died, it cannot be said that the fire barriers are no longer needed. Much valuable coal still remains in the fire area. Some of this will be removed. Likewise, there are valuable deposits of petroleum, clay, and other natural resources in the region. So it may prove worth while to attempt to smother out the fire rather than let it burn itself out, after the barrier project has been completed. Even if none of the coal within the bottled-up area could be saved, the barriers still would be a success, for they protect untold millions of tons of coal on the outside.

Questions:

Would "Wall Around Hell" do as a Sunday newspaper feature? Why—or why not?

Is the opening paragraph effective? Could you suggest alterations to improve it?

What should the opening paragraphs of an article like this try to accomplish?

What differences do you note between the style of writing here and in "Good News"?

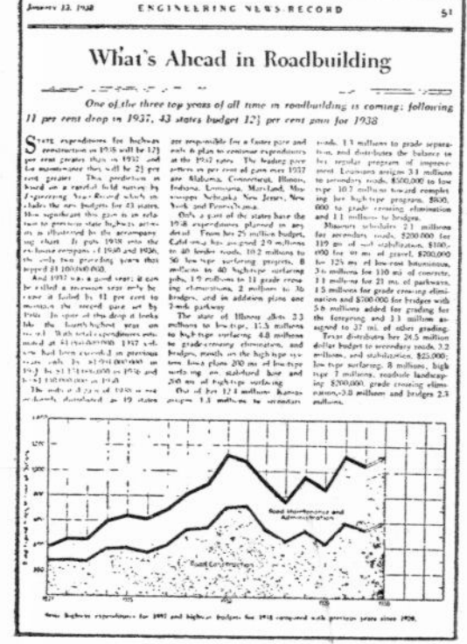
ENGINEERING NEWS-RECORD 51

What's Ahead in Roadbuilding

One of the three top years of all time in roadbuilding is coming: following 11 per cent drop in 1937, 43 states budget 12½ per cent gain for 1938

WHAT'S AHEAD IN ROADBUILDING

Reprinted by special permission from Engineering News-Record

Engineering News-Record is a *news* magazine of engineering. Naturally it runs a large number of articles of the news-feature type.

State expenditures for highway construction in 1938 will be 12½ per cent greater than in 1937, and for maintenance they will be 2½ per cent greater. This prediction is based on a careful field survey by Engineering News-Record which includes the new budgets for 43 states. How significant this gain is in relation to previous state highway activity is illustrated by the accompanying chart. It puts 1938 into the exclusive company of 1930 and 1936, the only two preceding years that topped $1,100,000,000.

And 1937 was a good year; it can be called a recession year only because it failed by 11 per cent to maintain the record pace set by 1936. In spite of this drop it looks like the fourth-highest year on record. With total expenditures estimated at $1,060,000,000, 1937 volume had been exceeded in previous years only by $1,091,000,000 in 1931, by $1,131,000,000 in 1936 and by $1,140,000,000 in 1930.

The indicated gain of 1938 is not uniformly distributed, as 19 states are responsible for a faster pace and only 6 plan to continue expenditures at the 1937 rates. The leading pace setters in per cent of gain over 1937 are Alabama, Connecticut, Illinois, Indiana, Louisiana, Maryland, Mississippi, Nebraska, New Jersey, New York, and Pennsylvania.

Only a part of the states have the 1938 expenditures planned in any detail. From her 25 million budget, California has assigned 2.9 millions to 40 feeder roads, 10.2 millions to 50 low-type surfacing projects, 8 millions to 40 high-type surfacing jobs, 1.9 millions to 11 grade crossing eliminations, 2 millions to 36 bridges, and in addition plans one 7-mile parkway.

The state of Illinois allots 3.3 millions to low-type, 17.5 millions to high-type surfacing, 4.8 millions to grade-crossing elimination, and bridges, mostly on the high-type system. Iowa plans 200 mi. of low-type surfacing on stabilized base and 200 mi. of high-type surfacing.

Out of her 12.4 millions, Kansas assigns 1.3 millions to secondary roads, 1.3 millions to grade separation, and distributes the balance to her regular program of improvement. Louisiana assigns 3.1 millions to secondary roads, $500,000 to low type, 10.7 millions toward completing her high-type program, $800,000 to grade crossing elimination and 1.1 millions to bridges.

Missouri schedules 2.1 millions for secondary roads, $200,000 for 119 mi. of soil stabilization, $100,000 for 30 mi. of gravel, $700,000 for 125 mi. of low-cost bituminous, 3.6 millions for 110 mi. of concrete, 1.1 millions for 21 mi. of parkways, 1.5 millions for grade crossing elimination and $700,000 for bridges with 5.6 millions added for grading for the foregoing and 1.1 million assigned to 37 mi. of other grading.

Texas distributes her 24.5 million dollar budget to secondary roads, 3.2 millions; soil stabilization, $25,000; low-type surfacing, 8 millions; high-type, 7 millions; roadside landscaping, $200,000, grade crossing elimination, 3.8 millions and bridges 2.3 millions.

Questions:

Is this article more or less like a newspaper story than the preceding examples of the news feature?

This story has no "embellishment." Why? Why will readers be interested in it?

MEXICAN BAD MAN

By Carleton Beals

Reprinted by special permission from The New Republic

One is tempted to flip a coin—heads, it's a news feature; tails, it's a personality article—to determine the classification of Carleton Beals' "Mexican Bad Man." To be sure, Cedillo is the central figure of the story, but the material is not restricted to a personality sketch of the "bad man"—it broadens out into a general discussion of the conflicting forces which are operative in Mexico.

Carleton Beals has spent years in the study of Mexico and Latin America. This article is a product of those years, of the background of his knowledge, as well as of a specific reporting job.

General Saturnino Cedillo is in revolt in central Mexico. Cedillo is the last of the big self-made barons of the revolutionary period, the product of twenty and more years of armed upheaval, which gradually canalized into a popular social revolution. He is the product of the clash of foreign versus Mexican interests, in which the struggle for petroleum took the center of the stage with proper melodrama—murder, battle, banditry, threatened war. Now, twenty-eight years after Francisco Madero, the first modern apostle of Mexican liberty, was jailed in this same San Luis Potosí, the scene of the present trouble, the Mexican people have triumphantly seized control of their most lawless industry. But of the social aims of the revolution of which he was so much a part, Cedillo knows little.

He merely rode upon the crest of disorder, matching his violent spirit with the violence of the times. Having ability, greed, courage and cruelty, he stamped his will on the lonely deserts, the rugged mountains and valleys of his native state. He was soil of its soil, a stocky, full-blooded Indian, through whose veins flowed the cold cunning of a race defeated and long oppressed, which also had acquired the ruthless personal ambitions of the oppressors.

Before the revolution even started, he had climbed out of the serfdom of his own people to become a petty rancher; and the rancher in Mexico, for centuries caught between the cultural thrust of the native folk and the competition of the large Spanish landholders, survived only by fierce, daring individualism. When revolution swept the land, such men had no alternative but to fight. Cedillo rode with the revolution. He rode with Villa. He helped Carranza oust Victoriano Huerta. He betrayed Carranza in behalf of Obregon, and became the dictator of his state.

An ignorant man, he had known his people well enough to stand for the new land program. According to McBride, before the revolution, 98.2 percent of the heads of rural families in San Luis Potosí were propertyless, paupers, serfs, without rights. But the cause of land reform was never deep within Cedillo. By 1920, after ten years of fighting, only four villages in his state had received lands. Cedillo was never in harmony with the village communal system. Ever the rancher, he clung fast to personal land ownership. Soon he was adding to his own holdings, enriching himself at the expense of the cause he was supposedly furthering. And he was absolute master of San Luis Potosí; his word was law. For eighteen years and more his word has been law there.

Some years ago, so busy was he raking in land, wealth and new concubines that he forgot to pay the school teachers for a whole year. When they went on strike, he branded them as "Communists," threw some into jail, and made others work in the sun on his vast estates at the point of the bayonet. Federal pressure forced their release—after many days. Some had to walk barefoot over the stones back to the capital. Some were never heard of again.

Cedillo has been supreme in San Luis Potosí. To his own armed followers he has given land and kept them armed like feudal retainers. They are organized into a fake agrarian league.

But he has permitted no labor unions in that mining state, where foreign capital gouges out the wealth of the hills. Every time an attempt has been made to hold a labor meeting, he has broken it up with armed thugs and bloodshed. When last year Cárdenas disarmed the Cedillo private militia, and sent in an agrarian commission to enforce the land laws, with orders not to exempt even Cedillo, an undeclared war was on. The local feudal barons decided to fight.

For some years now, Cedillo has been the principal white hope of the reactionaries. Many Catholics, who a few years before had denounced him as a bandit, came to look upon him as a savior, for he has steadfastly refused to enforce the religious laws in his domain. In Mexico City, I have heard American business men say, "Cedillo and Almazán are our only hope now." (Almazán, another old-line general grown wealthy, is close to the mine and steel interests of Monterey which several years back promoted an unsuccessful plot to oust Cárdenas.)

Of late, Cedillo has been known to have become an ardent admirer of Hitler and the Nazi doctrines. One of his right-hand men is Baron von Merk, former German army man, said to have a Gestapo record and to be in touch with Nazi and Fascist groups in Mexico and the United States. Cedillo is charged by the CTM, the national labor federation, with having smuggled German and Italian arms shipments across the border from Guatemala and other shipments from the United States. He acquired a whole fleet of airplanes, which President Cárdenas last year obliged him to sell to the federal government. Recently he has secretly obtained other planes, another Nazi agent being the intermediary.

If this sounds fantastic, it is merely because the American public is only hazily informed about the Nazi-Fascist *Putsch* in Latin America, active in every country and determined to cut England's life-line with the New World in case of war. The Nazis have been very busy in Mexico. They have had close relations with the Gold Shirts and other small organizations which, though their membership is minute, have plenty of funds and distribute much propaganda. The so-called Brown House on Uruguay Street is a center for many of these activities. The Gold Shirts specialize in anti-Semitic literature. Sometimes frightful cartoons of the Jews as enemies of the true Faith are printed on the back of pictures of the Virgin of Guadalupe.

But though ignorant folk are misled, the Catholic hierarchy itself does not seem to be falling for this delusion. A somewhat liberal trend has swept over the Mexican prelates. Catholic extremists, who look to men like Cedillo, are apparently for the moment not in favor. This is partly due to the political astuteness of President Cárdenas. While he has not set aside any of the restrictive legislation to which the Church so objects, he soon showed that within the legal framework, the Catholics would have full guarantees.

More and more, finding they had legal protection, the Catholics have desisted from their attacks on public education. And when Cárdenas took over the oil fields, the hierarchy, along with most of Mexico, so stirred by crusading pride, swung in behind him and agreed to raise several million pesos to help pay. This was a remarkable change of heart. Though Cedillo has the backing of local clericals, he will have to become more than an outlaw in the hills before the Church as a whole gives him aid or switches its allegiance.

Some people, no doubt, take it for granted that the Church and the oil interests are directly backing Cedillo. But no documentary evidence for such charges has been disclosed. Rodgríguez, head of the Gold Shirts, allied with Cedillo and plotting in the United States, has been receiving strange American agents. Only an official investigation—such as one by the United States Senate—could verify suspected tie-ups.

President Cárdenas has charged that the oil companies have been plotting armed trouble, a charge they have hotly denied. Certainly in the past, they and American mining companies have subsidized revolts—it is all on the record. One mining-company president once shipped a million rounds of ammunition to rebels in Mexico. The bandit Pelaez was on the payroll of American oil companies. San Luis Potosí borders on the rich oil state of Tamaulipas, said to be the goal of the Cedillistas. It was in Tamaulipas, some months ago, that the Gold Shirts staged an unsuccessful border invasion.

A few days after the Cedillo revolt broke out, the oil companies spread full-page advertisements over the Mexico City dailies, declaring they were entitled to fight for their rights. To place such ads at such a ticklish moment was certainly far from loyal to the government, to put it mildly, though quite in keeping with the long record of defiance of Mexican law, including the recent verdict of the Mexican Supreme Court.

The fact that Cedillo has a Nazi tie-up does not preclude also an American oil tie-up. Those who have followed closely Nazi activities in South America know that in many places, much to the perplexity of the State Department, the very companies which at home are demanding aggressive Pan-Americanism, are getting hand-in-glove with Nazi-Fascist groups and agents, are actively promoting our State Department's strange friendship with dictatorships which are half under the thumb of European agents. All this in the name of good will!

Cedillo and his revolt, and similarly the psychology and practices of the oil companies, have been the products of the same wild-cat era of lawless violence. Just as Cedillo feels himself above all law except his own will, so have the oil companies long considered themselves above Mexican law. For many years they ruled much of the state of Tamaulipas as an independent kingdom in much the same way that Cedillo has ruled San Luis Potosí. Not even government inspectors could penetrate those padlocked gates. Those who took their duties too seriously were fed to the buzzards.

Various oil companies fought every effort toward clearing up their titles, which were maintained at the point of the gun, fought every effort to tax them properly, every effort to make them take out drilling permits, every effort to regulate production. At a time when our Secretary of State, Bainbridge Colby, was fulminating that Mexican taxes savored of confiscation, our own government, in income, import and other taxes, was getting more revenue out of Mexican oil shipped to the United States than was Mexico.

The constant demand of the Mexican people for over twenty years has been for the nationalization of their oil fields. They have been balked by threats of armed intervention, by constant diplomatic pressure, by armed banditry supported by oil companies, by the agreements of 1923, by the Morrow compromise. But in the end their will has prevailed—fortunately, at a time when our good-neighbor policy made intimidation in the old style difficult. At no time have the Mexican people ever been more firmly united in their aims and less in a mood to be ruled by old-style military dictatorship, with all its brutalities, or by foreign capital, or by any combination of the two. Nor do they want Nazism anywhere in the land.

Questions:

If this story were written for *Liberty,* how would it differ from its present form?

What is the central theme of the story?

What contrasts do you find between this story and the way the same material would be handled in a news story?

Practice Suggestions

1. Make a list of meetings, conventions, and short courses to be held in your community during the next three or four months, which you think might provide material for news features.

2. What steps might you take, before the meeting takes place, to prepare yourself for covering it?

3. Look through an issue of a daily newspaper and list any items which you think might be elaborated into news features.

4. Why do trade journals use so many news-feature articles?

The Process Article

PREVIOUS discussions have dealt with experience stories and news features. Here we are to look at a third species of the magazine article. This is the sort of article, the main purpose of which (it may, of course, have subsidiary purposes) is to tell the reader how to perform a particular operation, how to make or do something. It is usually called the process article, although this term is not too accurately descriptive of it.

To this class of stories belongs that wide variety of articles, particularly numerous in women's magazines, farm papers, and trade publications, which describe a method or process. However much flesh there may be on the bone, the skeletal structure of these stories consists of the materials and steps that are essential to the process.

Note that not always is the process completely detailed. Often the purpose of the story may be to give the reader the general outline of the process or an introduction to it with the thought that he will supplement the story material from other sources.

Ten Minutes From Hollywood

"Ten Minutes From Hollywood" (Page 8) is a sort of stepchild of the FHA story. The only trouble with this comparison is that the child is considerably older than its parent. As has been indicated in the behind-the-scenes account of "Good News," "Ten Minutes From Hollywood" had won its place in the magazine as the lead-off article for April, and was shunted into second position only because of the news value of "Good News."

Whatever tutelary deities look out for the affairs of editors were thoroughly on the job when this April issue was in the making. For with no time to develop small-home material to illustrate how the National Housing Act would work, this article about the Cape Cod Cottage that migrated to California steps squarely and adequately into the breach. A bit of editorial inspiration puts an arrow at the bottom of Page 7, which points the reader over the page to "Ten Minutes From Hollywood"—an illustration of the type of home which the "Good News" article is especially designed to encourage.

But before you read "Ten Minutes From Hollywood," consider two harassing editorial problems that confront John Normile, architectural editor, month in and month out (they are problems that are far from being the exclusive property of Mr. Normile, but they are as well illustrated in connection with his work as anywhere else).

Problem Number One is how to get variety in a subject that has to be treated in some form or other in every issue. Put yourself in Mr. Normile's place. What would you do with the home-building material of the magazine? Should you give from issue to issue a series of small-home plans? Will such a program become monotonous? And consider, with this, Problem Number Two, which is: How to emotionalize the idea of home building—how to make it seem attractive, romantic, and attainable. For to do this last is one of the chief objectives of the editorial policy of the magazine.

Such an article as "Ten Minutes From Hollywood" is one way to meet these problems. The discussion of just how it does so we shall leave to the "Notes."

(The two problems mentioned are just as important to the writer as to the editor. Slightly restated they are: How to deal with old subjects in a new way; and how to humanize one's material. Many of the examples in this book point to ways in which writers—sometimes with editorial assistance—have solved these problems.)

Mrs. Head, the author, is the wife of a California architect. This is not the first time that she has had material in *Better Homes & Gardens*. In fact, she is a pretty regular contributor.

Originally "Ten Minutes From Hollywood" came to *Better Homes & Gardens* with snapshots and brief stories of three or four new houses. The Cape Cod cottage—both its floor plan and exterior appearance—appealed to Mr. Normile. The pictures which Mrs. Head had submitted were not entirely satisfactory; so letters were sent to her and a firm of photographers in Los Angeles which specializes in pictures of homes and gardens arranging for retakes according to the directions which Mr. Normile supplied. And Mrs. Head was asked to re-submit her manuscript in considerably more detail and with an attempt not only at impersonal description of the house but also of the reasons for its desirability. This second manuscript, with a considerable amount of editing and rewriting, is the one that appeared finally in the magazine.

Notes: One of the interesting things about this story is its evolution from the snapshots and brief original manuscript into the two-page-spread that it finally became. Here is the manuscript as it originally came to the editor:

"This little home situated ten minutes from Hollywood proves that Cape Cod can come to California and retain all of its picturesque and inviting appearance, yet gain at the same time the outdoor livability demanded by the sunshine of Southern California. This house, owned by Mr. and Mrs. Paul Power and designed by Leo F. Bachman, architect of Los Angeles, is constructed of white redwood siding and natural redwood shingles. The steeply pitched roof, green shutters, lattice work and white picket fence are all in keeping with the New England atmosphere.

"Every room has two exposures and easy accessibility is provided from each to the roomy rear porch, which may be used as an outdoor dining room due to its position in reference to the kitchen. Knotty pine has been used to excellent effect as a finish in the kitchen and as a wainscot in the charming New England dining room. The plan is compactly arranged, yet the retiring quarters are distinctly separate from the living quarters. A 60 foot lot will amply provide for both the house and the drive way."

The second version was somewhat longer than the story as it finally appeared. It contained all of the information and a good deal of the style of the final article. It was called "Cape Cod Cottage in California." Here are the first three paragraphs before they were revised and edited.

"This small white house is a definite success! Not on account of its New England forbears, though good heredity is as important to houses as to humans, nor because of its beautiful surroundings or even its pleasing appearance does it claim our attention. It is rather because this little house is a fine example of good architecture, good room arrangement and good construction. This trio of virtues,—sad to state,—is not commonly found in the small house.

"To architects all over the country, the house costing under $5,000 has been the problem child of the profession. If this problem child appeared attractive it was usually found to be quite refractory inside. On the other hand if the solidity of the structure were assured, the appearance of the house was utterly uninteresting and without any touch of imagination. To make a house appeal to the eye, satisfy the demands of efficient room planning and modern living, and withal make it proof against the onslaught of the years is not an easy job. But it can be done.

"This pleasant little house in California proves that even with budget limitations the trio of virtues may live amicably under the same roof. Delightful to the eye, comfortable to live in and immune to western sun and winter rains, it is compact without making the inhabitants feel as if they were living in a cracker box."

Questions:

Why was the title of this article changed from "Cape Cod Cottage in California" to "Ten Minutes From Hollywood"?

How does this story meet the "problem of monotony"?

Why was the beginning of the story directed at little houses in general rather than at the specific little house about which the article is to tell?

What do you think of the use of such words and phrases as "the house looked like Minnie the Moocher," "bratty," "come-hither"?

Compare the foregoing with the beginning of the story as it appeared in the magazine. Notice how the first three paragraphs of the printed story set the stage and pose the theme of this article. In this version the story is not merely about the Cape Cod cottage in California; it is rather about the problem of the low-cost house and how this problem has been solved in the particular instance of the Cape Cod cottage. By this change of emphasis the applicability of the story to any region is made more prominent, and the danger that the article may be discarded by the reader as just another example of California (or New England) architecture is minimized.

Why Families Leave Home

If all the correspondence which preceded the appearance of the story "Why Families Leave Home" (Page 14), were printed in this book it would take in the neighborhood of 20 or 30 pages. The story itself has four illustrations, two paragraphs of copy, and four paragraphs of legend. But before they appeared in the magazine, these two cottages were the subject of a year's correspondence.

Carl Sigman is a member of a firm of New York architects and illustrators. During the past few years he has done work for a number of magazines, among them *Better Homes & Gardens.*

This particular story started at a luncheon table in New York. Mr. McDonough makes frequent visits to New York, one of the major purposes of which is to keep in contact with the magazine's writers and illustrators. So there was a lunch with Sigman, in the course of which the architect mentioned summer cottages and the possibility of an article with summer-cottage plans for a future issue of the magazine.

A few weeks later letter number 1, accompanied by seven cabin designs, was dispatched from New York to Des Moines.

Letter number 2, from Mr. Normile to Mr. Sigman, is a commission to do the article. It read as follows:

"After giving your cottage designs very careful consideration, we have decided that we like numbers 2 and 3 best as they seem to contain a maximum of attractive design and workable layout for the average small family.

"The others for one reason or another we do not feel would be equally attractive. I would like to have you do a wash perspective of the exterior of each of numbers 2 and 3 and wash perspective of an interior feature of each. For number 2 a view which would clearly indicate the kitchenette arrangement with doors, and for number 3 a view showing the fireplace and bunks would be very good, I think.

"In addition we would like about 150 words of introduction and 125 or 150 words description of each of the two cottages. These will be published in a spread in one of our early spring issues."

The subsequent correspondence consisted of a continuous exchange of ideas, criticism, and suggestions. After they had looked over the plans Mr. Normile and Mr. McDonough decided that they would offer working drawings of these two cottages. Some of the correspondence with Mr. Sigman was concerned with the inclusion of these plans.

To the free-lance writer there is a further suggestion in this correspondence. Mr. Sigman took occasion, while writing about the article and the plans, which had been commissioned, to suggest three or four other subjects which he thought he could work up for the magazine.

Notes: Five-eighths of the amount paid to Mr. Sigman for this article was for illustrations and three-eighths for the manuscript. As a matter of fact, of course, it was the illustrations—and the ideas—that the magazine was buying. The manuscript itself was turned over to Mr. Adams, assistant to the editor, and when he got through with it not much of the original survived. His editorial work on this manuscript points to the magazine's policy in the handling of this kind of story. It wants the text to be sprightly, but it does not want to waste much space to secure this effect. Here are two pages assigned to the article. More than three-fourths of the space is to be occupied by the illustrations. More than half of the remainder goes to the legends, because, directly associated with the illustrations as they are, they offer a more convenient and effective place to point out details than the body of the text. And so there is little room left for the story—which actually is not a story at all but merely an introduction to the illustrations and legends.

With these things in mind, it is easy to see why the first paragraph of the original manuscript was killed out entirely. It went as follows:

"Are you one of those twice-cursed individuals who is forced to struggle for a place in the sun, in the midst of a great city where there is all too little sun and fresh air, and far too few trees and flowers? If you are, woe is you except during those enchantingly brief periods when the gods of business release you from your prison to the great outdoors. At such times to have a cottage by a mirrored lake or river or the waves of the ocean, is the perfect haven for your escape."

Whereas the opening paragraph of about eighty words is intended to orient the reader to the story and to give an air of spriteliness, the version as Mr. Adams rewrote it—"Here are two *Better Homes & Gardens'* cottages designed for families itching to get away from it all, but not so far away that father has to shave in cold water"—takes only a sentence to accomplish the same purposes.

The title of this article like those on many other stories in the magazine underwent an evolution. The author's title was "Better Homes for Better Holidays." This on the original manuscript has through it an emphatic black line. Above it but also crossed out with even greater emphasis is "Compact, Complete, and Simple." The final version, "Why Families Leave Home," ran the gauntlet of editorial criticism and was finally given a vote of confidence.

How to Tie Your Beds to Your Lawn

Each season as it rolls around drags with it the scraggly flock of "things that should be done." Whether one is editing a magazine for gardeners or sportsmen or farmers or construction contractors, one has the task of dealing with these recurrent problems. The story on Page 12, "How to Tie Your Beds to Your Lawn," illustrates how *Better Homes & Gardens* has dealt with one of these situations. No one had to "think up" this story—it was right there in front of your face when the green came out in grass and perennials in the spring. The difficulty here is not with the idea, for it is hoary with age and as recurrent as taxes, but rather how once again to project this idea in a form that will have effectiveness and originality.

Nor was there in this case much reporting to do, to get together the material for the story. The author, Mr. Hottes, is also author of a dozen or so garden books and for years has been an associate editor of *Better Homes & Gardens*. The facts that he must put into the story are an old, old song. The whole thing was one of presentation.

Notes: This story, like the one on lighting, seemed best served by illustrations. But what kind of illustrations? Should they be photographs or drawings? The trouble with photographs would be that they would show too much, that the one thing that Mr. Hottes wanted the reader's eye to fall on would be obscured by the variety and detail of the photograph. So the die was cast for drawings and for drawings so simple in technique that the reader's eye would follow without distraction the thing that he was supposed to see. The results of these cogitations and of conferences with Mr. Hainline, the art director, resulted in the commissioning of an artist to make the eight drawings finally reproduced with the story.

As for the text, it has to deal with a thoroughly practical bread-and-butter subject—how to keep the pesky grass from wandering into the flower beds and how to keep the pesky flowers from wandering about the lawn. What is needed here obviously is to tell the reader what you know about the matter as briefly, succinctly, and clearly as possible. To meet these specifications, Mr. Hottes' copy consists of a single paragraph of introduction and four following paragraphs, each dealing with a specific recommendation.

Questions:

Why are the scientific names of plants included with the common names?

How do you like the *Better Homes & Gardens* "stunt" of emphasizing one word in an article title—such as "Tie" in "How to Tie Your Beds to Your Lawn"?

Is there any point in attempting to get human interest into this kind of article?

Rooms for Boys and Girls

The two stories on Pages 20 and 23, "Plan for Miss Sixteen" and "Tommy's Room Is Washable," were in a sense accidents. Their origin and development illustrate graphically how material is developed by a magazine and how ideas are shaped and molded into magazine material.

A good many months before Miss Sixteen made her debut in the magazine, Mrs. Holbrook was called on as an interior-decorator consultant to supervise the furnishing of three model houses constructed by the Niagara Light and Power Company of Buffalo, New York. Mrs. Holbrook's plans for a young girl's room in one of the houses were executed by Miss Hastings, interior decorator with a large Buffalo department store.

When they had completed the girl's room, Mrs. Holbrook and Miss Hastings fell in love with their handiwork. Mrs. Holbrook had plans underway for a story about a boy's room. Why not make a companion story out of pictures and descriptions of this room for Miss Sixteen? The story as it finally appeared was a three-way collaboration, Mrs. Holbrook contributing the ideas and plans for the room, Miss Hastings executing the plans, and Jean Guthrie writing the copy.

The boy's-room story grew, really, out of an advertisement in a rival magazine. It was a Lux ad about a room for a youngster equipped with materials that could be washed—with Lux of course.

Helen Brooke is the pen name of a home-furnishing specialist with Marshall Field and Company, Chicago. Mrs. Holbrook, chatting with Miss Brooke, brought up the idea of a washable room for boys. Miss Brooke kindled to the suggestion and the upshot was a demonstration room set up in Marshall Field's and carrying out the plans that Mrs. Holbrook developed. The copy again was prepared by Jean Guthrie.

Notes: Here again pictures make the stories. The copy was designed largely as an introduction and framework for the pictures. There is a bit of fictionalizing in the copy about the girl's room. "Our Jean" and her birthday gift of a room all her own are figments of Miss Guthrie's imagination. This is not, as the explanation of its origin indicates, an experience story, but the fiction of Jean and her birthday personalizes the story and gives it a touch of human warmth and reality.

Dressing up the House and Garden

For several years *Better Homes & Gardens* has conducted a Better Homes Contest with substantial prizes for what are judged to be the best new houses (in various size and cost groups), the best jobs of remodeling old houses, and the best jobs of remodeling kitchens.

"Converted to Colonial" on Page 27 is a by-product of the remodeling contest. Before and after pictures were submitted by the contestant, but the after picture used with the story is a retake which the magazine had done by a commercial photographer. The three short paragraphs of copy were prepared by Mr. Normile.

"First Aid to Turf" on Page 24 is a satisfactory model for thousands of short process stories. There is here no waste of time or space in getting down to business. First the problem—and in this case the first paragraph is enough to put it before the reader—then the methods and materials clearly but briefly described, so that the reader can go through the steps of the process. And that is all.

About a year ago a package of no usual proportions arrived by mail at *Better Homes & Gardens.* Mrs. Holbrook chuckles when she thinks of that package. It contained twenty-five or thirty articles, some of them illustrated by the author with grim drawings. The package was from Jesse M. Pflanz, whom no one at *Better Homes & Gardens* had ever heard of before. Mrs. Holbrook confesses that the temptation was strong to re-crate the package and send it back—by freight. But instead she read the stuff.

Some of it did go back, but nine or ten of the stories stayed at *Better Homes & Gardens* and checks instead went to their author. The story "Magic" on Page 34 is one of these.

"He Annexes the Attic" on Page 28 is, like "Converted to Colonial," a by-product of the *Better Homes & Gardens'* remodeling contest. The pictures were taken by a commercial photographer and the three paragraphs of copy were written in the magazine office.

COFFEE DRESSES FOR TEA

BY ZORADA Z TITUS

COFFEE DRESSES FOR TEA

By Zorada Z. Titus

Reprinted by special permission from Household Magazine

A good many arguments could be brought out to prove that the foods editor of a women's magazine has the hardest job in the world. Month after month she has to say something new, interesting, exciting if possible, about the woman's eternal, three-times-a-day job of fueling the family engines. A tremendous lot of ingenuity, imagination, and research must be poured into the foods department. There isn't always much that is new to say—so the old things must be said differently. (Of course, there is a ray of sunlight in the gloom. Just because meal-making is a perennial task, women are eager to read about foods and are grateful for any light and guiding they can get. Reader-interest surveys of women's magazines almost invariably show the foods material scoring at the top.) Here is a foods article from *Household Magazine*:

Today coffee sits as majestically at one end of a tea table as its colleague in the beverage world, tea, sits opposite. It also dresses itself in disguise and appears, sometimes unnoticed, in the dainty accompaniments served on the modern tea table.

When tea hour was added to the other American meals at which coffee was king it helped the United States with the distinction of drinking one-half of the world's supply of coffee. Yet those who know differ about the best way to make good coffee. There are several methods, each with its special merit. You can take your choice. However, whether it is boiled with or without egg, percolated, dripped, or a combination of two of these, each method requires freshly ground coffee, tightly sealed to prevent exposure to air and consequent staleness.

A clean pot is essential to good coffee made by any method, and you can scrub, scour, rinse, and then dry to your heart's content, because a disagreeable taste is inevitable if sediment is allowed to collect. Use a brush for spout, grooves, and other difficult-to-clean places. Then wash carefully in hot soapy water, and don't skimp the rinses.

Accurate measurements are necessary even though we have made coffee for years on end. Measure both coffee and water. Measurements open the field for argument—for some persons like weak coffee and some like it strong, but in any case do not use less than one level tablespoon to each cup of water; use more if you like a stronger-flavored brew.

After you have enjoyed the luxury of sipping slowly that last cup of coffee, don't discard the portion which remains in the pot. Instead, use it in making puddings, icings, cakes, or candies to give a delicious intangible flavor to those tidbits you like to serve at four o'clock as well as with your daily meals.

Bran Cookies

½ Cup Sweetened Condensed Milk	2 Teaspoons Baking-Powder
½ Cup Melted Butter or Margarine	¼ Teaspoon Salt
1 Tablespoon Water	⅔ Cup Bran Cereal
1 Egg, Well Beaten	6 Tablespoons Chopped Raisins
½ Cup Flour	

Combine condensed milk, butter or margarine, water, and egg. Sift flour, measure, and sift with baking-powder and salt. Add to liquid mixture.

Mix thoroughly. Add bran cereal and raisins. Six tablespoons of coconut or 6 tablespoons of chopped nuts may be substituted for the raisins. Drop on to well-oiled baking sheet. Bake in hot oven (400° F.) 10 minutes.—The Household Searchlight.

Coffee-Chocolate Frosting

2 Squares Unsweetened Chocolate	1⅓ Cups Sweetened Condensed Milk
1 Tablespoon Coffee Beverage	Few Grains Salt

Melt chocolate over hot water. Add milk. Stir over boiling water 5 minutes or until thickened. Add coffee and salt. Mix thoroughly. Cool. Spread on cake.—The Household Searchlight.

Plum Pudding

1 Pound Seedless Raisins	2 Teaspoons Baking Soda
1 Pound Currants	1 Teaspoon Cloves
¼ Cup Nuts	1 Teaspoon Allspice
2½ Cups Flour	1 Teaspoon Nutmeg
4 Eggs, Well Beaten	1 Teaspoon Cinnamon
2 Cups Molasses	
2 Cups Buttermilk	2½ Cups Fine Dry Bread Crumbs
1½ Cups Ground Suet	
½ Cup Lemon Juice	2 Teaspoons Salt

Dredge fruits and nuts with 1 cup flour. Combine eggs, molasses, buttermilk, suet and lemon juice. Sift remaining flour, measure, and sift with baking soda, spices, and salt. Add bread crumbs and flour to liquid ingredients. Add fruits and nuts. Mix thoroughly. Pour into well-oiled individual molds, or two three-pound molds. Cover tightly. Steam 3 hours. Cool. Wrap in heavy waxed paper. Store until needed. Re-steam, cut in small pieces, garnish with hard sauce, and serve with coffee.—The Household Searchlight.

Hard Sauce

¼ Cup Butter or Margarine	¼ Teaspoon Cinnamon
1 Cup Powdered Sugar	¼ Teaspoon Grated Orange Rind
1 Tablespoon Molasses	½ Teaspoon Vanilla Flavoring
	Salt

Cream butter or margarine and sugar. Add molasses, cinnamon, rind, flavoring, and a few grains salt. Mix thoroughly. Chill.—The Household Searchlight.

Cocoa-Coffee Frosting

1 Cup Sugar	2 Tablespoons Coffee Beverage
1 Cup Sour Thick Cream	1 Teaspoon Vanilla Flavoring
3 Tablespoons Cocoa	Salt

Combine sugar, cream, coffee, and cocoa. Add few grains salt. Mix thoroughly. Boil to soft ball stage (236° F.). Add flavoring. Cool to room temperature. Beat until thick and creamy.—Mrs. Lowell Mattson, Dassel, Minn.

Caramel Coffee Cake

1½ Cups Cake Flour	1 Cup Brown Sugar
1½ Teaspoons Baking-Powder	1 Egg, Well Beaten
¼ Teaspoon Salt	½ Cup Chopped Nuts
⅓ Cup Butter or Margarine	Grated Rind ½ Lemon
	½ Cup Milk

Sift flour, measure, and sift with baking-powder and salt. Cream butter or margarine with sugar. Add egg. Add dry ingredients alternately with milk. Add nuts and rind. Mix thoroughly. Pour into well-oiled pan. Combine 1 teaspoon cinnamon, 1 tablespoon brown sugar, and ¼ cup rolled nuts. Sprinkle over top. Bake in moderate oven (350° F.) 35 minutes.—Gertrude Abrat, Dayton, Ohio.

Practice Suggestions

1. Why are process articles particularly prominent in technical, farm, women's, and home magazines?

2. If you were a reader what information would you want to get from an article on planning a Hallowe'en party; from one on building a canoe; from one on laying out a border of perennial flowers? Make a list of the items that you would want covered.

3. Why, ordinarily, is "embellishment" less desirable in a process article than in other types? Or is it?

4. Look at several process articles to discover whether or not there are any omissions (steps in the process or materials) which would stand in the way of the reader's performing the process.

XII

The Information Article

MAGAZINES and newspapers should hire a bright young person to think up new names for some of the well-worn and indistinct terms in journalistic nomenclature. For example, the word *feature* is used as a noun to describe a magazine article, a long special newspaper story, a short unusual newspaper story, and the outstanding aspect of a story.

The same sort of difficulty arises with some of the terms that are used to designate different kinds of newspaper and magazine articles. The descriptive word in the phrase "information article" is vague and ambiguous. The purpose of this kind of piece is to convey information, data, fact, description about a subject. This statement clearly demarks the information article from the personality story, but it does not clearly distinguish it from the news feature, the experience article, or the process story. This distinction can be made clear by example. A story about how bees gather honey would be an information story. A story about how Harvey Summers markets honey would be an experience story. A story announcing or explaining new federal quarantine regulations for the control of foul brook, a disease of bees, would be a news feature.

The outstanding thing about the article, "Light Where You Need It" (Page 10), is the use of pictures to tell the story and the shunting of the text to a very minor auxiliary role. A book of no mean proportions could be written on the evolution of the use of pictures by magazines. That evolution has, of course, reached a climax in the picture magazine. But other types of popular magazines have swum in the swift current toward pictorialization. Obviously those magazines which are primarily concerned with things have found a greater use for pictures than those magazines primarily concerned with ideas. Such magazines as *Popular Mechanics* and *Mechanix Illustrated* contain subject matter which can be presented with particular effect by means of illustration. The women's magazines, particularly in their foods, interior decoration, and fashions departments, have gone over in large measure to pictorialization. A corollary of all of this is that the magazine writer and editor must be picture conscious in the highest degree. If they can take good pictures, that is an asset, although it is not necessarily a prerequisite. (In the discussion of "He Pastures His Hobby-Horse in a Garden" and "Ten Minutes From Hollywood" we have seen that although the authors submitted pictures which they themselves had taken, the magazine employed expert commercial photographers to make retakes.)

A trip to Cleveland, another to Chicago, and scores of letters went into the making (the story was built rather than written) of "Light

Where You Need It." The traveler and writer of letters was not, however, the author, Miss Webber, but Mrs. Holbrook, associate editor of *Better Homes & Gardens.*

Just how long she held in the back of her head the idea for this story, Mrs. Holbrook doesn't remember. She does know, however, where the idea came from: it came from seeing pictures of lamps—*just* lamps without their use in relation to the furnishings of the home being demonstrated—and it came in the second place from hearing misused the names of different kinds of lamps.

In November, six months before the story appeared, Mrs. Holbrook took a trip to Cleveland, to the Nela Park Plant of the General Electric Company. She had a conference with the heads of the lighting departments of the General Electric Company. She told them what she had in mind and found, naturally, that they were as interested as she in a story on light in *Better Homes & Gardens.*

Miss Mary Webber is head home-lighting specialist at Nela Park. She was called into consultation and the up-shot was that on her shoulders was laid the responsibility of selecting the right lamps and showing their correct positions and uses.

It had been obvious to Mrs. Holbrook from the first that this must be a picture story. Her whole idea was that the story must picture not only lamps but lamps in association with appropriate home furnishings. Where then could such pictures be obtained? The answer was the Furniture Market to be held in Chicago the following January. (The Furniture Market is the annual showing of new furniture set up by the manufacturers, so that jobbers and dealers can survey the new offerings and study the trends of furniture styles.)

Back in Des Moines, Mrs. Holbrook made out detailed lists of the furniture and accessories which she would need as settings for each of the lamps that were to be photographed. Then she began writing letters to furniture manufacturers, arranging for the use of furniture that would be on hand at the Furniture Market. At the same time Miss Webber was making similar arrangements with the lamp manufacturers.

Questions:

Why was so much painstaking effort—the trip to Cleveland and the arrangements in Chicago—necessary to get the right pictures for this article?

What do you think of the way in which manufacturers are given credit for equipment used in the pictures?

Why is the picture of the "table study" lamp on the inside of the page rather than the outside?

Would it have been better to have had people in all of the pictures?

On the night of the opening of the Furniture Market, Mrs. Holbrook and Miss Webber, accompanied by one of the best photographers in Chicago, made the rounds of the furniture centers and took pictures of lamps in the settings that they had helped to arrange during the past two or three days.

The actual writing of the story was also a cooperative enterprise.

Miss Webber wrote two or three hundred words that constitute the running story. Mrs. Holbrook wrote the legends, and then all of the copy was sent to Jean Guthrie for editing and revision. After that it all went back to Miss Webber for final checking.

Discouragement may have darkened the soul of the prospective free-lance writer as he has read the accounts of the sources of *Better Homes & Gardens* material and has seen that much of it is commissioned to more or less regular contributors or worked out by members of the staff. But he can take a breath of renewed hope from the story, "Safe at Home but Are You" (Page 31).

Estelle H. Ries had a typical free-lance's experience in selling her story to *Better Homes & Gardens*. First she wrote a letter to the editor. It was a good letter and it contained four or five ideas for stories which she said she would like to work out for the publication. The letter was turned over to Mrs. Holbrook. She replied, asking Miss Ries to work out two or three of the suggestions. Of course, she made no promise to buy them. One of the stories that came back was "Safe at Home but Are You." It and two or three others were bought. Not only that but Miss Ries was asked to submit more ideas. Result: She has become a more or less regular contributor to the magazine.

Notes: This is in a sense the sort of story that anybody could write. The data can all be obtained from the American Red Cross or out of the head of the author. We have seen that some stories were bought because of the unusualness of the material they contained. Some were bought because of the personalities which they described. But here is a story about an old subject, unillustrated, and woefully deficient in human interest. Why was it used? The answer: The way it's written. Note that the story is essentially a series of "don'ts"—don't do this and don't do that, if you would avoid accidents. But note also how the imagination of the writer has transformed the stodgy "don'ts" into a lively and entertaining, as well as informative, essay.

We must not, however, give all the credit to Miss Ries. For an examination of her original manuscript shows that the editorial pencils of staff editors played a considerable part in brightening and pointing up the story. Here are some examples:

One sentence in the published story reads, "Or you can join the parade and fall down in your bathtub." In the original it was merely, "Another case of slipperiness is the bathtub."

Or "The embarrassed swain, who slips on the hall rug and lands at his lady's feet, may make good copy for the short story, but it's no joke when it's your own spinal column that's been injured for life." The original was: "Though as we shall see presently electricity can cause some serious mishaps, seventeen times as many people are killed by falling on rugs as from electrical accidents."

Again the final version has it: "There are a great many easy ways to set fire to your clothes, hair, home furnishings or your whole house." The original was: "Fire, of course, is a serious hazard."

Again from the published story: "Or you can start a good fire and

Questions:

What are half a dozen other "old" subjects that might be refurbished in the manner of this article?

What beginning would you put on an article for a popular magazine about automobile-driving safety rules?

There's an invisible line which divides the smart, light, and witty from the silly. Does this article keep on the right side of the line? If you think not, point out exactly where you think it sloshes over.

---

spread it by sloshing water on burning fat." The original was: "Never use water on burning fat, because it may spread the flames."

The drawings that illustrate the article were made by staff artists.

Old hands on the *Des Moines Register* will tell you that Gladys Denny was one of the best reporters and feature writers that ever adorned that paper's staff. As Mrs. Shultz, she abandoned newspaper work, but not her typewriter. Several years ago, her stories began to appear in *Better Homes & Gardens*—stories about children and the problems of their care and training. The occasional stories became more and more regular, and eventually Mrs. Shultz was Child Care and Training Director of the magazine.

But as a magazine writer, Mrs. Shultz has always remained a good reporter. You can trace through the story, "Watch Those 'Children's Diseases' " on Page 38, the trail of the news hound. For all the story says, the source of the material was a doctor in the State Department of Health. But back of that interview was a thorough job of preparation—reading up the latest information on the prevention of children's diseases, interviews with other doctors, and the author's experiences with her own boy and girl.

Notes: This information story might have been a dry and pedantic dissertation—but it isn't. The reasons it isn't are to be found in the devices that the author has used to give color and vividness to the story. Notice that "I" makes its appearance in the first sentence; that the account of the telephone conversation introduces action at the same time that it sets the theme of the story; that a touch of personal experience is introduced with Mrs. Shultz's reference to her own son and daughter.

Although the interview with the doctor in the State Department of Health was an actual one, the name of the state is not given. To have done so would have localized the story. That would be disadvantageous in a magazine of national circulation.

Several years ago Ray Giles, an experienced magazine writer, wrote a book on life insurance which was filled with case histories, and packed with facts. Later when *Better Homes & Gardens* wanted to do something about this subject, the editor, remembering Giles' book, got in touch with him. Together they planned a series of short articles on life insurance. Usually one is run each month, but sometimes when the magazine is tight the insurance article is left out. "Early-Bird Bargains" on Page 29 is one of this series.

Going on from 40

GOING ON FROM 40

By Constance J. Foster

Reprinted by special permission from Good Housekeeping

Assuming that the women who read *Good Housekeeping* range in age from fifteen to eighty-five, the forty-fifty decade would hit right at the center of the magazine's reader group. That may be one reason why *Good Housekeeping* published "Going on from 40." But more important was the vital, close-home nature of the subject matter and the thorough and authoritative way in which it was handled.

I don't mind telling you now that I'm going to have a fortieth birthday next year. March fourteenth, to be exact. That is an unusual admission—we used to call it confession—for a woman to make. But I have recently had an unusual experience.

A few months ago I set out on a personal pilgrimage. As an intelligent parent, I am preparing my children for adolescence. I decided to be an equally intelligent individual and learn *how to be middle-aged.*

All around me I saw women who regarded forty as the deadline. Some were bewildered and at loose ends. Others were discouraged about their prospects for the future. All of them were frightened at the thought of growing older, and resentful of losing their youth. I found exceptions, of course. There are glorious women in the world today whose usefulness and gallantry make them ageless. Among my friends I know a few happy though forty plus. But they can be counted on the fingers of one hand.

Must the forties be dangerous? Must they mean the beginning of boredom?

Need I spend them playing bridge or drifting forlornly from beauty parlor to motion picture? Why do so many people seem to think that forty is synonymous with such dreary words as "shelved," "divorce," and "gigolo"?

Soon my children will be leaving home for college and marriage. Can I wave them off cheerfully, refusing to be a "silver cord"? What new outlets may the middle-aged woman find to take the place of her long years of active mothering? I asked myself whether it was more important to take a lift in my face or a lift in my psyche. Should I stop at exercising middle-aged curves? Or is there some way to massage mind and spirit to new courage and activity?

I set myself to find out. Unlike Ponce de Leon's futile search for a mythical Fountain of Youth, my quest proved as full of rewards as a good child's Christmas stocking. It took me straight to the front doorstep of modern science. First I had to know whether there were enough years left to make it worth while for me to learn how to live them effectively. The statistician could tell me.

In his office on the twenty-third floor of the Metropolitan Life Insurance Company building, Dr. Louis I. Dublin had the latest figures spread out for me in the form of black-and-white charts. They do not encourage the delusion that life begins at forty. But neither do they indicate that it ends there.

"If you are white, forty, and a woman," Dr. Dublin told me, "your life expectancy is 32.15 years. That is three years more than it would have been if you had celebrated your fortieth birthday back in 1910. If you live out this allotted span, you will automatically earn a further dividend of nine years."

I added it up in my head. Forty plus thirty-two plus nine. It came to eighty-one years that the life-insurance statistics said I might reasonably expect to live! In that light forty took on new dignity and importance. The years ahead were not just so much time to be whiled away or wasted. They represented more than half a lifetime! They were the good years, the years during which I could enjoy and make use of what had been learned, often painfully, during the first half.

What could I do to make them count? School days were far behind me. Had I slipped enough mentally to make new achievements doubtful? I asked Professor Edward L. Thorndike of Teachers College, Columbia University.

In his little office tucked away in an obscure corner of the winding old buildings, Dr. Thorndike has been busy making important discoveries about those moot years after forty. His experiments in the field of adult learning and education have pinned orchids on middle age!

Professor Thorndike dotes on controversial

subjects and has been busy shocking the educational world for forty years. He devised a series of experiments to discover just how dull Grandma really is. His conclusions are startling. They completely demolish the old adage that you can't teach an old dog new tricks.

Hundreds of thousands of tests given over a period of years to subjects of all ages prove that mental powers fall off much more slowly than we imagined—only about one percent a year. Childhood is not, as we supposed, the best age for learning. Any age below forty-five is better than ten to fourteen. Nor is the decline of ability in later years rapid. A woman of sixty-five may expect to learn at least half as much per hour as she could at the age of twenty-five, and much more than she could at eight or ten.

"Any adult between twenty-one and seventy," Dr. Thorndike told me, "can learn anything in which he is really interested with little or no greater effort than at fifteen."

I glanced around the high-ceilinged, loftlike room whose walls are covered with shelves that hold manila envelopes crammed full of tests and data. Dr. Thorndike admits that he remembers what is in every last one of them! But he claims no special mental faculties to account for the feat.

"It's because I'm interested," he explained. "Interest is the vital factor in education. No one can learn with any facility what doesn't interest him, whether he is six or sixty. That's your real clue if you want to go on growing. We are all born with certain abilities. If you have a vital interest in anything from painting pictures to collecting butterflies, it's safe to say that you have an innate ability which is educable. The greater the interest, the easier you learn and remember. Age doesn't count much. Whatever differences exist between you and your children are moderate and will not prevent your doing anything at forty-five that you did at twenty-five."

Before my enthusiasm sent me rushing off to sign up for a course in current events or voice culture, I asked Professor Thorndike for a few tricks to make going back to school easier.

"Reward yourself for every achievement," he advised. "Human beings are like the trained seal in the circus. The trainer slips him a herring at the end of his act. Psychologically it's a sound procedure. The human animal requires 'satisfiers,' too. Often praise is enough. So pat yourself on the back. Take pride in your performance. Cultivate a few 'plus' gestures—treat yourself to a seat for a matinee or a new hat as a reward for work well done. Rewards are far more effective in learning than punishment."

"Anything else?" I coaxed.

"Yes. Another good rule is not to expect too much. It took you probably a hundred hours to master two or three simple books in economics or chemistry in high school or college. Don't be discouraged if you don't get much from ten hours of study now. Adult study groups and women's-club courses often attempt to go too fast and cover too much ground. Don't bite off more than you can mentally chew and digest at a sitting."

The conclusions for the middle-aged woman are obvious. Professor Thorndike's long and painstaking experiments on what make the cranial wheels go round prove that she can take on new skills *as long as she wants to!* The trouble is that she doesn't always want to.

A healthy curiosity about life, a wholesome skepticism, and a vital interest are necessary. She must stay open-minded, and she must say no to the temptation of all comfortable ruts. No one needs to be dull, stodgy, or boring. Those are states of mind which cannot be blamed on the mere physical procession of the years. They can be laid only to the individual's growing lack of desire for new ideas and new experiences. Hardening of the arteries may be due to old age. Hardening of the mind is not. It is self-imposed.

While I was in the neighborhood, I dropped in on Dr. Henry Clapp Sherman, professor of chemistry at Columbia University. Professor Sherman, in case you don't know, is the man whose name you see when you consult the statements of the vitamin content of foods and vitamin concentrates. His research in the fields of vitamins has established him as an authority on the subject.

I found him in his laboratory at Havemeyer Hall, where he and his rats have been making history in chemistry and nutrition. It is a history that is particularly pertinent to the middle years of life. For Professor Sherman's rats have been busy eating through forty rat generations for you and me. They have dutifully eaten certain diets just adequate to keep the family going—and died young. They have eaten certain other diets and waxed sleek, shown higher vitality, and lived longer than the life span of their kind. What possible connection has a rat's daily menu with the well-being of the woman at forty? A great deal. For it seems that the rat resembles the human being very closely in the chemistry of its nutrition.

But let Dr. Sherman himself explain what his experiments mean when translated in terms of men and women.

"The increase in the rat's life span, achieved by the use of a diet enriched in what we call the protective foods, is equivalent to an extension of about seven years in the human being."

In other words, the human family can eat its way to seven more years of life by following the guidance of the nutrition laboratory. But that isn't all. Merely living to a great age is in itself of doubtful advantage. But the newer chemistry of nutrition promises to enable us to look, act, and feel no older at seventy-five or eighty than we ordinarily would at sixty-five! It extends the prime of life cycle. For the individual this means not a longer old age. It means more years lived on a level of optimum health and happiness. Dr. Sherman put it scientifically for me:

"Starting with a dietary already adequate according to our current standards," he explained, "we may by enrichment of the diet in certain of its chemical factors, through an increase in the proportion of protective foods, induce higher adult vitality and postpone old age in the same individual."

The protective foods are *milk, green vegetables, and fruit!* In these you have the secret of long years that are full of buoyancy, a fresh complexion, and vivid charm. For these protective foods definitely tend to preserve the characteristics of youth; they supply the body with the minerals and vitamins it needs to keep resilient and active.

Dr. Sherman himself drinks a quart of milk a day and looks in the pink of condition. By actual count he found that he consumed 3259 servings of fruits and vegetables in the course of a year. (He kept a record for four years in a little notebook that he carries in his vest pocket!) This is equivalent to about 800 pounds of these foods as they are delivered to the kitchen door.

His diet gives less prominence to meats and sweets than the average American diet to which most of us are accustomed. It involves no significant change in the quantity of eggs and butter, and includes about the same amount of breadstuffs and cereals, but uses more than half of them in the less highly milled or whole-grain forms.

"A safe rule to follow, guided by the newer knowledge of nutrition," advised Dr. Sherman, "is to see that at least as much of your food budget is spent for milk, cream, and cheese as for meat, fish, and poultry. At least as much should also be spent for fruits and vegetables as you pass across the butcher's counter."

I wondered how this would appeal to the large number of women who go in for dieting. Would they fear that milk was too fattening?

"A good precept in reducing," insisted Dr. Sherman, "is 'no calories without vitamins.' Reduce your calorie intake among the foods that are not important sources of the needed mineral elements and vitamins. You can obtain this information from any good textbook on nutrition. Certainly milk is one of the foods that no one can safely cut out of the diet."

I stopped at the corner drugstore for a glass of milk! I decided to go to see my doctor. I had never before consulted him unless I had to. People usually don't! But I knew that a machine is no better than its individual parts. Sometimes a little thing can strip the gears or be the monkey wrench thrust into the mechanism. The years ahead, the years that were beginning to shine out as the bright ones, were mine to enjoy only if I brought them a healthy, sound body. I proposed to check up on my human machine.

"There's nothing wrong with me so far as I know," I admitted a little sheepishly to Dr. John E. Tritsch, who is one of New York City's leading gynecologists. "This time I'm not even going to have a baby—just a birthday! I'm a lady in waiting—for forty!"

"I wish more women would do themselves the favor of letting a doctor usher their birthdays as well as their offspring into the world," he grinned. "Middle age marks the beginning of the degenerative diseases. Especially after forty everybody ought to have periodic health examinations."

"Once a year?" I asked.

"Every six months is playing safer. It gives the doctor a chance to catch trouble in time."

He put me through the routine laboratory tests—blood pressure, urine analysis, hemoglobin. My blood pressure proved low. It probably accounted for my general feeling of lassitude. A series of injections of glandular extracts gave me new pep to get things done in the days that followed.

Modern medicine makes lagging glands behave themselves. Nowadays there is no need for a woman to put up with lack of energy on the grounds of her age. Let her tell her doctor about it, instead of taking it out on her family. He will enlist the new gland therapy to help her.

Lifting my eyelids, Dr. Tritsch flashed little lights into my eyes.

"The eye-ground test is important after forty," he explained. "Arteriosclerotic changes often show up first in the retina."

A complete physical examination from top to toe gave me a clean bill of health. Organically I was sound, with heart and lungs like those of a healthy young ox.

I was luckier than some women who have come to him—too late. There was the one who ignored a swollen, congested condition of the breast. It couldn't be cancer, she reasoned. Didn't cancer always start with a localized lump? But it *was* cancer. She's dead. Had she seen a good doctor six months earlier, she might have been saved. Six months isn't long—just the difference between life and death.

"Don't ignore any symptoms after forty," advised Dr. Tritsch. "Any little lumps, swelling, or tenderness may be benign. But don't take it for granted. Find out. Let your doctor be the optimist. I want especially to warn women not to ignore excessive menstruation at this age. Many think that it is merely a manifestation of the menopause. It may be. If so, glandular inoculations will help. Meantime the doctor has the patient under observation. Often vaginal bleeding is the first sign of cancer. That need not frighten you. The truth never killed anyone. Being afraid to discover it in time kills thousands."

He put me on the scales and added another medical warning for middle age.

"Don't allow yourself to become fat! Added pounds are dangerous after forty. It's a good idea to follow this general rule: A few pounds overweight during childhood and early youth; normal weight during the twenties and thirties; a few pounds underweight (about five percent) from then on. You'll live longer, feel better, and get more done. You wouldn't think of overfeeding your dog. Why not be as fair to yourself? Like dogs, human beings past middle age are better off if they're always a little bit hungry!"

"The wages of a chocolate sundae at sixteen," I mourned, "is only the price listed on the menu. But a sundae at forty-five is a double chin and a spare tire around the waist!"

"That's because there is a drop in the rate of basal metabolism in the late thirties or early forties," he explained. "After that happens the body requires less food to do its work. Two hundred calories a day, stored, mean seventeen additional pounds of body weight in a year. There are fifty calories in a single chocolate caramel. A sundae boasts about five hundred!"

"I have a friend who eats anything she wants and just takes a couple of little pills before each meal," I suggested hopefully. "She buys them at the drugstore. They're guaranteed to let you eat your cake and look as if you hadn't!"

Dr. Tritsch shook his head soberly. "Look out for patent reducing medicines," he cautioned. "Most of them contain extracts of the thyroid gland, which should never be taken except under a doctor's orders. The bath salts sold for the same purpose merely subtract fluid from the superficial tissues. Drink a glass of water, and you put it all back again. There's no royal road to anything—least of all to weight control. You can't drug or soak your way to slimness. If you value your health, keep thin after forty—by not eating any more calories than you need."

I knew that Dr. Tritsch had been instrumental in working out certain new combinations of pain-relief methods for childbirth. Tried recently on over six hundred cases at Metropolitan Hospital on Welfare Island, the ether oil and salts of barbituric acid proved highly successful. I asked why science couldn't get busy and do something to help women through the menopause. I was thinking of the hot flashes and dizziness, the disturbing mental and emotional states that make some women actual strangers to themselves and their families during this critical period.

"Science is doing things to take all dread from the menopause," he assured me. "No woman needs to approach the middle forties with fear. It is not necessary for her to suffer from the endocrine changes that distressed her mother and her grandmother. Of course not everyone requires help. Some women go through the experience with few or no symptoms. For the others there are newly discovered glandular extracts that definitely alleviate physical and emotional disturbances. This applies also to those cases where surgical interference has induced an artificial menopause. Injections of theelin, a hormone produced by the ovary and placenta, give relief. Clinical evidence is not complete, but there are some doctors who believe that in favorable instances theelin actually defers the menopause for several years. It is no longer the ordeal that it used to be. Modern gland therapy makes it a natural, uncomplicated process."

"What about all the so-called rejuvenators one reads about in the papers?" I puzzled. "You know—shots of this or that hormone to restore lost youth?"

He smiled. "The problem is much deeper than any artificial interference. Don't forget that the emotions influence the endocrines quite as much as the other way around. It's a highly complicated interrelationship. Better not tamper with it. Keep healthy and happy, and the chances are that your glands will take care of themselves."

Going to the doctor had been worth while, if only to discover that there was nothing wrong with me. But I was due for a jolt. Dr. Tritsch had one bit of professional advice left to deliver as I was leaving.

"See an eye man, I think he'll find that you need to wear glasses. And have your dentist X-ray those teeth. Better have them out if he discovers an abscessed root condition. There's nothing like bad teeth in the forties to cause rheumatism in the fifties!"

Have my teeth out? Wear glasses? It was a blow to my pride. Suddenly I found that I didn't *want* to be forty! I didn't *want* to be middle-aged! For a long, dark moment it began to look synonymous with crutches and a wheel chair!

I blurted out my sorrows to David Seabury, who is used to people's troubles. He's been listening to them for twenty years. As a practical psychologist who has helped thousands of clients to happiness, he knows how to fish folks out of hot water. I consulted him because I hoped that he could teach me to say yes to forty.

Tremendously big, with a gray Van Dyke and eyes that laugh a lot, he reminded me of a grown-up Pan who will always radiate a sense of spring and the first morning of the world. He's that vital and alive.

"False teeth!" he chuckled. "People waste enough psychic energy hating dental plates to solve the problems of technological unemployment. But it takes adults to remodel the face of our troubled world—not swingtime papas and hot mamas!"

"People hate being told to be their age," I reminded him.

"There are three ages," he told me. "They have very little to do with each other. It's their chronological age people hate being told to be. But at one and the same time you can be forty years old physically, three years old emotionally, and intellectually as ripe-minded as the philosopher of seventy! You have no choice about your chronological age. But you can select the other two for yourself."

"How?" I wanted to know.

"When she was eighty-five, my grandmother said to me—'David, I'm never going to be old.'" He smiled reminiscently. "And she never was. She had the pinkest cheeks and the reddest lips! She caught them like a contagion from living. She used to love to scramble down a steep river bank up in Maine where she lived. Many a woman of thirty-five would have hesitated to attempt it. Life was an adventure to her. You're old when you stop daring to live dangerously.

You're young, no matter what your birth certificate says, as long as you find life always opening up thrillingly ahead."

"But life is getting so much more complicated all the time," I protested. "Isn't that a part of the trouble?"

"That's where you're wrong," he corrected. "Life isn't more complicated. Life has always been the same. It's civilization that is complicated. It's what we've done to life that is making things difficult and confused for us. Spell 'live' backwards, and see what you get."

"E-v-i-l!" I discovered.

"Exactly. Anything that's against life—is evil. That's not a matter of morals or ethics. It's a natural law. Oppose it at your own risk. You wouldn't think of asking an apple tree to be accommodating enough to grow an orange for you. But a lot of women find themselves utterly confused at middle age because all their lives they've been turning themselves inside out, trying to be and do all the different things that everyone expects of them."

"We call it self-sacrifice," I laughed. "We've been brought up to believe that unselfishness is a virtue."

"If you'd lived a few thousand years ago, you might have felt called on to offer up your child on an altar. They called that a sacrifice, too," he commented dryly.

"Then you think the middle-aged woman needs to learn a basic philosophy of self-expansion," I prodded.

"Dare to be yourself!" he exploded. "Don't let other people nibble the edges off you as if you were a cookie. It will only give them spiritual indigestion and keep you living at half capacity."

"But the false teeth?" I murmured timidly.

"False teeth! They don't matter a tinker's dam. It's false sentiments about herself and her loved ones, false emotional attitudes toward life, that every woman of forty should hate and refuse to be aged by. Because they do age her. They hammer at her endocrine glands, etch lines in her face, and steal the resiliency from her body tissues."

I asked him what emotional conflicts the middle-aged woman was most prone to.

"Dozens of 'em!" he said cheerfully. "That's why the forties have such a reputation for being dangerous. As a woman approaches the menopause, any emotional conflicts that weren't resolved at adolescence automatically break through again. So we have a tremendous number of middle-aged nervous breakdowns and mental crack-ups."

The little white room was very still. A psychiatrist's inner sanctum always gives me a feeling of being on a different planet, detached from time and space. But David Seabury was talking about things that had to do with the here-and-now problems of every woman in the world. He went on thoughtfully:

"Too many women reach the forties still demanding to be what I call 'beloveds.' They want to be the adored little princesses that they were at three or four, sitting on a throne surrounded by an admiring audience who continue to shout, 'The Queen can do no wrong!' That sort of attitude makes an emotional parasite of a woman. She thinks it is her right to be loved, without doing anything to earn it.

"From my long experience in adjusting marital tangles, I can safely say this—*I have never seen any good come out of the desire to be loved!* The moment we demand love, the other person retreats. It's an instinctive reaction against being possessed. Jealousy and possessiveness are a hangover from the cave. Truly civilized individuals shudder away from it. It isn't until we *give* love that we meet success.

"All life, you see, comes down to a nice relation between the principles of *give* and *take*. Be able and willing to take—dare to take those things from life that nourish you as a personality. Be quick and glad to give those things that sustain those with whom you are in constant intimacy."

"You're rather famous for your quick cuts to happiness," I reminded him as I was leaving. "Will you give me a few aphorisms for the forties?"

Here they are:

The beginning of all reconstruction is *being willing to have it so*. Don't waste energy resisting what you can't change.

Get ready for middle age in youth. Get ready for old age in your forties.

Ignore gossip. There are always small souls who hate to see you happy and free.

Copies come cheap. Be an original model—of *yourself*!

Everyone has a saturation point. *This means you!* Set a limit on what you are willing to endure from others.

Love your family, but don't trade on the coin of affection.

Are the things you regard as your duties real or just states of mind?

Every woman needs to be needed—but not *kneaded* by her friends and relatives!

Never give up all your interests because they conflict with your husband's. It makes you dull to him. He loses the girl he fell in love with.

Don't have a series of set ideas that invalidate your thinking. It ages you.

Never be "unselfish" as a means of satisfying your ego. If you're a Lady Bountiful, you're no lady!

What were the things you used to like to do best? Travel? Paint? Write? Do them now. Do them adventurously.

What sort of fun do you crave for your old age? Start having it!

Get yourself a philosophy of life. Use it like a jack to change tires when life gives you a flat or a blowout.

A philosophy of life! To turn to the man of God for it was as natural as breathing. My father had been a minister. As a child I took my problems to his study. But his big chair is empty now.

I strolled up Park Avenue in the sunshine that slanted obliquely between the rows of tall white buildings. Christ Methodist Episcopal Church stands at the corner of Sixtieth Street. It is here that Dr. Ralph W. Sockman ministers to the intangibles of the human spirit that science cannot see through its microscopes or weigh on its most delicate scales.

Until recently Dr. Sockman was President of the Greater New York Federation of Churches.

I found him behind his desk, preparing one of the radio talks that have won him such a large unseen audience. If I had to characterize him in one word, I should have a hard time to choose between "tolerant" and "human." Perhaps they are the same thing. At any rate, he isn't concerned with the hereafter to the exclusion of being, like the Lord, "a very present help in time of trouble!" That was a comfort, since being forty was a problem that couldn't wait for eternity.

"A philosophy of life!" he exclaimed. "Finding it is half the fun of being forty! Maybe you've been looking at all the limitations and responsibilities of middle age. Turn the picture around and study it from another angle. It's like those puzzles where you hunt for things hidden in the trees and bushes. Forty has privileges, too—loads of them."

"Name one!" I challenged, like the little girl whose mother told her that lots of children liked spinach.

"More time to think things out," he contributed. "Before forty no woman has a chance to be an armchair philosopher. She's too busy, too rushed and hurried. But as the pressure relaxes and the children begin to get out from under her heels, she has an opportunity to revalue the things she has always taken for granted. She can dust off her mental shelves and get rid of the bric-a-brac and the whatnots that clutter up her thinking. Middle age is the time for spiritual house cleaning."

"How does one begin?" I wondered.

"Make a game of it. A game that you play with yourself," he suggested. "Project yourself impersonally on the screen of life and watch yourself perform as if you were your favorite movie actress. Study your actions, your thoughts, your motives. How much of what you say is genuinely kind? How much of it is what women call catty? You may be in for some startling surprises if you play fair and are ruthlessly honest. At least you'll discover what you're really like. Are you a scattered person? It means that you need to learn the wisdom of making choices. Have you a well-adjusted personality? Use it like a springboard from which to jump into new interests and activities that express the real *you.*"

He leaned back in his chair behind the great mahogany flat-top desk where his papers were spread out. Half-closing his eyes, he went on thoughtfully: "We sentimentalize about youth. It isn't the happiest time of life. If you could listen to some of the troubles young people bring to me! They're uncertain about everything. Middle age has lost that confusion. It's less angular, more mellow and serene. Sixteen is a lovely age to be—for a year! But it unfolds through progressive stages into something much more beautiful, like the butterfly emerging from the cocoon."

"Then a philosophy of life for middle age doesn't need to be a sort of consolation prize," I discovered.

"It should leave plenty of room at the top for glory," he smiled. "But remember that no one can serve you up a philosophy of life on a platter. Because then it wouldn't be yours. It would be like a hand-me-down dress. Maybe it would be too big for you. Maybe it would be too small. You must work out your own philosophy. It doesn't matter much what it is, so long as it 'speaks to your condition,' as the Quakers say. One woman may find it in church, another in the out-of-doors under the night sky, still another in the quiet of her own room. But if it works, for *you,* it's all one and the same thing. It's forty—*finding God!*"

We walked out together through the gallery that overhangs the lovely Byzantine interior of the church auditorium with its marble columns and crimson-velvet pews. I felt a sense of reverence that I did not leave behind me. It went singing up the Avenue with me.

Middle age was suddenly no burden. It was the blossom bursting into fruit. And, as everyone knows, ripe fruit is sweetest.

Forty is only a way station on the journey. No woman needs to take advantage of its stopover privileges for long. Resurgence is the law of life. The loveliest scenery, the most stirring sights, lie always ahead if we refuse to tarry behind.

My quest was over. But in my heart I knew that it was just beginning. And for a moment I was a girl, graduating again from high school. I was wearing a white dress, and I was sitting on a high platform listening to a beloved, gray-haired principal speak the lines with which he always closed our school Commencements:

"Grow old along with me!
The best is yet to be,
The last of life, for which the first was made:
Our times are in His hand
Who saith, 'A whole I planned,
Youth shows but half; trust God: see all, nor be afraid!' "

This time I understood what the words meant!

Questions:

To what elemental emotions in the reader does this article make its appeal?

Would you have liked the story better or less well if the personal element had been kept out and the results of the interviews presented impersonally?

How would you phrase the central theme of this story?

Why were drawings used instead of photographs?

Animals *Do* Think

No one ever taught Gunda, the elephant, how to hoodwink her keeper by robbing the cash box

by PAUL W. KEARNEY

ANIMALS DO THINK

No One Ever Taught Gunda, the Elephant, How to Hoodwink Her Keeper by Robbing the Cash Box

By Paul W. Kearney

Reprinted by special permission from Esquire

The newspaper assignment which sends a reporter to the zoo to get an animal yarn is almost an annual ritual. In early American newspapers the fabulous sea serpent was a newspaper standby. Kipling made a good share of his living out of the beasts of the jungle. And, currently, Frank Buck and Mrs. Johnson haven't lacked audiences for their animal stories.

Why?

Shall we take time out for a bit of Freudian speculation? To wit: We are animals too, but superior animals. And we are gratified by a demonstration of our superiority. Animals do think, but oh how little, we say, compared with us. By and large we are vastly supercilious toward animals, particularly those which have got themselves put into cages. But that isn't the whole story. No. Strange, complex creatures that we are, we entertain a suppressed envy of the beast's simplicity and courage, of his beauty, of his singleness of purpose. And withal, we say, we can learn much from beasts of how men can act when, in the frenzy of war or hunger or ambition, they themselves become bestial.

However all this may be, the animal story appears perennially in newspapers and magazines.

One day I stood idly in the Primate House at the zoo watching a man try to throw a peanut to an orangutan. The visitor's delivery was awkward and his aim very poor, and when the fourth successive peanut fell short of the orang's outstretched hand, the ape gave every evidence of deep disgust.

Relinquishing his grip on the bars, he rummaged around in the straw until he found an empty peanut shell. And then, with an easy, underhand toss, he pitched it directly into the man's hands.

"That's the way it's done," the animal seemed to say. And when my mind finally grasped the significance of an ape's teaching a human being a trick, I couldn't help chuckling at the many heated discussions I've heard on the theme of instinct versus reasoning in animal mentality.

I've seen bears at the zoo retrieve a piece of bread from the pool on a cold day without getting wet by the ingenious expedient of pawing the water until the swirling currents brought the food within grasp. I've seen an elephant snare a peanut beyond his reach by blowing a blast of air against the side wall so that the deflected draft carried the nut toward him. I even know of a grey parrot in a private home who, although he couldn't fly, repeatedly climbed up the forbidden window curtain over two feet away from his perch.

Nobody could figure out how he did it until the owner finally spied on him and discovered that the smart bird would flap his wings violently until the air current wafted the curtain within reach. Then he'd grab hold with his beak and climb right up.

If that isn't thinking out a problem, I don't know what is. But then I'm not a scientist and the dividing line between instinct and reason is often difficult to define.

Pursuing the question further, therefore, I paid a visit to a man who for thirty-five years has probably had closer contact with more different kinds of animals than any individual in the country: Dr. W. Reid Blair, Director of the New York Zoological Park. Aside from several thousand birds and reptiles, the Zoo normally houses from five hundred to six hundred different mammals ranging all the way from the two common house cats who live in the Bird House (and have been taught never to molest the birds!) to such rare creatures as the okapi and the duck-billed platypus.

"Do animals ever think?" I asked the affable Dr. Blair.

"Yes," he answered, "I firmly believe that they very often do. We have seen evidences of it here, through the years, that are very convincing: we have had scientists here, like Professor Yerkes and Dr. Haggerty and Professor Garner and others who have subjected various animals to elaborate mental tests in which instinct could not seem to play much of a role.

"Such experiments are pretty conclusive. But before we get to them, let me tell you two stories that have become classics in Park lore: one about an orangutan and the other about an elephant.

"Passing through the Primate House one day I noticed that the swing in Dohong's cage was broken. The nut had sheared off the eye bolt, allowing the bar to hang loose at one end; so I instructed the keeper to call the blacksmith in to repair the bolt.

"A few minutes later on my way back through the house I noticed that the orang was swinging merrily on the bar. Realizing that the blacksmith couldn't have gotten there and finished the job so soon, I was puzzled enough to investigate and I waited to see what could be seen.

"The simple explanation is that Dohong had figured out that if he held the bar with a sort of quarter-turn, it would not slip off the eye bolt, so that is the way he would grasp it. However, the bolt fitted so snugly into the hole that it was not easy to force it through. But the ape also figured out that when he moistened the bolt with saliva, the lubrication simplified matters.

"Those two things in themselves show a pretty fine brand of native intelligence, but they are only part of the story. Dohong knew from experience that visitors like a show, and this new situation gave him an idea. Gathering up all the straw in the cage, he made a large, soft bed of it at the proper spot on the floor: then he would climb up, repair the bar and begin to swing back and forth until his activity had attracted a goodly number of amused spectators.

"When the audience was big enough to suit him, Dohong, with the showmanship inherent in the apes, would relax his twist on the bar; it would slip off the bolt, and down he would come with a thump in the pile of prepared straw with every evidence of stunned surprise which made the public deception complete in every respect."

Naturally, as Dr. Blair explained in more formal terms, the act was a wow with the crowd and Dohong would repeat it fifty times a day if there was a "good house" as they say in show business. In fact, he got so much fun out of it that the director decided not to repair the swing—that is, not until the ape presently discovered for himself Archimedes' principle of the lever and began to pry everything loose that was fastened inside the cage!

Pretty keen reasoning, from beginning to end, for nobody showed that orangutan how to hold the bar securely, how to lubricate it, how to kid the public with the fake tumble, or how to pry out the brackets on the wall.

By the same token, nobody taught Gunda, the elephant, how to hoodwink her keeper into giving her unearned tidbits: she doped it all out herself.

It came about because the keeper thought it would be fun to teach Gunda to take pennies from visitors and put them in a cash box at the upper part of the cage. He rigged up a box with a bell in it which would ring whenever Gunda dropped a coin in—and whenever the bell rang, the elephant got some choice tidbit for a reward.

Gunda learned the trick in less than a day's tutelage, and hundreds if not thousands of children have got a great kick out of seeing the mammoth creature take a penny in its trunk, wave it gracefully aloft and drop it into the cash box. Gunda also learned very quickly, however, that when business was slack, she could slip her trunk quietly into the box, suck out a penny and then drop it in again so the bell rang for the reward.

Discovering this deception eventually, the keeper thwarted it by lining the bottom of the box with staples between which the pennies would fall beyond the suction power of the beast's trunk.

With the philosophic mien which distinguishes all elephants, Gunda accepted this setback with good grace and settled down to a decent, clean life again. Or so they thought for many months until one fine day the bell in the cash box tinkled and the keeper appeared somewhat more promptly than usual, with a favored morsel. To his astonishment, there wasn't hide nor hair of a single visitor in the Elephant House! But the bell had rung.

Gunda, her trunk extended beseechingly, stood there as the personification of four tons of sweet innocence. But the keeper knew there was larceny in the house and he decided to watch whenever the circumstances permitted.

What he discovered, after weeks of surveillance, was that Gunda was gypping him as neatly and as legally as any corporation lawyer could have contrived. On Sundays, when the crowds were large and pennies frequent, Gunda would not put every one in the cash box—she'd hold out every third or fourth one and bunk it up on the ledge above her head. Then, on pay days and rainy days when business was slow, she'd dip into the sock, as it were, for pennies which rang the bell and brought the reward!

Pretty shrewd, all right. And after you've searched the jungle life of the elephant for any precedent which might explain it on the theory of instinct, you've got to admit that it was pure reasoning.

The more you wander about the zoo and talk to the men who work there, the more impressed you are by their tales of the things these animals do on their own initiative. On a cool night, for example, all the elephants will close their own doors when herded into the pens for the night—when the weather is warm, they leave them open.

That might be imitation, to be sure, but it seems like more than that. So does the story about the chimpanzee and the dingo dog who were convalescing in the zoo hospital at the same time. One thing the chimp learned from observation was that when the dingo was exercised, a keeper took his chain and walked him. So a dozen times a day the chimp would unhook the chain and take the dingo for a stroll.

One thing nobody taught him, however, was that the dingo loathed music. And one of his favorite amusements was to sit the poor dingo on top of a toy piano some keeper had brought in, banging out a discordant jangle on the keys while the wild dog howled an accompaniment with the fervid agony of a lost soul.

Everybody in the zoo, of course, has some story about Buddy, the most accomplished chimp now residing there, but I think the most illuminating insight into the ape's intelligence is provided by the circus incident. Some scientists took Buddy to the circus four or five years ago when the Ubangi women with the "soup plate lips" were first exhibited in this country. Of all the interesting things he saw there, these freak women apparently made the greatest impression on the ape's mind. For, to this day, if you go up to his cage and ask, "What kind of women did you see at the circus?" he will thrust out his lower lip to its most generous extremity.

Even in the handling of sick or injured animals there are many occasions when the patients display an intelligent comprehension of the situation which would do credit to a human. One time they had a llama with an abscess on the gum which had to be lanced. They had such a battle giving the suffering beast an anesthetic for the job that, a week later, they approached the task of cleaning and dressing the wound with great forebodings. To their amazement, the beast stood motionless and let the doctor repack the dressing without any restraint.

On another occasion a tiger with a splinter of beef bone wedged between her teeth went into a rampage of panic and pain. A dozen men prodded her into a "squeeze cage," threw a rope around her neck and pulled her head up so the doctor could examine her mouth. While he got out the forceps, the 450-pound beast fought with the fury of her kind against this rude restraint. But the instant the instrument touched the offending chip of bone, she realized they were trying to help her and she stood stock still until it was removed.

In her own way, Janet, the gorilla, demonstrated her reasoning powers to the hospital attendants while she was there by a cute little trick of holding out her arms imploringly to any attendant who chanced to pass her "bed." Whenever any of them would pause for the invited cuddle, Janet would dismiss the sentimentality with a quick caress—then turn the man around firmly and give him a lusty shove toward the feeding room.

Certainly the obvious intent is well-known to every nurse and orderly who ever worked in a human hospital!

Naturally, the apes are particularly impressive, especially in the things they can be taught. One can go through a bunch of keys and select the proper one to unlock a certain door; all of them can eat with knives and forks as well as any eight-year-old child—and better than some I've seen!

One chimp was taught to sew; Ellen could dress and undress herself in feminine clothes; Buddy can spit with deadly aim, give the well-known "Bronx cheer," flip a stone with his thumb and middle finger with perfect accuracy—and can whistle, which is a rare accomplishment even for an ape. Some time ago one keeper taught him how to salute the flag and then, for the amusement of the visitors, hung a little flag in his cage. No matter how many hundred times a day Buddy would pass that flag, he'd wheel, stand erect and salute with the solemnity of a congressman. It went over big until some army officer took exception to this degradation of the national colors!

All these things, to be sure, are just the whims and fancies of the men who work around the apes and they are cited merely to show how adept the animals are at learning, not for any scientific weight such an accomplishment as, say, a "Bronx cheer" may carry. In the serious field of experimentation, Professor Garner once tested one of the chimps with differently shaped blocks and found that very quickly the ape would give him, on request, the ball, the cube, the diamond, the triangle, or anything else specified from the assortment.

In the Yerkes and Haggerty experiments mentioned earlier by Dr. Blair, more complicated problems were given which called for definite reasoning powers. In one, for example, a banana was placed outside the cage and beyond the animal's reach. Inside the cage and unknown to the ape, two sticks were hidden in different places under the straw and the beast was left to his own devices.

At first the chimp would try to reach the fruit with his arms, but he would soon give that up as futile. His next step invariably was to look for a straw long and firm enough to reach the objective, and then that would be discarded. Eventually, in his search for a tool, he would come across the hidden sticks.

Either one alone would not suffice for the task, but when joined together they would do the trick. No ape tested ever failed to join the sticks in fairly short order.

Another test was to hang a banana from the ceiling and leave a few boxes of various sizes in different parts of the cage. Left to his own devices, the chimpanzee or the orangutan will very quickly begin experimenting with the piling of the boxes and in a short time will succeed in stacking them in proper relation to size so that he can safely climb up to the fruit. Of course, if the experimenter shows him how to do it first, the ape will grasp the idea in a flash.

Still another experiment with an orangutan involved a secreted stick with a hook on one end and a banana thrust so far into a hollow iron pipe lashed to the cage bars that the beast couldn't reach it with his fingers. The search for some implement eventually disclosed the hooked stick hidden in the straw.

And after several futile attempts to get the large end into the pipe, the orang finally caught on to the idea, turned the stick around, and speared the banana as intended.

The first time the ape was confronted with this entirely strange problem he solved it in twenty minutes.

After that he would get the banana out in about as many seconds until he ultimately discovered an even better way to do it than the experimenter had figured on. That came about when he accidentally pushed the banana out of the opposite end of the pipe in one test. From that time on he would merely thrust the stick into the tube, give it a wallop with his paw, and shoot the fruit out like a bullet without any of the trouble of fishing for it!

All of this is constructive thinking: the ability to meet an entirely alien situation and reason out a solution. Mimicry, memory or instinctive skills have no bearing in tests that are conceived purposely to avoid those factors, and in such problems the apes excel.

That is not to imply, however, that the apes are the only smart animals in the zoo. Where, for instance, is the ape who could be taught the difficult balancing feats the seals master so readily—or the prosaic tasks the working elephant learns to do in such an amazingly short time?

That, naturally, leads to the question, which are the most intelligent animals and how do they rate. So for the sake of limiting them to the headliners, I asked Dr. Blair for his list of the "ten best brains" in the animal kingdom.

For obvious reasons already set forth, Dr. Blair heads that list with the chimpanzee whose brilliant but impetuous mind is somewhat childlike. The chimp is likely to learn a lesson in a flash of perception. But if the solution to a problem isn't forthcoming quickly, he is quite apt to drop it impatiently for something more amusing.

Rating No. 2 on the list, the orangutan, a very close second, is more mature and deliberate in his reasoning and more persistent.

No. 3 is the elephant which, as Dr. Blair emphasizes, is the largest and most difficult to capture of all wild animals yet is the most philosophic and adaptable of any. Fresh from the jungle wilderness, an adult Indian elephant can be taught in thirty days to respond to sixteen different tasks on command.

When you realize that the schooling of most other animals which doesn't begin very early in life invariably proves a long, tedious task, the contrast gives an eloquent insight into the mental alertness of the elephant.

No. 4 is the gorilla who, in common with the other great apes, displays an almost human faculty for grasping an idea quickly. "Perhaps when we know him better," says Dr. Blair, "he will rate higher in the scale."

No. 5 is the domestic dog whose achievements invariably require far more patience and "doggedness" in training than do those of his animal betters. Furthermore, the dog holds a great advantage over his wild contemporaries because of his centuries of association with man's culture.

The beaver, that phenomenal engineering genius of the woods, rates sixth on the list, one step ahead of the domestic horse who shares the dog's advantage of contact with man.

No. 8 is the sea lion; avid imitator; juggler par excellence and extremely adept at learning a wide range of tasks quickly. The best showman in the zoo, the sea lion performs for rewards in the form of fish tidbits.

In contrast, the bear, rating No. 9, is the zoo's outstanding clown who will perform tirelessly for nothing more than the applause of his public. This in itself may indicate a slight mental deficiency but we didn't go into that phase.

Tenth on the list, to the disgust of a good many feline lovers, is the domestic cat. But Dr. Blair hastens to explain, perhaps to retain the votes of that constituency, that the house cat is usually underrated by casual observers because, being self-sufficient, independent and intensely proud, the feline will not tolerate very many tricks which a good many vapid people think are cute for animals to know. "The cat," says Dr. Blair, "is complete master of himself and in that very quality displays an intellectual integrity which commands respect."

Certainly it is true that no self-respecting cat will put up with the abuse from man which almost any dog will suffer with that dumb quality we are prone to misname "loyalty." Yet when you begin to base comparative ratings on solitary traits or abilities, you are straying away from the main issue which is the ability to reason.

Every keeper in every zoo has some favorite animal who is the smartest of them all. Indeed, nearly every home which harbors a dog has the smartest dog in the neighborhood—except mine, perhaps, where we have a bull terrier who can't be taught anything! Since his early puppyhood various members of the family have tried to sell him on the stock idea of "shaking hands" when he is asked for his paw.

And now, after twenty-two months, you can't coax, cajole or browbeat him into doing it simply because he has no taste for tricks of that sort.

However, if you come home some evening and find a sofa pillow strewn all over the house—and you let loose a mighty bellow of wrath and scurry for the whip—what does our stupid "Wiggles" do? Why, he sits up on his hind legs and offers you his paw just as nicely as any trained circus dog who ever lived!

Is he so dumb, after all? Indeed not. He has reasoned out after months of observing the family's earnest efforts at training that this "give-me-your-paw" business is the one thing they want him to do most. And although he objects to that sort of exhibitionism as a general practice, he knows darned well what we want—and he is smart enough to save it for the critical emergencies, which are many.

That is certainly rudimentary reasoning and that is the sort of thing you've got to look for when you begin to make comparative ratings of animal mentalities.

As Dr. Blair puts it, "when you talk about animal intelligence, you must define exactly what you mean.

"An ordinary mule, for example, is not generally considered very bright, yet he has brains enough to refuse food when he is hot and tired—he is smart enough to slow down physically in hot weather—he has sense enough to stop eating when he's had enough, no matter how much food may be left.

"You can call that thinking or you can call it instinct, whichever you prefer. But the fact remains that the entire medical profession benefits because so few human beings have as much native intelligence as the mule in these respects. And humans are supposed to think!"

Questions:

Were you interested in this story? If so put down ten reasons why.

Is there too much or too little scientific material as compared to anecdotal material in the story?

If the story had been submitted to the following magazines, which of them do you think would have considered buying it: *Boy's Life, Business Week, Farm Journal, Collier's, American Mercury, Pictorial Review, American, American Home*?

Would this story be equally good in any issue of the year? (It was published in the July issue of *Esquire*.)

What do the Women of America Think About WAR

WHAT DO THE WOMEN OF AMERICA THINK ABOUT WAR

By Henry F. Pringle

Reprinted by special permission from Ladies' Home Journal. Copyright 1938, The Curtis Publishing Company.

What people think is, frequently, news. The importance of the newspaper interview story is witness to this fact. The reason is, basically, that thoughts in the minds of men are precedent to their actions. What a president or a governor or an important industrialist thinks is often the forerunner of a law, an administrative ruling, or a new production policy.

In the past newspapers and magazines have in large measure got their opinion stories either from men whose special training or qualifications gave them the right to speak authoritatively on a given subject, or from men whose positions gave their words special weight.

A third kind of opinion story—that which reports mass opinions—is not easy to get. With the development, however, of mass-interview techniques, largely by Dr. George Gallup (see Chapter XVI), there has in the past year or two been a marked increase in the number of mass-opinion stories in American newspapers and magazines.

The *Ladies' Home Journal* began in the winter of 1938 a series of such articles in which the views of women all over the country on significant current questions were polled. The article "What Do the Women of America Think About War" is one of these.

No camouflaged transports will again steam stealthily toward a war-torn Europe if the women of America have anything to say about it. Nor will the women consent to sending troops to the Far East, or anywhere else, to engage in an overseas war. This month, in the Journal's survey, the women give their outspoken views on war and peace.

"Would you ever favor fighting an overseas war?" they were asked.

From 88 per cent of all the women came a ringing "No" to this question.

Yet this does not mean that the women of America believe that war is never justified. A majority of them, 64 per cent, said "Yes" to a question as to whether war might ever be justified. To the specific question of whether this country should fight if the United States or her possessions were invaded, the answer was even more definite.

"Yes," said 87 per cent of the women.

War flared in a million headlines as the Journal investigators made their rounds from house to house in villages, cities and in the rural areas of the United States. Radios, too, were blaring the danger of imminent conflict. The armies of Hitler were on the march. Spain was torn by civil strife. Japan was pushing farther into China. With all this the women were all too familiar. What, then, of the United States?

"Do you think the United States will be drawn into another war soon?" they were asked.

"No," was the answer which came from 56 per cent of all the women. For the Atlantic and the Pacific oceans are still wide and the United States has designs on no nation in all the world. But 44 per cent were afraid that war was close.

"There's so much unrest in other countries and they are infringing on our rights all the time," said an engineer's wife in Salamanca, New York. A woman doctor in Chicago said that a war would surely have to be fought "to protect our own best interests here and abroad." A lawyer's wife in San Francisco thought that "greedy people who will profit" would, sooner or later, force the United States into some conflict. On the other hand an unmarried woman, employed as court clerk in Racine, Wisconsin, said there would be no war. "I think we learned a little from the World War," she insisted.

II

Twenty-one years have passed since the people of America, high with hope and believing their cause to be right, went into that war. The women, it is now apparent, have thought a great deal during those two decades.

In 1917, when President Wilson at last and reluctantly led his country into war, it was widely believed that the people of the Eastern and Western seaboards were behind him but that the Middle West was opposed. It is now clear that the majority of women of all sections of the nation believe participation in the World War to have been a mistake. In all the questions on war and peace, in fact, geographical lines play small or no part in the opinions of America's women. For instance:

"No," said 61 per cent of the New England women, in answer to whether we should have entered the World War.

"No," said 62 per cent of the Southern women.

"No," said 63 per cent of the Rocky Mountain area women.

"No," said 73 per cent of the women in Ohio, Michigan, Indiana and Illinois.

"No," echoed 72 per cent of the women who live on the broad prairies of Iowa, the Dakotas, Kansas, Missouri and Nebraska.

On the Pacific Coast, alone, were the negative answers substantially more in the majority. The women of California, Oregon and Washington returned an 87 per cent verdict against the folly of the World War.

Even greater agreement marked the answers of the various age, religious, marital and other classifications on "Should we have entered the World War?" Here is the vote:

Question: Should we have entered the World War?

	YES	NO
National	30%	70%
Urban	30	70
Farm	28	72
Small Town	30	70
Protestant	29	71
Catholic	34	66
All others	29	71
Married women and widows	30	70
Divorced	26	74
Single	30	70
Income Groups		
Under $1500 a year	32	68
Over $1500 a year	27	73
Age Groups		
Under 30 years	30	70
30-45 years	32	68
Over 45 years	27	73

Cynicism has mounted in the hearts and minds of the women in the twenty-one years since the bands played "Over There" and orators boomed forth that this was a glorious struggle to save democracy. "We were just the goat for the Allies," remarked, bitterly, a hat salesman's wife in Cleveland when asked to give her reason for believing that entry had been a colossal mistake. An insurance salesman's wife in Philadelphia branded the war a "waste of our man power and resources," and added that "no spiritual or material benefit" had been gained. There were, of course, affirmative answers. A farmer's wife in Frederick, Maryland, pointed out "they bombed our ships—we had to go in." Another farm woman in Leland, Mississippi, thought that the war "brought us into closer sympathy with other nations."

But these were minority views. Again and again the women said that money, trade, propaganda, Big Business, had been the actual forces which caused America to enter the war. A specific question applied to this. "Were Wall Street bankers chiefly responsible for getting us into the World War?" Most significant in the general affirmative answer to this—64 per cent of all the women said "Yes"—is the revelation that wealth and poverty had little bearing on what the women thought.

"Yes," said 67 per cent of the women whose incomes average less than $1500 a year.

"Yes," said 61 per cent of the women with more than $1500 a year.

Again there was substantial agreement among farm, city and small-town women. Again the age groups voted almost alike. True, the women old enough to have lived through the World War were most emphatic in blaming the financial interests; 67 per cent of the ones between thirty and forty-five years old said "Yes" to the question, and only 60 per cent of the women under thirty. As in the answers to whether the war had been a mistake, the women of the Pacific Coast were most certain that the bankers were behind it all; 71 per cent said "Yes."

"Revelations since the war have shown that money forces issued propaganda which got us into the war," said the wife of a clerk in Los Angeles. An unmarried typist in Detroit agreed: "Their expensive investments," she said, regarding the bankers, "needed protection."

"Do you think we gained what we said we fought for," the women were asked; "to make the world safe for democracy?"

There was an overwhelming "No," to this; 91 per cent of all the women said that the high purpose of 1917 had been thwarted. Only 9 per cent said "Yes." The highest affirmative answer, geographically, came from the women of the South. But there was, all in all, no substantial disagreement among any group.

"If we had, we would be at peace today," said a fifty-four-year-old widow of Wheatland, Wyoming, when asked to amplify her belief that democracy had not been saved. "The harsh treaties have actually paved the way for dictatorships," explained a schoolteacher in Breaux Bridge, Louisiana.

But a seamstress in Hazen, Arkansas, disagreed. "We made it safer for the time being, anyway," she said.

The World War, our most costly struggle overseas, was a failure, according to the women of America. This led logically to the question we have already noted—whether the women would endorse another overseas war.

"I would never favor going overseas again—fight only in self-defense," said a twenty-eight-year-old stenographer of Dillon, Montana. "We should live within our own boundaries and forget about those other countries," declared a civil-service employee's wife in Cincinnati. But in Miami a divorcee, a writer, expressed a forthright disagreement. "We should whip them before they all join and whip us," she said.

Only 12 per cent of women nationally voted "Yes" to the question "Would you ever favor fighting an overseas war?" Religious and geographical groups varied little in their answers—the only group which radically disagreed were divorcees, of whom 20 per cent would favor going abroad to fight.

III

And why has this change of viewpoint come? Twenty-one years, as time is measured, is but an electric flash. On April 2, 1917, President Wilson addressed the houses of Congress and called for war against "the Government of the German Empire." Not against the German People! The President chose his words carefully. "We have no quarrel with the German people," he said. "We seek no indemnities . . . no material compensation; we desire no conquest, no dominion. . . . The day has come when America is privileged to spend her blood and her might for the principles that gave her birth . . ."

To save democracy. To vanquish the German Kaiser and end dictatorships. But Hitler had not been heard of then, nor Mussolini nor Trotsky nor Lenin nor Stalin. Wilson's dream of a League of Nations would remain no better than a dream. The Treaty of Versailles would press down on conquered Germany, and the World War, to have ended in 1918, would continue in Europe and the Far East for twenty years.

IV

Women are denied the excitement of war. They give their husbands and sons to be slaughtered while they wait in misery at home. But the women of America, disillusioned though they are about the World War and opposed to any new overseas struggle, are not—as, again, we have already seen—pacifists at any price.

"Do you believe there are occasions when war is justified?" they were asked.

"Yes," said 64 per cent of all the women—and the variations, geographically or otherwise, were light. The women of the Pacific Coast, although more certain than their sisters elsewhere that the World War had been fought in vain, were 68 per cent affirmative on this question as compared with 60 per cent of the New England women. Small-town women were 68 per cent affirmative compared to 62 per cent in urban areas. Other age, marital and religious groups were strikingly uniform.

Individual answers among the 64 per cent who said "Yes" stressed the obligation of self-defense.

"In the history of the United States," said a youthful architect's wife in Carson City, Nevada, "we have had to fight to protect ourselves occasionally." War is justified, declared the sixty-eight-year-old wife of an iron-worker in Birmingham, Alabama, "when our flag or our soldiers are insulted." An advertising salesman's wife in Philadelphia included "defending principles of liberty" as a proper occasion for war.

The 36 per cent of the American women who said that war was never justified were equally definite in their reasons.

"It settles no troubles," said a cook in Wheatland, Wyoming. "War is never justified if you consider the thousands of lives it takes and ruins," was the reply of a sales manager's wife in Windsor, Missouri. "I don't think there's a cause in the world for war," declared a twenty-nine-year-old waitress in Newark, New Jersey.

A majority of her countrywomen do not agree even in general with the young New Jersey waitress, however. More of them would vote for war against an invading army. It might have been assumed that the women would return a substantial "Yes" as long as the invasion related merely to the territorial United States. Within recent years there has been a good deal of talk about letting the Philippine Islands go if any other power really wanted them. But the question put to the women of America was not phrased that way.

"If the United States, *or her possessions,* is invaded by a foreign nation," it asked, "should this country fight?"

Again agreement was so general that breakdowns by age, income, religion, and so on, show almost no variations.

The women who lived through the World War, by hearsay at least, returned a larger proportion of affirmative votes than their younger or older sisters; 89 per cent of the thirty to forty-five year group would go to war against an invader.

The variations in vote depended very little on geographical lines. "This is the only free country left; we should keep it free," said the twenty-one-year-old wife of a San Francisco salesman. "When our land is invaded we should fight," declared an eighteen-year-old schoolgirl in Racine, Wisconsin. A New England schoolteacher agreed. So did a broker's wife in Philadelphia.

Some of the women drew the distinction between invasion of the United States itself and invasion of her territories. "Our possessions are not worth the lives lost in a war," declared a widow in Rawlins, Wyoming.

A carpenter's wife in Broad Channel, Long Island, New York, voted "No" on the obligation of war in the event of an invasion. "Before I had a boy," she said, "I might have said 'Yes.' But when it strikes home, it's a different matter."

The women of America, it is now clear, will not be led into war by isolated insults to their country, no matter how grave those insults may be. "Remember the Maine!" today apparently would fall on deaf ears. The people of the United States, it will be recalled, were greatly aroused late last year when an American gunboat, the Panay, was sunk in China by Japanese aviator bombers. A number among her crew were killed, and for a few days excited war talk spread through the country. President Roosevelt and Secretary of State Hull handled the outrage calmly, however. Japan apologized and agreed to a proper indemnity.

"Should we have gone to war over the sinking of the Panay?" the women were asked.

A mere fraction of them—only 1.5 per cent—said "Yes" to that.

V

The women of America look with troubled eyes, in so far as the hope of peace is concerned, upon the world. For the war drums throb more ominously than ever. The battle flags wave above a dozen fields of war and a parliament of man—so the women say—is in the far, far future. Pessimism marked their answers to the question, "Do you think the time will ever come when war is outlawed?" Only 26 per cent of all the women—a fraction more than a quarter—said "Yes."

"There would probably be a war trying to outlaw war," said a salesman's wife in Chicago. Her answer was typical. Other women reiterated that peace might come "when the big shots have to fight," or that the capitalist system was behind war. A secretary in Bridgeport, Connecticut, said that "one country will always try to encroach on another."

No majority group of women anywhere disagreed with the conclusion that war would never be outlawed. An almost identical verdict was returned for a related question, "Do you think it will ever be possible to bring all nations into an effective world organization to preserve peace?" A 72 per cent majority replied "No" to this. An effective League of Nations and a World Court both seem improbable to the women of America. This is how they voted on whether one could be achieved:

Question: "Do you think it will ever be possible to bring all nations into an effective world organization to preserve peace?"

	YES	NO
National	28%	72%
Urban	30	70
Farm	22	78
Small town	26	74
Protestant	30	70
Catholic	23	77
All others	28	72
Married women and widows	28	72
Divorced	30	70
Single	29	71
Income Groups		
Under $1500 a year	27	73
Over $1500 a year	29	71
Age Groups		
Under 30 years	27	73
30-45 years	27	73
Over 45 years	30	70

"Not as long as Hitler and Mussolini are alive," was the significant explanation of a banker's wife in San Francisco.

It was essential, at this point, to find out whether, in the hearts of the women, hostility lurked toward the other countries of the world. Just half of the women said there was no country they did not like. But the 50 per cent who admitted a dislike for other nations made it clear it was the dictatorships now flourishing toward which their hostility is directed.

Germany, specified 40 per cent of the women who disliked some nation.

Japan, said 35 per cent.

Italy, said 12 per cent.

Russia, said 8 per cent.

The rest of the vote was scattered and insignificant.

"What country do you feel friendliest toward?" was then asked, and the answers gave overwhelming proof of how, in a few decades, public opinion can shift. For it was possible, virtually up to the World War, for American politicians to win thousands of votes by twisting the tail of the British lion. England was an object of vast distrust in the United States. But today, said 63 per cent of the American women, England is the nation toward which they feel most friendly. No group, geographically or on any other basis, disagreed.

France, said 10 per cent.

Canada, said 6 per cent.

Germany, said 3 per cent.

Scandinavian countries—Norway, Sweden and Denmark—said 3 per cent.

The balance of the votes, all by small percentages, were divided among Ireland, China, Finland, Switzerland and Russia.

VI

The women admit that there are occasions when war is justified. But let America's leaders beware against a war begun merely to protect commercial interests abroad. Let them tighten, if the views of the women mean anything, the embargoes against supplying money or munitions to nations engaged in war. For the circumstances under which the women believe war justified are strictly limited.

"Should we ever go to war to protect our commercial interests abroad?" they were asked.

There was an emphatic "No" to this; 84 per cent of the women so went on record. "Commercial interests should leave a warring country," said a stock buyer's wife of Willows, California. "What are commercial interests compared to torn nations, lost lives and an inevitable depression that follows war?" demanded a café proprietor's wife of Geneva, Alabama. "Those people are over there simply for money," said a farmer's wife in Caldwell, Ohio. "Let them look out for themselves."

"Should we lend money, send munitions or supplies to countries at war?"

The "No," this time, was even more unanimous; 87 per cent of all the women so answered.

It is significant, again, that the well-to-do women differed little from their less prosperous sisters on these questions. The well-to-do agree that we should not fight to protect our commercial interests, nor should we lend money or supplies to combatant nations.

"They'd have to quit fighting if we curbed supplies," said a garage superintendent's wife in Portland, Oregon. "Such actions get us entangled where we should remain neutral," declared a Chicago broker's wife. "It only helps to bring us in it," said a sales manager's wife in Detroit. Here are the tabulations:

Question: "Should we protect our commercial interests?"

	YES	NO
National	16%	84%
Urban	18	82
Farm	13	87
Small town	13	87
Protestant	14	86
Catholic	23	77
All others	17	83
Married women and widows	16	84
Divorced	16	84
Single	19	81
Income Groups		
Under $1500 a year	18	82
Over $1500 a year	14	86
Age Groups		
Under 30 years	19	81
30-45 years	16	84
Over 45 years	15	85

Should we lend money, send munitions or supplies? Thirteen per cent said "Yes," 87 per cent "No"—little variation in geographical or income groups here.

In the next war, so far as the women are concerned, there will be no enormous profits for industry, nor—although on this they are less unanimous—swollen wages for the workingman. For they declared, 81 per cent, that the profits of business should be limited—and it should be noted that the plus $1500 women agreed exactly with the less-than-$1500 women on this. Each returned an 81 per cent affirmative.

"Should the wages of workingmen be limited in wartime?" was the related question.

This time 59 per cent of all the women said "Yes." The less-than-$1500 group, containing a large proportion of workingmen's wives in their number, were a little less certain than the well-to-do that this was right. Yet they returned a 56 per cent affirmative answer, compared to 62 per cent on the part of the women whose incomes averaged more than $1500 a year.

VII

This is a changing world. It is just possible that one of the changes may be that in future wars the women will fight shoulder to shoulder with the men. They have already done so, to an extent, in the civil war in Spain. The women of America are not yet ready for this, however. Only 13 per cent of them said "Yes" to "If the United States had another war, do you think women should fight alongside the men?" The divorced women, for some reason, were far more willing; 25 per cent of them answered affirmatively. In general, however, there were only minor variations in opinion among the different groups.

"If we lost the war, the women would have to fight," explained one divorcee of Los Angeles, explaining why she voted "Yes." The wife of a furniture salesman in Wheeling, West Virginia, said that "in any future war we will need all the forces we can muster." A policeman's wife in Great Valley, New York, thought that "the wife should fight as long as she is allowed to vote."

But the women who said "No" had equally forceful reasons. They said that women were not trained, that they were needed at home, that they did not have the strength, that work behind the lines was best suited to them.

"The men would not keep their minds on fighting," protested, perhaps facetiously, a printer's wife in Newark, New Jersey.

The women declared, as we have seen, that war is sometimes justified. They voted, too, to turn back an invader by force. These answers, in part at least, were broadly objective. What would the women of America do in so far as their own sons and husbands were concerned? Would they try to keep them from going to war?

First, the sons. By a narrow margin—52 to 48 per cent—the women said they would not stop their sons from going to war.

Wide differences marked the answers to this question, however.

Yes—they would prevent their sons from going—said 53 per cent of the farm women.

The non-church members agreed; 51 per cent of them.

The married women and widows divided, 50 per cent to 50 per cent, on the question.

So, by the same vote, did the women of the Pacific Coast.

The individual answers indicated that many women would try to dissuade their sons from voluntary enlistment, but would not ask them to evade conscription. This was the statement of a letter-carrier's wife in Lancaster, New Hampshire. "In case of an invasion," said an electrician's wife in Burlington, Vermont, "I should feel that my sons and husband should do their part, God forbid!"

"They have to go, whether you object or not," was the fatalistic answer of a minister's wife in Delphi, Indiana.

What about trying to keep husbands from going? The problem of the wife depends vitally, of course, on whether there are children. So the first question was: "Would you prevent your husband from going to war if you had children?" To this, 64 per cent of all the women answered "Yes."

Not a single majority group disagreed. The fathers of America are not going to fight in the next war if the women have anything to say about it. East, West, North and South voted "Yes" on this. Here are the groups:

Question: "Would you prevent your husband from going to war if you had children?"

	YES	NO
National	64%	36%
Urban	62	38
Farm	70	30
Small town	65	35
Protestant	64	36
Catholic	59	41
All others	67	33
Married women and widows	65	35
Divorced	53	47
Single	60	40
Income Groups		
Under $1500 a year	64	36
Over $1500 a year	63	37
Age Groups		
Under 30 years	66	34
30-45 years	64	36
Over 45 years	63	37

Yet it would be dangerous to draw from these opinions the conclusion that the women of America will be pacifist in their views if war comes, that they will seriously interfere with the raising of an army.

"Would you prevent your husband from going to war *if you had no children*?" was the related question.

Only the farm women, by a 52 per cent vote, and the non-church members, with 51 per cent, said that they would do so. The total was a 53 per cent "No." This is the way the women voted:

Question: "Would you prevent your husband from going to war if you had no children?"

	YES	NO
National	47%	53%
Urban	46	54
Farm	52	48
Small town	46	54
Protestant	47	53
Catholic	40	60
All others	51	49
Married women and widows	49	51
Divorced	38	62
Single	41	59
Income Groups		
Under $1500 a year	47	53
Over $1500 a year	47	53
Age Groups		
Under 30 years	47	53
30-45 years	47	53
Over 45 years	47	53

Finally: "Would you rather have a son of yours go to jail as a pacifist than go to war?" Slightly more than a third of the women, 36 per cent, said "Yes." The youngest group, under thirty, was even more definite, and 42 per cent of them so answered. Not a few of the individual answers pointed to the obvious fact that a son, in jail for pacifism, would at least be safe.

"He would have committed no crime; if at war, he might be killed or injured," said an automobile worker's wife in Madison, Florida. "As long as it was principle and not cowardice," explained a bookkeeper's wife in St. Louis, she would rather see her son imprisoned.

The majority, though, disagreed. "Going to jail is a disgrace and to war is an honor," pointed out an unmarried woman in Rawlins, Wyoming. "If my son enjoyed the protection of his country," said a mechanic's wife in San Francisco, "he should help to maintain it."

Questions

To what elemental emotions does this story appeal?

To what source of material "zone" does it belong?

Why are the opinions of individual women quoted?

Is the story too "dry"?

The New York Times Magazine

BEHIND THE CONFLICT IN "BLOODY HARLAN"

BEHIND THE CONFLICT IN "BLOODY HARLAN"

By F. Raymond Daniell

Reproduced by special permission of the New York Times

Although "Behind the Conflict in 'Bloody Harlan' " had an obvious news peg (trial in federal court of charges that certain operators and operator-employees had violated the Wagner Act) the article is listed here as an information story. It is not a description of the trial or of the facts that led immediately to the trial. Rather it is a reporter's study of the economic and social aspects of Harlan County which have made it for years a hot-bed of employer-labor trouble.

Two things are worth noting about the story. First the wealth of factual material which it carries. Second the unbiased account of the situation.

Technically and legally the coal operators, corporations and peace officers of Harlan County on trial here at London are charged with a criminal conspiracy to nullify the Wagner act. Actually, however, it is the political and economic system of that rich soft-coal field which is at the bar. For in Harlan County, as nowhere else in the country, except possibly on the cotton plantations of the Deep South, the visitor encounters feudalism and paternalism which survive despite all efforts to break them down.

For years the county has been known as "bloody Harlan." It is feud country, and last year there were sixty murders, within its precincts. But Harlan has no monopoly on violence and bloodshed; its designation is due rather to the fact that much of the bloodshed has been directly connected with the struggle between miners and operators and with union organizations. Because of the national interest in that warfare its troubles have received more attention than other outbursts in the feud belt.

Within Harlan County, which lies in the southeastern corner of Kentucky on the Virginia border, are some 70,000 inhabitants. From 16,000 to 18,000 men work in the mines and produce from 14,000,000 to 18,000,000 tons of coal, worth $45,000,000 each year. This is more than a third of Kentucky's total bituminous production and, while only a drop in the national total, it is of sufficiently high quality and is produced so cheaply under existing labor conditions that it is a strong competitor with the product of other fields.

It is that fact, more than the hope of swelling its treasury with several thousand new members, each paying dues of $1.50 a month, which is responsible for the determined effort now being made by the United Mine Workers to organize the Harlan miners. Unless this effort succeeds, the union fears it will lose its recognition in neighboring coal fields, where operators are complaining that they cannot maintain union standards unless Harlan County's operators are brought into line.

Prior to 1911 Harlan County was a quiet rural community of small mountain farms. The chief industry was agriculture and logging, with a little moonshining. Even then it was known that beneath the ridges lying between Pine and Black Mountains, along the forks of the Cumberland River, there was wealth in the form of soft coal such as was needed for the manufacture of steel. There was no way, however, of getting it out to the Great Lakes. Then the railroad came.

Overnight the characteristics of the countryside changed. Here and there the beautiful green hills were defaced by the winding conveyors over which the mined coal is carried from the drift mouth or mine opening in the hillside to the tipple, where it is broken and sorted and sized alongside the railroad tracks. Great piles of black waste and excavated earth began making their appearance on the hillsides, and from neighboring counties there came a swarm of farm boys and men, lured by the hope of high pay. There were no towns, no houses for the miners, except those the coal operators built, and thus there came into being the company town and the company store.

As the coal industry grew in Harlan County, local capitalists got in on the ground floor. Among them was R. W. Creech, a patriarchal old gentleman with mustaches which spread a full eight inches on either side of his nose. He had been a lumberman before the railroad came, floating his logs down the river. To him his employes are like children, to be cared for and kept in order. He is one of the defendants in the conspiracy trial. Others among the defendants flocked into Harlan County in the early days of the industry. Among them were many who went there to escape labor troubles in other fields. They brought with them a bitterness against unions that has never died.

The camps they built for their laborers had moral standards on a par with the standards of the environment. Red liquor was drunk in Homeric quantities and fights were common. The county disclaimed responsibility for policing the mine camps, and there grew up the practice of hiring a special policeman and having him deputized by the Sheriff to lend the authority of law to his six-shooter.

Even now the mining camps of Harlan County are no week-end resorts for sissies. The industry of the peace officers in rounding up drunks on Saturday night is prodigious. The fine, usually amounting to $19.50, is often paid by the company employing the prisoner and then deducted from his pay. In the four years ended last Jan. 1 the records show that 14,000 persons went to the lock-up at one time or another—a profitable quadrennium for the jailer, who is allowed 75 cents a day for feeding each prisoner. A good manager can do it for considerably less.

For years the operators had everything their own way. But Harlan's position in the coal business and the number of unorganized miners there were not overlooked by the unions. There were repeated efforts to unionize the district, and for years the unionized miners and the operators have been engaged in a bitter feud, with not all the violence directed at the miners.

Back in 1931, when the United Mine Workers made an abortive effort to organize the Harlan field, there was competition for members among several rival unions, including one said to have been dominated by Communists and members of the I. W. W. In this period there was an epidemic of burglary of company stores and thefts of dynamite and copper from the companies, which was blamed on union members and organizers. The company put sheriff's deputies on their payrolls, and the killing of such deputies in a battle with strikers led to the "reign of terror" which union men say has been set up against them.

With the passage of the NRA, the Guffey act and, finally, the Wagner act, outsiders came in to organize the miners, and agents of the Federal Government stepped in. The world of the Harlan County coal barons began to topple. The United Mine Workers have succeeded in negotiating contracts with ten of the forty-two mines operating in Harlan County, and today the union has an office in the town of Harlan and its field workers travel about without molestation as long as they stay off non-union company property.

Although only about a fourth of the county's population works in the mines, nearly everybody in the county is dependent, directly or indirectly, on them. Only about 12,000 live in free, incorporated towns, and even there the influence of the coal operators is strong. The other 58,000 live in company towns, occupy company houses, walk on company streets, shop in company stores, go to company churches and send their children to company schools. Illness is treated by company doctors and justice is often administered by company magistrates, who hold court on company property. One of the big companies until recently had its own private jail.

The company towns range in size from little settlements of 100 or 200 houses to cities like Lynch, owned by a subsidiary of United States Steel, where more than 9,000 miners and their families live under rules and conditions laid down by a board of directors instead of a Common Council. Here the streets are surfaced, the houses painted and, though plumbing is almost as rare as elsewhere in the county, living conditions appear to be reasonably good. There are a private police force and a private fire department, a smart-looking new motion-picture theatre and a department store which might be a branch of a New York or Chicago store. Lynch, where a higher proportion of workers of alien stock are employed than elsewhere, has the only Roman Catholic church in the county.

In contrast to this tree-shaded little city, with its neat lawns and flower gardens, are the more typical towns of the smaller, locally owned companies. There the muddy, rutted streets swarm with pigs, raised to supplement the family larder when the cold weather comes. The dilapidated houses, standing frequently in pools of stagnant water, and the vacant faces of the inhabitants present a depressing picture to the visitor from outside. Yet shiny new automobiles, in improvised garages underneath the houses, washing machines on the back porch and electric refrigerators in the living room are as common as in the camps where housing conditions are better.

In the middle of the county is the town of Harlan, a rather shabby county seat of wood and brick buildings, hemmed in, almost squeezed, by the surrounding mountains. It is one of the three incorporated towns in the county, the others being Cumberland and Evarts. Harlan's Chamber of Commerce claims for the town a population of about 7,000, and Harlan is the shopping center for all the people in the county who have managed to scrape together enough cash to trade away from the company store. Even here, however, mine operators or their kinsfolk control most of the mercantile establishments in the town. A man can't even buy a headache remedy without patronizing the operators, for they own the drug stores, too.

Many of the county's people are mountain folk, quick to anger and quick to shoot. Men think no more of toting a gun than Englishmen do of carrying an umbrella. For a time, until the quaint inconsistency was corrected a few years ago, the Kentucky statutes provided a stiffer penalty for the man who merely fired at some one than for the man who wounded his enemy. Outside a little church in Harlan one Sunday night the writer saw two boys, not more than 12 or 13, with business-like .38-caliber revolvers in their overall pockets.

The people tend to resent intrusion in their affairs by "furriners," much as they would resent a stranger "messin' around" their women folk. During an inspection tour of the mines the writer ordered a photographer to take a picture of a "Tobacco Road" family—a mother sitting beside her cabin with a nursing baby and an old miner resting on the back stoop—and was about to ask the woman's permission when the local photographer intervened.

"Ask the man, not the woman," he said. "He might shoot if you ask her."

And then on our tour of the company towns our driver stopped suddenly in the road at High Splint and began backing up. At first, the reason was not apparent. Then a boulder, the size of a cabbage, rolled down the road in front of the car. Four boys stopped playing ball and retreated to the sidelines. From between two houses there came a man, his shirt torn and bloody, wielding an axe handle. Retreating before him was a man with a rock which must have weighed ten pounds. He threw it and the man with the axe handle had at him. When it was over the stone-thrower was unconscious in the road and the club-wielder was leaning against a fence, blood pouring from a crack in his skull. No one interfered or seemed especially interested.

The feud tradition is a strong factor in Harlan's way of life. For generations it has been the custom, when a man is killed by a member of a rival clan, for all the victim's family to go gunning for the killer and his kinsfolk. Honor is not considered avenged until the mortality score is even. Interference by the law and the courts is bitterly resented.

Relations between miners and operators have a similar directness. In the company towns the homes of the operators generally are alongside the three and four room dwellings of the miners, who pay between $1.50 and $2.50 a month per room. It still is a common thing for the children of the operator to go to the same company school as the children of the common laborers until they have reached high-school age. As a matter of fact, it is said with some justification that mine children in company towns get more schooling than the children of incorporated towns. The county provides only seven months' salary for the teacher, but the company town usually pays the teacher for keeping school open another two months. The schools are built by the company, but the teacher is appointed by the Superintendent of Schools.

The owners of the mines dress in khaki work clothes, go in and out of the mines and sit in an office, usually on the ground floor of the commissary, unguarded by secretaries. Any worker is free to come in with his problems whether they be financial, domestic or legal, and he usually can count on receiving help if he has kept clear of the United Mine Workers.

The mines pay off every two weeks in cash, and when times are good the miners of Harlan County make relatively good money, receiving from the open-shop mines a little above the union scale, but working longer hours than union men and having no means of checking company figures on the amount of coal they dig. Most of the financial transactions between the miner and the store are carried out by means of scrip issued to the employes against credit they have established by their labor underground. This scrip is non-transferable, and, generally speaking, can be spent only in the company store, where prices are slightly higher than in the cash chain stores downtown. Everything from the finest-quality meats and canned goods to the latest in overstuffed furniture can be bought there. Many of the commissaries sell liquor, which is legal in Harlan County.

Credit is available in almost unlimited amounts to regular employes of the mines, whether the mines are running or not. When they do run the operator knows his men will dig coal and he will sell it, deducting the amount he has advanced from the pay due the miners. Most of the company stores now have about an average of $20,000 outstanding in overdrafts of miners, but they are not worried.

In one camp this correspondent was permitted to inspect the ledger in which the miners' accounts are kept. One entry showed that one of the miners, after all the credit advanced to him had been deducted from his earnings for a month, came out exactly even with the company. Closer inspection showed that he was paying a lower rate of rent than the other miners. When the treasurer of the company was asked about this, he explained that the amount this man had earned last month was a little less than the credit that had been advanced him, so the company cut his rent by a few cents to make it come out even.

In Harlan a miner who "keeps shet" of union activities need not worry about keeping a roof over his head, nor need he concern himself much with where the next meal—or, for that matter, the next drink—is coming from, for the paternalistic employer provides a kind of social security.

Harlan's leading citizens are anxious that this side of the picture be presented.

Such are the setting and the background for the drama in the court room here in London which the whole country has been watching. Harlan today sees what may be the climax in the struggle between two sharply differing ways and philosophies of life.

Talk to the operators of the mines and you will hear that they want to protect their miners from being forced to join a union which they do not want and which, they say, for all the dues collected, cannot give them anything they do not now receive without the necessity of paying dues. You will also understand that the operators want to run their mines without outside interference.

Talk to the union leaders and you will hear that they are fighting paternalism of the operators. They charge that the one thing a miner may not do on company property is think for himself or speak out in public. They are fighting, they will tell you, to free the miners from an archaic system in which liberty has no place.

Questions:

Would this story have been handled differently for, say, the *New Republic*? For *New Masses*? In what ways?

What, at a guess, is the occupation of the author?

What do you think of the beginning of this story? If, in your judgment it is a good one, why do you think so?

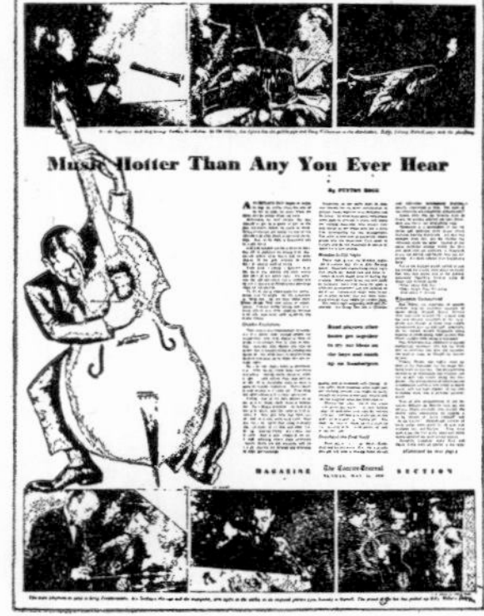

Music Hotter Than Any You Ever Hear

MUSIC HOTTER THAN ANY YOU EVER HEAR

By Peyton Hoge

Reprinted by special permission from the Louisville Courier-Journal

"How the other half lives" is a perennial subject-source for newspaper and magazine articles. The curiosity of readers to see the very rich at play, on the Riviera, at Palm Beach, at Newport; the very poor, in flophouse and "jungle"; the "queens" of Hollywood in their Klieg-lit privacy; the features under the circus clown's paint; the trivial intimacies of king, dictator, and president—this curiosity is insatiable. And it doesn't lessen its pull to rationalize it as merely an extension of the impulse to backyard gossip and as an ever-present nostalgia for greener—or at least different—pastures than those we now inhabit.

To the maw of this curiosity the *Louisville Courier-Journal* offered the article "Music Hotter Than You Ever Hear."

A musician's day begins at night. In fact, he works while the rest of us are at play, he plays while we sleep and he sleeps while we work.

Sometimes he will reverse the day enough to get in a game of golf in the late afternoon before he starts to work. Often rehearsals are called for late in the afternoon or after hours in the early mornings. But, at its best, a musician's life is topsy-turvy.

And like cabmen out for a drive on their day

off or postmen on hiking trips, musicians gather after hours and on their nights off for jam sessions, to make their distinctive kind of swing.

Their kind of swing is different from the music that crowds the ether waves and most of the dance halls. It's unrehearsed and unwritten, but as keenly felt by the musicians as Rembrandt's paintings were by the painter.

To these, slang expressions for instruments like "woodpile" for the xylophone or "doghouse" for the bass fiddle, come from people they call ickies or smart-alecks. And the words "swing" and "jive" have almost lost their meaning because they are incorrectly used to define too many things.

Dislike Exploiters

They dislike the exhibitionism of listeners who speak their strange jargon for amusement, and thus exploit a form of musical expression that to them is serious. Inwardly they dislike this type of notice, but to make a living at pleasing the customer they often have to swallow their distaste and play up to those who are always right.

Such is their day's work as entertainers. After hours, while their customers are sleepily setting alarm clocks in order to get to work before their boss arrives at the office, musicians want to have a little relaxation themselves. Then's when a jam session will come off. True ones are spontaneous and without spectators.

Perhaps one of the best definitions of swing ever made came from a famous New York Negro drummer. He said that swing in music was the same to him as when his best girl who had been out of town for a year came back home. Most musicians will agree that swing is mostly improvisations of rhythm and notes following a musical theme. It's a noun, not a verb. And a jam session is an informal gathering where these unwritten improvisations are the keynotes, and all the participants are relaxed and oblivious of their surroundings.

Louisville, in the early days of jazz, was known for its great contribution to popular music together with Memphis and St. Louis. In those days small restaurants were glad to provide a piano and space for visiting musicians, who bought beer and things to eat while they did a little free entertaining for the management. The same is now true in Louisville, where places like the Musicians' Club cater to hungry and thirsty musicians in search of space for a jam session.

Monday Is Off Night

There they gather on Monday nights (the musicians' day off) or after working hours. Musicians representing every night club, snack bar, dance hall and hotel orchestra in town might drop in during the evening. Some want to try out new ideas in harmony, some may have hit upon a different arrangement and are anxious to try it out. Others still might want to air an original melody that has been humming through their minds for several days.

The result isn't something stiff and rehearsed. It's music that has a different quality and is crammed with feeling. If you suffer from insomnia some night and are roaming around, you might be lucky enough to witness a real jam session and see for yourself what the difference is.

"There's the school which the ickies claim plays gut bucket—a slow foxtrot jungle rhythm associated with the colored orchestra," confided a trumpet player one night while munching a hamburger. "You might say that it's made up of a booming bass rhythm section with plenty of sock in the choruses.

Dixieland the Real Stuff

"Then you mustn't forget Benny Goodman and his followers. His time is usually straight 4-4 with a blaring brass section and individual instrumental choruses, usually improvised at first. But most of his selections are completely orchestrated."

Asked what was his favorite style of music, he quickly pointed out that Dixieland was really the true swing type.

"Dixieland is a descendant of the old circus and medicine show music which featured blaring trombones. All that has changed some now, but the rhythm has remained much the same. Instead of the usual rhythmic scheme where the first and third beat are accented, in Dixieland music the second and fourth beats are accented. It's more refined than Goodman's kind."

But as the trumpet player turned to join his friends for a little more music he found that they had joined him in the general discussion regarding favorite kinds of music and favorite bands.

"What about Red Norvo?"

"Don't forget Paul Whiteman."

"How about T. Dorsey?"

Whiteman Commercial

Red Norvo, the consensus of opinion showed, was an excellent example of sweet swing. Mildred Bailey, Norvo's wife, was made to order for his band and his own delicate treatment of the xylophone was enough to make most expert xylophonists give up and turn carpenters. As for Horace Heidt's Brigadiers being capable of sweet swing, most claimed that Heidt couldn't even swing a hammock.

Paul Whiteman was considered a typical commercial showman who did his level best to entertain and give the customer the kind of music he thought he wanted to hear.

Tommy Dorsey was highly rated by most of the musicians, but his music differed from all the rest. His arrangements seemed to be meticulous and brilliant, yet not so stiff that honest swing was forgotten. His arrangements of semi-classical compositions started a new trend in dance music, and the high register of his own trombone work was a personal achievement.

Talk of new arrangements of old favorites brought up Maxine Sullivan, the throaty Negro contralto who started the recent radio controversy by singing a swing version of "Loch Lomond" and "Annie Laurie." Phonograph records of these songs were made by Maxine and released late last summer. They were such a success that many important name bands imitated her style almost exactly.

Ellington, Lunsford, Andy Kirk and Chick Webb were all placed in the category of the Southern Negro musicians who still combine a plaintive melody with distinctive yet primitive rhythmic devices. The discussion over for the moment, actual playing took the spotlight of interest. Several exchanged instruments just to see what they could do that might be different.

A Breather and a Beer

They may have had present too many brasses or too many accordions, but that made no difference. Music was still the important thing. And how they could play it!

Back for a breathing spell and a beer, the trumpet player obliged with a few more definitions.

Skins were the drums and a skinbeater was the drummer man. The saxophone was dubbed the gobble pipe. The trombone boasted many names, among which "sliphorn" and "tram" are most used.

"'Jive?' Well, that's used to mean a lot of things, but mostly 'jive' refers to a player who is either talking about music or actually playing swing music.

"The clarinet is often called the liquorice stick or just the stick. 'Cats frisking their whiskers' is icky talk for swing musicians doing a thorough job of swing music.

In the Groove

"The colored boys seem to have the most talk about music. They have different names for almost everything you could think about. But most musicians don't try to keep up with that kind of language. In fact, we don't like to hear ickies spouting off with an exhibitionist vocabulary. As for me, it makes me sick."

Once again the informant joined the others around the piano. In the midst of a very torrid chorus of "Honeysuckle Rose" two new visitors rapped at the door for admission. Once inside—after convincing first the doorman that they were acceptable—they took a seat near the musicians at play. During a lull, the all-knowing gentleman remarked to his companion:

"Say, listen to dat solid jive. Them cats is sure gettin' tha kicks from beatin' it out. They're in de groove all right!"

Questions:

Can you think of half-a-dozen "how the other half lives" ideas that might make feature articles?

To what source of material "zone" does this story belong?

At a guess, what percentage of the readers of the *Louisville Courier-Journal*, will be interested in this article?

Practice Suggestions

1. Find a dozen subjects for information articles and write a 100-200 word statement of what each story would cover. In connection with each subject give the names of one or two magazines which you think might be interested in the stories.

2. The information article and the essay are close relations. Write a discussion of the characteristics that throw a piece of writing into one or the other of these two categories.

3. Read a half-dozen information articles. Decide which one of them you think is the best job (in view of the audience for which it is written) and write a paper giving your reasons for this decision.

4. Make a list of information-article subjects which could be told (like "Light Where You Need It") largely with pictures or drawings.

The Article About People

Old King Cole was a merry old soul,
And a merry old soul was he.
He called for his pipe,
And he called for his bowl,
And he called for his fiddlers three.

For king though he was—and not a hedged and puppet king, but a king of the old days of omnipotence and splendor—he had his enemies. They were the enemies not of his kingship but of his manhood. They were not his personal and private enemies, but the universal, permanent enemies of all men, at all times, everywhere.

King Cole's weapons against them were pipe, bowl, and fiddlers (wine, women, and song is another version). With these he tried with a desperate and fore-doomed bravado to keep at bay the foe of silence, the foe of passing time, and the foe of loneliness.

Was King Cole aware of his desperate plight, conscious of the grim struggle in which he was engaged? Probably not. History is not too explicit on this point. It shows us, as a matter of fact, only one glimpse of the King and reports that at that particular juncture of his career he was "merry." We have no reason to question this dictum of history. Can we not, rather, see in it a deep psychological insight, a clairvoyant revelation of the complexity of human nature? If the King had been really "merry," would he have needed the services of fiddlers, bowl, and pipe? And if he had not *thought* that he was "merry" would he have been in a mood to enjoy them?

Enough, you cry. Almost enough, not quite. There is still the moral.

Loneliness is the great enemy. What we want most of all is a shoulder beside our shoulder, a breast to lean upon. To know that we are not unaided if we should be attacked, not without help if we should be hurt—how tremendously have these desires worked themselves into the social structure that man has built—his family life, his organizations, his clans, and societies, and governments.

And wherever there is a deep need for communication, the writer, with his tools for building roads and bridges across space, appears upon the scene. He can help people our world. He can keep us always aware that we are not alone. He can support our faltering with pictures of the daring of Einstein, the courage of Lindbergh, the genius of Edison.

And that, at rock-bottom, is why we read personality stories.

But there are other, less solemn, reasons. We educate ourselves, out of such articles, as to how other folk live and work, talk, and play. We encounter their ideas and can swim in many intellectual currents. We are inspired to do likewise by their successes—and to avoid their mistakes. We are lifted, while we read, out of our own environments and given a chance to live, vicariously and briefly, in a thousand others.

About whom do we want to read?

About those whose lives glitter.

About those whose lives inspire.

About those whose lives are unusual, quaint, romantic.

About those who have conquered great odds.

The personality article (which is no newer than Homer and the Bible) is the attempt of the journalist to give us—"people."

In such articles the writer's chief purpose is to make the people described "live" for the reader—so to describe their appearance, their characters, their habits, hobbies, foibles, their ideas and achievements, that the reader can see and know them.

The personality story usually grows out of an interview, supplemented with material that can be obtained from reference books, newspaper stories, magazine articles, books, and other people.

Volume 103, Number 6 Scribner's MAGAZINE June, 1938

Grover Aloysius Whalen

BY HARLAND MANCHESTER

SCRIBNER'S EXAMINES *the greatest impresario of our times . . . the dictator of a $150,000,000 show for 50,000,000 guests . . his talents and his famed technique*

GROVER ALOYSIUS WHALEN

By Harland Manchester

Reproduced by special permission from Scribner's

The story which follows is an interesting example of the personality article. The story was timely because of Grover Whalen's part in the preparation of New York's World's Fair. But the story is not about the Fair—it is about Whalen.

Under the tireless hand of Grover A. Whalen, flamboyant master of countless civic ceremonies and for two decades New York's model of fashion and ubiquitous success symbol, "The World of Tomorrow" is rising from the ash dumps of the Flushing flats. Mammoth exhibition halls, towering temples, picturesque lagoons and a vast network of paved streets, shaded gardens, restaurants, theaters, and carousels swiftly take form as Mr. Whalen's co-ordinated army of fair-builders makes ready for an expected 50,000,000 guests.

Originally planned as a mere $30,000,000 show, the budget now runs to $150,000,000 due to Impresario Whalen's expert solicitations, and more millions may be coaxed before the grand opening next April. Sixty-four nations and most of the States have bought exhibition space, the Sixty Families will show their wares, there will be "villages," a "pirate castle," a musical comedy on ice, murals and heroic statues galore, and every gadget from television to the latest can opener will be spread before the eyes of potential buyers. Scouts are scouring the mountainsides for ten thousand full-grown trees which will be shipped, root, trunk and branch, to shade the Flushing fete; gardeners are setting out 1,000,000 tulips and 500,000 pansies, and the pick of American pulchritude is panting against the great day when judges will confer their accolade upon "Miss World's Fair."

Serene amid the apparent chaos of this epic adventure sits its gardeniaed Kubla Khan, guiding his minions toward the supreme moment in April, 1939, when 50,000 scrubbed and cockaded men-at-arms will start their inaugural march, and in the words of Mr. Whalen, there will be "festive bombs exploding, the crackle of fire-works in the sky, the touching of buttons that will throw into jewel-like brilliance the World of Tomorrow."

Meanwhile, the lover of pageantry has not been forced to wait for the grand climax. It has been two years since Whalen smashed the first champagne bottle, and what with formal luncheons and corner-stone layings, the ceremonial tempo has been steadily mounting toward the crescendo. A few weeks ago there was a "preview parade," to advertise the opening of the fair a year later. Whalen's plan was to send the hundred thousand marchers and numerous floats up Fifth Avenue and over the Triborough Bridge. Park Commissioner Moses refused a permit in the interests of regular traffic. The route was changed, but the World's Fair marches on.

A "theme center" has been designed for the exhibition—a spearlike tower and huge glittering ball, yclept in World's Fair language "trylon" and "perisphere." This novel architectural arrangement, which will stand near the middle of the grounds, is intended as a symbol for the entire venture. There is also a theme song—a jazz march by the late George Gershwin—which radio waves will carry to the ends of the earth. And there is "Mithrana," the shapely sculptured lady over the administration building, who "symbolizes the spirit of the fair," and "lifts the veil from the World of Tomorrow." Yet it has become clear to everybody that the "theme" of the big show will be, not a jazz ditty nor a lady lifting a veil, but the man sitting in the flag-decked office at the end of the long corridor—Grover A. Whalen himself.

Everyone connected with the fair agrees that Grover is the works. For better or for worse, the World's Fair is his baby. The tidings that emanate daily from his buzzing publicity department bring up memories of the welcoming trips of the *Macon*, the Lindbergh reception, the police parade, and a hundred other fiestas that have gladdened New York hearts since the radiant civic cotillion leader emerged from his East Side chrysalis.

"In presenting a new layout for a richer life," states a ukase from the Whalen camp, "the fair will not only predict, but may even dictate, the shape of things to come."

If this is true, it is time we looked into the matter. For it appears that the true nature of the World of Tomorrow can best be ascertained by a scrutiny of Mr. Whalen's past performances, his ideas, aspirations, and *modi operandi*.

There is no doubt that when it comes to showmanship, Grover Whalen is the whitest of white-haired boys. Since his first appearance at City Hall in 1918 as groom and mentor to the aspiring Mayor Hylan, he has seldom been far from a camera lens. Four times he has emerged from a lucrative business career to undertake a public or civic task. Whatever the job, the Whalen touch endowed it with spectacular importance. Mayors sulked while he stole their bows, and at times his very effulgence forced him back into the marts of trade. At each reappearance he shone with a brighter luster, and each new venture took him farther uptown. From his business on the lower East Side, he traveled in successive steps to City Hall, to Wanamaker's, and from the Ninth Street department store to the expansive Schenley offices in the Empire State Building. His private estate kept pace with his business and civic progress. Socially he has followed a northerly course from the parental hearth at 279 East Broadway up Fifth Avenue to Dobbs Ferry, where he is now pausing.

II

It was 1916 when Grover Aloysius Whalen, then thirty years old, tossed a modest but neatly brushed headpiece into the political ring. He organized a businessmen's league, of which he was secretary, and thus acquired a political following. Before that time, the Whalen record shows little more than perfunctory entries. He was born in the crowded lower East Side of an Irish-born father and a mother of Canadian extraction. Michael Whalen kept the family in comfort with his trucking company, which removed ashes and refuse from the streets. Grover went to the John F. Ahearn School around the corner. Years later his teacher was to remember the perfection of his pompadour. He commuted north to Fifty-ninth Street to attend the De Witt Clinton High School, and still farther north to the Clason Point Military Academy in the Bronx, where he acquired his life-long interest in uniform and parades. He studied for a time at the New York Law School. When his father died, he left to carry on the ash-removal business, which seemed to him not inconsistent with sartorial distinction. This attitude appealed to Miss Ann Dolores Kelly, who said he was the only man she knew who always wore a boutonniere. In 1913 they were married.

When John F. Hylan was elected Mayor, he picked Whalen, who had backed him, for secretary. Thus launched in public life, he was equipped with a square-jawed earnestness, shoulders that were a tailor's delight, a first-class mustache, strong white teeth, blue Irish eyes, an equestrian statue of Napoleon, no vices, no sense of humor and no policy.

His rise was rapid. Hylan made him Commissioner of Plant and Structures, and, later, head of the Central Board of Purchase, which supervised the spending of $25,000,000 annually. Soon Whalen controlled half a billion dollars' worth of public property, and directed the work of 6000 city employees. His salary was $10.000. He bristled with plans, and when he needed money, he got it. He suffered only one major disappointment—Comptroller Craig defeated his proposal to build a $42.000.000 bridge across the East River in the neighborhood of Wanamaker's department store.

The Whalen talent for pageantry found initial expression during this period. Hylan had been ill, and Whalen arranged a surprise welcome for his return. As commander-in-chief of New York's ferryboat navy, he had ordered grand new uniforms for the skippers. Now he called them in to add color to the chief's welcome. A forest of Christmas greenery was arranged, and when the rehabilitated Hylan hove in sight, someone blew a trumpet, the captains saluted, and a nervous stenographer read an ode.

The troops were returning from France, and Hylan asked his secretary to go down the harbor and welcome them. It was an almost daily chore, but the diligent Whalen did not fail. His reward came swiftly. As chairman of the Mayor's Committee for the Reception of Distinguished Guests, he was to welcome princes, queens, premiers, aviators and channel swimmers, and his face was to become as familiar to New York of the 1920's as the head on a postage stamp.

Wrote a chauvinistic admirer: "With his cane, his white spats, the rigid crease in his trousers, the flower in the lapel of his elegant black cutaway, the delicately striped shirt, the irreproachable necktie and the shining silk hat, even the ladies driving in the Champs Elysées would think it worth while to take a second look at him, and the Paris dandies would certainly regard him with a feeling akin to envy. . . ." A girl reporter assigned to a welcoming party simply wrote that Mr. Whalen was "shining like a silver teakettle."

Whalen called his boss "the greatest statesman since Lincoln," and Hylan reciprocated by backing Whalen to succeed him as Mayor, but the Hylan-Whalen love feast could not last. There was too much Whalen at City Hall. Hylan had a human liking for the pleasant perquisites of office, and when noted visitors dallied with the major-domo on the way to the throne, it griped him. It is even said that when he and Rodman Wanamaker discussed Whalen's potential abilities as a department-store executive, and Wanamaker demurred at raiding the Mayor's staff, Hylan said, "Don't mind me."

III

Thus the way was paved for a graceful exit, and Whalen packed his silk welcoming hats and accepted the Wanamaker offer. It was a triumphant retreat. His salary was said to be several times that of his city job, and later it was reported as $100,000 a year.

Mr. Whalen liked his new boss. Three years before he had said of him at a public dinner: "Rodman Wanamaker is one of the greatest men God ever put on the face of the earth. If an artist wished to do Mr. Wanamaker justice, he would require the assistance of all the great modern artists. An orator would require the combined eloquence of all the other great modern orators."

Whalen was still head of the Mayor's Committee for the Reception of Distinguished Guests, and his greeting technique quickly flowered to final perfection. Among those who received the authentic Whalen welcome were the King and Queen of the Belgians, Queen Marie of Rumania, the Prince of Wales, the Crown Prince and Princess of Sweden, Clemenceau, Foch, Joffre, Briand, Lindbergh, Byrd, Levine, Ruth Elder, and Gertrude Ederle. Foreign potentates reciprocated with decorations. The Whalen chest eventually bore the trophies of the Royal Victorian Order (Great Britain); the Order of Simon Bolivar (Venezuela); Chevalier (later Commander) of the Legion of Honor, and Officier d'Instruction Publique (France); the Red Cross (Germany); Commander-in-chief of the Order of the Crown (Rumania); Commander of the Crown of Italy.

Of all the Whalen festivals the Lindbergh reception was probably gayest and most memorable. It was also the most expensive, costing the city $71,850.87. What the world recalls is the bare-headed aviator riding up Broadway, the white maze of ticker tape, the smooth progress of the hero from triumph to triumph as with apparent spontaneity the city went giddy with joy. But behind the scenes, this was serious business. Two days before Lindbergh walked down the gangplank, eighty-two satraps of welcoming were summoned to final rehearsal in a Manhattan restaurant. Each was a squadron commander in charge of ten or fifteen people, and Grover A. Whalen put them through their paces until they were letter-perfect in details of radio, publicity, printing, luncheon speeches, and so on.

Now that all is ready, the Man With the Gardenia, correct and unruffled, greets his hero. The bands play, the crowds cheer, the speeches are made, and Whalen, like Addison's Marlborough, "rides the whirlwind and directs the storm."

But it was not until December, 1928, that he found full scope for his remarkable talents. His love of uniforms, his sense of drama, his flair for glamorous regimentation and his insatiable capacity for public attention were to be gratified as never before. The killer of Arnold Rothstein had not been apprehended, and the public clamored for official heads. Mayor Walker knew that something had to be done. Glamorous Grover could make them forget. So Walker appointed him Police Commissioner of the City of New York, commander of an army of 18,000, horse, foot and motorcycle.

Whalen knew nothing of police routine, but he had his statue of Napoleon, and a nightstick with his name in white, presented by Rodman Wanamaker, Jr. Wearing a yellow rose and two shades of blue, he shook up the force. He summoned his captains and commanded them to stamp out vice and the speakeasies. "There is a lot of law in the end of a nightstick," he said. "Strong-arm squads" went out to clear the city of "suspicious persons." In a few weeks, more than

3000 "criminals" had walked the police lineup platform. Most of them were released within a few hours.

Guardians of civil liberties began to mutter about constitutional rights. Whalen scoffed at them.

"I've studied law for a number of years," he said, "and nowhere in the lawbooks do I recall seeing anything about the rights of known criminals. We will continue to deal with them on the assumption that they have no constitutional rights."

His baffled critics strove in vain to explain that all persons were entitled to due process of law. Whalen smiled blandly and tried to take in more territory. "Young loafers" and "persons with criminal records" should be sent to the hoosegow, he said, charge or no charge.

It was then that the New York *World* suggested: "Commissioner Whalen would do well to go to some quiet place and think."

Once more the people asked about the Rothstein case. Whalen replied that the traffic situation in the theater district was terrible, and produced the theater traffic-control plan. This plan, suggested by a deputy during a previous regime, staggered theater openings and ruled out parking and right and left turns between 39th and 53rd Streets during theater hours. It was launched with a big conference, to which Florenz Ziegfeld, David Belasco, Lee Shubert, and other producers were invited. For days before inaugural night, the plan was blazoned across the city's front pages. Fourteen police booths were erected throughout the area, all connected by telephone with a central supervising booth at Times Square, which was painted a neat green, and bore the flags of the United States and of the New York Police.

The plan's opening night was attended with all the éclat of a smash hit. The Commissioner, in an arrangement of blue and black appropriately relieved by the thicksoled shoes of a patrolman, was the star, directing four hundred subordinates from the Times Square booth, while theater-bound crowds watched the show and the flares of cameramen struck a gala note.

This job was obviously more in Whalen's line than some of the more complex tasks of directing the public safety forces in the world's largest city. His approach was simple. He said that running the police department was like running any other business, and spoke with admiration of the Ford assembly line. Traffic responded to this treatment, after a fashion. It was like lining up dominoes and pushing them over.

IV

Every police commissioner must occasionally face a major crisis. Whalen met his on March 6, 1930, when a crowd of some 50,000 Communists, sympathizers and onlookers met in Union Square for an unemployment demonstration, and later attempted to parade without a permit. Feeling ran high because of the fatal shooting of a striker by a detective, and the Commissioner made extensive preparations. Two hundred and ninety policemen, fifty mounted police, one hundred detectives, a squadron of motorcycle police with armored sidecars and riot guns, and emergency wagons with machine guns and tear-gas bombs were assigned to duty at Union Square. Women and children were warned to stay away, and hospitals were requested to keep all available ambulances in readiness.

Speeches were made without disorder. The trouble started when leaders ignored the Commissioner's warning, and urged the crowd to parade. Hundreds moved toward Broadway and the police resisted. Now, highly trained military and police organizations the world over have a recognized technique for handling angry crowds. It involves close formation, inch-by-inch resistance, and above all, restraint. The British police, armed with nothing more deadly than their heavy raincoats, excel in this work, and United States Marines, particularly in China duty, have given magnificent demonstrations of the technique.

But when the Union Square crowd began to cross the Broadway deadline, Whalen's police cut loose. Swinging nightsticks, blackjacks and fists, they rushed into the crowd, hitting whatever heads presented themselves. They pursued fleeing men, and knocked people down and beat them with nightsticks after they had fallen. The melee lasted not more than fifteen minutes, but after the crowd had been dispersed, police were seen pummeling several fallen men whose positions in various parts of the square seemed unrelated to the attempted parade. The whole police performance suggested not preservation of order so much as retribution.

Whalen himself boasted of the activities of his *agents provocateurs*. The *Times* quoted him as saying: "I thought I would crack my sides laughing at some of the undercover men. . . . They were there as *Reds*, singing the *Internationale*. . . . They carried placards and banners demanding the overthrow of the government. . . . But the fun started when one of the undercover men started to razz a cop. He got a terrific punch in the eye and was knocked down before the cop was pulled off." The use of *agents provocateurs* as a stimulant to law-breaking is an ancient device, but few employers have been so frank.

There seemed to be no way of showing Whalen where the Police Commissioner's business left off and individual rights began. He followed up his Union Square victory by reporting to their employers the names of three hundred persons who, his undercover men said, were Communists. He had tried to use the city's license power as a weapon to force New York's 70,000 taxicab drivers to wear a standard uniform. A man of bustling activity, he has always loathed idleness, and he questioned the right of poolrooms, which are licensed by the city, to provide amusement for "young men who ought to be working or looking for jobs." Later, as local NRA administrator, he became concerned about workers whose hours were reduced, and appointed a Committee on the Use of Leisure Time. Raymond Fosdick, chairman, pondered and concluded that "our function might actually be termed impertinent."

Although Whalen had frequently been mentioned as Mayor Walker's successor, he had been Police Commissioner for less than a year when the effervescent Jimmy began to look around for someone to cut in. Two months after the Union Square fracas, Whalen resigned. Packing his landscapes, his draperies, his parchment-shaded lamps, his Corinthian columns, his mahogany desk, and his bronze Napoleon, he returned to Wanamaker's, where he was received with fanfares and floral pieces.

V

The archeologist is sometimes surprised, after clearing away thick layers of publicity releases, ticker tape and wilted gardenias, to find a stratum of solid accomplishment in the Whalen record. He turned the old police academy, which was little more than a gymnasium, into an up-to-date school in which all phases of modern police work were taught. He established classes for automobile drivers, and founded a crime-prevention bureau in which civic leaders and scientific specialists cooperated. He set up completely equipped homicide squads in the five boroughs, thus speeding the investigation of killings. The Board of Regents wouldn't let him use the word "college" for his school, and there was a laugh when his cadets paraded in sweaters and berets singing the Maine Stein Song, but the venture became permanent.

When Whalen left Police Headquarters for Wanamaker's, the boys and girls gaped as he went by, and an admiring cynic called him "a Greek god in the Irish manner." There were more greeting jobs and luncheon speeches. Then came the New Deal and the Blue Eagle. Whalen became New York's NRA administrator, and headlines told daily of his activities in enrolling industrial leaders beneath codes of employment.

When 100,000 dressmakers went on strike in August, 1933, it was Julius Hochman, union leader, who persuaded Whalen to call a conference of the industry and the union. As final arbiter of disputed points, Whalen was frequently able to bridge the gap, and the strike was settled with union recognition and improved conditions. This was the first of a hundred and thirty labor disputes which he helped to settle. Labor leaders say he did a good job, and Whalen himself says that of all his undertakings, he looks back upon this one with the greatest satisfaction. The dramatic climax came when he marched up Fifth Avenue bearing a Blue Eagle banner, leading a parade of 250,000 people—in Whalen language "The greatest mass demonstration of industry and commerce ever held in the world."

When the government took over the local NRA, the Schenley Affiliated Corporations made Grover Whalen chairman of their board of directors. He was not expected to understand the liquor business, any more than he was expected to understand merchandising when he went to Wanamaker's at a fancy salary with no previous experience. But crises often arrive in big businesses when it's handy to have someone around who can call all the political and business potentates by their first names. Repeal was young, and Schenley's needed a front man. This service commanded $75,000 a year, and did not interfere with the new chairman's civic and political activities.

Ever since the days of Hylan, budding "Whalen for Mayor" movements have been frostbitten for this reason or that. Last year, when a confused and divided Tammany sought a man to defeat LaGuardia, he came closer to nomination than ever before. The Whalen boom, months in the making, took definite shape in July, when he resigned from various business directorates and announced his political availability. Though he had a substantial backing of Tammany leaders, little popular enthusiasm developed, and the hard-hitting LaGuardia looked at Grover and licked his chops. After a few weeks, Whalen withdrew in favor of Mahoney. For all the applause and bouquets showered upon him, he is still untested as a vote-getter. "Grover Whalen couldn't be elected," said one of his early friends, "and I'll tell you why. It's all right to wear spats, but you've got to wink at the boys as you walk by. Grover keeps a straight face."

VI

In his big office in the World's Fair administration building, Whalen isn't worrying about votes. He sits at the controls of a huge, intricate, fascinating machine, which he drives with meticulous efficiency. His salary is $100,000 a year, according to printed reports which have not been denied. A few feet from his door is the long copper-paneled directors' room, where noted people gather to lunch and to hear reports of the World of Tomorrow. Foreign dignitaries come to see him about their concessions. There are frequent dedication ceremonies. There are big models of the grounds where carefully carved and colored miniatures of the fair buildings appear as fast as they are erected. There are huge picture calendars whose torn-off days gradually reveal next year's triumphant completion, and an alert publicity staff turning out statistical superlatives by the bale.

Of course, Whalen has had his troubles. His art committee had made no plans for a show of contemporary American painting and sculpture, and artists' groups protested. Whalen pooh-poohed "static displays," and said there would be art everywhere, "to the right, to the left, and even underfoot." Now plans have been changed, and a building has been earmarked.

When modern architects heard of the "World

of Tomorrow" motif, and of the model village to be called the "Town of Tomorrow," they expected that Frank Lloyd Wright would be asked to design a building, but it appears that the Whalen interpretation of "tomorrow" is quite literal, that while slogans and architectural trimmings suggest popular notions of a brave new world, the housing exhibits themselves will not depart from conventional current patterns.

At fifty-two, Grover Whalen has developed a comfortable thickness of the midriff, although Trainer Artie McGovern calls each morning at his town hangout on Washington Mews. When he has time, he rides, and is seen frequently at the smart Meadowbrook Club. Week ends he spends at Dobbs Ferry with his family, composed of Mrs. Whalen, Mary, a senior at Bryn Mawr, Grover, Jr., and Esther Ann.

When the writer talked with him, he wore the rosette of the Legion of Honor in place of his usual boutonniere. Casual and urbane in manner, he reached for a pad to illustrate the thematic origin of the exposition. He drew a small circle, and labeled it "man." This was the hub of the wheel, he explained. From it he drew spokes, and labeled them "food," "shelter," "clothing," "communication," "distribution," "science," "art," and so on. The diagram represented a preliminary examination into the present state of man, he explained. The research was financed by a $1,000,000 loan from the banks.

He closed the wheel with a sweeping circle. "All that we have today," he said, "is symbolized by that wheel. Now that we have all this, what's in the future? We have been spinning that wheel with relation to all industries, arts and sciences to interpret its influence on man's future development."

Whalen professes an idealistic hope that the Flushing exposition may contribute to international harmony. "Perhaps," he has said, "we will all be actors in a drama which will help to bring peace to this troubled world." He associates this aspiration with his plan for a military parade on opening day, with a composite force of 50,000 crack troops from various nations, who will thus display the "tools of peace which are so essential to a happy world."

The passion for neat pattern and the yen for unbuttoned hyperbole, both evident in the Whalen make-up, reveal themselves daily as buildings rise and plans unfold. Structures in the center of the prim geometrical arrangement of streets will be dead white, while the radial sectors bloom gradually into vivid colors, culminating in a "Rainbow Drive."

Other prospects paralyze the mind and blind the vision. Typical is Mr. Whalen's "so-called impossible" spectacle, "a Niagara plus a Vesuvius" in which towers of water and flame, wedded to fireworks and music, will regale the multitudes with "the nearest approach to chaos that man can contrive for purposes of sheer entertainment."

Questions:

Why will people be interested in reading this story about Grover Whalen? Or won't they?

How did the author get the material for this article?

Is it conceivable that the story was a publicity enterprise of the World Fair?

Would the story have been handled differently if it had been written for *Nation's Business*? For the *Saturday Evening Post*?

Women in the News

By GENEVIEVE FORBES HERRICK

WOMEN IN THE NEWS

By Genevieve Forbes Herrick

Reprinted by special permission from the Country Gentleman

It would be an interesting experiment to make a list of all the individual items of fact and observation that have gone into the making of the three-in-one personality story "Women in the News." It is this close-packed and detailed picture, plus the easy informality of the style, which brings these women before our eyes—not as paragraphs in *Who's Who* but as people. Note the details which made it possible for the author to make the women described "come alive" before the reader's eyes.

A lady who likes mice, in a laboratory; a lady who loves fat women, on paper; a lady who deserted Roman ruins, under the earth, for radio triumphs, over the air; and hundreds of ladies who read—and heed—the Country Gentleman—these are a few of the Women in the News to whom this past month I have said, and meant it—"Pleased to meet you."

The scientist who studies mice is Dr. Maud Slye, cancer research expert of the Sprague Memorial Institute, Chicago.

But I met her in Washington where she came to be one of the honor guests at the dinner and stunt party given by the Women's National Press Club. The artist is Helen E. Hokinson, New York cartoonist, who also came down for the party.

The ex-archaeologist, who found fame in the ether, is Lisa Sergio. I met her in Ithaca, New York, where we both took part in Cornell University's famous Farm and Home week.

And as for the women who like the Country Gentleman—why, I met them everywhere; at the Washington frolic; at the Cornell conference; up in Minneapolis, where I spoke to some 1500 club-women of the great Northwest; and back home in Evanston, Illinois, where I talked shop with the journalism students at my own Alma Mater, Northwestern.

But let's get down to personalities.

Of course, I had long heard of Maud Slye. For I grew up in Chicago, where for thirty persistent years, she has devoted her life, body and brain to research into the cause and control of cancer. Where, as a passionate pioneer along this rugged road of research, she has worked with more than 165,000 mice—think of that the next time you squeal when one little mouse rustles in the waste-basket—in an effort to learn the hereditary history of that dread disease. Where, too, she has won fame and not fortune, but something which is more precious to a scientist, the esteem of her colleagues.

I had, however, never met her.

So it was with real interest that I greeted her the night of the dinner. Here was no stiff and stern scientist, throwing cold water on merriment. Not a bit of it. I found a small wiry woman in an attractive black dinner dress; a woman with a fine face, magnificent eyes, distinguished head, and the ability to relax.

Two days later, when she was explaining her work to some of us, she was all business. She told her story the way I like to hear an expert talk to the interested layman. That is, she didn't patronize us by talking, so obviously, down to us. Neither did she confuse us by talking, so grandly, over our heads.

The result—she got her message across.

And what is that message?

Briefly it is this: Since the careful taking of complete case records of mice, with and without cancer, even unto the 20th generation, has shed so much light on the cause and control of cancer, let human beings institute a similar record-taking of their own hereditary histories.

"A business," she points out a bit ironically, "takes an accurate record of its transactions. Why should we not take equally reliable records of the people who are going to carry on the business?"

Back of this message are thousands of case histories. One hundred and sixty-five thousand histories, to be exact; for she has observed 165,000 mice since she first started her experiments. Today, more than 10,000 mice scamper merrily about her laboratory.

I say "scamper merrily" with reason.

For in this laboratory, Doctor Slye tells me, "the mouse is king, and we workers are but secondary."

They are kings because they are the key to her results.

Cancer attacks mice as well as humans in the full vigor of middle age. If, then, the mice were permitted to die in great numbers of other diseases before reaching the cancer zone of susceptibility, no truly scientific statistics on cancer could be computed. So, one of her main jobs is to prolong the life of every mouse in the laboratory.

"My laboratory," she says quietly, "is much kinder than nature. In nature, if a mouse lives to be one month old, he is a wise little mouse, and very lucky. In my laboratory, the average age is one year, and I have many entire families who live to be three years old.

"They live in clean cages. Once a week they get a steam sterilized bath. They eat good food."

Just what is good food for a mouse? I wanted to know. Limburger cheese? Not at all.

Doctor Slye's prescribed diet in her mouse-health resort is as follows—bread, milk, mixed birdseed and timothy hay.

The mention of milk prompted us to ask about the recent theory that milk is conducive to cancer.

"Ridiculous," was her comment.

"The mice," she continues, "don't smoke. They don't go to cocktail parties. They don't overeat. And the hot and spicy foods included in the diet of man kill any mouse I have ever tried them on."

Confident in the results of her years of experiment and experience, she asserts that:

"Two great facts emerge from my studies of mice.

"First, by selective breeding, it is possible to lengthen very greatly the span of vital life.

"Second, all diseases that occur in mice can be ruled out by selective breeding through knowledge of heredity."

Since the diseases of mice, "in both type and percentage," most nearly parallel those of man, and since "all of these results have been achieved in the laboratory," the next, and, to her, inevitable step, is that—"these results could be achieved for humanity."

And she points to her records, showing that some of her mice families have been completely free of cancer for over twenty-eight years. That, in terms of human life, is over 3000 years.

Three thousand years is a lot of years. But a young doctor, receiving his diploma this June, will presumably, she brings out, have three generations under his charge. And the records of those three generations, if taken everywhere in this country, would be a firm first step in cancer research, and, ultimately, in cancer control.

"Do not think that nothing can be done about it," here her voice vibrated with emotion. "Before Pasteur's work was accepted; before Florence Nightingale's work was done, nobody thought that infection could be controlled. Everybody scoffed at aseptic wounds and hospitals. Now these things are routine. The taking of scientific records must also become routine."

But to go back to the Press Club party for a moment. Or rather, to go back of it, by about seven years.

I had been living in Washington only a short time when I went to the Middle West to give a little talk on our national capital.

Just before I was introduced I was handed a note. It was from an old friend, contained a cordial greeting and a cartoon. The cartoon pictured a club meeting, with the president, plump and pompous, in these words—I have never forgotten them:

"Ladies, Mrs. Perkins has just returned from a three-day motor trip to Washington, D. C. She will now sum for us the entire political situation."

And there was I, about to make a speech on Washington.

Well, I started my speech, as I have started many since then, with a reference to that cartoon and with a pledge that I would not be another Mrs. Perkins. And I have always wanted to pay my respects to the lady back of the cartoon—Helen Hokinson.

I had my opportunity to do this at the Press Club dinner, for she, like Doctor Slye, was one of the honor guests. A demure lady with a devastating pencil is a good way to describe this famous artist. She is tiny and quiet. She dresses quietly; wears a fringe of bangs. And she carries a pencil, even at parties.

When I told her of her "influence on my life," she laughed and said the only other person she knew she had ever influenced was her own aunt. It seems Auntie was about to be persuaded by a zealous saleswoman to purchase an utterly silly hat. She had no sales resistance and was about to buy it when she suddenly thought of that other famous Hokinson character—the Fat Lady, who is always buying foolish things. And Auntie suddenly summoned up the will power to resist the hat.

"Aren't people afraid of you?" I inquired.

"Not my friends," she assured me. "But strangers are afraid of me. Sometimes they say, 'Please don't look at my hair.' "

It was all I could do to keep from fussing with my own hair at this point.

Speaking of hair, it was by her coiffure that a group of us at the dinner picked out Elizabeth Hawes, the famous dress designer.

Up at the speaker's table, either side of Number One Honor Guest, Eleanor Roosevelt, were a number of celebrated women: a distinguished nurse; a famous doctor; a Washington socialite; a widely known magazine editor; one of the founders of the Theater Guild; a wise and witty radio commentator; a successful New York business woman; the secretary of the Red Cross; and so on.

Over at our table we tried to fit the face to the name, amid much merriment. Sometimes we lost; sometimes we won. But all of us picked the right person for Elizabeth Hawes.

No, don't ask me what this fashion expert was wearing, for I can't remember. All I know is that she had that vague but valuable thing called chic. That she stood out in a roomful of 500 well-dressed women. That she didn't demand attention, but that she attracted attention. There is a difference.

I can't remember her gown. But I can remember her hair. It was done differently. Just how? I can't say. But we all immediately spotted her as the dress designer.

A few days earlier I had seen another woman possessed of that same clothes sense. She was Lisa Sergio, whose voice you may have heard on the radio, as one of the few women announcers in the world.

The reason there are so few women announcers, by the way, as she sees it, is that "so many of the radio audience in America are women, and women prefer to hear a man's voice." How about it?

Well, whatever your theory, I am sure in reality you'd love to hear this woman's voice, for it is rich and mellow and sympathetic.

Born of an American mother and an Italian father, she was brought up in Italy.

"Brought up very badly," she told the Farm and Home Week audience at Cornell, "for my teachers were so nice they did everything I told them to."

But she must have done some of the things they told her, for she grew up an excellent linguist; and she knew a lot about economics and music, and most of all, about archaeology.

The "fascination of Roman bones," as she calls it, sent her into archaeology, where she did very creditable work. Her friendship with Senator Guglielmo Marconi and his wife, took her out of underground activities in digging ruins, and sent her on to the air. It was the famous Marconi, inventor of wireless telegraphy, who first persuaded her to try her hand, or rather, her voice in radio. She walked into history as Europe's first woman commentator over the air.

Her voice won her the title, "The Golden Voice of Rome."

Last spring, again at Mr. Marconi's suggestion, she abandoned plans for a holiday in Europe and took a trip to America. While she was here, last July, her friend and mentor died. Within eight hours around-the-world tribute to its inventor was broadcast by radio, and Lisa Sergio was asked to take part. Her voice, tense with emotion, went over the air. Her fame quickly followed the voice, and she became one of America's few women commentators.

Speaking at Cornell, she urged the women not to keep their praise and criticism of radio programs "such a secret."

"Write in to the studio," she pleaded.

She lamented the differences in ear interest as illustrated by the following figures.

During an entire month, a certain large New York station received, she revealed, only 300 letters about an elaborate and expensive opera program it was broadcasting. But one thirty-minute period, offering a wishbone pin for a premium, drew forth 173,000 letters.

Radio, she maintained, has a particularly important function in rural communities.

It is true that centers of business and political activity have an influence on the rural community. But it is also tremendously true that the rural community has an increasing influence on centers of business and political activity. This was brought home to me with special statistical force when I read over a recent survey made by the COUNTRY GENTLEMAN.

Its figures were so surprising to me that I wondered if they might not also be news to some of the women to whom I was talking. I found that they were. Indeed, at Cornell, at Northwestern, and up in Minneapolis, I found that the women got out their notebooks and jotted down the statistics when I gave them these results of the research.

Here they are:

Sixty-one and six tenths per cent of our Representatives in the United States Congress come from districts in which more than one half the population lives on farms or in places of less than 10,000 population.

Seventy-five per cent of our Senators come from States in which more than one half the population lives on farms or in places of less than 10,000 population.

Spurred on by the women's interest in these figures, I usually gave them some more. By this same survey we learn that there are really only 12 urban states, using this same yardstick. These 12 are: California, Connecticut, Illinois, Maryland, Massachusetts, Michigan, New Jersey, New York, Ohio, Pennsylvania, Rhode Island and Washington.

Now I am usually well able to restrain my passion for statistics. But I found myself going on to other columns of figures; and I found the women taking notes with evident interest.

These other figures were compiled by the National Federation of Business and Professional Women. In a survey, made purposely in 1937 because it is an off-year politically, these facts came forth.

There are 140 women serving in the state legislatures in 35 states. Of these 140, only 14 are in state senates. The others are in the lower houses. New England, for all its conservative tradition, leads the feminine field, with the four states of Maine, New Hampshire, Vermont and Connecticut piling up more than one half the total number. Connecticut and New Hampshire tie, with 19 women in each state legislature. That's a pretty good number.

Out west, the states of Washington and Utah tie, with seven women apiece in their respective state legislatures. I was able to give that news, the other night, to Mrs. Elbert Thomas, wife of the junior senator from Utah, and she was pleased and proud. So was I, that I could give her news of her own state.

California, by the way, can boast of something more than climate. This sunny state smiles on more women in public offices, both elective and appointive, in all government units, than any other state in the Union. The number is 446.

A wise man, or maybe it was a woman, once counseled:

"Never stay home so much you don't want to go out. And never go out so much that you don't want to stay home."

Well, it was fun going off to New York, Minnesota and Illinois. It was also fruitful. For it is enlarging to the viewpoint to brush elbows with other arcs of the circle.

And everywhere I found women interested primarily in three things—peace and progress and politics.

I found them, too, interested in COUNTRY GENTLEMAN. And once the magazine saved "face" for me, as the Chinese say.

It was at a luncheon for Governor Lehman, at Cornell's Farm and Home Week. I was seated opposite an elderly, erudite gentleman who, I later learned, was a famous horticulturist.

He fixed me with a kindly but somewhat quizzical eye and he said:

"Pardon me, but I'm an old fellow with a lot of curiosity. And I'd like to know"—here a note of bewilderment crept into his voice—"just what connection you have with agriculture."

Well, to be honest, I was hard put for an answer, for a moment.

But only for a moment. Then I said: "Why, I write for COUNTRY GENTLEMAN."

He at once accepted me as a colleague.

And joyously recalled his teaching days in Michigan when one of his distinguished pupils was a boy named—Philip Rose.

But that's another story.

Questions:

Why is the title "Women in the News" better than, for example, "Interesting Women"?

Why do such magazines as *Better Homes & Gardens*, *Good Housekeeping*, and *Architectural Forum* use few personality stories?

Exactly how does Mrs. Herrick obtain the informal tone which marks this story?

HE'S SKINNER—AND A HOST OF OLD FRIENDS, TOO

HE'S SKINNER—AND A HOST OF OLD FRIENDS, TOO

By L. H. Robbins

Reprinted by special permission from the New York Times

Is it not "something" to be able, on your front porch of a Sunday afternoon, in San Pedro or Peoria or Worcester, to have a visit, a chat, a session of reminiscences, with Otis Skinner? No "serious" talk, no politics, or wars or economics. But a warm and friendly and intimate contact with a man of whom you have heard for many years, whom you have seen, perhaps, on the stage, the glamor and richness of whose life you have envied.

Such a visit a well-done personality article can give to you—as Mr. Robbins has done in the following:

Otis Skinner, dean of the American stage, will be 80 next Tuesday. In the last month he has been ill, but the invalid's role is strange to him. His habit is to keep as young in spirit and almost as vigorous in body as when he and John Drew, Ada Rehan, May Irwin and Edith Kingdon filled Augustine Daly's with fashionable crowds at first nights in the Eighteen Eighties.

Time has dealt kindly with Mr. Skinner. Perhaps the fellow with the sickle can't deal otherwise with a man who goes right on year after year being himself, serving his art and delighting in a world that reciprocates his feeling. As much as ever Mr. Skinner is a part of that world, though he might be expected to begin to weary of its noise and its jostling and to choose to be a recluse among his books and his art treasures.

Daily, in the Winter season, he leaves his apartment home in the East 60's to mingle with old friends at The Players, The Century and his other clubs, to do an occasional bit in civic affairs, and to drift often to the theatre. Summer finds him usually at Woodstock, in Vermont, where he has a fine old mansion facing the village green.

There he walks in the hills, plays a little golf, attends auction sales and drives the country lanes—he confides that he has exchanged his long car for a stubbier one on account of the hairpin turns in that rugged vicinity. He may even go brook-trouting, as he did in boyhood in those same Green Mountains where his father, a Universalist minister, of Cambridge and afterward of Hartford, took him on vacation in Civil War days. In Cambridge Mr. Skinner was born, and in Hartford he grew up, along with the late William Gillette; and rumor says that the key to the Connecticut capital city is his special possession.

Interview Mr. Skinner in his eightieth year and it isn't long before you are a happy captive of the charm of an urbane, forthright, humorous and finely speaking personality. A magical thing, that charm. Two chairs in a book-walled study, with Mr. Skinner in one, talking, and the room undergoes transformations.

Now it is the palace in "Kismet," and Hajj, the rollicking beggar—"Alms, for the love of Allah!"—lies prone on the floor, waggling his heels in air as he drowns the Vizier Mansur in the harem pool, a jolly murdering. Again, it is the dressing room at the arena in "Blood and Sand," and Juan Gallardo, the bullfighter, is cutting the splints from his broken leg to see whether he cannot yet stand upon it to slay one more bull. The customers used to faint right and left at that scene, though Mr. Skinner made the self-surgery as easy as possible for them.

It may be just the sentimental imagining of an old-time gallery god who remembers Mr. Skinner in "His Grace de Grammont," "Prince Otto" and "Rosemary"; but the man in the chair is much more than a famous retired actor. He is an old friend; in fact, a host of old friends, all as real as he himself.

He is the Napoleonic Colonel Philippe Bridau, in "The Honor of the Family," whacking the table with his stick. He is Hamlet and Petruchio, Romeo and Antony, Falstaff and Shylock—he likes to say that Shylock is the only gentleman in "The Merchant," and he played the part that way. He is Charles Surface, too, and Sancho Panza, and Tarkington's Tony with the hurdy-gurdy and the donkey cart. He is some 300 characters besides these, all of them romantic and many of them richly roguish. Time will need a lot of time yet to dim their memory.

Very much of today is Mr. Skinner, with a cigarette going and with a telephone, the latest "Who's Who" and the radio at hand—between fine music programs he tunes in on the fights and the ball games. Yet his recollections go back to Edwin Booth, Lawrence Barrett and John McCullough, to Janauschek, Lotta and Modjeska, with all of whom he faced the footlights, and to Barnum, who liked his father's preaching.

He can show you the identical letter that the circus man gave him, assuring whom it might concern that the bearer had a yearning for the stage and that his parents were "eminently respectable." It got the young man his first engagement—at the Arch Street Museum in Philadelphia in 1877. He went with a Shakespeare in his pocket, and they put him to work in blackface. The pay was uncertain. He knew what it was to be hungry.

Mr. Skinner remembers the time when stars toured in lonely grandeur, depending on local stock companies along the way for their supporting casts, and when a player in stock thought nothing of getting up six new parts a week. He had to be versatile, a pirate one night, a parson the next. It was great training.

By and by, as a lithe and lively juvenile, Mr. Skinner was studying in another exacting school, coached in light comedy by the iron-willed Daly, taking on polish, voyaging overseas to help Daly win European liking for American stage folk and stage ways. In time he was leading man for great women players, notably Modjeska.

At last an actor-manager, he led companies of his own through the country, playing "The King's Jester," "Villon the Vagabond" and Shakespeare. Maud Durbin, "imaginative, fair to look upon," played Juliet to his Romeo. One day in New Orleans he asked her to become Mrs. Otis Skinner, and she said yes.

Whimsically Mr. Skinner tells of his first seasons as a star. Although accepted in New England, the South and the West, "I couldn't get into New York," and "at times we traveled on a sea of red ink, with scarcely the means to get from town to town." Yet his day came, and Broadway at its palmiest was his oyster, and Charles Frohman's. It was under Frohman's management that he starred in "The Duel," "The Honor of the Family" and "Kismet"—"Kismet" ran here and on the road for three years.

Finally he saw theatre costs grow ruinous and a machine-made mass-production form of entertainment run off with the audiences, leaving the traditional theatre dark in large parts of the land. Yet on Broadway and on country-wide Shakespearean tours he kept the box offices busy, and before the Hollywood cameras nineteen years after his stage "Kismet" had set the world afire he made a screen version of the play and started another conflagration.

"The screen has its art, its good points and its uses," he admits readily. "Still, it is only the shadow of the real thing. The living personalities of the stage play aren't there. The vital contact of player and audience and their collaboration in the undertaking at hand—these the screen lacks and never will have. And the human fondness for that sort of effort can never be killed, as Broadway today and the little theatres and the Summer theatres prove.

"It takes player and beholder, working together," he explains, "to give conviction of life and reality to a play and to transport people out of themselves. Only that joint process can create the complete dramatic illusion; a two-dimension phantom on a sheet can never evoke the necessary response and cooperation from the people out in front." He tells of studying a part for weeks and still feeling uncertain in it until audiences had worked on the part with him for an equal length of time.

As Mr. Skinner looks back over eighty years, does he see any fundamental change in human nature? "Manners and morals are not what they were," he replies; "but then they are always changing. Look at the swing of the pendulum between the dour, joyless time of Cromwell and the gay days of the Restoration, and the swing back to primness in Victorian times, and the swing the other way today. We have lost, too, the leisureliness which the old days seem to have had. And we've grown pretty broad in our talking.

"Still I don't think there is any less decency in the human heart than there was when every play was chemically pure, when we dared not utter God's name on the stage, and a single 'damn' in a Clyde Fitch line set the pulpits to thundering.

"The stage reflects the superficial changes of the times, yet it also mirrors the deep and changeless truths of the human spirit. You have only to look at the stage today to see that the eternal spiritual values are still honored among us. Whenever a clean, simple, kindly play like 'Our Town' comes along, or a philosophical, soulful play like 'Shadow and Substance,' it always wins a following in competition with the welter of plays of the sordid sort. The popularity of the Shakespeare revivals is another sign that human nature is holding its own."

With a smile Mr. Skinner adds: "When I try to discuss the world in general I have to speak in terms of the stage. I always have to get back there and touch base."

What this actor regrets most about the present-day stage is its drift away from romance, heroism and sentiment toward literalism and the sheer, crass facts of life. He would have the theatre remain "a place of play, a place of fantasy and recreation and escape, where the audience would be expected to check its common sense at the door."

Political economy dramatized and propaganda plays about social problems leave him cold. He doesn't like the stage to ignore beauty and the gracious arts and go in for bald utilitarianism. Paraphrasing a French romantic dramatist, he says: "The garbage can is one of the most useful things in the world, but I don't care to see a play about it."

That provokes a query that has nothing to do with the theatre. Is it true that the tumult of the market place and the shouting of the forum cease to seem important to a man at fourscore years? Do the extraordinary governmental doings of the day disturb Mr. Skinner?

His answer comes instantly. "You don't suppose that I pick up the paper and read the headlines with any feeling of calmness, do you?"

Asked whether he would be a player again if he were to start over, Mr. Skinner looks back across sixty years of work and ups and downs, a rough-and-tumble mixture of stress, disaster, heartache, success and fortune, and replies, "I can't imagine doing anything else."

But the monotony of playing one part night after night for months at a stretch? "No profession can have less of humdrum. No day on the stage is ever like the day before," he says. "Though you may have trained yourself in a routine, you are still subject to the spiritual weather changes that affect all mortals. You are continually the victim of accident or mood, health or external conditions. So you never make your entrance twice with the same feeling toward the part you play.

"Often you are out of sorts and bowed beneath mountainous oppression. You look at the job before you and think, 'Have I got to go through with this awful pile of duty once more?' You try to lash yourself back into proper tone and temper.

"You yearn to be sprightly, avid, spontaneous again; to tackle the task with the old eagerness and excitement, and you yearn in vain.

"As you sit at the make-up table the feeling of futility may drop away, bit by bit, and the old feeling return. But if not, you learn in time not to be desperate about it. After all, you have worked out the mechanical details, you can go through the lines. It became my rule at last not to struggle to get back, but to let myself into the part in the exact mood I was in at the moment.

"Joseph Jefferson used to have the problem, and for years as Rip Van Winkle or Bob Acres he made a point of approaching his work at each performance as if he had never met Rip or Bob before; he would pretend to himself that it was a brand-new part he was undertaking, and you know how fresh his interpretations seemed.

"So it is with most players. The part is always played a little differently from the time before. Audiences, too, are never twice alike; they are as variable as the players who try to stir response from them. It means that every working night of a player's life is an adventure, a conflict with uncertainties, a little drama of its own. And who could ask for a livelier life than that?

"Perhaps it is this element of chance, this doubtfulness of the outcome, that explains the everlasting appeal of the living play. Certainly it contributes to the beholder's sense of satisfaction and to the actor's sense of triumph when the effort turns out successfully."

In "Footlights and Spotlights," Mr. Skinner's account of his career, and in his occasional public talks he has spoken often of the perennial thrill of the player's life. "Join the stage and stay young," and, again, "Sometimes I think that actors never really grow up; the years pass over their whitening heads and find them still Peter Pans and Topsies."

A friend of Presidents, a degree-decorated figure at college commencements and a man of the world honored by the distinguished in all the arts, Mr. Skinner is still youthful enough to enjoy a chuckle over the hard years and the mishaps before fame discovered him.

There was the night at Leadville, elevation 10,000 feet and the air very thin, when he rushed into Mark Antony's long speech and ran out of breath half way through. And there was the week when he was all but stranded in Lincoln, Neb., his misfortune being that a famous Wild West scout with a cowboy show was playing the town the same week. Yet the gloomy situation had its bright moment.

For the famous scout, whose manager knew his besetting weakness and kept him on short allowance of spending money, borrowed $10 from Mr. Skinner's impoverished manager, drank it up, then wandered into the almost empty theatre and could scarcely be restrained from taking the stage and berating the Lincoln public for so shabbily treating "my dear friend Skinner, the greatest actor in the world."

But plays that flopped and stars that were difficult; robberies, fires, blizzards, train wrecks on tour; moments of stage fright and forgotten lines; cold dressing rooms often and colder audiences now and then—these are only the shadows in the bright and pleasant picture that Otis Skinner looks back upon at 80.

Practice Suggestions

1. In your community are there any people who might be the subjects of personality stories? List them, describe briefly the articles that could be written about them and the magazines that might be interested in the articles.

2. Take one of these subjects and analyze in detail the qualities of the person and his achievements which would make a story about him of interest to other people.

3. Brush up on your reading of Dickens, Conrad, Dos Passos, Katherine Mansfield, Thomas Hardy,—or other able writers for whom you have a preference—to see how they make people and places come alive in their pages.

4. Look over a large number of magazines to see which ones make the most use of personality stories.

REFERENCES

BOOKS

A History of American Magazines, 1741-1850, by Frank Luther Mott. D. Appleton and Company, New York, 1930.

Magazine Article Readings, by Ernest Brennecke, Jr., and Donald Lemen Clark. The Macmillan Company, New York, 1931.

How to Write for a Living, by Trentwell Mason White. Reynal and Hitchcock, New York, 1937.

Magazine Publishing, by Lenox R. Lohr. Williams & Wilkins Company, Baltimore, 1932.

Why House Magazines? Business Journalist, Chicago, 1933.

Pulpwood Editor, by Harold B. Hersey. Frederick A. Stokes Company, New York, 1937.

Technical Journalism, by F. W. Beckman, Harry R. O'Brien, and Blair Converse. The Collegiate Press, Ames, Iowa, 1937.

See also *Magazine Article Writing* (Brennecke and Clark), *Modern Feature Writing* (Harrington and Watson), *Magazine Articles* (Crawford), *Writing Journalistic Features* (Reed), *Writing for Profit* (Wilhelm), *The Business Paper Editor at Work* (Woolf).

PERIODICALS

"Pocket and Pictorial Journalism," by Harry Shaw, *North American Review,* 243:2, Page 297, summer, 1937.

"Parade of the Pocket Press," by S. Claude Bartley, *Christian Science Monitor Magazine,* July 14, 1937.

"Controlled Magazines and How They've Grown," by Roy Sheldon, *Advertising and Selling,* 29:2, Page 29, May, 1937.

"Our 'Liberal' Weeklies," by Harold Lord Varney, *American Mercury,* December, 1937.

"The Women's Magazines," by Dora Copperfield, *Vanity Fair,* 41:5, Page 22, January, 1934.

"Sophisticated Vanity Fair," by John E. Drewry, *Quill,* 23:10, Page 9, October, 1935.

"How Cosmopolitan's Course Is Charted," by Daniel Henderson, *Quill,* 23:9, Page 6, September, 1935.

"Ties of the Atlantic," by Joseph Barber, Jr., *Quill,* 23:11, Page 8, November, 1935.

"Albert Shaw's Review," by David Page, *Quill,* 24:9, Page 8, September, 1936.

"Good Housekeeping's Story," by Daniel Henderson, *Quill,* 24:10, Page 8, October, 1936.

"The Magazine of Controversy: the Story of Forum Magazine," by Clementine Hall, *Quill,* 24:8, Page 7, September, 1936.

"Profiles: Henry Robinson Luce," by Wolcott Gibbs, *New Yorker,* 12:41, Page 20, November 28, 1937.

"Mencken and the Mercury," by John E. Drewry, *Quill,* 26:3, Page 10, March, 1938.

Magazine Departments

A POPULAR magazine is a good deal like a cafeteria. Laid out along the counter is a variety of foods. Soups and meats and salads and vegetables and pies and cakes. Suppose the counter displays a hundred items. There may be fish roe or sweetbreads, spinach for the puritanical, fried cucumbers or bananas for those who fancy the exotic, strange and alluring desserts—but there are always roast beef and potatoes and apple pie.

And a magazine is like that. It too has its staples. The food which it knows its readers want to buy month after month. Because they are staples doesn't mean that these standbys are stodgy or unappetizing. They may in fact be delicious and exciting.

The magazine's departments contain its staples. They line its counter because of the experience of the magazine, its letters from readers, its reader-interest surveys, show that these are foods that its public wants.

It would be hard to find a magazine without any regular departments. How many departments a magazine may maintain will depend largely upon the kind of magazine it is. In the *Better Homes & Gardens'* material reproduced in the front of this book, there are fifteen departments. They occupy about a third of the magazine's editorial space.

"Across the Editor's Desk," Page 1, is the special preserve of the editor. In such a department he can do two things: First, he can get acquainted with his readers or rather let them get acquainted with him. To meet his readers through his personal page, the editor of a magazine creates for himself the kind of personality, character, temperament, which he thinks is appropriate to the kind of magazine he is editing. He may be witty, a little sarcastic, and a specialist in the light touch. He may be straightforward and practical—the kind of chap upon whose judgment you can base an investment or a bet. He may be friendly and generous, a repository of the good old-fashioned virtues. He may be iconoclastic, the personification of the eternal question mark. In any case he must be—whatever his off-the-stage character—the sort of person that he thinks his readers think he should be—as the prow, not to say figurehead, of his magazine. His job in this department is to personalize, to make real and intimate, almost visual, through his readers' conception of him, the magazine that he represents. If his readers can be made to think of him as a fine fellow, a generous fellow, a brainy fellow, a witty fellow, then these characteristics are by transposition applied to the magazine itself; and it comes to be thought of not merely as paper spread with ink, but as a personality toward which one can make emotional gestures of loyalty, pride, and confidence.

The other thing that the editor can do in his department is to grind axes. Here he can bring before his readers the causes, the philosophies, the particular activities, for which the magazine stands.

Mr. McDonough's department is made up of short paragraphs. He wants them above everything else to breathe an air of friendliness. He wants them after that to be diversified, to pull an oar now and then for the things the magazine is interested in.

Where do the ideas and materials for these paragraphs come from? Mr. McDonough says, "Everywhere." He has in his desk a red accordion file. It has six compartments. Stick your hand into one of these compartments and it will pull out six or eight newspaper clippings, brief notes written on odd-sized pieces of paper, sheets torn from bulletins or magazines, letters from readers with red pencil marks around paragraphs here and there, memoranda from members of the staff who every month are asked to submit suggestions.

Mr. McDonough writes the stuff himself. For each issue he writes three or four times as much material as can be used. Then he whacks out and pares down, and the manuscript goes to others on the staff for their whacking and paring.

If, as a writer studying magazine markets, you want to get the "feel" of a magazine, the first place to go is to the editor's page. These pages vary greatly in externals—position, content, layout, style of writing—but they give a feeling of the "tone" that the editors want their magazine to maintain. The informal comment which many of them contain concerning material that is appearing in the magazine—or material to appear later—frequently holds valuable tips for the writer.

TOWN HALL

TOWN HALL

Reprinted by special permission from Pictorial Review

"Town Hall," the editorial page of *Pictorial Review,* is markedly different from the *Better Homes & Gardens'* editor's page, but it serves much the same purposes.

INTERNATIONAL NOTE: At last we know how some of those foreign diplomats feel when, after grave and secret conferences, their valiant efforts begin to jell. For now reposing in our vault is a manuscript, just arrived, for which we initiated heroic negotiations a vast long while ago. The manuscript is signed with the name of Booth Tarkington. It is a novel, and to it we attribute the distinction which marked Alice Adams for the Pulitzer Prize in 1922. Alice Adams was the novel by Mr. Tarkington which ran serially in Pictorial Review. This new novel of his will not be published serially—but complete, in one issue. We feel wonderful about it.

* * * * *

SPEAKING, as indeed we were, of things begun long ago, we remember clearly that summer day in 1935 when we bought a story called Mrs. Manning's Birthday. Written by Thyra Samter

Winslow, it was about an old lady and a Queen of England, and it ended with the Queen calling on the old lady for tea; though if you read the story when it appeared you won't need any memory jogging from us. After we got through swallowing our gulps we cheered madly. Then we sent for Mrs. Winslow and demanded more. "Next month," we said, "there must be another story, and the month after that, and the next month—." But no more came. From demanding we turned to persuading, from persuading to pleading. After a while we got tired.

Last New Year's Eve, doing our one and only annual toot, we landed at four in the morning in the home of Lilly Daché, the lady who makes very smart hats and was then giving a very nice party. Well, there we saw Thyra Samter Winslow again. "Look here," we said, "who (or whom) do you think you are? You can't go on like this, not writing stories." Finally Thyra admitted she had a theme in mind and we said Happy New Year.

Now it is another summer and in this issue you will behold Sophie Jackson, which has been so slow in coming. We think it is fine. And Romance at One, also by Mrs. Winslow, which will follow soon, is likewise fine. Just imagine—no stories for years, and then two in quick succession. "The thorn in the cushion of the editorial chair," Mr. Thackeray once wrote, and we think he must have meant authors who author all too seldom.

* * * * *

Social Note: Our fashion editor, Nancy White, will be on her honeymoon when this issue rolls off the press. If she sees this item over there in Norway she will know all of us are missing her.

Pugilistic Note: If our secretary doesn't remember to leave our phone connected every night when she leaves for home she is going to get a clip on the chin.

Gratitude Note: For two solid weeks now the woman who cleans our desk hasn't knocked over our pet donkey and broken off his weak right ear. If this record is continued we will give her a nice present.

* * * * *

"YOU'RE a flinty-hearted lot," protests Katherine Moorehead, of Sioux City, "if Fool Dog (May issue) only brought a lump to your throat. Personally I bawled a bucketful. Gosh, it's wonderful to have a cry like that, makes one feel so good. I loved that darn dog!"

For Miss Moorehead and others who, like us, are push-overs for dog stories, a friendly word of warning. Start now to practice laughing and crying in the same breath. For come the August number you will find therein a dog yarn that is a honey. By Arthur Tuckerman. Entitled The More I See of Men. 'S marvelous.

And being on the subject, Ruth Stewart Shenley has done a bit of verse which belongs exactly here:

MY EYES HAVE TOLD YOU SO

I'll never bark
Except when robbers come;
I'll never even beg for bones
Until you condescend to give me some.
I'll sit out front
And guard your house all day,
And never chase a falling leaf
While you're away.
I'll always brush my coat
And keep immaculate my paws;
And never scratch around the door
Without just cause.
And when we walk
I'll not embarrass you with trees,
But go as proud
As twenty pedigrees.
I'll listen when you talk,
And mind your every word;
I'll never jump on Things,
Or chase one cat or bird.
I'll be the nicest little dog
Oh, please, if you'll just say,
"Here, Boy, come in"—
And to your wife, "I guess we'll let him stay."

* * * * *

QUITE some to-do developed in the shop when Anton Bruehl handed us the photograph of the little flower girl that appeared on last month's cover. Everybody oh'd and ah'd and fell boldly in love, and no less than three male executives insisted on having the child's telephone number. Staunchly we refused to divulge it. What good would it do us if *other* people had it?

* * * * *

UNTIL Helen Welshimer's poem was opened we hadn't planned on going to the country for the weekend. Now, however, we have a sudden yearning to see a horse. The poem goes like this:

It isn't often that you meet
A horse upon a city street,
And when you do he's fastened to
A milkman's cart, for it is true
That mares and bays no longer go
In proud processional, and so
It's nice to know that on the farm,
Secure from taxicabs and harm,
They help to pull the plow and aid
In cabbage hauls and are repaid
By stalls in warm red barns where they
Can fill themselves with oats and hay.

* * * * *

So, as Ted Malone says, G'bye.

THE EDITORS.

Editorials

FARM SALES

Odds and Ends

The Song of the Lazy Farmer

EDITORIALS

Reprinted by special permission from Wallaces' Farmer and Iowa Homestead

The editorial page of *Wallaces' Farmer and Iowa Homestead* is an "idea" page. There facts and figures are driven home; legislation is discussed and advocated or condemned; the trends in the business of farming are analyzed. Yet the writing is no less interesting and graphic than that in less "serious" editorial pages.

Win Better Treatment for Butter

Corn belt dairymen will remember how Wallaces' Farmer and Iowa Homestead pointed out that the American Medical Association had not only refused its "seal of acceptance" to butter, but had given it to butter substitutes. And to make the situation even worse, the A. M. A. had allowed butter substitutes to use the "seal of acceptance" in connection with misleading advertisements of their product.

While running our articles on this subject, we discovered that physicians, as well as dairymen, were concerned over the situation. The Iowa Medical Association, under the leadership of Dr. Fred Moore, of Des Moines, passed resolutions asking for a change in the policy of the national organization.

The American Medical Association, meeting in annual convention at San Francisco, has now promised reform on both points raised by Wallaces' Farmer and Iowa Homestead. The resolution which was submitted recommended:

"That the House of Delegates request the Council on Foods to re-establish suitable standards for the acceptance of butter and the advertising associated therewith; and also

"That the House of Delegates request the Council on Foods to carefully scrutinize the advertising of accepted brands of oleomargarine or butter substitutes, to the end that no improper or extravagant claims of nutritional value be associated with the printing of the seal of acceptance of the Council on Foods of the American Medical Association."

This resolution was accepted unanimously by the House of Delegates, and a statement from Morris Fishbein, secretary of the A. M. A., tells us that "cordial reception by the council of the change in policy assures satisfactory results."

This is a real victory for public health and for dairy interests. Wallaces' Farmer and Iowa Homestead is glad to have had a part in it.

Corn Import Argument Is Out of Date

From Michigan comes one of the most fantastic of objections to corn acreage reduction for 1938. Ira Wilmoth, president of the Michigan Farmers Union, recently pointed to corn imports of 86,000,000 bushels for 1937, and said:

"Can you imagine how many farmers and how many acres of crop land could be put to work in this country producing that 86,000,000 bushels of corn? How can the farmers of this country have any confidence in Wallace when he seeks to limit our corn production in the face of that 86,000,000-bushel shortage in our last year's crop?"

The joker, here, as every reader of Wallaces' Farmer and Iowa Homestead probably sees at once, is that there was no shortage of any kind in last year's crop. The present stocks of corn are the highest since 1933. The 86,000,000 bushels came in to remedy the shortage in the 1936 crop, the year of the drouth.

As soon as the 1937 crop was harvested, imports slowed down. Here we give the figures for the imports and exports of corn (in bushels) for the four months following harvest in 1937:

	Imports	*Exports*
November	177,231	1,712,560
December	151,567	3,862,165
January	39,286	13,254,284
February	40,254	16,138,000

Imports of corn, therefore, are now—and have been since the harvest of the 1937 crop—at a rate considerably smaller than in any year of the period from 1924 to 1930.

Market Your Hogs Early This Fall

Hog prices surprised most farmers by being stronger than expected during most of June. It looks as though prices might continue strong through the next two months, although they will, of course, be considerably under last year.

If the corn crop continues to look good, and December corn continues to be quoted at 40 cents, Iowa farm price, a lot of farmers will hold out sows and gilts for fall farrowing. August shipments will be correspondingly lighter, and the run of early spring pigs may have a better chance.

With an increase in spring pigs this year, and plenty of feed, the chances are that the new crop will come on the market a little earlier than usual this fall, and in volume greater than last year. While there is a chance of a pick-up in consumer demand this fall, the increase in demand is not likely to balance the increase in supply.

It will probably pay farmers with early litters, therefore, to crowd them for the late August or early September market. This seems one of the years when early marketing will be more profitable than usual.

Marketing Quotas on Corn This Fall?

What is the chance of having marketing quotas on corn this year? We'll tell you the answer if you'll tell us what corn weather will be like in July.

The August 1 crop report will tell the story. If that report shows a crop of 2,450,000,000 bushels or more, and if the current estimates show a probable carry-over of 350,000,000 bushels, this will provide the total supply of 2,800,000,000 bushels which, under the law, forces the secretary of agriculture to call for a referendum on marketing quotas.

The secretary must make the announcement by August 15 as to whether marketing quotas will or will not be needed. And the referendum, in which all producers affected by the quotas can vote, must be held before September 4.

If one-third of those voting object to quotas, there won't be any. Moreover, if August weather shows a marked change in the crop, so that the September 1 estimate drops to 2,350,000,000 or to any point that carries the total of crop and carry-over below 2,800,000,000 bushels, then the secretary of agriculture, under the law, must announce by September 20 that marketing quotas are not needed and will not be used. Thus, even though quotas might be voted by September 3, a decrease in the corn crop could still abolish the quotas for the year.

If corn totals 2,450,000,000 bushels, and if a referendum is called for, will corn farmers vote to approve the marketing quotas?

That turns probably on the way corn prices look. If farm prices for the new crop, on the basis of December futures, are around 30 cents a bushel, and if cooperators can get a 55-cent loan on all corn and non-cooperators can get a 32-cent loan on the storage quota required, probably the referendum would approve the use of marketing quotas.

If corn prices are around 40 cents, cooperators would probably vote "Yes" to get the 55-cent loan, but some cooperators might balk, even though a big volume of corn stored might bring up the price materially for the corn actually put on the market. If only 15 per cent of the crop had to be stored, the favorable vote would naturally be higher than if 20 per cent were involved.

The size of the loan made on corn, of course, depends entirely on the size of this year's crop. If the crop is under 2,600,000,000 bushels, the loan to cooperators will be around 60 cents. If over 2,600,000,000 bushels, the loan to cooperators will be around 55 cents.

No loans will be made if marketing quotas are called for and are voted down. If quotas are called for, and are approved, then cooperators get loans on all their crop, and non-cooperators 60 per cent of the loan rate to cooperators, but only on the volume stored under the quota system.

Every one hopes, of course, that the corn acreage adjustment program of 1938 has been sufficiently successful so that the corn crop this year will be under 2,450,000,000 bushels. That would give cooperators a loan of around 60 cents a bushel and nobody would be bothered with marketing quotas.

ODDS AND ENDS

Pastures are looking fine this year. But many will look better now and do better next year if the weeds are cut before they go to seed.

There is still plenty of land in corn in Iowa that should be in grass or trees. The worst piece we saw in a trip in eastern Iowa recently was an up-and-down field near Anamosa which looked as if the corn had been planted with a shotgun. Or by a corn planter drawn by mountain goats. But we also saw, near Anamosa, the only field we passed in several counties, in which the corn was planted on the contour lines.

When the farmers put on the pressure these days, they can certainly get through with a pile of work in a few days. In mid-June, in the first dry days that followed two weeks of showers, everybody and his brother were out in the fields, cultivating corn or getting in hay. One Linn county corn field had in it a tractor cultivator, two riding cultivators and one walking cultivator.

It is hard to remember now that we used to think tractors were all right for plowing and for belt work, but not for much else. To see tractors galloping across a corn field, cutting hay, hauling hay wagons and loaders, is a revelation in the changes that have come in a few years. That's why a backward season doesn't handicap farmers severely any more.

In preparing the copy for "Its News To Me" (Page 2) Anna Olson creates some ninety dollars' worth of business for the United States Post

Office—all in three-cent bits for postage stamps. Her purpose in this department is to select, out of the hundreds of new gadgets, products, and processes that are put on the market every month, those that may be of some service or interest to the magazine's readers. She is on the mailing lists of hundreds of manufacturers to receive catalogs and announcements of new products. Obviously, manufacturers are anxious to get their products mentioned in her department. Her office, at times, has something of the appearance of a department store—floor and window and filing cases covered with samples that have been sent to her for inspection.

Out of all these materials plus additional suggestions which come to her from others on the magazine staff, Miss Olson makes a selection of the items that she wants to use. From catalogs, letters, mailing pieces, and the products themselves, she writes single-paragraph descriptions of each item. Then she writes to each of the manufacturers inclosing the proposed copy and asking them to check it. If she does not have information as to the selling price of the article and the retail outlets, she asks the manufacturer to supply this material.

When the okayed copy is back, she selects six or eight items and has the art department prepare drawings of the products. These drawings reproduced in a panel are each numbered and reference is made to them by number in the copy.

THE BUSINESS OUTLOOK

Reprinted by special permission from Business Week

Another "News" department—utterly different from "It's News to Me" in *Better Homes & Gardens*, but designed as all such departments are to meet the news wants of its readers—is "The Business Outlook," published each week as the lead feature in *Business Week*. It is made interesting and valuable to the magazine's readers by the bird's-eye glimpse that it gives of the week's developments in business and by its canny forecasts of trends and prospects.

This week the economic indexes continued to point downward. Steel production was off, security quotations were irregular, and commodity prices went to new low figures. There was little or no improvement in the political or international situations. For the next two or three months, as seasonal influences reinforce the cumulative effects of nearly a year of recession, business activity may be expected to slacken. If, however, the same months see the foundations for a revival laid in the fields of politics, money and business, the rebound after Labor Day may be rapid whether or not it carries far or proves enduring.

The most striking development of the week under review was the drop in the prices of basic agricultural and industrial raw materials. The huge carryover in cotton, the probability of a bumper American wheat crop, and the heavy metal stocks in the hands of producers were among the influences which exerted steady pressure on prices. Moody's index of 15 raw materials fell at mid-week to its 1934 low point, 43% below the peak of April 5, 1937.

Price Control Efforts

This continuing decline in commodity prices is a disturbing factor in the situation, and naturally leads to efforts to halt it by restricting supply. The wheat loans which the Commodity Credit Corporation is understood to be planning and the unexpectedly sharp reduction of rubber export quotas from 60% to basic allotments to 45% are examples.

Such moves, however, are not likely to have any controlling influence. It is seldom as a result of restriction of output or reduction of stocks that a period of price decline is brought to an end. Purchasing agents are likely to continue the strictest hand-to-mouth policy for the time being, confident that supplies are and will remain adequate if they should decide to buy. Prices, therefore, will hardly strengthen much in the immediate future.

Possibilities for Rally

It is from the side of demand that the impulse usually comes for an upturn in commodity prices at the end of a long decline. Just when stocks on hand are at their peak, buying starts, for one reason or another, and, if inventories in the hands of purchasers are low, a sharp rally may easily ensue. It would be reckless to make such prediction for the late summer and early fall of 1938, but it is becoming a distinct possibility.

Consumption Bulge

In connection with commodity prices, there are two basic factors on which reliance is placed for an upturn in the latter half of the year. One is the continuance of consumption at a rate greater than production, with a consequent depletion of goods in the hands of merchandisers and consumers, regardless of stocks in the hands of primary producers. This may be illustrated by the comparative rates of decline of national income paid out (including wages and salaries, dividends and interest, farm income, etc.) and industrial production.

What the Figures Show

In March of this year the former series was off 8%, the latter off 33%, from March, 1937. These figures are merely indicative: they take no account of such factors as changes in the percentage of income paid out which is actually spent by the recipient on goods or services. But of the gradual depletion of consumers' inventories there can be little or no doubt. The timing is another matter. Here the position has been taken that restocking movement is likely in the fall, and this guess still seems as good as another.

Monetary Stimulus

The second factor referred to in a preceding paragraph as giving grounds for an upturn this year is the new monetary and credit policy of the government. During 1937 Federal Reserve and Treasury policies were sharply deflationary, reflected (among other things) in a decline of nearly two billion dollars in the investment holdings of American commercial banks. In April, 1938, an entire reversal occurred. In accordance with the new policy, gold has been desterilized, reserve requirements have been reduced, the budget has been unbalanced.

These monetary influences require time before they affect commodities, but history supports the belief that sooner or later the influence will be felt. When combined with the effect of the new spending program—an effect which will probably disappoint the Administration but may easily add $100,000,000 to $200,000,000 to monthly government expenditures by Election Day—the power of the government is seen to have been turned in favor of higher prices.

The Political Factor

A third major factor which can prove bullish for business as well as prices in the autumn is the political campaign. There have been no important developments in evidence on this front during the week, but events in Washington show how the sides are lining up for the battle.

Here we have seen the President's verbal assault on the highly constructive tax bill followed by Senator Harrison's direct reply, the apparent slaughter of remedial railroad legislation in the cause of placating railroad labor votes, the progress of the wage and hour bill whose passage in very much modified form now seems not improbable, and the battle over use of PWA funds to finance competitive municipal power plants. Political rather than economic considerations seem to be controlling in these struggles.

Washington Viewpoint

The belief is spreading that the Administration looks on a time of depression as ideal for putting through reforms and feels, therefore, that recovery is a less than 100% benefit. Such a point of view necessarily assumes that unemployed voters will blame business rather than government when they go to the polls.

Labor Day Critical Date

In the other camp, a slow drift away from business-government cooperation toward hope for a swing to the right at the elections is apparently in process. This point of view assumes that voters in time of depression tend to oust the party in power. The outcome, one way or the other, will be a dominating influence on business after Labor Day—a date which is mentioned on the theory that straw votes, primaries and the Maine election will have shown by that time how the wind is blowing.

Midsummer Trough

Returning to the current trend in business, the pointers still look downward. Steel operations this week are off 10%, or three points in terms of capacity. Automobile production is declining. The cotton textile mills are pushing a shut-down movement. It begins to look as though industrial activity will not touch bottom until July or August.

Departments on This and That

For six or seven years, Harry R. O'Brien's "Diary of a Plain Dirt Gardener" (Page 6), has appeared in *Better Homes & Gardens.* O'Brien is a gardener-writer-teacher-lecturer. He conducts classes in journalism at the Ohio State University. He writes for *Better Homes & Gardens, Country Gentleman,* and other magazines. He gardens—abetted by his wife and two sons—on an acreage four or five miles from Columbus, Ohio. Between whiles, he travels up and down the country giving lectures before garden clubs and attending horticultural meetings.

The diary is a day-by-day record of garden work and happenings, set down just as they occur. It aims, first, to be a simple guide for timely work in the garden; second, to give as much news of the garden world as possible; and third, human interest is injected into it through relating incidents, mainly humorous, that concern the doings of the Plain Dirt Gardener and his family. The cartoon illustrations add considerably to the human interest.

For the most part, the diary is not planned. Whatever turns up or comes along is used for copy. Sometimes, however, a special trip will be made to a flower show or to a neighbor's garden, just to find something different to write about.

The diary is so written that each year some topics and plants will be introduced that are new to it. This is for the sake of variety. These new things must be provided for in advance by sowing the seed or buying and setting out the new plants at the right time. An effort is made to secure and grow seeds of new annuals, new roses, and the like a year ahead of their introduction, so, when mention of them appears in print, it will break as news at the right time for the reader.

To make the diary possible, O'Brien does the actual gardening work in his garden at home. The flowers and shrubs are grown. The spray is applied. The weeds are hoed out. A daily record is kept for every day in the year, in a looseleaf diary, written single space on the typewriter. At the end of the month, such portions of this as appear usable are written out on copy paper. This is edited and cut down to a little longer than can be used. This gives the editorial office a chance to make some selection of the material. Finally, a clean copy is made and sent to the editor.

To ask a question and to answer it—that is about as simple, direct, and efficient a way to present information as there is. The method is as old at least as the catechism. There are few magazines that do not resort to it once in a while. If the questions are bona-fide ones raised by readers of the magazine, so much the better. Most popular magazines receive a heavy mail from their readers, and most of them try to respond by letter, by the sending of service booklets, and by the use of questions raised by readers in the magazine itself. The department on Page 18, "Answering Your Spring Garden Questions," conducted by Arnold N. Davis, is a typical questions and answers department.

Note that the style aimed at in this department is one of simple and direct exposition. One point is raised by each question and it is answered by as few words as possible in a single paragraph. As a result nine items, which if they were handled as separate stories, would take considerably more space, are compressed to a single page.

"So Good Meals," the department on Page 19, conducted by Myrna Johnston, editor of the Better Foods and Equipment Department under the pen name "Helen Homer," is one of the important departments in the magazine. Almost all of the women read it, and it is not altogether scorned even by the men.

The plan of this department is to deal each month with a single food's problem, for example: desserts, Sunday-dinner menus, hot-weather luncheon menus. In the department reproduced on Page 19, it is Spring Breakfasts that get attention.

Opposite the department, as it appeared in the magazine but not reproduced in this book, was a full page, four-color photograph. An arrow pointing across the gutter from the department ties together the two pages.

Visitors to the Meredith plant are apt to be shown through the Tasting-Test Kitchen. If they get to the kitchen at the right moment, they will have a chance to sample an angel food cake or a piping hot roll, or a fancy canapé. In this kitchen every recipe that is used in *Better Homes & Gardens* is given a thorough tryout. The ingredients, the measurements, the processes of mixing and cooking are tested, altered, and retested until "Jean Byers" (the pen name for Helen Johnson), who is in charge of the kitchen, and Mrs. Johnston are satisfied that the recipes will work.

The "So Good Meals" department is a siamese twin to another department that appears farther back in the book. The latter, recipes for "So Good Meals" (Page 56), gives tested recipes for the dishes marked with asterisks in the first department.

Reader-interest surveys of women's and home magazines have shown almost without exception that meal plans and menus are of more interest to women readers than anything else in the magazine. Women demand of the magazines a continual flow of suggestions as to new and different ways of preparing foods, new combinations of foods for menus, and, because there are always new cooks coming into the circle of the magazine's readers, a certain amount of reiteration of standard recipes and principles of menu planning.

Where do the ideas for recipes and menus come from? Mrs. Johnston says that a great many are dug out of the letters of inquiry from readers and from that other group of reader letters whose authors volunteer information about their favorite recipes. Another source of suggestions and material is the literature of the food industries. General Mills, General Foods, National Dairy Council, California Fruit Growers' Association, the Institute of American Meat Packers, the Rice Institute, the Southern Citrus Growers Association—these are a few of the large commercial concerns and trade associations which employ staffs of home economists to develop and publicize uses of their products. Mrs. Johnston is not only on their mailing lists to receive any new materials that have come out, but she has a wide personal acquaintance with the home economists employed by these concerns. They are interested in having her use material about their products and she is interested in any new ideas she can come across.

Still another source of ideas is the other magazines that run foods material. A city editor of a newspaper does not follow more closely his rival sheet to see how it has played the news and whether or not it has beat him on a good story than a foods editor follows the work of her competitors. Added to these publications are the more technical journals in home economics and the bulletin publications on foods put out by the Bureau of Home Economics of the United States Department of Agriculture and by the experiment stations and extension services of the land-grant colleges.

A third foods department in *Better Homes & Gardens* is the "Cooks' Round Table" of indorsed recipes (Page 21). This two-page department is printed on heavier paper than the rest of the magazine and carries punch-holes so that when it is cut out it can be filed in the loose-leaf cook-book which *Better Homes & Gardens* sells to its readers. (Up to June 30, 1938, it had sold 896,000.) This is the department of recipes submitted by readers and paid for at a dollar apiece. Every recipe that is used is thoroughly tested in the *Better Homes & Gardens'* Tasting-Test Kitchen.

"The Question Before the House" (Page 26), a department which answers building and remodeling questions, is comparable in purpose and method of presentation to "Answering Your Spring Garden Questions."

Harlan Miller wrote his first column when he was a freshman at Iowa State College. He was too small for football and so he "went out" for the college paper. He was given a beat to cover, but that wasn't enough. He began turning in humorous paragraphs, gossip, foibles of faculty and students, shrewd comment on campus events. These were soon running regularly as Bally-Rot by Raconteur. After college Miller worked as a reporter for the *Des Moines Register,* was in New York a while on *The Post,* served three years with the Associated Press, and then came back to Des Moines as a feature writer and, soon, conductor of the column "Over the Coffee." His next berth was on the *Washington Post,* for which he conducts a column under the same title. It is widely syndicated to newspapers throughout the country.

A couple of years ago Miller arranged with the editors of *Better Homes & Gardens* to try out a magazine column to be called "The Man Next Door" (Page 32). The purpose of the column is purely and simply to entertain—the only feature in the magazine which has entertainment as its primary purpose. Even so, Miller slants his copy to conform to the general theme of the magazine, houses and gardens, and the human everyday folks who live in them.

THE NEW YORKER

THE TALK OF THE TOWN

THE TALK OF THE TOWN

Reprinted by special permission from the New Yorker

There is no more famous "column," if it can be called that, in an American magazine than "The Talk of the Town" which each week occupies the first front-of-the-book position in the *New Yorker.* It is read, reproduced, and quoted up and down the land.

The New England Telephone & Telegraph Company notified us last Tuesday that it would be possible to put a radiophone in our yacht so we could talk to people on shore. The advantages of this, they said, were apparent. Suppose, they said, we had been out cruising and were putting into port and one of the guests wanted a plane reservation—if there was a phone in our boat we could call up and make the reservation while still at sea. This situation, however progressive it seems to the phone company, seems of dubious merit to us. Anyway, we want to inform our friends that guest space in our yacht will continue to be reserved for persons wanting to catch flounders, not airplanes.

One thing we like about a boat is that when you are in it you don't have to talk to people on shore. There are, in fact, times when a phone might be considerable of a nuisance in a boat. Let's say you are trying to pick up the sound of a bell in a fog, listening with all six ears. We're pretty sure that this would be the moment the phone would ring, and who would it be? It would be Gladys, wanting to know where you put the key to the car.

The decline of the West: The Harvard Club is having the red furniture in its lounge done over in blue. . . . The gold braid that adorns the uniforms of officers of the armed services of the United States has to be imported from France. . . . The New York, New Haven & Hartford Railroad has removed the spittoons from the women's lavatories on the Merchants Limited. . . . A six-year-old bull named Alice is taking part in artificial-breeding experiments at New Brunswick, New Jersey.

When we were young and in our flower,
We got up with The Conning Tower.
This summer, quite the other way,
We'll go to bed with F. P. A.

We're sorry to learn that the main dining room of the Gotham Hotel is being converted into quarters for stores. It used to be pleasant to walk by and see the solid, English-looking people eating by the windows, a couple of feet lower and a trifle more accessible than the men in the University Club lounge next door. We doubt if we will ever be able to adjust ourselves comfortably to the march of progress, the passing of old landmarks. It is probably only a matter of months before the ground floor of the Vanderbilt house will be another Longchamps outpost and the back room of the Plaza a branch of Macy's. If anyone has definite information about these or other forward-looking projects, we don't wish to be told.

"I pledge to work actively to the preservation and extension of democracy and peace, for the defeat of Fascism and all forms of national oppression, and for the establishment of Socialism," runs the New Communist oath.

"Unless Republican party chiefs over-ride the clear preferences of their rank-and-file and nominate a right-wing Democrat, anti-New Deal Democrats will be faced with the choice of going along with the New Deal, attempting to nominate their own candidate, or crossing over to the Republican party," says the Times.

There can be little happiness for any party in these efforts to get complete coverage at the expense of political identity. In the old days, a Communist was simon-pure—a furious man, sworn to impose the Marxist philosophy on the world, let come what dreadful things might come. We cannot see him amiably swearing, presumably on a Bible, that he will work to extend a capitalist democracy in order to achieve Socialism. Nor can we see that much will be left in life for Democrats and Republicans, robbed of their old pastime of slinging mud and pointing to the record. Politics, in fact, seems to be degenerating into a confused game of ring-around-a-rosy, with everybody obliged to hold hands with the wrong people.

It seems rather a pity that the journalistic duel,

so fashionable in France, has failed to take hold in America. We have never had a challenge from even our angriest critic. Never has our receptionist announced, "A couple of seconds to see you, sir." We are embarrassed by the safe monotony of our days. There would be difficulties, of course. We would have to borrow a sword from a Knight Templar or a Noble of the Mystic Shrine. Our insurance agent would unquestionably disapprove. And where would we go for our sword play in the dawn? Central Park is the obvious place, although the children and the pigeons might be a false note. It is hard to picture cherubs and fat doves descending on the field of blood. But the hell with the difficulties. No one shall say we have been traitor to the fuller, braver life. Monsieur the editor of Time, you are a camel, a head of veal, a rolling nastiness!

Chairman

You have probably seen William McChesney Martin, Jr., in the newsreels and sized him up as an earnest young man with the embarrassed air typical of sweepstakes winners. Mr. Martin is, of course, no sweepstakes winner but the new chairman of the board of governors and president pro tem of the New York Stock Exchange, aged thirty-one. His embarrassment was due to the fact that he had never faced a movie camera up to his election three weeks ago. "I got bewildered," he says. He regained his composure in time to invite the cameramen to take pictures of the Exchange floor in action, which in turn bewildered them and also drew hoarse cries of horror from the more conservative members, who never dreamed that such a thing would come to pass. They'll have to put up with him till next May 16th, however, no matter what happens; his term as chairman runs until then, although his presidential duties will end as soon as the board appoints its first salaried president. It is now Martin's job to greet distinguished visitors, formulate policies, and attend meetings of the Exchange's subcommittees, all of which has kept him terribly busy. At present he is comfortably installed in Room 629 of the Exchange Building, the president's quarters. Yes, that used to be Richard Whitney's office. It's a large, panelled chamber, with a ticker ticking merrily in one corner, a secretary trying to drive away people who've just dropped by to shake hands, and an armed guard stationed in the corridor outside, suspicious of all comers.

Martin became a governor of the Exchange at the age of twenty-eight, breaking all precedent. He was a member of the liberal bloc of financiers that favored cooperation with the influential SEC and revolted against the haughty attitude of the Old Guard. The new chairman is anything but haughty; when we called at his office we found him a studious-looking fellow with a pleasant smile, dressed in a gray double-breasted suit and a brown tie. He's a bachelor, but his newsreel debut didn't result in a single offer of marriage—probably an indication of the times. Another unusual thing about him is that he's been in New York only seven years. He was sent here by the firm of A. G. Edwards & Sons, having previously worked in the statistical department of their branch in St. Louis, his home town. They've given him a leave of absence this year, with pay. The chairmanship is a non-remunerative job.

Until Martin left college (Yale '28), he'd never studied the social sciences, but he began to investigate them at night school in St. Louis and continued straight through this February, taking courses at Columbia and the New School for Social Research. At College he majored in English literature, never getting closer to the social scene than the pictorial editorship of the Yale News. He has had a thorough classical education, including five years of Latin and three of Greek, but at heart, he says, he's a romanticist. Romantically, he has such a passionate love for the theatre that during the past seven years he hasn't missed more than a handful of shows that ran for two weeks or longer. One season he saw a hundred of them. More often than not he goes by himself, buying cut-rate tickets and sitting happily in the balcony. He is probably the first president of the Stock Exchange who ever sat in the balcony. All these things have led his fellow-brokers to look upon him with incredulous awe, and matters aren't helped any by the fact that he's easily the best tennis player among them, too. From 1932 through 1934 he entered the national singles championships at Forest Hills and managed to reach the second round each time. He took on Tilden once. That was in 1928, in a local tournament at a Chicago country club, and Big Bill won handily, losing only one game in three sets. "He massacred me," says the chairman, whose avowed platform is to hide nothing from the public.

Of Mice and Men

Getting ready for some serious summer reading, a college girl went into Doubleday, Doran's the other day and asked for Plato's "Republic." "Plato?" said the salesgirl, wrinkling her brow. "Let's see—that would be in the children's department, with the Mickey Mouse books."

Pin Money

The fatherly president of one of the big publishing houses called one of his young men on the carpet the other day and gave him a lecture on extravagance. "You're dressing pretty expensively," he said, "and last night I saw you having supper at the Plaza. Don't you think that's flying too high for twenty-seven fifty a week?" "Oh, not at all," the young man said. "You see, I really make between fifty and sixty a week by raffling off my check to people in the office."

To the Ladies
BY PRINCESS ALEXANDRA KROPOTKIN

TO THE LADIES

By Princess Alexandra Kropotkin

Reprinted by special permission from Liberty

A third example of the magazine column, and a very popular one, is Princess Kropotkin's "To The Ladies" in *Liberty.*

If you think you would like to be an independent producer of Hollywood pictures, making movies entirely to suit yourself, let me introduce you to Fanchon Royer—one of the very few women in the world who do just that. While working on a picture she toils about twenty hours a day, falls asleep in her bath, and catches cold every time she eats a square meal. This goes on from ten days to two weeks at a stretch, with slightly less strenuous labor lasting several months. She has filmed crashing airplanes (Death in the Air) and racing midget cars (Ten Laps to Go), but her most dangerous picture, she tells me, was her latest release, Religious Racketeer, in which Madam Houdini, wife of the famous magician, exposes tricks employed by fake mediums to hoodwink the spook-credulous public. . . . "To induce us to lay off," says Fanchon Royer, "we have been offered bribes totaling nearly $300,000, and our lives have been threatened unless we consented to come to terms." So she has a couple of bodyguards trailing around with her now. . . . Meeting her personally, you never would take her for a movie executive who specializes in hard-boiled art. She looks too youthful, too attractive. I could scarcely believe my ears when she talked about her five children, including a son of college age. . . . Originally a Des Moines, Iowa, girl, she first worked in Hollywood as an extra, then edited a movie magazine, then spent two years making pictures in Mexico. She knows her Hollywood. . . . "While we were doing our film exposé of fake spiritualists," she said, "the members of the cast put in all their spare time telling ghost stories and exchanging addresses of their favorite mediums. You can't cure 'em."

Smartest novelty for summer adornment is the necklace of real flowers—roses or any small blossoms. Wire them close together on a length of narrow green ribbon. Tie the bow in back. Endures only one evening, but the boys will remember.

Skunk panic has long been a form of fear manifested violently by women who go camping in the summertime. Most girls are terrified of skunks—and I can't say I blame us much—but William Carr does. "All skunks are perfect gentlemen at heart," he says, "or perfect ladies, as the case may be. They're friendly by nature, and can be petted by any one who is fond of animals and knows how to handle them carefully." . . . Handle them, Mr. Carr? . . . No, thanks, Mr. Carr. . . . All we want to know is how to tell whether a skunk feels chummy toward us or not. . . . "As long as a skunk faces you," said Mr. Carr, "you and he are pals. Don't run unless he arches his back and starts turning sideways. If he does that, run *fast*." . . . William Carr has charge of outdoor experiments for the American Museum of Natural History. Has tamed and made pets of twenty-five skunks over a number of years, without depriving any of them of their aromatic weapon, and without once being sprayed.

All of which may be very reassuring—but I still prefer wildflowers.

The poet Byron had a wife who once ate twenty-one lamb cutlets at a sitting. Good as they are fixed the following way, with tongue and mushrooms, two apiece ought to be enough for you and your gang. . . . Trim a slice of white bread to fit each cutlet.

Fry the bread shapes in butter; drain them; dab sparingly with mustard; on each lay a thin slice of smoked tongue.

Arrange in a ring on a hot platter. Have ready a sauté of thinly sliced mushrooms mixed with a few green peas and heated well in a little thick cream sauce. Now broil your cutlets and place them on the *coasters* of fried bread and tongue.

Fill the center of the dish with creamed mushrooms and peas. Serve quickly.

A salad made with lettuce and watercress completes this excellent main course for a dinner party this summer.

Now that honey is being advocated for so many sweetening purposes, you may be interested in Dr. Bodog F. Beck's new book, Honey and Health, which tells the story of honey from its historic past to fashionable present. (Published by Robert M. McBride & Co.)

When we spell out names letter by letter to a

long-distance telephone operator or telegraph clerk, few of us understand how it really should be done.

Women get into extra-fantastic tangles. One girl I know, trying to spell out the name Avery, said: "A as in astringent; V as in velveteen; E as in earrings; R as in ruffles; Y as in Y. W. C. A." . . . Naturally, she had some trouble making her connection. . . . Since many of us do a considerable amount of summer-vacation phoning and wiring to out-of-the-way places, I thought the correct words to use in spelling out names might be useful to know. Here they are . . . A as in Adam; B as in Boston; C as in Chicago; D as in Denver; E as in Edward; F as in Frank; G as in George; H as in Henry; I as in Ida; J as in John; K as in King; L as in Lincoln; M as in Mary; N as in New York; O as in ocean; P as in Peter; Q as in queen; R as in Robert; S as in sugar; T as in Thomas; U as in union; V as in Victor; W as in William; X as in X-ray; Y as in young; Z as in zero. . . . I obtained this information over the phone from a Western Union man, and asked him to spell out *his* name. He said: "O as in omen; S as in suspect; L as in lunatic; I as in imperial; N as in Noel Coward."

Editors and Readers Talk

A great volume of reader correspondence finds its way to the desk of Associate Editor W. L. Benson. Out of it he fashions each month two departments—"Among Ourselves" (Page 35), and "Back Talk!" (Page 48). Mr. Benson takes a day off once a month and goes through 300 or 400 letters to get the comments and suggestions which seem worth passing on in the Among Ourselves department to other readers. Even more than its informative value, the department endeavors to build a confraternity of *Better Homes & Gardens* readers. To demonstrate that the readers are close and intimate friends of the magazine and the magazine of them, Mr. Benson's chief editorial concern with the department is to see that it represents a variety of subjects and that the letters used are well scattered geographically.

The purpose of "Back Talk!" is quite different from "Among Ourselves." "Back Talk!" is a forum open to readers for a discussion of the magazine and anything else on their minds. Welcomed in its columns are letters of criticism as well as letters of praise. The department has the effect of letting the readers feel that they have some part in the planning and making of their magazine. Such letters have some value to the editors as a barometer of reader reaction to the publication.

"We Parents" (Page 39), a department conducted by Mrs. Shultz, is an experiment tried out for the first time in the issue which is reproduced in this book. Here is the problem upon which the experiment was designed to throw light: Would it be better, from the point of view of reader interest, to handle the child care and training material in a department or to continue the practice of having one article a month on this subject? The trouble with a single article is that it will probably appeal to only a comparatively small portion of the magazine's readers. If the article concerns the pre-school child, readers who do not have children of this age will presumably not be interested. In a department, on the other hand, a wide variety of subjects can be handled briefly and so the interest of a larger proportion of the readers can be touched. Of course, the article has the advantage of more thoroughness, more detail.

The editors of the magazine were more than ordinarily interested in the results of the reader-interest survey of the issue in which this test was made. Exasperatingly, however, the test let them down. The reader-interest score for the two types of handling was practically identical.

The last editorial page in *Better Homes & Gardens* (it doesn't appear last in the reproduction at the front of this book. To print it in two colors as it appears in the magazine it had to be moved up a couple of pages) is the department "Along the Garden Path With the Week-End Gardener" (Page 62).

Suppose you had the job of designing an editorial feature for the last page of the magazine. What would you do with it? What subject matter would you deal with and what tone would you try to strike? Of course some magazines do not have any last page. The stream of editorial matter trickles away into the sands of advertising and disappears. But a good many advertisers have found that the back-of-the-book is a particularly good position if there is strong accompanying editorial matter.

In the case of *Better Homes & Gardens,* the attempt in "Along the Garden Path" is, in a sense, to summarize the whole point of view and tone of the magazine; so the department is written, in the first person, not by a member of the staff but by a gardener, an enthusiast, a practicer of what he preaches. The writing is warm and friendly and intimate. It seems to say, "We're all friends together in our love of the Good Earth and what it grows. We all stand alike upon that earth and draw from it our sustenance and our most substantial and abiding joys. We'll talk here on this page together once a month about our earth and its produce."

Practice Suggestions

1. Study a dozen editor's pages in magazines. Write a paper discussing the differences between them and what you think are the reasons for these differences.

2. What are the pros and cons, from the publication's point of view, of running letters from readers which criticize the publication?

3. Ask twenty people whether they read the letters in *Time*—and why.

4. Point out in detail the ways in which Harlan Miller's column, "The Man Next Door," is slanted for *Better Homes & Gardens'* readers.

XV

What to Write About

THE subject of an article has to be something about which people want to read. It seems fairly obvious, then, that a search for article subjects should start with people and their interests.

The first astounding thing to note about people is that they are all alike and they are all different.

They are alike because they are all human organisms which have to eat (and earn the wherewithal to eat), which want to go on living, which are so constituted that they fall in love—and out. And they are all different because this man has a wart on his nose, and is therefore self-conscious and introverted; this one is an only son, the pampered darling of an overly affectionate mother; this woman has been told so often that she is beautiful that she has come to believe it, with the result that her vanity is Napoleonic; and this other woman has had to drudge for years with never more than a dollar or two to her name, so that her view of men and things has taken on the drab dullness of poverty and strain; and so on and on for every single one of us.

How easy it is to think of "our readers"—the people for whom we are trying to find article subjects—in the mass, and to lose sight of what they are as individual human beings. But it is as individuals, not as "types," that they like or dislike the stuff that we write for them.

The strategy of this book has called, first, for a thorough, realistic description of the way in which articles get into print; second, for a painstaking study of examples of magazine and newspaper articles, their making and handling. These have been the service of supply, behind the front lines. The third step is the attack. And the attack should be more successful than it might otherwise have been, because, if the good soldier has gone conscientiously through Part I and Part II, he is mentally well-armed with a knowledge of the processes, the problems, and the methods of article writing, and is ready to move toward his objectives, not blindly, but along roads that have begun to look familiar and through a landscape that is no longer utterly foreign and forbidding.

Before we go a step farther, let's get acquainted with some *people*. And then, later, as we discuss subjects for articles we can keep these people, and others whom we know, in mind and can continually check our bright ideas against their probable likes and dislikes.

Clem Shakely owns a hardware store on Main Street—that is to say that he is the proprietor and nominal owner, although the bank has a mortgage which wouldn't pay out if Clem had to dispose of the business. He lives in a nine-room frame house, on the corner of Fourth and Arch Streets, and he has a wife who "isn't well," a son who plays football at high school, and two daughters, one of whom tap dances and the other of whom, being only six, has not yet shown any marked aesthetic proclivity. Clem is forty-six, has a Rotary button, and a bald spot. Once a year he and Cliff Samuelson and Art Arthur and Herby Gibbs go up North for a week of fishing. The fifty-one other weeks in the year are essentially only preludes and postludes to the week at the lake. The four of them go in Clem's Chevy. Clem confines what drinking he does to that week. He plays poker once in a while, but not for very high stakes because he can't afford it. Clem takes and reads the local daily newspaper. He subscribes for *Time* and the *Rotarian,* and Mrs. Shakely takes *Good Housekeeping* and one or two church papers. Clem gets a hardware trade journal at the store and usually he looks it through.

Emma Runkle is a waitress at the Star Coffee Shoppe. She is a brunette, twenty-two years old, five feet four. She has a ring with a blue stone and a comparatively new permanent wave. She has been in her present business since she was fifteen years old. Emma was brought up on a farm ten miles south of town. She attended country school and then came to town for high school. When things got tough for farmers in 1930 and '31, she quit school and went to work. She shares a room at a boarding house with her girl friend, Sadie Brown, who works at the five-and-ten. One week Emma goes to work at six o'clock and stays on the job until two. The next week she goes to work at twelve and doesn't get off until the Shoppe closes, which is anywhere from eleven to twelve. She usually looks through the local paper, leaning across the tobacco counter at the Shoppe.

Henry J. Harshbarger's name appears in neat white letters in the office directory beside the elevators in the lobby of the National Bank Building. He is the senior member of the law firm of Harshbarger, Stoop, and Arrowsmith. Besides these three, the firm employs a half-dozen unnamed young lawyers and a second half-dozen clerks and stenographers. Mr. Harshbarger is a graduate of Michigan Law School in the class of 1904. He has been married twice. First to Harriett Sellers with whom he fell in love while they were in school together. They had one son, Henry, Jr., who is now one of the six unnamed young lawyers of the firm. His second wife was Mary Courtland, the daughter of the senior member of a law firm for which Henry once worked. Henry and Mary have had no children. They live in a large apartment house on the lake front. As a lawyer, Mr. Harshbarger has specialized in tax cases. A good many large corporations and very wealthy individuals are among his clients. He has two avocations. One is yachting (he is an officer of the Chicago Yacht Club) and the other is history of the writing of the American Constitution. Mr. Harshbarger buys the *Chicago Tribune* in the morning and the *Chicago News* in the evening. Twenty-five or thirty magazines come to the apartment. The ones he always reads are *Yachting* and *Harper's* and, for some reason which even he can't explain, *Stage.* Mr. Harshbarger is nominally a Republican, but he belongs, he maintains, to the liberal wing. He even boasts in certain circles that he voted for Roosevelt in 1932.

Mrs. Jane Seyler has a husband and four children and her business is to keep the dust out of 927 McKinley Street and food three times a day before the mouths of her family. Her husband is a postman and while they don't make a great deal, yet, as Mr. Seyler says, it's regular. Three of Mrs. Seyler's children are boys and she sometimes thinks it would have been easier on her if they'd all been girls, except for the ironing. When she was a girl, she studied piano with Mrs. Wiggins and she has made up her mind that her children shall have advantages even if it means pretty hard scrimping. Joe, who has just entered high school, already plays the trombone pretty well, and Larry plays the trap drum in the junior high band. Mrs. Seyler belongs to the Longfellow Literary Society which meets every two weeks, and every week she attends one or two movies. She is a conscientious reader of the grocery ads in the local paper and she usually has time to look through the news. Mr. Seyler buys the *Saturday Evening Post* from the neighbor boy, and Mrs. Seyler takes the *Ladies' Home Journal* and *McCall's.*

Allen Parker farms 320 acres, five miles south of Centerville, Illinois. He is only thirty, but he has been farming for himself for ten years and he is already able to go to the bank in Centerville and make the kind of arrangements he wants to buy a bunch of feeders. He was brought up on the farm, attended country school, and the Centerville High School. He married a neighbor girl when he was twenty, just before he went to his first farm. They have two children. One hired man helps with the work. Parker is a member of the Farm Bureau, and he usually gets up to the university once a year for the farm short course. He raises Hampshire hogs and Angus cattle, and Mrs. Parker has a flock of 500 White Rocks. They live in a house that isn't all it ought to be, but the Parkers figure that they'll not only have a house but a farm of their own before many years. Parker subscribes for the *Centerville Excelsior*, the *Chicago Daily Drovers' Journal*, the *Prairie Farmer* and the *Chicago Tribune.* Mrs. Parker takes the *Farmer's Wife* and the *Woman's Home Companion.* The Parkers are also members of the *National Geographic Society* and subscribers to *National Geographic.*

Basic Emotions of People

Mechanics, stenographers, bankers, doctors, nurses, high school boys and girls, insurance salesmen, grocers, hotel men—for these and a thousand others in their infinite variety—you can fashion your own personality sketches. Note these things about all of these people:

1. People all work. Most of them work directly to earn money or to hang on to what they have. They are all tremendously interested in money. How to get it and how to spend it economically. This means that some or all of them are potential readers of newspaper or magazine articles on taxation, federal fiscal policy, world trade conditions, crop conditions and prospects, relative prices or efficiencies of products, men or businesses who have been successful in making money, devices or methods for saving money.

Clem Shakely is interested in articles about hardware merchandising, new hardware lines, hardware advertising, window displays, how to build up Christmas business.

Parker wants to know about any change in freight rates, about interest rates, about new farm machinery, about new strains of hybrid corn, about the national and world crop prospects and their probable effects on prices.

2. People all have to eat, but most of them have to take what is put before them and leave to Mrs. Seyler and Emma Runkle (or her boss) the business of food preparation.

Mrs. Seyler, with five mouths to feed three times a day and with motherly concern for the health of her family, wants to learn what she can about vitamins, carbohydrates, and fats and even more than that she wants to know what in the world she'll cook for dinner.

Now if we think of the ingestion of food as more or less symbolical of the wider functions of the home, then we find not only Mrs. Seyler but her husband and most of our other men and women interested in the multiple aspects of home—the house itself, its furnishings and equipment, the garden that surrounds it, the youngsters who inhabit it, family relations, sex problems. Emma Runkle may not be interested in all of this, nor, possibly, Lawyer Harshbarger. But most of our people will be. In fact, isn't it pretty largely to have a home and children that they are working for six or ten or fourteen hours a day?

3. People have to play. It is a pretty dismal lot—slavery of body or of mind—which doesn't make allowance in time and money budgets for recreation. But how diverse recreation is: traveling, reading, fishing, movies, clubs, woodworking, yachting, gossiping, dancing, swimming, golfing, listening to the radio.

A newspaper or magazine may itself be recreational. The unusual article, the humorous article, pictures which are looked at primarily for their entertainment value, satisfy this human need for recreation, but, more than that, articles can tell about recreational possibilities, about fishing in Canada or building ship models in the basement, or how Joe Louis trains for a fight, or what the outcome will be in the National League.

4. People have to educate themselves. The educability of human beings is an extraordinary thing. More than anything else it distinguishes men from animals. Animals can be educated too (See "Animals Do Think," Chapter XII) but at what a tedious pace and to what an infinitesimal degree compared to men. It is apparently almost a law of our being that we should want to know, and it is a law of our experience that we must know in order to get the things we want. Our desires set up certain goals for us—to make $3,000 a year instead of $2,000, to shoot 75 golf instead of 95, to build a house that will have plenty of closet space—and then we set about to learn how to reach these goals. Of course, we don't always get there, but that doesn't mean that we don't try. We try to make a million or win a certain girl or diet gracefully. And with a goal set up, the desire, the ambition, we study how to reach it. If we are

building our ideal house, we pore over plans. We go driving through residential sections looking at houses. We climb from cellar to garret through houses that are being built. We talk to contractors and to friends who have been through the ordeal. All this has nothing to do with money, with getting the means to realize our desires. It has to do with the innate curiosity of people and the innate desire to perfect themselves in one way or another.

Countless magazine articles draw our eyes and our interest because of this desire to know.

5. People have to give. Men do not walk alone. They are as gregarious as sheep. And gregariousness means eternal compromise—I must give something to others in return for the things I want the others to give to me. I want to be safe, so I contribute to the taxes which hire policemen and firemen. I want my children to have a better education than I could give them at home, so I contribute to the fund that buys school houses and pays teachers. I want the laws under which I live to be fair and favorable according to my lights and so I become a Republican or a Democrat or a Socialist and vote, perhaps even work, for candidates who, I think, will come nearest to passing the kind of laws I think should be passed. I join the Chamber of Commerce. I am a member of a church. I contribute to the Boy Scouts. And all these things I do because I recognize that there are many things desirable, the accomplishment of which can only come about cooperatively. And because I take part in various activities, they mean something to me. They have my interest. If I contribute $5 to the local Boy Scout Fund, I am pretty apt to read the story in the local newspaper about the boys from our town who attended the national encampment; or an article in a magazine about the encampment itself. If I am a Republican I am interested in political prognostications, in the personalities and records of the leaders of my party, in the political strategy of the G.O.P. in the coming campaign—and of its opponents.

6. People seek beauty. Standards of beauty change, but unchanging is people's preference of the beautiful to the ugly, their desire to see beautiful things, to make beautiful things, and to surround themselves with natural beauty and man-made beauty. A woman is buying curtains for her windows. They must control the light and keep people from looking in, but those aren't really the chief considerations. The main thing is how they will look. And so also with clothes, and houses, the pictures we buy, and the places we travel to see.

So here are six of the elemental emotions of people, emotions which propel them to action, which enter into their judgments, which determine their likes and dislikes. These are not, of course, all of the emotions, but they are probably the ones which are most widely played upon by the writer of articles.

A look at some of the stories in this book will show the basic emotions to which they make their appeal. For example:

"Mountain King" (Chapter IX) makes its chief appeal to our desire for money; "Light Where You Need It" (Chapter XII) to our interest in our homes and to our aesthetic sense; "Trout from Your Personal Pond" (Chapter IX) to our desire for entertainment; "Safe at Home but Are You" (Chapter XII) to our desire to go on living.

All of this is very fine, but how, the novice wants to know, does it advance one toward the finding of specific subjects for articles? Well it doesn't, but the writer is not in a very strong position to judge of the interest that inheres in specific subjects unless he is sensitive to the emotions which direct people's lives. When he has seen clearly the elemental wants and needs of people, then he is ready to see and evaluate subjects to write about.

Where, then, resides the elusive subject? Where shall the writer look for ideas?

1. In and About You

Let's take a walk. We know something about people, not only, it is to be hoped, from this book, but from our accumulated experiences of the past seventeen or twenty-five or fifty or seventy years. We know something of what people are interested in; and therefore about what they want to read; and therefore what we should look for if it is our business to supply their reading wants. So let's start from your house (in the city or town or country, it doesn't make much difference) and see what we can see.

We walk down the steps and onto the cement walk. The grass has just been cut, but there is a ragged, ugly fringe where grass and sidewalk meet. The mower won't touch it. It could, of course, be clipped by hand. You remember that you have seen a hand-clipper with long handles, so that a man can stand up while operating it. You remember, also, that

---

Please do not misinterpret the "possible markets" suggestions that are scattered through this chapter. There is no guarantee that the magazines suggested will buy the articles that are proposed. The whole point is: Here are *possible* subjects, lying all around one; and here are *possible* markets which should be investigated in connection with these story-ideas.

---

there is a power clipper. Some people dig a little trench along the walk with an edging tool, but it is hard to keep the trench clean and neat. What is the best way to handle this troublesome little problem, which bothers every man who has to cut his own grass? There may be a short process story in the available equipment for such a job and in the methods that are recommended by expert gardeners. (Possible markets: *Better Homes & Gardens, American Home, House Beautiful, House and Garden.*)

A car goes by on the street. It may be that your street has been recently paved, and you are very conscious of the cost of paving because of the assessment that you have to pay with your taxes. You are reminded of a short news story that you saw last week. It gave some figures from an engineering experiment station on the relative costs of driving different types of cars on different road surfaces. The story pointed to a considerable saving on tires, gas consumption and car depreciation, when cars are driven on a well-surfaced road as compared to a poorly-surfaced one. Would it be possible to get together figures on the cost of highway surfacing and on the economies in automobile operations that result from good surfacing? What would such figures show? The story could be conceived on the basis of your own town, your county, your state, or the whole country. (Possible markets: City newspaper, *Roads and Streets, Saturday Evening Post, Harper's.*)

Thinking about automobiles and paving suggests a really ambitious subject: The economic effects of the highway building program in the United States since the advent of the automobile. Even at first glance you can see a number of angles to the story—the amount of money that has been invested in roads and the effect of that investment on the money market; the labor required for the construction and maintenance program; the effect of roads on freight handling; their effect on retail buying centers; the auxiliary enterprises such as gas stations, cabin camps, etc., that have developed with paving. No, this isn't a little story. A book or several books could be written about it. A tremendous amount of data is available in a hundred different places. It is the sort of story that one would have to work on for a considerable period, gathering, filing, collating the material. Possibly, if one didn't tackle the whole story, he might handle some single aspect of it. (Possible markets: *Saturday Evening Post, Collier's.*)

As we walk down the street, you see a coal truck pulled up in the drive of a neighbor. You got coal yourself from the same company a little while back. After you sent the check, you got back a personal letter, signed by the president of the company, thanking you for your business, expressing the hope that the company's service was satisfactory. That is the only retail concern that you can think of that sends you that kind of a letter. It made you feel that you wanted to get your next batch of coal from the same place. It probably costs the coal company 10 cents a piece to send out those letters. You wonder if it is a worth-while business. Well, the president of the coal company, you know, recently built a fine new house. Maybe those letters helped to build it. Possibly the company has other practices of a similar nature with which it woos the patronage of customers. A call on the president or manager of the coal company would get the story. (Possible markets: *Coal Dealer, Advertising and Selling, Printer's Ink.*)

Old man Hinshaw, you notice, is digging out the hedge that goes around his corner lot. He is planting some new hedge material in place of the old. You wonder why. What was wrong with the old? What are the advantages of the new? Just what are the best hedge materials for your locality? How should they be planted and tended? (Possible markets: *Better Homes & Gardens, Garden Digest.*)

And that suggests another. Hinshaw has an evergreen on each side of the steps to his porch trimmed into the shape of vases. The word "topiary," which means the art of trimming shrubs into fanciful shapes, comes to mind. You've seen some pictures of English topiary. Would there be a story about it all, the history of topiary, and the topiary in famous old gardens? (Possible markets: *Coronet, Atlantic Monthly.*)

As you go on down the street, you pass Mrs. Burdette's house, a little white cottage set well back, and you know that back of the cottage is a garden that you've heard called the loveliest spot in town. Would that be a story—the loveliest garden in town, an experience story about Mrs. Burdette's garden and how she made it what it is? (Possible markets: Sunday newspaper, *Woman's Home Companion.*)

And that word "loveliest" sticks in your mind. It rolls around—loveliest this, loveliest that. It gets transposed into best—best this and best that. You begin to think of a half-dozen stories about the "best" in town.

It might be about the best-dressed girl (or boy) in high school. What is "best dressed" for a high school girl? What do the girls themselves think? And the possibility of a poll of twenty-five or fifty or one hundred of the high-school girls occurs to you. What do their mothers think? Again a poll might be a possibility. (Possible markets: Sunday newspaper, *Household Magazine, Farmer's Wife.*)

Another "best": the best kitchen in town. Not necessarily what the architects or the home economists call the best kitchen, but the kitchen the housewives themselves think is best. A little scouting and you could locate a half-dozen candidates for this distinction. With calls at these half-dozen places, you could get floor plans and the layout of the equipment. These, drawn up, could be laid before a number of women (some of the women's clubs would be willing to devote an afternoon to the subject) and you could get their ratings of the kitchens. Your story would be primarily about the kitchen that rated highest. Ideas and suggestions from some of the others could be brought in to give the story wider appeal and acceptability. (Possible markets: *Ladies' Home Journal,* Sunday newspaper.)

Across the street, as we head down town, is Central High School. Only last night, you heard two or three friends with youngsters in high school arguing bitterly about the extra-curricular program of the school. One of them thought the school was frittering away the students' time with all the fancy business of dramatics, school paper, chorus and orchestra, debating. But another said that her daughter *liked* high school just because of these things. And a third said that she didn't care one way or another, but that she thought it was going too far when Annabelle had to get to school at seven o'clock to practice folk dancing for the pageant. Up and down the country, the very rapid expansion of high-school facilities and personnel, with the decreased emphasis on the three R's, has made this problem of extra-curricular activities a burning issue in the minds of countless parents. What are the rights and wrongs of it, the arguments pro and con? What do the youngsters think, the parents, the educators? (Possible markets: *Parents' Magazine, Forum.*)

Ahead of us is the new viaduct. a complicated sifting out of railroads and streets to avoid the old grade-crossing and highway cross-traffic. Three hundred thousand dollars have gone into the project, and in another week or two it will be completed. (Possible markets: *Engineering News-Record, Public Safety,* newspaper.)

And this sets you thinking along broader lines. What is the status of grade-crossing elimination on highways? What has the federal-aid program accomplished in this direction? What are the data on grade-crossing accidents? (Possible markets: *Public Safety, Scientific American.*)

The construction of the viaduct has been the death tap to the moribund street railway. Electric cars haven't run for ten years, but the tracks have been kept open. You remember in one hundred towns you have driven through the unused tracks of electric lines or the scars where they have been. Might there be a story about this almost defunct industry, which in something like fifty years mushroomed to tremendous size and as quickly shriveled and died? (Possible markets: Sunday newspaper, *Collier's.*)

On down the street is the new ice cream factory, spotless with its white tile and chromium plate. But the chief thing you've noticed about it is that it has facilities for serving ice cream and fountain dishes to retail trade, and ever since it was opened a month ago the tables and booths in a large front room have been crowded with customers. Would there be a story for an ice cream trade publication in this enterprise? (Possible markets: *Ice Cream Trade Journal, Ice Cream Review.*)

And you think by contrast of the old drug store across the street. The only drug store you know which doesn't have a fountain, which doesn't serve meals and sell books, and yet for some reason it is the leading drug store in town. It's where you go to get your prescriptions filled. It's been a good business for fifty years—and it is still the best drug business in town. (Possible Market: *Drug Trade News.*)

The town library has been through a revolution during the past five years. The new librarian—new five years ago—exploded in our midst this novel sequence of logic: that reading is a good thing, that reading is pretty much a matter of habit, and that the earlier good habits are formed the better. So she went to work on the youngsters, even those who hadn't started to school yet. She has kept going a succession of exhibits in show cases and on tables in the lobby—dolls dramatizing fairy tales, historical costumes, exhibits about authors. And in the summer, when school is out, she has a reading contest that winds up with a celebration in the park. There is a parade, the grade-school band is out, and prizes are presented. The business has gone so fast and so far that you had to vote bonds the other day for an addition to the library. (Possible markets: *Ladies' Home Journal, Library Journal.*)

Speaking of the band suggests another story—about the small-town silver cornet band of yesteryear. What has become of it? Are there still any such bands in existence? Oh, yes, you have your municipal band, but the musicians now are paid. They play in the fine new municipal band shell. It's a different band from the old one—the old volunteer band that practiced on Tuesday nights in the Odd Fellow's hall. If you would see that old band, you must go to the old-fashioned photograph album that our grandmothers keep. (Possible markets: *Esquire, Etude.*)

That reminds you of another dead and gone institution, the volunteer fire department. In the old days the members were called out by runners. Later there were buzzers beside their beds. Many were the deeds of heroism and many were the humorous blunders in the annals of those volunteer companies. (Possible markets: *Vogue,* Sunday newspaper.)

We pass a man, tall, grey-haired, and he waves his hand in greeting. He is the mayor, but it is not for being mayor that he is famous. He is the best high school cheer-leader in the state, and this spring, when your high school team won the state tournament, the mayor by his presence and the cheers he led contributed to the victory. Back of that, of course, lies the fact that he is a friend of every boy and girl in high school, one to whom they go for advice and for help when they get into trouble. (Possible markets: *American,* Sunday newspaper.)

The mayor isn't the only interesting personality in town. There is the woman who last year was listed as one of the ten most influential women in the country. To be sure she no longer lives here, but she comes back once in a while to renew the friendships that have lasted through the years since she was a girl. And here about you are the people who know her and can tell of her girlhood, her school days, the books she read and the beaux she had. (Possible markets: *McCall's, Redbook.*)

There is the night watchman on the college campus. He is far from famous and now, after forty years of tramping the campus, he stoops a little as he makes his rounds, but he probably knows more about college boys and girls than twenty deans of men or women. He has tales to tell about them, and a very human philosophy that is the product of his night prowlings. (Possible markets: *Liberty,* Sunday newspaper.)

How bad (or good) are college boys and girls? Suppose for a moment that you are a college student. You are in a position, then, to see behind the scenes of college life and to answer this question, which is so important a one to fond parents whose John or Jane is thinking about going to college. How much drinking, how much gambling, how much church going, how much frivolity, how much seriousness? What is college life outside the class room? (Possible markets: *Good Housekeeping, Esquire.*)

We go into the bank to cash a check. You write it out and carefully fill in the stub in your checkbook. And that suggests the universal complaint of husbands against check-writing wives—that they never fill out the stubs. What could the banker up there behind the glass door tell women about how to handle their finances and their dealings with banks? (Possible markets: *Mademoiselle, Household Magazine.*)

Again one idea suggests several others. You have just had the banker in mind and that makes you think of the lawyer. Everybody ought to write a will, but most of us don't. We have the vaguest notions of the laws of inheritance and the complications that may result if no will is left. Wouldn't there be a story from one of your leading lawyers about wills and more particularly about the reasons for making wills? (Possible markets: *Pictorial Review, Cosmopolitan.*)

Our walk has been designed to point the obvious moral that there is story material all about us if we have the eyes to see it. It is a good bet that there are fifty magazine stories in every town of 1,000 population, and proportionately more in towns and cities that are larger.

But what about the country? This time let us take an automobile instead of walking and head down any of the roads that lead from town.

Not far out we come to a country schoolhouse. It happens to be white instead of red, but it's of the typical one-room variety. There are thousands just like it throughout the land. Suppose we get curious about this one-room school. What does it cost per pupil to run? How does this cost compare with the cost in city schools? How good or poor a job does a one-room school do? How does it compare on this basis with the city school? What have been the results of efforts directed toward the elimination of the one-room school? Here is, of course, a big and complex story. There is a tremendous amount of data bearing on it, and new data are being continually collected. The story has many angles, any one of which might make an article. (Possible markets: *School and Society, Country Gentleman,* state farm paper.)

Tom Elder, on the farm beyond the school, sells market milk at the new dairy plant in town. You happen to have heard (or maybe you made a point of inquiring) that Elder's milk has the lowest bacterial count of any that is delivered to the dairy. Might there be a story in the sanitary methods which Elder follows to keep his milk clean? (Possible markets: *Hoard's Dairyman, Capper's Farmer.*)

You may know of another farmer whose barns, milk-house, and dairy equipment are just as dirty as Elder's are clean. Perhaps the story might be a contrast between these two farms.

On our left, back from the road, under swinging elm branches, is a new house. "What a nice looking place," you say, and then it occurs to you that you couldn't make that same statement about a very large proportion of farm houses. This one isn't elaborate or costly, but it is architecturally well designed and it fits into the lovely setting of trees and grass. Why aren't more farm houses like it? There may be a story in the plans of this farm house. Or this house may be used as an instance to introduce one or a half-dozen farm house plans. Or this house, you find, was built with the help of Federal Housing Administration financing, and it might serve as a practical instance in a story on federal aid for farm homes. (Possible markets: *Successful Farming, Farmer's Wife.*)

If we keep our eyes open as we drive along, we may see a lot of little things: A really attractive and busy roadside market, a crop that is unusual in the neighborhood, a corn bin of new and inexpensive design. And if we stop to talk to farmers, we'll hear about their Farm Business Association, about the projects of the Smith-Hughes class in the consolidated school, about the boy who is in partnership with his father in building up a fine herd of Hampshire hogs.

How about the college campus? If this is the field of your search for subjects—assuming that you are a college student or a member of a college staff—try this device to bring close under your eyes the story possibilities of your campus. Write down on a piece of paper the name of a college department. If you know any of the people on the staff of that department, write down their names too. Now what does this department do, what do its staff members do?

Let's take an example. The mathematics department should be as good (or as bad) as any. Every mathematics department gets letters from home-made mathematicians, who have solved—just like that—some of the insolvable problems of the science. Some of these letters are humorous, some are pathetic, and one out of a million points toward a mathematical genius. Might there be a story in these letters? (Possible markets: *Mathematics Teacher, American.*)

The professor of statistics, in the mathematics department, may be the man to give you the story of the veritable revolution in research techniques which has been brought about by the introduction of statistical analysis of research data. This is not an easy or simple story, but it is an important and a timely one. (Possible markets: *Science, Atlantic Monthly.*)

With an idea or two from one department, go on to the next and the next. If your school is a large one it has under way an elaborate program of research. If it is a land-grant college it has its Agricultural and Engineering Experiment stations. From the heads of the research programs (or their secretaries) you can get a list of research projects.

From the office of the graduate dean, you can probably get the list of subjects for master's and doctor's theses that are being worked on. Not every one of these pieces of research will make a magazine or newspaper story, but many of them will.

At the college or university library, there are two especially useful sources of ideas (and material) for articles: the bound file of master's and doctor's theses and the incoming flow of bulletins from all over the world. The latter contain a running account of the findings and developments in the laboratories of every country. There are too many of these for a writer to follow them all, but he can watch the new publications in the one or two or three or four subject-matter fields in which he is most interested.

2. From the Other Fellow

There isn't very much that is new in the world. Most new things are adaptations of the old—new angles, new points of view, new combinations and interpretation, new instances of old truths.

And so what the other fellow sees and writes in newspapers, magazines, bulletins, books, should be a never-ending source of suggestion for things we ourselves can do.

Let's look at some of the stories reproduced in this book to see whether they suggest other stories that might be possibilities for magazines or newspapers.

"He Pastures His Hobby Horse in the Garden" (Chapter IX) is a story of a man and his hobby. It would be difficult to read it without thinking of other men—and women—and their hobbies. There is the college professor who started a small son on stamp collecting and who today is a world authority on stamps. There is the insurance-company executive whose hobby is boys, orphan boys, whom he helps through school, through college, and out into the world. There is the farmer whose hobby is tinkering in his woodshed machine-shop and who has a dozen patents registered in his name. There is the woman whose hobby is historical costumes and who has a collection of hundreds of dolls, dressed in the costumes of almost every time and every country.

To get back to Mr. Calkins, there is his other hobby, woodworking, and that suggests the possibility of a second story from him.

The fact of Mr. Calkins' deafness sets one's mind running along another line. Even deafness has its advantages. Might there be a story on the *benefits* of being deaf? Or another about people who have achieved marked success in spite of this handicap?

Such a story as "Mountain King," (Chapter IX) suggests the enormously wide range of possibilities for articles which recount the outstanding achievements of individuals or groups or institutions. For example, stories of the engineer who has completed an unusual bridge or dam or skyscraper or flood-control project; of the merchant whose business is unique and successful; of the high-school agricultural class which through its projects has been an influence for better farming in the community.

When one reads "Fairies Live in This Garden" (Chapter IX), he should be started off on a survey of his own experiences. He should say to himself, "Have I done anything that would be of interest or value for other people to know?" For example: One may be the first—or last, or middle—of thirteen children and have, in the adjustments of so complicated a household, material for a story on family relations. Or one may have built a canoe or a loom or a summer-house or an attic studio.

"Good News" (Chapter X) points to news events which may be made the subjects of magazine and newspaper articles. For example: annual meetings of scientific societies, or trade associations, of fraternal groups; short courses at the college, such as the garden short course, the dairy manufacturing short course, the bee-keepers' short course.

Scores of meetings, short courses and conferences are held each year on the college campus. The enterprising writer who wants to capitalize on these events should make himself a calendar of forthcoming meetings and, sufficiently ahead of the dates of the meetings, query magazines or newspapers that might be interested in having them covered.

"Ten Minutes From Hollywood" (Chapter XI) is the story of a house. As you read it there come to mind other houses that you know of that are unique in one way or another—in their low cost, in their novel design or arrangement, in some phase of construction, such as insulation, air conditioning, interior finish.

"Light Where You Need It" (Chapter XII) is the prototype of a hundred stories about home and office and factory equipment.

If there is a place for a story such as "Going On from 40" (Chapter XII) may there not also be for stories on "Getting Ready for 21 (or 6 or 13 or 70)"?

The poll of public opinion, popularized by the American Institute of Public Opinion and exemplified by the story "What Do the Women of America Think About War," (Chapter XII), suggests such subjects as these: "What Do College Students Think About Religion?" "What Do Farmers Think About Foreign Trade Agreements?"

One of the jobs of a feature editor of a newspaper is to scan the news columns of his own paper for items that might lend themselves to elaboration as feature stories and the columns of scores of exchanges to see what kind of features other papers are running. Most magazines are subscribers for a number of daily and weekly newspapers—*Better Homes & Gardens* takes thirty—which are gone through in a systematic search for article tips.

Let's look at a front page of a daily newspaper selected at random and see if it contains any suggestions for feature articles. Here is a copy of the *Kansas City Star*. The lead on the story in the right-hand column is: "Washington, May 12—The House beat down today a public attempt to turn the administration of relief over to the states. The standing vote was 106 to 39."

Suggestions: A newspaper feature on the amount or proportion of relief cost carried by the state in which the paper is published. An article reporting a study of the cost of relief administration under state and federal auspices.

Near the bottom of the same column is a paragraph story which reads: "Pittsburgh, May 12—The fate of the Reverend Father James R. Cox and four of his associates in the 'Monastery Garden Stakes,' which the government charges is a fraud and a lottery, was placed in the hands of a federal court jury this afternoon. Seven others have pleaded guilty."

Suggestions: An article on famous lotteries. An article giving a background of attempts to make lotteries legal in the United States. An article or articles on famous frauds and swindles.

In the same column: "E. D. Phillips, 85 years old, veteran teacher of English at Northeast High school, is at Research Hospital for observation. At his home at 3021 Forest Avenue, it was said that he was expected to return home in a few days."

Suggestions: An article on the extent of provision by public schools for retirement allowances for teachers. A personality study for a newspaper of "The Grand Old Man" (or woman) of the local schools.

In the next column is this story: "Henderson, Ky., May 12—Six members of the Elliot Gibson family burned to death last night when fire destroyed their tenant home near Poole, 20 miles south of here."

Suggestions: An article on fire losses on farms. An article on fire prevention practices, particularly in rural areas. An article on first aid for burns.

A story in another column has this lead: "An official report of a $2,379 loss suffered early yesterday at a robbery of the Katz Drug Company store at 8th Street and Grand Avenue was filed with the Police Department."

Suggestions: An article on local, state, or national losses from robberies. An article tracing the rise or fall of robberies in the city, state, or nation. A story comparing the statistics of robberies and perhaps other crimes with comparable statistics from other countries.

One can go in this way across the front page and up and down the inside columns of the paper and find in almost every news story the germ of an article.

Other repositories of the work and ideas of other men from which the writer of articles can skim suggestions are bulletins of the experiment stations, of the federal departments, of trade associations and industries; scientific journals, in which are locked quite out of reach of the general public new developments in every phase of research; books; reports of governmental bodies, investigating committees, and committees of professional and business groups. The writer who is on mailing lists and subscription lists to receive such materials is in contact with a continuing flow of ideas and material for articles.

3. From the Calendar

Timeliness and seasonableness are the pegs upon which are hung hundreds of magazine and newspaper articles. The calendar can be made the servant of the feature writer if he takes the trouble to use it.

Thinking always in terms of people—such people, for example, as those who are sketched at the beginning of this Chapter—let us ask ourselves what interests are paramount on:

January 1: Business and household budgets; mid-winter vacations; cropping plans for spring.

February 1: Plans for renovating the garden; plans for the new home that is to be built during the summer—or the old home that is to be remodeled; spring fashions.

March 1: Orchard spraying; new interior decoration.

April 1: Spring menus; summer clothes.

Of course, if a writer waits until January to think of subjects appropriate to January he will "miss the boat." He should think up January subjects in June or July or August (or in January this year for January next year). And get the stories to editors at the time *they* are thinking of their January issues. (See Chap. III for a discussion of the length of time magazines are planned ahead of publication date.)

And so on around the calendar. Each season has its peculiar interests and problems. These are important clues to article subjects.

Each season has, too, its special days, its anniversaries and holidays—Christmas, Thanksgiving, Fourth of July, Labor Day, May Day, and a host of others. On the basis of widespread interest in these holidays and festivals, magazines and newspapers build appropriate articles.

The biographical gazetteer in the back of the dictionary and textbooks of history—ancient, medieval, European, and American—are inexhaustible resources for the writer of articles. One can go through them and make a list of the anniversaries of the births and deaths of famous men and of important events that will fall during the coming months. There are stories for various types of magazines and newspapers in the anniversaries of inventions, battles, treaties, famous books, catastrophes, and declarations of war.

One final injunction to writers who would have always on hand ideas upon which to work: A bird in the hand is worth two in the bush; and this, translated, means that the writer must keep a systematic record of the ideas that he runs across or which occur to him.

A small "idea" book which one always carries, in pocket or pocket book, is a piece of essential equipment. Some writers use a card system for the more permanent recording and classifying of story ideas. Others use folders in which memoranda, clippings, and even bulletins and magazines can be filed.

REFERENCES

PERIODICALS

"If You Want to Write Magazine Articles," by Elmer T. Peterson, *Quill*, 22:7, Page 8, July, 1934.

"Know Your Ducks," by Ben Hibbs, *Quill*, 19:7, Page 5, July, 1931.

"So You Want to Break into the Magazines?" by Douglas Lurton, *Quill*, 21:4, Page 6, April, 1933.

"One Way to Make Crime Pay," by Douglas Lurton, *Quill*, 21:6, Page 6, June, 1933.

"Peek over the Farmer's Shoulder," by Loren E. Donelson, *Quill*, 21:1, Page 5, January, 1933.

"Want to Write for Boys?" by Franklin M. Reck, *Quill*, 21:4, Page 4, April, 1933.

"Write off the Depression," by Douglas Lurton, *Quill*, 20:8, Page 6, August, 1932.

"Your Stake in Junior Magazines," by George F. Pierrot, *Quill*, 22:6, Page 5, June, 1934.

"Make Your Small Change Count," by John F. DeVine, *Quill*, 21:12, Page 7, December, 1933.

See also *Magazine Article Writing* (Brennecke and Clark), *Modern Feature Writing* (Harrington and Watson), *Magazine Articles* (Crawford), *Writing Journalistic Features* (Reed), *Writing for Profit* (Wilhelm), *Technical Journalism* (Beckman, O'Brien, and Converse), *The Business Paper Editor at Work* (Woolf).

XVI

How to Get Material

THE writer of magazine articles and newspaper features is a reporter. He is *not* a writer of fiction, although he may employ many of the fiction writer's techniques. He is *not* a writer of essays, although the essay is not greatly different from some kinds of articles.

He cannot go up into the attic and pull the ladder after him—cut himself off from the world and produce articles out of his inner consciousness. The fiction writer or the essayist can do that, provided he has sufficiently stored his inner consciousness with experience.

Magazines exist because they purvey information and entertainment that people want to get—with an occasional dash of inspirational vitamins thrown in. A few magazines lean heavily toward the entertainment side. In most, however, information is paramount, although there is no law against this information's being presented in an entertaining way.

The job of a magazine is to look out over the area that it covers, spy the events, the ideas, the people which are report-worthy from the point of view of its readers, and to gather in for its pages accounts of those events, ideas, and people.

And this, to repeat, is a reportorial job. The editor of a magazine, like the city editor of a newspaper, sits at the center of a shifting and many-faceted scene from which it is his business to isolate the significant and the interesting for his readers. The scene of the city editor's activities is delimited geographically. The scene of the magazine editor is delimited by the subject-matter policy of his magazine.

The writer of articles is the magazine's leg-man—he is the lasso which the editor throws out around an event to drag it into the magazine. Members of the magazine staff who write articles do so usually on definite assignment of the editor. The free-lance writer gives himself an assignment which he thinks the editor would like, or ought, to have covered. Sometimes he proposes the assignment to the editor and gets a commission to cover it.

While ability to write effectively and entertainingly is important, the idea held by many novices that the writing is the whole job is pernicious and the source of many a heart-break.

An article is, in summary: First, an idea conceived editorially (this whole book is an attempt to show what the word "editorially" signifies and if the reader doesn't by this time have a vivid sense of its signification, he had best abandon for other pastures the field of article writing); second, the reportorial job of covering the story; and third, the employment of the techniques of the writer and the illustrator to tell the story.

Article Zones

By the term article zone is meant the "area" that must be covered in reporting a given story.

Some stories, from the point of view of coverage, are relatively simple—the area involved is small. The material for such stories can be secured from a single individual. The confession story, the personal experience story, and a good many third-person experience stories are of this sort. In the case of the confession story and the personal experience story, the reporting job consists of interviewing oneself. "Fairies Live in This Garden" (Page 16) is of this sort. So also is "A Professor Quits the Communist Party" (Chapter IX). Third-person experience stories require an interview with some other person. Examples: "He Pastures His Hobby-Horse in a Garden" (Page 4) and "Mountain King" (Chapter IX).

Stories like these, we can say, belong to zone 1.

In the next larger area, zone 2, several sources of information must be covered, but they are all close together. "Going on from 40" (Chapter XII) is a good example. In covering this story, it was not enough to interview only the doctor or only the psychologist or only the minister. To cover the story, the author interviewed not one but six people—insurance actuary, psychologist, food chemist, doctor, psychiatrist, and minister. To have omitted any one of these interviews would have deformed the story.

Many experience stories, even though they are concerned with the accomplishments of a single person, require not only an interview with that person but with others who are able to describe and evaluate his accomplishments. Other experience stories, dealing not with individuals but with groups of people or with organizations or with institutions, require coverage from a number of different angles.

You are getting, for example, the story of a farm record association. It is a group of farmers who have banded together to employ a farm-management consultant, who have agreed to keep detailed records of their farm operations, and whose program calls for the trying out of certain new ideas of farm management.

Here are the *obvious* sources of information for this story: The farm-management consultant and his records and reports; individual farm members of the association.

Here are *less* obvious sources of information: The county agricultural agent; the extension farm-management specialist at the state college who has worked closely with the association; agronomy and livestock specialists; bulletins and magazine articles.

How many of these sources one wants to cover depends upon the central theme of the proposed story. If it is to be a survey story of the association and its work then the story will be stronger if all these sources are tapped. It is conceivable, however, that the theme of the story might be what the association has done for Farmer Jones. And in this latter case, it might be enough to interview Jones and the consultant.

Some stories describe conditions or events over a wide area—a county, for instance, or a state or the whole country. Such stories belong to zone 2. They are usually covered in one of two ways. Either the reporter must travel widely, interviewing and observing, catching up with the different angles of the story in this place and that; or the material must be gathered by questionnaire or by a poll.

An example of the first of these two ways of covering a zone-3 story is "Behind the Conflict in 'Bloody Harlan' " (Chapter XII). Innumerable interviews, travel, and observation went into this article.

In the late '20's George Gallup wrote a doctoral dissertation at the University of Iowa on a method he had devised for measuring reader-interest in newspapers and magazines. This method was subsequently used very widely by periodicals. Out of his experience with reader-interest surveys grew in Dr. Gallup's mind the idea of scientifically controlled polls of public opinions. The American Institute of Public Opinion was organized to conduct such polls and to sell the material to newspapers for publication. The popularity of the Gallup polls has led a number of magazines, notably *Fortune, Ladies' Home Journal, Successful Farming, Wallaces' Farmer and Iowa Homestead,* to set up machinery for gathering similar surveys of public opinions. Less formal and elaborate polls and questionnaire surveys are standard methods of securing article material.

"What do the Women of America Think About War" (Chapter XII) is an example of the second of these two ways of covering the zone-3 story.

If we should formulate a zoning law on the basis of the foregoing, it would read like this: The writer of an article shall not be satisfied to cover a zone-3 story with zone-1 reporting, nor a zone-3 story with zone-2 reporting. The penalty for the violation of the law is an inadequate and unsuccessful story.

Interviewing

Estimated roughly, 90 percent of the material that goes into articles comes from interviews, 5 percent from published sources, and 5 percent from observation, out of the author's own head and from miscellaneous sources.

How does one get an interview? There are just two ways. One is to ask for it and the other is to sneak up on it.

Nine times out of ten the reporter will ask for an interview. If the request is made, not only in his own name but in the name of the newspaper or magazine for which he works or for which he is writing or to which he hopes to sell the article, so much the better. It is one thing to ask a busy man or woman to give his time to you personally—particularly if you are unknown to him—and it is quite another to ask him to give it to the *New York Times*, the *Saturday Evening Post*, or the *Farm Journal.*

Anything that is said about interviewing here, or anywhere else for that matter, must always make a wide allowance for the personal equation. What will work with one person may be exactly the wrong way to proceed with another. One's interview tactics should be based upon the best analysis that one can make, from what he knows or can learn, of the character and personality of the person to be interviewed.

It is a good general rule in arranging for an interview to tell as explicitly as possible what you want and why you want it. Your letter, telegram, or telephone conversation should explain who you are, what publication you represent or are writing for, and what you want to get from the interview.

Not always, however, can one be so forthright. There are times when you want to talk to people without their knowing that they are being interviewed. For example: The staff writer of a national magazine is sent out to get a dope story on the attitude of labor in various sections of the country toward the candidates in the presidential election. The bulk of his material will no doubt come from more or less formal interviews with labor and political leaders. But he will want to feel out for himself the sentiment of the men in the shops and factories and on construction jobs. And this he can do best informally by "rubbing shoulders" with the men themselves on street corners, in barber shops, and at the headquarters of workers' organizations. His method will be largely to listen and to put in a question now and then to point the conversation toward the topics in which he is interested.

One magazine editor says that the best place to interview a man is in the smoking compartment of a pullman car. There aren't two or three telephones at the man's elbow, his secretary can't stick her head in, there aren't pressing decisions to be made, letters to be signed, conferences to be prepared for. There a man lets down his guards, relaxes, becomes reminiscent.

Unfortunately all interviews can't be conducted in pullman smoking cars, but the interviewer can in many cases direct the interview toward the better rather than the worse time and place.

The morning is not usually the best time to interview a business man. He has his day's work to push along, the day's decisions to be made. Better to arrange to see him at luncheon, or late in the afternoon when his chores are mostly done and his tempo is slowing up, or at dinner, or at a baseball game, or on the golf course.

Stage the interview, if you can, at the place and at the time that the interviewee will be most at home, most at ease, and the least inconvenienced. The best place to interview a farmer is in his barn and the best time, if you can arrange it with the weather man, is a rainy afternoon. If he is plowing you can wait at the end of the corn row until he stops to breathe his horses. If he is in the hay field and dark clouds are rolling up the sky, pass him by and come another day.

Women are most at home in the kitchen, next in the back yard, next in the dining room, and least of all in the "parlor" (there are still millions of "parlors" in the land even though they may be known by other names). Unfortunately when you go to a person's home, it is the "parlor" to which you are taken. Find an excuse, if you can, to get your interviewee into the kitchen or the back yard.

When you ask a person for an interview, you are asking him for his time, for his knowledge, for his ideas. He gives you these things for several reasons. Most important of all, usually, is vanity. It is something to be sought out by a magazine or newspaper. It is something to get one's name into a periodical. It is something, even though one's name may not appear, to know that one has helped to make an article in a publication that will be read by thousands or millions of people. The interviewee as well as the interviewer may have an ax to grind. We are all propagandists for ourselves, for our ideas, and for our faiths. The interview and the subsequent article give a person a chance to speak out for the things he thinks and believes. He may on occasion have more specific reasons for wanting to get his views before the public. He may want to oppose a piece of legislation or advocate a theory or support a reform or justify his actions. And the article you are writing gives him a chance to do these things.

Besides these reasons for giving you an interview, there is the negative one that it is usually easier to accede to a request than to refuse it.

Now in these attitudes of the interviewee toward your request for an interview there are clues as to procedure. It won't be amiss—keeping always in mind the personal equation—to lay a little emphasis on the fact that the interviewee has been "selected" by your publication, that he probably knows more about the subject than anyone else you can think of, that you were told by So-and-So that he was just the man to see, that you've read his books or bulletins, or heard him lecture. And it may not be amiss to hint that if he wants to put certain ideas across, the article you are working on may be a means to that end. And it will never be amiss to indicate by manner and by words—perhaps by a note of thanks after the interview is over—that you are grateful for his time and sincerely appreciative of the help he has given you.

To repeat, you are asking for a man's time. You are also asking for his confidence. You are asking him to trust to you his ideas and his personality—his personal and professional reputation. It is only fair and wise, therefore, that you should take as little of his time as necessary and that you should so conduct yourself as to make him believe that he is safe in your hands. Put yourself in the place of the person being interviewed. What would you think of an interviewer who wasn't too sure of your name, or title, or position, or special interests; who had never heard of your books; who didn't evidence at least a working knowledge of the subject about which he is interviewing you; whose manner was too casual or too smart? To such an interviewer you would feel that you couldn't trust yourself. The less you tell him, the better.

But put it the other way around. The interviewer knows exactly who you are, he knows where you were born, where you went to college, to what fraternity you belonged, of what clubs you are a member, who your wife is, what prep school your son is attending. He knows that you were in the Rainbow Division during the World War, that you won three football letters in 1911, '12, and '13, that at forty-seven you still play a bang-up game of handball, that you are fanatical about Sibelius.

He knows too something about your economic theories and the employer-labor relationships that you have been working out in the industry with which you are connected. And he has read the article you wrote a couple of years ago for a trade journal, and the interview with you that was run last week in the *World-Telegram.*

In brief, he thinks, this fellow knows his stuff. One can talk to him and he'll know what you're saying.

But how can the interviewer get such information about a man he has never met and whom he may never have heard of before? To be sure, sometimes he can't—there isn't time, or the sources of information aren't available. But usually he can. First of all from the library, from *Who's Who,* from the *Readers' Guide to Periodical Literature,* from the *New York Times Index,* from the card catalog of authors; and, second, from people who know the man, from associates who are mutual acquaintances, from employes. You go about asking your friends, "Do you know So-and-So?" And one of them will tell you that he knows a fellow whose wife has a maid who used to work for Mrs. So-and-So. So you call up the maid.

But preparing for the interview is more than knowing what you can about the man or woman to whom you are to talk. Even more important is to know what you want to talk about, exactly what you want to get and how you propose to get it. You are going to interview the new national amateur-golf champion for a story on getting the right start in golf, for a boy's magazine. You have played a little golf, you know the language, and you are familiar with the careers of the leading golfers. But you wouldn't be able to give a very successful lecture on the fine points of the game. There are plenty of good books on golf and three or four hours with your nose in one will be a good investment.

Before you go for the interview, the story that you want to get should have taken tentative shape in your mind. You know the audience for which you want to write, the central theme that you want to present, and something of the detailed information that you want to obtain to round out the story. To be sure the interview may change all of this; it may give you some ideas that you hadn't thought of before; it may be desirable to shift the emphasis in the story; it may even become wise to handle the story for a different kind of audience than you had had in mind. So you don't want to be "sot" in your preconceptions of the interview. But with this in mind, it is wise to have elastic plans for the interview well worked out.

Questioning is a subtle and complex art. It can't be taught in a textbook. But these suggestions are, just the same, well worth minding.

Design opening questions to show that you know something about the subject of the interview.

Don't ask negative questions unless you want negative replies.

Ask specific questions rather than general ones (not, of a farmer, "How did you make out last year?"; but rather the series, "How many hogs did you raise last year? What did you sell them for? What was the margin?").

Ask general summarizing questions toward the end of the interview.

But talk isn't all of a successful interview. Seeing is almost as important. If your story is to be real and living to your readers, you will have to describe people and places. The smile with which a man answers a question may be as important as the answer itself. A trembling hand, a raised eyebrow, a two-days' growth of beard, these may be the dramatic highlights of the story.

A number of years ago Harry R. O'Brien wrote an article for the *Country Gentleman* which began like this:

"On an afternoon in late September, just as the sun was casting half-mile shadows from behind a distant shelter belt, I watched a tenant farmer on a 640-acre farm in the Red River Valley of North Dakota drive a reaper around a 70-acre field of sweet clover that he was cutting for seed.

"As he stopped at the corner where I waited, to unhitch and call it a day, I introduced myself and stated my mission. A man past middle age, he was, hair touched with gray and face brown and wrinkled.

"He listened to me, and as I talked a twinkle kept playing around his eyes. I paused for answer.

"First, he tinkered with a loosened bolt. Next, he relit his cob pipe and blew a cloud of smoke into the clear Dakota air without saying a word.

"Then his face broke out into a broad smile.

"That smile was the miracle of North Dakota.

"For it was as typical as anything I saw in 3,000 miles or more of travel throughout the Northwest in September and October, of a change that came over the states of Montana, North Dakota, South Dakota and Minnesota during the past summer and early fall.

"It was symbolical of the miraculous something that almost overnight turned the spirit of the people in this vast inland empire from the bottomless pit of discouragement and pessimism engendered throughout four or five long, lean, bitter years, onto the upland and mountain top of optimism and hope."

The North Dakota Farmer's smile may be taken as the symbol of the kind of seeing that should be a part of every interview.

Other Sources of Information

The writer of articles should be a heavy patron of the United States Post Office Department. Into his study should flow a steady stream of bulletins, reports, catalogs, mailing pieces.

There must be some method, however, in this madness. A fair-sized warehouse wouldn't hold all of the free stuff that a person could get if he put no brake upon his askings. Most writers of articles are in more or less degree specialists. They have fields of subject matter about which they are best prepared to write. It is within the limits of his special fields that one should attempt to secure this kind of material.

The woman interested in writing foods copy can get on mailing lists to secure bulletins from the Bureau of Home Economics of the United States Department of Agriculture; from the experiment stations and extension services of the land grant colleges; from trade associations and institutes, such as the National Dairy Council, Institute of American Meat Packers, the California Fruit Growers Association, the National Poultry Council; and from individual industries.

The man who is writing on labor relations can obtain bulletins and reports and periodicals from the Department of Labor, the Department of Commerce, the Bureau of the Census, the American Federation of Labor, the Committee for Industrial Organization, from employment relief agencies, from trade associations, and from individual industries.

Such receipts of printed matter will not do much good unless they are handled systematically. Much of the stuff can be glanced over and thrown away. For the rest there should be a well-maintained filing system.

A good investment for the writer is the subscription prices of three to a dozen daily newspapers. If they are from strategically selected spots about the country, they will bring him a very complete picture of the significant news and the political, social, and economic trends of the country. They should be used in these four ways:

To give the writer general background.

To supply him with story tips—clipped and filed.

To give him material on particular stories on which he is working.

To give him file material on topics upon which some day he may want to write.

To the free stuff and the newspapers there should be added a selection of magazines. These should include one or two authoritative, technical journals in the field of the writer's specialization, and several typical magazines of the sort for which he wants to write.

How It Is Done

A look at the stories reproduced in this book will give us clues to the ways in which writers have gone about getting material for newspaper and magazine features. The following tabular presentation offers a bird's-eye view of their chief sources of information.

Title of Article:	*Sources of Information:*
"He Pastures His Hobby-Horse in a Garden" (p. 4)	Books and articles by Mr. Calkins Two interviews with Mr. Calkins Picture retakes by commercial photographer
"Mountain King" (chap. IX)	Interview with Mr. Blakeslee
"Fire 1,400 Dozens of Dinnerware per Day in One Man Electric Kiln" (chap. IX)	Personal observation of the factory Interviews with factory officials
"Fairies Live in This Garden" (p. 16)	The author's own experience
"Trout From Your Personal Pond" (chap. IX)	The author's own experience

"Explanation for Albert" (chap. IX)	The author's own experience
"A Professor Quits the Communist Party" (chap. IX)	The author's own experience
"Good News" (p. 7)	Study of the bill passed by Congress Interviews with FHA officials
"Wall Around Hell" (chap. X)	Personal observation Interviews with engineers and mine officials
"Mexican Bad Man" (chap. X)	Largely from author's own knowledge Current newspaper accounts
"Ten Minutes From Hollywood" (p. 8)	Interviews with architect, contractor, and owners
"Why Families Leave Home" (p. 14)	Author's professional training
"How to Tie Your Beds to Your Lawn" (p. 12)	Author's professional training
"Coffee Dresses for Tea" (chap. XI)	Results of recipe testing in the magazine's test kitchen
"Light Where You Need It" (p. 10)	Author's professional knowledge Consultations with experts
"Safe At Home but Are You" (p. 31)	Printed material, probably from Red Cross
"Watch Those 'Children's Diseases' " (p. 38)	Interview with state health official
"Going on from 40" (chap. XII)	Six interviews with an insurance actuary, psychologist, food chemist, doctor, psychiatrist, and minister
"Animals Do Think" (chap. XII)	Interviews Personal observations
"What Do the Women of America Think About War" (chap. XII)	Nation-wide poll
"Behind the Conflict in 'Bloody Harlan' " (chap. XII)	Interviews Personal observation
"Women in the News" (chap. XIII)	Personal observation Interviews Reference material
"He's Skinner—and a Host of Old Friends, Too" (chap. XIII)	Interview Reference material

Practice Suggestions

1. Take a half-dozen different kinds of articles from different kinds of publications and analyze as well as you can the sources of information in them.

2. Outline the steps you would take to secure interviews with the following: A college president, governor of your state, James A. Farley, John L. Lewis, Joe Louis.

3. Glance through ten newspaper or magazine articles and indicate to which subject-matter zone each belongs.

4. If you were working up articles on early glassware in America, the anniversary of the battle between the Merrimac and the Monitor, the status of the livestock shipping associations in your state, how would you go about getting the information that you need?

5. Visit an office or a home. See what you can see. Afterwards put down twenty-five things you noticed (canary bird, dust on the table, copy of *The Young Joseph,* amazingly ugly picture, clean desk-top, etc.). Do this once a day for four years, more or less.

REFERENCES

BOOKS

Get That Picture, by A. J. Ezickson. National Library Press, New York, 1938.

News Pictures, by Jack Price. Round Table Press, New York, 1937.

See also *Magazine Article Writing* (Brennecke and Clark), *Modern Feature Writing* (Harrington and Watson), *Magazine Articles* (Crawford), *Writing Journalistic Features* (Reed), *Writing for Profit* (Wilhelm), *Technical Journalism* (Beckman, O'Brien, and Converse), *The Business Paper Editor at Work* (Woolf).

PERIODICALS

"Getting the Material," by Arthur H. Little, *Quill,* 20:2, Page 7, February, 1932.

"Building the Business Story," by Arthur H. Little, *Quill,* 20:3, Page 8, March, 1932.

XVII

The Writing Job

THE writing of an article is an adventure, an expedition, a sortie, into a new and undiscovered land. Neither you nor anyone else has ever taken the exact route that you will follow. Whether the expedition be a minor one—the tracing of the creek that runs by your home to its source in the hills a few miles away, or an attempt to reach the South Pole—there are in it the same necessities for foresight and preparation. A sandwich may be enough for the creek exploration. For the South Pole jaunt there are needed ship and men and planes and a thousand items of supply.

But in all three cases, creek, Pole, and article, there is the necessity of previsioning the goal, of anticipating the needs of the expedition, and of planning the route.

Defining the Goal

As with the explorer the first job of the writer of an article is to define very clearly for himself the goal which he is setting out to reach. This goal is just as real and must be made just as visible in the writer's mind as Mount Everest or the head waters of the Amazon.

This goal must always be defined in terms of:

1. The people for whom one is writing.
2. The idea which it is one's purpose to put into their heads.

The very first step, then, in the writing of an article is the decision as to what people it shall be written for. Is it for Mr. Harshbarger or Mrs. Seyler or Emma Runkle or Clem Shakely or Allen Parker? Or this question can be stated in another way: For what magazine shall this article be written? These two questions are roughly synonymous, because when one thinks of a magazine, he thinks, or should think, of the kind of people who comprise its reader group.

The second step is to formulate exactly what you have to offer the reader. With some stories this decision is simple; with others, it isn't.

Suppose you have been gathering material for an article on the changes that have come about in recent years in the textile industry as a result of the introduction of synthetic textile materials. You have data on the origin and development of rayon, on the processes of its manufacture, statistics on the production of silk, cotton, wool, and linen fabrics, on the development in Germany and Italy of lanatol, a wool substitute made from casein, material on tariffs, quotas, and embargoes, on cost of textile production in various countries, on experimental work with other textile substitutes, on sources of raw material, on the moves in international politics which have been based on the interests of various countries in textile production, raw material production, or textile consumption.

You feel confident that there is a story, perhaps a number of stories, in this wealth of material. You are faced now with the decision as to what to do with it all.

Question number one is:

What reader groups (or magazines) would be interested in this stuff or parts of it?

Answers:

1. Women, because of their interest in textiles. The magazines which could carry the story to this reader group are the general women's magazines.

2. People in the textile industry. The magazine possibilities in this case would be the textile trade publications.

3. Scientists and technicians in the textile field. For example, home economists who are specialists in textiles and clothing, and textile chemists. These readers would be reached through scientific journals, such as *Textile Research* and the *Journal of Home Economics.*

4. Farmers, and particularly cotton farmers, because of their concern with the marketing of natural raw materials. The *Country Gentleman* or *Progressive Farmer* might be interested in carrying such a story.

5. Laboring people in the textile field—reached through labor publications.

6. People with an intellectual interest in major economic, social, and political problems. These people would be reached through such magazines as *Harper's* and the *Atlantic Monthly.*

7. The great body of people who are citizens and taxpayers and who would be interested in this story because they are consumers, and because the textile situation has in it the possibilities of war, armament programs, national re-alignments—all of which touches them as citizens, taxpayers, and potential cannon fodder. Such magazines as *Collier's* and the *Saturday Evening Post* come to mind in this connection.

All of these possibilities lie in your material. Which shall be your goal? Now comes a process of weighing, comparing, and choosing. If your purpose is to get as much money out of the article as possible, you will aim at one of the general magazines or one of the women's magazines. If prestige in the textile field is more important to you than money, then you may want to write the story for a technical journal or a trade publication. If you are particularly interested in the producer's point of view, a farm journal may best be your objective.

You ask yourself some other questions. Granted that the story idea is of sufficient size and significance to rate publication in *Collier's* or the *Saturday Evening Post* or *Good Housekeeping,* will your material lend itself to the kind of handling that those magazines insist upon? Do you have the color stuff, the human-interest material, the realistic touches, which will make it possible for you to concoct a popular article? Do you have the particular kind of writing skill essential for popularization?

If you are thinking of a trade publication as a market, you need to ask whether it has already covered, from time to time as developments transpired, the material which you propose to put into the article. Would it be old stuff to it? Do you know enough, if you are thinking of a farm journal, about producer problems and techniques to slant the story toward that audience?

You would probably wish, in the case of a story of the scope of this one, to query an editor, or series of editors, as to his interest in your material.

These and a hundred other similar questions go through your mind and are argued back and forth, over and under. The upshot is, we'll say, that you decide to make a try at such a magazine as *Harper's*. That means that you will try to write the story for Lawyer Harshbarger and some 100,000 other people of similar intellectual capacities and interests.

The second question is: What exactly do you propose to give these people? What is the central idea that you want to lodge in their minds?

The answer to this question shapes the whole course of your future work with the story. Shall you deal with some one aspect of your broad material (for example, the textile situation in Japan as affected by synthetic processes, or Germany's effort to become self-sufficient in textiles through the development of synthetic processes)? Or shall you try to shape up the whole broad issue from the point of view, say, of American economic interests and international relations?

You can't do more than one of these things at a time. A story, like a house, to be effective and pleasing must be a structural unit. You can't start one way in a story and then, in midstream, turn about and go another way.

All of this sums up to this injunction:

Having determined at least roughly the audience for which you propose to write, you must next shape for your own guidance the central theme of your article.

It will be much the best for people who have not had extensive experience in article writing actually to put down in black and white a phrasing of their central theme. To be sure the experienced writer does not usually do this, but he does determine in his mind the theme of his article and selects his material and tone to project that theme.

How then shall we phrase the central theme of the textile article for *Harper's*? Something like this: The central theme of my story will be a description of the revolution that has taken place during the past twenty-five years in the world textile industry due to the introduction of synthetic textile materials and the effects of this revolution on world trade and world politics.

The central themes of some of the articles reproduced in this book will be worth exploring.

1. The central theme of the story, "He Pastures His Hobby-Horse in a Garden" (Page 4), is: How Ernest Elmo Calkins has pursued his garden hobby in his home in Connecticut.

Notice that the central theme of this story *might* have been quite different. It might have been: Developing a garden in uncongenial New England soil as exemplified by the experience of Ernest Elmo Calkins. Or it might have been: Garden plants for New England based on the experience of a New England gardener.

It is obvious that if Mr. Evans, the author, had chosen either of the last two central themes, he would have developed a quite different story from the one which appeared in *Better Homes & Gardens.*

2. The central theme of the article, "Mountain King" (Chapter IX), is: How Austin Blakeslee has made a phenomenal success on his Pennsylvania farm by studying the market and raising crops for which there is strong market demand.

3. The central theme of the story, "Fairies Live in This Garden" (Page 16), is: My miniature garden and how I built it.

4. The central theme of the article, "Good News" (Page 7), is: What the passage of the revised National Housing Act means to people who want to build or remodel houses, especially to people of limited means.

5. The central theme of the article, "Wall Around Hell" (Chapter IX), is: A description of the underground coal fires in the New Straitsville, Ohio, area and of the project to control the fires by means of underground barricades.

6. The central theme of the article, "Ten Minutes From Hollywood" (Page 8), is: Plans for a Cape Cod cottage which can be built for $5,000.

7. The central theme of the article, "Light Where You Need It" (Page 10), is: The proper names and uses of nine types of electric lamps.

8. The central theme of the article, "Coffee Dresses for Tea" (Chapter X), is: A number of new recipes which involve the use of coffee.

9. The central theme of the article, "Going on from 40" (Chapter XII), is: The status, physical and mental, of the woman of forty and what she can do to give significant value to the ensuing years.

10. The central theme of the article, "What the Women of America Think About War" (Chapter XII), is: To show, based on a scientifically conducted and analyzed poll, what the mass opinion of American women is on various subjects related to the general theme of war.

11. The central theme of the article, "Grover Aloysius Whalen" (Chapter XIII), is: An intimate picture of the character, personality, appearance, and activities of Mr. Whalen.

Supplies for the Expedition

With the audience determined and the central theme set down, we know where our expedition is heading. But to reach the goal we must utilize to the best of our ability the supplies of fact, data, anecdote, incident, and description that we have gathered together.

This is how it was done in a comparatively simple story, "How to Tie Your Beds to Your Lawn" (Page 12).

WRITING THE ARTICLE

The materials that Mr. Hottes had to work with, all out of his own experience as a garden specialist, were these:

- Edging operations
  - With special edging tool
  - With spade
  - With grass clippers
- Edging materials
  - Wood
  - Metal strips
  - Bricks
  - Tile
  - Concrete Curb
  - Rocks
  - Plants
    - Perennials
      - Harebell
      - Blue Fescue Grass
      - Iris
      - Pinks
      - Primroses
      - Stonecrops
      - Veronicas
      - Germander
      - Goutweed
    - Annuals
      - Sweet Alyssum
      - Ageratum
    - Hedges
      - Boxwood
      - Barberry
      - Cranberry
      - Wintercreeper

The proper selection and presentation of these data will "put across" the central idea. The design of the story, as Mr. Hottes wrote it, looked like this:

<table>
<tr><td colspan="4" align="center">Central Idea: Various ways
to put an attractive edge on the flower garden</td></tr>
<tr><td>Sub-Section:
Metal and
wood strips</td><td>Sub-Section:
Tile, bricks
and rocks</td><td>Sub-Section:
Annual and
perennial
plants</td><td>Sub-Section:
Hedges</td></tr>
</table>

The skeleton of every well-built story, however simple or however complex, looks just like this diagram.

Emphatic note: This is *not* an outline from which to write the story. The sub-sections may be presented in any *order* which seems most convenient and most effective. It is, purely and simply, an analysis of content—what to put in and what to leave out, in order that the purpose of the story (the "putting over" of the central idea) may be achieved.

Mr. Hottes' story is, merely, a thrifty elaboration of these four sub-sections, plus a paragraph of introduction, which hints at but does not phrase the central idea, plus a paragraph of conclusions, plus the drawings, which visualize and reinforce the points in the text.

"Good News" (Page 7) will offer a more complex example. The

central theme of the story is: What the passage of the revised National Housing Act means to people of limited resources who want to build or remodel houses.

The *materials* of the story are:
- Insurance premium lowered to 1/4 of 1 percent
- Twenty-five, instead of twenty year, mortgage term
- Down payment made lower
- Elimination of service charge
- FHA insurance lowered
- Details of carrying costs on $5,400 mortgage
- Details of carrying costs on mortgages up to $8,600
- Details of carrying costs on mortgages up to $16,000
- Remodeling loans
- Refinancing an existing home
- Rental-purchase plan
- Where to borrow money to build or remodel
- Analysis of significance of the act
  - Amount saved under the FHA plan
  - Easier to buy a home because of small down-payment
  - Security under the long-time amortization plan
- Owning vs. renting
- Why now is a good time to build or remodel

These are the materials that Mr. Hambidge put into his story. With these 15 sub-sections he *supported* the central idea. In this case the skeleton is considerably more complex than that of "How to Tie Your Beds to Your Lawn" but it is built on exactly the same pattern. It looks like this:

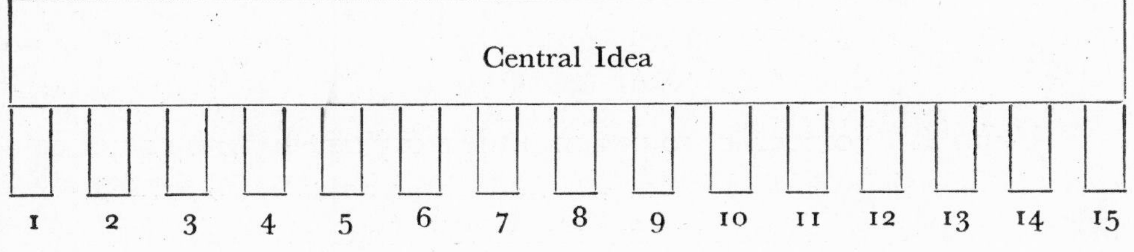

THE YOUNG AUTHOR WRESTLES WITH HIS JOB

Act I

Scene: Corner of a study. A desk, with typewriter, paper, pencils, etc. Filing case. Bookshelves. On the desk, two or three manilla folders, a magazine or two.

Time: Any time.

Characters: The Young Author
The Young Author's Muse, a dame uncertain of age, hard of visage, keen of eye, shrill of voice.

MUSE: You are doing—*what,* young man?

YOUNG AUTHOR (*with enthusiasm*): I'm writing an article. I'm hipped about it. It's got great possibilities. I think I'll send it to the *Saturday Evening Post.*

MUSE: Where did you say? Don't you know that at this very moment there are 19,736 other young authors writing articles for the *Post*? But let that pass. What's it about?

YOUNG AUTHOR: About our new viaduct. It's to open next week. It cost $300,000. It goes under seven tracks. Here, look at this picture. Six people were killed, right there, in the last five years. I've got a whale of a lot of dope. I've talked to the contractor, the city engineer, the divisional engineer—

MUSE: Yes, but—

YOUNG AUTHOR: Of the railroad. And I've got traffic counts from the state highway engineer's office. And figures on the number of grade-crossing accidents in the United States. And dope from the Bureau of Public Roads. The Governor will be here for the dedication.

MUSE: Yes, but—

YOUNG AUTHOR: I guess I've got too much stuff. I've been sitting here for an hour and I haven't got a word written.

MUSE: And for whom are you writing, young man?

YOUNG AUTHOR: Why—well—you know, for people—

MUSE: For Clem Shakely? For Emma Runkle? For Allen Parker? For people in New York? On ranches in Texas? College professors? Engineers?

YOUNG AUTHOR: Well—

MUSE: And all this stuff—what does it all boil down to?

YOUNG AUTHOR: Well—

MUSE (*still stern of visage but with the faint gleam of a smile in her eyes*): Give me a pencil.

(*Muse leans over the desk and scribbles on a piece of paper. She mutters to herself as she writes.*)

MUSE: These young punks. They have to learn, of course. They have brains—some of them. If they would only *use* their brains. All this stuff. Who really wants to know about it? Who are really interested in your viaduct, proud of it? Why, the people right here in this town, and, maybe, a lot of other people in the state. They're the ones to write it for, young man. . . . And here's a scheme of the piece—see?

(*Muse pushes the sheet of paper away from her, straightens up, lays a not-too-heavy hand on Young Author's shoulder.*)

YOUNG AUTHOR (*stuttering*): It's—it's an outline.

MUSE (*in disgust*): *Not* an outline. It's a plan.

The Route to Take

Up to this point *what* to put into the story has been the chief concern. Now it is time to look at the *how*—how actually to arrange our materials (already selected at least tentatively) in the story. Here are the possibilities:

1. The news-story arrangement. The most interesting and important material is put at the beginning, followed successively by materials of less and less importance. This might be called the shoot-the-chutes arrangement—you start at the top and slide down.

2. The chronological arrangement. The story starts with the first of the series of events that are to be recounted, and proceeds chronologically. This is the arrangement used in a history and normally in fiction and drama.

3. The logical arrangement. Because ideas and events have relationships—of cause and effect, for example, or of similarity—it is sometimes wise to arrange materials in a story on the basis of these logical relationships.

4. The flash-back arrangement. The story starts (as in the news-story arrangement) with the climactic material of the article and then goes back, in time, to present the antecedent circumstances leading up to the climax.

5. Combinations of 1, 2, 3, and 4.

To illustrate:

"Good News" (Page 7), the contents of which have been analyzed in some detail earlier in this chapter, follows closely the typical news-story arrangement. It starts with a summarization (paragraph 1) which contains the nub of the whole story. The major changes in the National Housing Act are given next (paragraphs 2, 3, 4, 5). The remainder of the article deals with the details of these changes and the ways in which they affect the man of limited means who wants to build a new house or remodel an old one.

"He Pastures His Hobby-Horse in a Garden" (Page 4) follows a "logical" arrangement. It goes like this: 1. Hobby idea is introduced; 2. Calkins, whose hobby is to be described, is identified; 3. a significant detail about Calkins—his deafness—is introduced; 4. here the story breaks away from the personal detail about Calkins, and begins the detailed account of his hobby (a logical relation to the hobby theme of the opening); 5. location of Calkins' "hobby" garden; 6. how the garden was started; 7. Calkins' work in the garden; 8. gardening as "the best of hobbies"; 9. vegetable gardening; 10. bees; 11. plan of garden; 12. details and features of garden.

This story *might* have been told chronologically. It *might* have employed the flash-back device. It would have been ruined if the news-story arrangement had been used.

"Mountain King" (Chapter IX) is a chronological story. It actually carries along two chronologies: the account of the author's visit with Blakeslee, and the account of Blakeslee's career. These two themes are handled like the first and second themes in a sonata—first one is heard and then the other and at times they go along together. The first theme starts at the bank where the author meets Blakeslee and proceeds chronologically through the events of the author's visit. The second theme (and the main one) begins at the potato-growers' banquet and goes forward through the subsequent events of Blakeslee's career.

The flash-back arrangement is illustrated by the article, "He's Skinner—and a Host of Old Friends, Too" (Chapter XIII). Given first is the picture of Otis Skinner as he approaches his eightieth birthday. Then the reader is taken back in time and given a series of glimpses of the man's career, of the achievements and successes that have built the reputation which he holds today.

A Sunday edition of the *Milwaukee Journal* ran a story which bore this head: "U. W., 100 Years Old, Celebrates Its 88th Birthday." The article, by Clifford F. Butcher, staff correspondent, appeared on January 23, preceding by a little over a week the celebration of Founders' Day by the University of Wisconsin.

We shall put ourselves in Mr. Butcher's shoes in that stage of the preparation of the article at which he had all of his material together and was ready to outline his story. The materials with which he had to work were:

History of the University—territorial "university" did not get started before Wisconsin became a state in 1848; provision for the University by the first state legislature; institution only a preparatory school at first; had 20 students first year; tuition was $20; students met in a rented brick building; one teacher; first chancellor was John H. Lathrop; by 1858 there were 7 faculty members; federal grant under the Morrill Act of 1862 marked beginning of University's growth; Civil War days; only one senior in class of 1864; no commencement exercises held; regime of President Chadbourne; expansion of the University; beginning of work in agriculture and law; women students accepted; presidents after Chadbourne; expansion of the University under Van Hise; research achievements of the University.

Growth in enrollment during 88 years.

Growth in buildings and other physical facilities during 88 years.

Facts about plans for the Founders' Day celebration—alumni clubs all over the country to meet; date, February 5; President Dykstra to address alumni in Chicago; national radio hook-up to broadcast Chicago program; University Band to play.

One-hundredth anniversary of first authorization of the University was January 19, just past; the territorial legislature passed the act in 1848.

Publication of bulletin telling story of history and services to the state of the University; bulletin an expansion of these words of Van Hise: "The boundaries of the campus are the boundaries of the state."

Outstanding services of the University today—state hygienic laboratory; Wisconsin general hospital; Wisconsin orthopedic hospital; psychiatric institute; electrical standards laboratory; distribution of legume cultures; distribution of Swiss cheese cultures; vaccines for farm animals; 4-H club work; state seed laboratory; state soils laboratory.

Those are the data with which we (substituting for Mr. Butcher) have to build a story. We figure out that the central theme should be: The University of Wisconsin birthday anniversary celebrates 88 years of growth and of service to the state. We know that the sub-sections of our material are the history of the University, what the University is today, the service of the University to the state, the plans for the Founders' Day celebration. But how shall we arrange these materials in the story—in what order shall we put them down?

Consider the possibilities. One is the following of the news-story arrangement. That means that we shall evaluate the *news* value of each item of material and arrange those items in the order of their news value, going from the more important to the less important.

And so we make this kind of an outline:

1. University to celebrate 88th birthday on February 5. (This goes at the top of the story because it is the news peg, it is timely, it is of interest to everyone who has any connection with or interest in the University.)
2. Details of the celebration. (Next in news weight, because many people will want to know the exact details—in order to attend, to listen to the radio.)

   a. Alumni club meetings.
   b. President Dykstra's address.
   c. National broadcast.
3. Why the University is really 100 years old instead of 88. (Next in value because of the unusualness of the "wrong birthday" angle.)
4. How the University has served Wisconsin. (Next in news value because of the many people this information will touch—people who have had contact with one or another of the University's services. But this information isn't new. It has all been printed time and time again in the past.)
   a. State hygienic laboratory.
   b. Wisconsin general hospital.
   c. Wisconsin orthopedic hospital.
   d, e, f, g, etc.
5. History of the University. (Next in weight because it has no current news value and does not touch the interests of the people generally as closely as does the service of the University.)
6. Status of the University today. (Last in news value because it is old stuff.)

With this outline before us we can begin to write our story. And the writing will be the filling in, the elaboration, of the outline.

But we might handle our material in chronological order. In that case our outline would look like this:

1. Founding of the University.
2. Early history.
3. Achievements of the University through the years.
4. The University today.
5. The anniversary celebration.

Of course, the weakness of this arrangement is obvious. This order takes no advantage of the strong news elements in the story. It is well to consider the possibilities of this arrangement, but there is no question that it should be discarded.

A combination of the news and chronological arrangements might, however, be desirable. We must consider that possibility. The outline, on such a basis, might look like this:

1. The anniversary.
2. Details of the anniversary celebration.
3. History of the University—chronological narrative beginning with the "first" founding of the University and following through with its story up to the present.
4. Service of the University to the state—arranged chronologically in the order in which the services described were initiated.
5. The status of the University today.

Still another possibility is the flash-back arrangement. With it, we could focus on the University today, its size, scope, services, and the *news* of the anniversary celebration; and then go back to pick up the antecedent material, the history of the University. This arrangement would not, in this case, be greatly different from the news-story arrangement, but it would not be identical.

1. The anniversary as a symbol of the University as it is today.
2. What the University means to the state today.
   a. State hygienic laboratory.
   b. Wisconsin general hospital.
   c, d, e, f, g, etc.
3. Details of the celebration.
4. Flash-back to founding of the University and its history.

We have not so far considered a "logical" arrangement of our material. We are dealing in this story largely with facts rather than with ideas. A close "logical" relationship between the parts of our material is not, therefore, so important as if we were dealing with a subject in which the connection between causes and effects had to be clearly shown. There is, however, a minor place for "logical" arrangement even in this material. We won't want to scatter material on the achievements of the University in the field of research (for example) throughout the story; we'll want to group that material into one section because of the logical (subject-matter) kinship that it has.

Which of the arrangements that have been outlined is best in this instance? Probably the news-story arrangement. With other stories, other arrangements will be more effective. But this much can be said with considerable dogmatism:

The writer should make for himself, before he starts to write, an outline. This outline should employ the order of material which best fits the particular story circumstances. The decision on this point should follow some such "thinking through" process as has been illustrated with the University of Wisconsin material.

For very short articles it may not be necessary actually to write down an outline. But if the story is at all complex, an outline is highly desirable.

THE YOUNG AUTHOR WRESTLES WITH HIS JOB

Act II

Scene: Same as Act I.

Time: The next day.

MUSE: Industry, young man, is a noble virtue.

YOUNG AUTHOR: Maybe *you* think so, but—

MUSE (*looking at the first of several sheets of paper which she has picked up from the desk*): Well, I'm not so sure—now. So this is what you've written. Listen to this, young man. "In the olden days when the trails of Indians and wild animals threaded the forests and the hills of America there were no traffic accidents." Why didn't you begin with the flood—that was a little earlier.

YOUNG AUTHOR: I thought that was pretty—

MUSE: You didn't think at all. That's just the trouble. What *are* you writing anyway—a treatise on the history of transportation?

YOUNG AUTHOR: No. But I didn't think—

MUSE: Exactly. You're writing a story for the Sunday paper to appear three days before your beautiful viaduct is dedicated. And that means— Here, give me a sheet of paper.

(*She leans over the desk and mutters as she writes.*)

MUSE: The big thing is first. This is a news story. What this viaduct means in saving lives and injuries—that's the main thing. Then back to how it started and who started it. And then . . . and then.
(She pushes the sheet of paper away from her, straightens up, lays a not-too-heavy hand on YOUNG AUTHOR's *shoulder.)*
YOUNG AUTHOR *(stuttering)*: I—I be—begin to see.
MUSE *(in disgust)*: I hope so.

Before You Write

What has been said previously in this chapter concerns chores that must be gone through with before one puts his hands to the typewriter keys. To summarize, these chores are:

1. To get a clear conception of the people (or the magazine) for whom you intend to write.
2. To phrase carefully the central theme of your article.
3. To determine the sub-sections of your material which you propose to use in elaboration or support of the central theme.
4. To determine the arrangement of your material as you propose finally to present it in the written article.

Now it will be a good idea to step back thirty paces and take a bird's-eye look at the way people read articles. First we see that there is no law which requires people to buy newspapers and magazines. They do it because they want to.

We see in the second place that there is no law which requires that people read any particular article in the newspapers or magazines which they buy. They do so because they want to.

But that phrase, "want to," isn't so simple. A magazine comes to your house. It takes time to open and look at it. And time is a valuable commodity. You have to take time for your business, for eating, for sleeping, for going to the movies, for listening to the radio, to talk to your wife, to visit with friends, to take jaunts in your car. How, then, can the magazine buy a fraction of your busy days?

It buys your time only if it offers you something that is worth the time you sell—only if it offers a good bargain. You sit down and take up the magazine. What in it can you be induced to read? What selling arguments does the magazine have to offer?

The first of these is the magazine's general reputation and character. Next is its physical appearance. As you leaf through the magazine you are "sold"—or not "sold"—by the subject matter which you see presented, and which, for one reason or another, may be the sort of thing in which you are interested; by the illustrations, which draw your eye and lead you on to sample the story; by the arrangement of illustrations, type, white space, and color—the format and layout—which makes an impression of attractiveness or the opposite; by the names of the authors which, if they are known to you, may determine you to read the articles to which they are attached; by the titles which not only give you an idea of the content of the article, but, if they are attractively phrased, predispose you to read further; by the beginnings of the articles, which, if they are attractive, graphic, impressive, induce you to read on.

Every article, then, is engaged in a grim competition for the reader's time with every other article in the magazine, with other magazines, newspapers, and books, and with a thousand other consumers of people's time. This statement indicates the importance of the showmanship expressed through title, beginning, and style of writing.

Effective Writing

That writing is good writing, effective writing, which is best adapted to convey the writer's message (ideas, facts, descriptions, opinions) to the readers whom he has envisaged.

The qualities of effective writing are clarity, color, variety, tempo, tone, and concreteness.

The instruments which the writer uses to construct his message are the instruments of language—words and word combinations.

Words, which are man-made, are very like their creator. They, like he, have a brain and a heart. Their existence, like his, is a fusion of ideation and emotion. The characters of words are as varied as the characters of men. In the word-kingdom there are aristocrats and drudges, pedants and rich roisterers. There are words which can halt the reader imperiously as a traffic light, words that can invigorate, words that can soothe and, sad to say, words that are as soporific as a sleeping draught.

What of all this? Simply that one can not use tools very well unless he understands them, unless he senses the fine distinctions between them and, perhaps, unless he loves them.

Example: You want to say that an old woman, fat, rather shabbily dressed, wearing a ludicrous hat, comes through the door into the store. You can say that she walked in, teetered in, barged in, rolled in, marched in, waddled in, pranced in. Any one of these words will get her into the store—but with a difference. They all denote locomotion. They differ in the exact type of locomotion which they represent, but their great difference lies not so much in what they say as in what they make us feel.

The very foundation of all writing is a keen, sensitive discrimination between the meanings and, even more important in popular writing, the emotional overtones of words.

But words do not, any more than men, live isolated lives. They do their work and play in association with other words. The writer has not only to use words individually but to associate them into patterns or constellations. We can say of our fat woman that she rolls through the door. Or we can say that she rolls through the door like a wave-weary freighter. Here we have associated three or four other words with "rolls" to make an idea and emotion pattern so precise and detailed that it can be clearly seen and deeply felt.

By such discriminating use of words are clarity and color obtained.

Variety is manifested too in the selection of words and word patterns but beyond that is the contribution of sentence structure. Consider the resources of sentence structure that are available to the writer: the simple sentence, the compound sentence, the complex sentence, the imperative, sentence fragments, sentence inversions, sentences introduced with different kinds of phrases and clauses, sentences broken up with interjected material between dashes and parentheses, questions, exclamatory constructions.

For example, we want now to say that our old, fat woman; a slim, Adonis of a youth; and a freckle-faced boy all came through the door. We can say: "A fat old woman walked through the door. A slim young man walked through the door. A freckle-faced boy walked through the door." And that, we'll agree, is monotonous. Our resources are not limited, however, to a series of identical, simple declarative sentences. We can say, "A fat old woman rolled narrowly through the door. After her a moment later strode, Adonis-like, a slim young man. To make it three, a boy whose face was a freckled mask sneaked over the threshold."

Every piece of writing has a tempo or pace. It moves swiftly or calmly or excitedly or thoughtfully. Pace is a product of the choice of words and word patterns, of sentence structures, and of the presence or absence of elaboration. If a sense of speed or excitement is what one wants, he drives straight at his goal without paying much attention to minor issues. He used words which connote speed. He uses short sentences which snap and sparkle. He leaves out details of description and minor incident. A leisurely tempo has room for longer and more varied sentences, for more adjectives and adverbs, for figures of speech. It can loiter along the wayside and take account of the way things look, of incidental happenings, of trivia.

The thing to be sure of in this connection is that the tempo shall be appropriate to the subject matter. The pace of an exciting news account should be swift. What the reader wants here is to get the facts, to get the *news* just as quickly as possible. Swift too, should be the pace, usually, of a process story. The personality story, on the other hand, will usually proceed at a more leisurely gait.

It should not be inferred from what has been said that a story necessarily maintains the same tempo throughout. Even within a story, the tempo should be sensitively adjusted to the nature of the material that is being presented.

The tone of a story is its emotional key. The tone may be solemn or facetious or ironical or practical. As with tempo, the tone must be appropriate to the subject matter.

One other quality of effective writing needs to be noted—and then underlined. Ordinarily the more concrete, the more specific, a piece of writing is, the more effective it will be. This is simply because of the way the mind works. All that we know gets into our heads through the channels of the senses as itemized bits of experience. With the experience that the mind has stored in memory, it can make combinations, syntheses, and generalizations. But to do so is hard work. We apprehend most words by a process of visualization. We learned the word *dog* when we were a year old by having someone point to something and say: "Dog. Dog. See the dog." We did not learn it by being told that a dog is a carnivorous mammal (*Canis familiaris*) of the family *Canidae*, kept in domesticated state by man since prehistoric time.

In short we read with our eyes—and in a deeper sense than that our eyes see the printed marks on the paper. If the words employed are easy to visualize, they are by and large easy to read. No one was ever able to point to something and say: "Freedom. Freedom. See the freedom." We can't visualize it, and it is by that token a harder word than dog. It follows that a piece of writing which is preponderantly comprised of such words as *freedom* will be difficult to read and that a piece of writing comprised preponderantly of such words as *dog* will be easy to read.

Please do not jump to the conclusion that you are being advised not to use the word *freedom* and its ilk. You are being advised of two things: 1. If you do write in general terms, do so with malice prepense, in full recognition that your audience is intellectually equipped to follow you. 2. Usually a generalization will be more effective if it is translated into visual terms, made specific and graphic. You may conceivably wish to write: "Freedom is a priceless heritage." But ninety-nine times out of a hundred it will be better to say: "A ragged, hungry pauper not even for a million dollars would surrender his right to feel the sun, to walk under the trees, to say what comes into his mind to say."

There are many devices by which one can make the reader see. The choice of words has already been mentioned. There are figures of speech. Particularly the simile and metaphor. You illuminate, visualize, the word *freedom* by saying that freedom is like the air, boundless and uncontrolled. Or that mercy "droppeth as the gentle rain."

A specific instance or anecdote can be used to visualize an idea. A few words of description bring a scene or person before the reader's eye. Conversation gives a sense of actuality. Exact dimensions, weights, ages, are more graphic than approximations.

The characteristics of effective writing constitute a sort of score card, with which one can evaluate his own writing or the writing of others. That score card has on it these points: clarity, color, variety, tempo, tone, and concreteness. With this score card in mind we are ready to look at specific examples of article writing and to see the ways and means by which they obtain effectiveness.

Look back at the article, "Explanation for Albert" (Chapter IX). Test it out with our score card. But first note that it is reprinted from *Stage*, which is subscribed for by a few thousand people with leisure to be interested in the stage and its doings and with money enough to gratify this interest.

Clarity: The story's purpose is not primarily to define. Rather it is to convey an emotional situation. While the words are simple, they are chosen for connotative power rather than for simple definition. Notice, for instance, the overtones in the three-word pattern "very unsuccessful indeed," in the second sentence. Or the flip turn that is given to the same sentence by the colloquialism "right off."

Clarity is not the chief virtue of this story, because clarity isn't its chief purpose.

Color: The colors are subdued, but they are far from gray. This isn't tragedy that requires deep reds and black nor a story of young love that should be painted in springtime greens and yellows. This is a whimsical and ironic reminiscence, pastel tinted.

Variety: Obtained by a very wide range of sentence structure, by wit, by phantasy, by colloquialisms, by burlesque.

Tempo: The story has all of the time in the world. Note how the tempo is set in the first sentence with its loose, strolling series of clauses.

Tone: One of witty, ironic retrospection.

Concreteness: Albert himself is created to dramatize an abstraction. The audience is shown to the reader in its tails and ermine. The argument of the piece is put into the form of a dialogue between the author and Albert.

Look next, for purposes of violent contrast, at "What's Ahead in Roadbuilding" (Chapter X). This story is for engineers, particularly those engineers who may be engaged in work related in one way or another with highway construction.

Clarity: The whole purpose of this story is to convey information as clearly, concisely, and accurately as possible. No overtones are wanted—just the hard and fast, pre-shrunk meaning of the words.

Color: Almost colorless. Color here would get between the reader and the facts. And the facts—not emotion—are paramount.

Variety: Not much variety here. For example, the four sentences in the first paragraph are very similar in length. They contain, respectively, 26, 21, 18, and 19 words. While they are not identical in structure, they do not vary greatly.

Tempo: Rapid. The facts pound along on each other's heels. There is no time to dally by the wayside. This is for busy men. They come for facts. They want to get them and be gone.

Tone: One of single-minded practicality.

Concreteness: The story gets this quality in high measure from the figures. There is, however, very little visualization.

Another way to get at the secrets of effective writing is to study how articles have been edited before they get into a magazine. The accompanying illustration shows a page of edited copy that was used in *Better Homes & Gardens.* This page is from an original manuscript edited by a member of the *Better Homes & Gardens* staff. It was recopied, of course, before it went to the printer.

It is interesting to compare for clarity the two short experience stories, "Grassland Farming Gaining" and "Count Your Peaches," on Pages 167 and 168. The writing problems in the two are almost identical, but note how much clearer the second is than the first. The reader might well try his hand at editing "Grassland Farming Gaining." And wouldn't you want to do something about the title?

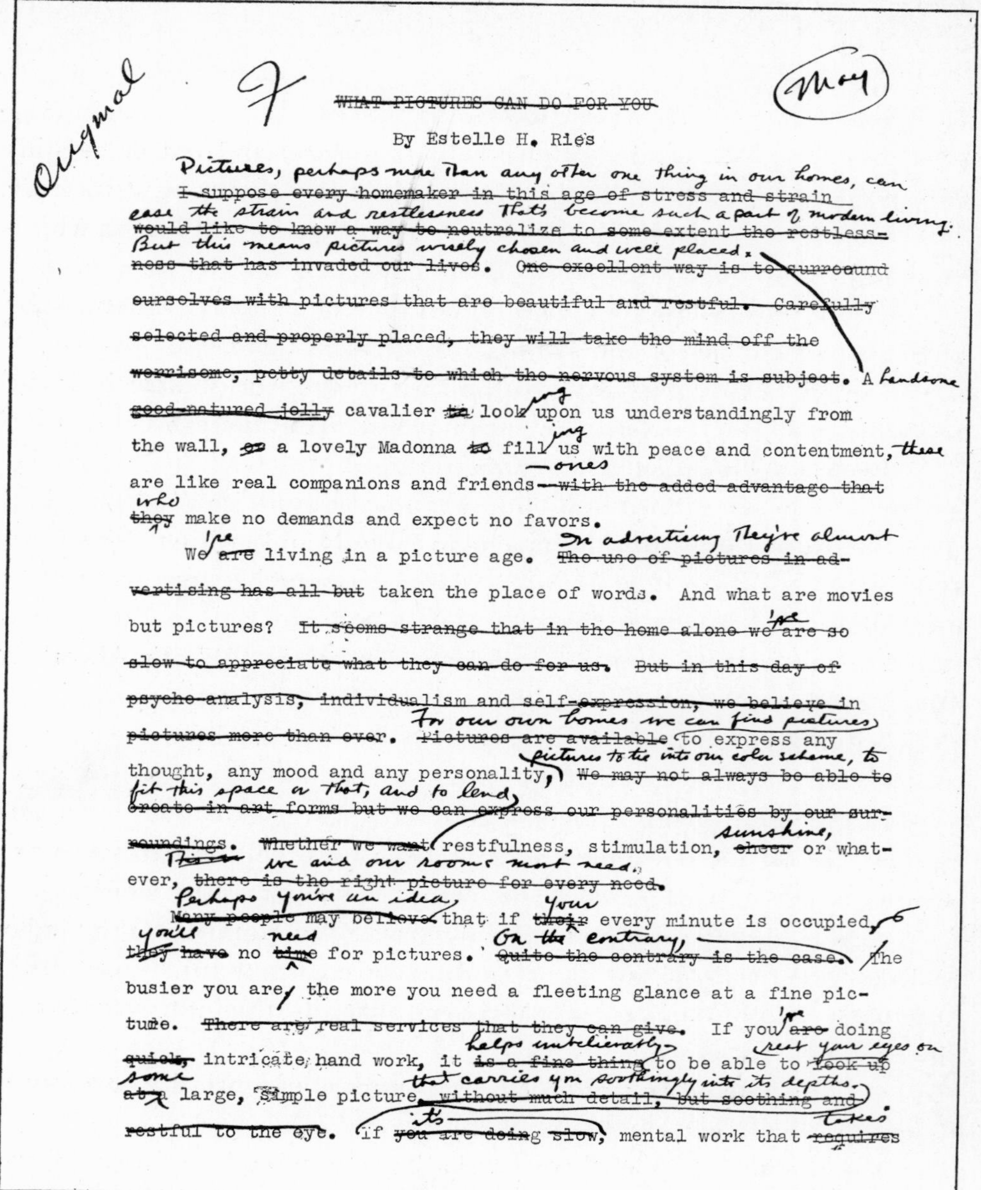

Original 7 ~~WHAT PICTURES CAN DO FOR YOU~~ May

By Estelle H. Ries

Pictures, perhaps more than any other one thing in our homes, can ~~I suppose every homemaker in this age of stress and strain~~ ease the strain and restlessness that's become such a part of modern living. ~~would like to know a way to neutralize to some extent the restless-~~ But this means pictures wisely chosen and well placed. ~~ness that has invaded our lives. One excellent way is to surround ourselves with pictures that are beautiful and restful. Carefully selected and properly placed, they will take the mind off the worrisome, petty details to which the nervous system is subject.~~ A handsome ~~good-natured jolly~~ cavalier ~~to~~ looking upon us understandingly from the wall, ~~or~~ a lovely Madonna ~~to~~ filling us with peace and contentment, these ones are like real companions and friends ~~--with the added advantage that they~~ who make no demands and expect no favors.

We're ~~are~~ living in a picture age. In advertising they're almost ~~The use of pictures in advertising has all but~~ taken the place of words. And what are movies but pictures? ~~It seems strange that in the home alone we're so slow to appreciate what they can do for us. But in this day of psycho-analysis, individualism and self-expression, we believe in pictures more than ever. Pictures are available~~ For our own homes we can find pictures to express any thought, any mood and any personality, pictures to tie into our color scheme, to fit this space or that, and to lend ~~We may not always be able to create in art forms but we can express our personalities by our surroundings. Whether we want~~ restfulness, stimulation, sunshine, ~~cheer~~ or whatever, ~~There~~ we and our rooms most need. ~~there is the right picture for every need.~~

Perhaps you've an idea ~~Many people may believe~~ that if ~~their~~ your every minute is occupied, you'll ~~they have~~ no need ~~time~~ for pictures. On the contrary, ~~Quite the contrary is the case.~~ the busier you are, the more you need a fleeting glance at a fine picture. ~~There are real services that they can give.~~ If you're ~~are~~ doing ~~quick,~~ intricate hand work, it helps unbelievably ~~is a fine thing~~ to be able to rest your eyes on ~~look up at a~~ some large, simple picture that carries you soothingly into its depths. ~~without much detail, but soothing and restful to the eye.~~ If it's ~~you are doing slow,~~ mental work that takes ~~requires~~

Page of original manuscript as edited for publication in *Better Homes & Gardens*. Frequently a manuscript is so edited, then copied, and again edited and copied before it is ready to go to the composing room to be put into type.

Note these things about the editing: The far-away generalization of the first sentence is thrown out, and the word "pictures" is put at once under the reader's eye. The generalization in the second sentence is eliminated, but the specific instances in the third sentence are retained.

Also in the third sentence, the threadbare phrase, "with the added advantage that" is deleted. Instead of "we are" at the beginning of the second paragraph, the contraction "we're" is used. The philosophizing in the middle of the second paragraph is taken out. In the first sentence of the third paragraph, the "you" of direct address is substituted for the third-person pronoun. In the original the page contained 309 words. As edited it has 201.

Getting the Story Started

Not many will take exception to the statement that the beginning is the most important part of the article. It is the front yard. As people pass, they see it first and from it form an idea of the whole establishment.

The first requirement of the beginning is that it shall be interesting—that it shall catch the eye, that it shall "sell" the article to the reader.

The second function of the beginning is to give the reader a clue to the central theme of the story. Obviously we don't want always to begin articles by saying, "My purpose in writing this article is to do so-and-so"—although occasionally a story does begin this way.

But we do need to give the reader a broad hint as to the country he will explore with us if he reads on into the story.

The third thing that the beginning should do is to set the tempo and the tone of the article. If it is to be a serious article then the beginning should advise the reader of that fact and put him in the proper frame of mind to read on. If the article is a practical, straightforward one, the beginning, too, should have those characteristics.

Beginnings can be roughly classified into four sorts:

1. The summary beginning. Such a beginning gives a bird's-eye view of the salient facts of the story.

2. The incident beginning. This beginning employs an incident, an anecdote or a bit of conversation, which foreshadows the theme.

3. The climactic beginning. This beginning employs the incident or facts which are the high point of the article. It may be similar to the summary beginning, but it differs in that it does not summarize the story's material.

4. The descriptive beginning. This beginning starts the story with a description of a person, place, or thing.

More profitable than classification will be a close scrutiny of the beginnings of stories which editors have bought and paid for.

The first three paragraphs of "He Pastures His Hobby-Horse in a Garden" (Page 4) give a clear foreshadowing of the story's central theme. The second half of the first sentence, "wrote an authoritative treatise that had nothing to do with advertising," is an important clue to the tone of the story. The impression that it gives is strengthened by the second sentence in the third paragraph.

While the beginning is not an exciting one, it is anything but dull. The hero of the story is introduced at once so that we know that we are going to read about a man. The whimsical idea of the "hobby horse" sets the reader's imagination going.

This beginning is a very dilute summary. It tells you that the story is to be about the garden hobby of Mr. Calkins, but it gives you no other details.

The beginning of "Mountain King" (Chapter IX) starts with an incident, the dinner of the 400-Bushel club. The attention and curiosity of the reader are aroused by the first sentence, "It was the biggest moment of Austin Blakeslee's career." And there is another superlative, "greatest," in the second sentence. And notice how the reader's curiosity is piqued by the paradox in the next to the last sentence in the first paragraph—a great potato grower, Blakeslee decides to raise no more potatoes.

By the time one has read the third paragraph, he has a definite conception of the theme of the story.

The beginning of the story "Maine Potatoes Put on Airs to Attract Customers" (Chapter IX) is an interesting example of a summary. The summary is there but it is stated obliquely, so that the reader feels that he must read on to make sure what it is all about.

The beginning to "Grassland Farming Gaining" (Chapter IX) is also a summary.

So too is the beginning to "Count Your Peaches" (Chapter IX).

And another summary is the beginning to "Fire 1400 Dozen Dinner Ware per Day in One Man Electric Kiln" (Chapter IX).

The beginning to "Fairies Live in This Garden" (Page 16) is largely descriptive. The first four paragraphs picturing the miniature garden whet the reader's curiosity. The fifth paragraph contains the transition into the body of the story. It says in substance, "I have given you a sample. If you would like to learn more, come along with me."

Note how the child-like fairy tone of the story is established in the first few sentences. The opening question and the answer—they might be a child talking, or an older person talking to a child.

When the problem of the beginning of the story is solved, then comes the question: What of the ending?

The ending is not, of course, of any great importance as a "selling point" for the story—as the beginning most certainly is. But the writer who wants to do a workman-like job, who wants his piece to have structural unity, will be concerned with the way in which it ends.

Usually a brief summarizing paragraph, which gathers together the major threads of the story is desirable, particularly if the story is a long one. Such a summary may take the form of a re-statement of the high points, or it may be presented more dramatically as an incident which symbolizes the central idea of the story, or a bit of conversation which performs the function of a summary.

Notice in the following examples how the central theme of the story is neatly summed up in the final paragraph or so:

"Ten Minutes From Hollywood" (Page 8) ends: "All in all, the little Cape Cod cottage has settled down in the shadows of the mountains as if it had been there always. Could our austere New England forebears see it today, gleaming white behind its picket fence and rose bushes on a quiet, sunny street, they'd choke up with pride and admit they'd been pretty smart lads to have created anything so splendid."

The last paragraph of the brief "Light Where You Need It" story (Page 10) is: "So here they are—nine types of lamps, suitably scaled, and developed to do duty with any sort of furniture grouping."

The one sentence—"Result—the perfect room for the boy"—is the summary ending of the story, "Tommy's Room Is Washable" (Page 23).

The ending of "Fairies Live in This Garden" (Page 16) is practically an itemization of the sub-section topics of the article: "But a Fairy Garden! It isn't necessary to have a large space for it. It's within the reach of everyone's space and purse. Here is a place where the children may first experience the wonderment and thrill of a garden. The plants are small and easily cared for in a Fairy Garden so that it may be truly the child's very own. If a doubting adult would but supply the space and plants, any little child could bring a Fairyland of his own into his own backyard!"

The ending of the article "He Pastures His Hobby-Horse in a Garden" (Page 4) illustrates a device that can, on occasion, be used very effectively. It is the refrain. A phrase, an incident, a bit of description or a character, used early in the story, possibly referred to in the title, can be repeated or alluded to in the ending. The effect is one of rounding-out, of unity, of having got back to the place where we started or to the goal that we set out to reach. This is the way Mr. Evans ends his article: "A little later I took my leave of Ernest Elmo Calkins. As I went out the door I seemed to feel something brush by me; and there, believe it or not, was the hobby-horse, streaking down the hall—apparently in the general direction of Connecticut. But doubtless he'll come back to keep Mr. Calkins company.

"In the meantime, I think I'll agree that Ernest Elmo Calkins, as master of the art of living, knows how to ride 'im."

Titles

The title is the banner that waves above your story. It will be a good title if it catches the reader's fancy, if it stirs his interest, and if it tells him what he will find in the story over which it flies.

In the title more than anywhere else full value must be squeezed out of words. The four, six, or eight words for which there is space carry a heavy weight of responsibility. For on them, in a considerable degree, depends whether or not the story will be read.

The title is a matter of major concern in the editorial offices of a magazine. The story is told of a magazine which a few years ago paid $500 for an article not because it wanted the article but because it wanted the title.

A good title has action in it. Some editors insist that the title must always have a verb, either actually present or very definitely implied.

A good title should have eye-value. It should paint a picture for the reader.

A good title should use colorful words, words with strong emotional connotations, words which have not become drab and dull and commonplace through over-use. A cliché is as unenterprising as a dead fish.

One of the best titles reproduced in this book is "Fairies Live in This Garden." Why is this a good title? It has a powerful, active verb and that verb gives the title life and movement. The pronoun "this" plays an important part. It points like a finger. "Look," it says, "at *this* garden." The word "garden" relates the story to the general theme of the magazine and defines what this particular article is about. But there is one more word which is more significant than any of the others—"fairies." This word starts at once a stream of associations through the reader's mind—childhood memories, imponderable longings. It brings visions of peace and quaintness and simplicity. Suppose the story had been entitled "A Miniature Garden." As a matter of fact that title *defines* the story more exactly than the other. But, in comparison, how dull and lifeless it is.

Consider these questions: Would "elves" be better than "fairies"?

Would "A Garden for Fairies," be better or worse?

Would "Fairies Dance in This Garden" be better or worse?

How do you like "A Little Garden for Little Folks"?

In the above questions is a clue to the tracking down of good titles. Unless a title, which passes your critical judgment, comes easily to mind, try jotting down as many possibilities as you can think of. Make a list of twenty or thirty titles. Approach the idea from different angles. Try different words. Usually such a list will suggest new combinations and out of all the possibilities you have jotted down, the right one will spring into your mind.

THE YOUNG AUTHOR WRESTLES WITH HIS JOB

Act III

Scene: Same as Act II.

Time: A day later.

MUSE (*reading the last page of the manuscript*): Aren't you the proud young author!

YOUNG AUTHOR: No, of course not, but I do believe they'll use it.

MUSE: We'll hope for the best. By the way, do you believe in insurance?

YOUNG AUTHOR: Why—yes.

MUSE: Wouldn't it be a good idea to take out insurance on your story?

YOUNG AUTHOR: I didn't know you could get insurance on—

MUSE: There's much you don't know. Here, give me a pencil.

(*She leans over the desk and mutters as she works.*)

MUSE: Only half done when it's written. Revise, revise. This will pep up the title. Switch these paragraphs. Six words gone and all the better for it.

(*She straightens up, hands the pencil back to the young author and lays a not-too-heavy hand on his shoulder.*)

YOUNG AUTHOR: I—I believe that does improve it.

MUSE: And how!

[CURTAIN]

Practice Suggestions

1. Read ten articles and phrase for each of them what you think are their central themes.

2. Rewrite each of these ten central themes as you think it should be phrased if the article were to be submitted to a different magazine than that in which it was published. (If it appeared in *Harper's* re-state it for *Esquire*; if in *Liberty*, re-state it for a Sunday newspaper.)

3. Analyze the chief sub-sections of each of these ten articles.

4. Brief a number of articles to show the outline the writer followed in putting down his story. Indicate the type of arrangement employed in each case.

5. Write as many articles as the exigencies of eating, sleeping and taking care of your other duties permit.

6. Read a number of articles. Describe the tempo and the tone of each.

7. Copy out a thousand words or so of an article in triple-spaced type-script. Go over this material with minute care, looking at every word, every phrase, every figure of speech. In keeping with the tempo and tone of the article, edit it to give it more color, more effective and interesting words, more pleasing word patterns, more pungent figures of speech. Repeat this exercise until the habit of critically scanning copy becomes so ingrained that you can apply it with thorough impersonality to your own stuff.

8. Clip and paste up ten article beginnings. Rate them in order from one to ten on the basis of their effectiveness, and explain the reasons for your ratings.

9. Do the same (as 8) with titles.

REFERENCES

BOOKS

It's the Way It's Written, by Henry Justin Smith. Sterling North, Chicago.

How Writers Write, edited by Nettie S. Tillett. Thomas Y. Crowell Company, New York, 1937.

What a Word! by A. P. Herbert. Doubleday, Doran and Company, New York, 1936.

Something about Words, by Ernest Weekley. E. P. Dutton and Company, New York, 1936.

See also *Magazine Article Writing* (Brennecke and Clark), *Modern Feature Writing* (Harrington and Watson), *Magazine Articles* (Crawford), *Writing Journalistic Features* (Reed), *Writing for Profit* (Wilhelm), *Technical Journalism* (Beckman, O'Brien, and Converse), *The Business Paper Editor at Work* (Woolf).

PERIODICALS

"Your Story Must Interest," by Arthur H. Little, *Quill,* 20:4, Page 11, April, 1932.

"Watch Your Style," by Arthur H. Little, *Quill,* 20:5, Page 8, May, 1932.

PART THREE

Aids to the Writer

It does not appear that the earlist printers had any method of correcting errors before the form was on the press The learned The learned correctors of the first two centuries of printing were not proofreaders in our sense they were rather what we should term office editors. Their labors were chiefly to see that the proof corresponded to the copy, but that the printed page was correct in its latinity that the words were there, and that the sense was right. They cared but little about orthography, bad letters or purely printers errors, and when the text seemed to them wrong they consulted fresh authorities or altered it on their own responsibility. Good proofs in the modern sense, were impossible until professional readers were employed men who had first a printer's education, and then spent many years in the correction of proof. The orthography of English, which for the past century has under gone little change, was very fluctuating until after the publication of Johnson's Dictionary, and capitals, which have been used with considerable regularity for the past 80 years, were previously used on the miss or hit plan. The approach to regularity, so far as we have may be attributed to the growth of a class of professional proof readers, and it is to them that we owe the correctness of modern printing. More erors have been found in the Bible than in any other one work. For many generations it was frequently the case that Bibles were brought out stealthily, from fear of governmental interference. They were frequently printed from imperfect texts, and were often modified to meet the views of those who publised them. The story is related that a certain woman in Germany, who was the wife of a Printer, and had become disgusted with the continual assertions of the superiority of man over woman which she had heard, hurried into the composing room while her husband was at supper and altered a sentence in the Bible, which he was printing, so that it read Narr instead of Herr, thus making the verse read "And he shall be thy fool" instead of "and he shall be thy lord." The word not was omitted by Barker, the king's printer in England in 1632, in printing the seventh commandment.

- ⊙ Period.
- , Comma.
- - Hyphen.
- : Colon.
- ; Semicolon.
- Apostrophe.
- Quotations.
- □ Em quadrat.
- One-em dash.
- Two-em parallel dash.
- Push down space.
- Close up.
- ✓ Less space.
- ^ Caret—left out, insert.
- Turn to proper position.
- \# Insert space.
- Dele—take out.
- Broken letter.
- ¶ Paragraph.
- No ¶ No paragraph.
- Move to left or to right.
- Move up or move down.
- tr. Transpose.
- ----- or stet. Let it stand.
- w. f. Wrong font.
- or eq. # Equalize spacing.
- ≡ or caps Capitals.
- = or s. c. Small capitals.
- l. c. Lower-case.
- Superior or inferior.
- —— or ital. Italic.
- rom. Roman.
- [/] Brackets.
- (/) Parentheses.

XVIII

Printed Sources of Information

Two free-lance writers, Jones and Smith, attend an evening lecture by an industrial leader. Among his remarks the speaker presents new data concerning the relationships of capital and labor, and both Jones and Smith, working quite independently, get the idea that here is the germ for an article that ought to interest a national business magazine.

After the lecture each writer procures from the speaker's secretary a copy of the lecture, then goes home and turns out on his typewriter a plan for a brief article. Each finds that, although the main body of his article will come from the talk, he must supplement his information with other data.

Up to this point their procedures have been exactly alike. Now they differ.

Jones realizes that he can go no further until he gets from standard source books the information he needs. That means waiting until the next day. Jones goes to bed, planning a visit to the library the first thing in the morning.

Smith, however, remains at his desk. From the bookshelf over it he takes down the latest *World Almanac* and finds most of the additional facts he needs. From a drawer he pulls a late copy of the *Monthly Labor Review*, a Department of Labor publication that he receives regularly, and gets other necessary data. Then he turns to his typewriter, and in two hours he has finished a rough draft of his article.

Next morning he gets up early, polishes his script with a pencil, and rapidly types a final copy. About the time Jones is setting out for the library, Smith drops into the corner mailbox a big envelope marked AIRMAIL.

Smith gets a check. Jones gets his manuscript back. Is Smith merely lucky, and Jones luck's victim?

Not at all. Smith is probably the more experienced free lance of the two, but no better writer than Jones. His experience shows itself in his having had available a few standard reference materials that he has found useful in writing previous articles. Over a period of years he has built up a small reference library of his own; he adds certain periodicals to it from time to time, and new volumes of annual reference books. And he discovers that the time he saves while Jones is going to the library for the same information more than makes up to him, in increased production and steadier income, the cost of maintaining it.

Some day Jones will meet Smith, and when they compare notes Jones will find out why Smith's article beat his to the goal. Then he will commence building his own reference library. What will he put into it?

Let us grant at once that he will start with a good dictionary, so that he can know that *weird* is right and *wierd* wrong and the date of George Washington's death. It need not be an unabridged. The Pocket Oxford, the Winston Simplified, the Webster's Collegiate, and other desk dictionaries are satisfactory.

He has other writing aids. Among the common ones are Roget's *Thesaurus,* Fowler's *Modern English Usage,* Woolley's *New Handbook of Composition,* Bartlett's *Familiar Quotations,* one of several books on synonyms, Weseen's *Words Confused and Misused.*

Then he starts on books for factual reference. The *World Almanac* is a good first; or the *National Almanac and Yearbook,* or the *New International Yearbook.* Useful largely for current or recent information, a book like this also provides, Jones finds, a surprising body of background material. The *World Almanac,* for example, presents a list of recent labor disputes, population data, postal information, a description of the White House, instructions for the display of the American flag, and many thousands of other facts.

Jones will want to add to his list, if he hopes to save more trips to the library, a book on mythology—Brewer's *Dictionary of Phrase and Fable* is a good one; a Bible; a good atlas; perhaps *Who's Who in America* and other more specialized biographical books; perhaps an encyclopedia such as the *Britannica,* the *Americana, Nelson's,* or an-

---

If Jones is a strictly up-to-date free lance, he has one or two books on a highly specialized subject: Photography. Much free-lance article writing today involves photographic illustration, and competition for the good picture is keen enough that the writer who uses his own camera—which means most writers—must equip himself to do first-rate work. From a professional photographer or a camera supply house he can learn what books and other literature will suit his particular needs.

---

other; perhaps, if his checks are coming nicely, the *Dictionary of American Biography* and other more expensive reference-luxuries.

If he has all of these, Jones will soon be rivalling the public library. If he has only a few of them, carefully selected, he will have ready at hand sources of standard and often-used information that will save him many hours of time. But before he gets them all he will find it necessary to add periodical literature.

His favorite daily newspaper, preferably a city newspaper with good wire and cable coverage, is a "must." He will find such a paper as the *New York Times,* seven days a week or Sunday only, of wide benefit. He may add a news magazine such as *News-Week* or *Time,* several publications in the field for which he prefers to write, and at least one weekly or monthly magazine devoted to critical discussion of current affairs. Among these are not only the "quality group"—*Atlantic Monthly, Forum, Harper's, American Mercury,* and *Scribner's*—but also magazines such as the *Nation* and *New Republic* and others such as *Current History* and *Foreign Affairs* (a quarterly).

By this time his study is crammed to the doors. Not only are his bookshelves groaning. His desk drawers and the top of it are littered with magazines and clippings, and he is finding it increasingly difficult to locate what he wants when he wants it. And so he goes to an office-furniture dealer and procures a filing-cabinet for 9″ x 12″ manilla folders—a second-hand cabinet, with two or three drawers, will do—and to the stationer for a supply of the folders themselves.

The cabinet he divides into two sections: One for filing reference material in properly labeled and alphabetized folders, one for article ideas. In the idea section he has a folder for each "hunch" that has come to him. Suppose a news story about the increased number of visitors at the local art institute has suggested to him a possible magazine article for which he sets down a number of tentative titles—"Selling Art to the Layman," "Art Goes Popular," "Art for Everybody." He puts the clipping into a folder which he labels "Art Article" and adds a hasty memorandum on the nature of the article that may grow out of it (Jones learned long ago that he couldn't hope to carry all his hunches in his head). From time to time, he adds clippings, memos, and other data. Perhaps he writes to several art museums for annual reports, or for answers to germane questions. All material goes into the file.

And some day he pulls it out, finds it bulging, and gets to work on the article.

Perhaps, too, he keeps a small file for 3″ x 5″ cards, alphabetized. This is an index file to references that he may need—an article in *Fortune,* a book on a subject in which he is interested, a note of a series of newspaper features that would be too bulky to clip in their entirety for the larger file. He confines the references in the small file to those easily obtainable in his city library or elsewhere; into his personal file goes material he's not likely to find in the library, or that he'll need frequently.

References for Special Purposes

Neither Jones nor Smith, nor the two of them put together, is likely to have all the reference materials so far suggested. Each will have the selection that will best serve his special needs. And the needs of no two free-lance writers are exactly alike. The fact is that, if Jones and Smith are typical of American free lances, each will have started on the road that distinguishes him from all other free lances long before he completes his list of general reference material. He will have commenced to specialize.

For most men and women making their living, or a part of it, by writing articles for the magazines and features for the newspapers have found that nothing is more productive of results than the establishment of a specialty. Not only does the possession of a more or less expert knowledge of a given field aid a writer in the production of articles; it almost always yields returns in special assignments from editors who know of his special capacity. *Collier's* asks Grantland Rice, a sports writer, to manage the annual All-America selection and write the article about it. *Scribner's* gets Thomas Craven, the author of many popular critical works on art, to do a series of articles on his subject and thereby satisfy the magazine's need for this kind of article. Magazines in the Northwest, desiring outdoor articles about their own area, ask Robert Page Lincoln, an expert in the field, to do them.

Young Jones, the beginning free lance, learns early that specializing is desirable. Perhaps his particular field is one of long-standing interest; perhaps he falls into it by accident. Let us say that he has sent an article on hybrid seed-corn experiments, a subject of which he learned something during his agricultural college years, to a farm magazine. He gets back from the magazine not only an acceptance but also a letter suggesting that he become the magazine correspondent in his territory. He is glad to take the assignment, for he can see small but regular checks coming his way if he does so. And, as he makes the rounds to collect material for the farm magazine, he shortly finds himself picking up more stories than his regular market can use. Why not sell them to other publications in the agricultural field? He decides to equip himself as a minor expert.

One's ambition does not need to be satisfied with "minor" expertness. For those who have a scholarly, rather than an "amateur" interest and ability in a field of specialization, there is the possibility of becoming a leading interpreter of that field through the writing of articles and books. Paul de Kruif was a bacteriologist before he became an author, and his success is perhaps as much due to his scientific training as to his skill as a reporter and writer. J. S. B. Haldane is a great English biologist, and he is also one of the most effective interpreters of his science to intelligent laymen. Stuart Chase has made economics his specialty. Carleton Beals is an authority on Mexican and Central American affairs. The list of outstanding interpreters is not very large. There is always room for the man or woman with thorough training, a scholarly bent of mind, and skill as a writer to make for himself a place of eminence in this kind of work.

His first step is to procure a number of basic books on various fields of agriculture. The dean of his state agricultural college will be glad to give him advice on these and on other materials he will need. Next, he seeks one or more books on agricultural and technical journalism.

Now he lays in general agricultural reference books: the *Yearbook of the United States Department of Agriculture*; the *Drovers' Journal Yearbook*; *RUS* (Rural Who's Who); the *Census of Agriculture for 1935*; and other similar publications. These he may supplement with the *Abstract of the Fifteenth Census, Agricultural Statistics,* the *Yearbook of the International Institute of Agriculture,* and so on.

He wants agricultural publications. He sends $1 to the Superintendent of Documents in Washington, D. C., for a year's subscription to the *Monthly Catalog of United States Public Documents,* in which are listed all the publications of every government department. Here he has an up-to-date list of hundreds of pamphlets, bulletins, and other information, most of it free or available at low cost.

He has his name put on mailing lists: Those of his state's Agricultural Experiment Station, Farm Bureau, Department of Agriculture, cooperative marketing organizations. He finds publicity releases from the USDA and the AAA especially helpful. He asks agricultural manufacturers and wholesalers to send him material when available.

And he subscribes for a number of leading trade and class publications.

Has Jones found it hard to bring this kind of reference library into being? Neither hard nor expensive. Each new publication he acquires suggests others—he knows from the start of many more than he can use. And, beyond the cost of a few basic books and periodical subscriptions, he has not had to spend much money. Almost every organization, whether in agriculture or inorganic chemistry, has some kind of ax to grind, and that means that it is glad to get its literature into the hands of anybody who asks for it.

Now let us suppose that the free-lance writer wishing to specialize is neither Jones nor Smith, but Miss Brown; and that, a graduate of a college of home economics, she wants to make clothing and textiles her field. She has started with the same broadly basic reference books and aids to writing that appear on Jones' and Smith's shelves, and her procedure as she seeks more restricted material is very similar to Jones'.

She gets from a member of her college faculty suggestions as to books on fundamentals of textiles, clothing, and design. She finds in library bibliographies and card catalogs names of allied publications she needs or should know about. She subscribes for the *Monthly Catalog of United States Public Documents,* for many publications in her field appear regularly under governmental auspices. She asks to have her name put on Extension Service and other mailing lists for material of interest to her. She perhaps subscribes for the *Textile World,* and certainly for other trade and fashion journals.

And she finds that, by writing to manufacturers', wholesalers', and retailers' associations in the textile and clothing field she can assure herself of a daily mail large enough to gain the respect if not the active dislike of the mail carrier.

What Jones, Smith, and Miss Brown are doing is precisely what thousands of free lances in every corner of the country are making daily practice. The number of fields open to specialization is untold: To list them would be to list all but the more esoteric occupations, vocations, and interests.

All of which is not to say that every magazine writer must style himself an expert. Many do not. But it is safe to say that more checks go each week to the specialists than to those who do not equip themselves for specialized work.

The Public Library

To urge free-lance writers to build their own reference libraries is by no means to suggest that they ignore the public library. The library has thousands of minor references to which every writer resorts occasionally, and an important collection of major sources that no private reference collection can supplant.

A few of the most useful among the major sources are:

Periodical and newspaper guides—Poole's Index to Periodical Literature (1802-1906); *Reader's Guide to Periodical Literature* (1900 to the present); *Magazine Subject Index* (1907 to the present); *New York Times Index* for reference to the invaluable files of this paper; *London Times Index*; and the individual indices of many magazines.

Biographical material and names—Who's Who in America; *Who's Who* (English); similar contemporary books in many other countries, states, and other geographical and political regions; similar books, often issued periodically, in many businesses and professions (*Who's Who in the Theatre, American Men of Science, Directory of Agricultural and Home Economics Leaders, Leaders in Education,* etc.); *Dictionary of American Biography, Biographical Dictionary of the United States,* etc.; *Burke's Peerage; Statesmen's Year Book;* social registers, Army register, Navy register; *Lloyd's Register of Shipping*; telephone and city directories.

Encyclopedic works—Encyclopaedia Britannica, Encyclopedia Americana, Lincoln Library of Essential Information, Nelson's Loose-Leaf Encyclopedia, etc.; *Bailey's Encyclopedia for the Farmer; Grove's Dictionary of Music and Musicians; Cruden's Concordance to the Bible; Farrow's Military Encyclopedia*; and many other specialized works.

Year books—American Year Book, Europa, Music Year Book, Year Book of Agriculture, League of Nations Armaments Year Book and other League publications, *American Labor Year Book, Aviation Year Book,* etc.

Business references—Dun's *Review,* Poor's and Moody's Railroads, Public Utilities and Industrials, etc.

Learned and specialized journals—Journal of the American Medical Association, Journal of Applied Sociology, Public Opinion Quarterly, American Political Science Review, Annals of the American Academy of Political and Social Science, Journal of Forestry, etc.

Such a list as this is hardly more than a poor beginning. It suggests rather than describes the rich resources that even a modest public library's reference room holds for the free lance who cares to prospect in it. But since the mere listing will do nothing for a writer—he must do his own exploring and make his own discoveries—and since a complete bibliography of major references alone would doubtless fill all the pages of this book, there is no need to carry it further.

Directly allied to a discussion of the riches Jones, Smith, and Miss Brown will find in these printed sources of information, however, is the subject of the technique of making use of them. How, in other words, should they go about taking notes?

Notes on copy paper, notebook leaves, the backs of envelopes, and last month's grocery bill are to be shunned. Such notes are often waste motion. They are easy to lose and sometimes, because they become dog-eared and smudged, hard to use. At best, unless they are to be put into manuscript form at once and thrown away, they must be transcribed.

The experienced free lance usually finds that 3″ x 5″ cards of light cardboard are his most successful note-bases. There are a number of reasons:

1. These cards are easy to handle and to carry. They fit into a pocket or a purse. They are durable—not often do they become dog-eared. They take ink cleanly (don't take notes in pencil, for pencil notes smear and become illegible if they are jogged very long in a pocket).

2. They lend themselves to classification and analysis.

3. They are of "filable" size—they fit into a standard filing cabinet.

The writer who uses 3″ x 5″ cards takes a new card for each new topic, each illustrative anecdote, each additional subhead under which he is gathering information. Making his notes in as small and neat a hand as he can manage, he can cram a surprising amount of information onto one card (use of only one side is desirable, though the only objection to using both sides is a slightly greater difficulty in turning notes into manuscript).

He always observes this rule: NEVER put notes on more than one subject or subhead or anecdote onto one card. If the notes on a subject demand two or five or ten cards, all right; but when a subject has been covered and a new one is to be taken up, start on a fresh card. This rule offers several advantages. First, notes on one card or on one batch of cards clipped together can readily be placed in their proper place among many sets of notes; if two subjects are included on one card, arrangement is at once made difficult. Second, the notes on one subject may be discarded as used (if the writer has no further need of them) without risk or inconvenience of destroying unused material. Third, cards may be easily filed in a cabinet after use if the writer thinks they contain information for which he may have later need.

House Organ

A magazine or newspaper, published by an industrial concern, a trade association or an institution, for dissemination to its own employes. Its chief purposes are, usually, to serve as a channel through which news and announcements can reach the staff, and as a builder of morale in the organization. Some house organs are handsomely prepared magazines.

Clip Sheet

A printed or mimeographed publication put out by an institution, an industry or some other enterprise to send to newspapers and magazines in the hope that they will reproduce (free of charge) the material contained. This is a widely used form of publicity dissemination.

Syndicate

A syndicate is an organization for the sale, to newspapers and magazines, of editorial and pictorial matter. Syndicates buy, edit, and disseminate feature articles, serial and short fiction, editorials, pictures, cartoons, comic strips, material for various kinds of departments, such as the beauty department, fashion department, sports department. A number of the larger newspapers run syndicates which sell material prepared by their foreign correspondents, Washington correspondents, special writers, columnists, photographers, artists, and cartoonists. A list of American syndicates can be found in the *Yearbook* published each January by Editor and Publisher.

XIX

Studying the Market

FREE-LANCE writer Jones, being no longer a novice, would be insulted if anybody asked him whether he makes it a point to study his markets before sending his manuscripts away—indeed, before writing them. Of course he does.

"You have to know what kind of thing a magazine wants, and what its 'slant' is, and how long to write your piece for it," he says. "Any writer knows that."

Any writer who sells enough scripts to keep himself alive, he might add. For, as has appeared some scores of times in this book, the primary reason that 97 percent of all the manuscripts submitted to magazines go piping back to their owners is that their owners haven't taken the trouble thoroughly to acquaint themselves with the magazines. They have failed to come to a full realization that most magazines, in order to reach special audiences, must offer material tailored to special tastes and needs. Obviously, if they hope to get checks instead of rejection slips, they must inform themselves of these tastes and needs *before* they start to write. An automobile salesman does not attempt to sell a five-ton truck to a florist; from his study of the florist's business, of the commodity the florist has to sell and of the demands of customers, he knows that a light, fast delivery truck is the thing to offer. Most writers, the statistics of rejection indicate, would not make good automobile salesmen.

Jones is not among this group. He has learned the primary lesson. But let him be asked a second question, and—because he is still not as experienced as his friend Smith (or possibly because he has not yet had a chance to read this book)—he is likely to stumble:

"How do you go about studying a market?"

His obvious answer is a simple one: Get a copy of the magazine and read the articles in it. It is simple, and it is partly right. But will reading the articles in it tell Jones exactly who the readers are? where

---

Copies of many magazines may be found in libraries or on news stands. Trade journals are not always so easy to locate. Writers needing copies of them and unable to find them in libraries have a standard method of finding them: They go to probable subscribers. If a free lance needs to find a retail shoe dealer's magazine, he goes to retail shoe shops. He is likely to find not only the periodicals he seeks, but also to pick up stories for them.

---

they live? what the magazine's current needs are? what special demands it makes? Will it inform him as to whether the magazine pays good rates or poor ones?

To these questions and many others a mere reading of the magazine will not supply the answers. Jones will have to improve his technique considerably before he knows all the things about his market that may be helpful to him in preparing his article.

How does Jones or any other free-lance writer go about a thorough, comprehensive study of a magazine, once he has decided that it is a likely market for the feature he proposes to write? More specifically, how does he undertake a study of, say, the *Country Gentleman* when he has data on rural living standards that he thinks may make an article of interest to that magazine's readers?

Why has Jones chosen the *Country Gentleman* in the first place as a probable market for his article? Here is the reason. His data are *about* men and women living in rural districts; therefore they are *of interest to* these same men and women. His first thought is to find a publication reaching this kind of audience.

There are several breakdowns of periodicals into many classifications: That in the N. W. Ayer & Son annual *Directory of Newspapers and Periodicals,* or those in any of the many "market lists" (described later in this chapter). Here he finds the names of several publications that may be good markets for him. The *Country Gentleman* is one—a likely one, he thinks, because of its large circulation and broad scope. To make sure that he is right, he goes through the procedure outlined in succeeding pages.

His first step is not to go to the magazine itself, but to explore external sources of information. One of the first among these is the *Standard Rate and Data Service,* a compendium of information issued monthly for advertisers who buy newspaper and magazine advertising space. He finds a recent copy of the Service in the public library or local newspaper office, and he turns to farm papers in the magazine section.

On its first page he finds his first guide post. The *Country Gentleman* is listed under "general" rather than under a specific agricultural heading. Turning the page to the first table, he finds circulation figures that bear out the "general" classification. It has more than 1,600,000 "net paid" circulation. From the same table he finds that almost half of this circulation is in the north central states, the next largest group in the Atlantic coast states, the third in the south central states and the fourth in the mountain and Pacific states. And the table tells him finally that half the circulation goes to subscribers on R. F. D. routes (almost all the other farm publications, he notes, have larger R. F. D. percentages), a quarter of it to towns of more than 2,500 population, and the remainder to smaller villages.

From the detailed data in the succeeding section of the *Service* he learns that an issue of the magazine is on sale the third Tuesday of the month preceding its date; that it has less than 10 percent of its circulation in news stand sales; that it sells for 5 cents a copy or 25 cents a year; that its advertising rate is $4,800 a page. Here, too, he finds the name of the editor and other executives, the address and other information of less importance to him.

Should the *Standard Rate and Data Service* not be available to him, he can get total circulation figures, subscription price, and other less detailed information from N. W. Ayer & Son's annual *Directory of Newspapers and Periodicals.*

Now he goes to one of several "market guides"—Jones has one on

---

> Among the "market guides" are the following: The quarterly "Handy Market List" in *Author & Journalist,* a monthly writer's magazine; similar listings in the *Writer's Digest,* the *Editor,* and like magazines; the *Writer's Market,* an annual publication; the *Manuscript Market Guide,* published several times a year; *How and Where to Sell Manuscripts,* a most complete book of which several editions have been issued; and other such publications. Free lances usually find most useful the guides issued at relatively short intervals, because they are most up-to-date.

---

his own desk. In the "Handy Market List," for instance, he finds this notation:

> Country Gentleman, (Curtis) Independence Sq., Philadelphia. (M-5) Short stories up to 6500; serials; articles 3000-4000; articles for women; humorous sketches; jokes. Philip S. Rose. First-class rates. Acc.

Translated, this means that the magazine is published by the Curtis Publishing Company; that it appears monthly at 5 cents a copy; that it is in the market for the materials listed, short stories and articles at the lengths (in words) suggested; that Mr. Rose is the editor; and that it pays a "general average around 5 cents a word or better" on acceptance.

This is all external information. Now Jones is ready to follow his own advice—to go to the magazine itself.

What the Magazine Tells

First, its physical appearance. *Country Gentleman* is a large-page magazine, of the same size as the other Curtis publications, *Saturday Evening Post* and *Ladies' Home Journal.* The cover illustration, in full color, shows a pioneer farmer striding beside his covered wagon; its general tone is one of vigorous dignity. This tone is carried out in the typography, layout, and illustration of the magazine. Its layouts are modern, but neither modernistic nor freakish. Major editorial pages, without advertisements, are set in three columns; others in four. All major features and many minor ones are liberally illustrated, either with photographs or with drawings or diagrams. Color appears on many pages, both editorial and advertising; it is not blatant, but rather in soft shades and tints.

The editorial staff listed on the masthead above the table of contents is large; ten associate editors are named. This suggests not only that the magazine is carefully edited but also that a good share of its material may be supplied by the staff. The table of contents in the issue under examination, however, shows only three features signed by staff names.

What types of material does the magazine use?

Jones would expect, from the things he has already learned about the *Country Gentleman,* that there would be a heavy emphasis on subjects of agricultural interest. He is right. He would expect, however, that the topics would be of broadly rural nature rather than of the dirt-farming type, for the magazine's circulation is too broad for it to tie itself down to the techniques of farming; it must appeal to small-town residents as well as farmers. Right again. And he counts on finding material for every member of the family. Right a third time.

The lead article is a discussion of the United States merchant marine and its shortcomings. No farm angle here—but it is brought in by the author when he talks about the sons of the farm in the crew of the freighter whose voyage furnishes the backbone of the article. "Putting New Life in World Trade" is a subject of vital interest to farm communities, and the writer lays special emphasis on the relation of trade treaties to agricultural exports. Another major article discusses the migration of farm labor to California; a fourth the agrarian situation in Mexico. The fifth major article plunges directly into agricultural method: "Plant Breeding Grows Up."

The four pieces of fiction in the issue show varying characteristics. One of them is a tale of a Dutch farmer. A second is a story of a farm community that might lie anywhere in the agricultural West. The third and fourth, one of them a serial, are out-and-out adventure stories; but they concern people whom the *Country Gentleman's* readers can understand.

"The Country Gentlewoman" is the title of a "second magazine" in the center of the issue. Introduced by a full-color cover page, it covers many topics of seasonable or general interest to the rural woman. Meals and meal-planning, clothing problems, household hints, gardening, child care, home furnishing—all these and more are here.

A page in this section is devoted to "Girls' Life"—a set of short features for older girls. Another page is dedicated to "The Outdoor Boy." And two regular departments discuss livestock and dairy interests and poultry problems.

So, concludes Jones, the *Country Gentleman* seeks to be of interest not only to agricultural specialists such as poultrymen and stock raisers, but to all farm and small-town residents. It seeks not alone to inform, but also to entertain. It attempts to give, along with its discussions of specific farming problems, light on the broader aspects of American rural life.

From all of this he can come to certain conclusions as to the magazine's needs and desires. He makes up a list:

General articles of wide reader interest, with their application to rural life stressed where possible
Practical farming hints
Practical home-making hints
Special articles on new farm practices
Special short articles on subjects of interest to women—beauty hints, entertainment in the home, cooking, child care and so on
Special short articles for older rural boys and girls
Vigorous fiction, often with a rural background

Jones can make this list as long and as detailed as he thinks desirable. He will take special note, however, of the subjects on which he feels himself qualified to write. And he may make a few additional notations as a result of his analysis:

> Seasonable material in demand. "Big names" apparently not of as much importance as authority. Many regular features probably prepared by staff members or regular contributors. Considerable demand for practical, directly useful material.

While he has been analyzing subject matter and types of material, he has been making mental notes on another aspect of the problem: The treatment of articles. Setting down his findings on this aspect, he gets something like the following:

> Length of articles—majors run to about 4,000 words. Back-of-the-book features shorter—1,500. Practical farming tips, boys' and girls' material, etc., always short.
>
> General tone—informal and friendly, though not unduly breezy and never slangy nor cheap. Diction and sentence structure simple and direct. Technical jargon seems to be frowned on, even in semi-technical articles. Clarity and brevity are "musts."
>
> Special style characteristics—incidents, anecdotes, and specificity are desirable. No stereotyped form for articles. Original (not freakish) treatment desirable.
>
> Authority—material for technical pages usually comes from experts. Some shorter stuff apparently from non-experts.
>
> Illustration—photographs usually appear with articles. Diagrams used when they will save words or add to clarity.
>
> Humor—not much in major articles, though it appears in entertainment features occasionally. One page devoted to short humorous bits, probably from free lances.

One revealing portion of the magazine has not yet been examined—the advertising columns. Its advertisements tell a great many things about a magazine's readers (and, ultimately, it is to find out precisely who and what the readers are that a writer goes through this whole process).

What do the *Country Gentleman's* advertising columns reveal?

For one thing, the advertisements are by no means entirely for products of a strictly agricultural nature or use. Important among them are automobiles; in fact, perhaps the largest proportion goes to passenger cars, trucks, tractors, and such accessories as oil, tires, and piston rings. Other large percentages advertise prepared foods, health aids, up-to-date home equipment, even cigarettes. A page is devoted to classified advertising, mostly for poultry (the amount of poultry and seed advertising is much heavier in winter than in summer).

Interpreting the Data

What does all this mean to Jones about the reader to whom he hopes his article will appeal?

This reader is the "average farmer" or rural resident, or his average wife or son or daughter. He is neither provincial nor unschooled. He has many interests outside the boundaries of his own immediate life; he gives his attention not only to his own poultry yard but also to international economy as it may affect him. He has money to spend. He wants radios, mechanical refrigerators, and tailor-made cigarettes just as does the reader of the *New Yorker.* His wife is just as interested in scientific child care and a balanced menu as is her sister who went to Chicago to do social service work. In short, the farm family to whom this magazine talks is living a very modern kind of life—no life of luxury, to be sure, but one characterized by a breadth of interest, activity, and convenience that Jones had not suspected.

Here, then, is what the free lance has learned through his detailed analysis: He has a picture of the interests, the background, the life, of the reader for whom he hopes to write; and he knows the special appeals and devices that the editors of the magazine and its advertisers have found effective in reaching these readers. Without this knowledge he cannot hope to satisfy either editor or reader. With it—provided he observes all the cautions offered elsewhere in this book—he has a very fair chance of succeeding.

The analysis just outlined is a lengthy and an arduous procedure, and Jones asks himself whether he must go through it each time he starts thinking about an article. Theoretically, the answer is yes. Practically, he will frequently make his study less complete, especially when he is familiar with the magazine he has selected as a market. He may not commonly resort to a study of the *Standard Rate and Data Service.* But he will find the *Service* useful when his article-idea seems to suggest that the finished product will be of regional appeal.

Every free-lance writer soon learns that keeping up with his market is a day-by-day business. Magazine needs and demands change with the seasons, with changes in policy, with changes in staff, with the ebb and flow of material received. A magazine that publishes an article on food-preparation and meal-planning in every issue may have in its files enough such material to last for a year and a half. If this is the case, it is not likely to wish to add similar material to its inventory for some time. Often notations in the writers' magazines serve to keep free lances posted on specific overloads, and on specific shortages as well. Sometimes they can be discovered only through correspondence or the submission of manuscripts.

In any case, the free lance should never forget the necessity of watching the magazines themselves. *Scribner's* since 1936, with its photographs, slick paper, and modern type-dress and format, is not the *Scribner's* of old. The *Ladies' Home Journal* would not likely have presented a discussion of the pros and cons of feminine smoking in the days of Edward Bok; but it has had a succession of editors since Mr. Bok retired, and with each have come new policies and demands. H. L. Mencken would hardly recognize as the magazine of which he was the first editor the *American Mercury* as it appeared when Paul Palmer took the chair; a manuscript Mr. Mencken considered suitable for publication might cause Mr. Palmer to despair. For many years the title *Life* meant a humor magazine. Now it means a picture book. The *Farm Journal* has entered on a policy of emphasizing last-minute agricultural news, and has developed a production schedule which greatly reduces the time between deadline and publication.

A Magazine Information File

No free-lance writer can hope to carry in his head all the information he ought to have before attempting to write for a specific magazine, and the market lists, convenient and necessary though they are, can hardly be inclusive enough. A writer doesn't care, and can't afford, to go through an entire analysis each time he writes an article. The obvious solution is that employed successfully by some free lances: An information file.

A practical type is that shown in the illustration. It employs 5″ x 8″ filing cards of light cardboard—cards large enough to bear a considerable volume of information, but not too large for convenient filing.

The illustration shows a suggested division of space on such a card. Divisions may differ according to the special needs or desires of the writer—the fiction writer looks for somewhat different information from that of interest to the article writer; the man whose specialty is short news-features for the trade publications has needs varying from those of the science-article expert.

Uniformity in a file, however, is desirable. Once a uniform "layout" is adopted, cards may be typed as they are needed, or mimeographed (a lot of 100 should last anybody less prolific than, say, George Jean Nathan, a very long time).

Date October 1, 1938

Country Gentleman	Independence Square	Philadelphia, Pa.
Name of magazine	Street address	City and state
Philip S. Rose	Curtis Pub. Co.	Monthly, 3rd Tues.
Editor.	Publisher	Time of publication

Rates 5 cents up Payment Acceptance

Audience General rural audience, both men and women, upper middle economic level. Rural boys and girls.

Subjects treated Fiction with farm slant; adventure of general interest; politics, economics, etc., from rural angle; technical farm material; home making.

Special types of articles See above.

Departments and special sections Boys'; Girls'; humor page; livestock and dairy; poultry; women's.

Length of articles Majors up to 4,000; shorts 200 to 1,500.

Style Simple, clear, informal, non-technical. Uses much incident.

Illustrations Photographs or diagrams with most articles.

Seasonable material Yes. Heavy emphasis is throughout magazine.

Advertisements Farm and home equipment, seeds, feed, stock, foods.

Suppose Jones is using the card illustrated. He records first the date on which the record is made; then the name of the magazine, beginning with its first significant initial to make alphabetical filing easy, and its address. The name of the editor is always important; that of the publisher, ordinarily, only when the magazine is one of several issued by one firm such as Curtis, Crowell, or Fawcett. "Time of publication" includes the frequency of issue and the day of week or month—"Monthly, 20th" or "Weekly, Tuesday."

"Rates" means rates of payment—information to be found usually in a market list. Under "payment" go data as to the time at which the magazine pays for accepted material—on acceptance, on the first of the month following acceptance, on publication. Or, in a few sad cases, rarely, never, or upon litigation.

The illustrated card, filled in with information about *Country Gentleman,* indicates the general types of data the free lance may want to keep. Under "special types of articles" are listed topics which are not indigenous to the interests of the magazine's special audience: Travel, humor and so on.

On the back of the card may be recorded certain additional information: Notes on the amount of material, and the particular types, apparently furnished by regular contributors or staff members; comment on special needs; enlargement on some of the listings on the front. Since one side of 5″ x 8″ filing cards is usually ruled, it isn't difficult to record such miscellany. It may frequently be convenient to paste on the back clippings of recent market-listings from the writers' publications.

Finally—if the writer is very serious about his free-lancing, and decently optimistic—it may be wise to provide space on the back of the card in which to record sales. No particular form for this listing is suggested. Included in it should be the article's title, the date of sale, and the size of the check. And, perhaps, some short and highly personal comment, such as "At last" or "Now I can eat!"

REFERENCES

"News of the Magazine Markets" (monthly department), *Matrix Magazine.*
"Lines to the Lancers" (monthly department), *Quill.*
See also *Magazine Making* (Bakeless).
See also references to periodical discussions of individual magazines at end of Chapter IV.

Relations with the Editors

By this time free-lance writer Jones is becoming well-versed in his craft. He has built up his own small reference shelf and file. He knows how to go about selecting and studying his markets. And he has dispatched enough manuscripts to market and—whether they were purchased or rejected—has observed what happened to them acutely enough so that he knows a good deal about editors: How to deal with them, what to expect from them, what their attitude toward him is likely to be.

If Jones were asked to name a primary rule for dealing with editors, he would probably say something like this:

"Be sure that their first impression of you is right."

Now, Jones has never seen an editor face to face in his life. He lives, let us say, in South Bend, Indiana, where the only publication aside from newspapers is the *Eagles' Magazine*, a fraternal publication for which he has never tried to write. His first impression on editors, therefore, is made by way of the United States mails—by nothing more intricate than the appearance and form of his manuscripts when they reach the editorial offices.

The rules-of-thumb by which Jones and some of his brother and sister free lances follow this first injunction are obvious and simple. Kindergarten stuff, in fact. Yet thousands of would-be free lances fail to observe them; which is one of the reasons that most would-be writers never reach their goal.

How to Prepare Manuscript

Rule Number One is as old as the craft of putting symbols together with the hope that they will convey a message to somebody else. The ancients when they carved their hieroglyphs observed it: Make it clear, neat, and legible.

In modern terms, this means these things: Never send to an editor anything but a typewritten script on 8½" x 11" paper. Make it double-spaced, with adequate margins—perhaps an inch all around. Be sure that the typing, if not letter perfect, is always perfectly clear. Never leave doubt in the editor's mind as to a single letter in the script. If an error in spelling appears in the typing, do one of three things: Erase and retype; xxx out and retype; or edit carefully and clearly with ink. Pencil-editing is likely to smudge.

How "clean" should a script appear? The cleaner the better, Jones or any editor will answer. A letter-perfect script undeniably makes the best subconscious impression on the editor. Few scripts, in practice, attain perfection; and they need not do so, as long as they are entirely legible. But it is always wise to retype a page that has been badly cut up by editing or poor typing.

Jones has learned that the habit of making a carbon copy of a finished manuscript is a necessity. Occasionally manuscripts get lost; occasionally it is necessary to make changes after the master copy is in the editor's hands. The carbon copy protects against such occasions.

A good grade of white bond paper should be used for the master copy of a manuscript. Good paper makes a good-looking script, and it stands a lot of handling without getting dog-eared or crumpled.

Some other rules Jones has learned about script preparation:

ALWAYS put full name and address in the upper lefthand corner of the first page. Thus:

Manfred Q. Jones
2729 West Minnehaha Drive
South Bend, Indiana

ALWAYS number succeeding pages. Many writers put name and page number at the upper left of each page. Thus:

Jones—2

Put a title on a manuscript, and be sure that it is the kind of title that the editors of the magazine to which the script is going are accustomed to use. If an article describing the brevity of the careers of Hollywood stars were to go to *Harper's,* it might bear a title like this: "The Tenure of Movie Stardom."

In *Collier's*: "Life Is Short in Hollywood."

In *Esquire*:

"The Path of Glory
It leads but to the grave
in Hollywood—and it's
a short path, at that"

Note that a subhead is added to the *Esquire* title. Why? Because *Esquire* uses subheads on all its articles.

Many writers add another line under their name and address at the top of Page 1: "Submitted at usual rates." This is a polite way of saying that the script is offered for sale, not as a gift. Usually this isn't necessary. Editors know that free lances are not sending manuscripts around purely for the love of licking stamps.

A final writer-aid to the editor is an estimate of the manuscript's word-count, usually typed in the upper righthand corner of Page 1. Editors don't care much whether a writer furnishes this estimate or not. If they decide to purchase the script on a word-count basis, they will make their own count anyway. But there's no harm in including it.

So much for the preparation of the manuscript. Next comes the business of getting it to the editors.

Two things Jones has found he has to think about in this connection: Presenting the script to the editors so that it will be easy to handle and read; and getting it back promptly and surely if they don't want it.

To achieve the first, he does a number of things. He folds the manuscript as little as possible. If it is very short—four pages of typewriter paper or less—he may fold it twice, the typing inside, so that it will go into a No. 10 business envelope. A brief manuscript thus folded is not difficult to handle. But if it runs to greater length—from five to, say, thirty pages—he folds it only once, horizontally through the middle, still with the typing inside. This he will mail in a 6″ x 9″ envelope. And if the script is of more than thirty pages he will probably send it flat.

Often Jones puts "packing" into the envelope with the manuscript—a sheet of stiff cardboard cut to the folded size of the script so that, in handling in the mails, it will not become unduly crumpled. If photographs, diagrams, or other such enclosures go with it, he uses heavy cardboard packing. A cracked photograph is useless.

Free-lance rules for the preparation of photographs to go with a manuscript:

Always identify each photograph. For identification, use a typewritten "caption" or explanation pasted to the back of the photograph. Do not write on the photograph (unless in very soft pencil, on the back). Handwriting on the back of a photograph often makes an indelible impress on its face, one that cannot be eliminated in reproduction.

Never use a paper clip on a photograph. The clip may make marks on it more damaging than those caused by handwriting on its back.

Always use plenty of cardboard packing with photographs.

If the photographs are small, enclose them in an envelope to aid the editor in keeping them together.

"To whom should the envelope be addressed?" ask beginning free lances. Usually to the magazine itself, rather than to the editor or a subeditor. In most cases it will go through the routine manuscript-receipt procedure, no matter to whom it is addressed: Recording by the mail clerk, consideration by the "first reader," progress to other editors' desks if it merits further reading. If a writer has had previous correspondence with a particular editor about a manuscript, or about other matters, he may address the envelope to the editor. But it will probably go through the routine nevertheless.

The cardinal rule that must always be observed is the old one about enclosing return postage. The only question is whether merely to put in stamps to the right amount or to include a self-addressed, stamped envelope. The return-envelope procedure is more convenient for editors and mail clerks, and it is surer. If stamps alone are enclosed, they should be clipped to the first page of the manuscript, or put into a small cellophane or waxed paper envelope obtainable at stationery stores.

"But doesn't the enclosure of return postage prejudice the editor against you? Doesn't it tell him that you *expect* the manuscript to come back?" ask beginning writers. Not at all. The fact is that the prejudice, if any, works in the opposite direction. Editors are prone to call a strike on the script unaccompanied by return postage before they have read a word of it.

Typewritten or hand written manuscripts, when accompanied by printed proofs of the same matter, may be mailed third class (or if over 8 ounces, fourth class). The proofs may contain corrections of typographical errors as well as marginal instructions to the printer. Part of an article may be entirely re-written, if necessary for correction. Note: Manuscripts when not accompanied by proofs must pay the first class rate. In the case of bulky manuscripts, shipment by express is sometimes an economy.

One other trick Jones has learned in connection with this problem: That of keeping an adequate record file to show where his wandering scripts are. Having tried a number of systems, he finds a 3″ x 5″ card file most satisfactory. When he completes a manuscript, he types its title and such other information as seems necessary (such as the date of its completion) at the top of a card. Under this he writes or types the name of the magazine to which it is first sent, and the date of dispatch. If it comes back, a second date is added. Similar records of the script's other travels are kept on the same card. When a sale is made, the date and amount of the check are added. Jones, a fulltime free lance with many scripts in editors' hands, files the cards according to the date on which the manuscripts were last sent out. A daily check-up tells him which manuscripts have been out a month and suggests that it is time to do something about them. Other writers with fewer manuscripts in the mails sometimes file the cards alphabetically according to title.

What is it that Jones does when a script has been out a month without his having heard anything about it?

He knows that few magazines profess that they need more than four weeks to come to a conclusion about a manuscript. In complete agreement with other free lances, he thinks that none should take that long. Manuscripts are the free lance's bread and butter; he can't afford to wait endlessly for decisions. Moreover, some scripts may have timely or seasonable value that will disappear if editors hold them too long. So, when a script has been out a month or thereabouts, Jones writes a letter. A very polite letter, something like this:

> On August 16 I sent you my 3,000-word article, "Making the Old Auto Last Another Season." In lack of word from you about it, I fear that it may have been lost in the mails. If you have not received it, will you please let me know so that I may send you another copy?

That is what the letter says. But both Jones and the editor know that, translated, it means this:

> My article has been in your shop a month now. That's long enough for any editor to give it a reading and a decision. Will you be so kind as to get on the horse and let me have some action?

Usually it achieves its purpose. If by any chance the story has been lost, Jones finds out. If the editor is considering its purchase, the letter spurs him to action. If he hasn't got around to reading it, he will do so.

Rarely does such a letter irritate an editor. If he has been dilatory, it is usually by force of circumstance rather than by desire. He agrees that no writer should have to wait longer than a month for a decision.

When a manuscript comes back, the experienced free lance examines it carefully to see whether it needs renovation. A script well prepared in the first place will usually stand up for four or five trips to market without renewal. But if it becomes dog-eared or wrinkled or thumb-printed, the writer should have it retyped (often retyping first and last pages, those that bear the brunt of handling, will be adequate. But new typing and old should be reasonably well matched).

And if the script has come back ten or a dozen times, its author may well consider a major operation on it, or its decent burial. Tales of scripts that sell on their fortieth trips are told whenever free lances get together; but they remain the exceptions. If an article is carefully written in the first place, if its markets have been carefully chosen, it doesn't take forty editors' rejections to indicate that there is a major deficiency in it.

Some suspicious novices employ tricks to tell them whether editors have read their masterworks thoroughly. Among such tricks: Turning Pages 18 and 19 upside down; pasting two or more pages lightly together; even tying a long hair or a light thread around several pages. "This," says the novice, "will let me know whether the ogre in the editor's office has given me a fair break. I'll catch him!" Sometimes he does. But the fact that the pages remain upside down, or pasted or tied together, does not mean that the author has been unfairly treated. More often it means that Pages 1 to 4 were so very bad, or so completely unsuited to the editor's needs, that he didn't have to go farther to come to a decision. . . . It is only fair to warn the suspicious that most editors discovering these sophomoric tricks are irritated by them. "Please note," wrote one editor to such a writer, "that I have pasted back together the pages which I carelessly tore apart. I found, as you did, that the script read better when they were passed over."

Letters to the Editor

When should a free lance write to a magazine editor?

One occasion has already been described: When he thinks a report on a manuscript is due. There are two other common occasions for letter communication:

When he wants to "query" an editor about his interest in an article-idea, or a group of them.

When something about a manuscript he is offering needs to be explained more fully than the script itself can do.

Jones, like every other free lance, has found that the "query" procedure is a valuable one. It saves the writer work that may in the end turn out to be fruitless; it sometimes gives him instructions as to the slant his article ought to take, if the editor approves the idea and comments on it. A typical "query," say to the editor of a motor-boat magazine, goes like this:

> I have material for an article of about 2,000 words on giving the old cabin cruiser a new paint job. It would tell exactly how the job may be done without too great expense, what kinds of paint to use, when to apply it and how an amateur can do a good job of it; it would suggest several good color combinations. I would base the article on my own experience, but would add short anecdotes of other similar jobs on which I have data.

> I can turn out the article in a couple of days after I get word from you, if you want it. I have a number of good photos to go with it.

And the response:

> We like the paint job article you suggest, and we should like to see it. Please hold it to 1,500-1,800 words if you can. We suggest that you tell your story as a personal experience yarn, bringing in the other brief anecdotes as needed. We think we'll illustrate the piece, if we can use it, with drawings, but send along the photos. They may offer suggestions.

The result of this is likely to be an article sold—and with a minimum of effort on the part of the writer, and a minimum of risk of wasted time. The risk is rarely completely obviated, for few magazines commit themselves definitely to the purchase of an article described in a query. Rather they say, as in the letter above, that they would "like to see it."

Writers often describe a number of possible articles in a query letter. Sometimes none of them strikes the editor's fancy; sometimes several. In any case, the query is one of the free lance's most useful devices, and one that most experienced free lances employ constantly. Beginners may well use it more than they do, at least as soon as they have learned to construct and write articles properly, and to study markets so as to fit products to demands. Most editors welcome it.

A manuscript resulting from a query should be accompanied, when it goes to the editor, by a brief letter referring to the previous correspondence. Letters should go with a manuscript, too, when the material presented in the script is not altogether self-explanatory. If a writer is "ghosting" an article, he should explain the circumstances under which he procured the material, and let the editor know that he has authority to present it under a name not his own. If he wishes to use a

---

Evidence is that "ghost-writing" may play a less prominent place in American magazines in coming years than it has in the last decade. Many magazines are adopting the practice of using joint by-lines. One issue of the *Saturday Evening Post,* for instance, contains these three by-lines: "An Interview With Daniel Willard, as Reported by Donald Wilhelm"; "Robert C. Zuppke, With L. M. Tobin"; and "Irwin (Ike) Hoover, Edited by Wesley Stout." Two factors appear to be influencing editors in this direction. First, it is at least mildly less than honest to present in a by-line the name of a man who has not written the article (and who perhaps couldn't write two consecutive intelligible sentences); and often the reader is not fooled. Second, the writer's most valuable asset is his reputation as a writer, and to conceal him under the anonymity of ghost-writing is to deny him the opportunity to achieve or add to a reputation.

---

pseudonym, he should explain why. If some of the facts in the article need more authority than the article presents, or if statements or situations need clearing up, a letter is necessary. (But in this kind of case, the writer should always ask himself whether the material in his letter does not perhaps belong in the article itself.)

Except in situations like these, however, the letter with the manuscript is usually as much a handicap as a help. It is obviously not necessary to write to an editor that "I am enclosing with this letter my article about such-and-such, and I hope you will buy it." Moreover, no manuscript was ever sold to a magazine on the basis of a sales letter. Sales letters, like tricks to check the editor's thoroughness, more frequently irritate him than not.

Some sales letters that accompany manuscripts into editorial shops are unbelievably naïve. This one is from the files of a national monthly: "If you want to increase your circulation, publish my story in your next issue. I know of seven people in my own neighborhood who have promised to buy a copy if you publish it. I have read the story to my grandfather, who used to work in a printshop when he was a boy, and so he knows a lot about stories. And he says it is one of the best stories he ever read. And he has read a lot of them. Please answer promptly."

The rules that tell a free lance when to write to an editor, and when not to, serve as a guide in answer to the question, "When should I call on an editor?"

If Jones, going from his home in South Bend to New York, misses the opportunity to have informal chats with New York editors with whom he has had dealings, he is doing himself an injustice. And if there are other editors in New York with whom he would like to do business—if he has article-ideas to suggest to them, or if he thinks that talking with them would clear up for him problems about their slants or needs that have prevented him from selling to them in the past—he will do well to make appointments for conferences. He will aid himself, and the editors will welcome him.

But there is no more reason for taking up editors' time with unnecessary calls than there is for writing the "I am enclosing with this letter my story" type of letter. Editing the magazine is, to its editor, a business (for most editors a pleasant one, since few men and women remain long in editorial work unless they enjoy it) just as much as writing is to the free lance. It is a business that makes heavy demands on its workers—demands on time, patience, and energy. And the writer can choose no more effective method of getting himself "in Dutch" in the editorial office than making unnecessary demands on editors' crowded time.

Perhaps the best broad rule is this: Don't call on the editor if a letter or a telephone call will do as well. Neither will serve to establish personal relationships between writer and editor who have met only by typewriter; and neither will accomplish certain types of business as well as a face-to-face meeting over the desk. But one or the other will meet demands of most situations.

Magazine and newspaper editors are convinced, with some justification, that practically every young man or woman in America decides at one time or another to go to Europe, Patagonia, or the Grand Canyon and to confer on editors the privilege of paying for his trip. Literally hundreds of willing young writers write to or call on editors each year—the favorite season is June, about the time summer vacations begin—to suggest some variation on this procedure. Editors can offer no answer but one: The idea is an old one, and egregiously overworked. "Go make your trip," they say, "and write your pieces. If you have anything new to say, we'll be more than glad to see it."

The Literary Agent

Free-lance Jones has never made use of the services of a literary agent. Asked why, he replies, "An agent is not of much value to the beginning free lance, largely because the beginning free lance—especially if he's a non-fiction writer—isn't of much value to the literary agent. A free lance who sells mostly short articles to the trade magazine field, or to markets where rates are relatively low, doesn't offer the agent a very promising income. For it takes about as much effort on the part of an agent to sell a $10 short as to market a $200 major article."

Jones might add other facts about the work of the literary agent: That fiction writers are the preferred clients of most such agencies; that a few of the larger agencies make special effort to place non-fiction, but that they prefer to work with non-fiction writers who have at least the beginning of reputations and who turn out mainly long articles that bring good prices; that relatively few free-lance non-fiction writers market their products through agents.

The literary agent works usually on the basis of a "reading fee" which is returned to the writer in case the agent sells the manuscript for which the fee was paid. Agents take a standard 10 percent commission on sales prices; for writers whose manuscripts they handle regularly and successfully they cancel the reading fee. But, as Jones has pointed out, 10 percent on a small check isn't enough to pay costs. And since there is a far bigger market for unsolicited fiction than for unsolicited non-fiction, and since the average sum paid for a fiction story is larger than the non-fiction fee, the agent favors the fiction writer as much by necessity as desire.

Many successful fiction writers turn their entire marketing problems over to agents, and usually to their financial advantage in spite of the 10 percent commission. Agents are in position to keep in intimate touch with magazine needs, and they can often procure better prices for their clients than can the writers themselves. Moreover, they are of great value to fiction writers in secondary sales—sales of book, motion picture, dramatic and radio rights.

To repeat: The literary agent, valuable as he may be to the fiction writer and to the topflight "arrived" essay or article writer, is not often in a position to aid the beginning free lance. As to all rules, there are exceptions to this one.

For years it was a familiar saying in New York authors' circles that one of the leading literary agents was as closely in touch with the needs and policies of the *Saturday Evening Post* as the editors themselves. Later he became an official member of the *Saturday Evening Post's* staff, relinquishing his work as an agent.

Some place in the back of every writer's head as he works at a manuscript—and at times very much toward the front of it—is this question: "How much will I get for it?"

This question points to a curious phenomenon of the writing craft.

The writer produces a salable commodity much as does a dressmaker. Both put energy, a certain amount of creative effort and imagination, and at least a degree of professional skill into their products.

The dressmaker usually knows, when she starts a piece of work, for whom it is intended and precisely how much it is worth in dollars. The writer may have only a hope as to the market, and no idea at all as to its salable value.

Writing is, in other words, distinctly on a gambling basis. "Here is my script," the writer says, in effect, to the editor. "I am offering it to you for whatever you choose to pay for it."

Not even does he say, "How much do you offer for it?" Theory is that he may refuse to accept what the editor offers; and in rare cases he does. Usually, however, he submits his manuscript "at usual rates" and accepts the editor's interpretation of just what this phrase means.

To the not uncommon query of the beginning free-lance writer, then—"How much shall I charge for this when I get it finished?"—the experienced man has only one answer: "You don't charge. You just take what you can get, and be thankful!"

The situation is not quite as fortuitous as this reply indicates. The writer always can discover, from the market listings and from the magazine itself if he wishes, something about the rates usually paid for material of the type he is writing. There is no compulsion for him to offer a manuscript to a magazine that pays at a rate lower than he thinks his work is worth, and there is nothing to force him to accept an offer or a check if he doesn't like its size. To the credit of the magazines, it must be added that they rarely take advantage of the author. Their rates are usually as high as possible, and sometimes that is high indeed.

REFERENCES

BOOKS

The Americanization of Edward Bok, by Edward Bok. Charles Scribner's Sons, New York. 1923.

Forty Years—Forty Millions, by George Britt. Farrar and Rinehart, New York.

The Golden Age of Authors, by W. W. Ellsworth. Houghton Mifflin and Company, Boston.

My Autobiography, by Samuel S. McClure. Frederick A. Stokes Company, New York.

The Autobiography of Lincoln Steffens. Harcourt, Brace and Company, New York. 1931.

This Trade of Writing, by Edward Weeks. Little, Brown and Company, Boston. 1935.

Free-Lancing for Forty Magazines, by Edward Mott Woolley. The Writer Publishing Company, Cambridge.

See also *Magazine Making* (Bakeless), *Pulpwood Editor* (Hersey) and *The Business Paper Editor at Work* (Woolf).

PERIODICALS

"A Literary Experiment," by Alan Devoe, *Atlantic Monthly,* April, 1934, Page 472.

"Hard Times and the Author," by Edward Weeks, *Atlantic Monthly,* May, 1935, Page 551.

"Bargaining With Writers," by Curtis Brown, *Harper's,* June, 1935, Page 26.

"The Literary Worker's Polonius," by Edmund Wilson, *Atlantic Monthly,* June, 1935, Page 674.

"Good Times for Authors," by Roger Burlingame, *Esquire,* May, 1936, Page 46.

XXI

The Rights of an Author

An old saying has it that "nothing is so peculiarly a man's own as the product of his own mind." The principle laid down by this statement is the basis of law and practice governing property rights in writing in the United States and most of the rest of the literate world.

What does this mean to free-lance writer Jones when he writes an article? How much of the article does he own, and how long does he own it? What rights have others to its use? What rights does Jones surrender when he sells it to a newspaper or magazine? Who owns it after it appears in print? And what can Jones do to protect his rights or obtain redress if somebody who has no right to it makes use of it?

These are simple questions. The answers are not always simple or brief. Laws give Jones a fairly complete technical protection, and adequate avenues of redress if his literary rights are violated. Unfortunately, however, actual cases involving infringement of literary rights are rarely as simple as the principles governing them. Identical cases seldom arise, and each one is hedged about by so many "special circumstances" that it is likely to become a case unto itself. Moreover, customs and habitual practices as often govern such situations as do codified laws.

With this brief prelude, let us answer some of the questions about Jones' rights in the articles that he produces.

"Nothing is so peculiarly a man's own as the product of his own mind." And the writings that Jones turns out are, essentially, the products of his mind. The information on which he bases them may come from many sources; but the arrangement of them, the wording of them, the "literary style" of them, are his. These, then, belong to him.

They belong to him until he does one of two things:

1. Sells, gives, or otherwise transfers ownership of them to some other owner for such use as the new owner cares to make of them, with or without restriction.

2. Makes them public without restriction.

Suppose that Jones writes his article about rural living standards, basing it on facts derived from a college bulletin. If he writes the article and then puts it into a drawer of his desk, offering it to nobody to read and making no further use of it, it remains entirely his property. He could keep it there forty years and it would still be his. If he offers it to a very limited number of friends to read and criticize for him, on the understanding that it is his article and that they are being asked merely to read and criticize, it remains his property. He has not offered it to them for use, nor has he shown it to enough persons so that he has "made it public."

And if he sends it to an editor for consideration, or to a large number of different editors, one after another, and if each editor rejects it, it is still his. Neither the editors nor the others who have seen it have any rights over its use, for he has not technically fulfilled either of the two conditions that would release it for general use.

Suppose, however, he sends it to an editor who wants to buy it. The editor makes an offer; Jones accepts, and cashes the magazine's check. By doing so he gives up certain rights, usually specified, to the magazine. As a rule a magazine purchases "first serial rights," which means the right to print the article once in periodical form (it does *not* mean that the article must be published serially, in installments). Sometimes a magazine purchases all serial rights, which gives it the privilege of publishing the article in as many periodicals as it wishes, and even of selling it to other periodicals without reimbursing the author if it wishes (occasionally a sales contract specifies that author and magazine will share proceeds of sales after first serial publication, though this is not common). Jones will likely retain rights other than serial rights

---

In 1937 the *Saturday Evening Post* published in installments Eve Curie's biography of her mother, Madame Curie. Then Doubleday, Doran and Company issued the biography in book form. Third, the *Ladies' Home Journal* published in its July, 1938, issue an abridged edition of the biography. How did it happen that two magazines published the same material within so short a time, and what were the rights involved? The answer: That both the *Saturday Evening Post* and the *Ladies' Home Journal* are Curtis Publishing Company publications, and that the Curtis company buys all rights to every bit of material added to its copy list. This is done with the proviso that upon publication and on the request of the author all rights revert to the author except American (including Canadian and South American) serial rights. In this case the *Saturday Evening Post* used its serial rights for the biography's first use; it assigned book rights to the author on her request; the *Ladies' Home Journal* took advantage of Curtis ownership of serial rights for second magazine publication.

---

when he sells a manuscript to a magazine—book, dramatic, radio, and such rights are rarely purchased by periodicals (though the Curie case is an example to the contrary).

Thus Jones has fulfilled the first set of conditions laid down for the disposition of his ownership in his article. He could also dispose of it by giving it away, and if he did the rights he would surrender would probably be only first serial rights.

Contracts for the sale of manuscripts to magazines are not often formally witnessed and notarized documents. They usually consist of nothing more than the notice on check or on voucher accompanying it to the effect that endorsement of the check by the writer turns certain rights over to the magazine. As has been noted before, these rights commonly include not only right of publication but also the right to at least minor revision.

We have said that Jones would not fulfill the second set of conditions—making his manuscript public without restriction—merely by showing it to friends for comment and criticism, nor by offering it to editors for sale. How might he "make it public"?

It would be made public—published—if Jones had it mimeographed or otherwise copied and sent it around to what the law books define vaguely as a "considerable number" of persons, with the intent that it be "dedicated" to this portion of the public. If he did this, he would lose all right in the script, and anybody else could offer it to a magazine and receive payment for it should the magazine wish to buy. He could similarly make it public property by delivering it as a speech before a fairly large public gathering ("fairly large" may mean no more than a score); but his reading it in his home to a group of friends would not constitute publication. His *intent* is the governing factor in cases of this kind.

Ownership of "Literary Style"

These, then, are the manners in which Jones may give up his rights in a "product of his own mind," or refuse to give them up. But another question arises: Precisely what are the rights of ownership that inhere in the manuscript as long as Jones does not sell, give away, or publish it?

The answer: Its "literary style." This means that what Jones owns in the manuscript is his manner of expression. He does not own the facts he has stated in it. In the example we are considering, he has gathered the data from other sources; the mere fact that he has put them into his manuscript does not give him control over their use. What he does have is control over the form in which he has stated the facts. In other words, the material in the manuscript may be considered public property. But the style in which it is handled is Jones' own. Nobody has the right to that unless Jones gives it up.

And so, basically, it is the style that he is selling to the magazine. Since this is the case, it is obvious that the magazine editor might go to the bulletin from which Jones has gathered his material, take the material, and get up his own article. He doesn't thus cut Jones out of the picture for one of two reasons: He likes the way Jones has presented his article, and is willing to buy the presentation; or he feels that Jones should be recompensed for calling the material to his notice, even when he has to have the article rewritten and amplified before publication.

Jones would be able to defend ownership of a body of information that he has gathered himself and that he has not "dedicated" to the public. A newspaper, according to most court decisions, is the legal possessor of facts its reporters have gathered until a few hours after they have been published. This does not mean that the newspaper can prevent a competitor from going to the same sources and gathering the same facts; but it can obtain legal satisfaction if a competing reporter steals its own facts from its own reporters' notes or copy before they have been released. Similarly, Jones can take legal action to restrain another writer's use of the product of his own efforts. He has, however, no control over the other writer's comparable efforts.

Suppose Jones' rights have been infringed—that his presentation of certain material has been copied or his unreleased facts "stolen." What redress does he have? The specific answer to this question depends on the laws of the state in which he brings action. In the broad, his course is to sue for damages under the laws of unfair competition. It is "unfair" for one author to make use of the literary property of another without full permission.

So far this discussion has not taken into account one of Jones' chief safeguards against infringement of his rights: The laws of copyright.

What the copyright law does for an author or a publisher invoking it is, briefly stated, this: It insures to him for a period of twenty-eight years a full protection against the reprinting, in full or in part, of a piece of writing he has copyrighted. Copyright protects nothing but the form of presentation (literary style), however. A critic may retell the whole plot of a copyrighted story or the whole argument of a copyrighted essay; a writer may make full use of the facts in a copyrighted article the rights to which he does not own. What a writer may not do is reprint *exactly* enough of a copyrighted piece of writing that his use of it will substantially damage its financial value to the copyright owner.

If Jones wishes to protect his article under the copyright law, he must furnish a full and exact copy of it to the Register of Copyrights, Library of Congress, Washington, D. C., together with an application for copyright on the proper official form and a $2 money order to pay the fee. With that done, he may spread the article on the four winds, secure in the knowledge that nobody may reprint it without rendering himself liable for a suit to restrain infringement of copyright and for the payment of damages.

In practice few writers take out copyright in their own names. Perhaps more would do so if periodicals were not trustworthy. Since they are—since the number of cases of theft of uncopyrighted writings offered to editors for consideration is practically negligible—writers rarely bother with the procedure.

Almost all magazines, however, and a few newspapers copyright each issue. To do so, a periodical must deposit with the Register of Copyrights two complete copies of the issue, along with the application and $2 fee, at a time coincident with the appearance of the issue; and each copy of the issue must bear the notice of copyright followed by the year in which it is obtained and the name of the copyright owner (this notice must be on any copyrighted material—manuscript, book, magazine, photograph, song, or anything else). At the time of its expiration a copyright may be once renewed for another twenty-eight year period in the name of the original author or of a member of his family.

What does it mean to Jones that the article he sells to a magazine is copyrighted in the magazine's name rather than his? Technically this gives all reproduction rights not to Jones but to somebody else. In practice a magazine is usually ready to re-assign to the author what rights he asks for further publication of a piece of writing, if such publication will not decrease the writing's value to the periodical. Often provision for such re-assignment is included in the sales agreement made between author and magazine.

The classic copyright story in American literary history concerns the book *In His Steps* by the Reverend Charles Monroe Sheldon. Mr. Sheldon wrote the novel, a story of fifty church members who guide their lives for a year by the precepts of Jesus Christ, with no expectation that it would have more than a modest sale. It appeared in a religious periodical, and the periodical failed to register it properly for copyright, so none was issued. Book publishers took it up, and in the thirty years after its first appearance 8,000,000 copies were sold in the United States and more than 12,000,000 in other countries. Mr. Sheldon received almost nothing for writing the best-selling book of modern times—because of lack of copyright.

The Right to Gather Material

What other writers cannot do in the way of using Jones' writing for their own purposes, he cannot do in using theirs for his. Which is to say that literary property rights work both ways: The rules that protect Jones against unfair competition, lifting, theft, and other literary sins also protect others against him.

The statement of what Jones' rights are is, in a sense, a negative statement. It presents the list of the things others cannot do in respect to his work. There is a positive side to it as well. Let us look, then, at the things Jones can do in respect to others' work.

As has already been said, Jones or any other writer has complete right to use the factual material, the thoughts expressed, the conclusions reached, in any published piece of writing, copyrighted or not. From uncopyrighted publications, or work on which the copyright has expired, he may take as much verbatim material as he wishes, without even bothering to give credit, for such work lies "in the public domain." From copyrighted material he may extract all of the *content* he desires, so long as he avoids copying or mimicking *literary style*—the individual pattern of words by which the author has chosen to express his meaning. For example: A writer is preparing an article on Germany's *Drang nach Osten*. He seeks everything published on the subject—articles in *Current History, Foreign Affairs,* and other periodicals, books such as John Gunther's *Inside Europe* and Hitler's *Mein Kampf,* newspaper correspondence, and so on. Much of this material has been copyrighted. But he uses as much of the factual material it presents to the public as he wishes, being meticulously careful not to say what he has to say in the words of any of the writers from whom he draws. Working on this basis, he is in no danger of violating any literary property right.

This case arose a few years ago: Writer A wrote a book on a narrowly limited period in American history, and the book was published and copyrighted. A few years later Writer B decided to write a book on the same period. To get his material he not only read Writer A's book but also went to virtually all the same original sources that A had used (in this case there were but two important bodies of original source material, and naturally both writers used both of them). Writer B was able to add to his material a limited amount of "new" material—

material to which A had not had access. Both A and B made extensive use of uncopyrighted publications, or publications on which copyright had expired.

When B's book appeared, A complained that "B has merely rewritten my book" and talked of litigation. He named several passages in which the two books appeared similar. But B pointed out that in such passages both writers had used the same original material, and that in some of them both had borrowed freely not alone from facts but from literary style. The upshot of the matter was that A's advisers told him that no literary rights had been violated, and A withdrew his objections.

There are relatively few cases of outright plagiarism. But many writers think themselves the victims of plagiarists. The reason usually is that the "plagiarist" has happened, quite independently, to conceive and develop an idea that has already been conceived and developed by another writer. The second writer does not know of the existence of the first writing; his only method of idea-theft would therefore be occult. In cases such as this the courts have often held that chance similarity of material is not plagiarism. If the second writer has probably not had access to the first writer's work—especially if he can prove that he has not seen it nor heard of it—he is usually absolved.

An unusual recent case of idea-similarity: A non-professional writer submitted to a magazine a humorous story the basis of which was the casting up of two young men on a curious South Sea island inhabited by spring-tailed monkeys, balloon-footed water birds, and other imaginary beasts. The magazine bought the story. Hardly had the deal been completed when the editor received from a professional writer—one who lived 1,500 miles from the first man and had never heard of him—a suggestion that he write a story almost identical, even to the spring-tailed monkeys and balloon-footed birds. The editor replied that he had a similar story in stock. When it appeared in the magazine later, the second writer shot at the editor a sizzling letter charging theft of his idea; and, if he is like most writers, he is probably still unconvinced that there wasn't "something funny" about the situation.

If, however, a court can be shown that a writer has employed a plot-idea from a copyrighted fiction story as the basis for a play, or has similarly used such base-material so that its sale-value to the original author is injured, the original author can recover damages. In this respect the law differs from that covering factual material. Factual material is available to everybody; imaginative material, if protected under common law property or copyright laws, is not.

There are two other sources of information to which free-lance Jones may go without anybody to say him nay: The man or woman possessing data of value to Jones who is willing to release it to him for what use he may choose to make of it, and the tremendous gold mines of public records.

And Jones and all other free lances use these sources perhaps more assiduously than they do the other more restricted sources. Probably a majority of free-lance articles is based on interviews with authorities. There is no legal problem connected with procuring information in this manner beyond that involved in the permission of the interviewee. If Jones is granted an interview, and if his informant gives him data in the full knowledge that it is to be used for publication, he has every right to base published articles on it. If he uses information which the interviewee asks him to withhold, however, he may be liable for damages if the informant can show that its release has worked to his pecuniary disadvantage.

There is not even this restriction on public records. It is a basic principle of law that most of the records of Congress, of the courts, of almost all legislative and judicial bodies, are open to every citizen (some jurisdictions hold that writers and reporters have a special pecuniary interest in records and so are entitled to special advantages in examining them). Similarly any citizen has the right of attendance at most official assemblies, and in some cases at any public assembly.

And so an immense body of material with thousands upon thousands of articles for the periodicals in it is at all times available to the free lance.

What About Libel?

One basic principle Jones needs to follow to avoid liability for whatever libel he may commit in his writings: Truth is a complete defense in a vast majority of cases.

If Jones says that a man has been convicted of burglary and the man *has* been convicted of burglary, the man has little chance of legal recourse. If Jones casts any kind of aspersions on the character or business ability or reputation of any individual, and if he can prove the factual soundness of the aspersions, he need have no sleepless nights. But if he is in error in any such statement or aspersion, or if he cannot prove its truth, he may be liable for payment of damages; for the burden of proof rests on the defendant in a civil libel suit.

Three elements are necessary to establish a civil suit for libel:

1. Publication of the allegedly libelous material. This means that the material must be circulated to a considerable number of readers in such form that it may be read and observed by them. If it is in a newspaper or magazine issue, publication is automatically established. If it is merely a manuscript offered to a few editors, it may be considered published legally, if not in the popular sense.

2. Identification of the person libelled. This means that the material must be of such nature that a number of readers will consider it as attaching unmistakably to a given individual. Omission of a name, or misspelling of it, does not defeat identification if other statements lead readers to identify a person as the one to whom the statements apply (even when the writer has intended them to apply to somebody else).

3. Defamation. This element may be constituted by words that are in themselves defamatory—words like "scoundrel," "skunk," "thief," "villain," "wife-beater"—or by words innocent in themselves but defamatory because of circumstance. It is not defamatory *per se* to say of a woman that she is a mother. But if she should be unmarried, the words would become defamatory.

With these rules in mind, Jones avoids libel primarily by being very sure of the truth of the things he says, and of the accuracy of names and other identifying material. He must bear in mind, too, that even though he has carefully veiled defamatory remarks so that they apply to no single identifiable individual, he may still become a defendant in a prosecution for criminal (as distinguished from civil) libel if an identifiable group is libelled. To say a certain social organization is a body of corrupt nincompoops may not libel any individual; but a criminal prosecution on the ground that the organization as a whole has been libelled might grow out of such a remark. In criminal libel proof not only of truth but also of lack of malice, or "good motives," must be presented by the defendant as a defense.

Libel suits based on magazine material grow as commonly out of inadvertent circumstance as from intentional defamation. Such a suit

---

In England some 5,000 men and women have formed an organization for the "sale" of their names to writers. Their names are listed; a writer picks such names as he needs, and pays a sum of about $15 to the owner of each. For this payment he is legally granted the right to use of the name, and no charge of libel may be based on such use.

---

might develop if, quite by chance, a writer uses as a name for a reprehensible character that of an actual person. It would be easy for the person to establish the elements of publication and defamation. If, in addition, he can show that a considerable number of readers attach the supposedly fictional name and the defamatory words, remarks or incidents to him, the writer is in trouble. It is as a guard against this kind of situation that many books and magazines carry some place in their front-matter a sentence such as this: "All names in this book (or in this magazine, or in the fiction in this magazine) are fictitious, and resemblance to or duplication of the names of living persons is purely coincidental." (But such a disclaimer is not complete defense against libel; it serves merely to show lack of malice or evil intent, and will be accepted in court "in mitigation of damages.")

There are circumstances, of course, under which Jones may say exceedingly unpleasant things about actual persons. One of these is the circumstance that he has provided adequate safeguards to insure that the persons cannot be identified. Another, as has been said, is the case in which he has complete and adequate proof of the truth of his libel, and in which he can show good motives for publishing it.

Finally, he may make the most uncomplimentary of remarks about men and women who, in one way or another, are offering themselves "for public approval." This is interpreted to include actors, singers, authors, and all such individuals who present their words or talents to the public; and also candidates for public election and in some cases public officials. But if Jones chooses to write an article pointing out that, in his opinion, nobody should read Mr. So-and-so's new book, he must take care that his remarks confine themselves to the merits of the book and Mr. So-and-so's qualifications as a writer. The law holds that it is not germane that Mr. So-and-so is a drunken sot and steals candy from little children as well. So Jones leaves So-and-so's personal life strictly out of his script, and writes only about the faulty logic, the illiteracy, and the literary sloppiness of the book, or the failure of its author to equip himself adequately to write it.

Laws governing "fair comment and criticism"—the term lawyers apply to this type of writing—vary considerably from state to state, as do many other laws of libel and of access to public records. It is possible that an assertion libelous in one state will be unexceptionable in another (and the libel laws of England are far stricter than those of the United States). Jones cannot know all laws; his best safeguard, therefore, is to conform to the broadly general principles that apply in most jurisdictions.

REFERENCES

The Protection and Marketing of Literary Property, by Philip Wittenberg. Julian Messner, Inc., New York. 1937.

The Rights and Privileges of the Press, by Fredrick S. Siebert. D. Appleton-Century Company, New York. 1933.

XXII

Production Biography of Your First Accepted Story

WHAT happened during that long gap between the day your article was accepted and the moment it appeared? We need not repeat its editorial history, since that has been covered in the foregoing pages. This is the place to tell what happened during the complicated process of translating your typewritten manuscript into the finished magazine product.

1. The layout department has done its work on the article and it is ready to be set. What type will be used? Will it be set in a *Gothic*? Not very likely, since Gothic types (marked by an absence of serifs and by a uniform weight of strokes) are seldom used as body type. A serif is a smaller line used to finish off a main stroke of a letter, as at the top and bottom of M. Perhaps Gothic will be used for the title of your article (as it was used on Page 19 for the top line "Better Foods & Equipment—Edited by Helen Homer"). If your article is not too long, it may be set in a type family similar to Gothic but called *Sans Serif*. This name is given to recently designed faces, widely available, and extremely useful. (The chapter headings in this book are "Sans Serif Light"; the running page titles, "Sans Serif Bold"; the chapter subdivisions, "Sans Serif Light Italic.") In the vast majority of cases your article will be marked up for one of the *Roman* types—by far the most widely used types for body matter. Roman type is vertical, its letters have serifs, and the strokes are not mechanically uniform in weight. Roman types are available in an enormous variety of styles and sizes, and are usually distinguished by some family name. (The body type in this book is Baskerville. Other widely used Roman types are: Caslon, Garamond, Granjon, Old Style, Cloister, Bodoni, Elzevir, etc., etc.) Once in a great while an entire article is set in *Italic*—a slanted letter which is used in conjunction with a *Roman* type of the same family. (The words "Roman" and "Italic" in the previous sentence are italicized.)

2. Let's say that your article has been marked for "10 on 12 Garamond, 2 columns, 18 picas each, flush first paragraph, other paragraphs indent 1-em." What does all this mean to the foreman of the composing room?

First he has to decide whether the article will be set on a line-casting machine or a Monotype. (A line-casting machine, usually either a *Linotype* or an *Intertype,* is equipped with a keyboard—similar to a typewriter keyboard— which "taps out" matrices of individual characters and assembles them into lines. A given line of "mats" is then impressed in molten metal, and a full line, or "slug," is cast.) Line-casting is used in newspaper composition and in many magazine composing rooms since it is faster and less expensive than Monotype. When many changes are envisaged—for reasons either of difficult composition or shifting make-up —Monotype is preferable. (A Monotoype machine is equipped with a keyboard which perforates a paper ribbon. The ribbon then runs through a caster which actuates that machine to cast individual characters.) Pages 1-65 in this book were cast on the Monotype; the text of the book is Linotype.

Assuming that your article will be set on a Linotype, the foreman of the composing room will turn the manuscript over to an operator whose machine is equipped with a magazine of 10 point Garamond. He sets his machine to cast a slug 18 picas long. (A *pica,* originally a designation which meant a 12 point type, is a "12 point" space. There are approximately 6 picas to an inch—and a "point" is approximately one seventy-second of an inch. Your article, then, will be set about three inches wide per column of type.) The operator will note that the text is to be set "10 on 12"—which means that there will be two points of space between lines. He will set his machine to cast a 10 point face on a 12 point body. If by any chance it is decided later to "open up" the text and set the type "10 on 14," the composing room will insert a 2-point *lead*—a metal space 2 points thick—between the lines.)

Before he begins tapping out the first lines, the operator will note that the first paragraph is marked "flush"—that is, there will be no indention. For the remaining paragraphs, to be set 1-em indention, he will tap out a space 10 points high by 10 points wide. (Later on, the cost department of the magazine will figure the composition expense on the basis of the number of ems. If the article were composed outside the magazine plant, the charge would be made on the basis of a rate per thousand ems.)

The operator will set up the article in lines and these will be placed in a *galley*—a metal tray. A galley proof will be pulled and used for the first readings and revisions. (When the article has been made up into pages, the page proof will be taken.)

After the type has been set, revised, and okayed for make-up, it may prove desirable to put more space between paragraphs. If an additional 6-point space is decided upon, the make-up man will add a *nonpareil*—originally a term for 6-point type, now commonly used to designate a metal space 6 points thick.

3. Assuming now that your article has gone through all the preliminary stages and is ready for printing, what method will be used? Printing processes fall into three broad groups: letterpress, planography, and intaglio. In *letter press* the impression is made from raised surfaces—type or engraved plates. (This book is printed by letter press.) *Planography* is a generic term for a variety of processes of "contact" printing. The image to be printed is ink-attractive, the non-printing areas are chemically made ink-repelling. (*Fortune* and *Country Home* are printed by *planography*. See also insert "Case History" in Chapter III.) *Intaglio*

might be called the "opposite" of letter press inasmuch as the image to be printed is below the surface of the plate. The depressions are filled with ink and the surface wiped clean. The paper then "sucks" the ink out of the depressions. Because the depressions are of varying depths, and so contain varying quantities of ink, many differences in tone can be obtained. (*The New York Times Sunday Magazine,* the rotogravure sections, are examples of intaglio printing.)

Assume that your article will appear in a magazine printed by letter press. The press room will receive either the type matter locked up into forms or electrotypes. (Electrotypes are produced by making a wax or lead mold of the page of type, upon the surface of which is deposited, by electrolysis, a thin shell of copper. The shell is then backed up with a lead mixture. Such plates can be flat—for "flat bed" printing—or curved, for rotary presses.) Most magazines use electros because of the necessity for speed. Books are usually printed on flat bed presses, but electros are widely used so that subsequent printings can be made without the necessity of storing and rehandling heavy pages of type. (The *Better Homes & Gardens* section of this book was printed from electros on rotary presses.) Newspapers usually make stereotypes—a printing plate made by taking an impression of the type page on a papier-mâché composition matrix, from which the lead mold or plate is cast. Stereos are

TEMPO LIGHT
TEMPO MEDIUM
TEMPO HEAVY
TEMPO INLINE
Tempo Medium Italic
Tempo Heavy Italic
KARNAK LIGHT
KARNAK MED.
KARNAK BLACK
KARNAK OBELISK
GARAMOND LIGHT
Garamond Light Italic
GARAMOND BOLD
Garamond Bold Italic
CONDENSED GOTHIC
BODONI BOLD

Bodoni Bold Italic
BODONI BLACK
Bod Black Italic
EDEN LIGHT
EDEN BOLD
Coronet
Old English
SQUARE GOTHIC
CAMEO
Mandate
CHELTENHAM
LINING PLATE GOTHIC
ENGRAVERS
DELPHIAN
UMBRA

commonly used for printing daily newspapers. They are quicker and cheaper to make than electros, but the printing surface is less refined and less durable.

4. Your article may be illustrated with *halftones* and/or *line etchings*—that is, by photo-engravings. Photo-engraving reproduces photographs, drawings, paintings, etc., etc., on metal for printing purposes. The chief steps are: (1) preparation of a photographic negative from the original copy, (2) printing of the negative on a metal chemically sensitized, (3) etching of the metal plate with acid—to remove surfaces of the plate which have been exposed to the light, (4) mounting of the plate on a wood or metal base.

If your article contains diagrams, charts, pen and ink drawings—any such copy which consists of lines and solid areas but which has no gradations in tone—line etchings will be made (on zinc or copper). If your article is accompanied by a photograph or by other copy which has gradations in tone, halftones will be used. (Halftones are made by the same processes as those used to make a line cut except that the copy is photographed through a screen. A screen is a piece of glass ruled with extremely fine, opaque lines, usually running at right angles. A 50 line screen is one with 50 lines to the inch. It is a "coarse" screen halftone. Newspapers printed on rotary presses usually use from 65- to 85-screen halftones. Magazines normally use halftones of from 100 to 180 line screen.)

Sometimes it is found desirable to shade a given area in a line etching; in which case a Benday screen is ordered (a mechanical application of a line tone or pattern). Sometimes a halftone requires highlighting to give greater contrast between gradations of tone. (In such cases the light tones are made pure white by "dropping out" the screen from these highlighted areas.) Sometimes solid lines are needed in the same plate with tone (in which case a "combination plate" is made). It may prove desirable to silhouette a halftone (as, for example, the picture of a chair in the advertisement on Page 44). In certain cases a halftone should be made to fade out gradually (in which case a vignette is ordered).

Your article may contain square halftones (example: Pages 7, 9, 10, 11, 12, 13, 16, 17). It may have bleed halftones (example: Pages 3, 21, 22). Perhaps the art department had prepared a hand-lettered title (as on Pages 3, 7, 10).

If color is to be used, a tintblock may be ordered (in order to give a solid area of color—see Page 2, for example). When paintings or color photographs are used, the copy is photographed through color filters, and a separate halftone is made for each of the several colors used in the printing process (usually one for yellow, one for red, one for blue, and sometimes one for black. The printed plates combine to give the intermediate shades of the original).

5. Now before the printing begins, a preliminary make-ready process is undertaken, by which the press is "prepared" for the type and plates. Without proper make-ready, the minute differences in the height of the type or plates would lead to uneven impression. Low areas or

"spots" in the type or plates are compensated for by padding. When the make-ready is completed and a satisfactory sheet is run, the pressman may begin the actual printing.

6. And after the sheets have dried and are ready for folding, they are sent to the bindery for the final operations prior to shipping. The sheets will be folded into signatures (the folded sheets produced from a single press form; they consist of two, four, eight, sixteen, thirty-two, or sixty-four pages). What happens next depends on the style of binding used. The magazine may be *saddle stitched* (as, for example, *Theatre Arts Monthly,* the *New Republic,* the *Nation, Readers Digest, Saturday Evening Post*—stapled through the center and folded once to open flat). It may be *side stitched* (as, for example, *Better Homes & Gardens*), a method which will take care of a large number of pages, but does not permit the page to lie perfectly flat when opened. It may be sewn in the standard book style (as, for example, this book). It may be bound in one of the several spiral-binding styles (as, for example, *Inland Printer*).

7. Important in the binding as in every other production operation is the paper. Made from cotton or linen rags, from wood pulp, or from other cellulosic materials, paper may be obtained in a wide variety of qualities, surfaces, weights, bulks, colors, etc. *Newsprint,* the cheapest kind of printing paper, is made from wood pulp and delivered in flat sheets or rolls. *Book Paper* is the general term applied to printing papers which have not been "coated." *Machine finished book* (m.f.) has a fairly smooth surface, which is obtained by running the paper through the calender stack of the paper-making machine. *English Finish* has a somewhat firmer and more even surface than m.f. *Sized* and *super-calendered* (s. and s.c.) has a glossy, polished surface, having been "sized" and run through the calender rolls.

Antique finish, widely used in books and pamphlets, has a rough or mat surface. *Eggshell,* similar to antique, has something of the dull, unpolished surface of an eggshell.

By applying a coating of clay or other material, manufacturers produce papers with an extremely smooth surface—*coated paper. Plate finish* is obtained by applying pressure to paper which has been interleaved with metal or cloth to give finishes resembling vellum, linen, lawn, crash, ripple, etc.

The importance of selecting the right paper arises from more than reasons of taste or impulse. There is a specific interdependence between the type of printing and the paper used. Coarse-screen halftones may be used on newsprint; but the finer the halftone screen, the more polished a paper surface is required. In planography and intaglio, specially made papers are required.

Index

INDEX